The marketing economy

Holt, Rinehart and Winston Marketing Series

PAUL E. GREEN, Adviser
WHARTON SCHOOL, UNIVERSITY OF PENNSYLVANIA

PHILIP KOTLER, Adviser
NORTHWESTERN UNIVERSITY

JAMES F. ENGEL, DAVID T. KOLLAT, ROGER D. BLACKWELL,
All of The Ohio State University
  Consumer Behavior
  Cases in Consumer Behavior
  Research in Consumer Behavior

RONALD R. GIST,
University of Denver
  Marketing and Society: A Conceptual Introduction
  Readings: Marketing and Society

CHARLES S. GOODMAN,
University of Pennsylvania
  Management of the Personal Selling Function

PHILIP KOTLER,
Northwestern University
  Marketing Decision Making: A Model-Building Approach

JOHN C. NARVER,
University of Washington
RONALD SAVITT,
Boston University, National Economic Research Associates
  The Marketing Economy: An Analytical Approach
  Conceptual Readings in the Marketing Economy

THOMAS R. WOTRUBA,
San Diego State College
  Sales Management: Planning, Accomplishment, and Evaluation

THOMAS R. WOTRUBA,
San Diego State College
ROBERT M. OLSEN,
California State College, Fullerton
  Sales Management: Concepts and Viewpoints

The marketing economy

AN ANALYTICAL APPROACH

John C. Narver
University of Washington

Ronald Savitt
Boston University
National Economic Research Associates

HOLT, RINEHART AND WINSTON, INC.
New York · Chicago · San Francisco · Atlanta · Dallas
Montreal · Toronto · London · Sydney

Dedicated to

Betty Jane,
Gregory, and
Allison Ann Narver and
Naomi Savitt

Foreword

The Advisory Editors of the Holt, Rinehart and Winston Marketing Series are pleased to publish this fresh and distinctive new text in marketing. Drawing on the intellectual heritage of great marketing scholars, such as Alderson, Breyer, Cox, Grether and Revzan, the authors manage to create a long-needed neo-classical synthesis of marketing principles. They see the marketing economy as susceptible to rigorous concepts, definitions, relationships and methods of analysis, all of which are often ignored by the more managerially-oriented introductory texts.

Their book presents marketing as an intellectually important discipline that deserves a place in the *general* education of business and other students in both their intellectual development and training for managerial, citizen-consumer, or public policy responsibilities. As such, it develops the student's understanding in a way that should increase his capability of dealing with social as well as specific managerial issues facing individuals, government agencies, or companies in a marketing economy.

—*Paul E. Green*
—*Philip Kotler*

Preface

This book is born from a certain deep-seated frustration. It is the frustration we have experienced both as students and as professors of not having in the literature of marketing a textbook addressing itself solely to the question of *why* of the structure and behavior of our marketing economy. The current and continuing emphasis on marketing decision-making, a "how to" approach has left aside unfortunately most all analysis of the "what" and "why" of marketing.

The present book is addressed precisely to the *why* of marketing, rather than decision-making. The book will serve ideally as a preface to decision-making analysis, or equally well as simply an analytical text—especially suitable for a student's sole exposure to marketing. Such an analytical, non-managerial text, to our thinking, has long been needed both as a prelude to managerial analysis and simply as a part of a student's liberal education.

Thus, the book is addressed to the many professors and students in marketing, agricultural economics, and economics departments who have long felt the need for an analytical treatment in marketing that is not oriented to decision-making.

Our basic premise is that an understanding of the marketing economy is a vital part of everyone's education. We shall briefly discuss our reasoning.

AN UNDERSTANDING OF
THE MARKETING ECONOMY

Effecting transactions is the end toward which marketing is directed and is the basis of seller and buyer behavior in our economy. The seller and buyer structures and behavior comprising marketing are extremely complex. Even so, complexity alone does not justify its study. Why is an *understanding* of the marketing economy, as we attempt to provide in this book, important?

Prelude to Enlightened Citizenship and Professional Activity

Every reader of this book is at the minimum an ultimate consumer of goods and services provided by our marketing economy. If any person is to be both an effective consumer and citizen in our democracy, he must insofar as possible, understand the society in which he lives. First, as a citizen, if one understands the major determinants of marketing behavior, he can better judge both firms' actions and governmental economic policies.

Second, a consumer in the marketing economy benefits from a greater understanding of the determinants of marketing structure and behavior. For example, with this background, the reader will better appreciate some of the forces underlying efficiency and prices in the economy. Moreover, he will recognize the possible trade-off between private and social efficiency, for example between sellers gaining some control over demand and supply which may permit them to develop new products and engage in research, and sellers gaining so much control over demand and supply that the pressures for new products, research, and efficiency may be lessened.

Third, beyond the role of citizen and consumer, an understanding of marketing will assist one in any other decision-making in marketing. If one is a manager in a firm, he will have a sharper framework in which to relate his firm's activities both internally and to the environment and ultimately by which to optimize the firm's value. Or if he is involved with public policy in government, a comprehensive understanding of the relationships between his immediate field and other areas in the marketing economy is extremely valuable to him. Or if he is a lawyer in private or government practice, this understanding obviously will provide him keener insight. We could continue, but the preceding examples illustrate the point.

In short, sophistication in marketing is an important element in one's liberal education whereby one becomes a more enlightened member and consumer in our society, and/or from a professional standpoint, is a vital foundation for decision making in private management, the law, or public agencies.

UNIQUE FEATURES OF THE BOOK

Aside from the uniqueness of a short, analytical, non-managerial text, there are several specific features of the book that would appear to have virtually no counterpart in current marketing texts. Specifically, the book:

1. Removes marketing from the unfortunately typical conceptual box in which it is seen merely as "selling in product markets," and broaden the concept to relate to transactions in *any* markets in the economy.

2. Relates the marketing economy of the real world to its intellectual antecedent—the pure market economy.

3. Relates structure and behavior within and between the individual consumer or firm level and the market level. By viewing marketing structures at two levels of aggregation—firm (individual) and market—the analysis permits an explicit relationship between the field of "marketing" and the field of "industrial organization," fields too long artificially separated.

4. Derives a framework for a general theory of marketing structure and behavior.

5. Considers public policy in marketing in a broader context than virtually any other marketing literature, and moreover, focuses on one aspect—antitrust—in more analytical detail than virtually any other marketing text.

6. Devotes substantial emphasis to consumer welfare in today's marketing economy, including such issues as the price discrepancies between branded and non-branded prescription drugs, whether the poor pay more, and whether *abundance* of goods, including by-products such as pollution, necessarily means in total a higher quality of life for consumers.

USES OF THE BOOK

As stated, a short, analytical, non-managerial marketing text permits use in conjunction with a managerial book, *or* provides the basis for a completely non-managerial course. With an eye to both possible uses, we have offered sufficient additional sources including a separately published readings book to satisfy either objective. Among undergraduate and graduate schools of business, as well as economics and agricultural economics departments, we perceive a variety of uses for such a short conceptual marketing text.

A prime area of need for the present analysis is the first marketing course in graduate schools of business. A closely related area is agricultural economics departments, as their analyses increasingly consider differentiated offerings, concentrated markets, and consumer issues. This book is applicable also in the upper-division level of undergraduate schools of business and departments of economics in which one desires an analytical marketing book for either the introductory marketing course in the junior year or specialized upper-division courses such as marketing theory or industrial organization.

THE SEQUENCE OF ANALYSIS IN THE BOOK

Part I
The Marketing Economy and Some Basic Concepts

Part I introduces and discusses "marketing," "analysis," and "theory," the current state of theory in marketing and approaches to marketing, including what we call the analytical approach.

Then there is an analysis of transactions and want satisfaction in the pure market economy of classical economic theory contrasting it to the real world economy—the marketing economy—and highlighting the several ways in which the real economic world is "incomplete." The discussion then turns to the institution of sorting, after which, the analysis specifically considers the meaning and some implications of wants, offerings, markets, products, market diversification, and so on.

Part II
The General Structure and Behavior of Marketing

The analysis in Part II begins with a general framework of marketing structure and behavior—a framework that provides a possible basis for a general theory of marketing. It relates firm (or individual) structure to behavior and in turn, to market structure and behavior. By comprehending both firm and market levels of aggregation, the concept "marketing structure," permits analysis at either level of detail. Subsequent analysis throughout the book retains the structure-behavior framework.

Part III
Buyer Structure and Behavior

The analysis, relating theory and empirical studies, is of the determinants of buyer (demander) behavior. Structure, including several economic, psychological, and sociological dimensions is considered first. The behavior of demanders is then analyzed with particular attention paid to buyer learning including both intermediate customers and ultimate consumers.

Part IV
Seller Structure and Behavior

The analysis initially establishes a framework for perceiving firms as sellers. The framework encompasses planning and information-gathering aspects. The subsequent three chapters analyze both conceptually and empirically decisions relating to products and channels, promotion, and pricing.

Part V
Social Perspectives of the Marketing Economy

The section analyzes three important sets of social issues in the marketing economy—productivity and efficiency, public policy, and consumer welfare.

AUTHORS' PERSPECTIVE IN SUMMARY

The present book analyzes the processes and implications of buyers and sellers seeking satisfaction in markets. The analysis is of buyer and seller structures and behavior and the private and social aspects and implications of buyer and seller behavior. The overriding purpose is to create an understanding, a sophistication, of a marketing economy.

Our fundamental hope is that the present book sharpens the reader's analytical perspectives of marketing and through the dual consideration of concepts and empirical findings heightens his understanding of the *why* of real-world marketing structure and behavior.

We have derived the contents of this book through our own teaching and research as well as graduate study. We believe this analytical material constitutes a required minimum for a basic understanding of marketing.

If this book requires some effort on the part of the reader, we hope it is due largely to having to think one's way along. If such is the case we shall be amply rewarded.

Seattle, Washington   —J.C.N.
Boston, Massachusetts   —R.S.
January 1971

Acknowledgments

The present book is the result of a long period of informal discussions, personal class lectures, correspondence, and formal drafts of text material. The authors, one-time classmates at the University of California at Berkeley, in the Graduate School of Business Administration, conceived of the present book in the early 1960s in part from Professor E. T. Grether's careful appraisal of the literature in marketing and analyses in two seminars, and in part from the authors' many intellectually provocative contacts with Professor David A. Revzan. The spirit of this book may be traced essentially to our relationships with this pair of very able scholars. We are unstinting in our respect and admiration for these two tireless and intellectually stimulating professors, both of whom are well versed in the historical development and contemporary literature of marketing, institutional economics, and economic theory.

Professors Paul Green and Philip Kotler were extremely helpful sounding boards as the basic arguments of the book were put into final form.

Our former student colleagues at Berkeley and Wharton, and also faculty colleagues at our respective institutions and elsewhere have substantially contributed in both direct and indirect ways. Discussions and exchanges of papers with them on various subjects in and out of "marketing" enhanced this project. We wish to recognize some of these individuals to whom we are indebted: Professors Lee Preston, Willard Mueller, Sumner Marcus, Douglas Egan, Ahmet Koc, Bill Alberts, Joseph Monsen, and Delbert Duncan.

We also wish to recognize the assistance of several graduate students, especially Merlyn Kent, Dennis Dunlop, and Douglas Brooks, and also several graduate marketing classes at the University of Washington and Boston University.

The really unsung heroes (heroines) in the publication of a book are they who man the typewriters during the drafting and re-drafting. In this case it is with great appreciation that we cite especially Mrs. Mildred Butler for her very generous help and willing assistance, and also Miss Mary Gosieske, Mrs. Elizabeth Watson, and Mrs. Madilyn Wisnia.

Finally, we wish to recognize the generous willingness of our families as well as parents and in-laws to allow us over the past four years the many long hours and days for the work—the necessary result of which was fewer games of catch and fewer hikes, and innumerable late dinners and absences. It is our immediate families, and especially our patient and loyal wives, Betty Jane and Naomi, to whom we dedicate this book.

Seattle, Washington   —J.C.N.
Boston, Massachusetts   —R.S.
January 1971

Contents

Preface   vii

Acknowledgements   xiii

PART I/   The Marketing Economy and Some Basic Concepts   1

Chapter 1/   Marketing and Analysis   3

Chapter 2/   The Pure Market Economy, the Marketing Economy, and Want Satisfaction   22

Chapter 3/   Markets, Products, and Want Satisfaction   53

PART II/   The General Structure and Behavior of Marketing   83

Chapter 4/   Marketing Structure and Behavior   85

Chapter 5/   Functions and Flows in Marketing   118

Chapter 6/   Agencies and Channels   134

Chapter 7/   Time and Distance in Marketing   151

PART III/   Buyer Structure and Behavior   171

Chapter 8/   Buyer Structure   173

Chapter 9/   Buyer Behavior   198

PART IV/   Seller Structure and Behavior   223

Chapter 10/   Marketing Management and Information   225

Chapter 11/   Product and Channel Decisions and Performance   254

Chapter 12/   Promotion Decisions and Performance   286

Chapter 13/   Price Decisions and Performance   311

PART V/   Social Perspectives of the Marketing Economy   343

Chapter 14/   Marketing and Public Policy   345

Chapter 15/   Marketing Performance: Productivity and Efficiency   371

Chapter 16/   Marketing Performance: Consumer Welfare   398

Subject Index   419

Name Index   427

I The marketing economy and some basic concepts

1

Marketing and analysis

Ours is a market-based or marketing economy. It is a complex system of markets, that is, a complex system of communication, negotiation, and transactions. At the heart of the market-based or marketing economy are demand (buyers and lessees), supply (sellers and lessors), and markets—the nexuses of demand and supply. Whatever is being acquired, whether a factor of production or a final good or service, the process is the same: demanders search for relevant suppliers, and suppliers search for prospective demanders. And because most goods and services are owned, both parties—those who have items to sell or rent and those who wish to purchase or lease them—seek satisfaction through an exchange, that is, a transaction.

Why call our market-based economy, a "marketing economy"? Why not simply a "market economy"? Choosing our words advisedly, the former term distinguishes contemporary market-based economies from the name typically associated with the *pure* market economy of classical economic theory. The "pure" market economy establishes the principles of want satisfaction through markets, but is solely an analytical framework rather than a portrayal of the real world. Thus, to distinguish the real world of markets and market behavior from the classical pure market economy, we employ the term "marketing economy."

Briefly, for now, markets in the real world, unlike the pure market economy, are characterized typically by buyers and sellers *not* fully informed of trading opportunities, resources *not* completely mobile into and out of markets, buyers and sellers *not* unable to affect price, and government *not* absent from the markets.

We turn now to the definition of marketing. The remainder of the chapter consists of a discussion of the meaning of theory, theory in marketing, and approaches to the study of marketing.

DEFINITION OF MARKETING

"Marketing" means all activities, both pre-purchase and post-purchase, in any way related to transactions of ownership or use rights to any factor, good or service.

Discussion of the Definition

1 / All Activities Related to Transactions

The concept "all activities" embraces all commercial and noncommercial tasks which in any way relate to past or future sales or leases of factors of production, goods, or services. Embracing as it does all pre-purchase and post-purchase activities related to transactions, marketing obviously includes such functions as the movement of goods, advertising, pricing, storing, grading, purchasing, and so on, for all of these and similar tasks are clearly related to transactions of factors, goods, and services.

Not only does "marketing" include all commercial activities in any way related to transactions, but also includes any transaction-related noncommercial activity, such as government providing product information or regulating trade, as well as the activities of consumers acquiring information. Moreover, the concept understandably includes, along with any pre-purchase and post-purchase activity of commercial parties and the federal, state, and local government, any activities of organizations such as nonprofit consumer advisory groups which relate to transactions by providing demanders and/or suppliers with market and product information pertaining to shopping and use suggestions, possible injurious effects of products, and so on.

The raison d'être of marketing in a private-property economy is the effecting of transactions, for thereby suppliers and demanders—all types: firms, noncommercial units, and individuals—satisfy some of their goals. But associated with transactions in an "impure" or incomplete world are numerous directly and indirectly related activities that must be incorporated in the concept "marketing" for a realistic view of all that is involved in the transfer of legal rights in our economy.

2 / Transactions of Ownership or Use Rights

The institution of private (and public) ownership of property and resources is a distinguishing feature of our society. At any time, virtually all factors of production, goods, and services are within the legal domain of an individual, firm, noncommercial agency, or government. Thus, access to factors, goods, and services is gained only by obtaining the ownership or use rights, an act which very frequently requires a market exchange, that is, a transaction. The transfer of legal rights is the most substantive element of a transaction, and it is for this reason that we frame our definition of marketing in terms of transactions. Supply, demand, and transactions (and implicitly information and negotiations): these are the vital sum and substance of the marketing economy.

3 / Factor, Good, or Service

Factor markets, although concerned simply with special kinds of "goods," are explicitly included in the definition to remind one that "marketing" refers to all markets—factor-of-production markets as well as product markets. There is no logic in excluding the factors of production, that is, land, labor, and capital, from "marketing." Of course, the particular marketing activities vary among markets. In factor markets, for example, the promotional element may be minimal in that the demand for labor, capital, and other factors is a derived demand, derived from the demand for "ultimate" goods and services. Consequently, it is a demand over which the owners of the factors have little control. There may, however, be competition between types of factors as well as among the suppliers themselves, for example, among various suppliers of capital in the capital market. Debt and equity capital are supplied by several sources such as banks, investment companies, and insurance companies as well as savings and loan companies and Small Business Administration agencies.

Goods and services, which for convenience we may generalize as "products," are sold or leased in both intermediate and ultimate markets. In an intermediate market, the product may be a good which is purchased for further processing such as grapes for wine-making, cream for butter, or steel for automobiles. Many intermediate products constitute inputs in the production (or sale) of other products. In some intermediate markets, the buyer is a wholesale middleman or retailer purchasing the products for resale. In yet other intermediate markets, the purchaser is a public or private agency such as a hospital, university, federal government, or city hall, and the products are supplies or other inputs required in the activity of the agency. A government agency is a buyer in an *intermediate* market in that its demand is derived from an ultimate market—the "dictates" of the citizenry.

Markets in which goods and services are purchased for purposes of personal consumption are termed "ultimate" markets. Ultimate consumers, the name given demanders in ultimate markets, acquire goods and services solely in the satisfaction of private noncommercial wants. The products are purchased neither as inputs nor for resale. Of course, additional refinements and modifications may occur. The consumer may further refine or shape the product, such as a do-it-yourself consumer using lumber, prefinished panel-ing, and composition tile to build a recreation room in his house. These purchases are nonetheless ultimate consumption.

We explicate goods *and* services rather than "products" simply to indi-cate that wants may be satisfied (1) in some instances by goods, (2) in some instances by services, (3) in some instances by goods and services (for example, a new suit and an evening on the town), and (4) in other instances by goods or services (for example, the desire for relaxation for some consumers may be satisfied either by buying a good such as a yacht or by buying a service such as a trip to Europe).

"Wholesale" and "retail" sales are concepts directly related to the two levels of markets. A wholesale sale is any non-ultimate-consumer sale—*all* intermediate-market transactions are "wholesale" transactions. A retail sale is *any* sale to an ultimate consumer. Manufacturers and wholesalers typically sell at *wholesale* (that is, to non-ultimate consumers), but in certain industries and circumstances they also sell to ultimate consumers. Retailers primarily sell to *ultimate consumers*, but on occasion they sell at wholesale, for example, to other retailers.

Additional Comments on the Definition of Marketing

Wherever there is a market, there necessarily is marketing, for some minimal number of pre- or post-transaction activities must *always* be per-formed. As we have stated, transactions and the implicit "satisfaction of wants" are the raison d'être of marketing.

We have taken pains to point out the pervasiveness of marketing in our economy. For reasons not entirely clear, in the past few decades there has been an unfortunate *conceptual limiting* of marketing to an activity somehow existing only in product rather than product and factor markets. An even more serious error is the curious tendency by some to see marketing as primarily "ultimate-consumer oriented." We stress that if marketing has to do with markets and transactions, then *all* markets must be included.

Our definition avoids the mechanistic and narrow sense of the definition of marketing of the American Marketing Association. The Association defines marketing as "the business activities that direct the flow of goods and services from producer to consumer or user."[1] Perhaps it is uninten-tional, but the impression left a reader of the "official" definition is that marketing not only "starts" on the supply side, but moreover, specifically with the "producer." We would argue that marketing starts with an actual or potential demand, and then, producers or other agencies respond to the wants. For the present, it is immaterial to consider how the want arose. It's enough that it exists. Secondly, we disagree with the AMA definition

[1] Committee on Definitions, *Marketing Definitions* (Chicago: American Marketing Asso-ciation, 1960), p. 15.

in that it suggests that marketing merely steers the movement of goods and services, rather than in part at least, initiating and/or stimulating the flow. Finally, the Association definition seemingly narrows the conception of marketing to merely the physical flow of goods and services rather than implicitly including the several types of activities—such as information, negotiation, physical handling, and so forth—associated with transactions.[2]

UNDERSTANDING MARKETING: ANALYSIS AND THEORY

An Understanding of Marketing

An analytical approach to marketing seeks understanding of the *why* of marketing, specifically the why of marketing *behavior.*

What is an "understanding" of marketing? It is necessarily more than description, for description does not get to cause-and-effect relationships. By simply enumerating the phenomena, one cannot separate symptoms and causes. Obviously, if everything is accorded equal importance, one must dutifully observe and record every single element. Rather than shedding light on the determinants of behavior, the result is a meaningless labyrinth of facts.

To attain understanding, that is, the comprehension of *why* phenomena are as they are, one must establish the relative importance and relationship of facts.

Facts and Theory

Understanding—the relating of facts—implies "theory." Theory and facts are closely connected. First we shall define "fact."

A fact is an empirically verifiable observation.[3]

The meaning of "empirically verifiable observation" is complex; a full clarification would require an extensive treatment. However, the implications for our purposes will become clear in subsequent passages.

[2] The emergence of the narrow view of marketing might be explained by either of the following:
  1. To the promotion-oriented writer, there is no "marketing" in factor markets because there is, he assumes, an atomistic seller structure and the items for sale are physically homogeneous. Thus, in such markets, promotion is irrational, and hence there is no "marketing."
  2. To some writers the broad groupings of the factors of production—land, labor, and capital—are completely the domain of other academic disciplines. Writers of this opinion, therefore, cede the marketing aspects to the other disciplines, leaving to the field of marketing, the residual, which is some set of product markets.

[3] See William J. Goode and Paul K. Hatt, *Methods in Social Research* (McGraw-Hill, 1952), p. 8 ff.

In any analysis, facts must be fitted into a systematic pattern. The "systematic pattern" in which facts are related is another name for *theory*. Specifically,

A theory is the meaningful relationship between facts.[4]

"Theory" appears to be an extremely misunderstood concept. Contrary to a popular but incorrect opinion, theory does *not* mean "armchair speculation" or some such notion. Rather to us, as to the scientist in general, theory means *realism*—namely, the ordering of facts in some meaningful way. Theory as the relating of facts is a central part of science.

> Facts, or empirically verifiable observations, could never have produced modern science if they had been gathered at random. One scientist might count the grains of sand in a sand pile; another might survey the range of size and shape of leaves on a maple tree; still another might record the variations in color of rainbow trout taken from a particular river eddy. The infinity of possible procedures, objects for observation, and of ways to make those observations would effectively prohibit any substantial progress from one generation to the next. Without some system, some ordering principles, in short *without theory*, science could yield no predictions. Without prediction there would be no control over the material world. . . . The facts of science are the product of observations that are not random but meaningful, i.e., theoretically relevant. Thus, we cannot think of facts and theory as being opposed.[5]

To one school of thought including the present authors, the test of a theory's validity is its usefulness in illuminating reality. The elegance of the logic of the theory is irrelevant. In our conception, when the reader next hears the inevitable statement, "That's all right in theory but not in practice," he will know that what should have been said is simply, "*This theory is not valid.*"

Theory necessarily involves abstraction. This makes some who claim to be "realists" uneasy. But why should it make them uneasy? Everyone acknowledges that some facts are more important than others in explaining any phenomenon. Thus, one *must* abstract from the whole of reality if he is to understand and avoid a clutter of facts. And, therefore, theory—the

---

[4] Goode, *et al., op. cit.*, p. 8. As David A. Revzan has said, "(Theory) is not a description merely of things as they are, but also of why they are . . . ," *The Journal of Marketing*, XV, No. 1 (July 1, 1950), p. 101.

Samuelson, in pointing out the connection between facts and theory, says that true analysis incorporates facts, description, explanation, and relationships. See Paul A. Samuelson, *Economics: An Introductory Analysis* (5th ed., McGraw-Hill, 1961), pp. 8–9, and p. 12.

[5] Goode, *op. cit.*, p. 8. In speaking of science itself, it is useful to remember that science is a method of approach to the empirical world: it is a *mode of analysis* rather than merely an accumulation of systematic knowledge.

making sense of facts—necessarily requires abstractions. We repeat: This should not be discomforting even to the staunchest "realist." In that the test of a theory is its ability to illuminate *reality*, who could ask for more?
In summary,

> Every theory, whether in the physical or biological or social sciences, distorts reality in that it oversimplifies. But if it is a *good* theory, what is omitted is greatly outweighed by the beam of illumination and understanding that is thrown over the diverse empirical data.[6]

Marketing and the Types of Theory

In marketing (as in any field), it is useful to distinguish among positive theory in marketing, normative theory in marketing, and the art of marketing.[7] Positive theory explains what *is*. An understanding of phenomena is gained from positive theory. Positive theory is often also called "descriptive theory," though it by no means is merely description.

Normative theory states how *best* to attain a given goal. Normative theory because it prescribes, is often called "prescriptive theory." Normative *theory* exists only insofar as there is a meaningful relationship between facts. If there is no theory, the prescriptions then are called "art." Thus, marketing-management rules that do not meet the criteria of normative theory constitute simply the *art* of marketing.

Relationships between Positive Theory and Normative Theory

Normative marketing theory cannot successfully be independent of positive marketing theory.[8] The relationships among positive theory, normative theory, and art appear so obvious as not to warrant mentioning. The point repeatedly appears in the economics literature, and more recently in the marketing literature, that positive theory is indispensable in normative matters.[9]

[6] Samuelson, *op. cit.*, p. 12 (emphasis added). Dorfman concurs: "If you want literal realism, look at the world around you; if you want understanding, look at theories," Robert Dorfman, *The Price System* (Prentice-Hall, 1964), p. 11.

[7] The distinction among a "positive science," a "normative or regulative science," and an "art" was drawn by John M. Keynes in *The Scope and Method of Political Economy* (London: Macmillan, 1891), pp. 34–35, and quoted approvingly by Milton Friedman in his well-known *Essays in Positive Economics* (Chicago: University of Chicago Press, 1953), p. 3. For related comments *see* Lee E. Preston, "The Role of Economic Analysis in Research in Marketing," Graduate School of Business Administration, University of California, Berkeley, 1963 (mimeo.). See also the distinctions drawn by H. A. Simon, *Administrative Behavior,* (2d ed., Macmillan, 1957), Chapters 1 and 3.

[8] A statement of fundamental, general connections is found in Friedman, *op. cit.*, p. 5. Support in the marketing literature for the positive-normative relationship is found *inter alia* in Revzan, *loc. cit.*, p. 101 ff.

[9] As Samuelson says, "Ultimately, understanding [positive theory] should aid in control and improvement." Samuelson, *op. cit.*, p. 9. But the benefits flow both ways: Positive theory is refined and improved by actual experience.

Managerial and public policy are both concerned with the normative questions of controlling and improving various types of performance. But policy without underlying positive theory is risky indeed. Positive theory is the basis for helping answer such questions as, "What are the economic effects of the expansion of chain stores?", "What are the economic effects of resale-price maintenance?", and "What is the efficiency in specified markets in our economy?". Positive theory, though an aid in policy matters, does not substitute for the judgment of the decision-maker.

Consider the managerial questions of "How shall we price our product?", "Shall we extensively or exclusively distribute our product?", and "How much shall we spend on advertising versus other forms of promotion?". The answers to all of these normative questions rest in part on such positive-theoretical questions as, "How do the markets operate?", "What determines the level and location of market demand?", and "What is the 'production function' of advertising?". Regardless of the sophistication of the measurement techniques, only the relevant facts as indicated by positive theory will be of assistance in answering normative questions.[10]

The State of Marketing Theory

What is the state of theory in marketing? What is the relative development of positive and normative theory? Does one find the attempt to develop normative theory in the absence of a basis of positive theory? We can only touch briefly on these very involved questions.

First, there is an important distinction between "theories in marketing" and a "theory of marketing." Recalling that theory means an ability to explain and predict some portion of reality, most assuredly there are theories *in* marketing, just as there are theories in economics, psychology, sociology, physics, and all other disciplines.

Although marketing has theories, these theories are frequently of small segments of the total field of marketing. Thus, these theories are correctly referred to as "theories in" rather than a "theory of marketing." The latter, implying one grand, explanatory theory encompassing the whole field of study, is not imminent.

For an ultimate *theory of* marketing we must first develop a conceptual framework embracing all the fundamental aspects of marketing. The authors, in Chapter 4 of the present book, suggest one possible basis for a general theory of marketing.

Second, only relatively recently have marketing scholars devoted substantial effort to develop positive theory (perhaps finally from a recognition that positive theory must precede normative managerial theory). Alderson sums it up,

---

[10] See Preston, *op. cit.*, pp. 18–19 for a related discussion.

Perhaps its [marketing's] greatest weakness, until recently, has been that it had concentrated on the attempt to establish control without giving adequate attention to the companion steps of explanation and prediction. This has tended to make marketing research an opportunistic approach to concrete problems.[11]

The preoccupation with control in the absence of an adequate understanding of underlying processes meant that progressive, alert companies were often more advanced in rudimentary normative theory than were the leading normative textbooks in the field.[12] However, this reverse-leadership situation is changing. Systematic research by marketing scholars as well as university and industry research is producing positive theory which in turn is enabling a substantial body of sound, normative theory.

Two rough indicators of the current state of theory in marketing are the two volumes of *Theory in Marketing*, published under the sponsorship of The American Marketing Association. The first volume of readings was published in 1950 and the second volume was published in 1964.[13]

Cox, one of the editors of both volumes, sets the historical perspective:

The appearance of a second volume of essays concerned with the theory in marketing offers a welcome opportunity to see how far and in what directions we have moved since the first volume appeared in 1950. . . . (T)he conscious effort to establish a sophisticated theory or set of theories as a joint effort of students in the field is about twenty years old.[14]

Many will disagree that the "conscious effort" toward theory dates back only 20 years or so. If theory is the meaningful relationship of facts, the effort certainly exceeds 20 years.

A comparison of the two volumes suggests that contributions of a positive-theory nature were present as much or more in the first volume. However, as Grether notes, the second volume is substantially normative

---

[11] Wroe Alderson, *Marketing Behavior and Executive Action*, (Irwin, 1957), p. 9. See also p. 7 ff.

[12] John A. Howard, *Marketing Theory* (Allyn and Bacon, 1965), p. 9. *See* pp. 1–3 with respect to the increased use of theory by managers.

[13] Reavis Cox and Wroe Alderson, *Theory in Marketing* (Homewood, Ill.: Richard D. Irwin, Inc., 1950), and Reavis Cox, Wroe Alderson, and Stanley J. Shapiro, *Theory in Marketing* (Homewood, Ill.: Richard D. Irwin, Inc., 1964). Two insightful essays in response to the respective volumes are David A. Revzan, "Review of Theory in Marketing," *Journal of Marketing* XV No. 1 (July 1950), pp. 101–109; and E. T. Grether, "An Emerging Apologetic of Managerialism?: Theory in Marketing, 1964," *Journal of Marketing Research* II (May 1965), pp. 190–195.

[14] Reavis Cox in Cox, Alderson, and Shapiro, *op. cit.*, p. 1.

due in large part to its frequent turn to functionalism and other concepts of Professor Wroe Alderson.[15]

The second volume of essays in theory in marketing is clearly a greater admixture than the first volume, both in terms of normative-positive as well as particular perspectives—economics, quantitative, abstract-logical, behavioral science, and so on. It would be fair to conclude that if the second volume is representative, there is recently a recognition on the part of many marketing scholars that positive theory must precede normative theory. Also, one may conclude that today a greater variety of—and frequently more rigorous—analytical tools are being brought to bear on the development of positive theory in marketing. As Cox says in the second volume, "Unquestionably the level of sophistication of the volume is much higher than that of the first volume."[16]

In the following section we shall consider several approaches to the study of marketing. Each approach has contributed to positive theory in marketing. The reader may wish to reflect on the unique contributions to positive theory each approach can make.

APPROACHES TO THE STUDY OF MARKETING

An "approach" to the study of marketing is simply a particular perspective of marketing chosen because it best highlights the aspects desired for investigation. There are in principle as many approaches as there are perspectives or views of marketing. However, over the years marketing scholars have primarily employed four approaches: managerial, commodity, institutional, and functional. The reader will recognize that they are *not* mutually exclusive. These four we may call the traditional approaches. In addition there are several other approaches which simply are focuses on more narrowly defined aspects of marketing, such as for example, consumer welfare. We shall discuss the traditional approaches first.

Traditional Approaches

1 / Managerial Approach

Of the four traditional approaches, the most normative is the managerial approach. Many managerial decisions are necessary in market behavior and

[15] Grether, *op. cit.*, p. 192. Functionalism is briefly described, and reference is made to Alderson in the "Functional Approach" described in a subsequent portion of this chapter.

[16] Cox, *et al.*, 1964 *op. cit.*, p. 13. Even though many marketing scholars recognize that positive theory must underlie normative theory, the second volume suggests a confusion on the priorities of these tasks. Cox says marketers have not yet settled the question of "whether we seek a theory for operating managers, for their staff associates and advisers, or for the academicians." We would respond that we seek both positive and normative theory, but not necessarily simultaneously!

hence in effecting the transaction. The managerial approach primarily focuses upon the marketing manager and considers the variables available to him in the various decisions to be made. The approach assists a marketing manager in selecting the best combination of marketing emphases and expenditures for any particular situation.[17]

2 / Industrial Organization (Including Commodities) Approach

The industrial organization approach to marketing analyzes the relationship between marketing (especially market) structure, conduct, and performance. It is essentially the application of economic theory to the empirical evaluation of real world markets. Taking hypotheses and deductions from economic theory, it assesses the determinants of market behavior —specifically, it analyzes the implication of the concentration of sellers, the ease of entry into a market by new sellers and buyers, the concentration of buyers, the rate of market growth, the degree of product differentiation, and other elements, and their association with profit levels, efficiency levels, progressiveness and innovation levels, and so on. (These issues and topics are discussed more fully in Chapter 4, "Marketing Structure and Behavior.)

Whereas economic theory is a framework relatively abstracted from specific markets and contexts, industrial organization on the other hand, is very much a specific-context approach. Industrial organization is largely empirical analysis of the abstractions of the theory.

The typical industrial organization analysis is in one of two veins. One is cross-sectional analysis, wherein the analyst takes a structural variable, such as the concentration of sellers, and views this particular variable across several markets establishing its mean value. Against this he takes performance in terms of, for example, profit levels of the several markets and establishes its mean value, attempting thereby to see the relationship between the structural element and the performance element. Typically, it is even a more complex analysis in that several structural variables are taken simultaneously, and then, through multivariate analysis, their association with performance of one type or another is determined. The second type of industrial organization analysis is commodity study or industry analysis in depth. In this version the particular good, service, or industry is analyzed exhaustively as to the nature and conditions of supply and demand, distribution channels, and processes involved, promotional methods, and pricing patterns, and so on. This latter approach is frequently highly

---

[17] Some current managerial-approach textbooks are: John A. Howard, *Marketing Management* (Irwin, 1963), Philip Kotler, *Marketing Management: Analysis, Planning, and Control* (Prentice-Hall, 1967); Alfred R. Oxenfeldt, *Executive Action in Marketing* (Wadsworth, 1966); E. Jerome McCarthy, *Basic Marketing: A Managerial Approach* (Rev. ed., Irwin, 1964); Richard H. Buskirk, *Principles of Marketing: The Management View* (Rev. ed., Holt, Rinehart and Winston, 1970); William J. Stanton, *Fundamentals of Marketing* (2d ed., McGraw-Hill, 1967); and Martin L. Bell, *Marketing: Concepts and Strategy* (Houghton Mifflin, 1966).

descriptive—at times extensively pointing out marketing similarities and differences in one industry versus another, or one commodity or product versus another. Comparative marketing analyses are somewhat of the commodity version of the industrial organization approach. The commodity approach in emphasizing particularities arrives at generalities only after exhaustive case analyses and comparisons. For this reason the commodity approach is not well suited to briefly covering the entire field of marketing. On the other hand, it is extremely well suited to penetrating in depth a particular product or industry, leaving generalizations for other approaches.

The analytical approach to marketing—of which this book is one example—relies very heavily on the industrial organization approach, in particular, the cross-sectional form of this approach. This industrial organizational approach to marketing, though surprisingly little utilized by many marketing scholars, serves very well to bridge the gap between what many people see as "marketing analysis" on the one hand and "economic theory" on the other. We would not be inclined to favor such a distinction, but if the distinction between "economic theory" and "marketing analysis" is to be made, then surely industrial organization does lie between them. At any rate, the industrial organizational approach is one of the most important approaches to the study of marketing, in terms of heightening marketing theory—our ability to explain and relate facts—in its emphasis on empirical relationships in real world markets.[18]

3 / Institutional Approach

The institutional approach analyzes the emergence of marketing structures. In its most complex form, the institutional approach attempts to explain marketing structures by beginning with the actual institution, that

---

[18] The industrial organization approach in the form of cross-sectional analyses has a broad and well-established literature. Two leading books in the area are Joe Bain, *Industrial Organization* (Wiley, 1959); and Richard Caves, *American Industry Structure, Conduct, Performance* (2d ed., Prentice-Hall, 1967).

For a very useful summary of empirical analyses in industrial organization of market structure and performance, see Norman Collins and Lee E. Preston *Concentration and Price-Cost Margins in Manufacturing Industries* (University of California, 1968). Also see William Comanor and T. A. Wilson, "Advertising, Market Structure, and Performance," *The Review of Economics and Statistics*, LXIX, November 1967, pp. 423–440.

Included in the commodity or in-depth industry-study version of the industrial organization approach are such examples from the literature as J. S. Bain, *The Economics of the Pacific Coast Petroleum Industry* (Three volumes, Berkeley University of California Press, 1944, 1945, and 1947); B. P. Pashigian, *The Distribution of Automobiles* (Prentice-Hall, 1961); E. A. Duddy and D. A. Revzan, *The Supply Area of the Chicago Livestock Market* (Chicago: University of Chicago Press, 1931); Jesse Markham, *Competition in the Rayon Industry* (Harvard, 1952); and James McKie, *Tin Cans and Tin Plates: A Study of Competition in Two Related Markets* (Harvard, 1959).

is, the performance of a task in accordance with societal prescriptions, whether it be a task such as "retailing," or more specific tasks such as "credit," "physical distribution," and so on. Beginning with the actual institution, the institutional approach then considers the forms in which the institutions are found. This approach, accordingly, presents the logic of marketing structures at the individual firm level, the market level, and the overall, economy level.[19]

The institutional approach in its most complex form, not only sets the logic of agency, price, and geographic structures, but empirically examines various structure and behavior patterns. It is useful in explaining the roles and relative significance of the retail and wholesale sectors. It also relates the legal and other social institutions which comprise the environment of marketing.

A more limited version of the institutional approach is simply a description of the various agencies who do the work of marketing, but this does not represent the true (complex) institutional approach.[20]

4 / Functional Approach

In the functional approach the emphasis is on the tasks performed by the marketing system and the functions performed by the individual marketing agencies. The functional approach, like the institutional approach, leads from the task or activity to be performed to the agencies performing them. However, unlike the institutional approach, the functional approach's major emphasis is more on the activities themselves than on the structures and structure-behavior relationship (although Alderson's work, cited in footnote 21, is one exception). As pointed out before, it is difficult to pursue any one approach to the strict exclusion of all the other approaches.

---

[19] For readers not versed in sociological theory, the institutional approach is no doubt hazy. In the present book we employ, in part, the institutional approach and the reader may wish to look ahead for clarification. See Chapter 2, where the logic of the overall structure in a marketing economy is established. As we analyze the determinants of marketing structure and behavior in the chapters that follow, we shall continually stress that marketing consists of sets of purposive activity and that the structures selected to perform the activity are *intendedly rational* individual selections. The reader must remember that in this book "institutions" refers to customary performance of activities. It does not refer merely to a physical entity, as for example, a building.

[20] For the best-known recent attempt to employ fully the complex approach, see E. A. Duddy and D. A. Revzan, *Marketing: An Institutional Approach* (2d ed., McGraw-Hill, 1953), especially pp. 16–18 and Chapter 2, for an elaboration of the elements of the institutional approach. Another book utilizing in part the institutional approach is R. S. Vaile, E. T. Grether, and R. Cox, *Marketing in the American Economy* (Ronald, 1952). Almost every marketing principles book (see below) to some extent employs the *limited* version of the approach.

So it is with the functional approach. Clearly the institutional and functional approaches dovetail.[21]

Other Approaches

We have said above that there are conceivably as many approaches to the study of marketing as there are possible perspectives. The following are some additional approaches to marketing.

1 / Legal Approach

A so-called legal approach may be divided into two parts, each a useful approach to the study of marketing.

A. Statutory and Common Laws Affecting Marketing. This emphasis focuses on the local, state, and federal legal frameworks in which marketing occurs. Among other elements, it focuses on the law of property and the transfer of ownership or use rights; the laws against deception and fraud, as well as the laws safeguarding other rights of buyers and sellers; and the laws for preserving competition, commonly called the antitrust laws.

B. Flow of Ownership or Use Rights. Because the transfer of legal rights to possession is the end to which all of marketing is directed, a specific focusing on the flow of ownership or use rights of goods and services as they move into intermediate and ultimate markets is clearly another valid approach. Of course, to focus strictly on the transfer of title or use rights omits among other things the psychological and sociological elements.

2 / Consumer Approach

A so-called consumer approach (or better, "customer approach" to include all demanders) to the study of marketing has at least two emphases: (1) analysis of buyer behavior, and (2) consumer welfare.

A. Buyer Behavior. Part III of this book reveals the interdisciplinary nature of the analysis of buyer behavior. High-quality conceptual and empirical analyses are increasing, improving the buyer-be-

---

[21] A recent book utilizing in part a functional approach is George Fisk, *Marketing Systems: An Introductory Approach* (Harper and Row, 1967). Fisk's book, as is frequently the case, also incorporates the managerial approach. P. T. Cherington, *The Elements of Marketing* (Macmillan Company, 1920), one of the early marketing texts, was largely an analysis of the functions in marketing.

The marketing literature has benefited greatly from a particular extension of the functional approach. The late Professor Wroe Alderson of the University of Pennsylvania developed an integrated functional analysis which we may call, "functionalism." His basic conceptual work is found in *Marketing Behavior* and *Executive Action* (Irwin, 1957), and subsequent refinement in his *Dynamic Marketing Behavior* (Irwin, 1965). For discussion of Alderson's work relative to other approaches, see F. M. Nicosia, "Marketing and Alderson's Functionalism," *Journal of Business*, October 1962, pp. 403–413.

havior theory. An approach to marketing in which the focus is on the formation and expression of wants obviously is an extremely valid one.[22]

B. Consumer Welfare. In the *pure* market economy, but perhaps to a lesser extent in the marketing economy, consumers are completely sovereign: they alone determine what goods and services will be produced. For the better part of the twentieth century in this country there has been a strong, consumer movement—a series of efforts intended to make the consumer a wiser buyer and user of goods and services. (The Consumer Movement will be discussed in Part V, Social Perspectives of the Marketing Economy.)

One approach to marketing is that of the welfare of the consumer, an approach assessing and examining the implications of marketing for consumer well-being. Legislative activity in the late 1960s has punctuated the importance of this approach, for example, the Truth in Packaging bill, The Wholesome Meat Act, and the Truth in Lending bill. Moreover, the Federal Trade Commission continues to probe alleged misrepresentations in advertising and promotion and to investigate other unethical behavior of sellers. President Johnson's elevation to a sub-cabinet position of a Special Assistant for Consumer Affairs further highlights the timeliness of such an approach. Obviously, related to a consumer-welfare approach are emphases on efficiency and productivity in marketing and on antitrust. The latter, the maintenance of competition, promotes market efficiency, and hence helps assure increased value to consumers.[23]

"Principles" of Marketing

"Principles of marketing" are an attempt to illuminate what are believed to be the underlying, and enduring relationships in marketing. The earliest systematic marketing literature attempted to suggest invariable propositions or principles relating to the selling and buying goods and services in our economy.

It is safe to say that very few marketing scholars, let alone other social-science scholars, would assert that there are *invariable* behavioral relationships. In the social sciences the development of positive theory has led to

---

[22] One recent study of this nature is Francesco M. Nicosia, *Consumer Decision Processes* (Prentice-Hall, 1966). See also J. F. Engel, D. T. Kollat, and R. D. Blackwell, *Consumer Behavior* (Holt, Rinehart and Winston, 1968). The buyer-behavior approach may be limited merely to the consumer, or to the industrial customer, or may include both.

[23] For some recent discussion of consumer well-being see Carolyn Bell Shaw, *Consumer Choice in the American Economy* (Random House, 1967); and Senator Warren G. Magnuson, and Jean Carper, *The Dark Side of the Marketplace* (Prentice-Hall, 1968).

increasing emphasis on probabilistic models in which human beings are seen as limitedly rational entities content with satisfactory (not necessarily maximum) levels of performance.[24]

The principles concept in marketing as it is found today is a synthesis of the functional and institutional approaches. Books incorporating marketing principles have also included some discussions of managerial decisions from a normative viewpoint. Virtually no principles books on the market today uses "principles" in its literal sense—rather each one speaks in conditional terms.

As work in marketing progresses in testing hypotheses and accumulating theory, one may expect increased development of principles of marketing. Until we know more, however, the use of the word "principles" will be in a quite modest vein.[25]

AN ANALYTICAL APPROACH TO MARKETING

The present book is an analytical approach to marketing. It attempts to create understanding of the what and especially the *why* of marketing in a market-based economy. Because the emphasis is on explanation, the analysis is at times abstract, but "theoretical" in the proper sense of the term. Because the present theories attempt to explain rather than prescribe behavior, the thrust is *positive* rather than normative. Hence, the analytical approach to marketing embodied in this book is a *positive theoretical* analysis of marketing.

As the reader now knows, to be "theoretical" is in no sense to ignore facts—indeed, as pointed out, theory is completely involved with facts: In particular, it is meaningfully relating facts.

To relate facts meaningfully—that is, so one can explain and understand the real world—the analytical approach focuses on the interrelationships of structure and behavior. Thus, the analysis attempts to highlight

---

[24] Various scholars at the Graduate School of Industrial Administration, Carnegie-Mellon University, have contributed substantially to the reformulation of theories of human behavior. These contributions are rapidly finding their way into the marketing literature as well as the literature of other social sciences. Some of the books with many implications for marketing analysis are Herbert A. Simon, *Administrative Behavior* (2d ed., Macmillan Company, 1958). (This book is now virtually a classic.); James G. March and H. A. Simon, *Organizations* (Wiley, 1958); Richard M. Cyert and J. G. March, *A Behavioral Theory of the Firm* (Prentice-Hall, 1963); Oliver E. Williamson, *The Economics of Discretionary Behavior: Managerial Objectives in a Theory of the Firm* (Prentice-Hall, 1964); and Kalman J. Cohen and R. M. Cyert, *Theory of the Firm: Resource Allocation in a Market Economy* (Prentice-Hall, 1965).

[25] An example of a well-known, unpretentious principles book, combining managerial and nonmanagerial approaches is C. F. Phillips and D. J. Duncan, *Marketing: Principles and Methods* (5th ed., Irwin, 1964); another long-established principles text is T. N. Beckman and W. R. Davidson, *Marketing* (8th ed., Ronald, 1967).

causal relationships by noting first various structures, that is, the elements which shape or condition behavior, and then the behavior which emanates from the structures. The relationship between structure and behavior as we shall see is dynamic. Over time, not only do various structures determine behavior, but behavior tends to influence the initial structure, and thereby affect subsequent behavior. For example, in analyzing a retail gasoline market, one frequently observes among the initial set of service stations some service stations outcompeting others. Ultimately the superior competitive techniques of some stations relative to others may change the structure of the market. Some of the less efficient or otherwise less successful stations may go out of business. Unless new firms completely replace the demised firms, one aspect of the market structure will have been changed— there obviously will be fewer firms, and accordingly gasoline sales will be more concentrated. When market concentration reaches certain levels, more personal forms of behavior ensue, owing to the heightened interdependency among sellers.

The analytical approach employs the structure-behavior framework to analyze marketing at the level of (1) individual customers' "structure" conditioning their "behavior" and over time the reverse as well; (2) similarly, individual sellers and their structure and behavior; (3) groups of buyers and groups of sellers and their respective structures and behavior; and (4) the structure and behavior of entire markets, embracing all buyers and sellers. Thus, the structure-behavior framework is general and permits one to analyze in parallel fashion various levels of aggregation in marketing. (Chapter 4 discusses the structure-behavior framework in detail.)

The analytical approach draws upon theory—economic theory, organization theory, and the behavioral sciences—to identify structures and the emergence of new elements of structure. This approach, distinguishable more by the fields of theory it draws upon than by any methodological uniqueness, is a linkage between much of formal economic theory which is highly general and abstract, and much of marketing research which is highly particular and empirical. It is thus close to the industrial organization approach but incorporates more elements into "structure" than is the tendency of many industrial organization scholars. As a result the more comprehensive structure—including elements from both unit and market levels—more fully explains marketing behavior than can *either* the traditional economic analyst (that is, traditional industrial organization) looking primarily at market level elements, or the traditional marketer looking primarily at firm-level elements in conceiving of decision constraints.

To summarize, the analytical approach manifested in the present book is characterized by two features—both of which are present in varying degrees throughout the entire treatment. First, as we have said, the analytical approach is *positive theoretical*, drawing upon postive theory and citing relevant studies to corroborate evidence. Second, the analytical approach stresses structure-behavior relationships in trying to understand marketing. The structure-behavior framework is not, however, a rigid, lockstep treatment. Rather, the framework is an acknowledgment that at any given time, the behavior possibilities open at any marketing level to any marketing participant are constrained by various elements or "structure." The structure-behavior framework forces one to try to identify the relevant structures, that is, the behavioral determinants which, in a dynamic world, tend to change quantitatively and even qualitatively over time. Thus, the structure-behavior framework insists on analytical flexibility and sensitivity if one is to explain and predict real-world marketing behavior.

TOPIC SEQUENCE

Following the present chapter, the book discusses some basic principles and concepts pertaining to marketing and our marketing economy. In this section we establish the meaning of markets, wants, products, want satisfaction, and competition.

The analysis then, employing the concepts developed in Part I, considers carefully in Part II the relationship between marketing structure and behavior, and examines accordingly flows, functions, channels, and spatial relations in marketing.

Part III of the book considers the structure-behavior relationships with respect to demanders (buyers and lessees). One chapter focuses on the determinants of demand—that is, demand structure—and a second focuses on demander behavior.

In Part IV, the discussion turns to the structure and behavior of sellers. This part of the book analyzes some determinants, effects, and implications of seller behavior, including product, distribution, promotion, and pricing decisions.

Finally, in Part V, the present book treats some social issues in marketing. In largest part emphasizing the structure-behavior relationships, the analysis is of marketing productivity and efficiency, public policy in marketing, and consumer welfare.

SUGGESTED READINGS

The reader is encouraged to investigate readings cited in the footnotes. In addition, the following works are suggested, for they point up the type of breadth and empirical content which we wish to emphasize in the analytical approach.

Kenneth E. Boulding, "The Legitimacy of Economics," *Western Economic Journal*, September 1967, pp. 299–307.

Boulding considers the ascendency and limits to the legitimacy or acceptance of the field of economics in our society. He cautions against the tendency toward over-abstraction and over-specialization which legitimacy encourages. All social sciences, even economics, which is the most prestigious, are studying the *same* system, the "sociosphere," the total sphere of all human beings, their organization, behaviors, and so on. Too successful abstractions may lead to the neglect of the other elements of the system. (See also his "The Legitimation of the Market," speech given at Midwest Economic Association, 1967.)

Kalman J. Cohen and Richard M. Cyert, *Theory of the Firm: Resource Allocation in a Market Economy* (Englewood Cliffs, N.J.: Prentice-Hall, Inc., 1965), Chapter II, "The Methodology of Model Building."

E. T. Grether, "A Theoretical Approach to the Analysis of Marketing," in Reavis Cox and Wroe Alderson (ed.), *Theory in Marketing* (Homewood, Ill.: Richard D. Irwin, Inc., 1950).

Professor Grether's paper underscores the importance of analysis in marketing which stems from and builds upon positive theory. Unless analysis relates the firm to its markets and other contexts, yet does so selectively, guided by formal economic analysis, one has either some results which cannot be linked to other analytical systems or he has merely a logical construct without relevance to reality. Grether's framework stressing the physical and spatial relationships of firms and groups of firms provides a feasible approach to positive analysis.

Philip Kotler, *Marketing Management: Analysis, Planning, and Control* (Englewood Cliffs, N.J.: Prentice-Hall, Inc., 1967), Chapter X, "Marketing Models and Systems."

The chapter in Cohen and Cyert and the chapter in Kotler are useful introductory discussions of systematic approaches to and uses of models. Cohen and Cyert, the more technical of the two chapters, deals with the role of models in scientific analysis and the meaning and relationship of assumptions and conclusions. In his chapter, Kotler describes the types of models in marketing analysis. Cohen and Cyert should be read before Kotler.

George W. Stocking, "Institutional Factors in Economic Thinking," *American Economic Review*, Vol. 49, March 1959, pp. 1–21.

Much has been made of the technological dynamics of corporate capitalism and the implications for efficiency and consumer welfare. Stocking urges careful, systematic empirical investigation of these and other claims, which sometimes are taken for granted by those who prefer the realm of purely abstract analysis.

Additional Readings

Kenneth E. Boulding, "Economics as a Moral Science," *American Economic Review*, March 1969, pp 1–12.

Robert E. Emmer, *Economic Analysis and Scientific Philosophy* (New York: Humanities Press, Inc., 1967).

2

The pure market economy,
the marketing economy,
and want satisfaction

We begin now the analysis of want satisfaction in our economy—how demanders and suppliers satisfy their respective interests through markets. Chapters 2 and 3 present an overview of markets, marketing, and want satisfaction. The present chapter establishes the meaning and logic of the "market solution" and marketing with respect to a society's economic problems. It discusses and contrasts the pure market economy of classical economic theory and the marketing economy of the real world.

In Chapter 3, we shall examine closely markets as the "points" at which demand and supply come together, and we shall introduce among other topics some fundamental aspects associated with the concepts of "want," "product," and "competition."

AN ECONOMY

Each of us knows—or thinks he knows—what an economy is. But this concept is not easily put into words. One reason for the difficulty is that an economy is not a tangible entity; rather it is an aspect of society, or indeed, perhaps it is a society looked at from a particular point of view. In any case, an *economy* is all-embracing, for it includes the whole set of social rules, customs, and in short, the institutions that control how the members of a society cooperate in making, trading, and using exchangeable goods and services. Thus, each and every activity performed in accordance with these institutions is an economic activity, and all exchangeable goods and services are economic goods or commodities.[1]

Let us turn briefly to the rules, customs, and institutions controlling the exchange of goods and services. Institutions are the societally accepted ways of resolving recurrent problems. Within any economy, there are various institutions—which superficially take many forms. We shall not concern ourselves with many implications of institutions at present—saving some of the discussion for later in this chapter and other discussions for Part II. At this point what is important is that an economy may be understood as a *set* of component institutions—that is, a collection of prescribed behavior for performing required tasks.[2]

Division of Labor: A Basic Economic Institution

The division of labor is the most fundamental of all the institutions that constitute an economy. Specialization or division of labor is universal and very ancient: archeologists and anthropologists have not yet encountered a society that was so primitive that its life was not enriched by having some members function as hunters, some as priests, some are warriors, some as builders.[3]

Division of labor is not necessarily an all-or-nothing proposition, for frontier families of early America (and yet today in certain parts of the country) were self-sufficient to the extent of providing shelter, food, and clothes. Within virtually any society today one finds a substantial range of economic self-sufficiency—at the upper end of which, families choose to depend on "specialists" such as cooks, butlers, maids, chauffeurs, as well as a range of other retail agencies for all of their consumer requirements.

Relatively affluent families have the pleasure of choosing the degree of self-sufficiency they wish, whereas the low-income levels in our society (or any society) obviously *must* depend on their own resourcefulness, public aid, or both. Significantly, most of the inhabitants of the poorer countries of the world today live in a so-called "subsistence sector" where individual families are nearly as self-sufficient as the historical pioneer or frontier family. In general and across all countries, the greater the specialization of production and exchange of commodities among specialists, the greater is the cultural and economic advance. Division of labor is the sine

---

[1] Much of this section of the chapter is drawn on the spirit of Robert Dorfman, *The Price System* (Prentice-Hall, 1964), p. 2 ff. Two other works provided important background for the chapter: Robert L. Heilbroner, *The Making of Economic Society* (Prentice-Hall, 1962); and Robert H. Haveman and Kenyon A. Knopf, *The Market System* (Wiley, 1966).

[2] See A. W. Gouldner and H. P. Gouldner, *Modern Sociology* (Harcourt, Brace & World, 1963), p. 483 ff; Talcott Parsons and Neil J. Smelser, *Economy and Society*, (Free Press, 1956), p. 102; and also see Chapter 4 of the present text.

[3] Dorfman, *op. cit.*, p. 2, is the source of several points in the immediate section.

qua non for the rise and maintenance of cities. And specialization begets further specialization. With the rise of the arts and technologies, ever more specialization is required to take advantage of expensive, highly specialized equipment and fields of knowledge and skills demanding many years of study. Efficient specialists constitute one type of external economy to any participant in marketing.[4]

Can we summarize with numbers some idea of the specialization our economy has developed? One set of statistics is provided by the U.S. Census. At present, the government recognizes more than 15,000 trades, occupations, and specialties. As to "separate industries," at only a moderate degree of detail, there are over 400 different manufacturing industries. These are in addition to scores of branches of agriculture, mining, construction, distributive trades, and services of many types.

Risks and Problems of Interdependency

There is a curious dichotomy attendant with the division of labor in as highly advanced an economy as ours. We recognize that specialization affords us an opportunity for an ease of material life. But there are several other implications of this extreme dependence of the individual in his search for the means of existence. Left to our own devices, few Americans could—short of stealing—sustain themselves by individual effort. The overwhelming majority of Americans have never grown food, caught game, made clothes, built homes, and so on. Indeed, for urban, dependent man, one of the attractions of camping, or otherwise "roughing it" is a demonstration of sorts of his ability to confront and conquer wildness. (With sufficient mosquito repellant, dehydrated food, and plenty of dry matches modern man can eke out limited victories over nature.) For that matter, even minor repairs are beyond the knowledge and abilities of most Americans. Thus, we vitally depend on other members of the community.

What are the risks of interdependency? With our sophisticated technologies and substantial economies of scale in many industries, it takes relatively few individuals to provide us fully with various goods and services. For example, we approximately 200 million citizens of the United States depend on only 180,000 men to provide us with our coal; fewer than 75,000 men to run the locomotives which haul the freight and passengers; and less than 15,000 total of pilots and navigators for our commercial aircraft.[5]

---

[4] We shall discuss external economies in the form of commercial specialists in our analysis of agencies and channels of distribution. For a useful summary discussion of specialization and external economies, see George Stigler, "The Division of Labor is Limited by the Extent of the Market," *The Journal of Political Economy* (June 1951), Vol. LIX, No. 3, pp. 185–93, reprinted in Perry Bliss (ed.), *Marketing and the Behavioral Sciences* (Allyn and Bacon, 1963).

[5] R. L. Heilbroner, *op. cit.*, p. 4.

Labor unions frequently need not be large to shut down a complete industry, and management counters by bargaining with labor through industry associations representing all the firms in the industry. In this atmosphere the dependent citizens wait out the power-bloc bargaining. Freedom of bargaining is consistent with the ideas of free society—but our economic interdependency understandably induces Congressmen and Senators to try to ward off the ability of any one labor or management group to affect for any period of time large areas of the economy.

Heilbroner has highlighted the complex web of our interdependency:

> We are rich not as individuals, but as members of a rich society, and our easy assumption of material sufficiency is actually only as reliable as the bonds which forge us into a social whole.[6]

How do we effect coordination of the literally thousands upon thousands of specialists in our society? We shall turn now to this question.

THE FUNDAMENTAL ECONOMIC PROBLEM[7]

The basic problem of economics and hence the basic problem of positive analysis in marketing is the problem of how societies forge and maintain the bonds which guarantee their material survival. The necessary struggle for existence is *the* economic problem in any society. The economic problem derives ultimately from the scarcity of nature, for if there were no scarcity, goods would be as free as air and the struggle for existence would cease.

Yet, while nature's stringency underlies scarcity, man also is a source of many of our economic problems. In an industrialized, wealthy society, man and nature combine to create scarcity.

> If Americans today, for instance, were content to live at the level of Mexican peasants, all our material wants could be fully satisfied with but an hour or two of daily labor. We would experience little or no scarcity, and our economic problems would virtually disappear. Instead, we find in America—and indeed in all industrial societies—that as the ability to increase nature's yield has risen, so has the reach of human wants. In fact, in societies such as ours, where relative social status is importantly connected with the possession of material goods, we often find that 'scarcity' as a psychological experience and good becomes more pronounced as we grow wealthier: our desires to possess the

---

[6] *Ibid.*

[7] For several of the central ideas in this section the authors are indebted to Heilbroner, *op. cit.*, and Haveman and Knopf, *op. cit.*

fruits of nature race out ahead of our mounting ability to produce goods.[8]

We see that *the* economic problem—the struggle for existence—derives from scarcity which is the joint result of nature and humans. What then are the functions which social organizations must perform to bring both humans and the stringency of nature into social harness? Or, what amounts to the same thing, what are the functions which social organization must perform to coordinate its many specialists in the face of scarcity? This fundamental problem involves the solution of three important component problems: *What* goods and services shall the society produce? *How* shall society produce the goods and services?—since there are alternative techniques and different combinations of resources which may be used to produce a good or service; and *For Whom* shall the goods and services be produced?—that is, who receives what quantity of the goods and services? The first two problems, those of What and How, we shall call the "production problem" and the latter problem, For Whom, the "distribution problem."

Production Problem

Somehow a society must organize a system for producing the goods and services it needs for its own perpetuation. The problem is to devise social institutions which will mobilize human energy for productive purposes. A viable economic society is one which can overcome the stringencies of nature as well as the intransigence of human nature.

What to Produce?

The choice of what to produce is the first of the two production problems within the total economic problem. At any time, a society has a fixed amount of resources available to produce the things its citizens may want. That is, at any time, it has a fixed amount of land, labor, factories, machinery and so on, which it can use to produce goods and services. Clearly, if all of its resources are employed, a society can produce *more* of any good or service only by producing *less* of some other good or service. It is just as clear that if all of its resources are *not* fully employed, the society, in principle, can produce more of all goods and services—up to the point of full employment of all resources—before a choice-problem arises.

---

[8] Heilbroner, *op. cit.*, p. 5. Heilbroner's point is true especially if "to live at the level of Mexican peasants" implies little or no demand for public goods such as education, good roads, inexpensive electric power, unpolluted streams and so on. That increased personal wealth incites further desire for material expressions of wealth *as well as* even more wealth is an essential point in John K. Galbraith's *The Affluent Society* (Houghton Mifflin, 1958). Galbraith decries the allocation of so many resources to the satisfying of private needs when it means that many public needs such as education and aid to poverty will be underemphasized.

In a society in which resources are fully employed there obviously are trade-offs between the additional production of a good or service and all other goods and services. Analytically, these trade-offs are illustrated in "production possibilities curves" wherein a curve concave to the origin indicates the various outputs of two goods or services. Figure 2.1 illustrates the "guns or butter" trade-off, a contemporary illustration suggesting the kind of choice in allocating resources to defense purposes or domestic programs.[9] It is *not only* capacity which determines what to produce. Later in the chapter we shall discuss the three major types of economic organizations and how in each the *what* problem is solved.

FIGURE 2.1

A HYPOTHETICAL PRODUCTION POSSIBILITIES CURVE SHOWING HOW SOCIETY CAN SUBSTITUTE "BUTTER" FOR "GUNS," ASSUMING A CONSTANT STATE OF TECHNOLOGY AND A GIVEN TOTAL STOCK OF RESOURCES.

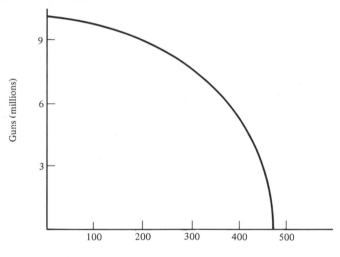

Butter (millions of pounds)

How to Produce?

To ensure a sufficient quantity of effort and hence output, the society must assure the proper allocation of effort. The problem of *how to* produce

[9] For elaboration of production possibilities or transformation curves see Paul Samuelson, *Economics: An Introductory Analysis* (5th ed., McGraw-Hill, 1961), pp. 19–24. For an example more rich in economic implications, see the discussion of the production possibilities curve between capital goods and consumer goods, Haveman and Knopf, *op. cit.*, pp. 4–8. A decision to forgo some production of consumer goods by producing more capital goods, is of course, a decision in favor of *future* consumer goods. In its post-war push to catch up to Western economies, the Soviet Union minimized the allocation of resources to consumer goods so as to develop capital-goods strength. The decision, while immediately distressing to consumers, permitted the Soviets a broader capital base on which to produce capital and consumer goods. In recent times, the Soviet economy has become considerably more consumer oriented.

is the problem of choosing the most efficient combination of resources for the production of any good or service. Again by simplifying what is a complex decision, we can illustrate the character of this choice.

We observe that in a society in which there is scarcity, that is, one in which there are competing claims made on all resources, each resource has a cost to the user. Thus, labor may be "purchased" at so many dollars per hour, machinery may be purchased at so much per unit, and so on. The particular price of any resource is the result of the complex supply and demand forces—the availability of the particular resource and the amount and intensity of desire for the resource.

A second fact, which was implied above, is that any particular level of output—for example, 100,000 pairs of a particular grade of men's leather shoes—may be produced with various combinations of resources. In general, any given level of output of virtually any product may be produced by various combinations of capital and labor, the two basic factors. Figure 2.2 illustrates the *how* choice, showing the equal-product (or isoquant) curve.

FIGURE 2.2

CHOICE OF HOW TO PRODUCE: THE EQUAL-OUTPUT CURVE. ALL THE POINTS ON THE CURVE REPRESENT THE DIFFERENT COMBINATIONS OF CAPITAL AND LABOR THAT CAN BE USED TO PRODUCE THE SAME 100,000 PAIRS OF SHOES. AT THE EXTREMES, IT TAKES VERY LARGE CHANGES IN LABOR PER REDUCED UNIT OF CAPITAL, AND VICE VERSA, TO HOLD OUTPUT CONSTANT. THE LAW OF VARIABLE PROPORTIONS (DIMINISHING RETURNS) UNDERLIES THESE RELATIONSHIPS.

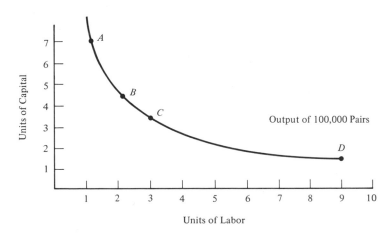

With various factor-of-production combinations possible and with each combination uniquely associated with a corresponding factor cost, the *how to* problem is precisely that of selecting the least-cost factor combination to attain the given *output* level. The problem of maximizing efficiency can also be stated as attaining the greatest output level with any given level of *cost*.[10]

As we shall discuss in Part IV, marketing-management decisions essentially are decisions as to various combinations of the use of price variations and promotion, product, and distribution-channel expenditures to attain the firm's market goals. Just as Figure 2.2 suggests, a marketing manager may attain a sales goal for example, by using more and more promotion and less and less product improvement and distribution channels, *but* because of the law of diminishing returns, for the manager to attain the same sales level, beyond some point he will have to spend *disproportionately* on promotion *per decrease* in expenditures on product and distribution channels.

Demand or the Distribution Problem

The distribution problem is *for whom* goods and services are produced. To ensure its steady material replenishment, a society must parcel out its production so as to maintain not only the capacity but the willingness to go on working. In the case of the peasant who feeds himself and his family from his own crop, the requirement of adequate distribution may seem simple enough. But beyond the most primitive society, the problem is not always so readily solved.

> In many of the poorest nations of the East and South, urban workers have often been unable to deliver their daily horsepower-hour of work because they have not been given enough of society's output to run their human engines to capacity. Worse yet, they have often languished on the job while granaries bulged with grain and the well-to-do complained of the ineradicable 'laziness' of the masses. At the other side of the picture, the distribution mechanism may fail because the rewards it hands out do not succeed in persuading people to perform their necessary tasks.[11]

Any society must have some institutional arrangement to answer the question: For whom are the goods produced? That is: Who has the ability (means) to purchase goods and services? There may be different answers in different societies, with the product uniformly distributed among the members in one, or with varying degrees of inequality in others.

A Lorenz curve in general is an analytical tool used to describe degrees of inequality within any population. Figure 2.3 is a Lorenz curve indicating the degree of inequality in the distribution of income. Through the past

[10] For a discussion of the theory of production and equal-product curves see Samuelson, *op. cit.*, Chapter 26 and appendix; and for a briefer introduction see Haveman, *op. cit.*, pp. 8–10.

[11] Heilbroner, *op. cit.*, p. 8.

few decades in this country, income inequality has been lessening; graphically, the curve has become less bowed.[12]

FIGURE 2.3

CHOICE OF FOR WHOM TO PRODUCE: HYPOTHETICAL EXAMPLE EMPLOYING THE LORENZ CURVE. IF THE CURVE IS BOWED TOWARD THE PEOPLE AXIS, AS IN THE FIGURE ABOVE, THE DISTRIBUTION IS UNEQUAL. THE MORE BOWED THE CURVE, THE GREATER THE INEQUALITY— AT THE LIMIT, THE CURVE IS A 90° ANGLE, INDICATING ABSOLUTE INEQUALITY. AND OF COURSE, PERFECTLY EQUAL DISTRIBUTION OF INCOME IS REPRESENTED BY THE DIAGONAL LINE WHICH BISECTS THE ORIGIN.

Distribution of Income in the United States, 1964 (Lorenz Curve)

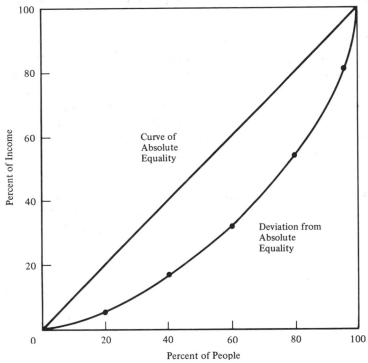

SOURCE: Paul A. Samuelson, *Economics: An Introductory Analysis*, 7th ed. (N.Y.: McGraw-Hill Book Co., 1967), p. 110.

THE THREE SOLUTIONS TO THE ECONOMIC PROBLEM

The economic problem in all societies is the struggle for existence—a struggle necessitated by scarcity. Essentially society is an elaborate mecha-

[12] For a discussion of the *for whom* problem see, Samuelson, *op. cit.*, Part IV, which deals with the pricing of the productive factors, and also Chapter 6, "Individual and Family Income," where he discusses the distribution of income in the U.S. and utilizes a Lorenz-curve diagram. The principle of the Lorenz curve is briefly described in Haveman, *op. cit.*, pp. 10–11.

nism for survival, in large part a mechanism for accomplishing the complicated tasks of production and distribution necessary for social continuity.

Among the diverse contemporary societies as well as among societies
throughout all history, there are (and have been) but *three* principal ways
in which man has succeeded in solving the production and distribution
problems. That is, within the many different actual social institutions which
guide and shape the economic process, there are only three general types
of systems which separately or in combination enable societies to solve
economic problems. These three types are economies run by *tradition*,
economies run by *command*, and economies run by the *market*.[13]

Tradition

Tradition-based social organization is perhaps the oldest and, until
recently, the most common way of solving the economic problem. In the
tradition solution, production and distribution are based on procedures
devised in the distant past. These historic procedures have been rigidified
by a long process of trial and error and have been maintained by heavy
sanctions of law, custom, and belief.

The tradition solution is a very "manageable," but also is a very static
solution to the economic problem. It is manageable because the production
problem of assuring that necessary tasks will be done is solved by assigning
the jobs of fathers to their sons. Thus, one was born to the soil or to a
trade, and on the soil or within the trade, one followed in the footsteps of
his forebears.

Tradition has been the stabilizing and impelling force behind a great
repetitive cycle of society, assuring that society's work would be done very
much as it had been done in the past. Until recently, India had a caste
system which predestined one to an occupation of the particular caste. The
Bhagavad-Gita, the great philosophic moral poem of India, preached:
"Better thine own work is, though done with fault, than doing other's work,
even excellently."

A solution to the distribution problem is also provided by tradition.
Many societies, for example, primitive societies which depend on their
hunting prowess for their livelihood, have traditional patterns of dividing
the kill.[14] And tradition has often allocated to women, in nonindustrial
societies, the most meager portion of the social product.

Even in America, tradition plays a role in solving production and
distribution problems. For example, much of the actual process of selecting
an employment in our society is heavily influenced by tradition, as in
families in which sons follow their fathers into a profession or a business.

---

[13] This discussion is based in part on the excellent treatment by Heilbroner, *op. cit.*,
pp. 9–17.

[14] See Gouldner, *op. cit.*, on Malinowski's study of primitive cultures.

Tradition also dissuades us from certain employments. By tradition, sons of American middle-class families do not usually seek factory work, even though factory jobs may pay better than office jobs, for "bluecollar employment" is not in the middle-class tradition.

We have said tradition is a static solution to production and distribution. It is obvious why this is so. A society which follows the path of tradition is necessarily *backward* looking—it regulates its economic affairs at the expense of large-scale rapid social and economic change. When change occurs in tradition-bound societies, it is due mainly to externally induced causes; hence, typically it is *not* self-generated change.

Command

Under the command solution, the problem of economic continuity is solved by imposed authority, by economic decree. This solution, possessing an ancient lineage, is based not so much on the changeless reproduction of a system as was tradition; rather it is based on the organization of a system according to the orders of an economic peak coordinator, an economic commander-in-chief. Frequently, one finds this authoritarian economic control superimposed upon a traditional social base. For example, the Pharaohs of Egypt exerted their economic dictates above the timeless cycle of traditional agricultural practice on which the Egyptian economy was based. By their economic command, the rulers of Egypt marshalled the effort which built the pyramids, temples, and roads.

One finds the mode of authoritarian economic organization in ancient China in, for example, the building of the Great Wall; in the works of ancient Rome; and today, in the dictates of the communist economic authorities. And in less severe form, we find economic command today in our own society—for example, in the form of *taxes* (a preemption, albeit through legislative processes, of part of our income by public authorities for public purposes).

Economic command is far less static than the tradition solution. Indeed, in times of crises, such as war or famine, it may be the only way in which a society can organize its manpower or distribute its goods effectively. Following a great natural disaster, we often declare martial law.

Unlike tradition, command has no inherent effect of slowing down economic change. For that matter, authority is *the* most powerful instrument society has for enforcing economic change. Through the command solution Russia and China, for example, were both able to bring about radical alterations in the systems of production and distribution (so far, at least, with dissimilar results).

No modern society is without its elements of economic command, just as no society has eliminated all vestiges of tradition. Clearly, economic command exercised in a democratic society is far different from that exercised in a totalitarian society. If tradition is the brake on economic change, so economic command can be the great instrument of change. In achieving social stability and change, both tradition and command have their places. Through history, tradition and command solutions have been the primary approaches utilized to solve the production and distribution problems.

Market

The third of the three solutions to the economic problem is the *market* organization of society. The market solution allows society to solve the problems of production and distribution with a minimum of recourse either to tradition or command.

The essence of a market economy is that each and every person is allowed always to pursue the best economic opportunities open to him. Collectively, the self-seeking society through the impersonal, intangible "market" solves the economic problem. What precisely is the market-economy solution to the economic problem?

A market economy is an economic system controlled, regulated, and directed by markets alone; order in the production and distribution of goods is entrusted to this self-regulating mechanism. An economy of this kind derives from the expectation that human beings behave in such a way as to achieve maximum money gains. It assumes markets in which the supply of goods (including services) available at a definite price will equal the demand at that price. It assumes the presence of money, which functions as purchasing power in the hands of its owners. Production will then be controlled by prices, for the profits of those who direct production will depend upon them; the distribution of the goods also will depend upon prices, for prices form incomes, and it is with the help of these incomes that the goods produced are distributed amongst the members of society. Under these assumptions order in the production and distribution of goods is ensured by prices alone.[15]

Some Elements of the Pure Market Economy

The first and most fundamental element of a pure market economy is of course the centrality of "markets." In the pure market economy, it is through markets that every good or service and every factor of production—land, labor, and capital—are valued in terms of *prices*. A market economy, in short, is a system of markets and prices. Indeed, many economists use the term "price system" as a synonym for the market economy.[16]

---

[15] Karl Polanyi, *The Great Transformation* (Beacon Press, 1957), pp. 68–69 (paperback); Polanyi's statement, quoted from an earlier edition of *The Great Transformation*, may be found along with other comments on the market economy in E. A. Duddy and D. A. Revzan, *Marketing: An Institutional Approach* (McGraw-Hill, 1953), pp. 2–6.

[16] See for example, the excellent, brief survey of the market economy in Dorfman, *op. cit.*, (We shall analyze thoroughly the meaning of "market" in Chapter 3.)

A second element of a market economy is that not only is all production for sale on the market, but all incomes derive from such sales. Every member of a market society necessarily relates to the market either for goods and services with which to satisfy his wants or for the sale of commodities or factors of production he owns.

Third, the market mechanism need have little recourse to tradition or command for it utilizes the motive of *economic self-interest*, or maximization of well-being and income, in a society based on the monetization of tasks and mobility of the factors of production.

Fourth, the motive of self-interest drives the factors of production into those employments where they will fare best. As the impersonal forces of supply and demand, operating through markets, raise or lower the rewards, land, labor, and capital are automatically directed to uses society desires most.

Fifth, a market society depends for control not only on the motive of self-interest, but also on the institution of competition. Seller competition— the rivalry among sellers—protects the customer by driving prices down toward costs of production. Competition exerts a similar restraint on buyers. Bidding between buyers keeps prices from going below costs of production. The competitive mechanisms work not only in the market for products, but also in factor markets—where the roles are reversed. Thus, the competitive struggle assures that prices will control behavior. In the give and take, prices of goods and of factors will tend to swing back and forth, but in the long run, competition among buyers and competition among sellers will bring prices back toward costs of production. Competition is an economic balancer, for it tends to prevent rewards in one field from being out of line with rewards in another.

Sixth, the customer in a pure market society, exercises a final sovereignty in determining the goods which will be produced. It is customers' collective spending in the market place which gives the price signals that guide society's producers. It is precisely so in the model of the pure market economy—the customer is *sovereign*; he truly reigns.[17]

MARKET FORCES

The market price of any good or service is determined by the interaction of demand and supply—portrayed by the intersection of DD and SS in Figure 2.4. We must remember that supply and demand in the real world *always* determine price; the caveat is that in some markets supply or demand are under some control—hence there may be a personal rather than impersonal character to S or D. But, whatever the market structure,

[17] The preceding list of important elements of a market economy is drawn in part from the statement of Polanyi and from Heilbroner, *op. cit.*, p. 68.

the general statement holds. In perfect competition supply and demand cannot be influenced by any seller—hence, markets at times adjust quickly and impersonally to changes in input prices and demand functions. On the other hand, in some markets in the real world, there are only a few or perhaps only one seller controlling supply and demand. Nevertheless, there is *still* supply and demand, and they *interact* to determine price. For example, the old axiom among some retailers, "Charge what the traffic will bear" implies adjusting supply to correspond to the inelastic portion of the consumers' demand curve.

Thus, to summarize supply and demand as underlying all market behavior,

> (T)he patterns of demand and supply include and reflect the degree of competition and monopoly in any market—the idea of a price 'other than that set by supply and demand' is simply a verbal misunderstanding. Price is *always* set by supply and demand, but either or both may be under monopoly control.[18]

In Figure 2.4, from the intersection of *DD* and *SS*, the resulting price and quantity are respectively the equilibrium price (P_E) and equilibrium quantity (Q_E), so called because neither the price nor the quantity traded is under pressure to change. P_E is the price at which buyers are willing to go on buying and sellers are willing to go on selling, for demand precisely equals supply.

But what does this mean? Is not the quantity one man sells precisely the quantity another man buys? Is there not always "equilibrium" in the sense the amount sold always equals the amount purchased? Yes, of course: What is bought and what is sold is always a *statistical identity*. But equilibrium is a special condition.

> [The] important question is this: at what price will the amount that consumers are *willing to go on buying* be just matched by the amount that producers are *willing to go on selling*? At such a price where there is equality between the scheduled amounts that suppliers and demanders want to go on buying and selling, and only at such a P, will there be no tendency for price to rise or fall. At any other price such as the case where P is above the intersection of supply and demand, it is a trivial fact that whatever goods change hands will show a statistical identity of measured amount bought and sold.[19]

[18] M. A. Adelman, "Pricing by Manufacturers" in *Proceeding of Conference of Marketing Teachers from Far Western States* (University of California, 1958), p. 147 (emphasis added). Pricing in imperfect markets is largely a problem in acquiring and interpreting information. "(A) price is determined in a market and . . . a market is a system of information on cost and demand, a set of signals which the business firm must learn to read as best he can." *Ibid.*, pp. 147–148.

[19] Samuelson, *op. cit.*, p. 71.

FIGURE 2.4

EQUILIBRIUM PRICE AND QUANTITY.

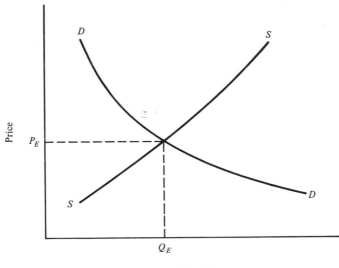

Quantity

It is this balancing of forces, this perpetual tendency toward equilibrium, which is known as the "law of supply and demand." A market may be said to be "cleared" when all traders are satisfied with the market price—that is, when there is no seller bidding down the price nor any buyer bidding up the price. We come then to the meaning of "shortage" and "surplus" or respectively "excess demand" and "excess supply." For example in Figure 2.5, P_E is the price at which demand and supply are equal, the price at which the market is cleared. P_1 is a price above P_E, and is a price which leads to a quantity supplied, Q_S, exceeding the quantity demanded, Q_D. The difference in the two quantities ($OQ_S - OQ_D$) is the amount of the excess supply, the surplus. The price will be bid down to P_E (or S will decrease in the L-R), but the important point is that there is a "surplus" or a "shortage" *only when* the market price is respectively above or below the equilibrium price. (The reader should consider also the case of "excess demand" that is, a "shortage," and consider why and how price will be bid up to P_E.)

Why do we bring in at this point the concepts "shortage" and "surplus"? We do so primarily because they are illustrative market aspects to be understood if one is to appreciate market forces (and absence of forces) in our own *impure* market economy. For example, one hears much about "water shortages," but unfortunately the demand concept is often ignored or overlooked with the result that public policy becomes confused. The typical view is to the so-called "need" for water, not to the demand for it. From our review the student can appreciate Watson's statement:

Obviously, if the price of water were higher, less of it would be used in households, in industry, and in agriculture. When the price of water is adjusted so that the amount available is equal to the demand *at that price*, there can be no shortage. The future might hold the prospect of more expensive water, but proper pricing policies will prevent 'shortages.'[20]

Having reviewed briefly the manner in which price rations supply and demand and hence the way market forces generally solve the Production and Distribution problems, we shall turn to the role of the customer in a market economy.

FIGURE 2.5

EXCESS SUPPLY.

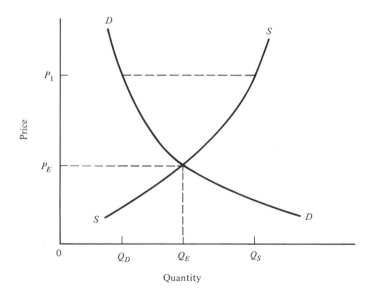

Quantity

Consumer Sovereignty

When we discussed the Production problem earlier in the chapter, the *what to produce* problem was couched largely as a capacity problem— production-possibility curves. *What* to produce is only a minor problem in the premarket economies, for what one produces in a tradition society is largely already established. Technological and political considerations are paramount in command societies. However, in a market economy the decision of what to produce is transmitted to the suppliers by the actions of demanders in markets. Suppliers and potential suppliers of goods for which there is a demand, respond to the demand. The resulting interplay

[20] D. S. Watson, *Price Theory and Its Uses* (Boston: Houghton Mifflin, 1968), pp. 26–27.

of supply and demand determines the price that they receive and that which demanders must pay. With the price high relative to other opportunities, the resources are attracted to this market. Their entry—an increase in the number of suppliers—increases supply, that is, shifts the supply curve to the right, making for a lower price.

In the *pure* market economy, the customer is absolutely sovereign: Supply responds to the wants of society, to the millions of daily as well as anticipated votes in the market, the economic voting booth.

> In this way the market society catapults the consumer into a position of extraordinary importance. On his ability and willingness to buy hinges the schedule of demands which confront society's producers. If consumers do not want a good or service, or if they do not wish to buy it at its offered price, that good or service will go unsold. In that case, the production effort needed to supply it will not pay for itself and will soon terminate. *In a market society the consumer is the ultimate formulator of the pattern of economic activity.*[21]

We single out consumer sovereignty for two reasons. First, in a market economy, in principle, consumer sovereignty determines what will be produced. Second, in our own culture wherein personal freedom is highly valued, the question of the *degree to which* the consumer (each of us) is truly sovereign is an extremely important question in which no one is (or should be) uninterested. Consumer well-being is so important a set of issues that we devote the entire last chapter of the book to it.

THE PURE MARKET ECONOMY IS NOT THE REAL WORLD

The real world, the world in which we live, is *not* a pure market economy. Although we in the U.S. rely in large part on the market solution, our economy is a mixed or "impure" market economy. It is what we call a marketing economy.

The *pure* market economy implies a basis of perfect competition—a situation in which the complete competitive checks and balances are present. In general, it is a case in which no farmer, businessman, or laborer has any personal influence on market price. Technically, perfect (or complete) competition is a market structure characterized by many firms selling completely homogeneous products such that no firm can perceptibly affect price; the firms and consumers have perfect knowledge of the market; and resources are perfectly mobile. This clearly is *not* the real world.

Our Mixed or Impure Market Economy

Our economic society is impure—specifically, *mixed* in two senses. First, the prevailing mode of competition is imperfect or monopolistic

[21] Heilbroner, *op. cit.*, p. 67, (emphasis in original). Also see Haveman, *op. cit.*, pp. 144–150.

competition, *not* perfect competition. With the exception of the many farmers who produce but a negligible share of the total crop, virtually all businessmen have some ability (although perhaps minimal in many cases) to affect the price in a market. Indeed, it is rational for them to try to do so. As we shall discuss in Part IV, the essence of marketing management is the attempt to shift *outward* and as well as increase the *inelasticity* of the demand curves for most or all of the firm's products.[22] Competition in the real world is not that of perfect competition, because in many markets there are few, not many firms; and/or most firms are not selling perfectly homogeneous products—rather, in one or more senses they are differentiated; and/or neither the firms nor the customers have perfect (complete) knowledge of the market; and/or resources are not perfectly (immediately and frictionlessly) mobile.

The second sense in which ours is a mixed economy is that elements of governmental control are intermingled with market elements in solving the production and distribution problems. Democratic countries that are not satisfied with the market solution to the problems of production and distribution in providing more public services such as roads, hospitals, and libraries, let alone national defense, maintenance of law and order, and the guarantee under law of equal opportunities and justice effect solutions through nonmarket means. Government is also empowered to set restraints on the economic activity of firms, prohibiting acts such as price-fixing, and fraudulent and misleading product claims.

The logic of the pure market economy is straightforward and compelling. Little wonder that it serves as the analytical ideal to which real-world results are compared. But, once again, the pure market economy *does not and never did exist.*[23]

Let us, in passing, make an important point, to which we shall return in the chapters on social perspectives of marketing. The most critical element

---

[22] As we shall discuss in Part IV a firm may increase demand for some of its products by increasing and/or exploiting the elasticity of other of its products—so that the latter are used as traffic or demand builders.

[23] For a summary of some departures of our economy from a *pure* market economy, see the preceding chapter and Robert Dorfman, *The Price System* (Prentice Hall, 1964), p. 13. Professor John Kenneth Galbraith in his book, *The New Industrial State* (Houghton Mifflin, 1967), argues that, if anything, our economy will move even *farther* from reliance on markets as the solution to the economic problem. Moreover, he believes that public policy, such as antitrust, is completely futile, because, in view of "technological imperatives" *inter alia*, small-firm competition is no longer possible. In short, the market is dead.

Galbraith's arguments are stimulating, but not always supported by hard facts. For a strong rebuttal to Galbraith—a rebuttal representative of many economists—see the comments of Dr. Willard F. Mueller, Director, Bureau of Economics, Federal Trade Commission, before the Select Committee on Small Business, United States Senate, June 29, 1967, and also those of Assistant Attorney General Donald Turner and Professor Walter Adams, *loc. cit.*

See also E. T. Grether, "Galbraith Versus the Market: A Review Article," *Journal of Marketing*, Vol. 32, January, 1968, pp. 9–13.

in the *pure* market economy is that human beings act in order to maximize money gains or utility; thus, as owners of factors and/or products they will sell only in the market of highest bidding. In reality, most people, owing to human nature, do not "maximize" anything (even if they had the information and ability to calculate precisely).[24] Even so, economic organization *can* come close to the classical ideal. In our mixed or marketing economy, *if* there is sufficient information and ability of factors to move into and out of markets in response to information on opportunities, rivalry *can* be maintained, resources *can* be efficiently allocated, and our marketing economy *can* solve the economic problem. There are many varieties and degrees of "imperfection"—therefore the reader must not be too hasty to cast judgments on the "workability" of our mixed economy—simply because the *pure* market economy does not, in all senses, exist. The real (impure) economy, coupled with some judicious public policy, may allocate resources surprisingly efficiently. One will want to weigh the facts carefully so as not to underestimate its innate capacity.

IMPURITIES AND THE NECESSITY FOR MORE COMPLEX FORMS OF MARKETING

We shall now show how the various departures from the ideal have necessitated complex activities associated with transactions—that is, complex marketing. In the *pure* market economy, markets perfectly solve the economic problem. Buyers and sellers fulfill their desires without difficulty because in that framework of complete information, complete mobility of resources, and undifferentiated factors and products, supply and demand easily and fully are matched. Although there necessarily is "marketing" in the pure market economy, it is different in scope, as well as partly in type, from that evidenced in the real-world or marketing economy.

We recall from the preceding that all of the real-world "impurities" fall into either of two categories: (1) government replacing or supplementing private enterprise; and (2) markets which are not complete, that is, perfectly competitive.

The major marketing implication of "impurities" is that want satisfaction is not automatic. The impurities necessitate some marketing tasks not required in the pure model. For wants to be satisfied, in our economy, resource frictions and technological, spatial, and temporal gaps must be overcome. In short, to effect transactions various specific tasks are necessary. For example, in our economy virtually no buyer or seller is perfectly informed about his market opportunities. Participants in the economy require information to know where they, as buyers, can obtain greatest value or as sellers the greatest market return on their sales. But information is not free—one must expend energy and dollars to acquire it. Thus, buyers

24 H. A. Simon, *Administrative Behavior* (2d ed., Macmillan, 1958).

or sellers desiring more information can develop techniques and acquire information themselves, *or* they can purchase it from firms who specialize in the acquisition and sale of information.

Take a second example of an impurity, and hence friction, which must be overcome for want satisfaction to occur. As we recall from the discussion in Chapter 1, specialization of labor is an institution common to all societies. Frequently the specialization in the production of a good is at a location far removed from the customers desiring the particular good. Moreover, frequently, because of the unique scarce resources required, no additional producers can produce other than at the same location. The task clearly is for one or more types of specialists to bridge this physical gap by providing an efficient flow of the product from point of production into the intermediate and ultimate markets.

A third example is directly related to the preceding one. Suppose a consumer wants a new automobile, specifically, a latest model Ford Mustang. The Ford Motor Company in producing Mustangs will, in anticipation of strong demand, produce enough units to attain all possible economies of scale. With respect to the consumers, there will be not only a probable spatial gap between the nearest assembly plant and the consumer, but a quantitative gap as well. The buyer desires one Mustang; the company will have turned out many hundreds of Mustangs. The marketing task on the supply side obviously is that of sorting the supply in qualitative and quantitative terms so as to match appropriately and fully each consumer's demand. One or more types of specialists (including Ford) perform the required tasks, at one or more levels of the marketing channels. We shall return to this point later in the chapter.

THE INSTITUTION OF WANT SATISFACTION

We have discussed the fact that impurities in an economy constitute frictions and hence tasks that must be performed if wants are to be satisfied. Impurities are the logical connection between the pure market economy and the marketing economy—that is, the basis for the more complex forms of marketing in the real world in contrast to the pure market economy.

Let us establish further the concept of the *institution* of want satisfaction. By perceiving want satisfaction as an institution—indeed, a complex hierarchy of institutions—the reader will more easily understand why there are so many types of marketing structures.

Component Institutions

The *marketing institution* in the aggregate, is the creation of utility in all markets in the economy. The creation of utility for specific demanders in specific markets implies component institutions. We have mentioned some of the impurities which distinguish our economy from that of the pure market economy. Conceptually, each *task* that is necessitated to effect transactions is the basis of an institution.

An example will clarify the idea of component institutions. Let us take the institution of *contract*. The institution of contract subsumes the component institutions of *sale* and *lease* (rent), each with various types of agencies at wholesale and retail. The institution of sale in turn subsumes the component institutions of *cash* sale and *credit* sale, with specific structures at wholesale and retail performing them. Credit may be subdivided into the component institutions of *buyer credit* (the product or factor is exchanged for the promise to pay) and *seller credit* (payment to the seller is made prior to the supply of a product or factor). Each may be further specified in terms of component institutions, and so on, finally on down to an irreducible component institution.

What about the performers of the task(s)? The concept *institution*, whatever the level of aggregation, implies agencies, and in particular, agencies in credit in the case of consumer appliances. In the wholesaling institution is the visible form, for example, a wholesaler, but such is *not* the true institution—only a form in which the functions are performed. If we are speaking of the institution of *want satisfaction* in the total economy, the corresponding participants in the institution are *all* business firms, public agencies, and individuals who participate in markets.

For a more specific example, let us take again the institution of credit, a component of the institution of contract. We will look at marketing agencies in credit in the case of consumer appliances. In the wholesaling sector, the institution of credit sales of electrical appliances is performed by various types of agencies. Some of the agencies are the manufacturers selling on credit to wholesalers or directly to the retailers; some are wholesalers selling on credit to the retailers; and a few even are retailers selling on credit to other retailers.

In the retail sector, credit sales of electrical appliances are effected typically by retailers such as department stores, large specialty shops, and manufacturers' retail branches. Drug stores and discount houses are other retailers who frequently sell electrical appliances but who typically do *not* offer credit. Thus, in the wholesale and retail sale of electrical appliances, the institution of credit is engaged in by several but certainly not all agencies. Moreover, among the agencies performing in this or any institution, there will be considerable differences in their internal structures and market behavior.

MATCHING SUPPLY AND DEMAND

The impurities or frictions and the activities to overcome them distinguish the essentially frictionless and therefore relatively simple pure market economy from the marketing economy. We have noted that transactions occur in our economy in many instances only by marketing participants performing one or more tasks which overcome the impurities or frictions.

In the logic of profit maximization, firms overcome impurities as necessary to attain their goals, but in the process create other impurities. As Alderson says, a firm or individual will behave so as to promote the power to act.[25] For example, a firm will attempt to develop the product or factor it is selling such that buyers perceive it as possessing more want satisfaction than other offerings. A favorable customer perception means a firm has gained a differential advantage over its rivals. It means the firm now enjoys, to an extent, some control over demand and supply, which in the short run creates restrictions for other firms. There is in general an incessant effort by firms to overcome impurities to satisfy wants, and to satisfy them better than the competition. The rival firms in turn not only contend with the original impurities and the competitive frictions but strive to create some to their own advantage. In this way competition is the safeguard to customers. Without competitive pressure upon the firms, the particular institutions performed and especially the manner of performance would be solely at the discretion of relaxed, secure sellers (buyers).

Sorting Processes

A useful perspective of marketing is that of *sorting* to which we now turn. Marketing, as all activities relating to transactions, essentially consists of efforts to match supply and demand.[26]

Meaningful and Meaningless Heterogeneity

Customers and consumers acquire factors and products singly and in combination to satisfy their wants. The marketing economy is the complex of institutions through which want satisfaction is effected. Let us now open up the marketing economy or marketing institution to see more clearly the matching of supply and demand.

An assortment is a collection of two or more types of factors or products which either singly or jointly possess want-satisfying ability. Among *all*

[25] Wroe Alderson, *Marketing Behavior and Executive Action* (Irwin, 1957), p. 51. Professor David A. Revzan has described it as the effort of participants in marketing to "maximize their alternatives." It is a completely logical endeavor in a rivalistic system, and leads (in principle) via Adam Smith's concept of the "invisible hand" to the maximum number of feasible alternatives to demanders.

[26] This discussion is based in part on Wroe Alderson, *Marketing Behavior and Executive Action, op. cit.*, pp. 199–227. For additional insight in the institutional complex of matching supply and demand, the interested reader should see F. M. Nicosia, "Marketing and Alderson's Functionalism," *Journal of Business*, XXXV, Oct. 1962; Alderson, "The Analytical Framework for Marketing," in D. J. Duncan (ed.), *Conference of Marketing Teachers from Far Western States, Proceedings* (University of California, 1958); and Alderson, "Factors Governing the Development of Marketing Channels," in B. E. Mallen (ed.) *The Marketing Channel* (New York: Wiley, 1967).

demanders in the economy or among those in any intermediate or ultimate market, or even for any single customer, the total assortments of products is a diverse collection—a heterogeneity. There is great dissimilarity among the assortments as to the particular goods, services, and factors and the wants to which they relate. But let us note, these are not randomly collected by any demander or demanders; they are selected in each instance by customers as items or services possessing want-satisfying ability. In short, each assortment selected by a demander has meaning to him. Generalizing for the entire economy, we may consider the total collection of all assortments held or desired in any all markets as constituting a *meaningful heterogeneity*.

On the supply side, the total collection of land, labor, and capital and products is also an extremely diverse collection. There is great discrepancy among all extant or potential supply items as to the locations, quantities, and combinations in which they either occur naturally or are produced. Accordingly we may describe the radically dissimilar total collections on the supply side as a heterogeneity as well. However, while there is a heterogeneity of collections in both demand and supply, the supply heterogeneity by contrast is *meaningless*, that is, meaningless in terms of utility as the supply *initially* occurs in nature or immediately upon production. In the particular combinations, quantities, and locations in which supply exists either naturally or upon production, supply typically has no necessary immediate form, time, place, and possession utility. There is truly a *gap* between the heterogeneities of supply and demand, a gap composed of information, form, time, space, and technology. Figure 2.6 portrays the gap between the heterogeneity of demand and supply. Marketing must transform meaningless heterogeneity into meaningful heterogeneity. The transformation is the institution of "sorting." Four component institutions are required.

FIGURE 2.6

THE GAP BETWEEN SUPPLY AND DEMAND.

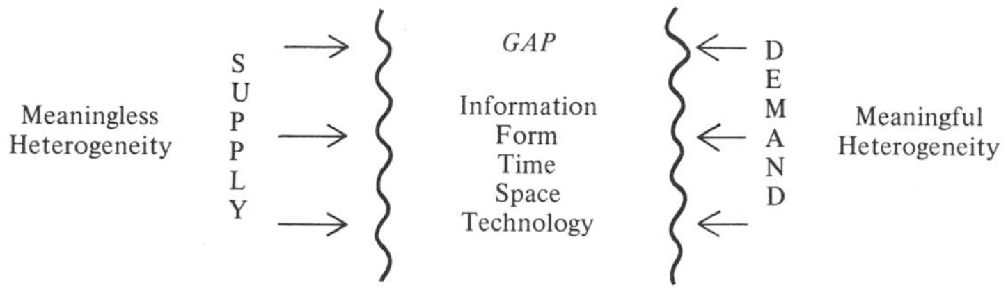

The Component Institutions of Sorting

(1) Sorting Out. The first process in transforming meaningless to meaningful heterogeneity is that of breaking collections into various ho-

mogeneous classes of goods. The breaking down of the collection into homogeneous supplies is based on qualitative and quantitative criteria. For example, in commercial salmon fishing, the catch is broken down along such lines as species, size, and type of subsequent processing; in agricultural commodities, the breaking down of fresh produce is by color, size, freshness, and so on.

What is the explanation for sorting out into homogeneous supplies? Among other reasons, (a) some items must undergo further processing and moreover must be sorted out for particular processing activities; and (b) homogeneous supplies facilitate physical handling, storing, and shipping due to the uniformity within the collection and permit inventory and production efficiencies in subsequent processes.

(2) Accumulation. Given homogeneous supplies, it is possible to create larger supplies by combining homogeneous lots, thereby realizing economies in the handling, storage, and transportation of the item. Because products or factors meeting standard specifications may be combined, the output of different suppliers, such as wheat from all ranches in one area, may be assembled and combined by a single agency. Mass production requires steady flows of the inputs and the outputs. The convenience and economies of steady streams of homogeneous supplies, accumulated into the necessary total supply, are essential elements in mass production and mass marketing.

(3) Allocation. Homogeneous supply is broken down into smaller quantities in conformity with the requirements of each use situation. The relationship between accumulation and allocation for example, is illustrated by a full-service food wholesaler. The wholesaler's warehouse receives carload lots of, say, Tasty brand, canned peas. These homogeneous supplies are accumulated in anticipation of demand for Tasty peas by grocery retailers, restaurants, and other customers of the wholesaler. As demand arises, the homogeneous collection is broken down into smaller quantities as desired and shipped from the warehouse to the customers.

(4) Assorting. The respective homogeneous supplies from several sources, or several different homogeneous supplies from one source, make up a heterogeneous collection intended to match the wants of one or more types of demanders. If the information on the specific demand is accurate and effectively communicated through the supply levels, the building-up or assorting phase of sorting provides the desired *assortment*. Thus, if demand is correctly interpreted and if all processes are accurately carried out, meaningless heterogeneity will have been transformed into meaningful heterogeneity—meaningful in the sense of potentiality for want satisfaction. Matching of supply and demand will have occurred.

Discussion of Sorting

In Figure 2.7 we depict the sorting processes by means of a double-funnel diagram. The double-funnel shape suggests economies in the physical flow: Between the largely qualitative aspects of sorting out and assorting, there occur the two largely quantitative aspects of accumulating and allocating.

FIGURE 2.7

SORTING PROCESSES: MATCHING SUPPLY AND DEMAND. THE CONCEPTUALIZATION IS GENERAL—IT PORTRAYS EITHER A MACRO-VIEW OF GOODS MOVING ACROSS MANY MARKET LEVELS OR A MICRO-VIEW, I.E., A SINGLE MARKET.

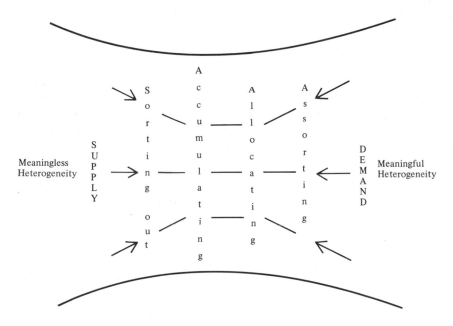

The four institutions of sorting occur time and again in the economy. They can be analyzed at a very aggregate level, spanning many markets, such as wheat moving from ranches to the flour mills, or they can be analyzed in any market, such as a wholesale-grocery firm sorting out, accumulating, allocating, and assorting products for retailers as well as such other wholesale customers as restaurants.

The double-funnel is placed horizontally rather than vertically to connote purposive effort by *both* sellers and buyers. We recall that frequently both sellers and buyers exert effort to effect transactions.

The complete transformation of meaningless to meaningful heterogeneity may occur within a single firm, that is, complete vertical integration, or the sorting processes may be effected by transactions and shipments among a series of firms. Thus, sorting may span several markets or only one.

An example of the latter is a vertically integrated wood-products firm where the firm owns the timber, conducts its own processing of the timber, does its own wholesaling, and owns its own retail lumber yards. For such a firm, the only *external* market is at retail in selling to the ultimate consumer. But the institution of sorting remains the same.

Sorting out, accumulating, allocating, and assorting generally occur in the order listed, although there are variations, depending on competitive constraints and opportunities, internal and external economies, and other internal and external factors.[27] The steps of sorting may occur in other sequences due to additional processing, seasoning, aging, and packaging occurring enroute to intermediate customers and ultimate customers.

The sorting processes are sometimes performed solely by sellers and at times solely by buyers. For example, cash and carry grocery wholesalers charge lower prices than some other agencies because the retailer-customers in effect perform most of their own sorting processes. Retailers pick up the items they require from the wholesaler, paying cash at time of pick up. They simultaneously effect sorting out, accumulation, allocation and assorting. On the other hand, full-service wholesalers perform the bulk of the four institutions for retailers. The ultimate consumer performs one or more sorting processes for himself in retail agencies of the self-service variety.

Discrepancy of Assortments

The most convenient or economical combination of products typically varies at each production or marketing stage in the flow of goods to intermediate and ultimate demanders. This fact of differing optimal assortments has been generalized in the term "discrepancy of assortments."

A product or factor has very different meanings for the seller and the buyer. A consumer views a product in terms of its possession and use utility; whereas, a rational producer, although continuously sensitive to the demand for the good or service, views a product as a *technological* element in his operation. The ideal specifications of a product from the standpoint of a producer would be those which made most effective use of his plant capacity, his labor, and other resources. Managers will attempt to maximize the productivity of their extant resources. This desire frequently leads firms to diversify into other goods and services which more fully utilize production and marketing capacity. Some products are happenstances—produced as by-products in the production of other products. For example, either mutton is a valuable by-product of producing wool, or wool is a valuable by-product of producing mutton. They come together. Examples of both economical production combinations and joint products are numerous.

A product belongs largely to the "technology of production" at the

---

[27] See Chapter 6 with respect to external economies and agency and channel structures.

supply stages and belongs to the "technology of use" at the customer end of the stages. Discrepancies or differences in optimal assortments are not "undesirable" phenomena to overcome. The reader will recall that the process of accumulation is the building up of homogeneous stocks—in some senses serving to increase discrepancies. The reason, as we pointed out, is that in many tasks there are possibilities for economies of scale; hence, specialization in the task provides the increasing returns to scale. Goods are combined for transportation because of handling characteristics as well as common origin and destination. Intermediate inventories of goods frequently are created because of similarities in storage requirements, additional processing, financing arrangements, and so on. Hence, discrepancies frequently are effected and even enlarged in exploiting economies.

Discrepancies of assortments whether for reasons of convenience or economies limit to an extent the possibilities for vertical integration. If the optimal scale including assortment is approximately similar in successive stages—there is an economic opportunity for vertical integration. However, successively smaller scales or successively larger scales sometimes create substantial difficulties for single control or ownership of all stages.

It is also true however, that scale economies are not necessarily the sole or even primary determinant of vertical integration.[28] Vertical integration is but one structural pattern which may increase a firm's productivity and efficiency. Firms under strong competitive pressure must increase their efficiency, and they continually consider various structural arrangements for increased savings. Frequently, firms will *dis*integrate, that is, retract from on-going vertical integration believing that contracting out to specialists is more efficient, less risky, or both, than performing personally the larger number of activities.

An advanced marketing economy is characterized by a diverse set of vertical and horizontal patterns—ranging from complete vertical integration to single-level firms, from broad assortment to narrow or single-line assortments, from far-flung and extensive diversification to concentrated and intensive diversification, from many-establishment chain stores to single-establishment operations, and so on. Specialization need not necessarily require an independent agency, for large firms can specialize within divisions. This point is frequently overlooked in assessing diversified firms. Advanced societies tend to have more specialization of labor than the less advanced, and as a consequence they possess a vast array of structures in which the specialization is embodied.[29]

---

[28] The determinants of vertical integration and other marketing-channel structures are discussed in Part II.

[29] Thus we believe the following statement by Alderson is too *limited*:

"An advanced marketing economy is characterized by intermediary sellers who intervene between the original source of supply and the ultimate consumer."

Marketing Behavior and Executive Action, op. cit., p. 211.

The fact of specialization occurring *within* multiprocess or diversified firms is a

SUMMARY

An *economy* is all embracing for it includes the whole system of social rules, customs and institutions that controls how the members of a society cooperate in making and trading goods and services. Division of labor is the most fundamental of all the institutions constituting an economy. From primitive societies to the present, specialization of activity has occurred in each and every known society. With specialization, however, come risk and other problems stemming from interdependency. The more specialized the society, the fewer are the number of specialists in any one particular activity. The more, therefore, other people must depend on this few number for the particular tasks they perform.

The fundamental economic problem in a society is the struggle for existence deriving from scarcity. Society must, therefore, organize itself with respect to its total scarce resources. It must decide *what* goods and services shall be produced, *how* they shall be produced, and *for whom* they shall be produced. These elements are the three central issues in the basic fundamental economic problem.

Throughout history, societies have adopted essentially three major solutions to the economic problem: One is *tradition*, in which the procedures for dealing with scarcity have been arranged by the ancestors and continued by their succeeding generations. In many societies under the pattern of tradition, one was born to the soil or to a trade, and all progeny followed in the footsteps of their forebears with respect to these particular activities. *Command* is the second solution found in many societies. It is the solution by which imposed authority and economic decree organizes economic activity. From the building of the pyramids and temples of ancient Egypt to the organization of activity in autocratic countries today, such as is typical in Communist countries, command is a well-known and widely used solution. The third of the three solutions to the economic problem is the *market* solution which allows society to solve the problems of production and distribution with a minimum of recourse either to tradition or command. The essence of a market economy is that everything is assessed in markets, and relative values induce efficient resource allocation. Each and every person is allowed always to pursue the best economic opportunities opened to him. Through this self-seeking, the society solves its problems via the intangible market.

The market price of any good or service is determined by both the

---

partial explanation why many firms do not become less vertically integrated when economic times are good. Moreover, frequently a department in a vertically integrated firm will supply not only intrafirm demand but external demand as well. Hence, modern firms behave not inconsistently with Adam Smith's well-known theorem that the division of labor is limited by market size. The internal market plus the external markets may make opportunities for many internal specialists. See George Stigler, "The Division of Labor Is Limited by the Extent of the Market," *The Journal of Political Economy,* (June 1951), pp. 185–193.

supply and demand. In each and every market there is always supply and demand, and hence, the latter always determines price—however, in some markets of the real world either or both supply and demand are under some monopoly control. The pure market economy, a fiction but nevertheless a useful construct for analysis, is a world in which prices completely determine resource allocation and a world in which there is no government, nor any control over supply or demand in any market. Moreover, it is a world in which the consumer is sovereign—his wishes are completely met by supply responding precisely to his demands.

The real world, the world in which we live, is not a pure market economy. The "imperfections" are in large part that government has a role in the economy, information is not complete, resource mobility into and out of markets is not complete, and supply and demand are under some or considerable control in many markets. Because there are incompletenesses in the ways mentioned—there are jobs to be done in effecting want satisfaction. It is these various activities to effect want satisfaction that are the basic role for what we have defined as "marketing." These would be some activities relating to transactions (that is, marketing) even in a pure market economy—but it would be a relatively simple set of tasks, unlike the complex tasks required for marketing in the real world.

A useful perspective of marketing with respect to frictions in the economy is that of *sorting*. Marketing, as the activities relating to transactions, essentially consists of efforts to match supply and demand. The heterogeneity of demand in the economy we may call meaningful heterogeneity, whereas the heterogeneity on the supply side, that is, differences in supply relative to what is demanded, we may refer to as meaningless heterogeneity. It is the task of the marketing system to convert the meaningless heterogeneity into meaningful heterogeneity. The concept of sorting in the economy includes four subset activities: First, *sorting out*, which is the process of breaking collections of disparate items into various homogeneous classes of goods; second, *accumulation*, in which the homogeneous lots previously sorted out are combined to effect economies in handling storage and transportation; third, *allocation*, in which homogeneous supplies that had been accumulated are broken down into smaller quantities to conform to the requirements of each use situation; and fourth, *assorting*, in which the different homogeneous supplies in the allocation process are combined into heterogeneous combinations but meaningful collections which intend to match the wants of one or more demanders.

If the information on specific demands is accurate and effectively communicated through supply levels, the building up or assorting phase of sorting provides the desired assortment. Thus, if demand is correctly interpreted and if all processes are accurately carried out, meaningless heterogeneity will have been transformed into meaningful heterogeneity, that is, meaningful in the sense of potentiality for want satisfaction. Accordingly, demand will have been matched by supply, and, in principle, wants satisfied.

SUGGESTED READINGS

The Concept and History of the Market-Based Economy

Robert L. Heilbroner, *The Making of Economic Society* (Englewood Cliffs, N.J.: Prentice Hall, Inc., 1962).

George Hotchkiss, *Milestones of Marketing* (New York: The Macmillan Company, 1938).

Henri Pirenne, *Economic and Social History of Medieval Europe* (New York: Harcourt, Brace and World, Inc., 1937).

Karl Polanyi, *The Great Transformation* (Boston: The Beacon Press, 1957).

David A. Revzan, "Some Evolutionary Aspects of the Wholesaling Sector," Essay 6, *Perspectives for Research in Marketing: Seven Essays* (Berkeley: Institute of Business and Economic Research, University of California, 1965).

On the Market Economy and Modern Society

Edward H. Chamberlin, "The Chicago School" in Chamberlin (ed.) *Towards a More General Theory of Value* (Oxford University Press, 1957).

Milton Friedman, *Capitalism and Freedom* (Chicago: University of Chicago Press, 1962).

Elementary Theory of Supply and Demand

Robert Dorfman, *The Price System*, Chapters 1–3 (Englewood Cliffs, N.J.: Prentice Hall, Inc., 1964).

R. H. Haveman and K. A. Knopf, *The Market System*, Chapters 1–5 (New York: John Wiley & Sons, Inc., 1966).

Paul Samuelson, *Economics: An Introductory Analysis*, 5th ed., Chapters 3, 4, 20–24, 26–30 (New York: McGraw-Hill, Inc., 1961), or *see* equivalent chapters in subsequent editions.

Institutions

A. W. Gouldner and H. P. Gouldner, *Modern Sociology* (New York: Harcourt, Brace & World, Inc., 1963).

Talcott Parsons and Neil J. Smelser, *Economy and Society* (Glencoe, Ill.: The Free Press, 1956), p. 102 ff.

Matching Supply and Demand (Variations on the Concept of Sorting)

Wroe Alderson, *Marketing Behavior and Executive Action* (Homewood, Ill.: Richard D. Irwin, 1957), especially Chapter 7.

Wroe Alderson, "The Analytical Framework for Marketing," in D. J. Duncan (ed.), *Conference of Marketing Teachers from Far Western States* (Berkeley: University of California Press, 1958).

Wroe Alderson, "Factors Governing the Development of Marketing Channels," in B. E. Mallen (ed.), *The Marketing Channel* (New York: John Wiley & Sons, Inc., 1967).

Fred E. Clark and Carrie P. Clark, *Principles of Marketing* (3d ed., New York: The Macmillan Company, 1942), especially Chapter 1.

The interested reader will want to compare and contrast the concepts in Alderson, Vaile, *et al.*, and Clark, *et al.*, to consider which best portrays two-way search through markets, which best portrays adjustments of supply to demand and demand to supply, and which is most relevant to both factors *and* goods and services.

David R. Craig and Werner K. Gabler, "The Competitive Struggle for Market Control," *Annals of the American Academy of Political and Social Science*, May 1960.

David A. Revzan, *Wholesaling in Marketing Organization* (New York: John Wiley & Sons, Inc., 1961), Chapter 1.

Roland S. Vaile, E. T. Grether, and Reavis Cox, *Marketing in the American Economy* (New York: The Ronald Press Company, 1952), especially Chapter 6, "Collecting, Sorting, and Dispersing."

History of Marketing

Robert Bartels, *The Development of Marketing Thought* (Homewood, Ill.: Richard D. Irwin, Inc., 1962).

George Hotchkiss, *Milestones in Marketing* (New York: Macmillan Company, 1938).

David A. Revzan, *Essays*, Berkeley: Institute of Business and Economic Research, University of California, 1965.

Jacob Viner, "The Intellectual History of Laissez Faire," *The Journal of Law and Economics*, Vol. 3, October 1960.

Comparative Marketing

Robert Bartels, *Comparative Marketing: Wholesaling in Fifteen Countries* (Homewood, Ill.: Richard D. Irwin, Inc., 1963).

Marshall I. Goldman, *Soviet Marketing* (Glencoe, Ill.: Free Press of Glencoe, 1963).

Simon Kuznets, *Modern Economic Growth: Rate, Structure, and Spread* (New Haven: Yale University Press, 1966).

G. Warren Nutter, "The Structure and Growth of Soviet Industry: A Comparison with the United States," *The Journal of Law and Economics*, Vol. 2, October 1959.

3

Markets, products, and want satisfaction

In the preceding chapter, we discussed the essentials of the pure market economy and its real-world counterpart, the marketing economy. Our overview of want satisfaction now takes us to a consideration of "markets," the specific contact of supply and demand. At times this supplier-demander contact is an exceedingly complex matter. We acquire a beginning understanding of "market" if we think simply of suppliers searching for interested demanders, and demanders searching for interested suppliers.

To understand markets fully, one first must understand the central and related concepts, "need" and "want."

NEEDS AND WANTS

There is for us no value judgment in the terms "need" and "want." The present framework is neutral, for it simply relates the two concepts in an analytically useful way. Some authors contrast needs and wants, assigning an "essential" quality to the former and a "contrived" quality to the latter. This distinction, whatever its merits, is best left to one's personal reflection, for the judgments are arbitrary. We therefore avoid value judgments and simply adopt a neutral framework in which to define and relate needs and wants.

Needs

A *need* is a condition—physical, psychological, or social in origin—requiring satisfaction.[1] The most important aspect of need is that it is a state of unrest or tension which, from the individual's standpoint, requires satisfaction. For any type of demander, satisfaction of this tension-state implies, clearly, that the individual achieves a greater internal harmony—the desired state.

Needs are either or both "biogenic" or "psychogenic."

Biogenic Needs

Biogenic needs, the first of the two general categories of needs, are those arising from tension-systems, physiological in nature, such as hunger, thirst, shelter, and sex.

Psychogenic Needs

Psychogenic needs are based upon tension-systems existing in the individual's subjective psychological state as well as in his relations with others. There is considerable difference of opinion as to a list of specific psychogenic needs; however, the various lists can be grouped into three broad categories:

1. Affectional needs—the need to form and maintain warm, harmonious, and emotionally satisfying relations with others.
2. Ego-bolstering needs—the need to enhance or promote the personality; to achieve; to gain prestige and recognition; to satisfy the ego through domination of others.
3. Ego-defensive needs—the need to protect the personality, to avoid physical and psychological harm, to avoid ridicule and loss of "face," to prevent loss of prestige, to avoid or to obtain relief from anxiety.

Want

A *want* is the total set of physical and nonphysical elements believed by the demander necessary to satisfy the need. The relationship between needs and wants is straightforward. The *relation* of wants and needs is that a want is simply a perceived need. In our framework, every want stems from a need, and therefore, needs and wants are complementary rather than contrasting.[2]

---

[1] See Martin L. Bell, *Marketing: Concepts and Strategy* (Houghton-Mifflin, 1966), p. 179 ff., and James A. Bayton, "Motivation, Cognition, Learning—Basic Factors in Consumer Behavior," reprinted in Perry Bliss, *Marketing and the Behavioral Sciences* (Allyn and Bacon, 1963), pp. 44–56.

[2] Wroe Alderson has presented a needs-wants relationship similar to the present argument. He has said:

> To need something is to be dependent upon it as an essential factor in maintaining or enhancing a way of life. The individual is not always conscious of his

However, there is considerable disagreement on the urgency of various needs in a society in which, among other things, there are persistent poverty, slums, and hunger.[3] A democracy attempts to reconcile different judgments of needs through the electoral process and other means of expression of opinion.

Some needs may exist for a period of time in the subconscious. But until one is conscious of a need, there is no want. It is the want rather than the underlying need which is the action or drive element that seeks satisfaction of the condition.

As Alderson has pointed out, an individual is not always conscious of his needs. To want a good, service, or factor is to "recognize" it consciously or unconsciously as a means of fulfilling a condition requiring gratification.

For example, objectively one may have a *need* for medical attention, or for emotional reassurance, or for relaxation, but none of these becomes a want until perceived (and as well until there is the economic means to acquire the good or service). Obviously, the more *intense* the condition, the earlier will be its perception and the more insistent will be the effort to satisfy it. Thus, in our sense, a so-called "urgent need" or "insistent need" is a physical, social, or psychologically based condition creating very substantial tension. To reduce the tension and thus gain greater internal harmony, one is induced urgently to seek a good or service which will satisfy the pronounced condition. And it follows that the more urgent the need, the more urgent the searching for the good or service best able to match the condition and thereby satisfy it.

Marketing creates wants, but only in the sense that "creating" is simply the facilitating of the perception of need.[4] One's needs, especially the psychogenic, are acquired through experience and exposure to various

---

needs. To *want* a product is to recognize it explicitly as a means of meeting a situation which is regarded as both probable and important. Marketing creates wants by making [customers] aware of needs and by identifying specific products as means of meeting these needs. [Emphasis added]

See Wroe Alderson, *Marketing Behavior and Executive Action* (Irwin, 1957), p. 280 ff. To Alderson, there is throughout the world no deficiency of needs; rather, it is wants that are lacking. Marketing helps evoke them.

[3] For some indication of the magnitudes, *see* the *Report of the National Advisory Commission on Civil Disorders* (1968) and Michael Harrington, *The Other America* (Macmillan, 1963).

In Part V we will consider these and other aspects of consumer welfare as they relate to marketing and the marketing economy.

[4] The suggestion that marketing creates wants not needs is supported by considerable empirical analysis which we will discuss with related issues in Chapters 8 and 9. It suffices for now to indicate that studies point up the *inability* of persuasion, especially of the mass media variety, to create wants in the absence of needs. Indeed, evidence suggests that the more important the issues involved, the less able are mass media to alter behavior. See George Katona, *The Mass Consumption Society* (McGraw-Hill, 1964), pp. 58–61, and n. 2, page 59.

stimuli over time. An individual's total environment—his impersonal communications sources as well as his family, friends, professional contacts, and
other groups to which he intellectually or emotionally relates—uniquely
shapes his needs. As Katona points out, they are neither instantaneously
formed nor altered.

The preceding discussion of wants focuses on perception by a customer
of the conditions requiring satisfaction and of the potentiality of goods and
services to match them. Satisfaction implies both transaction utility and use
utility. Transaction utility means a customer believes he will increase his
well-being by acquiring a good or service. For a transaction to occur, the
perceived want-satisfying ability of the good or service must exceed the
utility to the customer of the dollars, time and other scarce resources he
must give up to acquire the good or service. If he does not anticipate a
gain in his total satisfaction, he rationally will not purchase.[5]

Use utility is the second part of the satisfaction of a need. Once the
customer possesses the good or service, he utilizes (consumes) it in whatever manner he believes most likely will match the condition requiring
gratification. If the good or service fails to fulfill the need, there is little or
no use utility. And with supply alternatives on the next purchase occasion,
the customer probably will not purchase again the particular product or
brand which failed to satisfy.

Let us turn now more specifically to the content of wants. It is helpful
for an understanding of want satisfaction to conceive of wants as mathematical sets. A set is any "well-defined collection of objects."[6] A want, as
already defined, is the "total set of physical and nonphysical elements
believed by the demander necessary to satisfy the need." The concept is
completely general in that it applies to any type of customer in any type of
market.

We need not be concerned at present with precisely what physical and
nonphysical elements a buyer believes necessary to satisfy the need. For
now the important point is that a buyer's want is composed of some number
(n) of elements he believes necessary for want satisfaction and hence for
need satisfaction.[7]

Braces are the customary notation for denoting a set. Let E stand for
an element in a want. A three-element want may simply be noted as $\{E_1, E_2, E_3\}$.

Using the notion of sets, one can meaningfully speak of "simple wants"
and "complex wants." A simple want is a set of desired elements few in

[5] See the discussion of the meaning of "price" in Chapter 13.

[6] John G. Kemeny, et al., Finite Mathematics with Business Applications (Prentice-
Hall, 1962), p. 53 ff.

[7] It may be helpful for the reader to anticipate a complexity we will introduce later in
the book: Namely, what if a buyer can only partially specify the desired elements? One
role of promotion, a socially productive role, is its assistance in want specification. We
defer discussion of such roles to a later part of the book.

number. Thus, "m" is some small number, $\{E_1, \ldots, E_m\}$. And similarly, a complex want is a want containing some large number of "n" elements as for example, $\{E_1, \ldots, E_6, \ldots, E_n\}$.

Another useful conception of wants as sets is the use of Venn diagrams. We shall use a circle to represent the set of elements constituting a want. Thus, a want with n elements, which we shall call Want A, can be expressed conceptually two ways: First, Want A is $\{E_1, \ldots, E_n\}$, and second, simply depicted as Want A. The advantage of Venn diagrams

Want A

will be seen when we consider the matching of products and wants. Let us reemphasize that the concept of sets is useful because of its complete generality. The simple Venn diagram of a constant size, can be used to represent a very simple want, that is, one of very few elements, and on the other hand can be employed to represent a very complex want.

Perhaps it is already clear that it will take a complex product to match a complex want. We will discuss the matching of wants later in this chapter. For now, our analysis of want satisfaction turns to the meaning and several aspects of "markets."

MARKET

A *market* is the contact between demanders (buyers or lessees) and suppliers (sellers or lessors) for transferring ownership or use rights to a factor, good, or service.

Demanders and Suppliers

Demanders are consumers or customers with wants and the financial ability (cash or credit) to acquire legal rights to the desired factor, good, or service. Suppliers are the individuals or firms offering the factor, good, or service.

Transfer of Ownership or Use Rights

"Transferring ownership or use rights" refers to either a sale or lease. In our society, virtually everything, or at least the access to it, is owned by private individuals or public agencies. Clearly then, for one to own or use a good or service in the satisfaction of a want, he must legally acquire the good or service or access to it from someone else. Thus, he must either buy or lease it.

The Meaning of Contact

If "market" refers to the coming together of suppliers and demanders must both of the principles (or their agents) be present? Must all or part of the good be present in some physical "marketplace"? For that matter, must there be some physical marketplace? With respect to all three questions, the answer is, "Not necessarily."

The legally important component of a market is the agreement between a buyer or lessee and a seller or lessor. A legally binding agreement can be effected whether the principles or their agents are face-to-face or miles apart communicating by agents, letter, telephone, or telegraph. And the goods themselves? It follows that if neither the buyer nor the seller need always be at some specific place, neither must the good always be at some particular physical place. The reader can easily consider many examples where he as a consumer, or firms as customers, purchase or rent goods and services with neither the goods, service, or supplier physically present at the transaction.

Bases for Transactions

There are some conditions in which the goods, and representatives of suppliers and demanders are present at a particular place. We will consider the three bases for transactions: (1) inspection, (2) sample, and (3) description. From this discussion, the circumstances requiring a "physical" market will become clear.[8]

The three bases for transaction are distinguishable by the extent to which the goods to be bought and sold are required to be physically present. Each basis has implications for (1) the kinds of marketing agency required, (2) the type of physical facilities required, (3) the nature of the sales promotional program, and (4) auxiliary marketing facilities.

Transactions by Inspection. This basis, in which the goods are inspected by the buyer (or lessee) or his representative, derives from product characteristics and marketing situations in which there is (1) a lack of standardization, (2) a high degree of perishability (as in the wholesale or retail sales of fruit and vegetables), or (3) an emphasis on a high degree of self-service by the buyer or his representative.

Transactions by Sample. Seller's (lessor's), buyer's (lessee's) or third party's samples are frequently the basis of sale when the sample is representative of all units of the product to be sold. For example, extractive agricultural commodities frequently incorporate this basis, permitting traders to observe the (representative) samples of grain, poultry, seafood, wheat, corn, rye, and so on and thereby discern the quality of the entire lot.

Transactions by Description. Selling or leasing by description is by means either of a supplier's description of the good or service, or a demander's description of the good or service he desires. What attitudes and conditions

[8] This section is based on E. A. Duddy and D. A. Revzan, *Marketing: An Institutional Approach* (McGraw-Hill, 1953), pp. 49–50; and R. S. Vaile, E. T. Grether, and Reavis Cox, *Marketing in the American Economy* (Ronald Press, 1952), pp. 378–80.

permit transactions by description? Customer confidence in the accuracy of description underlies selling by means of supplier's description. And, of course, a supplier is better able to describe accurately the entire lot of goods to be sold when the goods are completely standardized as to size and quality. Hence, the development of standardization of product through tighter production, handling, and packaging controls has facilitated seller communication and its heightened credibility—accordingly reducing buyer risk.

Thousands upon thousands of consumer and industrial goods are sold by description. The reader should consider, for instance, all of the consumer goods offered for sale and sufficiently described for (most) buyers in newspapers, circulars, and catalogues, not to mention descriptions received in word-of-mouth telephone, radio, and television communications.

Suppose a law was passed whereby sales could only be made on the basis of inspection or sample. (As we all recognize, there unfortunately are numerous deceptions and frauds perpetrated by false descriptions of goods and services.) What would be the implications of *no* sales by description? If customers, sellers, and goods all had to be present in some physical marketplace, what would be the implications for our standard of living, and for our daily patterns of life? Also, what would be the implications, for instance, for the kinds of firms in marketing, the location of retail stores, the average size of stores, and the character of product assortment in these stores? The implications of such a requirement truly would be numerous as a careful consideration will reveal.

A Factor, Good, or Service

We have said that a market is the contact between demanders and suppliers for transferring legal rights to a "factor, good or service." For simplicity, the term "good or service" will imply *all* intermediate and final goods and services.

Our analysis of the meaning of "good or service" will effect a bridge between the concepts of "want" and "product." For the present, we may say that the meaning of "good or service" in our definition is simply the supplier's offering for which ownership or use rights are passed.

For now let us speak only of the physical and explicit elements of the offering recognized by both customer and supplier. The offering in terms of physical attributes can be simple, for example, a package of nationally branded cigarettes obtained in a vending machine. In this case, a consumer is aware of the physical product through the brander's information and perhaps through previous experience with the product. In buying from a vending machine, the consumer in large part creates the time, place, and possession utility. The whole matter is relatively straightforward and simple. Ownership passes from vendor to buyer with the release and presentation of the package.

As the reader may well recognize, it is hardly as elementary in many other transactions. For example, the good or service for which ownership or use rights are passed may be precisely definable only upon the analysis of the quality and quantity of the offering. The good is affected as well by the terms of shipment and terms of sale. Iron ore from Lake Superior is priced on the assumption that it has 51.5 percent of iron.[9] Upon analysis of the ore, an appropriate adjustment in price is made.

In the brief, preceding discussion, we have implied that the good to which legal rights are passed may possess intangible want-satisfying attributes as well as certain obvious physical attributes. We have also alluded to the interrelationship between "price" and the good or service. The complexity of "price" will be fully developed in a later section of the book. Let us now look further into the meaning of "product." Product is one of the most important and complex topics in marketing.

PRODUCT: A DETAILED ANALYSIS

What precisely do we mean by "product"? Of course, we have an immediate, intuitive notion of "product" as the good, factor, or service which is sold or leased. However, can we give a meaning as precise as we gave for "want"?

We obtain a uniform perspective of wants and products by retaining the perspective of customers attempting to satisfy their wants. We recall that the market economy *in principle* is built upon consumer sovereignty, the manifestation of wants by consumers and the economy's response in providing goods and services to satisfy those wants. As we have noted, our economy is of course an impure market economy, or what generally is called a marketing economy. The viewpoint of the customer establishes both for him and a fortiori for any group of firms attempting to sell or lease to him (1) the character of his want, and (2) the good or service able to satisfy his want.

The Meaning of "Product"

What the demander believes in terms of wants and fulfillment of those wants is for him reality. If a buyer for whatever reason believes one good or service is better able to satisfy his want, then this is also necessarily reality for suppliers of relevant goods or services. The protests of a firm's high-salaried engineers and product technicians notwithstanding, if the customer believes a good or service not to be want-satisfying, then given any alternative he will take another course of action, or will choose not to take any action at all.

As we shall consider more carefully later in this chapter, a seller to

[9] R. S. Vaile, *et al., op. cit.,* p. 378, ff.

make a sale, must present a good or service so that a buyer perceives his own want as being fully satisfied (or at least, more so) by the particular good or service. If two sellers are competing, the one who more completely matches the customer's own perception of what he wants is the seller who gets the sale. We see already the outlines of the link between seller rivalry, the resulting supply alternatives, and consumer sovereignty. Clearly, a consumer in a totally monopolized market (no supply alternatives), for example, is a very weak sovereign indeed.

The most useful definition of product is: A *product* is a demander's total set of percepts of the want-satisfying elements a supplier is offering for sale or lease.

Recall in the same vein, our definition of "want:" "A *want* is the total set of physical and nonphysical elements believed by the demander necessary to satisfy the condition requiring gratification."

These two very important concepts permit us to analyze suppliers and customers in terms of the perceived requirements for tension reduction, and the perceived offerings. Thus, as a customer considers the offerings of several sellers, the products are what he believes to be the total want-satisfying ability of each of the several offerings. The customer who is trying to be rational, compares the several offerings and decides which of the offerings best matches his want. And that one, all other things equal, is the offering he acquires.

In our immediate discussion, the reader may substitute "brand" for "offering." For example, consider a thirsty consumer deliberating among a milk shake, a popsicle, and a soft drink, and/or between two brands of soft drinks. In either case it is the same: He will choose that offering which he believes best matches his want.

"Total Product"

Let us be more specific about "product." As we shall discuss more fully in Part III, what one sees is largely determined by his psychological state, his repertoire of experience, his environment, the intensity of his want, and other factors. For example, if one selects ten students at random and asks them to describe the potential want-satisfying ability of a specific good or service, the chances are he will get ten different answers. Why? Because each person, being different, would tend to see a different set of physical and nonphysical want-satisfying elements.

Let us take a particular good, such as a man's suit. If ten male students, randomly selected, describe the want-satisfying ability of this particular good, the responses in all probability will constitute a spectrum of percepts —a spectrum ranging from many perceived want-satisfying elements down to perhaps but one want-satisfying element. At the lowest end of the spectrum, one or more of the sample of students may believe the particular suit of clothes possesses want-satisfying ability *only* in terms of a physical garment regardless of style. And thus, for such a customer, the "product" is essentially the physical good, no more and no less.

On the other hand, another potential buyer considering the same suit of clothes may see this good as offering want satisfaction in terms of a physical garment with at least some minimal level of style *as well as* some emotional fulfillment and other utility derived from the perhaps national brand name, also some emotional fulfillment from the friendliness of the salesman, the attention paid by the tailor, the opportunity for delivery and a return privilege, the ability to buy on credit, the pleasant surroundings inside the store, and other factors. For the latter buyer, the "product" is a set of percepts in which the physical product is but one element.

From this point on, let us implicitly substitute "total product" for "product." By "total product" we imply that the "product" may be more than merely the physical good or the service. "Total product" reminds us that *reality* in want satisfaction is whatever the customer *believes* to be both his want and what will satisfy his want.[10] In as many cases as not, in our increasingly affluent, sociologically and psychologically complex society, buyer's wants stem from a combination of biogenic and psychogenic needs. And, therefore, only in the minority of instances will merely the *physical* product fully satisfy the want.

Two Offerings: One Product or Two Products?

What if a demander holds equal percepts of the offerings of two different firms? The answer, of course, is that the two offerings with respect to this particular buyer's desires are the *same product*. This holds whether the offerings are two brands of the same physical offering or two different physical offerings such as sail boats and motor boats. It necessarily follows

---

[10] Chamberlin was one of the first economists to articulate the concept of products as "bundles of utility" in which the physical offering was but one element. In 1933 Chamberlin said:

> "Anything which makes buyers prefer one seller to another, be it personality, reputation, convenient location, or the tone of his shop, differentiates the thing purchased to that degree, for what is bought is really a bundle of utilities, of which these things are a part." Edward H. Chamberlin, *The Theory of Monopolistic Competition* (8th ed., Harvard, 1962), p. 8.

Professor Chamberlin's analysis contributes to the development of positive marketing theory. Throughout, he emphasized demander perception as the determinant of whether offerings were the same or different. Again, as we are stressing, what is important is what a demander believes:

> "[A basis for distinguishing offerings] may be *real* or *fancied*, so long as it is of any importance whatever to buyers, and leads to a preference for one variety of the product over another. Where such differentiation exists, even though it be slight, buyers will be paired with sellers, not by chance and at random (as under pure competition), but according to their preferences." (Emphasis added) *Ibid*, p. 56.

that two offerings are *different products* when one or more customers view them as substantially different in their ability to satisfy a given want.

There are no absolute rules as to when two offerings no longer are two products, but become the same product. There is, however, a useful conceptualization of this matter of offerings, products and wants: It is to conceive of offerings arrayed in terms of their want-satisfying ability.

Take for instance, a consumer-beverage company which bottles its good for sale in vending machines, supermarkets and other retail outlets. Clearly such a company has a want for containers that, among other things, will adequately safeguard the good, permit some simple branding or identification, prove easy to handle by the retail merchants, at the lowest possible cost. The total set of elements believed by this company necessary to satisfy the need are the four listed above plus the container's relationship to the physical-handling equipment on hand, personal preferences of management, and perhaps other elements. The set of elements comprising the want can be fully listed. Thus, this particular want is $\{E_1, E_2, E_3, E_4, \ldots, E_n\}$. The company considers all or most of the offerings potentially able to satisfy this want, and ranks them in terms of their specific ability to match this want.

At one end of the spectrum are the offerings best able to satisfy the want, and at the other end, those offerings least able. When all the elements of the want are considered, it may well be that among the highest potential want satisfiers are aluminum cans, nonreturnable glass bottles, and plastic bottles. Farther down the spectrum may be returnable glass bottles and tin-plated cans. The first three offerings in their perceived similar ability to satisfy the want are the same product. The latter two, in their perceived lesser ability to satisfy the want, are but imperfect substitutes for the first three offerings, and hence, vis-a-vis the first three are not precisely the same product.

Where is the dividing line? As we stated above, no one can offer an absolute rule, except to say that two or more offerings are different products when a buyer believes they are substantially different in their ability to satisfy a want. The commercial world abounds with examples of inter-industry competition where technically different processes and materials become behaviorally the *same product.* Consider the competition between the aluminum and lumber industries in the market for exterior siding for houses. In the eyes of many buyers these disparate physical materials are highly substitutable in satisfying the want for attractive, durable, exterior siding. Or consider the inter-industry penetration made by lumber in invading the historic domain of steel in the structural-beam market. There are many instances today where laminated, wooden beams have been purchased rather than steel beams. Two examples are the Astrodome in Houston, Texas and the Coliseum in Portland, Oregon.

Products and Some Want-Satisfaction Implications

Let us note briefly some customer and supplier implications of the concepts "offerings" and "products." When a buyer views several offerings as equal in their ability to satisfy his want, he is absolutely indifferent as to which one he buys. The reader may reply, "But suppose one of the offerings is a local brand, and the buyer is sympathetic to local firms?" The reader has simply indicated a case in which our hypothetical buyer's percepts of the offerings are *not* equal; therefore, intrinsically, the local-brand offering possesses more want-satisfying ability, and therefore, it is preferred over the others.

Remember, two or more offerings may differ slightly in their relevance for satisfaction of a want and still be the same product. It is when the differences become *substantial* that conceptually they become a different product.

The reader can relate this discussion to the conventional economic-theory models of markets. One basis of perfect or pure competition is complete homogeneity of the offerings. Hence perfect competition describes a situation of all offerings being the same product. The student will recall this same-product state is characterized by a horizontal demand curve, which implies perfect substitutability—that is, infinite demand elasticity.[11]

Another implication of several offerings being the same product is that any customer is of course very well off when at any one time he may choose from several offerings each of which completely satisfies his want. He pays no heed to brands, for in this situation they are immaterial. He can simply with assurance pick the offering which is physically most convenient (closest to pick up).

A buyer is less well off when confronted by several offerings, each essentially identical in want-satisfying ability, but *none* fully satisfying his want. Obviously, he is still indifferent as to brands, but his want is only partially satisfied by any offering on the market. As we shall discuss later in the book, a situation in which there is only partial want satisfaction is an opportunity for an alert seller to market an offering more closely matching the buyer's want. To the extent that any seller becomes more relevant than his competitors in terms of want satisfaction, that seller, of course, gains the custom of some number of additional buyers.

We may summarize the above by using Venn diagrams. Let us suppose there is a want with some "n" elements which we shall call "Want A." And let us suppose there are two offerings, which we shall call "O_1" and "O_2" with "J" and "K" percepts respectively. In Figure 3.1 Want A is the total set of physical and nonphysical elements believed by the buyer to be necessary to satisfy the need. And "O_1" and "O_2" are the buyer's total set of perceptions of what sellers 1 and 2 are offering.

[11] See for example, Paul A. Samuelson, *Economics: An Introductory Analysis* (McGraw-Hill, 1961), pp. 413–18.

FIGURE 3.1

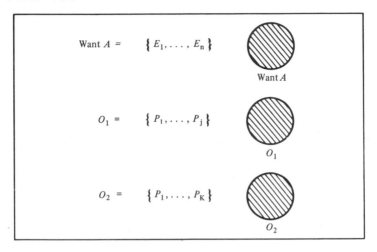

Want A = $\{ E_1, \ldots, E_n \}$

O_1 = $\{ P_1, \ldots, P_j \}$

O_2 = $\{ P_1, \ldots, P_K \}$

For a buyer rationally to purchase a particular offering, he must perceive a greater matching of product attributes and the elements desired than in any other offering. How do we show this perception of a matching of attributes offered and elements desired? We indicate the degree to which the want-set and offering-set contain common elements by the *intersection* of the sets. For any two sets, for example sets G and H, the intersection is denoted by $G \cap H$, and is the set which contains only those elements which belong to both G and H.[12]

Perceived Ability to Satisfy Wants

In the instance where both offerings are *equal* in want-satisfying ability, we show $A \cap O_1$ equal to $A \cap O_2$ in Figure 3.2.

FIGURE 3.2

PERCEIVED EQUAL WANT SATISFACTION

Want A O_1 Want A O_2

Obviously if $A \cap O_1$ is greater than $A \cap O_2$, then by definition, O_1 is preferred to O_2. Figure 3.3 indicates the perceived greater ability of O_1 to satisfy the want.

A want is potentially fully satisfied when the offering set is perceived as completely matching the want set. "Want A" is the want set which must

[12] Kemeny, *et al.*, *op. cit.*, p. 57.

be fully matched for maximum gratification of the need. *Complete* satisfaction from, for example O_3, is described by the set Want A identical to O_3, or as depicted in Figure 3.4. By contrast, absolutely *no* perceived want satisfaction from O_4 is shown in Figure 3.5.

FIGURE 3.3

PERCEIVED DIFFERENCES OF SATISFACTION

FIGURE 3.4   FIGURE 3.5

PERCEIVED COMPLETE SATISFACTION   **NO PERCEIVED SATISFACTION**

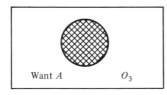 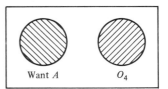

Perceived Potential versus Actual Want Satisfaction

All of our discussion so far has been in terms of a buyer perceiving a need and perceiving the want-satisfaction *potential* in one or more offerings. The most important implication of an a priori perceived matching of a particular offering and a want is, clearly, that the buyer will purchase such an offering. We have not discussed, however, the satisfaction the buyer *in fact* experiences once he purchases the offering, that is, use utility.

What about one's perception of *actual* satisfaction derived from the purchase of a good or service? How do we incorporate it with the perception of potential want-satisfying ability? The Venn diagram concept remains useful. Suppose a buyer purchased O_1 believing it promised the greatest amount of want satisfaction; thus, perceived, $A \cap O_1$ was greater than any other set. However, upon purchasing O_1 and actually experiencing its abilities to satisfy Want A, the buyer believes that in fact the set $A \cap O_1$ is far *smaller* than he initially perceived it to be. What are the implications? Clearly, one implication is that on the next purchase occasion, the buyer will not necessarily repurchase O_1, but will more carefully consider alternative offerings. If no alternatives exist, he may sublimate his desires, perhaps postponing the purchase.

A large discrepancy between a buyer's a priori and expost perceptions of an offering is a condition marketing managers attempt to avoid. Rational marketing management, if oriented to long-run profit maximization, creates brand images *consistent with* brand quality so that a buyer's expectations are fulfilled. It tries to ensure that the promised want satisfaction does not exceed the intrinsic want-satisfying ability of the offering.

We shall analyze in Parts III and IV of the book additional aspects of customer perception and implications for offerings, products, and wants. Let us now relate "product" and "market" and introduce the concept "competition."

MARKETS, PRODUCTS, AND COMPETITION

We have defined a market as "the contact between demanders and suppliers for transferring ownership or use rights to a factor, good, or service." From preceding discussions, the reader knows that the contact is in no sense automatic or costless. Rather, in a marketing economy self-interested suppliers attempt to find demanders to whom they can sell or lease their offerings, and self-interested demanders attempt to find suppliers from whom they can buy or lease offerings.

Offerings in the Same Product Market

Two or more offerings are in the same product market when one or more demanders believe the offerings possess substantially the same ability to satisfy a given want. Thus, when two or more offerings are perceived as the same product, they are in the same market.

For example, if a family wishes to go out to dinner (the want), and they consider as equal alternatives a drive-in restaurant and a conventional restaurant, then the two types of restaurants for these demanders are in the same market. The buyers perceive essentially the same utility from these two physically different offerings.

For obvious reasons customer perceptions are central to the planning of marketing managers. Also, the analysis of monopoly in antitrust turns on the number of types of offerings which can satisfy a demand. For example, if only one firm can match a want, then clearly that supplier has a monopoly. However, if the want is not insistent—the need is not urgent—then the single seller may have only a weak monopoly, for if he tries to raise the price of his "monopolized" good or service above the buyer's demand schedule, the buyer will simply switch to some imperfect substitute, postpone his purchase or sublimate his desires.[13] Moreover, there may be but one current seller—yet, if other firms could easily satisfy the want, the "monopolist" will be induced to behave competitively to forestall entry by additional sellers. Salt is an example of a unique product: There are no substitutes. However, the technology required to supply salt is sufficiently simple and the costs sufficiently low, that many suppliers sell salt. Hence, an offering such as salt for which there are no substitutes, is not monopolized because of ease of entry and many different sellers.

The demand for postal service is a want which can best be satisfied by only one supplier. Thus, postal service is a "natural monopoly" in which the government is the sole supplier. Because of decreasing-costs (increasing returns to scale) or because competition among suppliers would lead to chaos, offerings such as telephone service and utilities are granted conditional monopoly rights within specific geographic regions.

Arithmetic relationships can suggest when two offerings are the same product. Suppose one wanted to determine product markets within "children's shoes." For example, when would data on purchases and price suggest that children's sandals and children's tennis shoes were the same product? Or when would the data suggest that Buster Brown boys' medium quality oxfords compete with Paul Parrott's boys' medium quality oxfords? Conceptually, two offerings A and B are the same product if there is a high positive cross-elasticity of demand between them.[14] The closer two offerings are perceived by buyers as substitutes, the greater is the cross-elasticity coefficient. At the limit there is infinite cross-elasticity.[15]

---

[13] The issue of breadth of product market is especially critical in antitrust cases in which one is attempting to determine the number of offerings in a market. The broader the definition of the market, the more offerings in any product market.

For example, in the famous "cellophane" case of U.S. v. E.I. du Pont de Nemours, (1956), 351 U.S. 377, Du Pont allegedly had a monopoly in cellophane in that it produced some 75 percent of all cellophane in the country. However, the Supreme Court held that cellophane was interchangeable with other flexible wrapping material, and hence the appropriate product market in which to assess the question of monopoly was all flexible wrapping material rather than the more narrow market of cellophane. DuPont produced only 17.9 percent of the broader market, and thus, the majority of the Court held that the company did not monopolize the relevant market.

[14] That is, $\%\Delta Q_A / \%\Delta P_B > 1$. For a review of the basics of elasticity of demand/supply, see for example, Paul A. Samuelson, Economics: An Introductory Analysis (5th ed., McGraw-Hill, 1961), pp. 413–18; for a discussion of cross-elasticity of demand, see Donald S. Watson, Price Theory and Its Uses (Houghton-Mifflin, 1963), pp. 99–101. For one example and discussion of the use of the cross-elasticity concept in antitrust analysis see George W. Stocking and Willard F. Mueller, "The Cellophane Case and the New Competition," American Economic Review, Vol. XLV, No. 1, March 1955, pp. 29–63.

[15] Negative cross-elasticity of demand—more of offering A is purchased when the price of B is reduced—implies complementary products. For example, beer and pretzels for many consumers are complements: The lower the price of beer, the more beer is purchased and the greater the demand for pretzels.

We have carefully distinguished between offerings and products—two or more offerings become the same product when perceived as essentially equal in utility. What is the same thing, two or more offerings are in the same *product market* when perceived as substantially identical in utility. From the present point on, we shall be implying the offerings-product relationship whenever we speak of two or more factors, goods, or services as being in the *same* market. Thus, the important but somewhat complicated distinction between offerings and products will be replaced by the synonymous concept of *product market*. For example, when we frequently speak of inter-industry competition, we shall mean offerings produced in separate industries but nevertheless competing in the same product market—that is, attempting to match the same want. Illustrations are rugby and baseball competing for the patronage of the spectator of collegiate spring sports; glass, tin-plate, plastic and aluminum containers competing for the custom of bottling companies; paper and wooden boxes competing as containers for fresh fruit; and ocean liners competing with airlines for consumers in the market for inter-continental travel.

Demanders in the Same Product Market

Two or more demanders are in the same product market when they have the same want, that is, if the elements comprising their wants are essentially the same. For example, two demanders are in the same broad product market if they both desire a luxury automobile whether it is a Rolls Royce, Jaguar, Lincoln Continental, or Cadillac. If, however, the want is more narrowly defined such that one demand is for a luxury American automobile and the other a luxury European automobile, then clearly they are in separate product markets.

Suppliers in the Same Product Market

The determination of when two or more firms as suppliers are in the same market is at times complicated. Firms currently supplying offerings perceived as approximate alternatives by the same demanders are in the same market. Thus, if at least some consumers in a city perceive the same utility in purchasing gasoline from major-brand oil companies and the lower-price gasoline from private-brand service stations, then to this extent, the major and private branders are in the same market.

When one assesses the *current* goods and services of two or more firms, the determination of whether they are in the same or different product markets turns simply on buyer perception of current output. Technically, the analysis implicitly or explicitly turns on the cross-elasticity of demand. The analysis of *current* goods and services of firms is, however, completely a *short-run analysis*: Specifically, firms are conceived of in terms of their current sets of products, and the firms are in the same or separate markets as buyers perceive the respective substitutability of the current offerings.

A more complicated but in many ways more useful analysis ensues if a firm is conceived of in more dynamic and what we believe more fundamental terms. What precisely is a firm? A firm realistically is one or more pools of productive resources—labor, plant, equipment, management know-how, liquid assets, good will, and other assets. These productive resources, within limits, are capable of producing (or supplying, if a middleman) a range of types of offerings. That is, most firms' resources permit them to vary the composition of output and engage in specific offerings new to them, but within the capacity of the resources. Thus, firms—pools of productive resources—can and do supply a range of types of offerings.

Data indicate that many firms continually alter their mix of offerings. The marginal cost of adding an offering is typically low for firms with idle capacity or high fixed costs. On the other hand, the character of resources and higher variable-cost structures of many of the smaller firms may frequently preclude some immediate variability of offerings.[16] There are exceptions, for resource flexibility permits firms in some lines to vary output easily.

Given the fact of resource flexibility, a firm not currently producing a particular offering may nevertheless be considered "in" the product market *if* it could easily supply the offering. The ease and immediacy with which it could supply the good is the test.[17] If among a certain group of firms there is a high cross-elasticity of supply with respect to any product market (whatever their current output, they all could and conceivably would supply the product if prices rose in that market relative to the firms' other opportunities), all of such firms are effectively *in* that product market. Aggregate objective data on diversification and mergers provide implications for real-world relationships and hence, actual breadth of markets.[18]

[16] The essentially long-run and very useful characterization of firms as pools of resources is well treated in Edith Penrose, *The Theory of the Growth of the Firm* (Wiley, 1959). Penrose is one of a few economists who has elaborated on the resource flexibility feature of firms. Formal economic theory incorporates little of the dynamics of firms, in large part because of the extremely complex formulations required for precise models. For this, among other reasons, Penrose's theory is presented completely in literary rather than mathematical form. Arguments parallel to hers are found in J. M. Clark, *Competition as a Dynamic Process* (Brookings Institutions, 1961).

Empirical evidence on the multiproduct characteristics of large firms is offered in Michael Gort, *Diversification and Integration in American Industry*. (Princeton: National Bureau of Economic Research, 1962).

The relative ease with which many firms can add products without incurring substantial incremental costs, because of idle capacity and/or high fixed costs, is discussed in Joel Dean, *Managerial Economics*, (Prentice-Hall, 1951), Chapter 3. Richard Holton cites the virtually zero marginal selling cost of supermarkets' adding another product to their shelves, in "Price Discrimination at Retail: The Supermarket Case," *Journal of Industrial Economics*, Vol. VI (October 1957), pp. 13–32.

[17] Ease of potential entry is uppermost in the minds of current sellers. In concentrated markets, potential competition induces more competitive behavior from current sellers to deter entry by additional firms. See the discussion of "Competition" below.

[18] For a discussion of the concept and measurement of supply space—*viz.*, firms as one or more pools of productive resources and the range of demands to which they easily could respond—see John C. Narver, "Supply Space and Horizontality in Firms and Mergers," *St. John's Law Review*, Special Edition, Spring 1970, pp. 316–340.

For example, the large and marketing-sophisticated firms selling food and related nonfood items in supermarkets are *currently* in many product markets subsumed by supermarkets, and in addition in a "supply-capability sense," are "in" many if not most of the remaining food and nonfood markets. Thus, the fact that a firm is currently producing some set of goods and services represents nothing more than its current choice of how best to use its resources. Analytically, the critical question is the range of offerings the resources *could* easily produce. Most large grocery-products firms could enter, with relative ease, additional product markets in supermarkets. At any one time, the fact that firms are in some markets and not in others has more to do with relative current profit opportunities than resource inflexibility.

Procter & Gamble is an illustration of a sophisticated, resource-flexible, grocery-products firm. Although best known for its broad line of soaps, cleansers, and toiletries, the company has moved into additional product markets in grocery stores, such as food products, paper napkins, paper towels, and other paper goods. Procter & Gamble and firms similar to it adeptly employ their resources in selling high-turnover, low-markup products in supermarkets and other large-volume outlets. When Procter & Gamble entered the liquid bleach market—an offering new to it—one P & G executive underscored the firm's resource flexibility:

> While this is a completely new product for us, taking us for the first time into the marketing of a household bleach and disinfectant, we are thoroughly at home in the field of manufacturing and marketing low-priced, rapid turn-over consumer products.[19]

Again, many firms certainly have varying degrees of resource flexibility and, therefore, may accurately be characterized as essentially pools of resources, the short-run output of which is determined by managerial decision. Many of the issues are too complex for an introductory text, but let us consider another example in passing. Today, most large companies historically in the paper industry are also engaged widely in one or more aspects of the lumber and wood products industry. Examples are International Paper Co., Crown Zellerbach Corp., and St. Regis Corporation. These and other large paper and lumber companies attempt to obtain the highest yield of their basic input, timber, by shifting its usage among their paper and lumber producing activities according to shifts in the relative demand and cost structures. By 1966, three of the largest lumber companies —Weyerhaeuser Corp., Georgia-Pacific Corp., and Boise Cascade Corp.— also engaged extensively in paper products. Thus, most of the largest "paper" companies were substantially also in lumber, and three of the four largest "lumber" companies were substantially as well in paper.

[19] Commerce Clearing House, *Trade Regulation Reporter*, paragraph 16,673, p. 21,566.

In 1966, the fourth of the four largest lumber companies, U.S. Plywood, was only modestly in paper, and that was in Canada. One of the largest paper companies, Champion Papers Corporation, was not in lumber.[20] In 1967, U.S. Plywood Corporation purchased Champion Paper Corporation, thereby combining a company which had been almost active exclusively in lumber and wood products with a company exclusively in paper. Does this merger represent an acquisition between two *different* markets or is this a merger within the *same* market? If one takes a static view and observes only what the two companies are currently producing—the firms as sets of products—then one logically concludes that this is a so-called conglomerate merger, a merger in which the acquiring and acquired firms are in different markets. On the other hand, if one takes a dynamic view and observes the supply capability of the *resources*, coupled with the fact that virtually all of the *other large firms* in the forest industries are engaged (for rational, profit-seeking reasons) in *both* lumber and paper, he logically must conclude that this is a horizontal merger, one in which the acquiring and acquired firms are in the same market—"forest products." [21]

Product and Geographic Markets

There are two major reasons why a demander might not buy a particular offering. First, it may have virtually no perceived ability to satisfy his want. That is, it is in another product market.

Second, a buyer will not buy an offering if it is available to him only at a location beyond the distance that it is economical for him to travel. Clearly, for goods sold by mail order, there is little or no travel required of the customer. However, many goods do not lend themselves to, or for other reasons are not sold by mail order. Hence, there is a geographic/time limit for each customer with respect to any want.

When a good or service is sold only at a location farther than the buyer wishes to travel (or can afford to travel because of the cost and time), that offering is in a different market, in particular, a different *geographic* market. Offerings in separate geographic markets, just as offerings in different product markets, reveal virtually zero cross-elasticities of demand. (Chapter 7 discusses space and time aspects of marketing.)

Market Diversification

What is meant by "market diversification"? As we shall see, virtually every firm in our economy is market-diversified to some degree.

---

[20] One may obtain a broad outline of the product structures and plant locations of the larger publicly held U.S. manufacturing companies, in *Plant and Product Directory*, published by *Fortune*.

[21] We shall have more to say in Parts IV and V about the managerial and public-policy implications of mergers.

The definition of market diversification: Market diversification is the simultaneous selling by a firm in more than one product or geographic market.

If diversification is the simultaneous selling of two different products in the same geographic market or the same product in two geographic markets, diversification is indeed a wide-spread phenomenon. Literally, a supermarket may be in as many as 10,000 product markets. Or, to emphasize the number of markets, for example, suppose a person has a want specifically for a package of king-size, menthol, filter-tip cigarettes. There are many cigarettes such as regular, nonmenthol cigarettes or even menthol, regular-size cigarettes which the consumer definitely believes will not satisfy his want. For him, all of the preceding offerings, not to mention cigars and pipe tobacco, are essentially in other product markets. Moreover, vending machines or other retail outlets selling packages of menthol, filter-tip cigarettes (his want) located substantially beyond his daily points of habitation and travel are in different geographic markets. Consider the potentially many product and geographic markets in this simple example. (Of course, if this tobacco want is sufficiently intense, and if his most convenient retail outlets cannot satisfy his want, this buyer under "duress" may enter another product market or venture farther afield into another geographic market.)

Although market diversification is a topic we shall take up in Part IV and in particular in Chapter 11, we will point out now a couple of important aspects of diversification. The reader must be very clear on the point that market diversification is the *simultaneous* selling in *two or more* markets. The definitional test is simply that the markets are *different* product and/or *different* geographic markets.

Conceptually—namely, zero cross-elasticity of demand—it is just as much diversification for a supermarket to add a noncompetitive consumer household product, such as a toaster, to its assortment as it is for it to sell deep-sea cabin cruisers. Or, conceptually, it is no less diversification for an automobile manufacturer to manufacture and sell another noncompeting style of automobile as it is for it to begin selling surfboards.

We note that although all four cases are market diversification, there are more economic relationships in the respective first examples. Because of more numerous common costs, it undoubtedly costs the supermarket less to enter, and also because of demand interrelationships it costs less to compete, in the first market than the second, and the same is true for the automobile manufacturer. However, this situation in no way alters the fact that all four instances are "market diversification."

Firms may enter new product and geographic markets through internal investment, or they may acquire another firm already marketing in the market they wish to enter. The term given diversification through the avenue of merger is "conglomerate" merger, but this rather awesome word may be replaced by "diversification," for the meaning is the same. Call it conglomerate or diversification, it merely means the firm has entered a new (for it) product or geographic market. We shall have more to say about the economic relationships and competitive implications of diversification in Parts IV and V.

New Products

One comes across countless admonitions in the business literature that a firm must add new products or face economic death. So-called "new" products pour onto the market.[22]

What exactly is a "new product"? Our analysis in this chapter of the meaning of "product" and "market" gives us a solid basis for defining "new product." There are three contexts in which the term "new product" is typically used. Two of them are of analytical importance, for they have a buyer-perception basis. The first of the three, however, is a nonsubstantive usage.

The first usage, and perhaps the most common, is of no consequence either for the firm's customers or competitors. This usage of the term "new product" means simply that a company is changing its offering, but demanders still perceive the *same* utility as before the change. Hence, it is still the same product. For example, the company says it is marketing a "new product" because the physical offering now has more chrome, or is a color the company never has before marketed, or in short, there is a modification of some aspect of the offering new to the particular supplier; however, if none of these substantially alters a *buyer's perception*, nothing has changed. Many an annual report to the company's stockholders relates the "new products," in this usage, that the company is marketing.

The second and third uses of "new product" utilize a *market perspective* rather than an internal-company perspective. The second meaning of "new products" is that a firm enters a *product market* new to the firm. The firm is now selling an offering in virtually no degree a substitute for any good or service it has previously sold. (Remember, the criterion of "different" products is that no buyer perceives this new offering as a substitute for any of the firm's current offerings.) In entering a product market new to the firm, we imply that one or more extant firms are already in that particular product market. The firm in entering the product market is adding one more alternative to the set of alternatives already perceived by the buyers.

The third meaning of "new product" is the development of a good or service for which demanders perceive there is no substitute offering by *any* firm. Thus, this third meaning implies that for some period of time (perhaps only very short), the firm will be the *only* seller in the product market. In

[22] For example, the president of the Toiletry Merchandisers Association stated that in the last 5 years TMA members have been offered approximately 10,000 "new" products. *Marketing Insights*, February 20, 1967, p. 3.

subsequent analyses in this book, "new product" will be used only in either the second or third sense, with the distinction indicated at the time of usage.

Competition

Competition in the real world is rivalry. It occurs in and only in markets. "Competition" has no meaning outside the context of a market. Buyers compete among themselves for preferred sources of supply just as sellers compete among themselves for the custom of demanders. For any two buyers or any two sellers to be in competition they must be in one or more of the same product and geographic markets. However, "competition" is also used by many economists to denote "pure competition"—a state of *no* personal rivalry.[23] Thus, the reader must be alert to an author's usage.

The market-based economy, founded on suppliers and demanders acting completely out of self-interest, means that the ensuing competition among sellers and among buyers serves to drive costs and prices down. Thus, active competition—complete rivalry—produces desirable economic performance in the form of profits that are not excessive and in the form of induced innovation, thereby increasing consumer satisfaction.

Some authors distinguish between "price competition" and "nonprice competition" but in light of all factors this distinction is extremely difficult— if even possible—in many instances. The complexities of "price" and "non-price" are discussed in Chapters 10 to 13 where we analyze competitive policies and effects.

Direct and Potential Competition

Competition produces satisfactory performance in two ways—one direct, and one more subtle. The obvious way in which competition produces acceptable performance in terms of innovation, efficiency, and "normal" profits is *direct* competition among firms in a market. For example, the competition among Procter & Gamble, Colgate-Palmolive, Lever Brothers and supermarkets' own brands of soaps and detergents exerts downward pressure on the prices of these products.

The more subtle aspect is *potential* competition. Firms not currently in a market but with the capacity to enter relatively easily, exert pressure upon the firms already in the market (this is especially true in concentrated markets). Firms currently in a market recognize that if they price above a certain level, or if they earn profits in that market exceeding some minimal

[23] The real-world meaning of competition as rivalry conflicts in terminology with the economic model, "perfect competition." The latter is a state of *no* rivalry, yet usefully serves as an idealized norm of the structure and performance required for optimal resource allocation. The reader must be on guard not to confuse the rivalistic meaning with the structure meaning. Throughout this book, we utilize "competition" in the sense of rivalry. The distinctions are briefly but well treated in Robert H. Haveman and Kenyon A. Knopf, *The Market System* (Wiley, 1966), p. 114.

level, other firms will enter, thereby reducing the profitability of all. Thus, because of strong potential competitors, the extant suppliers are induced to keep their prices below the entry-inducing level.[24] In that firms continually search for new and more profitable ways to employ their resources, potential competition and potential competitors are widespread. The result, especially in relatively concentrated markets, is economic performance closer to the competitive ideal than would otherwise be the case.[25]

Differential Advantage

Competition among suppliers is the rivalry in effecting larger inter-sections of the offer-set and the want-set. If all other things are equal, the seller whose offering effects the largest perceived satisfaction gets the purchase by the demander. Let us define "differential advantage," the objective of any supplier in his rivalry with others.

> Differential advantage is the belief of a demander that one supplier's offering possesses more want-satisfying ability than other suppliers' offerings.[26]

Clearly, rational marketing management seeks to develop a preferred position in the buyer's perception, thereby gaining a differential advantage over rivals. How does one gain a differential advantage? In brief, he must be different from his rivals but still relevant to the demander. At this point we will suggest only a couple of implications.

In attempting to gain differential advantage, a seller can manipulate the physical product thereby differentiating himself from his rivals. He can change the physical product by altering its shape, its components, or in general, altering its functional, tangible attributes. Frequently, however, a seller may be unable to alter the physical product—for example, if he sells coal—or for other reasons he may choose not to alter the *physical* offering. Instead he alters the *total* product by differentiating the firm or other non-physical aspects of the product. This is "enterprise differentiation" rather than "physical-product differentiation" and is effected, for example, by changing the product appeals, by changing the meaning conveyed by the firm's institutional advertising, by changing the character and quality of the

---

[24] Joe S. Bain discusses "limit" or "keep-out" pricing in *Price Theory* (Wiley, 1966), pp. 213–218. For a more detailed analysis *see* Bain, "Pricing in Monopoly and Oligopoly," *American Economic Review*, March 1949, pp. 448–464.

[25] In many markets potential competition is absent or at least too weak to be the sole means for bringing about improvement of performance. Structural remedies sometimes are effected by public policy, in particular, antitrust. See Chapter 14 for a discussion of antitrust policy.

[26] The concept will be more fully developed in Part IV. For a greater understanding of differential advantage at this point, see Wroe Alderson, *Dynamic Marketing Behavior* (Irwin, 1965), p. 184 ff.

sales force and outlets through which the firm distributes its offering, and by other related efforts.[27] Corporate philanthropy may be related to attempts for differential advantage. Some evidence strongly suggests that corporate contributions are "motivated by a striving for competitive advantage."[28]

SOME ADDITIONAL DIMENSIONS OF MARKETS

Markets Classified by Similarity of Behavior

Markets may be classified according to the activities of suppliers or demanders performing the same general sets of activity such as sellers of goods to nonultimate consumers, the wholesale market; or sellers selling to ultimate consumers, the retail market.[29] The description may be employed analogously with respect to demanders: Buyers in the wholesale market, and buyers in the retail market.

Markets may also be classified according to other homogeneous behavioral aspects. The homogeneity of behavior may center on the activity of buyers and sellers of a single commodity, for example, the wheat market, cotton market, lumber market, and so on. The descriptive use of "market" in the present sense applies also to services. Thus, one can speak of the vacation market, the travel market, and so on because much of the selling and buying of these kinds of services is becoming institutionalized in specific agency structures, characterized by homogeneous patterns of behavior.

Time Aspects of Markets

Much of the behavior of suppliers or demanders is in anticipation of a future market. Products require time to be made and to be invested with time, place, and possession utility. Demanders, especially with respect to a substantial purchase, plan ahead including storing-up purchasing ability in advance of entering the market.

In some agricultural and industrial commodities traded on organized exchanges, one may distinguish between the "cash market" and the "futures market"—two markets with separate institutional organizations. Transactions

[27] The concept of "enterprise differentiation" can be traced to Professor E. T. Grether, and less formally to Professor E. H. Chamberlin. Professor Chamberlin in his 1933 book, *The Theory of Monopolistic Competition* (Harvard University Press), was the first to introduce to economic theory the aspect of product differentiation and also the first to introduce what we have called differentiated "total product." See Chamberlin, *op. cit.*, (Harvard, 8th ed., 1962), Chapter IV for physical-product differentiation and p. 8 for products as differentiated "bundles of utilities" in the perception of buyers.

[28] Orace Johnson, "Corporate Philanthropy: An Analysis of Corporate Contributions," *Journal of Business*, October 1966, pp. 489–504, p. 503 (quote).

[29] The material in this section is drawn from E. A. Duddy and D. A. Revzan, *Marketing: An Institutional Approach* (McGraw-Hill, 1953), pp. 10–11.

in the cash market are those in which immediate delivery is contemplated. A future trading or futures market is one in which contracts are entered into in the present, with delivery and payment in the future, and where the transactions are governed by the rules of a trading exchange.

Buying Markets and Selling Markets

The terms buying markets and selling markets are used in two senses. The first refers to a supply-demand imbalance at a particular point in time. Thus, if demand exceeds supply ("excess demand" discussed in Chapter 2), it is a sellers' market. The sellers' bargaining power dominates that of the buyers. (In the long run we would expect the price to fall as the result of increased supply attracted into the market to participate in the current high profits. The added supply capacity conceptually is a shift of the supply curve to the right, making for a lower market price.) A buyers' market occurs when supply exceeds demand, and buyers can exercise a dominant influence on market price.

The second sense in which the terms "buying markets" and "selling markets" are used is that of a buying market as a physical location to which sellers ship their products. The flows are centripetal; for example, Chicago for a long time was the buying market for livestock, and sellers throughout the Midwest shipped their livestock to the buyers and auction yards at Chicago. Where scattered buyers buy from a central point or goods are shipped out from fixed plants, and so on, the flows are centrifugal—the pattern typifying selling markets.

Organized and Unorganized Markets

An organized market consists essentially of a specialized group of wholesale middlemen operating under membership and trading rules and certain government restraints. An example is the Chicago Board of Trade, the world's largest commodity exchange, on which are traded wheat, corn, oats, soybeans, cotton, and so on. Trading at the Chicago Board of Trade is increasing: In 1966 the volume reached $81.4 billion—only moderately below the $98.5 billion volume on the New York Stock Exchange, the largest of the nation's financial markets.[30] Organized markets conform closely to the model of perfect competition, for no participant can influence price, and information on demand and supply is highly complete.

Unorganized markets are simply all markets not operating under centralized trading rules including membership requirements. Clearly, most markets and most of marketing are *unorganized* in the sense used *here*.

There is, however, another meaning of "organization" with respect to markets and groups of individuals and firms within markets. This latter

[30] "Booming Bedlam in Commodity Trading," *Business Week*, March 4, 1967. *See also* the discussion in D. A. Revzan, *Wholesaling in Marketing Organization* (Wiley, 1961), pp. 227–230.

sense of organization, to which we turn in Chapter 4, refers first and fore-most to the specific influence and coordination of activity among partici-pants—and the formality of such organization is only of second significance. The implications of this latter type of organization far exceed those of "organized markets" in the previous sense of membership and rules.

SUMMARY

A need is a condition—physical, psychological, or social in origin—requiring satisfaction. A want is the total set of physical and nonphysical elements believed by the demander necessary to satisfy the need. The relationship between need and want is that a want is a perceived need.

A market is the contact between demanders (buyers or lessees) and suppliers (sellers or lessors) for transferring ownership or use rights to a factor, good, or service.

A product is a customer's total set of percepts in terms of want-satisfying elements of what a supplier is offering for sale or lease. The *total* product is all the want-satisfying elements perceived by a demander, whereas the *physical* product is merely the perceived physical want-satisfying elements from among the entire set of perceived want-satisfying elements. The offerings of two or more firms are the *same* product if they are perceived by any demander as possessing essentially the same want-satisfying ability. Similarly, two offerings are *different* products when any demander perceives them as possessing essentially different want-satisfying abilities.

Want satisfaction is the degree to which the elements one is aware of in his want are matched by the elements one perceives in a firm's offering. *Complete* want satisfaction is the complete matching of want elements with offering elements.

Two offerings are in the same product market when they are the same product, that is, viewed as essentially identical in their want-satisfying ability. Two or more demanders are in the same product market when they have the same want, that is, they seek essentially the same elements of utility. Two suppliers are in the same product market when either they currently produce offerings that are preceived by the same demander as substitutable, or in a long-run sense, when the pools of resources constituting the respective firms are capable of supplying the same good or service *regardless* whether the particular good or service is currently being produced by either firm. The assessment in this latter case turns on the fact of resource flexibility (characterizing most firms) and the willingness of profit-maximizing managers to add to or alter the product mix as demand and cost structures change. Thus, the essential element is the capability of a pool of resources to produce, rather than the less interesting fact of how the resources are currently being utilized.

A geographic market is the spatial or time limits to which a buyer or seller will move (or the good will move) with respect to engaging in a transaction.

Market diversification is the simultaneous selling by a firm in more than one product or geographic market. Most firms in the economy by dint of being in more than one product or geographic market are diversified firms. The terms "conglomeration" and "conglomerate merger" are simply synonyms respectively for "diversification" and "diversification merger."

A new product, in an analytically important sense, is an offering that is perceived by the market demanders as being different in want-satisfying ability from any other offering currently offered by a given firm. Thus in this first sense, *new* product means a firm has entered a new product or geographic market. Secondly, a new product is an offering by a firm that is perceived as being different from all current offerings by *all* firms across all markets. In this sense, "new" means "unique" supply. But in both cases, "new" is determined by buyer perception.

Competition in the real world is rivalry, and it occurs in and only in markets. Competition (rivalry) produces satisfactory performance in the economy in two ways: one, by direct competition among the firms *in* a market and the other, by potential competition from firms *outside* the market who threaten to enter if prices rise above certain levels.

Differential advantage is the belief of a demander that one supplier's offering possesses more want-satisfying ability than other suppliers' offerings. This simply says that competition among suppliers is the rivalry in effecting larger intersections of the offer set and the want set. Rational, profit-maximizing firms strive continually for differential advantage.

Markets may be classified by similarity of behavior, time, whether they are buying or selling markets, and finally whether they are organized or unorganized markets (in the sense of codified trading rules).

SUGGESTED READINGS

Wants, Products, and Differentiation

James A. Bayton, "Motivation, Cognition, Learning—Basic Factors in Consumer Behavior," reprinted in Perry Bliss, *Marketing and the Behavioral Sciences* (Boston: Allyn and Bacon, Inc., 1963).

Bayton discusses the concept of needs and relates needs to wants. The framework is general, and applies equally to intermediate and ultimate demanders.

Edward Hastings Chamberlin, *The Theory of Monopolistic Competition* (8th ed., Cambridge, Mass.: Harvard University Press, 1962).

Chamberlin's analysis points up products as bundles of utility defined by the perception of demanders. The utility one perceives in an offering may derive from either or both the physical and non-physical elements in the offering. Chamberlin's framework relates to Bayton's in that both wants and products with respect to *want satisfaction* have essentially a subjective base. The Chamberlinian framework accords logically with differentiation as the effort to alter consumer perception of utility by altering either or both physical and nonphysical aspects of an offering. Selling costs are explicitly included in the analysis.

Chamberlin is best known for incorporating both competition and monopoly elements in his model—pointing out that most firms have a limited monopoly through some (frequently slight) uniqueness in their "total product."

Edward Hastings Chamberlin, *Towards a More General Theory of Value* (New York: Oxford University Press, 1957), especially Part II, "Nonprice Competition."

This book of articles by Chamberlin, includes a section (three chapters) dealing with the "product" and "advertising" as important economic variables. It is these discussions by Chamberlin that appear to us as his most significant contribution to marketing and competition theory. "Nonprice" and "price" competition are carefully considered and are seen as closely related concepts. (We discuss these issues, among other places, in Chapter 13 of the present book.)

Kalman J. Cohen and Richard M. Cyert, *Theory of the Firm: Resource Allocation in a Market Economy* (Englewood Cliffs, N.J.: Prentice-Hall, Inc., 1965), Ch. 11 "Monopolistic Competition."

Cohen and Cyert present a penetrating description and analysis of Chamberlin's monopolistic competition. Whatever the merits of some individual aspects of the model, when Cohen and Cyert consider it as a whole, they find little substantive distinction between "monopolistic competition" and oligopoly. Their arguments, a counterpoint to Chamberlin, are essential reading for the serious student.

Firms and Markets

John C. Narver, "Supply Space and Horizontality in Firms and Mergers," *St. John's Law Review*, Special Edition, Spring, 1970.

The article discusses firms in terms of their dynamics—conceiving of them as one or more pools of productive resources capable of responding to a range of demands. Accordingly, firms occupy one or more supply spaces, that is, their effective supply capability. The fundamentally important aspect of firms is not what they are making/selling at any instant of time, but rather the total range of what they could easily do. In this supply-space framework, many firms otherwise considered "dissimilar" in a static conception, are by dint of their identical supply capabilities, correctly to be considered as *in* many of the same markets.

Competition

Paul J. McNulty, "Economic Theory and the Meaning of Competition," *Quarterly Journal of Economics*, November 1968.

      McNulty distinguishes between competition as a structural concept and competition as a behavioral or process concept. Originally —in Adam Smith—competition meant a process, but today to many economists, the concept of competition is a state of affairs epitomized by particular structures.

Some Additional Related Readings

Morris Adelman, "The Product and Price in Distribution," *American Economic Review*, May 1957.

A. Alchian, "Uncertainty, Evolution, and Economic Theory," *Journal of Political Economy*, LVIII, June 1950.

M. A. Copeland, "Competing Products and Monopolistic Competition," *Quarterly Journal of Economics*, Vol. 55 (November 1940), pp. 1–40.

E. R. Hawkins, "Marketing and the Theory of Monopolistic Competition," *Journal of Marketing*, April 1940.

Jack Hirschleifer, "The Exchange between Quantity and Quality," *Quarterly Journal of Economics*, LXIX, November 1955, pp. 596–606.

II

The general
structure and behavior
of marketing

4

Marketing structure
and behavior

In Chapter 1 marketing was defined as any and all activities, both pre-purchase and post-purchase, related to transactions. The activities that comprise marketing range from activities by *individual* sellers and buyers to those of *groups* of sellers or buyers, and even groups of both. Thus, marketing may be perceived and analyzed at the level of individual units such as ultimate consumers or individual firms, or as well may be perceived and analyzed at the level of collections of individuals—such as groups of individual or firm buyers, groups of sellers, or both. It is critical in the following analysis always to remember that marketing may be perceived at these *various* levels of aggregation.

We now effect a synthesis of the preceding separate aspects of marketing as well as a basis for subsequent analyses. The purpose of this chapter is to understand the determinants of marketing behavior and the processes by which the determinants change. A general framework is provided by which one may relate various levels of aggregation in marketing and thereby link the structure and behavior of individual consumers and firms to the structure and behavior of aggregates. Moreover, the general framework permits linking one market to another within a given system of markets, such as, for example, in the canned and frozen vegetable industry, relating

The preceding chapters treated various aspects of marketing, including sorting, markets, wants, offerings, and products. By contrast, the current extractive, processing, wholesale, and retail markets.

chapter concentrates on a few strategic dimensions and ties the parts of marketing into a unified whole. Of course, any framework capable of relating both complex parts and various levels of the marketing economy necessarily must be presented rather abstractly at the outset. Thus, the reader must patiently accept a general treatment of the argument until we have identified the critical variables. Then we shall be more specific and show some implications of the general structure-behavior model.

In this chapter, we shall indicate (1) that marketing is essentially a collection of interacting participants, both individuals and groups; (2) that the concepts of structure and behavior are analytically useful at the level of individual units, and at the level of various aggregates, that is, groups of individuals, seller firms, buyer firms, all firms in a market, or groups of markets; and (3) that typically to explain the behavior of any specific level in marketing, one finds that "structure" includes elements not only from the subject level—the individual or the particular group—but also from one or more other levels. Thus, for example, if one is trying to explain the market behavior of a conglomerate, he must include one or more intrafirm aspects (division and corporate elements) as well as various elements within one or more of the firm's markets. We stress: One *cannot* understand marketing behavior by focusing only on consumers and individual firms (unfortunately the tendency of many business administration scholars) *nor* only on markets (the equally unfortunate tendency of many economists). Frequently, to understand the real structure, the analyst must comprehend elements from within the units as well as elements from the market(s).

THE NATURE OF HUMAN DECISION-MAKING

Humans, whether in the context of marketing or any other field of action, make decisions in terms of choosing the means to attain a goal. The particular decision may be that of a buyer attempting to find the means to satisfy a want, or of a seller attempting to find the means to maximize his profits. Thus, whether we are speaking of individual buyers or sellers or collections of buyers and sellers, the process is the same—the participants implicitly or explicitly select an objective and then determine the means to attain it. "Rationality" is the name given the activity of aligning means to ends. Human beings frequently do not have sufficient information to be objectively rational, that is, to be able to assess all alternative means and select that which is superior to any other alternative for everyone concerned.[1] Rather, because of limited information, people generally tend to behave in terms of subjective or personal rationality rather than objective rationality. Even if one intends to be objectively rational, it is virtually

[1] See Herbert A. Simon, *Administrative Behavior* (2d ed., Macmillan, 1958), p. 243, and *see also* H. A. Simon and James March, *Organizations* (Wiley, 1958).

impossible, because humans can see primarily only some portion of all the factors impinging on themselves.

There are two important points: (1) decision-makers in attempting to be rational take into account various elements in choosing how to attain their ends; and (2) because of their incomplete information, time, and calculating ability, they only deal with a *few* "strategic" or "limiting" factors *at a time*.[2] Precisely what they take into account, that is, the elements they consider as "strategic" or "limiting" for the attainment of the end will vary depending on the decision context—including the uniqueness of the decision, the importance, the time permitted, and so on. We focus most importantly on the elements themselves—those things taken into account in deciding how to attain ends—such as one's own budget or economic resources of other types; or an element such as one's ethnic heritage, or geographic location, or nearness and strength of competitors, and so on. These elements constitute the *structure*. Thus, the term "marketing structure" simply means the elements which a decision-maker, whoever "he" is and whatever level of aggregation, takes into consideration either implicitly or explicitly.

THE MEANING OF MARKETING STRUCTURE

Structure in marketing or in any other area of human decision-making represents the elements a decision-maker takes into consideration, explicitly or implicitly, in making a decision, or in general, in performing an activity. It follows that structure affects behavior. Many authors define structure precisely as the slowly-changing elements that affect behavior, implicitly recognizing that they affect behavior because they enter into the *decision process*.

Structure has a behavioral implication. It is in no sense a static concept. Rather, it is precisely those elements in any situation which, by *being taken* into consideration by the decision-maker, affect his behavior. The purpose of marketing theory, as we discussed in Chapter 1, is to help us understand marketing behavior by pointing out in any situation the elements that *most probably* will comprise *structure*. Knowing these elements in advance permits us to anticipate the type of behavior that will ensue. As we shall discuss more fully later, at any one time there is a long list of elements that *could* conceivably enter into structure. For example, an individual consumer *may* possibly, but not necessarily, be affected by the size of his income, his ethnic heritage, the location of his home and his place of business, his friends, and so forth. But because of lack of information, time, and so on,

---

[2] March and Simon, *op. cit.*, p. 169. *See also* Simon, *op. cit.*, p. 79 for a related discussion on the "limits of rationality."

the structure of any one decision probably consists of some relatively small subset of all conceivable elements.[3]

We see that structure being so intimately associated with behavior is the set of elements which are the "determinants" of behavior. If we are able fully to conceive of all elements taken into consideration by a decision-maker, then in principle, we are in a position fully to explain and predict behavior. However, in the real world, it is usually impossible for any analyst or student to realize completely all of the elements comprising a structure. Hence, our prediction of behavior is usually not entirely accurate. Obviously the better is our theory the better we are able to anticipate what elements will be in a structure and thereby more accurately predict behavior.

A common definition of structure is that it is "an orderly arrangement of elements."[4] Although an abstract notion, this meaning makes sense because in our usage, in which structure is associated so closely with behavior, there *is* "an orderly arrangement among elements"—*but* the orderly arrangement comes about by the decision-maker's adapting his behavior to the elements of structure. This sense of structure as implying adaptive behavior is even more vivid in a dictionary definition of structure as "the interrelation of parts as dominated by the general character of the whole."[5] Thus, we see structure as explicitly or implicitly serving to coordinate and influence human behavior—hence, there is an "orderly" arrangement among elements. It would follow that the more constricting, severe, or stringent are the pressures on the decision-maker from the structural elements, the more "orderly" is the ensuing arrangement (behavior) among the elements. Hence, in such instances, the better the predictability.

What influences orderliness of behavior? It is interesting to consider whether a smaller number of highly constraining and influencing elements creates more orderly arrangements, that is, more predictable behavior than a larger number of less constraining elements. Whatever the answer, it is sufficient for us to see in the concept "structure" precisely the spirit of

[3] Our definition of structure as the determinants of behavior—that is, the elements taken into consideration by a decision-maker—is a perspective widely used in economics. Richard Caves in speaking of participants at the *market* level of aggregation uses essentially the same language as we, for he defines *market structure* as "the economically significant features of a market which affect the behavior of firms in the industry supplying that market." Caves, *American Industry: Structure, Conduct, Performance* (1st ed., Prentice-Hall, 1964), p. 15. *Also see* Joe S. Bain, *Industrial Organization* (1st ed., Wiley, 1959).

[4] *See* William Scott, *Organization Theory: A Behavioral Analysis for Management* (Irwin, 1967) who says structure implies system and pattern, and that within a firm, structural elements are *effected* to provide an orderly arrangement among functions, p. 107. *See also* March and Simon, *op. cit.*, p. 170. This implication of controllable and uncontrollable elements within structures anticipates a subsequent discussion.

[5] *Webster's New Collegiate Dictionary* (2d ed., G. & C. Merriam, 1956), p. 841, fourth meaning.

"orderly arrangement among elements." The better we are able to understand the components of structure, the more we as analysts shall see orderly arrangements among the elements. And moreover, the stronger the compulsions by any element on the decision-maker in a structure, the more one can see orderly arrangement.

In terms of the constraints on the decision-maker, let us consider two somewhat far fetched extreme examples. Take the situation of the prisoner in a jail. His is a highly "structured" situation. His behavior is obviously constricted by very stringent influences and sanctions on him. All other things being equal, his behavior is rather predictable, at least in the short run. On the other hand, consider someone who, having worked long and hard through the year's employment, goes on vacation, and chooses to ignore the everyday compulsions under which he has labored, and enter a more intuitive, free-form existence. He purposefully establishes an "unstructured" mode of life. Few constrictions, by his choice, impinge on his behavior. From this unstructured situation, his patterns of activity are difficult to anticipate in this short (and, we might add, delicious) period.

For individual buyers or sellers some situations are highly constricting. For example, there are very strong social pressures on a college student aspiring to become a member of a social organization which he believes to be terribly concerned with his manner of dress and mode of behavior. For him, his structure consists of a few prime factors defined by the term "social pressures," manifested in the form of dress, conversation topics, choice of friends, and so on.

An example of a highly constraining structure for an individual firm is that experienced by a leading firm in a highly concentrated market where there are, let us say, two other leading sellers equally large. It is clear in this instance that with a slow rate growth one seller will gain only at the expense of one or both of the other sellers and hence there are very strong interdependencies among the sellers. These interdependencies act to restrain aggressive behavior on the part of any one firm—in the full and understandable recognition by all three of them that cooperation will be more profitable than aggressive individual behavior. Because of the character of constraints, the "orderly processes" emanating from this structure are cooperative rather than competitive.

THE SOURCES OF MARKETING STRUCTURE

The set of variables or elements that affect one's decision arise from various sources. Some of the elements are "controllable" whereas, others are "uncontrollable." Moreover, some of the elements are located at or within the decision unit; whereas, others are located at other levels of aggregation. Most but not all controllable structural elements are intra-decision-unit variables. Let us look at the controllability issue first.

"Controllable" / "Uncontrollable" Elements of Structure

As Scott implies in his *Organization Theory*, some elements of structure are created or established to provide a more orderly arrangement. But, clearly, other elements of structure (or sets of elements) are in no sense purposely created; rather, they are exogenously determined. Nevertheless the latter may have just as much or more a constraining influence than if they were created.[6]

Let us take as an example a firm's decision with respect to selling its goods and services. Some elements of its structure are elements effected by the firm itself. That is, it establishes certain policies and acquires what it considers appropriate resources in attempting to attain certain ends. Its resources, including both production and marketing resources with their capabilities and limitations, obviously are structural elements in many of the marketing decisions. But, also, some elements of its structure are *not* effected by the firm itself—such as the rate of market growth, the nearness and strength of the competition, the ease of entry into the market, the short-term tastes and preferences of customers, and the policies of the government with respect to antitrust and other trade regulation policies. The firm's decisions must be made in full recognition of *both* the internal structure elements, some of which are created and others of which are given constraints, and those structure elements outside the firm, most of which are not created directly by the firm. It follows that a rational decision-maker, whether he is an individual buyer or seller, or collections of buyers or sellers, will strive continually to enlarge his *control* over the nature of his structure. Thus, increasingly, an individual, if rational, is trying to enlarge his influence over elements so that he can make and carry out effectively precisely the decision he wishes. This desire "increasingly to control one's environment" has been pointed out by Alderson and Galbraith as well as by others.[7]

Of course, the desire to increase control over the elements in one's total structure is implicit in economic theory. It is expressed in terms of a firm's wishing to increase the inelasticity of its demand curve, an aim which implies an increased control over the supply of a good or service and thereby increased control over the pricing patterns for the good or service. And, of course, in terms of market competition, the desire to enlarge one's control over his structure is implicit accordingly in the effort of the firm to differentiate itself meaningfully from its current and potential competi-

[6] For a discussion of purposive structure and the associated concepts of problem solving and learning, *see* March & Simon, *op. cit.*, p. 170 ff., and Simon, *op. cit.*, p. 94 ff. A more precise discussion of the controllability of variables is found in Chapter 10 of the present book.

[7] Wroe Alderson, *Marketing Behavior and Executive Action* (Irwin, 1957) and John K. Galbraith, *The New Industrial State* (Houghton Mifflin, 1967).

tors—thereby gaining this increased control over supply. Thus, knowledge of structure not only assists analysts of marketing in predicting behavior of firms and individuals, but obviously such knowledge facilitates rational planning in the firm. That is, for rational utilization of resources and full anticipation of future requirements for resources, a firm or an individual would very much like to increase the certainty of the future events. Accordingly, he wants to be able to predict more accurately, and to do so, he strives always to improve his ability to "act" in the next period,[8] which means the drive to control both the number and type of his constraints.

At the market level of aggregation, there is a well known example in which the structure is largely beyond the control of any firm, namely, pure competition—a situation in which any one seller has virtually no control over his environment. The structure in the case of pure competition consists of several very constraining uncontrollable elements: market price, input costs, production function, and information.

A pure monopoly on the other hand, is a situation where there is relatively large control over structure. Much of the relevant structure in principle is completely or very largely controllable. The firm, which in this case is the sole supplier in the market, utilizes its resources according to perceived profitability and, among other things, has some control over input prices and market price on the output side, an ability to acquire more information, an ability to change production functions—an ability in short, to move from one economic short run to a new economic short run as it wishes. That is, in large part the monopolist can voluntarily structure his activity in whatever manner he deems appropriate. In "controlling" his price he has some influence over the ease of entry of new competitors as well as perhaps the rate of market growth. Hence, for the monopolist, the elements which he takes into consideration—that is, the structure— are to a large degree controllable by him; in that he controls supply, he necessarily has influence over the market price. And in controlling price he has some influence over the attractiveness of the market for potential entrants.

Thus, we may conclude that structure, the elements affecting behavior, is either or both (1) effected (purposeful and "controlled") or (2) involuntary ("uncontrolled"). Most firms (and groups of firms) in the real world are in neither purely competitive nor purely monopolistic markets. Hence, for most firms their structure is some combination of controllable and uncontrollable elements. As we shall discuss in the portion of the book analyzing managerial behavior, firms attempt continually to gain more control over their elements (that is, over their structure). Every firm rationally would like to be a monopolist in that it thereby would have considerable control over the elements to be considered in a market decision.

[8] Alderson, op. cit.

Structural Elements from Different Levels of Aggregation

The reader may ask, "What elements comprise structure?" It is difficult, although it is *the* crucial question in analysis, to determine before the fact what the relevant structure is. As we recall from Chapter 1, the whole thrust of theory is to suggest precisely what the behavior determinants, that is, the elements of structure, are. In the real world we never know the determinants of behavior for certain, but scholarly activity is always attempting to understand them more carefully. We *can* say with certainty that the relevant structure for any decision-maker—be he an individual or group of buyers or sellers—consists of some number of elements we can list in the abstract. In the absence of a complete theory, we do not know fully which elements will be evoked, nor the significance of any element. For example, the buying structure of an individual buyer (such as an ultimate consumer) may consist of the individual's income, occupation, social contacts, race, religion, geographical location (in part because of climatic and local differences), and so on. Thus, an individual buyer at any point in time has some set of elements he takes into consideration because for him they are important. These elements are the "buyer structure." Though different among different buyers, they are drawn from the totality of all elements, some of which are within himself and others that stem from groups to which he relates.

Consider another situation. What is the structure with respect to a firm and its selling decisions? We would suppose that the elements comprising the structure consist, in part, of the following: the number and closeness of competitors, the ease with which new firms can come into the market (obviously a consideration for the ease which the firm can raise its price above its average or marginal cost), the degree of product differentiation, the rate of market growth, the tastes of the customers, and so on— all of which are potential structural elements. But for any seller firm there are also other structural elements *within* the firm itself constraining its decision.[9] Thus, the structure of the selling decision consists *not only* of market-level elements but also intra-firm elements, such as organizational policies with respect to resource utilization, technological capabilities both in production and marketing, the personnel currently employed, the cost of capital to the firm, the communication network in the organization, and so on.[10]

[9] Cyert and March agree that to understand contemporary economic decision-making, one needs to supplement market factors with an examination of the internal operation of the firm. That is in our language, to include in structure, elements from both the market and the firm. See R. Cyert and James March, *A Behavioral Theory of the Firm* (Prentice-Hall, 1963), p. 1.

[10] Typically, many economists of the conventional profit-maximizing traditions ignored organizational considerations in their theories of firm behavior. One notable exception is R. H. Coase, "The Nature of the Firm," *Economica*, New Series, Vol. 4, 386–405. Also see Almarin Phillips and Oliver Williamson, *Prices: Issues in Theory, Practice, and Public Policy* (University of Pennsylvania, 1967), pp. 32–33, and 41.

We see, therefore, that for an individual or a firm as a buyer or seller, or for a group of buyers or sellers, the structure may consist of elements neither solely at the market level nor exclusively at the unit level but in some combination. Suppose one wanted to explain the behavior of a division of a large diversified firm, for instance, the Chevrolet Division of General Motors. Obviously some of the Chevrolet decision-makers' structural elements would consist of policies and resources at the level of the Chevrolet Division itself. But also clearly some of the considerations facing the Chevrolet Division would be policies and resources at the corporate level. In addition, there would be the market-level considerations, such as the number and substitutability of competitive products, the condition of entry for new competitors, the rate of market growth, and so on. In summary, structure typically consists of elements at both the firm or individual level, as well as the market level (and sometimes at *more* than one market level, such as an independent retailer vis-à-vis two or more wholesale market levels). It is the job of theory to tell us precisely which will apply.

Complexity of Structures

Repetitive Decisions

The question to which we now turn is not what elements may be in a structure but *how many* elements comprise a structure? If a decision-maker took into account but one factor, we would say the structure is extremely simple. On the other hand, if the decision-maker took into account many factors, whether from the unit level itself or one or more levels greater than the unit, we may say the structure is complex. As we shall discuss in chapters dealing with buyer behavior as well as seller behavior, there is considerable evidence that the structure of *repetitive decisions* for a given decision-maker tend to be increasingly simplified with experience and over time.[11]

For example, in the area of buyer behavior, as a buyer experiences continued satisfaction with a particular brand or source of supply, he tends increasingly to react habitually (that is, less consciously) toward this brand or source of supply, creating thereby an increased predisposition or loyalty toward it. This phenomenon, called "buyer learning," is simply evidence of an increasingly simplified buyer structure—fewer things explicitly are taken into account in the decision process. (See Chapter 9.)

It is equally so with sellers and what we may call "seller learning." As a seller continues successfully to attain his goals in putting together the marketing variables of price, promotion, distribution, and product features, he tends increasingly to rely on his successful experience, that is, the successfully known mixes of the variables, and thereby limits his search for alternatives. At the limit, a buyer or seller, by this learning process, is

[11] For a general discussion of long-run adaptiveness (learning), *see* March and Simon, *op. cit.*, pp. 9–10 ff. and pp. 170 ff.; Simon, *op. cit.*, p. 94 ff.

entirely habitual in his response to a given stimulus. The case is obviously one in which the structure is extremely simple, consisting essentially solely of one's repertoire of successful experience. (The reader must note that memory, although but a "single" element of structure, is nevertheless a complex composite of elements. Thus from outward appearances such a structure may be simple in terms of numbers of explicit elements, but it may also be an extremely *constraining* and insistently *reinforcing* structure.[12]) Obviously, however, the world would have to remain unchanging for one to be able simply to rely on his experience—and, unfortunately, a consistent world is not one that most decision-makers can anticipate. Hence, learning is seldom complete. (See Chapter 9.)

Nature of Decision Problem

The complexity of structure also varies in accordance with the *nature* of the decision problem. If the decision-maker, as we implied above, embarks on a new decision—one he has never faced before—he will be more extensive in his information search, analysis, and problem solving (assuming a nontrivial decision). Thus, the structure in such a decision typically is more complex than when the decision relates to already experienced or what he considers to be analogous problems.[13] The point is that a strategic decision (long-run planning horizon) structure differs from a tactical decision (near-term) structure.

Time

Time affects the complexity of structure. First, the complexity of structure varies according to the *time available* for decision. If rushed, a decision-maker of necessity relates fewer elements—hence, a more simple structure. Each of us can think of personal examples of forced simplification. Second, from an analytical standpoint, the complexity of structure depends among other things upon the interval of time we select for our observations of decision-making. In very short intervals of real or planning (economic) time, the decision stimuli and cues will be very few. By contrast, over a longer real time period or economic long-run, a large part of the memory content may be evoked during some portion of that interval. A large part of the psychological set and a correspondingly large number of environmental aspects may become a part of the stimuli that influence behavior.[14] Thus, from this second point, we stress that the implications of time for *complexity* of structure are identical whether one speaks in terms of real time or economic time (the character of adjustment implied respectively in the economic "short run" and "long run").

[12] March and Simon, *op. cit.*, pp. 9–10.
[13] *See* March and Simon, *op. cit.*
[14] March and Simon, *op. cit.*, p. 11.

Character of the Market

The complexity of the structure also varies according to the *character of the market*. In a market characterized by numerous small sellers selling essentially a homogeneous total product with relatively easy entry for new competitors and in which buyers are highly informed as to alternatives, no seller has much control over price. In this type of market—essentially the purely competitive market—the structure is relatively simple. Prices are beyond the control of the individual seller, and also virtually all other elements are essentially beyond both his control and immediate concern. The prevailing considerations are simply the input prices, the production function (which includes both "production" and "marketing") and market information and price.

However, as one moves to more concentrated markets—that is, fewer sellers accounting for total sales—sellers are not essentially independent one from another. Disproportionate increases in sales by one come at the expense of the sales of one or more others (of course, this assumes the market is relatively static in growth). The degree of interdependence increases with concentration. As a result, the complexity of the structure increases because not only is a firm having to consider the number and strength of competitors, entry conditions, and so on, but also it must anticipate the competitor's reactions to one's own behavior (the classic oligopoly problem). In the concentrated markets, as is widely recognized, there is a great conflict-cooperation phenomenon among the participants. The pressures for cooperation with competitors may exceed those for rivalry with them.

Economic theory has insufficiently delineated the relevant structure in oligopoly; hence, oligopoly behavior is not determinate—that is, we cannot, based on current theory and models, predict firm behavior in markets where there is a high degree of interdependence. The theory is simply inadequate. In the real world, a considerable number of elements are taken into consideration by decision-makers in concentrated markets, or in general, whenever there is a great amount of interdependence (which comes from multiple-market as well as single-market contacts) among the participants. Hence the structure in interdependent situations is sometimes very complex.

Structure in Terms of Organizations

We have stressed that the essence of structure is the affecting of behavior. And as we have also stressed, the degree to which the structure is either purposive and controllable, or exogenous and uncontrollable, in a sense is immaterial. Essentially all that matters to us as analysts is that the elements taken into consideration to some extent *affect the behavior* and thereby constitute for us, *structure*.

Structure, as the influencing of behavior, sometimes includes one or more *organizations*. The essence of an organization is specific influence directed to the members, as well as a coordination of their activities.[15]

We see then that some of the elements comprising a decision-maker's structure at one time may in fact represent one or more *organizations*. Because both "structure" and "organization" relate to influencing and coordinating behavior, there is a close relationship between structure and organization. If one by choice or otherwise is in some active sense a member of an organization, whether a family, a car pool, a fraternity, or local Democratic club, the organization at least in some decisions is a part of his decision structure. But the reverse is not always true: Structure does not always consist of organizations.[16] Thus, an organization vis-à-vis its members is structure, but structure is not always one or more organizations.[17] To label *all* structures as organizations—albeit true in a conceptual sense—overly extends the conventional meeting of the term organizations which pertains to both formal and informal, and voluntary and involuntary social groups. Usually one will find a substantial portion of a structure consisting of one or more organizations, but that does not entitle us to label any structure an organization.

The apparent test, admittedly subjective, of whether a structure in part or whole is an organization is the durability of the particular set of elements. If the elements were either only briefly to be found in the same combination or together only on a random basis, there is a strong temptation to consider the elements simply a structure not constituting an organization.

[15] James G. March and Herbert Simon, *Organizations* (Wiley, 1958), pp. 2–3 ff. *See also* A. L. Stinchcombe, "Social Structure and Organizations," in J. G. March (ed.), *Handbook of Organization* (Rand McNally, 1965), p. 142.

The implications of organization theory for marketing are numerous. The authors of the present book have drawn from several sources in developing the arguments in the immediate sections of this chapter. We acknowledge our debt to the very thoughtful presentations of several authors including, Herbert Simon, *Administrative Behavior* (Macmillan, 1958); March and Simon, *op. cit.*; Richard Cyert and James March, *A Behavioral Theory of the Firm* (Prentice-Hall, 1963); Mason Haire (ed.), *Modern Organization Theory* (Wiley, 1959); and Phillips and Williamson, *op. cit.*

Two related works, long considered important arguments on the organization of market activity, are Frank Knight, *The Economic Organization* (A. M. Kelly, 1951) and Ralph Breyer, *The Marketing Institution* (McGraw-Hill, 1937). A short essay suggestive of the organization of marketing is Edward A. Duddy and David A. Revzan, *Marketing: An Institutional Approach* (2d ed., McGraw-Hill, 1953), Appendix C. *See also* David A. Revzan, *Perspectives for Research in Marketing: Seven Essays* (Institute of Business and Economic Research, University of California, 1965).

[16] A reference group, in general terms, is an organization frequently of an implicit, tacit form to which a decision-maker relates. We will discuss reference groups more specifically in Chapter 8.

[17] One, of course, could say that the elements comprising a structure at any time constitute a unique *organization*—itself perhaps a complex of more typical organizations such as one's church, family and car pool.

As we noted, some structures are purposely effected as when one "structures a problem," or in the instance of a firm's policies constituting a purposeful set of constraints. It is the same with organizations: Some are the result of conscious efforts to create influencing and coordinating activity, and others are involuntary, such as certain reference groups based on one's race, family, sex, and so on. Organizations which are characterized by explicitly and overtly arranged communications channels are called "formal" organizations; whereas those (nonetheless influential) that are not explicitly created, at least in accordance with agreed upon rules of behavior and coordination, are called "informal" organizations. *But* all types of organizations, voluntary and involuntary, formal and informal, lead to the same result—influence and coordination.

Within many firms, or in general in all social organizations, one tends to find various types of both formal and informal organizations. In firms, one finds, for example, formal organizations such as the sales force, the accounting department, the computer programming department, and so on. With respect to the sales force, it is a formal organization with component formal organizations—all responsible to a sales manager. The sales division is responsible to the marketing manager, and the marketing division in turn to the executive vice-president in charge of marketing, who in turn is responsible to the chief executive officer.

Informal organizations abound in formal organizations. Informal organizations are groups such as those arising from friendships at the water-cooler, car pools, coffee-break groups, people with similar interests such as fishing partners, bowling teams and so on. Some personal reference groups are formal organizations and others are informal.[18]

There is a simple principle as to when a person, firm, or group in our framework becomes a member of any formal or informal organization. It is with whom he (it) identifies. Specifically,

An individual acts as a member of a group when he applies the same general scale of values to his choices as do other members of the group, and when his expectations of the behavior of other members influence his own decisions.[19]

When there are one or more strongly constraining organizations—formal or informal—among structure elements, the implication is that the organization rather than the subject individual becomes the decision-maker.

[18] *See* Tamotsu Shibutani, "Reference Group as Perspectives," *American Journal of Sociology*, May 1955, pp. 562–569. We hold that organizations, both formal and informal, pervade marketing and that organizational identification provides a primary key to understanding marketing. Organizational identification has long figured prominently in analyses of consumer behavior, as we shall discuss in our analysis of buyer structure and behavior in Chapters 8 and 9.

[19] Simon, *Administrative Behavior, op. cit.*, p. 151. *See also* Shibutani, *op. cit.*

It is entirely legitimate (1) to consider organizations as decision-makers in and of themselves, and (2) to conceive of an organization deciding for (constraining strongly) the subject individual. With respect to a collection of units as a single decision-maker, Cyert and March point out:

> Organizations make decisions. They make decisions in the same sense in which individuals make decisions. The organization as a whole behaves as though there existed a central coordination and control system capable of directing the behavior of the members of the organization sufficiently to allow the meaningful imputation of purpose to the total system.[20]

In summary, we are saying that because of individuals' (units') strong identification with a reference group (one or more other individuals or units), the latter aggregate in effect is the decision-maker. The more pronounced the coordination and control system, the greater the substitution of the aggregate for the individual.

Markets As Organizations

A market is always an organization, for it always impersonally or personally influences and coordinates supply and demand. Specifically, it coordinates particular supply to particular demand. Of course, the degree of formality of this organization varies. The most obvious example of the market as a formal organization is the formally organized markets such as commodity exchanges, discussed in Chapter 3. Less obvious examples of organization are "weak oligopolies." In some circumstances, the influencing and coordination on either or both the demand and supply sides are highly formalized and personal; whereas in other circumstances, they are highly informal and impersonal. The degrees of formality and personalness do *not* affect the validity of perceiving of markets as organizations, but they do, however, provide different implications for the behavior we may expect from the organization. In principle, a market as an organization is composed of two primary sets of members—all sellers and all buyers (including both current *and* potential sellers or buyers).[21] The behavior of the market organization is determined fundamentally by the power relationship between and within the two composite sets of members—the sellers and the buyers. The market as one total organization will behave differently when the member relationships are (1) characterized by sellers dominating the buyers; or (2) the buyers dominating the sellers; or (3) neither side dominant; or (4) asymmetries among either side.

---

[20] R. M. Cyert and J. G. March, "A Behavioral Theory of Organizational Objectives," in Haire, *Modern Organization Theory, op. cit.*, p. 76.

[21] *See* the discussion in Chapter 3 pertaining to suppliers in the same market.

Two or More Sellers and Two or More Buyers as Organizations

Dominance is a function of the relative degree of organization characterizing the two membership sets. Let us turn, therefore, to levels of aggregation immediately lower than the entire market—that is, to the seller and buyer groups themselves. There are various types of potential and actual organizations among the sellers and buyers. In general, a group of sellers or a group of buyers may constitute an organization. This means that if there are among the sellers specific influence processes and coordination (either of a formal or informal nature) then the sellers may be perceived as an organization. A tight oligopoly may lead to rather formal organization. A joint venture—a legal arrangement—is an obvious example of a formal organization among firms. Interlocking directorates may lead to organization of varying degrees of formality. A price conspiracy among sellers stems from an organization, sometimes relatively formal, of sellers. Similarly, there may be organization among buyers and hence organized behavior.

In a purely competitive market—characterized by atomistic seller (and buyer) structure—the relationship between the sellers is extremely impersonal. It is, therefore, improbable that there exist specific influence processes and coordination emanating from within the total group of sellers. Thus, in purely competitive markets, the "seller organization" is virtually or completely nonexistent. Witness the difficulty of even *explicit* efforts to organize agricultural supply. And, we may conclude similarly with respect to the existence of buyer organization in purely competitive markets. This is not to say that supply in a purely competitive market is not well ordered nor responsive vis-à-vis a given want. Nor is it to say that demand is not well ordered in such a market. It merely says that the organizing forces—that is, the influence and coordination—stem from impersonal forces originating from points *other than* within the group of sellers, or within the group of buyers. A long standing goal of government antitrust policy has been precisely to maintain this rule of impersonal market forces rather than personal influences between firms. (See Chapter 14.)

By contrast, a market characterized by only a few sellers (buyers) is one in which each seller (buyer) is aware of his competitors. In markets with high concentration, each firm recognizes that he and the other firms are extremely interrelated, for any disproportionate increase in sales (purchases) by one lessens some other firm's share. Frequently, therefore, considerable personalness—inter-firm specificity of influence and coordination arises in such a context. Such organization of sellers (buyers) may remain only informal and tacit, and each firm attempts individually to anticipate the character of rivals' responses before it changes its price or engages in more promotion, and so on. On the other hand in some highly concentrated markets, the interrelationships among the firms may be such as to encourage a formal organization among the sellers (buyers)—for rational firms soon discover that cooperation invariably yields higher returns than conflict.

The Formality of Organization

In markets characterized by pure competition, the complexity of the structure is less than in some more concentrated markets. Because of the degree of *independence* of participants, the organization in purely competitive markets is impersonal and informal. However, with increases in *interdependence* arising from increasingly concentrated markets or from the increased contacts between large firms diversified into many of the same product or geographic markets, the increased degree of personalness frequently heightens the potential for and actuality of formal relationships between the firms. Note that the many contacts between *highly diversified firms* increases personalness *no less* than single market concentration. Though overlooked by many economists, firms are *global* maximizers, and the multimarket relationships, and hence interdependence between large multimarket firms, may well effect the same sort of personal "competition," which in the single market case encourages increased nonpriced competition, live-and-let-live behavior, and in short, a substitution of cooperation for intense impersonal rivalry.[22] Public policy on conglomerate mergers, for example, only recently has begun to address itself to the competitive implications of the interdependencies arising from multimarket relationships rather than simply, as in the tradition of economic theory, looking only at single market relationships (see Chapter 14 and specifically, consider the U.S. Antitrust Division's challenge of Ling-Temco-Vought's acquisition of Jones and Laughlin Steel Company). In general, with higher degrees of interdependence among firms, the relationships—whether in a single market or across many markets—typically become more formalized. However, once again, whether the organization is explicit and overtly arranged or simply partially explicit, does not matter from an analytical standpoint. The result is the same—"organization" means influence, coordination, and increased cooperation.

Empirical evidence indicates both increased influence and more formality in the influence process, the greater the interdependence between firms. Accordingly the degree of rivalry is less in many highly concentrated markets and among similarly highly diversified firms because of the interdependence and the mutual realization, aided and abetted by *explicit* arrangement, that cooperation is more profitable than aggressive competition. Thus, with increased concentration in a single market, or increased

---

[22] See John C. Narver, "Supply Space and Horizontality in Firms and Mergers," *St. John's Law Review*, 1970, especially text at pp. 9–23, and 44–51. *See also* Federal Trade Commission, *Economic Report on Corporate Mergers* (1969), Chapters 2, 3, and passim; and Peter C. Dooley, "The Interlocking Directorate," *American Economic Review*, June 1969, pp. 314–23.

contacts between firms that are diversified, one finds tendencies for higher profit rates, which suggests therein a reduction of intense rivalry between the firms.[23]

There are additional aspects to which we will now turn. Consider the role of differentiation in conjunction with increased market concentration as factors with respect to the degree of formality of organization. In the preceding sections, we argued that all other things being equal, the greater the interdependence among either sellers or buyers, the greater the probability of organization and, at the limit, formal organization. However, if, for example, the seller firms are differentiated, that is, demanders perceive substantial utility differences among the several offerings in the market, the sellers, whatever the level of concentration in the market, are less interrelated than if they sold homogeneous total products. One sees thereby possibly offsetting tendencies—*increasing* interdependence stemming from increasing concentration (or in general, increasing contacts, however they arise), but *decreasing* interdependence stemming from increasing differentiation. The very interesting question is which will prevail—and whether and how much organization among sellers will result? Will increases in seller concentration (or contacts among diversified firms) and the concomitant increases in interdependencies swamp the possible decrease in interdependencies stemming from demanders perceiving substantial differences among the several offerings? We have noted earlier that firms if rational are continuingly trying to obtain more control over their structures. One way to do this is to differentiate oneself from his competitors so that one has increasing control over supply and hence, that portion of the structure. Also one must include the fact of potential-entrant buyers or sellers. Clearly

---

[23] This discussion of the probable formality of "organizations" as a function of concentration (proximity) paraphrases the oligopoly and oligopsony theory found in any price theory text. The preferability of joint cooperation to conflict, even in the absence of formal communication between the parties, is well documented in research on human behavior in many economic and other contexts. There is considerable research on individual choice and the decision whether to engage in cutthroat tactics or cooperate with a known but physically separated partner. One classic example of this research with many economic implications is the so-called "prisoner's dilemma." *See*, for example, Lester Lave, "Factors Affecting Cooperation in the Prisoner's Dilemma," *Behavioral Science*, Vol. 10, January 1965. An excellent discussion of the formality of interfirm organization is in Almarin Phillips, "A Theory of Interfirm Organization," *Quarterly Journal of Economics*, Nov. 1960, pp. 602–613.

The 1961 pricing conspiracy among electrical manufacturers was the behavior of a formal organization—that is, formally established channels for influencing and coordinating the group. *See* John G. Fuller, *Gentlemen Conspirators: The Story of the Price Fixers in the Electrical Industry* (Grove Press, 1962).

There is considerable evidence of the increasing interdependence and hence, reduced rivalry among firms as a result of increasing market concentration in a single market. This evidence is implicit in evidence of a positive relationship between concentration and price-cost margins. *See*, for example, Norman Collins and Lee Preston, *Concentration and Price-Cost Margins* (University of California Press, 1968).

concentration alone is not the sole determinant of interdependence. A firm could be the only seller in a market but if entry were relatively easy that firm would have relatively little control over its structure in that if it were to price above the average-cost level to any appreciable degree, it would undoubtedly attract new entrants.

Clearly, analysis of market behavior must include several variables, especially those types of pressures tending for organization among sellers and buyers as well as those types of pressures tending away from organization among sellers and buyers. It is not surprising, therefore, that in most markets the single variable of the *market* concentration of sellers or concentration of buyers is unable to explain statistically very much of market behavior.[24]

Focal Organizations

We have noted that typically a decision-maker is impinged upon by one or more organizations of which he voluntarily or involuntarily is a member. The organization (the constraints) to which he relates at any one time, we shall call the "focal" organization. As the decision-maker's attention turns from one organization in the structure to another, he is, we would say, simply changing his focal organization.[25] We must recognize that individuals belong simultaneously to many different organizations. Moreover, there are multiple and overlapping "organizations of organizations" all relating quite directly to goals and purposes accomplished through essentially economic and market activities.[26] According to Cyert and March, the focal organization varies with the nature and locus of the achievement problems of the human participants. The focal organization may be one or more of the sub-organizations of a firm or the overall organization of the firm itself, or some seller (buyer) organization of which the firm is a formal or informal member.[27]

The focal organization may be the total firm for certain classes of problems, but for other classes of problems, will incorporate interfirm as well as intrafirm organizations. The full overlay of *various* organizations' influences must be considered for full explanation of marketing behavior.[28]

---

[24] There are only two market structures in which the single variable market concentration is significantly ex ante determinative—pure competition and pure monopoly. However, neither pure competition nor pure monopoly enjoys very many real world examples. *See* Norman Collins and Lee Preston, *op. cit.*, for the evidence of the general relationship between market concentration and profits. *Also see* George Stigler, *Capital and Rates of Return in Manufacturing Industries* (Princeton University Press, 1963).

[25] Almarin Phillips, "An Attempt to Synthesize Some Theories of the Firm," in Phillips and Williamson, *op. cit.*

[26] *Ibid.*, p. 38.

[27] *Ibid.*, p. 36.

[28] *Ibid.*, p. 41.

In inferring the appropriate focal organization(s) in the structure, the point obviously is to select the organization(s) with which the decision-maker *identifies* or to which he relates in making a given decision. When one can identify the decision-maker's focal organization, one then can comprehend the relevant decision constraints and thereby more accurately predict the behavior. We repeat a basic fact: For any decision-maker such as, for example, a firm making a pricing decision, there may be several elements of structure only some of which are organizations. They may be one or more subgroups of the firm, the seller organization in the market, or the total market organization (sellers and buyers). For another example, consider a purchasing agent in a firm. The possible relevant focal organizations for him are perhaps the management group of the firm, the purchasing department, the buyer organization, and the market organization—but also various informal organizations with which the purchasing agent identifies, such as his peer group of other purchasing agents, various social groups such as the country club to which he may aspire, (thereby influencing the placement and/or size of orders), and his family (potentially very significant influence on his purchasing behavior).

The most subtle and hence most difficult task in the analysis is trying to identify the focal organizations—which necessarily requires the analyst to see the world as the subject decision-maker sees it. Unfortunately, it is tempting to impose our own beliefs as to what the decision-maker's reference groups are or what they should be. In analyzing the buying behavior of a particular black consumer, one or more aspects of black society may *or* may not constitute a reference group. If a black consumer does not identify with the black society in a given decision, then it clearly is pointless in analysis to incorporate aspects of that society. The essence of organization—specific influence and coordination—for *this* individual does not emanate from black society. Rather, in his case, there are probably one or more *other* reference organizations which the analyst must identify.

RELATION BETWEEN STRUCTURE AND BEHAVIOR: A DYNAMIC VIEW

We have stated in the preceding passages that structure affects behavior. Thus, all other things being equal, the structure, for example, of the buyer conditions his behavior. So it is with sellers, and so it is with any other level of aggregation or any other participant—such as all buyers in the market or all sellers in the market. They frequently are a "single" decision-maker; that is, a collective decision-maker.

Analysis becomes more realistic and necessarily more complicated when we recognize that all other things frequently are not equal. For example, a buyer structure may lead the buyer to desire certain things that the sellers, because of the seller structure, do not provide. Specifically, a buyer structure may lead a buyer or a group of buyers to desire, for example, a convertible compact automobile with all the trimmings of a sports-style car, but the seller structure may induce the sellers, as they consider what they believe relevant to their profit maximization, *not* to offer such a car. The sellers are, in this case, content in the belief that the less-than-fully satisfied buyer still will take the offered automobile in that he has no good alternative, and potential competition cannot enter to provide him the more desired offering.

We see that although buyer behavior is determined in largest part by buyer structure, it also is affected by seller structure. And in parallel fashion, the sellers' range of alternatives is determined by both seller structure and the constraints of buyer structure. The essential point at this juncture is that in largest part buyer or seller structure affects respectively buyer or seller behavior, but that the structure on the opposite side of the market also affects behavior. This is especially true with respect to seller behavior, for unless a seller corresponds in some degree (as we have discussed in Chapter 3) to the wishes of the buyer, his offering is obviously meaningless. Virtually no amount of energetic activity can sell his products if the offering is perceived as totally irrelevant to the want of the demander. (A subsequent section of the book dealing with the behavior of the firm will have more to say about the interrelationship of buyer structure on seller behavior.) In short, we say that the more substantive alternatives a buyer has to choose from, the more the sellers must and will be conditioned by the buyer structure. In intensively rivalistic markets, the sellers must respond precisely to what is wanted or forego the sale to some competitive seller. This is simply the performance of *active complete competition.* On the other hand, in a market in which buyers have fewer options, the seller can steer a more independent course. Accordingly, in the extreme—a monopoly— the seller structure almost completely determines seller behavior, in that he need pay little heed to the wishes of the virtually *un*sovereign customer. Thus, the greater the real rivalry among sellers, the more choices are open to buyers and, therefore, the more the sellers have to pay close attention to buyer structure.

Our analysis has begun with the notion of structure leading to behavior. Let us add further complexities. Behavior can be broken down into two parts: (1) *conduct*, the actual decisions of the decision-maker, and (2) *performance*, the outcome of those decisions usually expressed in terms of profits and efficiencies for sellers, and profits and utility for customers and ultimate consumers respectively. At any one point in time there is a total set of structure elements with respect to a given decision-maker and this leads to behavior. Over time, the participants' behavior will affect those structure elements both as to number and type. We have already mentioned buyer learning which is simply satisfaction leading back to the structure itself so that increasingly the structure is simplified. This obviously is but one of many possible examples of a return influence of behavior on structure.

Another example of behavior affecting structure is seen at a higher level of aggregation than the individual unit. Consider a market of five sellers, each aggressively competing against the others. If the behavior of one seller is superior to that of one or more of his competitors, sooner or later his greater efficiency or more aggressive behavior or other superior aspects may ultimately decrease the position of one or more of the other firms. Let us take another example at the level of the individual firm. If the firm has not performed as profitably as it had desired, the unsatisfactory results will induce the decision-makers to alter some elements in their structure in the attempt to improve performance.

We see from these few simple examples a continual interreaction between structure and behavior. At any one time there are definable structures for any decision-maker which lead to definable (in principle) types of behavior, but the one or more various aspects of behavior *in turn* tend to affect structure and thereby create new structures. Thus, we are saying, structure leads to behavior which in turn leads to alterations of the initial structure. The more active the competition among either or both buyers or sellers, the stronger the interaction between structure and behavior.

Behavior affects structure in another sense. Specifically, marketing functions become institutionalized in structure.[29] That is, in a dynamic context, one perceives activity emanating from structure leading to *new* forms and other elements of *new* structure. The concept of form following function or derived from function is, of course, the notion held by Alderson in his concept of "marketing functionalism."[30] Thus, the interrelationship of structure and behavior is truly a complex matter and we repeat: At any time, in principle, one can define the relevant structure with respect to any decision-maker. From this structure there emanates behavior which, in conjunction with changing elements in a dynamic world, will lead over time to new structures. To be complete, the analyst will want to consider simultaneously the structure-behavior relationships and the behavior-structure relationships. Structure to behavior is essentially the framework of the traditional industrial organization approach; whereas, the behavior leading to (new) form or structure is essentially the framework of the institutional theory school. In his own framework, one will want to consider and comprehend both, and thereby appreciate the dynamic and always evolving character of structure and behavior.

[29] See E. A. Duddy and D. A. Revzan, *Marketing: An Institutional Approach* (2d ed., McGraw-Hill, 1953), pp. 17–19. Also see Chapters 1 and 2 of the present book for references to institutions and institutional theory.

[30] See Wroe Alderson, *Marketing Behavior and Executive Action* (Irwin, 1957).

A FURTHER SPECIFICATION OF MARKETING PARTICIPANTS, STRUCTURE, AND BEHAVIOR

In this section we shall elaborate on some previous discussions. (Refer to "The Sources of Marketing Structure.") Analytically, there are four important levels of aggregation of marketing participants: (1) individuals (units), (2) groups of sellers, or groups of buyers, (3) all sellers and buyers in a market, and (4) collections of two or more markets or inter-market aggregation.[31]

Individuals (Units) and Structure

The structure of the "unit" (includes individuals, firms and nonfirm organizations such as government agencies) is by definition its set of decision considerations. At this individual or unit level of aggregation, it is analytically useful to divide the units into two types—(1) unit buyers and their structure and (2) unit sellers and their structure.

Unit Buyers and Structure

Buyer structures at the unit level consist of the decision elements of the individual buyer. Thus, for example, unit-level buyer structure with respect to ultimate consumers pertains to the constraints on behavior of any individual consumer such as the individual's economic resources, the sociological and psychological influences impinging on him, his stage in his life cycle, the size and age of his family, his ethnic background, and so on.[32] However, as noted, some elements in unit buyer structure may come from higher levels of aggregation—such as social-group influences.

With respect to individual firms as buyer evidence suggests that a firm's buying is affected by the budget constraints of the firm; the buyer's market share in the buying market (that is, the degree of monopsony power); the production flexibility and excess capacity of the firm which affects the

---

[31] For a discussion of firm structure as a determinant of firm behavior *see* for example, Richard Cyret and James March, "Organization Structure and Pricing Behavior in an Oligopolistic Market." *American Economic Review*, March 1955, pp. 129–39.

For a discussion of groups of sellers and groups of buyers constituting collective decision-makers and also with respect to their implications for structure, refer to the discussion on pp. 99–102 of the present chapter.

See Joe S. Bain, *Industrial Organization* (Wiley, 1959), pp. 7–9, and Richard Caves, *Industry Structure, Conduct and Performance* (Prentice-Hall, 1964), Chapter 2, for discussions of the minimum structure elements required to constitute a base for predicting market behavior.

The most inclusive aggregation, the inter-market level, may include only two or at the upper limit, includes *all* markets in the economy. The latter is the total marketing system.

[32] Buyer structure for consumers, firms, and nonfirm organizations as well as buyer structure at the market level are considered in Chapter 8.

"make or buy" decisions of the firm and hence its buying behavior; the self-perception of the role of purchasing agent or other individual or individuals who make the purchasing decisions, and so on.[33] Similar types of components comprise the buyer structure of nonfirms such as educational institutions, hospitals, libraries, etc. The considerations with respect to buying—that is, the buyer structure—of the Defense Department or other such units includes among other things policies such as the character of bidding permitted potential suppliers, the budget limitations of the buying unit, political pressures, and so on.

Unit Sellers and Structure

Individual sellers include private individuals such as a person selling his car to a used-car dealer, plus the whole gamut of commercial firms of one type or another, as well as nonfirm units such as a governmental agency selling the cutting rights to some of its timber or a post office selling unclaimed parcels. Unit-level sellers and structure are most clearly analyzed by dividing structural elements into three groups: (1) intra-agency aspects, (2) price/product aspects, and (3) space/time aspects.

Intra-agency Aspects.   Agency aspects are the unique constraints within the various *types* of sellers—businesses, governmental units, nonprofit units and individuals—in the marketing system. They range from large complex private enterprises such as Procter and Gamble or Sears & Roebuck, to the Department of Agriculture, to Consumers' Union (which provides product information to consumers), to the neighborhood "mom and pop" corner store. They also include agencies providing other functions such as transportation companies, insurance companies, banks, and manufacturing firms.

Perhaps the most visible commercial set of agencies is the retail establishments with which we as consumers deal on a daily basis. However, these are only a small portion of all commercial agency types, let alone all agencies in marketing.

Price and Product Aspects.   "Price" includes the resources given up and the utility received. Specifically, price is the total resources expended to acquire a given good or service. (See Chapter 13.) "Product" is an *offering's total* utility perceived by customers. (See Chapter 3 and Chapter 11.) And as we shall discuss in Chapter 13, "price" and "product" are extremely interrelated concepts. For our present discussion, customer perceptions constituting "price" and "product" are important considerations in a firm's selling decision. Hence, price and product aspects are a substantial set of elements

---

[33] Some aspects of purchasing agents' intra-firm bargaining and political behavior are discussed in George Strauss, "Tactics of Lateral Relationship: The Purchasing Agent," *Administrative Science Quarterly*, Vol. 7, September 1962; and see also the discussion of the structure and behavior of industrial purchasers in Chapters 8 and 9.

in the structure of a selling unit. Price structures are interlinked with agency structures.

Consistent with our usage of "structure," the concept "price structure" is the terms and conditions for sale or lease of a given good or service— obviously, considerations for both sellers and customers. Price structures as enunciated by a seller or a buyer specify (at least some of) the total scarce resources a customer must expend to buy or lease a given good or service.[34] One may perceive price structure at the inter-market level of aggregation in which it has a vertical dimension. That is, there are variations in the price of a product as it begins from some raw form to some finished state, or in general as it moves through channels of distribution. Thus it is clear that price structures can be defined for a unit, a market, an industry, or in principle for the economy as a whole.[35]

Space-time Aspects.   Spatial and time dimensions of the supplying and demanding of any product or service clearly are elements of both seller and buyer structure. Spatial-time factors are translated into and expressed in terms of the *costs* (including opportunity costs) which are required to move either the goods and services or the customers over distance. It is obvious that the *time* required for movement is frequently an important element along with the physical costs themselves.

For a firm, for example, a supermarket, the spatial structure with respect to selling is the distance which consumers (based on their own exception of personal costs) will travel to reach the enterprise; and with respect to buying, it is the least-cost distance for its purchase of goods and services. Different products as well as different agencies have dissimilar geographic structures. For example, chewing gum, television sets, and antique silverware have geographic structures of various dimensions depending how consumers and suppliers view the importance of the transaction as well as the supply alternatives and the efficiency of supply.[36]

Groups of Sellers or Groups of Buyers

When among the sellers or buyers in a market, an organization emerges, there is a collective decision-maker. The argument is qualitatively the same whether the organization is informal or formal. The basic discussion of a

[34] The term "scarce resources" is used advisedly, for as we make clear in Chapter 13, the "price" of an item includes far more than dollars given up by the customer.

[35] Some authors have discussed the concept and examples of price structure in considerable detail. *See*, for instance, Duddy and Revzan, *op. cit.*, Chapters 25 and 26 and R. S. Vaile, E. T. Grether, R. Cox, *Marketing in the American Economy* (Ronald, 1952), Chapter 23.

[36] We examine some of the many issues and subtleties of the space and time aspects in Chapter 7 and also in the discussion of customer structure and behavior, Chapters 8 and 9.

group of sellers or a *group* of buyers as a decision-maker in and of itself is found at pp. 99–100 of the present chapter. The fundamental point is that as interdependence increases among firms, the units tend to identify with the group—that is, it becomes their focal organization.

Market Buyer Structure

Oversimplifying, the most important aspects of the structure of demanders in a market are their tastes, their purchasing power, and the concentration of the buyers. All three aspects are determinants of buyer behavior with respect to both nonultimate consumers and ultimate consumers.

Taking demander concentration first, the more concentrated the purchases among a group of firms, the more the buying side may tend to interdependence, that is, oligopsony, and at the limit, to monopsony. Economic theory suggests and observation corroborates that collusion among buyers is far more probable when buyers are few, that is, buying is concentrated.[37]

As to ultimate consumers, the more they are concentrated, or what is the same thing, the more interaction among consumers—the more rapidly innovations are accepted and spread, the greater is the likelihood of emulation. In general, the greater the interaction among consumers, the more pronounced are many sociological and psychological influences.[38]

In recent years researchers increasingly have been successful in isolating and measuring the critical elements of market buyer structure such that predictions of buyer behavior are at times very accurate. One such example is the success achieved in predicting the acceptance of a new brand of concentrated orange juice in Chicago.[39]

Market Seller Structure

Perhaps there has been even more success in beginning efforts to isolate important determinants of seller behavior. Market behavior subsumes both the price and nonprice decisions as well as the net results in terms of market profit rate, efficiency and progressiveness in the use of resources, and

[37] The conspiracy in bidding among electrical contractors in 1961 occurred in concentrated markets—a not-surprising fact in that coordination among "rivals" is far easier when the number of interested parties is few, *City of Philadelphia v. Westinghouse Electric Corp.*, 210 F. Supp. 483 (E. D. Penn., 1962).
   See also the discussion in Chapter 14.

[38] *See* Elihu Katz and Paul F. Lazarsfeld, *Personal Influence* (Free Press, 1955); James Coleman, Elihu Katz, and Herbert Manzel, "The Diffusion of an Innovation Among Physicians," *Sociometry*, December 1957, pp. 253–270.
   See also Tamotsu Shibutani, *op. cit.*

[39] Alfred A. Kuehn, "Consumer Brand Choice—A Learning Process?" in Ronald E. Frank, Alfred A. Kuehn, and William F. Massy, *Quantitative Techniques in Marketing Analysis* (Irwin, 1962), pp. 390–403. The model used in the study is essentially that of learning—that is, systematic changes in behavior resulting from exposure to a succession of experiences with a particular product or brand. The basic learning model is discussed in Chapter 9 of the present book.

so on. The decision portion of market behavior typically is called market conduct and the net results, market performance.[40]

Research suggests that the most important determinants of market performance, especially profit levels and rates, are seller concentration, and condition of entry. Within the condition-of-entry aspect, an apparent critical determinant of profit performance in a market is the degree of product differentiation. That is, in concentrated markets, the more customers perceive differences among the offerings of the sellers in the market, the higher tend to be both the profit levels and profit rates. Other important causes of barriers to entry are scale economies and absolute cost advantages.[41]

Market-Level Participants (All Sellers and Buyers in a Market)

The legitimacy of perceiving a *collection* of units as a decision-maker was pointed out in previous sections of this chapter. If an analyst is interested in all sellers *or* all buyers in a market, he would focus on the preceding level of aggregation. However, if he is interested in conceiving of the *entire* market as an organization embracing both buyers and sellers, then he analyzes at the market level of aggregation. In practice, there is no clear line between the two levels of analysis.

Market structure is the total constraints on the collection of buyers and sellers in a market. It is the totality of the three firm-level structures within unit structure *and* other elements such as the number and size of firms, the ease of entry by new demanders and suppliers, rate of growth of the market, and so on. These latter are part of structure in that they affect behavior.

Specifically, in addition to unit-level structure, the most important elements of total market structure are seller concentration, buyer concentration, tastes and purchasing power of buyers, condition of entry by new sellers and new buyers, differentiation of products in the market, rate of growth of the market, and ratio of variable to total costs.[42]

Thus, market structure is an aggregation of agency structures, price

[40] Bain, *op. cit.*, Chapter 1 on conduct and Chapter 9 on performance. *See also* Caves, *op. cit.*, Chapters 3 and 6.

[41] Though there are exceptions, high levels of seller concentration and high barriers to entry, and especially high product differentiation, are positively associated with profits. This implication of economic theory has been supported by several researchers. *See* Joe S. Bain, *op. cit.*, Chapter 10 on market structure and performance; Caves, *op. cit.*, pp. 94–108; William S. Comanor and Thomas A. Wilson, "Advertising, Market Structure and Performance," *Review of Economics and Statistics*, vol. 49 (November 1967), pp. 423–440; and H. Michael Mann, "Seller Concentration, Barriers to Entry, and Rates of Return in Thirty Industries, 1950–1960," *Review of Economics and Statistics*, vol. 48, August 1966, pp. 296–307. A summary of relevant studies as well as additional evidence of market seller structure-performance relationships are in Norman Collins and Lee E. Preston, *op. cit.*

[42] See Joe S. Bain, *op. cit.*, and Richard Caves, *op. cit.*

structures, and geographic structures and certain additional structural elements. Clearly, structure at the market level is more comprehensive than that of the unit or firm level—although as pointed out, the "structure" for any one unit may include elements from both levels of aggregation.

Summary of Marketing Participants and Structures

To summarize, units specifically are the individuals, firms, and other participants in marketing. However, to understand unit behavior it is necessary to perceive marketing in terms of more than one level of aggregation.[43] Thus, the elements comprising the structure of units may come not only from the units themselves but from other levels as well. For example, if one wants to explain the average profit level of sellers in a market, he will look at the sellers. Or, for example, if one is focusing on the performance of a total industry, he will tend to analyze all the industries' component markets, examining in them the seller-buyer relationships.

Marketing Behavior

We have mentioned that for every level of aggregation there is a structure, and that behavior emanates from every structure whether at the individual-unit group, market-level, or inter-market level of aggregation. The behavior of units we may call "unit behavior," and that of groups, "group behavior," and so on. Behavior may be divided into *conduct*—the policies and decisions; and *performance*—the net economic results in terms of profits and efficiency and so on for commercial agencies, utility for consumers, political attainment for government agencies, and so on.

Marketing Conduct

Unit-level Conduct. At the unit level, conduct is the activities of decision-making including both establishing goals and policies and implementing them. More specifically, in principle, there are two separable sets of conduct at the unit level. One is essentially the choice of long-range goals, technology, and capital composition—intra-agency constraints of a strategic nature. This first set of "conduct" approximates the economic long run, for it is the choices of technology, basic policies, and capital that substantially define the behavior feasibility for a unit for some ensuing period.

The second set of conduct, separable in principle, but definitely complementary to the first set, is the recurring information, price, product, promotion and distribution decisions—activities of a tactical nature. These

---

[43] As we mentioned in Chapter 1, marketing scholars traditionally have focused primarily on "unit" level, a very particular emphasis; whereas many economists of the traditional industrial organization analysis have focused only on the one or more aggregate market levels, a sometimes equally oversimplifying emphasis. The present analytical approach obviously attempts to overcome the shortcomings of either polar extreme.

are more in the economic short-run than the former, for in total they comprise the responses a unit makes to changes in its environment including changes among competitors' conduct. This second set is frequently called the eight marketing functions, one or more of which any one unit performs (see Chapter 5).

Group-, Market-, and Inter-market Conduct. At levels of aggregation above individual units, conduct is necessarily the sum of the conduct of the units and/or groups of units. If there are many diverse types of units and if there is little or no organization among units, conduct at aggregation levels may be difficult to predict with any accuracy. That is, the particular choices with respect to long-run and short-run decisions described above may be a priori unpredictable.[44] Diverse unit structures create the possibility of varying types of market conduct, for within each structure there may be many possible policies.[45] On the other hand, the greater the interdependence among units or groups of units the greater the predictability of conduct. Seller and buyer concentration and barriers to entry will be among the primary determinants of the diversity of market conduct.

Marketing Performance

Unit-level Performance. Performance is the net result of the conduct, and is usually measured and expressed for commercial units in terms of net profits; rate of return on owners' equity; efficiency with which plant, equipment and other resources are used; progressiveness; and so on. The performance of nonprofit agencies such as governmental bodies is measured in terms appropriate to their goal, such as the efficiency with which tasks were performed with the given budget, the extent of new, more productive approaches, voter satisfaction, and so on. For ultimate consumers, the appropriate measure and expression of performance is want satisfaction, or simply "utility."

At the market level, performance is expressed in terms of the average profitability, level of efficiency, progressiveness, and so on for all units in the market.

Group-, Market-, and Inter-market Performance. Performance of levels of aggregation above the unit level is expressed as the average performance of the units and/or groups of units.[46] We have discussed some of the structure-performance relationships in previous sections of this chapter. An overall analysis of performance at various levels of aggregation is the focus of Chapter 15.

[44] Bain, *op. cit.*, Chapter 8, and Caves, *op. cit.*, Chapter 3.
[45] See Caves, *op. cit.*, Chapter 3.
[46] See Bain, *op. cit.*, Chapters 9 and 10.

Summary of Marketing Behavior

Marketing behavior may be separated in principle into two parts: conduct and performance. Conduct is the policies and decisions of marketing participants, and performance is the net outcome of the decisions.

A basic point, to be recalled constantly, is that at any one time structure affects behavior. However, over time behavior affects structure. One type of conduct itself is the choice of certain structural elements believed essential to effect stated goal. Competitive conduct and dissatisfaction with actual performance are two other ways in which behavior affects structure.

SUMMARY OF THE STRUCTURE AND BEHAVIOR OF MARKETING

Marketing, as all the prepurchase and postpurchase activities related to transactions, is a complex of interacting participants. The participants in marketing range from individuals as sellers and buyers, to groups of sellers, groups of buyers, and even groups of sellers *and* buyers. Marketing can be perceived and analyzed at several levels of aggregation—individuals (units), groups of units, entire markets, or even groups of markets.

In human decision-making the rational decision-maker first selects a goal and then decides upon the means to obtain it. In choosing among alternatives, the decision-maker will, in focusing on his goal, estimate the effectiveness of the various means, taking into account some or all elements that are going to affect his decision. The elements or considerations he takes into account are what we call the "structure." Thus the structure for a buyer or the structure for a seller or the structure for any other participant, is simply the elements the particular decision-maker takes into account in making a decision. For a buyer, the elements in his structure may include his income, his ethnic background, his geographic location, his occupation, his age, his family, his friends, his social reference groups, and so on.

Structure by definition is closely associated with behavior. Behavior in turn may be broken down into two parts: (1) conduct, which is decisions and the policies themselves, and (2) the performance, that is, the net result of the decision in terms, for example, of utility for consumers, and profits, efficiency and so on for commercial decision-makers.

A static model points up that structure influences behavior. The static model of structure affecting behavior simply emphasizes the relationship from a given structure. Thus, at any one time there are definable structures from which behavior emanates. However, *over time* the relationship is dynamic and any structure is, in turn, affected by behavior. If one is speaking of an individual unit, the structure of that unit—that is, its policies, its resources, its markets, in short, its total set of constraints—will determine, in large part, its behavior. However, the performance aspect of behavior may be deemed insufficient given the unit's goals and thus, the unit may choose to change insofar as possible some of its structural elements in order to improve performance. For another example of behavior affecting structure, consider the market level of aggregation, such as five firms in competition with each other. The competitive tactics of one or two may be superior to those of the others, in which case over time the others will be lessened in their market position, and ultimately perhaps even extinguished in that particular market, thereby changing the structure of the market (the elements that remaining decision-makers would take into account).

The elements of structure for any one decision-maker typically arise not only from its own level of aggregation, that is, within the decision-maker itself, but also from other levels. Thus, for example, a firm in many decisions may take into account aspects of its *own firm* such as its resources, its personnel, its policies but also aspects from the *market* level of aggregation, such as the number and nearness of competitors, the ease of entry into the market, and so on. Also, some elements of marketing structure are relatively controllable whereas others either at the same or other level of aggregation are essentially uncontrollable. All firms continually try to gain greater control over the elements in their structure.

The number of elements in a structure is a function of many factors. The complexity of structure is determined in part by the issue of whether it is a repetitive decision being made. A decision once having been made may tend to be simplified in subsequent trials given reasonably satisfactory performance in the initial trial. The complexity also varies according to the time available for the decision and the character of the market, that is, the degree to which the firm by differentiation or otherwise has control over supply and hence price.

Structure—the elements taken into consideration in a decision—frequently consists of organizations. The essence of an organization is a specificity of influence directed to the members. Individuals are members of many organizations, both voluntarily and involuntarily, where "organization" means simply a group which influences their activities. The group may be a family, a car pool, a bowling team, a coffee group, or it may be a formal organization as a sales force, a political party, a church, and so on. One is a member of a formal or informal organization when he identifies with it, that is, when he applies the same general scale of values to his choices as do the other members of the group. The organization to which one relates at any one time is called the "focal" organization. The most subtle task and hence most difficult feature in marketing analysis is trying to identify the focal organizations of the decision-maker—which necessarily requires the analyst to see the world as the subject decision-maker sees it.

Groups of sellers and buyers in a market can, at times, be seen as organizations themselves. That is to say, when the interdependence among sellers or the interdependence among buyers becomes sufficiently pronounced there tends to arise informal if not ultimately formal organization among the sellers and among the buyers. In general, interdependence increases for reasons of increasing concentration among either the sellers or the buyers, or even because of increased contacts between firms, as happens when diversified firms increasingly encounter each other across many markets. As a result there tends to arise implicit and even explicit organization among the firms.

As stated, structure and behavior, dynamically viewed, relate as follows: structure at any one given period of time affects behavior, which in turn over time affects structure. In the long run, the functions or the activities in marketing become institutionalized in structure. That is, the activities become expressed in particular patterns or structural forms. This suggests that due to society's sanctions, preferences, and legal stipulations, functions end up being formed in particular consistent ways. These technically are the real institutions, whatever their outward appearance or form. For example, the institution of credit is engaged in by a variety of forms—banks, savings and loan associations and insurance companies to name a few.

SUGGESTED READINGS

The Concepts of Structure, Rationality and Organization

Richard Cyert and James March, *A Behavioral Theory of the Firm* (Englewood Cliffs, N.J.: Prentice-Hall, Inc., 1963), Chapter 1 and *passim.*

Herbert A. Simon, *Administrative Behavior* (2d ed., New York: Crowell-Collier and Macmillan, Inc., 1958).

Herbert A. Simon and James March, *Organizations* (New York: John Wiley & Sons, Inc., 1958).

Marketing Structure: Unit and Market-Level

Joe Bain, *Industrial Organization* (1st ed., New York: John Wiley & Sons, Inc., 1959). See especially Bain's discussion of market structure and its relation to performance.

Perry Bliss, "Non-Price Competition at the Department Store Level," *Journal of Marketing*, XVII (April, 1953). An interesting discussion of the firm's conduct affected by elements of structure from both the firm and market.

Richard Caves, *American Industry: Structure, Conduct, Performance* (1st ed., Englewood Cliffs, N.J.: (Prentice-Hall, Inc., 1964). *See* Caves' discussion of market structure and its relation to performance.

Norman Collins and Lee Preston, *Concentration and Price-Cost Margins* (Berkeley: University of California Press, 1968). A useful discussion and summary of empirical analyses of the association between market-level elements of structure and performance.

Richard Cyert and James March, "Organization Structure and Pricing
   Behavior in an Oligopolistic Market," *American Economic Review,*
   March 1955, pp. 129–39. Discusses aspects of a firm as elements of
   structure and the implications for behavior.
Alfred A. Kuehn, "Consumer Brand Choice—A Learning Process?" in R. E.
   Frank, A. A. Kuehn, and W. F. Massy, *Quantitative Techniques in
   Marketing Analysis* (Homewood, Ill.: Richard D. Irwin, Inc., 1962),
   pp. 390–403. Discusses aspects of a buyer's experience with a product
   as an element of buyer structure.
J. R. Moore and R. G. Walsh (eds.), *Market Structure of the Agricultural
   Industries: Some Case Studies* (Ames: Iowa State University Press,
   1966). Empirical data on essentially market-level elements of structure
   in several agricultural industries.
Almarin Phillips, "An Attempt to Synthesize Some Theories of the Firm,"
   in Almarin Phillips and Oliver Williamson, *Prices: Issues in Theory,
   Practice, and Public Policy* (Philadelphia: University of Pennsylvania
   Press, 1967).

Structure in Terms of Organizations

Federal Trade Commission, *Report on Corporate Mergers* (1969), Chapter 3.
   Discusses rising interdependence among firms as in part the outgrowth
   of interlocking directorates, joint ventures, and increasing aggregate
   concentration.
Almarin Phillips, "An Attempt to Synthesize Some Theories of the Firm,"
   in Phillips and Williamson, *op. cit.* A notable, recent analysis of
   various elements of structure, treated both singly and in combination.
Almarin Phillips, *Market Structure, Organization and Performance*
   (Cambridge: Harvard University Press, 1962). An overlooked book
   analyzing market structure in terms of formal and informal organization
   of the participants.
Studies by the Staff of the Cabinet Committee on Price Stability. (January,
   1969). Empirical analyses of various aspects of the structure of
   markets and implications for performance.

Interrelationship of Structure and Behavior

Wroe Alderson, *Marketing Behavior and Executive Action* (Homewood,
   Ill.: Richard D. Irwin, Inc., 1957). A stimulating book discussing
   the emergence and behavior of specialists and other participants in
   marketing. The thrust of the argument essentially is "functionalism"—
   the evolving of various forms from activities designed to solve
   marketing problems. The major conceptual focus primarily is on
   "macro" forms and behavior.
Wroe Alderson, *Dynamic Marketing Behavior* (Homewood, Ill.: Richard
   D. Irwin, Inc., 1965). A conceptual framework of marketing—

published posthumously—which by treating more extensively various "micro" behavior in marketing, is a sequel to Alderson's *Marketing Behavior and Executive Action*. The two books, taken together, are provocative (although not necessarily complete) conceptual discussions of the interrelationship of structure and behavior in marketing.

E. A. Duddy and David A. Revzan, *Marketing: An Institutional Approach* (2d ed., New York: McGraw-Hill, Inc., 1953), Chapter 2 and Appendix C. Two brief, provocative (and largely overlooked) discussions of marketing structure-behavior interrelationships and the concept of an "organic whole" are found in Chapter 2 and Appendix C. There are certain parallels between Alderson and Duddy and Revzan, though nominally the former is "functionalist" and the latter, "institutionalist."

David A. Revzan, *Perspectives for Research in Marketing* (Berkeley: Institute of Business and Economic Research, University of California, 1965). Essays 1 and 2. Revzan considers further certain aspects of the "holistic" ("organic whole") approach. A close, critical reading and appraisal of the Alderson books, Duddy and Revzan, and Revzan are extremely rewarding in terms of implications for the analysis of marketing structure-behavior interrelationships.

5

Functions
and flows
in marketing

INTRODUCTION

The purpose of this chapter is to provide a detailed understanding of the role of functions and flows. In Chapter 4 we discussed market conduct by participants at various levels of aggregation. "Functions" are simply the activities comprising conduct. Functions are critical, for they are the groups of activities necessary for want satisfaction to occur. In Chapter 2 we concerned ourselves with the discussion of functions aggregated in terms of sorting. We shall in effect disaggregate the sorting processes into the separate activities which are performed by various marketing agencies. Also we shall examine the functions with respect to their movement or flow between various agencies "Flows" are simply a different perspective of functions. Specifically, flows are the sequential path of marketing functions. Moreover, in some instances they are best visualized as composites of various functions.

The basic marketing functions are:
Functions of exchange
    1. Buying (including leasing)
    2. Selling (including leasing)
Functions of physical supply
    1. Transportation
    2. Storage
    3. Standardization and grading

Facilitating functions
1. Financing
2. Communication
3. Risk-bearing

FUNCTIONS OF EXCHANGE

Relation of Buying (Leasing) and Selling (Leasing)

The functions of exchange consist of buying and selling, along with which are included nontitle transactions—leasing. For simplicity we shall speak primarily only of "buying" and "selling," but the discussion relates as well to leasing. These two functions are closely related in two ways. One, every transaction has both buying and selling elements. In order for a transaction to take place there must be someone willing to offer a good or service, and someone willing to acquire it. The conventional language is "supplier" and "demander." Two, in every instance what is purchased readily affects what can be sold. For example, a firm must purchase raw materials, semi-finished goods, finished goods, and the required labor and other factors to have an assortment of goods and services to offer for sale. In this perspective, how successful a business is in satisfying wants of intermediate or ultimate cutomers is in part a function of how well the firm prepares itself for meeting those demands. For example, a supermarket that runs out of milk early on a Saturday afternoon has not correctly related its purchases to buyer demand. In other cases, we find examples of producers purchasing specific component items to be included in their final product as a means of satisfying a specific demand. Consider the case of KLH Research and Development Corporation which uses Garrard of Great Britain turntables as part of its stereophonic reproduction system.

Buying

Buying is the activity through which ultimate and intermediate buyers obtain necessary inputs to meet operational goals whether they be health and well-being for the individual or merchandise for resale or use by the business firm. Included in this activity is the acquisition of operating supplies for all types of enterprises as well as capital investment projects for business and governments and nonprofit agencies, the latter instances exemplified by new plants, highways, and hospitals.[1]

Although the analysis of buyer structure and behavior is treated in subsequent chapters, it is necessary at this point to indicate the five elements which make up the buying activity. The first element is the estimation of

[1] Edward A. Duddy and David A. Revzan, *Marketing: An Institutional Approach* (2d ed., McGraw-Hill, 1953), pp. 46–48.

demand. It includes for the ultimate consumer the estimation of what and how much of each individual good or service will be required for a given period of time; for the reseller it includes the analysis of what and how much his customers will require. The methods for estimation of demand run the gamut of complexity from simply extrapolation of current usage rates to sophisticated econometric models, to anticipating changes in tastes and consumption in the future. The second element of the buying function is the searching for information, first about the possible offerings which may satisfy a given demand, and second the suppliers of such offerings. The negotiation of the transaction is the third element. It ranges in complexity from simply agreeing to accept the stated price of a given item, to extensive bid description of what is desired and the terms on which it will be purchased. Fourth is the transfer of title or use rights, including payment and delivery. And, finally, there is the element of evaluation of the purchase decision in terms of actual product performance compared to expected performance.

Selling

The selling function is basically concerned with discovering and influencing demand. Selling has several elements which are mostly the counterparts of the buying elements. The first element is the discovery of and contact with potential customers. It entails a search for those firms and individuals which may currently or in the future require the offering of the seller. Consequently it entails acquiring information of how to adjust the total product to better match the want. To the extent that buyers and sellers, respectively, are searching for information about want-satisfying goods and services and are offering information about ways of satisfying wants we can, as in Chapter 2, talk about double-search in the market. The second element contains persuasive activities which can be examined in terms of nonpersonal selling, that is, advertising and promotion, and personal selling, meaning salesmen.

Advertising is also part of discovery and contact insofar as it includes the transfer of information to buyers. Advertising may permit substantial contact economies in that it makes the offer simultaneously to thousands or even millions of potential consumers at one time. Obviously personal selling cannot effect this type of economy. Advertising can also be regarded as part of the negotiation activity insofar as it makes an initial offer and aids the salesman in terms of the number of items that he must be concerned with in making the sale. Personal selling provides certain information to buyers—especially in cases of technical offerings—which cannot be relayed as easily by advertising or in matters in which sellers may be willing to negotiate, such as price. It is obviously more expensive than mass-media advertising in terms of the individual contact; however, its effects in obtaining sales for many types of goods, especially technical goods and those of high value, make it occasionally an important element of selling. Although most transactions have some elements of advertising and personal selling, it should be noted that some sellers rely solely on one or the other, as in the case of direct mail advertising or telephone selling.

The final elements of selling essentially parallel those of the buying function. In the selling function, the negotiation of transaction terms (price), the transfer of title or use rights, and delivery, are simply the reverse of the buying elements. However, in one aspect of delivery—post-sales activities—there is a difference. This element relates to the service and warranty activities which a seller engages in after all the other steps are finished. Post-sales evaluation, which we have termed a buying element, is an evaluation of how well the seller guaranteed and stood behind what he sold.

FUNCTIONS OF PHYSICAL SUPPLY

Transportation

"Transportation" is the activity which moves goods and customers through time and geographic space. It is a function undertaken by sellers and buyers alike although frequently it is performed by specialist agencies who effect economies in the function. Airlines, railroads, trucklines, steamship companies, pipelines, and canals are representative of such agencies.

It is important to note that the transportation function includes the movement of both goods and customers. That is, intermediate and ultimate customers as well as sellers engage in the function. Perhaps the dual performance is most clearly seen in the retail sector, where department stores deliver merchandise, sometimes "free" and sometimes at an explicit cost. At the same time, customers, some of whom have travelled to the store to effect the purchase, self-deliver a great many of the goods purchased at such agencies. But two-way movement is not limited to ultimate markets alone. The movement of buyers to sellers is found in such intermediate markets as furniture and hardgoods. This movement, for example, can be observed by the notices found in newspapers such as the *New York Times* indicating the buyers and buying agents who have arrived in town. Primarily, this movement of buyer to seller arises because of the terms by which the goods or services are sold. (See the section "Bases for Transactions" in Chapter 3.) When inspection of the merchandise is requisite, then buyers or their agents may necessarily be required to travel to view the goods. As part of the movement of people one must not forget the movement of companies' salesmen or sales agents (with or without goods in hand) in search of customers. The sales force used by a firm thus represents in effect a geographic extension of the firm through time and space.

Performance of the transportation function and improvement in the performance of the activity have three major implications for want satisfaction. One, improvements in the speed and mode of transportation lead to a reduction of the volume of goods in transit. This type of reduction has an impact on the level of inventories which must be carried; it increases the rate of turnover in production and distribution; and it lessens risks of losses in the value of inventories due to spoilage and other depreciation. Reduction in the gaps of time and space also enables sellers to forecast market demand more accurately; hence, increasing the ability to react to changes in demand. Two, better and more efficient transportation leads to a reduction in the cost of transporting people. In terms of consumer welfare, reduction in the cost or time of travel, lowers the "total" price of goods and services, thereby raising real income. Buyers are also enhanced by transportation improvements in two additional ways: (1) they are able to purchase goods and services which were not formerly available since reduction in time required for transportation creates the conditions by which firms can expand their geographic markets (consider the air-freighting of orchids—a world wide market); (2) as market areas become large and intersect, any one firm may have to compete with a greater number of firms. "The wider the market, the more generally does competition exist and the less can any producer depend upon local fortuitous advantages of either production or distribution."[2]

Storage

"Storage" is the activity by which goods are protected from deterioration and surplus commodities are held for future consumption. Marketing always involves some storage because there are always some gaps in time between periods of production and periods of consumption. For example, sometime during each summer, toy manufacturers have completed their production of goods for the coming Christmas. Since production and distribution are not instantaneous, toys must be produced in appropriate types and quantities far enough in advance to meet the anticipated demand. In general, many goods must be produced and/or stored in anticipation of demand. The stage function is perhaps most easily seen in the agricultural sector where the production schedules are for the most part a direct function of nature. Blueberries, for example, have a relatively short growing season in contrast to year-round demands for blueberries in pancakes. The only way in which seasonal production can satisfy continuous demand is by storage. If blueberries are to be available in the depths of winter, they must be stored in one form or another, as for example, by freezing, flash-drying, canning or packing as preserves.

There are other important reasons for the storage function.[3] One, storage

[2] Wroe Alderson, *Dynamic Marketing Behavior* (Irwin, 1965), pp. 134–135.

[3] *See* Frank H. Mossman and Newton Morton, *Logistics of Distribution Systems* (Allyn and Bacon, 1965), pp. 285–310; Norton E. Marks and Robert M. Taylor (eds.) *Marketing Logistics: Perspectives and Viewpoints* (Wiley, 1967).

creates value in that some items increase in value according to the length of time which they are stored. One need only consider how storage affects liquor, tobacco, cheese, and wines. Storage may also be used as a means of reducing risks of price flunctuations which arise because of alternating periods of high demand and high supply. For example, a profit maximizing firm might not want to sell all its output when supply is high and when demand is low. The firm might hold back some of its output as a means of keeping prices high, hoping that over the time period that they are higher on the average than by selling low when output is great and selling high when output is low. In most instances a monopolist is an example of a supplier withholding some supply. Holding back some production from the market obviously creates the need for storage. Of course, such goods would be stored only so long as the revenue from expected future sales is greater than the costs of holding the goods to the future period. Three, goods are stored because the sizes in which they are produced and transported differ from the sizes demanded. For example, there are major economies in the production and transportation of plumbing pipes in lengths which differ greatly from those used in normal installation. Since demand for specific work is usually specified in shorter dimensions, pipes must be stored near the place of use. The concept also holds true to the extent that there are economies in using production facilities for long production runs such as, for example, sun tan oil for an entire year's demand is made over a short period and hence must be stored.

It is evident that the physical and chemical characteristics of products affect the storage function. Products such as ice cream or delicate cut glass require special storage conditions. Other products because of their usage patterns must be stored in many locations rather than only one or two. For example, prescription drugs are stored near the great number of ultimate consumers because of the immediacy of need which might arise; whereas large bulky goods such as milling equipment, sold by inspection, may be stored in relatively few locations. These types of variations have great impact on the number and types of marketing agencies as well as the costs and prices for many goods and services.

In the firm, the "storage decision" represents the sum total of management decisions regarding the why and wherefore of storage. The various decisions include the following: (1) the type of storage facility to use, (2) the location of the facility, and (3) whether to own the facility or lease.[4]

Standardization and Grading

"Standardization" is the creation of measures of a recognized value which are generally acceptable to those using them. Such measures provide information about the intrinsic qualities or characteristics of a product or

[4] See Frank H. Mossman and Newton Morton, op. cit.

service. While many of the measures are purely subjective as in the case of fashion merchandise, standards in the main can be expressed quite objectively. For example, the dictates of the "mod" look of London or those of the fashion designers of the House of Dior reflect subjective standards, whereas objective standards such as weight, color, size, and degree of purity, may be stated for butter, wheat, or iron ore. Simplification, a concept closely related to standardization, involves product design. It is the adaptation of form to function and the elimination of all unnecessary parts and excrescences. To the extent that it creates specific standards of measurement simplification is part of the standardization activity.

"Grading" involves the physical sorting of goods into the various categories established by the standardization process. Recall the "sorting out" process in sorting, discussed in Chapter 2. For example, oranges may be graded by their diameter; hence all oranges of a diameter of three inches, a standard of measurement, are placed in a specific collection. Grading takes place as well when sizes are placed on garments, when wines are tasted, or when spectroscopic analysis is used to test the components of an alloy.

Standardization and grading affect marketing in at least four ways. First, they provide an ethical basis for marketing transactions. "As long as no objective standard prevails, there is opportunity for the strong to take advantage of the weak and for the clever and unscrupulous to outwit the unwary and trusting."[5] Second, they facilitate economies in physical handling and transportation. For example, uniform boxes, crates, and other shipping containers facilitate the use of uniform materials and handling equipment, allow maximum use of available space in transportation media, and allow for minimum numbers of display equipments, such as in groceries. Third, standardization and grading facilitate sale by description. Goods which have been subjected to these functions allow buyers to make comparison among a number of offerings without having to inspect each of them. In this way, these activities create information which aids in the operation of markets and reduces risk. "To the extent that the buyer can rely on grade and pack at the shipper his risk of loss from unsalable merchandise is reduced."[6] Finally, these activities provide a basis for financing inventories. To the extent that inventories can be offered as security for loans of various description, standardization and grading provide a base for evaluation.

FACILITATING FUNCTIONS

Financing

The function of "financing" arises from certain obstacles which retard the exchange of goods. Financing—in general, the extension of credit—operates in three ways. One, it is a means by which production can be adjusted to

[5] Duddy and Revzan, op. cit., pp. 82–85.
[6] Ibid., p. 84.

demand. By the availability of credit, production facilities can be put into operation well in advance of demand. In this way it plays a role similar to that of storage. For example, consider the production of color television sets. The sets are produced well in advance of demand, and orders are given for all of the various elements and component parts stemming from expected demand. The range of items required varies from sand for glass and tubes, to rare metals for color dies. Since the production of these items takes place long before the receipt of any revenues from the sale of the sets, the various producers require funds to operate.

Two, examples of financing are also found in products which have seasonal or other patterns of demand differing from the time of production. In this case certain specialized marketing agencies, public warehouses and field warehouses, provide credit against merchandise in storage. The owner of the inventory can deposit the goods in such an agency and receive a negotiable receipt against the inventory.[7] Financing, also plays an important role in the promotion of sales to resellers. This is accomplished by three methods: (1) the financing of open accounts, in which the seller establishes a limit, often called a credit line, on the amount which any buyer is entitled to purchase and a given period of time in which the obligation must be paid; (2) consignment selling, in which the seller retains title to the merchandise after it is in the physical possession of the reseller who is then able to sell it without the need to pay for the entire inventory, but is obligated to pay for what he sells in a specific period; and (3) accounts-receivable financing. Accounts-receivable financing, in contrast to either of the others, is provided by specialized financial agencies. This type of financing contains a continual relationship between the seller and a financial agency known as a factor, who purchases the accounts receivable of the seller at a discount of their face value and usually without recourse for any loss.[8]

Three, in allowing the purchase of goods and services by ultimate buyers, before income is earned, consumer credit takes three important forms. Mortgage credit for home financing allows consumers to purchase an item which is so singularly expensive that if one had to wait to accumulate requisite funds only a few people would ever be able to own their own home. Among the most important agencies in the extension of such credit, in addition to banks and savings institutions, are the Federal Housing Authority, Home Owners Loan Corporation, and the Veterans Administration. Installment credit is used in the financing of most other consumer durables. Of these the most important and certainly most familiar is that of automobile financing, however, it includes boat, refrigerators, television sets, and the like. Finally, short-term credit is extended through the use of charge accounts. These range from the credit plans offered by retail merchants,

---

[7] David A. Revzan, *Wholesaling in Marketing Organization* (New York: John Wiley and Sons, Inc., 1961), pp. 453–457.

[8] Duddy and Revzan, *op. cit.*, 96–97.

including the thirty-day charge accounts, to the more complex revolving charge accounts. Also included here are the national charge plans as extended through banks, *BankAmeriCard, Inter-Bank,* and others, *Diners' Club,* and *American Express.* The following table presents consumer credit data for a number of categories for recent years.

Frequently buyers finance sellers. One example is large packers of produce or fish who finance the growers or fishermen prior to harvest or catch.

Communication: Three Perspectives

The communication function has three important perspectives, the first of which is persuasion. As seen earlier, communication is part of the selling function insofar as market information is necessary to locate buyers and inform, if not convince, them of the merits of a particular good or service. In most conditions, it will be the seller that is attempting to inform and convince the buyer, although and one should not loose sight of those circumstances in which buyers solicit sellers. Firms that specialize in the disposal of damaged merchandise or "seconds" actively scout the market for sources of such goods. Second communication is an integrating force in that it bridges gaps in knowledge among the various marketing agencies. It links all the agencies concerned with the production and distribution of a product, from raw material extraction to the ultimate buyer. It also helps competitors discover what each other is doing. An example is the process of "competitive shopping" by which retail merchants discover what goods their competitors handle and the prices they charge. Although a great amount of such information is generated within the confines of the firm there are specialized agencies which gather, prepare, and distribute such information. Trade associations, news gathering services, and governmental bodies all provide necessary information; these are exemplified respectively by the National Wholesale Druggists Association, Associated Press International, and the Department of Agriculture.

Third communication is an instrument of control for management in that it provides the inputs for decisions by providing statements about the effectiveness and efficiency of the business organization.[9] With respect to the latter usage, the flow of information is the managerial directive through which other functions are evaluated and the way in which they are changed. This type of information, for example, can be the bills of lading which direct the physical movement of goods or the sales orders which provide information about demand. As an instrument of control there is feedback. For example, information to the effect that a certain motor freight carrier continually damages shipments can be used as the basis for arranging for a new carrier or reexamining methods of packaging or materials handling.

[9] *See* Herbert A. Simon, *Administrative Behavior* (Free Press, 1957).

TABLE 5.1

CONSUMER CREDIT: 1940 TO 1968

In millions of dollars. Prior to 1960, excludes Alaska and Hawaii. Estimated amounts of credit outstanding as of end of year or month; extended and repaid, for entire year or month. See also *Historical Statistics, Colonial Times to 1957*, series X 415–422.

Type of Credit	1940	1945	1950	1955	1960	1965	1966	1967	1968, Mar.
Credit outstanding	8,338	5,665	21,471	38,830	56,028	87,884	94,786	99,228	97,875
Installment	5,514	2,462	14,703	28,906	42,832	68,565	74,656	77,946	77,581
Automobile paper	2,071	455	6,074	6,074	17,688	28,843	30,961	31,197	31,380
Other consumer goods paper	1,827	816	4,799	7,641	11,525	17,693	19,834	21,328	20,692
Repair and modernization loans[1]	371	182	1,016	1,693	3,139	3,675	3,751	3,731	3,636
Personal loans	1,245	1,009	2,814	6,112	10,480	18,354	20,110	21,690	21,873
Noninstallment	2,824	3,203	6,768	9,924	13,196	19,319	20,130	21,282	20,294
Single-payment loans	800	746	1,821	3,002	4,507	7,682	7,844	8,267	8,370
Charge accounts	1,471	1,612	3,367	4,795	5,329	6,746	7,144	7,595	6,263
Service credit	553	845	1,580	2,127	3,360	4,891	5,142	5,420	5,661
Installment credit									
Extended	8,219	5,379	21,558	38,972	49,560	75,508	78,896	81,263	7,100
Repaid	7,208	5,093	18,445	33,634	45,972	67,495	72,805	77,973	6,846
Net change	1,011	286	3,113	5,338	3,588	8,013	6,091	3,290	254
Policy loans by life insurance companies[2]	3,091	1,962	2,413	3,290	5,231	7,678	9,117	10,059	10,362

[1] Holdings of financial institutions; holdings of retail outlets are included in "Other consumer goods paper."
[2] Source: Institute of Life Insurance, New York. Year-end figures are annual statement asset values; month-end figures are book value of ledger assets. These loans are excluded in consumer credit series.
Source: United States Department of Commerce, *Statistical Abstracts of the United States*, 89th ed., 1969, p. 461, derived from Board of Governors of the Federal Reserve System: *Federal Reserve Bulletin*.

Risk-bearing

"Risk" is the possibility of loss which arises from uncertainty. More generally, the greater the variance of possible outcome of a decision or action, the greater the risk.[10] Risk in marketing arises from the phenomenon of change in both supply and demand.[11] The causes of risk are: (1) uncertainty about natural phenomena, (2) imperfections in the performance of marketing functions, (3) the inability to forecast the future course of human behavior. In order for risk to be borne the probability of risk must be known. When individual risks are assigned probabilities, risks can be shared and shifted, as is the case in insurance. Risk can be minimized in several ways. One is to minimize the conditions which create it. As we have seen previously, standardization of packing containers allows for uniform handling systems; hence, minimizing damage from odd sizes and shapes. Marketing research, especially that in the area of buyer behavior, can reduce the risks of product failure. And in general, more complete information increases ones ability to predict outcomes—and thereby reduces risk. Also, risk can be borne by shifting it to other agencies as is done through insurance, the establishment of contingency funds, and the use of hedging, as is most common in commodity transactions.[12] Risks involving price movements can be diminished as we have seen by storage and also by forward buying at an assigned price level.

FLOWS

Introduction

Flows, the sequential perspective of functions, originate from the performance of marketing functions. When a function is performed it concomitantly initiates a flow which relates one marketing participant to one or more other participants. Flows exist even when market transactions do not. A vertically integrated firm "internalizes" many flows, as the func-

[10] The pure theory of risk defines it as the range over which an outcome may occur. A more narrow business usage is the probability of decreased or negative profits. An interesting and heated controversy arose over whether the prescription drug industry is a "risky" industry. From the pure-theory side, it is risky, for profit levels occur over a broad (albeit positive) range, but from a business view, it is *not* risky, for among the leaders, profits are *vitually never low*, let alone negative. See *Hearings on Present Status of Competition in the Pharmaceutical Industry*, U.S. Senate, Select Committee on Small Business, *90th Congress, 1st and 2d Sessions, Part V*, especially Professors G. R. Conrad and I. H. Plotkin, who take a pure theory of risk approach and Dr. W. F. Mueller, who focuses on the absolute level of profits as the measure of risk. For an historical treatment of risk, *see* Frank H. Knight, *Risk, Uncertainty and Profit*, Houghton Mifflin, 1921.

[11] George Fisk, *Marketing Systems: An Introductory Analysis* (Harper & Row, 1967), p. 399.

[12] For a discussion of hedging—in its formal sense a practice limited in large part to organized commodity markets—*see*, Duddy and Revzan, *op. cit.*, Ch. 22.

tions are performed by various divisions of the firm. This represents an internalization of the market, and consequently does *not* alter the substantive content of the concept of flows. Flows include all of the functions, although in the description and analysis of flows it is useful to categorize some of them in terms of a combination of one or more functions. For example, when the functions of buying and selling are consummated, title or use rights pass and hence the flow of ownership (legal rights) is created. Sometimes prior, sometimes simultaneously, and sometimes subsequently, other functions are performed, such as movement of goods from warehouses by motor freight carriers, and payment by the buyer. The concept of flows permits selective analysis. For example, analysis of how and where title passes, without regard to the other flows is possible. In all, there are eight flows, each of which relates to a specific set of functions: ownership; physical possession; communication; financing; risk-bearing; ordering; payment; and promotion.[13]

The relationship between functions and flows, indeed, the all-pervasiveness of functions and flows, can best be appreciated by example. Take the case of a supermarket which, through one aspect of the communication function, discovers that its inventory of a certain brand of crackers is low. Transmitting the "recognition" to its chain store warehouse, an interal communication, elicits a response from the warehouse—an order is placed with the appropriate supplier if the warehouse is not able to supply the merchandise. An order in a situation such as this might be sufficient for the seller to arrange immediate movement of the crackers from his warehouse to the supermarket. This assumes that the functions of buying and selling have become so routinized that all the steps of these functions do not have to be performed each time an order is placed. At some point after delivery, payment will be made. Although this example has not touched upon all the functions or subsequent flows, they are present and functions such as risk-bearing, financing, and promotion and the associated flows could be overlaid on the ones discussed.

Such analysis obviously becomes quite complex if there is a desire to trace each of the flows for all of the functions for a number of marketing agencies. Consider the network of graphic arrows which would be necessary to trace all the flows in the above example if financial agencies, advertising agencies, and business supply houses were added, let alone primary levels of production involving the sequence of wheat to flour to crackers. Payment from the buyer to the seller would need to be accounted for as well as payment of the seller to a freight lines if the baker did not have his own trucks. Because of complexity, flow analysis tends to concentrate on a single flow such as physical possession, which itself is a combination of a set of functions. The observer should continually reflect on the primary, secondary, and third-order functional flows which arise.

It must be noted clearly that flows have more than one direction; that

[13] *See* R. S. Vaile, E. T. Grether, and R. Cox, *Marketing in the American Economy* (Ronald, 1952), Chapters 6 and 7.

is, whereas, orders generally flow from buyers to sellers, ownership flows from seller to buyer. Moreover, some, such as risk-bearing, flow two ways. For the entire group of flows, we can see the direction the components can take. In Figure 5.1, "Flows in Marketing," the direction of the various flows are shown for a simplified collection of agencies. Besides flows occurring only between buyers and sellers, there are cases in which flows occur between buyers *or* sellers, such as the communication flow which arises when a trade association collects and distributes information among its members.

FIGURE 5.1

FLOWS IN MARKETING

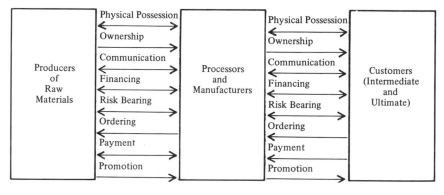

Measurement of Flows

One of the most important analytic features of flows is that they can be measured. Such measures are arrived at by counting the number of marketing agencies through which the various flows pass. For example, in Figure 5.2, "Red Meat: Physical Flows—United States, 1963," the flow of physical possession can be observed. Note the detail given, including the number and types of marketing agencies between the meat packers and the retail stores. In 1963, 72 percent of the meat sold by packers was resold by retail stores. Half of the output went directly to the retailers while the remainder passed through various middlemen including branch houses and wholesalers. Approximately 35 percent of the volume went through hotels, restaurants, schools, hospitals, government facilities and other institutional outlets.[14] Although most flow charts in the marketing literature have focused primarily on the measurement of the physical flow of goods and services,[15] the Federal Reserve Board has pioneered analysis in the flow-of-funds for use in national income accounting. This is simply a measurement of the

[14] National Commission on Food Marketing, *Organization and Competition in the Livestock and Meat Industry*, Technical Study No. 1 (June 1966), p. 42.

[15] Reavis Cox and Charles S. Goodman, "Marketing of Housebuilding Materials," *Journal of Marketing* XXI (July, 1956), pp. 36–61. This article reports on the classic use of flow analysis. It describes methods and problems of measurement and use in the analysis of marketing.

flow of funds among a number of sectors of the economy which can be decomposed into the respective firms.[16]

FIGURE 5.2

**RED MEAT: PHYSICAL FLOWS
UNITED STATES, 1963**

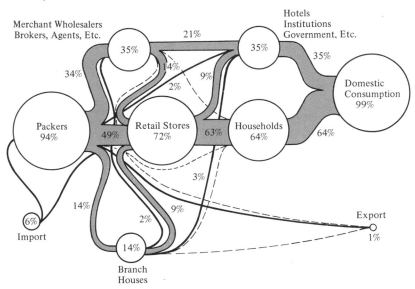

Source: National Commission on Food Marketing. *Organization and Competition in the Livestock and Meat Industry*: Technical Study No. 1. (June 1966), p. 43, derived from U.S. Department of Commerce, Census of Business, Wholesale Trade, Census of Business, Retail Trade, Census of Manufacturers.

To measure flows, substantial detail is required for the statistical breakdowns, for example, by firms, industries, geographic areas, and time periods. The complexity of flow analysis is so great that to trace each flow for each transaction would require extensive storage capacity on the largest computer. Hence, flow analysis is usually limited to general description for an industry or for separate activities for the individual firm.[17] Quite clearly even the most detailed data available are not at the level of detail desired and hence we are left with only the most superficial of data.

SUMMARY

Functions are the homogeneous groups of activities necessary for want satisfaction to occur. The eight functions at the level of the firm or

[16] William I. Abraham, *National Income and Economic Accounting* (Prentice-Hall, 1969), Chapter 6, "Flows-of-Funds Account." A discussion of the use of flow-of-funds approach and national income accounting.

[17] Reavis Cox in association with Charles S. Goodman and Thomas C. Finchandler, *Distribution in a High-Level Economy* (Prentice-Hall, 1965), pp. 27–28.

market can be classified as the functions of exchange, the functions of physical supply, and the facilitating functions. When we examine the functions in the manner of Chapter 5, we are simply looking at the individual activities of the matching of supply and demand.

Flows are the sequential patterns that originate from the performance of the various marketing activities and the nucleus around which the variety of marketing agencies develop. For purposes of managerial analysis, flows can be measured in a number of ways, although an attempt to account completely for all the flows arising for one transaction would be complex. Most studies of marketing flows concentrate on physical activities in and between agencies.

SUGGESTED READINGS

Books

Reavis Cox in association with Charles S. Goodman and Thomas C. Finchandler, *Distribution in a High-Level Economy* (Englewood Cliffs, N.J.: Prentice-Hall, Inc., 1965). An extensive treatment of flows insofar as measurement of the cost and value of marketing is concerned.

Edward A. Duddy and David A. Revzan, Marketing: An Institutional Approach (2d ed., New York: McGraw-Hill, Inc., 1963). Chapters 2–7 provide an extensive view of the various marketing functions.

Roland S. Vaile, E. T. Grether, and Reavis Cox, *Marketing in the American Economy* (New York: Ronald Press Company, 1952). Chapters 6 and 7 connect the functions and flows in marketing, both at the level of the economy as well as in terms of firms and markets.

Articles

Paul L. Farris, "Uniform Grades and Standards, Product Differentiation and Product Development," *The Journal of Farm Economics* XLII (November, 1960), pp. 854–863.

Mark R. Greene, "Market Risk—An Analytical Framework," *Journal of Marketing*, 32 (April, 1968), pp. 49–56.

Charles H. Kriebel, "Warehousing with Transhipment under Seasonal Demand," *Journal of Regional Science* 3 (Summer, 1961), pp. 57–70.

Charles L. Leven, "Regional and Interregional Accounts in Perspective," *Regional Science Association: Papers and Proceedings* 13 (1964), pp. 127–144.

Edmund D. McGarry, "The Contactual Function in Marketing," *Journal of Business* 24 (April, 1951), pp. 91–113.

Allan R. Pred, "Toward a Typology of Manufacturing Flows," *Geographical Review* 54 (1963), pp. 65–84.

Paul Smith, "Cost of Providing Consumer Credit: A Study of Four Types of Financial Institutions," *Journal of Finance* XVII (September, 1962), pp. 476–498.

Fred J. Weston and Rupert Craig, "Understanding Leave Financing," *California Management Review* (Winter, 1960), pp. 67–75.

P. A. Zusman, "A Theoretical Basis for Determination of Grading and Sorting Schemes," *Journal of Farm Economics*, 49 (February, 1967), Pt. 1, pp. 89–108 .

6

Agencies and channels

INTRODUCTION

The discussion of Chapter 5 focused on functions and flows. Little attention was paid to the agencies which performed the various functions and initiated the resultant flows. We remember that marketing participants or agencies include a range of *types* from individual consumers, to firms, to nonprofit entities; and, as well, a range of *levels of aggregation*. Specifically, in this chapter, we are concerned with the nature of the commercial participants— the firm. In particular, our interest is in why it exists, how it chooses to perform one or more sets of functions, and how it is related to a single market as well as how it is arrayed to a series of vertical markets. In Chapters 8 and 9, we shall consider in detail consumer participants, and return once again to firms in Part IV.

THE FIRM

Definition

The "firm"—the commercial agency—is a collection of productive resources, the disposal of which between different uses and over time is determined by administrative decision.[1] The major question faced by the administration of any agency is the age-old question of how to best use the resources it has at its disposal. Hence the managerial process is one of con-

[1] Edith T. Penrose, *The Theory of the Growth of the Firm* (Wiley, 1959), p. 24.

tinually examining a series of "make or buy" decisions.[2] The firm constantly examines its internal cost structure to determine whether it should perform a specific function or whether it should delegate it to another (in effect delegate it to "the market"). A firm exists because its management believes that it can organize its productive resources in such a manner that it will be able to perform a function or a set of functions with respect to a target revenue at costs lower than others, or with respect to given costs, at a higher revenue than others. Further, it believes that the performance of such activities can be sold in a market to return profit. Obviously, when this latter condition does not prevail and the function is still demanded, other firms must absorb the activity themselves or prevail upon governments to provide such functions. The national highway system is a classic case of this. And indeed users do pay for the performance of the function but not directly as in the case of a market transaction.

How a Firm Decides Which Functions to Perform

What activities a firm will choose to perform besides the one it was organized around is a function of what economies or in general, profit possibilities, are associated with the new activities. We are asking, then, why a firm which specializes in the performance of the credit function, such as banks, for example, offer for sale a communication in the form of data transmission. In one case, we see that a firm may choose to perform a function when there is no other agency available to perform it, such as when a grocery store in a small village must deliver its own goods instead of contracting with a delivery service.[3] A major factor in the determination of whether a firm performs a specific function or delegates it to others is the existence of external economies in the form of other more specialized agencies. For example, the existence of export agents, a specific type of wholesale middlemen, is an external economy to a manufacturer of adhesives desiring to sell in the European Economic Community. Instead of having to maintain a sales force to sell to this market, the firm can use the services of the export agent. Of course, this is dependent on the assumption that the total costs involved in engaging the external agency to perform the requisite functions are lower than those of performing the function internally.[4]

The essence of external economies and how agencies arrange their resource expenditures is developed in the following example. Assume that a firm has three functions to perform, financing (Y_1), storage (Y_2), and

---

[2] R. H. Coase, "The Nature of the Firm," *Economica*, New Series (November 1937), pp. 386–405. This is one of the few discussions of the theory of the firm which does not ignore organizational considerations.

[3] George J. Stigler, "The Division of the Market is Limited by the Extent of the Market," *Journal of Political Economy* XIV (June 1951), p. 187. Much of the following analysis is based on the arguments developed in this article; no further citation will be made.

[4] C. E. Ferguson, *Micro-Economic Theory* (Irwin, 1966), p. 393.

transportation (Y_3). In Figure 6.1, the respective average cost curves for performing each of these activities as well as the average cost curve (AC) for the firm are shown. Over the range shown Y_1 is a decreasing cost activity (increasing returns to scale); Y_2 is an increasing cost activity (decreasing returns to scale); and Y_3 is U-shaped, indicating first increasing and then decreasing returns to scale. So long as the firm performs all three activities, the point at which average total costs are minimized is Q_m.

FIGURE 6.1

EXTERNAL ECONOMIES

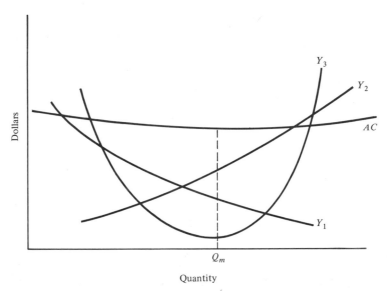

Now assume that other firms in the economy organize to perform Y_1. This is a reasonable assumption to make if the shape of Y_1, decreasing costs, holds for all firms in the industry. If the firm contracts out Y_1, the financing activity, and purchases it back at P_1, there is a downward shift of all or part of the firm's average cost curve as indicated by the broken segment in the figure. The minimum cost output becomes Q_m. If all firms abandon the Y_1 function to a firm specializing in its performance, such a firm is a monopoly, but one who obviously must set his price for performing the function in line with internal costs of his various customers. Because this line of analysis applies equally to the other curves, it can be said that when sufficient demand exists for the performance of a function, special agencies will emerge to perform the activity, seeking profits from exploiting increasing returns to scale, or, if demand is sufficient, *reorganizing* decreasing-return activities to *effect* economies, and thus conferring an external economy upon its customers. Instances of external economies are plentiful. For example, some firms contract out the maintenance of buildings, others advertising and promotional activities, collection of accounts receivables, training of employees, and others, even the manufacturing of products they sell.[5]

Besides the previous, there is no one comprehensive theory for explaining what governs the range of activities engaged in by a firm.[6] There is the overall principle of enterprise differentiation which suggests that firms attempt to differentiate themselves by taking advantage of location or product offerings or by influencing the impersonal forces of supply and demand. (Refer to Chapter 3 with respect to differentiation and differential advantage, and to Part IV for detailed analysis of managerial decisions designed to effect differentiation.) "The pressure for differentiation stems very largely from two sources: first, the fundamental competitive selling drive in our economic system, especially when there is excess capacity, and second, the enormous variety of wants and needs that can express themselves in effective demands in our prosperous country." [7]

There are, however, certain more precisely identifiable factors which are relevant in understanding why a firm chooses to perform certain functions and why it contracts others out. One, certain functions can be contracted out to specialized agencies because the nature of the activity is exceedingly general and comparable from firm to firm. Provision of credit by banks illustrates this. Two, the size of the firm and the extent to which it may have surplus resources undoubtedly plays an important role in the selection of functions. For example, the larger the selling area for a retail establishment, the greater may be the assortment of products offered or the larger size the more frequently the firm might engage in activities of storage and transportation. "But the relationships between size and number are complex. Small retailers may not need sufficient quantities of many services to attract potential contractors, and thus may be forced to perform (or omit) many activities that large retailers contract out."[8] Three, the contracting of certain functions is required because of the great proficiency which is required. Four, some activities are feasible on a group basis as is the case for credit information. Finally, certain legal requirements may exist which call for contracting out even when it may be more economical to perform the activity internally. Outside audits of publicly-owned corporations are an example.[9]

[5] *Ibid.*, p. 392. A classic example of an external economy is the service of cross-pollination which occurs when a bee keeper and a apple orchard are situated side-by-side.

[6] Stanley C. Hollander, 'Who Does the Work of Retailing?" *Journal of Marketing* 28 (July, 1964), p. 20.

[7] Roland S. Vaile, E. T. Grether, and Reavis Cox, *Marketing in the American Economy* (Ronald, 1952), p. 353. The origin of this line of analysis is found in Edward H. Chamberlin, *The Theory of Monopolistic Competition* (6th ed., Harvard, 1948).

[8] Hollander, *op. cit.*, p. 21. The discussion in this section is based on a synthesis of Hollander's points.

[9] An extremely useful empirical analysis of diversification and integration patterns is Michael Gort, *Diversification and Integration in American Industry* (National Bureau of Economic Research, Princeton University Press, 1962). *See also* the extensive discussion of firm growth and product assortment in Chapter 11 in the present book.

Functions and Integration

If we examine firms distributed along any given flow, it is easy to see that some firms by the nature of functions they perform extend further along the flow than others. For example, one finds that large retail chain drug operations extend further along a flow by the fact that they operate wholesale facilities which the small neighborhood pharmacy does not. This example has developed two dimensions—the extent along a flow and the width at any point along the flow. The width along the flow is "horizontal integration," that is, the duplication of a given function as in branches of an agency, or the performance of a number of functions at one geographic location, or the performance of several functions at a number of geographic locations, or all three. For example, a retail hardware integrates horizontally when it offers a wider product assortment than is usually associated with such a store, that is, it adds new items for satisfying wants. It may also integrate by either establishing or merging with other firms in other locations.[10] From the discussion in Chapter 4, it is clear that horizontal integration and vertical integration have both structural and behavioral elements. "Vertical integration" describes the resultant change in market structure from one period to the next as well as the process by which the transformation occurs.

Vertical integration takes place when a firm chooses to perform a function which has been performed by preceding or succeeding firms in the flow.[11] In the first instance one speaks of backward vertical integration as in the case of a steel mill acquiring a coal mine; the latter is forward vertical integration as exemplified by Firestone Rubber and Tire Company operating its own retail outlets or two-way vertical integration by Aluminum Corporation of America which acquires bauxite ore, refines it, extrudes metal, and forms cooking utensils which it then sells to retail establishments.[12] Vertical integration may be accomplished by acquisition or new investment in the flow or through a number of legal arrangements such as joint ventures which while not giving the firm control of the ownership flow nevertheless confer operational control. Also among the most important of the latter are exclusive dealing contracts and franchising agreements.[13] The former has

---

[10] William F. Mueller and Leon Garoian, *Changes in Market Structure of Grocery Retailing* (University of Wisconsin, 1961), p. 18.

[11] M. A. Adelman, "Integration and Anti-trust Policy," *Harvard Law Review* 63 (November 1947), p. 27. *See also* Eugene M. Singer, *Antitrust Economics: Selected Legal Cases and Economic Models* (Prentice-Hall, 1968), Chapter 18.

[12] Donald Wallace, *Market Control in the Aluminum Industry* (Harvard, 1937); and Merton J. Peck, *Competition in the Aluminum Industry: 1945–1958* (Harvard, 1961); and R. D. Hale, "Cookware: A Study in Vertical Integration," *The Journal of Law and Economics* 10 (October 1967), pp. 169–80.

[13] This discussion indicates the close relationship between agency structure and channel structure—in part an *identity* when a firm is highly vertically integrated, thereby becoming in many respects "the channel." A graphic portrayal of integration is shown in Figure 6.3.

much the same effect as integration by ownership since the reseller becomes a "captive" of the seller as it must purchase all its merchandise from the seller and offer it at his terms.[14] Franchising arrangements are characterized by a contract in which a seller supplies all the goods to the franchisee and other services as well, including site selection, building, promotion, and management skills.[15] Some of the most common franchise operations are Howard Johnson, McDonald's Hamburgers, and in the industrial market, Snap-on-tools.

In passing it should be noted that there is a relationship between vertical integration and horizontal integration. Vertical integration beyond being a function of alternative firms is also a function of size. Vertical integration can arise when a firm specializes for example in the sale of newspaper ink. At some point in time the "make or buy" decision will arise. When its size and resources, both capital and managerial, are of a sufficient size, it may decide to produce its own ink. Horizontal size is a variation of this to the extent that the firm is large because it operates in a series of locations or because it sells a number of products.

KINDS OF AGENCIES

Reasons for Numbers of Types

There are many kinds of commercial agencies because there are numbers of opportunities to specialize around the performance of specific functions at various positions along the flows and because there are numerous varieties of products requiring such activities. Beyond these reasons, certain agencies exist because of legal requirements or as the result of legislative directive. In a short book, it would be inappropriate to attempt an analysis of all the specific reasons which exist for each of the many agencies related to the various functions. Our immediate concern is middlemen—those agencies predominately associated with marketing, specifically, wholesale and retail middlemen.[16] However, this is not to deny the importance of consumers, manufacturers, banks, insurance companies, security markets, transportation companies and all the other marketing participants.

The existence of a set of specialized middlemen agencies can be appreciated by an understanding of two interrelated propositions: (1) the principle of minimum transactions, and (2) the principle of massed reserves.[17]

[14] Parts of this discussion are augmented in the analysis of channel decisions in Chapter 11.

[15] An excellent treatment of franchising is found in E. H. Lewis and Robert Hancock, *The Franchise System of Distribution* (The University of Minnesota Press, 1963).

[16] Recall the definition of wholesale middleman and retail middleman (retailer) in Chapter 1.

[17] Margaret Hall, *Distributive Trading: An Economic Analysis* (Hutchinson's University Library, 1946), pp. 80–81. "Massed reserves" is often designated "pooling of resources" as well.

The principle of minimum transactions states: The total number of transactions in a market with a given number of goods can be substantially reduced by the infusion of a specialized agency between sellers and buyers so that a few large transactions occur between the seller and the agency and between this agency and the buyer in place of the number of transactions which formerly took place.[18] For example, if the transaction directly incorporated financing, the seller might have to perform this activity for each of the many buyers to whom he sold. Suppose in a market there are ten such sellers, a single product, and one hundred buyers. If financing were required by all buyers, the function would have to be performed 1000 times. If instead there are two financial intermediaries or two wholesale middlemen performing the financing, only 120 contacts would be required. This arises from the fact that now each seller would have to perform the function twenty times with the new agencies who in turn would have to perform financing fifty times assuming that each serves one half of the total. The principle of massed reserves is an extension of the minimum transaction concept insofar as it relates to other functions. For example, if in a market ten retail appliance dealers each sold 1000 portable television sets a year, it is conceivable that they would maintain an inventory of 300 to prevent stock-outs. If there were a middleman such as a wholesaler between the retailers and the producer, the retailers might maintain an average of only 100 sets and let the wholesaler maintain an average of 1000 sets. Even if demand were highly erratic among the various retailers, the wholesaler should be able to prevent stock-outs.[19]

Classification of Wholesale Establishments

There are five types of wholesale establishments. They are classified primarily by the following criteria: (1) degree of managerial control including ownership of merchandise; (2) the number of marketing functions performed; and (3) the kinds of goods and services handled.

Merchant Wholesalers

These wholesale middlemen take title to goods they sell and perform most if not all of the marketing functions. This is the one type of wholesale middleman for whom "wholesaler" is a correct synonym. Included in this category are: (1) full-service wholesalers, including jobbers, (2) cash-and-carry wholesalers, (3) industrial distributors, (4) drop-shippers and desk-jobbers, (5) importers and exporters, (6) chain-store buying offices, and (7) wholesaler-sponsored, retailer-sponsored buying cooperative. Most interesting in terms of the merchant wholesaler group are drop-shippers and desk-

---

[18] *Ibid.*

[19] Hall, *op. cit.*, 81–82. For examples in electric power and military supply *see* E. A. G. Robinson, *The Structure of Competitive Industry* (The University of Chicago Press, 1958), pp. 26–27.

jobbers, chain-store buying offices, and wholesale-sponsored, retailer-sponsored buying cooperatives. Drop-shippers specialize in the products handled as well as in the functions performed. Occurring mainly in low-value, bulky products as clay, coal, and gravel, and lumber, where transportation rates are high, they serve as an intermediary that seeks out buyers and sellers, offering them knowledge of transportation services, and charging for shipment. They, however, do *not* take physical possession. Chain-store buying offices and the associated warehouses perform collection and sorting activities for the various units which constitute a retail chain. For example, in food it is common for a large chain to have facilities near railroad yards where the chain's entire needs for a region are collected before being moved to individual supermarkets.

Wholesale-sponsored buying cooperatives are a result of the pressures exerted by large chain operations on wholesale middlemen. In drugs, for example, Kiefer-Stewart, Inc., Indianapolis, Indiana, has organized independent retail pharmacies in a voluntary arrangement in which all the druggists carry a common name and promote the private merchandise lines of the wholesaler.[20] The retailer-sponsored arrangement has arisen from the same pressures, and performs the same role for the retailers involved. Here, however, the stimulus for development arises on the part of the retail agencies instead of the wholesale agencies.[21]

Manufacturers Sales Branches and Sales Offices

These are wholesale establishments which are owned and operated by manufacturers. They reflect the vertical integration of manufacturing into the wholesaling sector. Sales branches are distinguished from sales offices in that the former maintain inventories while the latter do not.

Agents and Brokers

Agents and brokers are usually compensated in the form of commissions rather than by receiving profits from the sale of goods. Typically, they do not take title. For many of the types, their operations mirror those of merchant wholesalers. Other types are: (1) auction companies, (2) selling agents, (3) manufacturers agents with and without stocks, (4) resident buying offices, and (5) purchasing agents.

Petroleum Bulkplants, Terminals, and LP Gas Facilities

Petroleum bulkplants, terminals, and LP gas facilities specialize in one product area although there are independent, agent, cooperative, and integrated types.

[20] "Helps Rx Man to Locate Next to Supers," *American Druggist* 145 (September 27, 1965), 27.
[21] For an interesting history of changes in wholesale market structure in which those we have discussed are included, *see* Ralph Cassady Jr., and Wylie L. Jones, *The Changing Competitive Structure in the Wholesale Grocery Trade: A Case Study of Los Angeles Market, 1920–1946.* (University of California Press, 1949).

Assemblers

Assemblers operate in agricultural commodity groupings. They are primarily engaged in buying and selling of farm products. In contrast to other wholesale establishments they purchase in small amounts and sell in large amounts. Assemblers are a clear example of the accumulating phase of sorting discussed in Chapter 2. As in the case of the last group, there are independent, cooperative, and integrated operations.

We can observe the magnitude of each of these groups in the following table.

TABLE 6.1

WHOLESALE TRADE STATISTICS

Type of Opration	1963	1958	1963	1958	Percent change
	(numbers)		($1000)	($1000)	1958 to 1963
Merchant wholesalers	208,997	190,492	157,391,769	122,060,171	28.9
Manufacturers' sales branches and sales offices	28,884	25,420	116,443,312	87,819,865	32.6
Petroleum bulk plants, terminals	30,873	30,520	21,485,414	20,252,116	6.1
Merchandise agents, brokers	25,313	26,666	53,245,009	46,589,318	14.3
Assemblers of farm products	14,110	14,125	9,820,245	9,005,434	9.0
Totals	308,177	287,043	358,385,749	285,726,904	25.4

Source: *Census of Business: Wholesale Trade, 1963*, Table 1.

Classification of Retail Establishments

Retail agencies can be classified according to product offerings, location, or consumer perception. In terms of products offered, by conventional designation, there are eleven major sub-sets of the retail sector ranging in diversity from lumber, building materials, farm equipment, and hardware dealers, to nonstore retailers. Figure 6.2 provides a list of the eleven as well as a comparison of sales for 1958 and 1963.

Although this approach to classification of the various retail agencies appears to have few disadvantages, the observer realizes that retail establishments classified as pharmacies or food stores, for example, are an either/or situation. For example, there are numerous drugstores that have added a wide assortment of products including bread, milk, delicatessen items, and hardware so as to decrease the percentage of sales accounted for by prescription items. These, of course, were the original criteria used, but how many of us can recall an apothecary in contrast to what we conceive of as a contemporary drugstore, stocking as it does beachballs to brassières,

FIGURE 6.2   **UNITED STATES RETAIL TRADE: 1958 AND 1963 SALES**
In Millions of Dollars

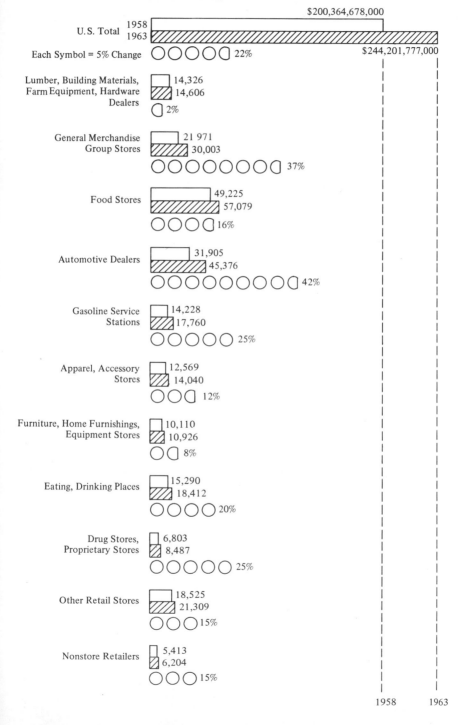

and flea powder to household cleansers. Also, the product assortments of supermarkets have gone well beyond food items. Among those that have been added are hardware, software, proprietary medicines, magazines, phonographs, and books.

Further, this classification scheme does not take full notice of most service agencies or governmental services which are as much a part of retail agency structure as those listed above. Among the service establishments which must be included in the classification are: (1) hotels, motels, tourist camps, and trailer camps; (2) personal services including laundries, barber shops, beauty shops, shoe repair service, and funeral homes; (3) auto repair; (4) miscellaneous repair services including electrical, locksmiths, and the like; and (5) amusements including motion pictures, dance halls, theatres, bowling alleys, racetracks, and amusement parks. Among the governmental services provided as part of the retail structure, we find a wide range of activities running from postal services and highways to water supplies, electrical services, and credit. Further, the classification is not wholly consistent with the product criterion because of the inclusion of nonstore retailers which include establishments which deal in like products with others. The three categories which are part of the nonstore retailers are mail-order houses, merchandise vending machine operators, and "house-to-house" selling operations. Finally, this scheme does not include a most interesting class of retail establishment, the "consumer cooperative." These types of retail stores, while often carrying the same product offerings as other retailers, differ because of the kind of ownership and philosophy of business operation. Consumer cooperatives operate by attracting members with the promise of lower cost of merchandise and services because of lower operating costs by the elimination of profits and by the concentration of purchases. Consumers are "rewarded" for their patronage at the end of each year when rebates are paid in some proportion to the purchases made by each consumer.

There are three patterns which characterize the location of retail transactions. These are: (1) those transactions taking place in the location of the establishment, which are a result of the consumer going to the retailer; (2) the retail agency consummating the transaction at the location of the consumer, which is the result of an employee or legal agent of the retailer going to the domicile of the consumer; and (3) a combination of (1) and (2) where the seller provides sufficient information for the sale to take place by description.

Finally, retail establishments are classified by buyers in terms of how they perceive them for specific sets of wants. For example, a buyer may classify one store, depending upon what is to be purchased, in terms of all three of the following, or in terms of two or of only one. By this scheme retailers can be classified as:

> *Convenience stores*: Those stores for which the consumer, before his need for some product arises, possesses an indifference map that indicates a willingness to buy from the most accessible store.

Shopping stores: Those stores for which the consumer has not developed a complete preference relative to the product he wishes to buy, requiring him to undertake a search to construct specific preferences before purchase.

Specialty stores: Those stores for which the consumer, before his need for some product arises, possesses a preference map that indicates a willingness to buy the item from a particular establishment even though it may not be the most accessible.[22]

THE MARKETING CHANNEL

Definition

The "marketing channel" is the collection of agencies and flows associated with the transactions of any *given* good or service.[23] A channel is formed when trading relations are established between or among agencies making possible the passage of legal rights and/or possession (usually both) of goods and services.[24] Although the channel is usually expressed in terms of "*M*," "*W*," "*R*," and "*C*," for manufacturer, wholesaler, retailer, and consumer and thought of as a "bucket brigade" that passes goods from manufacturers to consumers, the concept has greater complexity.[25]

Agencies as Linkages and Blockages

In terms of physical analogies one could compare the channel conceptually to a water canal.[26] However, the analogy has *little value* since the various agencies in the channel are *not* inert walls through which goods and services pass. Most important the various agencies are linked together as a function of past trading relationships and often by legal arrangements such as exclusive dealing or franchising contrasts. A channel may be composed of a number of agencies linked together, or merely one or two agencies. An assortment of some combinations is shown in Figure 6.3.

The various links are also regulators of the flows in that some agencies have control over the initiation or the performance of the various functions. For example, in the right-hand portion of Figure 6.3, we see the horseshoe-

[22] Compare the customer-perception classification of stores to the customer-perception classification of offerings in terms of convenience goods, shopping goods, and specialty goods in Chapter 11.

[23] F. E. Balderston, "Design of Marketing Channels," in Reavis Cox, Wroe A. Alderson, and Stanley J. Shapiro (eds.), *Theory in Marketing* (Irwin, 1964), p. 176; and David A. Revzan, *Wholesaling in Marketing Organization* (Wiley, 1961), p. 107.

[24] Ralph F. Breyer, "Some Observations on 'Structural' Formation and the Growth of Marketing Channels," Cox, Alderson, Shapiro, *op. cit.*, p. 163.

[25] Hollander, *op. cit.*, p. 18.

[26] Revzan, *op. cit.*, p. 108. "The word 'channel' has its origins in the French word for canal."

shaped figures which designate the agency that has control over the respective channel. Control can be exercised in the channel by several methods in addition to ownership. Probably the most important is promotional activities such as advertising, sales promotion, packaging and branding of products in attempts to create and maintain loyalty by intermediate and ultimate buyers. The more successful the promotion process the more assured is the agency of a power position.[27] Also as we have indicated, control is established by legal means.

FIGURE 6.3

PROGRESSION FROM SIMPLE TO COMPLEX CHANNELS

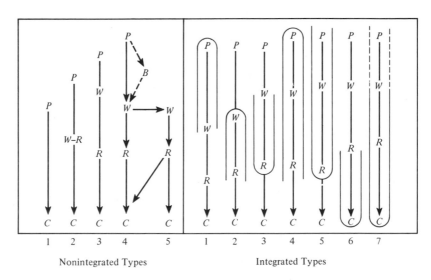

Nonintegrated Types   Integrated Types

In general, one would expect more problems for channel control for any agency where there are numerous links. Hence, a producer using a channel such as "4" on the left-hand side of Figure 6.3 would have more agencies to deal with than is the case with "4" on the right-hand side. If the producer were desirous of controlling such a channel, it would be necessary to cement relation with all the members. As one might expect, this could be a most expensive process especially when one considers that there will be numbers of agencies at wholesale and retail levels. This suggests that channel control by a producer is a function of size and availability of resources. If the producer has neither, there are only limited chances that channel control will be available. There are cases, however, when channel control may be a difficult task even when there are limited numbers of channel members

---

[27] Bruce Mallen, "A Theory of Retailer-Supplier Conflict, Control, and Cooperation," *Journal of Retailing* (Summer, 1963.), p. 23. This article suggests that there may be more than one purpose for ultimate consumer advertising.

(vertical). A prime case of this is the so-called "bilateral oligopoly" where giant retail chain stores in drugs, foods, and appliances oppose manufacturers of like goods.[28]

Once a set of links is established among firms in a channel, either as a result of the influence of a single agency or as a result of mutual need, the agencies in the channel may attempt either individually or collectively, or both, to set up obstructions to the formation of competitive linkages. These may be made effective by one or more of the following: "by means of exclusive-dealer franchises; by resale price maintenance agreements or other price control measures; legislation barring the free movement of goods; membership requirements; trade association activities; establishment of fighting brands in the channels; creation of special subsidiaries not identified with the parent corporation; or similar devices."[29]

When Functions Are Performed in the Channel

It is not possible to isolate and discuss all the possible points at which functions may be performed in the channel. The following example is limited; nevertheless it provides insight into where two of the less-obvious functions may be performed. Assuming that the American buyer is willing to pay a premium for large eggs and given that chickens do not always lay eggs of uniform size, it benefits the farmer to grade eggs into size categories. In so doing, he recognizes the price-size sensitivities of the various market segments. The farmer discriminates in price, that is, assigns a different percent mark-up over cost to each segment. The result is greater profits than if the eggs were sold without grading. While this explains why standardization and grading occur, it does not explain why these functions take place at this point. Eggs are graded at the production level because the market is the "widest," that is, the number of units is the largest. Therein we see the inextricable interrelationships between the various functions. As eggs leave the farm, it is easier to match specific grades of eggs with the various demands, and accordingly place them in various marketing channels. For example, those channels which process the eggs or combine them with other products will have less concern about size, hardness of shell, color and the like. Local bakeries or food processors such as Pillsbury convert eggs into part of another product, bread and cake mixes for example, and do not express the same demands as a chain store buying office concerned with meeting the wants of ultimate buyers.

It is important to recognize that at some point the performance of the grading function may become uneconomic for the farmer. At this point, the function might be contracted out to a firm which specializes in the performance of this function. Of course, we are assuming two things: (1) that

---

[28] See Richard C. Heflebower, "Mass Distribution: A Phase of Bilateral Oligopoly," *American Economic Review*, XLVII (May, 1967; Papers and Proceedings), pp. 274–285.
[29] Revzan, *op. cit.*, p. 20.

the function has increasing costs associated with it (although even here a sufficient demand may induce specialization), and (2) that there are specialized firms in the market which perform this function. In this example, there are instances in which this very phenomenon is taking place. To the extent that certain retail agencies contractually support the breeding and raising of chickens and eggs, designed to meet the demands of ultimate buyers, the function of grading becomes part of the production process itself. This, while prevalent in many manufacturing industries through establishment of standards or brand and labels, has future prospects in agriculture. "A growing development has been the formation of large-scale specialized egg-producing units, resembling much specialized automatic equipment which reduced unit egg-producing costs and increased egg quality control. Some of these units were developed and operated by specialized egg-producing or egg-distributing firms. Others have been run by firms whose major economic activities were in different areas, principally feed manufacturing or food retailing." [30]

Channels As External Economies

It should be noted that the marketing channel as a set including the agencies, functions, and flows becomes in principle an external economy for any firm within it. If in fact it ceases to be, the firm will alter its channel arrangements. In the same way that we consider a single agency performing one function as an external economy, so can we extend the line of analysis to the channel. A manufacturer, for example, who is developing a new product for a market in which he has had no experience will not be required to establish a complete new set of relationships with each and every one of the possible agencies through whom his product may possibly be sold. When he contracts to use the distribution facilities of a wholesaler in one city, the net effect has been to establish direct relationships with the customers of that wholesaler. The same may be said for each of the other resellers with whom the manufacturer may engage for distribution. There are circumstances, however, when the nature of these pre-established relationships may work to the detriment of the manufacturer. Such would occur when the outreach of the wholesaler, for example, is so great that sufficient attention cannot be paid to the needs of each of the customers and suppliers. Also, there are cases when the wholesaler carries competing products which may be perceived as more profitable and thus have greater demands on the resources of the wholesaler. Accordingly, the product of the manufacturer receives less attention than at least he thinks it should. A manufacturer may find an external economy in the wholesaler relationship only in the initial stages of product introduction into a market. Thus, a ready established

[30] National Commission on Food Marketing, *Organization and Competition in the Poultry and Egg Industries, Technical Study No. 2* (Washington, D.C.: U.S. Government Printing Office, 1966), p. 9.

channel may not offer the same potential and the manufacturer may consider either the establishment of his own channel by negotiating for the performance of the functions with a group of agencies across the market or supplement the activities of the channel members with extra resources such as providing the channel member with promotional allowances of one sort or another. Or he may buttress the channel members by the creation of a sales force or other task force to take up the functions not adequately performed by channel members. The development of dual distribution—an arrangement in which a manufacturer sells both through an independent channel *and* through his *own* outlets—is one possible result.[31]

SUMMARY

Marketing agencies are the organizations which perform the marketing functions and create the resultant flows. The firm—the commercial agency—is a collection of productive resources. The central concern of the management of any agency is the allocation of the resources through a series of "make or buy" decisions. The firm decides whether it will perform a function or a set of functions in accordance with its desire to differentiate itself from other firms and in relation to the internal cost of performance in contrast to the market price. To the extent that agencies perform functions above it or below it in the flow, they are vertically integrated. Agencies are horizontally integrated to the extent they perform a set of functions at different places—geographic—at the same level in the flow.

The marketing channel is the collection of flows associated with the transactions of any good or service. The channel is formed when trading relations are formed among agencies so that passage of title, possession rights, and physical possession can take place. The channel is much more than a simple linear "bucket brigade" between and among various agencies. It is the mucilage which links agencies as goods pass from raw extraction to production and to consumers. Although the channel is primarily established for linking agencies, it is also an instrument of competition as organizers control them to establish blockages for competitors. Such devices run the gamut from complete vertical integration to exclusive dealership agreements to extensive promotional campaigns which are designed to build loyalty.

SUGGESTED READINGS

Books

Helmy H. Baligh and Leon E. Richartz, *Vertical Market Structures* (Boston: Allyn and Bacon, Inc., 1967).

[31] See the discussion of dual distribution and dual merchandising in Chapter 11.

Louis P. Bucklin, *A Theory of Distribution Channel Structure* (Berkeley, Cal: Institute of Business and Economic Research, University of California, 1966).

Richard M. Clewett (ed.), *Marketing Channels for Manufactured Products* (Homewood, Ill.: Richard D. Irwin, Inc., 1954).

Bruce E. Mallen (ed.), *The Marketing Channel: A Conceptual Viewpoint* (New York: John Wiley & Sons, Inc., 1967).

Louis W. Stern *et al., Distribution Channels: Behavioral Dimensions* (Boston: Houghton Mifflin Company, 1969).

Articles

Kendall A. Adams, "Achieving Market Organization through Voluntary and Cooperative Groups," *Journal of Retailing* (Summer 1966), pp. 19–28.

J. E. Faris, "Structural Changes and Competitive Relationships among Buying and Selling Firms," *Journal of Farm Economics* 46 (December 1964), pp. 1238–1245.

R. A. Miller, "Exclusive Dealing in the Petroleum Industry: The Refiner-Lessee Dealer Relationships," *Yale Economic Essays* 3 (1963), pp. 223–247.

H. L. Moore and C. Sherwood, "The Franchise and Market Structure: A Case Study," *Journal of Farm Economics* 45 (December 1963), pp. 1375–1379.

7

Time
and distance
in marketing

INTRODUCTION

The analysis of previous chapters has implicitly been built on the interrelationships of time and distance. In fact, the basic relationship between functions and flows, on the one hand, and agencies and channels, on the other, is based on the occurrence of an activity at one point in time and location and the subsequent sequence of events which result in other activities occurring at other points in time and location. In this perspective we examined functions and agencies in terms of discrete locations where activities take place and flows and channels as the sequences of activities traversing both time and distance. Quite clearly, time and space are interdependent concepts insofar as space or distance is measured in time. That is, from the standpoint of both supplies and customers, time implies costs—delays, forgone opportunities, and deterioration. Distance is of analytical significance insofar as it implies time. Thus time and distance through their costs aspects are analytically closely related.

MARKET AREAS

Definition

A "market area" is a market defined to incorporate the elements of time and distance. It is the geographic area in which buyers and sellers come in contact with each other for the transferring of ownership or use rights. One geographic market can be differentiated from another when a good or service is sold only at a location farther than the buyer wishes to travel; hence offerings in separate geographic markets have zero cross elasticities of demand.[1]

Levels of Market Areas

There is a series of market areas which can be discerned. For example, a market area can be defined for an economy, a specific geographic region, a city, a firm, or for any product purchased or sold by the firm.

Let us examine the market area for a geographic region such as New England. An "economic region," for purposes of analysis, may be defined as a relatively large geographical area with the following four characteristics: One, it is an area where there is a center of economic control such that it can be differentiated from other such areas, and for market participants because of convenience and other cost aspects, there are preferences for one such "center" in contrast to another. Such control, though it may in no way be absolute, arises because of the unequal distribution of resources versus the location of users of those resources. A case in point for this is the lobster industry of Maine. Two, it has greater homogeneity in terms of the economic activities than would be the case if the area were merged with continuous areas. New England for example contains a much different assortment of manufacturing activities from the contiguous Middle Atlantic area. The former has no steel plants while the latter has several. Three, the New England region imports a wide assortment of goods and services which it does not produce, it being a deficit area for them. And conversely, New England exports a series of goods and services which it produces in quantities too large to be consumed by New Englanders.[2]

Price and Markets

In order to appreciate fully marketing in terms of time and distance, it is useful to begin with a simple example. Assume there are producing areas as shown in Figure 7.1 in which there are the following conditions: homogenous product; complete information; no consumer mobility, but product mobility; and linear transport costs from high price market to low price market. Note that the supply and demand curves for Region A are shown in the traditional manner and that those for Region B are reversed and positioned adjacent to the diagram for Region A. The transfer costs between the two regions are shown by the "offset," Tab, of the individual market diagrams. Since the flow of product would be from B to A, the

---

[1] Chapter 3, pp. 68, 73.

[2] Roland S. Vaile, E. T. Grether, and Reavis Cox, *Marketing in the American Economy* (Ronald, 1952), p. 488. For the original discussion *see* Bertil Ohlin, *Interregional and International Trade* (Harvard, 1935).

Region B diagram is elevated so that any horizontal line of the back-to-back diagram indicates prices in the two markets that differ by exactly the unit costs of transfer, Tab.

FIGURE 7.1

DETERMINATION OF EQUILIBRIUM PRICES AND PRODUCT FLOWS IN THE TWO-REGION, COMPETITIVE CASE, USING A BACK-TO-BACK DIAGRAM WITH POSITIVE TRANSPORTATION COSTS

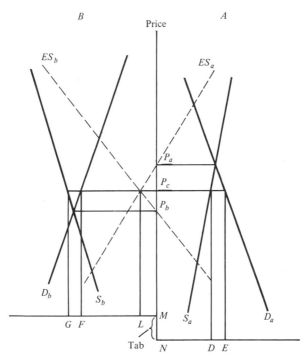

Quantity (Region *B*)   Quantity (Region *A*)

"Excess supply" curves are plotted for each region by subtracting the amount demanded at any given price from the amount of the regional supply at that price. The resulting curves show, in regard to price in both markets, the amount by which the regional supply exceeds regional demand. The intersection of the two excess-supply curves equates the combined-market supply and demand functions of the two regions and specifies the combined-market equilibrium price as well as the amount of interregional product flow.[3]

This price is NP_c in Region A and MP_c in Region B. The amount of product shipped into Region A is ML which is equal to the surplus in

---

[3] C. C. Dennis and L. L. Sammet, "Interregional Competition in the Frozen Strawberry Industry," *Hilgardia* 31 (December 1961), pp. 509–510.

Region B of DF or the deficit of GF in Region A. It is important to recognize that if the transfer costs are equal to or greater than the difference in the market price, assuming all other things constant, trade will not occur. What this means is that prices in one region can differ from those in another by an amount plus or minus the transport cost without giving rise to trade.

An example of this is the basing point pricing system or delivered price system.[4] This system creates a fixed, well-defined price structure over distance, with the delivered prices of all sellers identical to that of all consumers at each specific location. Under a single basing point, the buyer is charged a price that includes both the cost of a good at a geographic location designated the basing point, "Pittsburgh-plus in the steel industry, plus the transportation charges from the basing point to the buyer's location."[5] "The effective operation of this system requires basing points and base prices publicly known (in the trade), and uniquely defined freight costs from every basing point to every possible consuming point."[6] This can occur when: (1) There are standardized products, that is perfect substitution, and hence in equilibrium the prices charged by two sellers are the same; (2) The product is low in value per unit weight so that shipments except for short distances result in transportation costs which form a substantial amount of the delivered price; hence there is spatial differentiation of the product.[7] Under the plan in the steel industry, a customer was charged the Pittsburgh price plus railroad transportation even if the steel was delivered from a nearer location such as would be the case of a purchaser in Chicago. The result of this system was to create an identical price for any buyer regardless of his location, by any steel supplier in the United States.[8]

More complex variations of the basing point system include "zone pricing," which is a scheme whereby the entire country is divided into a number of geographic areas and all buyers within a specific zone pay the same delivered price although prices may differ between zones. What this tends to accomplish is the creation of unique geographic market areas for each seller in a zone and by this the seller becomes isolated from competitors in other zones.[9]

---

[4] The basing point pricing system has been held to be illegal. See: *Corn Products Refining Company V. Federal Trade Commission* 324 U.S. 726 (1945); also, Chapter 14.

[5] Eugene M. Singer, *Antitrust Economics: Selected Legal Cases and Economic Models* (Prentice-Hall, 1968), pp. 228–29.

[6] Carl Kaysen, "Basing Point Pricing and Public Policy," in Richard B. Heflebower and George W. Stocking (eds.), *Reading in Industrial Organization and Public Policy* (Irwin, 1958), p. 155. Originally published in *Quarterly Journal of Economics*, XLIII (1949), pp. 289–314.

[7] *Ibid.*, p. 154.

[8] Singer, *op. cit.*, p. 228.

[9] *Milk and Ice Cream Can Institute v. Federal Trade Commission* 152, F. 2nd 478 (7th Cir., 1946).

Exchange Between Areas

Exchange between two geographic market areas, transport costs not withstanding, will be a function of all or several of the following factors. First, an area which is in a deficit position must offer a money price or its equivalent in goods and services sufficient to generate flows of the needed goods and services from a surplus area. This exchange then is determined in part by the differences in available resources and, as we shall see, the differences between supply and demand in specific areas has an important impact on the boundaries of market areas. Second, exchange is based on the managerial policies of various agencies as they pertain to the selection of functions to be performed, and the location of such functions in terms of time and distance in the context of the marketing channel, that is the type of operation and its location.[10] The third factor is consumer preferences for certain goods and the amount of energy they are willing to expend in searching for goods insofar as they classify them in terms of convenience, shopping, and specialty goods.[11] Four, some goods and services are simply not transportable or if they are, the costs associated with transporting them are not realistic in terms of the alternative, namely, consumers moving to the location of the goods and services themselves. Recreational and tourist areas are examples of the former while services or professionals, doctors and over-the-counter retailers are examples of the latter. Five, the perishability of a product limits the distribution it may have within a particular area. Even with the availability of high-speed transportation media and the development of methods of preserving goods, fresh bread, ice, dairy products and daily newspapers remain in the confines a specific area. Yet, through jet airfreight service, highly perishable and valuable items such as Hawaiian orchids have attained a world-wide market. Six, the high cost of transportation for highly homogenous products with a relatively low value and which are available near a location, such as sand and gravel, cement, and fresh milk, limit the extent of the market from anyone location. In contrast, where the value of the product is high, in relation to its bulk and weight, the area of distribution is wide because the percent of transportation cost on a single unit will be small. Seven, the existence of political barriers, either explicit prohibition or taxation, will prevent the movement of goods across market boundaries. For example, we are familiar with the effect of tariffs on prices. Movement can also be restrained by more informal means, for example, we are all familar with "Buy American." Also, there may be inducements to purchase or to sell in certain market areas such as the efforts of the Small Business Administration to help small businessmen in urban areas.[12] When there are formal means by which goods and services are

[10] David A. Revzan, *A Geography of Marketing: Integrative Statement* (Institute of Business and Economic Research, University of California, 1968), p. 13.

[11] See Chapters 3 and 9.

[12] See Chapter 14.

restrained this is not to imply that such goods or services will not move through what can be termed "illegal channels" such as in the case of alcoholic beverages, narcotics or even margarine transported in past times into Wisconsin.[13] Finally, there will be no movement if there is an absence of advantages in obtaining goods from exterior sources as is true of many products produced in market areas with diversified resources and little concern by customers as to their origin.

Boundaries for Market Areas

The previous discussion implicitly indicated that conceptually and actually a boundary separates markets. The following analysis, shown in Figure 7.2, provides a means for establishing boundaries between market areas. We are assuming again a homogenous product, perfect market information and linear transportation rates, that is, increasing at an equal rate from the location of the seller. In the upper part of the figure, the two sellers are identified by A and B while in the lower part they are represented by 1 and 2. The distances AC and BD represent the prices (costs) for the product at A and B respectively, that is, a purchaser would pay that amount for the product if purchased at the location of the seller. The arms beginning at C and D and moving out in two directions indicate the transportation costs from the two locations and as we have said they are linear. Total product cost to any purchaser including transportation increase as a linear function from the center of the market area. The boundary between the two market areas is formed by the locus of points as which the delivered product price from and B is equal. This is shown in the lower portion of the figure where x and y are isotims of the areas 1 and 2, respectively, and where EF is the boundary of the two areas. It is formed by the intersection of isotims of equal value. The market area of 2 with the lowest non-transport costs is the largest, with the boundary of equal delivered costs between the two regions bending around the supply region of higher costs as indicated by EF.

Other possibilities exist as well. For example, if transport costs were equal, the boundary of equal costs would be the perpendicular bisector of a straight line joining (1) and (2). Another alternative is the possibility of varying transport costs. "If transportation cost increased with distance at a decreasing rate, the equal cost boundary would eventually envelop the region of highest nontransport costs."[14]

[13] T. J. Wales, "Distilled Spirits and Interstate Effects," *American Economic Review* 58 (1968), pp. 853–863.

[14] Dennis and Sammett *op. cit.*, p. 512. Also see: Frank A. Fetter, "The Economic Law of Market Areas," *Quarterly Journal of Economics* 38 (May 1942), pp. 520–529; and *The Masquerade of Monopoly* (Harcourt, Brace & Co., 1931), Chapter 20.

If we remove the assumptions on which the previous analysis is based, the possibility of establishing boundaries still exists though to be certain the task becomes more complex. First, it must be recognized that transportation rates do not have the linear qualities described in the previous example. There are many variations both in regard to the method used and the interrelatedness of time and distance, as we will discuss later, as well as to specific products and the form in which they are found when moved from place to place. Second, there is great variability in the rate structure of the various transportation media used in the movement of goods and services and the costs which accrue to buyers as they move over distances from one point to another. Given these premises it is possible for the management of an agency to establish a geographic market boundary although the elements for this may indeed be different identification and measurement problems for each type of agency. If we assume that a city is an agency,[15] it is possible to identify and measure the elements which effect the position of the boundary. For example, Howard L. Green, in a study of the market areas dominated by Boston and New York, concluded that the boundary between the two cities was a function of the following factors:[16]

1. Railroad coach purchases by commuter to the major city;
2. An estimate of truck freight movement to New York and Boston;
3. Metropolitan newspaper circulation;
4. Long-distance telephone calls;
5. Metropolitan origin of vacationers;
6. Business addresses of directors of major industrial firms; and
7. Metropolitan correspondents for hinterland banks.

This analysis for complete realism needs to include two other factors: (1) the causes of boundary movement; and (2) market thickness. The latter of the two will be discussed in a later section. Boundaries for a region or market or trading area are directly related to the performance of several functions, most notably transportation, storage, and communication, although changes in the cost of any other will have effects as well. For example, a decrease in transportation costs can extend the market area for a given firm. In Figure 7.3 we see two firms located at A and B, each selling at the same price and with linear and equal transport costs. Under these conditions the market boundary between the two is reached at the intersection of price

[15] See Reavis Cox, et al., *Distribution In a High-Level Economy* (Prentice-Hall, 1965), Chapter 6, "Cities as Agencies of Distribution," pp. 85–97.

[16] Howard L. Green, "Hinterland Boundaries of New York City and Boston in Southern New England," *Economic Geography* 31 (October 1955), pp. 283–300. Reprinted in Jack P. Gibbs (ed.), *Urban Research Methods* (Van Nostrand, 1961), pp. 286–309. Although Green did not use the concept "dominance," one must note in passing the entire line of analysis developed by Bogue. *See* Donald J. Bogue, *The Structure of the Metropolitan Community: A Study of Dominance and Subdominance* (Horace H. Rackham School of Graduate Studies, U. of Michigan, 1949).

plus transport functions from which a perpendicular to the horizontal axis
equally divides the area between the two. If for some reason there is a
reduction of transport costs for B such that the arm ED arises, B will now
be able to extend its market area by the area FC; at this point the delivered
price of the two sellers will be once again equal.

FIGURE 7.2

**MARKET AREA BOUNDARIES OF SUPPLY REGIONS OF UNEQUAL TRANSPORTATION COSTS AND
EQUAL TRANSPORTATION RATE-DISTANCE FUNCTIONS**

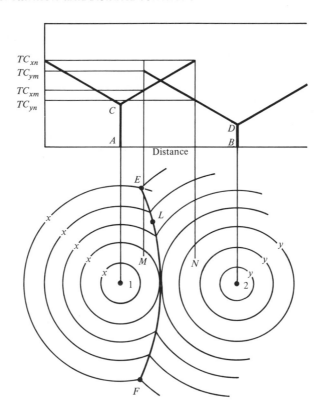

On the other hand, a similar result is possible if the price at B's location
drops from P_1 to P_2. Even with transportation costs at E^1G^1 (the same as
EG) the market has increased by the amount HC. At the same time it must
be appreciated that an increase in the speed, time which distance is crossed,
will have the same effect even if transport rates are constant. If for example
it takes a train one hour to move the merchandise from B to C and it takes
one hour for a truck to move the same merchandise from B to H, the
market area for B is larger by the use of the second medium.

FIGURE 7.3

THE SPATIAL DEMAND CURVE

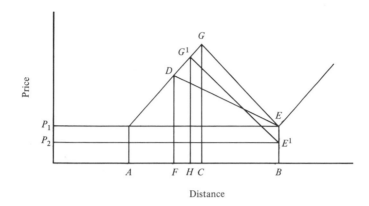

Another variation on transportation services, known as "in transit privileges," is illustrated by Figure 7.4. This is the arrangement whereby a raw material is shipped from point A to point B, there subjecting it to some processing and then shipping the processed product on to the consuming point C. The following example illustrates the manner in which the rate structure of railroads provides for the equalization of competition between two flour-milling companies both drawing their supplies of wheat from the same area and selling flour in the same consuming area. A flour miller at point B competes with a local mill at X, which is adjacent to the source of wheat at point A. The mill at X has the advantage of a through freight rate of twenty-five cents per hundred pounds on flour, which is equal to the rate on wheat, from X to the consuming market C. Without the advantage of a transit privilege, the mill at B must pay a combination of local rates; that is, the total of the local rate on wheat from A to B (twelve cents) and the local rate on flour from B to C (sixteen cents), or a total of twenty-eight cents per hundred pounds. If a transit privilege exists at point B, the mill pays the local rate on wheat of twelve cents into B. When the shipper presents a freight bill showing freight paid on the flour equivalent to wheat from B to C, the mill is entitled to a refund from the inbound carrier of three cents per hundred pounds. The total freight paid by the mill located at B is twenty-five cents, which is equal to that of the mill at X in reaching the market at C. This principle works equally effectively when the competing mill is at a distance from the source of supply and adjacent to the consuming market. Assuming that there is no through rate from the origin point X to the consuming point C, as illustrated in the following figure, the miller at B would have an advantage of three cents per hundred pounds over a miller at *A*. With the transit allowed at *A*, the transportation rate through the two milling points may be equalized.[17]

FIGURE 7.4

IN TRANSIT PRIVILEGE

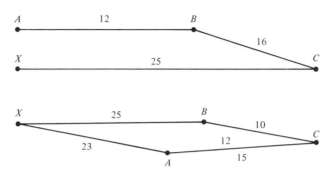

12 = Transit Balance from *A* to *C*

Market areas can be extended by a scattered location of inventories throughout a geographic area provided of course that there are economies of scale in performing warehouse and selling functions at several locations. Economies may develop, for example, from a firm's ability to take advantage of full carload shipments, public or other types of leased warehouse arrangements, and the marketing services of certain agents and brokers. The use of public warehouses and leased facilities can clearly allow a firm to experiment with a territory when there are questions about entering the market because of the seemingly low pay-off given the high investment required. Concomitant with the use of public warehouses in such circumstances is the employment of intermediate agencies, especially if the firm normally sells directly to its customers. The public warehouse service, in addition to those presented in a previous chapter, offers the manager two important advantages: flexibility and professional competence. The circumstances under which public or private warehousing may be favored in market expansion can be summarized in the following table.[18]

Market Thickness

Analysis of geographic market areas up to this point has been based on the assumption that the market areas are flat, that is, there has been a

[17] E. A. Duddy and David A. Revzan, *Marketing: An Institutional Approach* (2d ed., McGraw-Hill, 1953), pp. 63–64.

[18] John F. Magee, *Industrial Logistics* (McGraw-Hill, 1968), p. 153.

uniform distribution of customers over distance. In fact, frequently this is not the case and there tend to be numbers of buyers at or around some points and none at other points in the spatial plane. Market areas have, therefore, a "height" dimension in that buyers are more likely to be concentrated in specific locations in the market area.[19]

TABLE 7.1

CIRCUMSTANCES FAVORING PUBLIC OR PRIVATE WAREHOUSING

	Private Warehousing	Public Warehousing
Market:		
Geographic location	Concentrated, stable	Dispersed, shifting
Level of demand	Stable	Volatile
Seasonality	Uniform	Seasonal
Product line:		
Promotional items	Limited in number or importance	Frequent and important
Physical characteristics	Require special handling and storage	Standardized packaging, handling, storage
Transportation media:		
Technique used	Stable	Subject to changes

If we assume that identical buyers, distributed at uniform densities over an unbounded plane, can move freely in any direction they want, the price paid for a good from a seller will be the basic selling price plus the cash required to reach the seller. A buyer living nearer the seller will consume more than one living some distance because the price for the latter includes the cost for movement to the seller. "Since travel is equal in all directions, it is possible to draw a *demand cone* around the store, according to which quantity consumed drops off with distance because of price increases to the consumers due to increased transport costs."[20] Where the outreach of demand is equal to zero, we have found the trade area of the seller as is shown by r, the radius of the perfect circle in Figure 7.5.

[19] See Lee E. Preston, "Restrictive Distribution Arrangements: Economic Analysis and Public Policy Standard," *Law and Contemporary Problems* 30 (Summer, 1965), pp. 512–19. Preston offers a two-dimensional model of depth with market locations along the horizontal axis and potential customers, at each location, ranked by size along the vertical axis. Along a lower horizontal axis are distributed the potential customers not reached. From two points, say A and H, one perceives a triangle showing depth, that is, the number of customers reached from one location.

[20] Brian J. L. Berry, *Geography of Market Centers and Retail Distribution* (Prentice-Hall, 1967), pp. 60–61.

FIGURE 7.5

SPATIAL SUPPLY AND DEMAND CURVE

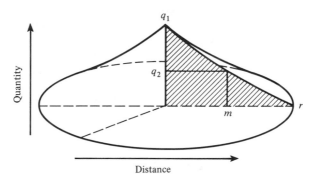

Source: Brian J. L. Berry, *Geography of Market Centers and Retail Distribution* (Prentice-Hall, © 1967), p. 61.

The total quantity of the good demanded within this maximum *r* may be obtained by calculating the area, *D*, beneath the demand cone. "Since quantity demanded, *q*, varies in response to the level of retail price plus transport cost, $p + mt$, *D* is found by integrating the function $q = f$ $(p + mt)$ out to the maximum radius *r*, and multiplying by the population density."[21]

If this calculation is repeated for a variety of different store selling prices, p_1, cones of varying heights and maximum radii will result, and different levels of total demand D_1 may be calculated. If these values of p_1 and D_1 are plotted in a graph and a line is fitted to the results, an aggregate demand curve *D* for the market area can be drawn, as in Figure 7.5. At price p_1 the total demand beneath the cone will be D_1, but if this retail store price drops to p_2, aggregate demand increases to D_2, because the demand cone is much larger. If the retailer's long-run average cost curve *C* is now added to Figure 7.6, the conclusion is that the maximum possible size of store is one providing for an aggregate demand for good *x* of exactly D_m, offered to consumers at a store price of p_m. Only if the demand curve *D* and the supply curve *C* intersect will it be possible to operate a retail store offering good *x*. Only where *D* and *C* cross is some optimum achieved, for elsewhere, at any given price, there would be unmet demands or excess supplies. The resulting price at the retail store, p_m, will yield a particular set of prices $p_m + mt$ to consumers at their place of residence. Since, by

[21] *Ibid.*, p. 61.

$$D_i = S^{2\pi} \int_0^{} \left[\int_0^{M = r} f(Pi + mt)\, m\, dm \right] d\theta$$

assumption, each consumer has the same individual demand curve, the demand cone that can be drawn will have height q_m determined by store price p_m, and a maximum radius r where $pm + rt$ leads to zero demand.[22]

FIGURE 7.6

AGGREGATE DEMAND AND SUPPLY CURVES

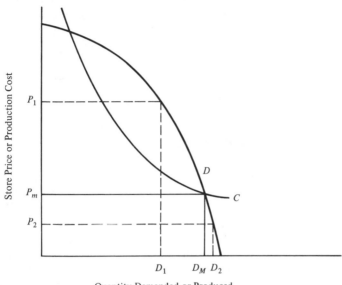

Quantity Demanded or Produced

Source: Brian J. L. Berry, *Geography of Market Centers and Retail Distribution* (Prentice-Hall, © 1967), p. 63.

What this suggests is that in general sellers follow buyers in that for competitive reasons their locations attempt to minimize the total price. From this we would expect to find a positive relationship between buyer density and sales. However, at this time, no study has discovered a concept of population density appropriate for analyzing of distribution.[23] Hall, Knapp, and Winsten, in an international study, which examined population as one of several environmental studies thought to affect retail sales in Canada, Great Britain and the United States, concluded: "There is no single concept of density of population suitable for the analysis of distribution."[24] Revzan, on the other hand, using a different approach, where concern of density of population was measured by wholesale/retail sales ratios, discovered a definite relationship between density of retail sales and wholesale sales. For

[22] *Ibid.*
[23] Margaret Hall, John Knapp, and Christopher Winsten, *Distribution in Great Britain and North America* (London: Oxford University Press, 1961), p. 4.
[24] *Ibid.*, p. 136.

example, in 1963 the distribution of wholesale trade was such that large percentages were concentrated in cities of 500,000-or-more persons, or over three times the national ratio. The ratio for the 250,000–499,999 group was 1.76, or somewhat above the national level. The successive lessening importance of wholesale trade coupled with the greater locational dispersing of retail trade led to below average ratios as follows: 100–249,999, 1.19; 50,000–99,999, 0.92; 25,000–49,999, 0.96; 10,000–24,999, 0.49 2500–9999, 0.25. The "remainder" group had a ratio of 0.83 due to the location of wholesale middlemen oriented to agriculture and other extractive industries.[25]

MOVEMENT IN TIME AND OVER DISTANCE

Introduction

The previous analysis has perhaps given the impression that movement in time and space is somehow a function of sellers alone and that market or trading area boundaries are related to factors of costs and prices in and between areas. This is not entirely so because buyers and the degree to which they expend resources have an effect on the establishment of market areas and boundaries. The analysis of this section is concerned largely with the ways in which consumers express preference for goods and services insofar as they are willing to expend energy in the movement over distance.[26] It should be noted that the principles regarding changes in the movement over distance have the same effect on the establishment of boundaries and the movement of boundaries as the principles discussed previously. Having laid that foundation, we allow the reader to make the necessary relationship.

Charactereistics of Goods and Gravity Models

In Chapter 3 and earlier in our present discussion, we pointed to the fact that markets represent points of contact between buyers and sellers. That point as defined in terms of a specific location is related to the fact that we are able to classify goods and some marketing agencies, notably, retailers, in terms of the effort the buyer was willing to exert in searching for the best want-satisfying choice. From that, three categories of goods were developed: (1) *convenience goods*, those goods which the buyer purchases frequently, immediately, and with the minimum effort; (2) *shopping goods*, those goods which the customer in the process of selection and purchase characteristically compares on a basis of quality, price, and style; and (3) *specialty goods*, those goods for which a significant group of buyers are habitually willing to make a special purchasing effort. Given this perspective, two factors must be understood. One, although we used this categoriza-

[25] Revzan, *op. cit.*, p. 117.
[26] This is one part of the more general analysis of buyer behavior; *see* Chapter 9.

tion system for retail goods in previous discussion, it is equally applicable at the most general level of analysis for all goods and services. We shall bring to bear greater complexity later when buyer structure and behavior are fully developed. Two, effort is defined in terms of moving through space at this point and not to the complete process of buying which, too, is examined later in greater detail.

The most interesting and certainly controversial attempts to relate the characteristic of goods and movement through space by buyers is W. J. Reilly's "Law of Retail Gravitation."[27] The "law" stated in mathematical notation indicates the means by which a boundary can be established for two retail trading areas as a function of fashion and shopping goods. The law states that "two cities attract retail trade from any intermediate city or town in the vicinity of the breaking point, approximately in direct proportion to the populations of the two cities and in inverse proportion to the square of the distances of these two cities to the intermediate town."[28] The formula is

$$\left(\frac{Ba}{Bb}\right) = \left(\frac{Pa}{Pb}\right)\left(\frac{Db}{Da}\right)^2$$

where: Ba is the proportion of the trade from the intermediate city attracted by City A
Bb is the proportion attracted by City B
Pa is the population of City A
Pb is the population of City B
Da is the distance from the intermediate town to City A
Db is the distance from the intermediate town to City B

The law has been the basis of numerous studies, some of which have tested the validity of the proposition while others have attempted to improve on the law itself.[29] These studies have proceeded along the lines of adding other variables to distance, the most important of which we have noted being time. "Specifically, where population depends on public transportation, retailers tend to locate in areas serviced by public facilities. Customers then

[27] W. J. Reilly, *The Law of Retail Gravitation* (The University of Texas, 1931). The controversy, if from nothing else, has stemmed from the choice of the word "law." A. J. Wolf's definition is "in its scientific sense, the word *law* means nothing more than a regularity or uniformity in the character or relation of certain classes of facts or events." (A. Wolf, *Essentials of the Scientific Method* (Macmillan, 1930), p. 108.)

[28] Paul D. Converse, "New Laws of Retail Gravitation," *Journal of Marketing* (October 1949), p. 379.

[29] E. Douglas, "Measuring the General Retail Trading Area—A Case Study" *Journal of Marketing* XIII (April 1949). R. B. Reynolds, "A Test of the Law of Retail Gravitation," *Journal of Marketing* XVII (January 1953); A. F. Jung, "Is Reilly's Law of Retail Gravitation Always True?" *Journal of Marketing* XXIV (October 1959). G. Schwartz "Law of Retail Gravitation: An Appraisal," *University of Washington Business Review* XXII (October 1962).

will be attracted from large areas, and the extent will depend in part on accessibility."[30]

Behavioral Formulations

Most recently attempts to synthesize gravity models with more precise formulations of behavioral traits have been developed. The most important of such efforts have been developed by W. J. Baumol and E. A. Ide and David Huff. Baumol and Ide establish a solution for determining how far a buyer will travel for a single good within the context of a set of goods. The maximum distance buyers are willing to travel is:

$$r = \frac{e}{mt} p\ (T) - \frac{1}{t}\ (Cn\sqrt{T} + Ci)$$

where: $P(T)$ = the probability that a consumer will find the goods he needs to make his trip a success in the center that offers T goods.

mt = the costs of travelling m miles to the center at t per mile.

$Cn\sqrt{T}$ = the difficulty of shopping, emerging out of size and congestion, defined as costs proportional to the square root of the size of the shopping center T.

Ci = the opportunity costs of alternative activities foregone, including other shopping opportunities.

Given, that the consumer will not shop at a store unless $f\ (t_1 m) = e[p(t)] - l\ (mt + Cn\sqrt{T} + Ci)$ is positive where constants e and l are respectively the subjective weight functions assigned by the consumer to his expectation of excess.[31]

Huff's model of buyer behavior in space assumes that buyers: (1) isolate a set of "alternative shopping center choices" from a much larger group consisting of all possible alternatives; (2) calculate a positive measure of utility for each of these alternatives; (3) distribute their patronage spatially in a probabilistic fashion.[32] The probability of a person moving to a specific location for shopping is proportionate to the utility of that location in relation to the utility of other locations which in turn is a function of the size of facilities at that location and the time required to reach it; or:

---

[30] Jac Goldstucker, "Trading Areas" in George Schwartz (ed.) *Science in Marketing* (Wiley, 1965), p. 298.

[31] Berry, *op. cit.*, p. 46. *Also see* W. J. Baumol and E. A. Ide, "Variety in Retailing," *Management Science* 3 (October 1956), pp. 93–101.

[32] David L. Huff, "A Probability Analysis of Consumer Spatial Behavior," in William S. Decker (ed.), *Emerging Concepts in Marketing*, Proceedings of the American Marketing Association (Chicago: December 1962), pp. 443–461.

$$P_{ij} = \frac{\dfrac{S_j}{(T_{ij})^\lambda}}{\displaystyle\sum_{j=1}^{n} \dfrac{S_j}{(T_{ij})^\lambda}}$$

where: P_{ij} is the probability of a buyer at i traveling to the shopping
center j,

S_j is the size of the shopping center j,

T_{ij} is the travel time to move from i to j, and

λ is a parameter reflecting effect of travel on various kinds of
shopping trips.

The numerator represents the ratio of the size of the center to the travel
time necessary to reach it raised to a power. The denominator represents
the sum of the values of the ratios for all shopping centers in the area.
Hence, the probability of shopping in one area in contrast to another is
directly related to the size and inversely related to the time necessary to get
there. Travel time is the cost or "effort" to the buyer making the trip and is
increased by a series of exponents which vary with the type of goods.[33]

IMPLICATIONS

Analysis of geographic market areas suggests that marketing agencies,
in order to serve the requirements of buyers and sellers, must be able to
position themselves at some optimum point in time and space. The problem
of location in time and space, to be certain, is a most complex one because
it requires analysis of the opportunities and costs which prevail at any one
location in relation to others. What this implies is that firms must be able
to gather inputs for the basis of offerings in the market which can be
differentiated on a geographic basis at a price which will attract potential
buyers.[34] This means that elements of geographic markets must be included
as part of the offering in such a manner that the inputs can be combined
at a cost that will attract buyers. In the most general sense, firms are confronted by the simplistic locational question: Should the agency be located
closer to the loci of supply of any one or a set of factors and inputs or should
it be located closer to the loci of demand? This question in part is answered
by the following: One, location is a function of how buyers perceive its

[33] David Huff, "Ecological Characteristics of Consumer Behavior," *Papers and Proceedings of the Regional Science Association* 7 (1961), 19–28; and "Defining and Estimating
a Trading Area," *Journal of Marketing* 28 (July 1964), 34–38.

[34] These problems are given considerable attention in Part IV of the present book, especially, *see* Chapter 10 for a discussion of the basis for differential advantage.

offerings. If they are perceived as convenience, shopping, or specialty offerings, there will be different patterns of locations by agencies and different cost expenditures by buyers. In general, specialty goods have the largest market areas, with shopping goods and convenience goods respectively smaller. Agencies carrying combinations of the three types will have mixed patterns, including interoffering "external" economies—a point discussed in Chapter 11. Two, the location of the productive inputs, their importance, and the costs of transporting raw versus semifinished versus finished goods, in relation to their final value will also dictate locational alternatives. For example, for marketing agencies whose offerings are resource bound such as steel mills, and especially where the transportation costs of moving iron ore is much more on a proportionate basis than the costs involved in moving finished steel, location is closer to the source of raw materials and inexpensive transportation services. As can be imagined, there are a substantial number of possible combinations of firm location because of the value-relative-to-weight factor. Three, there are a number of legal restrictions which affect locational alternatives, most common of which are zoning laws; and water and air pollution guidelines also establish priorities for the location of agencies.

Of great importance in the implications of geographic markets is the price structure which is part of the time distance equation. As we have seen, price, in the specific dollars and cents terms as well as the total value sense becomes a means by which firms establish boundaries for the geographic market areas around them. Since we have defined market boundaries by the use of cross elasticity of demand, costs for enterprise differentiation translated into price necessarily affect the degree of elasticity. And as we shall see later in this volume, differentiation, that is, effecting low cross elasticity of demand, is a critical part of marketing strategy.

SUMMARY

Time and distance in marketing are concerned with the basic relationship between functions, flows, agencies, and channels—which is to focus on the occurrence of an activity at one point in time and at one location and the subsequent activities which occur at other points. The concept which allows time and distance to be incorporated in the analysis is geographic market areas. This is a basic expansion of the concept of a market. Market areas can be identified and measured for every marketing agency or for any offering of an agency, and in fact, every offering has a different market area insofar as there are different costs associated with the movement of the offering or buyers, and insofar as buyers have different perceptions about offerings and the resources which they will expend. Conceptually these areas are not flat surfaces but are three dimensional, reflecting the fact that agencies and customers concentrate around certain places because of economies such as, for example, provided by waterways. The boundaries of market areas are continually changing insofar as costs change, or buyers are willing to expend further resources or agencies are able to differentiate themselves.

Location of agencies becomes an important element in this process and is a function of several elements: (1) market demand, (2) supply costs, (3) buyer preferences, and (4) legal constraints.

SELECTED READINGS

Books

Brian, J. L. Berry, *Geography of Market Centers and Retail Distribution* (Englewood Cliffs, N.J.: Prentice-Hall, Inc., 1967). A concise treatment of market area analysis; traces historical development suggestion of the ways in which the various techniques can be used in marketing and regional planning.

Edward A. Duddy and David A. Revzan, *Marketing and Institutional Approach* (2d ed., New York: McGraw-Hill Book Co., Inc., 1953), Chapter XXIV, "Market Areas: The Wholesale Market." Classic discussion developed here.

Walter Isard, *Location and Space Economy: A General Theory Relating to Industrial Market Areas, Land Use, Trade, and Urban Structure* (Cambridge, Mass.: M.I.T. Press, 1956). A major work in regional science analysis; theory is fully developed; sets out general conceptual problems and is understandable to the uninitiated.

David A. Revzan, *A Geography of Marketing: Integrative Statement* (Institute of Business and Economic Research, University of California, Berkeley, 1968). A comprehensive treatment of the geography of marketing; treats various topics including: Locational Determinants, Locational Patterns, Commodity Flows and Barriers.

David A. Revzan, *A Geography of Marketing: Resource Bibliography* (Institute of Business and Economic Research, University of California, Berkeley, 1968). Volume contains almost 3700 entries from various disciplines, dealing with all geographic aspects of marketing. It is cross-indexed for easy reference. A must for any research in this area.

R. S. Vaile, E. T. Grether, and Reavis Cox, *Marketing in the American Economy* (New York: The Ronald Press, Inc., 1952). Chapter 25, "Marketing Areas for Primary Producers and Manufacturers." Chapter 27, "Retail Market Areas."

Articles

W. J. Baumol and Philip Wolfe, "A Warehouse Location Problem," *Operations Research* 6 (March-April 1958), 252–263.

David L. Huff, "A Probabilistic Analysis of Shopping Center Trade Areas,"

Land Economics 39 (1963), pp. 81–90. An interesting article combining behavioral notions with trading area analysis.

————, "Defining and Estimating a Trading Area," *Journal of Marketing* 28 (October 1964), pp. 34–38.

John F. Magee, "The Logistics of Distribution," *Harvard Business Review* 38 (July-August 1960), pp. 89–101. A classic article containing channels, logistics, and locational problems.

A. S. Manne, "Plant Location under Economies of Scale-Decentralization and Computation," *Management Science* XI (November 1964), pp. 213–235.

George S. Tolley and Lloyd M. Hartman, "Inter-Area Relations in Agricultural Supply," *Journal of Farm Economies* 42 (1960), pp. 453–473.

Rutledge Vining, "Delimination of Economic Areas: Statistical Concepts in the Spatial Structure of an Economic System," *Journal of the American Statistical Association,* 48 (1960), pp. 189–220.

Buyer structure and behavior

8

Buyer structure

This is the first of two chapters devoted to the analysis of buyers. We recall "buyer" includes "lessees" as well. Our discussion is consistent with the framework established in Chapter 4. In the present chapter, we examine buyer structure; in Chapter 9 we examine behavior, although, as in Chapter 4, we recognize the interrelationship of structure and behavior. Any prolonged separation of structure and behavior is unreal, so on occasion in this analysis of customer structure, we have had to introduce behavioral aspects as part of our discussion. The behavioral essence implicit in "structure" does not allow otherwise.[1]

Structural Analysis

The structural elements which concern us in the present discussion are, by definition in Chapter 4, those elements which affect buyer perception and hence behavior.[2] In Chapter 4, we discussed many of the elements of structure. This chapter will "disaggregate" and elaborate some of the structural elements with respect to buyers. For example, buyers will be examined in terms of the importance of psychological, sociological, and demographic characteristics, along with economic aspects.

[1] Chapter 4, pp. 92, 104.
[2] Introductory comments were presented in Chapter 2.

It should be clearly remembered that aside from buyer structure-behavior relationships, seller structure has an important effect on buyer structure.[3] This takes place to the extent that sellers by offering only specific sets of goods limit what buyers perceive in the market. For example, tire manufacturers do not offer yellow "white wall" tires; hence buyers in the short-run may not expect such an item, or buyers in fact desiring such a tire will be frustrated in their efforts to acquire such an offering and may have to take a close or distant substitute. This example suggests in general the relationship of seller structure to buyer structure; obviously, there are many more overt instances as well, such as price-fixing among competitors, which clearly affect buyer choice.

Initially, our approach to the analysis of buyer structure is static in that we examine one of the elements at a time holding all others constant. We have chosen this method as a means of focusing on the importance of each of the elements. It is clearly recognized that some of the studies in the buyer area use techniques such as multiple discriminant analysis as a means of measuring various structural elements. This technique assigns weights to the various elements such as age, income, occupation, social class, and so on as a means of determining what combination of factors is the best predictor of behavior. At this point, it is beyond the scope of the analysis.[4] At the end of this chapter a number of references are listed which will give the interested reader some idea of the work in this area.

BUYER STRUCTURE: INDIVIDUAL BUYERS

Introduction

In this section we describe in some detail various elements of buyer structure which affect the behavior of individuals. Our discussion examines the following elements: (1) economic resources including income, (2) psychological elements, (3) sociological elements, (4) life cycle and family status, and (5) demographic elements including education, national background, religious background, and racial characteristics. The analysis begins with economic resources; this choice was arbitrary. However, since income, or wealth in general, is a major ingredient in effective demand, it is obviously a fundamental determinant for understanding buyer behavior.

---

[3] The reverse is also true; Buyer structure affects structure, see the discussion in Chapter 4, pp. 104–105.

[4] Thomas S. Robertson and James N. Kennedy, "Prediction of Consumer Innovators: Application of Multiple Discriminant Analysis," *Journal of Marketing Research* V (February 1968), pp. 64–69. For a discussion of the techniques, *see* Maurice G. Kendall, *A Course in Multivariate Analysis* (Charles Griffin and Co., 1957).

ECONOMIC RESOURCES

Definition

Economic resources, include both current income and beliefs about future income flows, as well as wealth in inventory and the power to borrow. Obviously, "economic resources" is a broader concept than "income." How buyers perceive the future in relation to expected income and such phenomena as inflation has great impact on how they dispose of current income, that is, consume or save.[5] Here it is obvious that we are including two important elements, namely, income and beliefs about the future; later these are a function of several things including psychological as well as sociological aspects. More important in this line of analysis is the recognition that we are forced into a situation in which actions in several periods is included. Simply, current expenditures and/or savings will have an impact on what can be spent in future periods. Of course, this is linked to income expectations. One may spend or commit himself to more now if either or both of the following are true: Prices will be higher in the future or his own income will be larger in the future.

Income and Consumption

To assert that consumption is a function of current income is an oversimplification of a complex set of relationships. Keynes formulated the basic premises: (1) real consumption expenditures are a stable function of real income; and (2) the marginal propensity to consume is positive, but less than one; that is, as income increases a proportionate amount of income will be spent on consumption. The consumption function tells how consumption expenditures change as a result of changes in income, that is, what happens to the quantity and quality of goods and services purchased when real income changes.[6] What is important to recognize is that buyers can be categorized by income groups, each with its own marginal propensity to consume, and then when income change takes place some estimates of differences in consumption can be made. A case of this is described by Engel's Law.

Engel's Law

Engel's law proposes that as income increases the proportion of income spent on food decreases, the proportion spent on household operation, rent,

---

[5] Indeed many hold that the fight against inflation centers on the psychological expectations of demanders. See George Katona, *Psychological Analysis of Economic Behavior* (McGraw-Hill, 1963), Chapter 12, 'Attitudes and Behavior in Inflation," pp. 257–270; and, Paul Davidson and Eugene Smolensky, *Aggregate Supply and Demand Analysis* (Harper & Row, 1964), pp. 203–205.

[6] John Maynard Keynes, *The General Theory of Employment Interest and Money* (Harcourt, Brace and World, 1936), Chapters 8, 9, and 10. *See also* George Katona and Eva Mueller, *Consumer Responses to Income Changes* (The Brookings Institution, 1968).

fuel, and light, and housing remains reasonably constant, and the proportion spent for clothing, transportation, recreation, personal care, and education increases.[7]

Permanent Income

Other changes in income as one of the structural elements for the individual buyer have more subtle aspects. Of greatest interest is the permanent income hypothesis.[8] This hypothesis, put forth by Milton Friedman, is based on the assumption that consumption can be subdivided in two parts—permanent consumption and transitory consumption. Likewise income can be examined in the same manner. This hypothesis establishes a minimum standard of living which is enhanced with additional transitory income. Each time transitory income becomes permanent, for example, when a man's yearly bonus for company performance becomes part of his income without regard to the firm's sales, his standard of living increases. In general, transitory income is expended on goods and services not in the normal assortment of goods and services in the given standard of living. When transitory income declines as one would expect during periods of recession, for example, transitory consumption declines. When transitory income disappears and permanent income decreases, dissavings in one form or another takes place as the buyer attempts to maintain his standard of living. Such dissaving may also occur for other reasons, such as the inability to meet current expenditures out of current income and desires to make unusual expenditures. What is important is to be able to relate quantitative and qualitative changes in the assortment of goods purchased to changes in income.

PSYCHOLOGICAL ELEMENTS

Introduction

In Chapters 2 and 3 we discussed demand and supply in the marketing economy and the concepts of needs and wants. In Chapter 2 our concern was the examination of the reasons for a marketing system and how this system served as a responsive mechanism. In Chapter 3, we closely considered wants, products, and markets. This section is directly related to that analysis, but here our concern is with the individual and his specific wants and needs. In Chapter 3 we made an important distinction between the so-called biogenic needs and the psychogenic needs and further sub-

[7] H. S. Houthakker, "An International Comparison of Household Expenditure Patterns, Commemorating the Century of Engel's Law," *Econometrica* 25 (October 1957), pp. 531–51; George Fisk, *Marketing Systems: An Introductory Analysis* (Harper & Row, 1967), p. 161; and, Benjamin S. Loeb, 'The Use of Engel's Laws as a Basis for Predicting Consumer Expenditures," *Journal of Marketing* XX (July 1955), pp. 20–27.

[8] Milton Friedman, *A Theory of the Consumption Function* (Princeton, 1957), p. 138.

divided the latter into: (1) affectional needs; (2) ego-bolstering needs; and (3) ego-defensive needs.[9]

The Problems of Psychological Analysis

Psychological analysis of buyer structure is in part a deductive process, that is, theory suggests some determinants but also other elements of structure are deduced afterwards from the behavior itself. For example, if one purchases a station wagon, the possible structural elements included by theories of human behavior vary from the point of view that the buyer who has a large family is manifesting a rational motive to the theory that he was a deprived child and desires a vehicle which will allow him to collect things. Given these alternatives, the following two caveats must be kept clearly in mind when psychological analysis is used. One, the buyer is subjected to a great many influences which trace a complex path through his psyche and lead eventually to overt purchasing responses.[10] And two, there are a great number of suppositions which are used to explain various responses and the structures which accompany them; and there is no easy way of dealing with the subtle, and yet often critical distinctions which mark the numerous psychological theories. What we then find are several theories, some of which have greater predictive value than others, each with its own framework, assumptions, and structural elements. Kotler has explored the various approaches of Marshall, Pavlov, Freud, Veblen, and Hobbes with an intention to finding applications in understanding the psychological elements as they pertain to marketing. Summarily, he suggests that each has some contribution to make, though as individual theories they do not provide a complete explanation of the deterministic elements.[11]

> *Marshallian* man is concerned chiefly with economic cues—prices and income—and makes a fresh utility calculation before each purchase.
>
> *Pavlovian* man behaves in a largely habitual rather than thoughtful way; certain configurations of cues will set off the same behavior because of rewarded learning in the past.
>
> *Freudian* man's choices are influenced strongly by motives and fantasies which take place deep within his private world.
>
> *Veblenian* man acts in a way which is shaped largely by past and present social groups.
>
> And finally, *Hobbesian* man seeks to reconcile individual gain with organizational gain.

[9] See, Chapter 3, pp. 53–54.

[10] W. T. Tucker, *Foundations For A Theory of Consumer Behavior* (Holt, Rinehart and Winston, 1967), p. 5.

[11] Philip Kotler, "Behavioral Models for Analyzing Buyers," *Journal of Marketing* 29 (October 1965), p. 45.

The Psychological Elements

Although the several theories have a great diversity of elements, at minimum it seems fair to state that most have as a nucleus certain critical features, namely, the external stimulus, the internal state, the behavior itself that often requires an object, and some effective reaction that makes the behavior more likely to recur or less likely to recur in the future. The basic psychological model presumes the presence of a dynamic psychophysical system such as the human body or enterprise which is continually moving out of balance. For example, for the individual we can easily observe situations when thirst requires some type of satiation through the consumption of liquid refreshment. This concept in the biological context is known as homeostasis. It refers to the tendency of a physiological system to maintain internal stability due to the coordination of its parts in any given situation or a reaction to a stimulus tending to disturb its normal condition or function.[12] The classic example in physiology is the automatic role of perspiration as a cooling mechanism. It is the means by which the body temperature is stabilized. It is obvious that this concept does not fully serve the purposes of buyer analysis since it is solely concerned with the automatic readjustment of physiological affairs. However, the concept has been modified in psychological terms.

The psychological counterpart of homeostasis is cognitive dissonance. It refers to an uncomfortable psychological state produced by external factors, especially changes in the environment, and changes in the internal balance which singly or together cause disquiet in the individual.[13] For example, the feeling might arise when there is a difference between an individual's own belief on a matter which for the most part he is committed to and some new piece of information he has accepted. The individual must relieve the disquiet either by changing his own views about the matter or by rejecting the new information which he has come across.

Stimuli

Stimuli are the signals which evoke responses from the individual. They are the means by which the individual is notified about the state or states of disequilibrium which develop from various parts of the body in relation to the environment. Such stimuli as the individual's recognition of hunger

---

[12] See Walter B. Cannon, *The Wisdom of the Body* (rev. and enlarged ed., Norton and Co., 1939) for the most definitive statesmen on homeostasis and social systems (reprinted as Norton Library paperback N-205, 1963). *See also* Jules Henry, "Homeostasis, Society, and Evolution: A Critique," *Scientific Monthly*, 81 (December, 1955), pp. 300–309. For a general discussion of the role of biological analogies in economics, *see* Edith T. Penrose, "Biological Analogies in the Theory of the Firm," *American Economic Review* XLII (December, 1952), pp. 804–819.

[13] Leon Festinger, *A Theory of Cognitive Dissonance* (Harper and Row, 1957), and J. W. Brehm and A. R. Cohen, *Explorations in Cognitive Dissonance* (Wiley, 1962), Chs. 1 and 2.

can be as far apart as the feelings by the Englishman who expects tea and crackers in the late afternoon to those of the Finnish farm-worker who has his tea break early in the day. Stimuli can be categorized in terms of the sensations that they elicit, for example, pain, thirst, hunger, or just the desire for an object. They can be measured in terms of heat or light by such devices as thermometers or light meters when expressed in purely physical terms.[14] However, when they are expressed as desires they can be estimated only by behavior; for example, the amount of time an individual will spend searching for a product, the amount of money that is spent, or the amount of care taken of it.

Motivation

Motivation refers to the action undertaken by the individual to over-come the disquiet and in fact arises out of the tensions which have created the state. "This triggers a sequence of psychological events directed toward the selection of a goal which the individual *anticipates* will bring about release from the tensions and the selection of patterns of action which he anticipates will bring him the goal."[15]

Although the definition is quite simple, it should be recognized that the concept is complex. This arises because the term is linked to a physical analogy which underlies motivation. For example, an object does not move unless force of some kind is applied. Balls on a pool table move only as the result of some energy being exerted and in relation to the amount of friction which must be overcome. By analogy, it is presumed that all human actions are in response to the appropriate motivation. It is reasonable to conclude that hunger leads to certain appropriate actions which assuage the need and are more or less common to the human species. "But it is fairly clear that eating can be used similarly as a process to assuage anxiety, loneliness or boredom—crudely described drive states or tensions that may be thought of as driving toward action without driving toward any particular behavior or class of behavior."[16]

One of the major problems with this approach is that there is no one single list of motives to which all will agree; different motives can lead to identical buying behavior and, conversely, different buying behavior can be traced back to the same motives. For example, if we use A. H. Maslow's list of basic motives, we find a safety need.[17] One buyer might install and

---

[14] Tucker, *op. cit.*, p. 6.

[15] James A. Bayton, "Motivation, Cognition, Learning—Basic Factors in Consumer Behavior," *Journal of Marketing* XXII (January, 1958), p. 282. The student should see that the same concepts are equally applicable in viewing the operations of the business firm and the non-profit organization.

[16] Tucker, *op. cit.*, pp. 6–7.

[17] A. H. Maslow, *Motivation and Personality* (Harper & Row, 1954), pp. 80–101. Maslow's list also includes physiological needs, belonging and love needs, esteem needs, and need of self-acutualization.

use seat belts in his automobile; another might increase his automobile insurance; and a third might sell his car and take the train.[18] A second problem with the motivation approach is the lack of a fully acceptable research methodology. Motivational research, which has been used in advertising and marketing research in an attempt to discover basic motives, is not held in the highest regard by everyone in the field.[19]

The basic model which best describes the relationships between these elements is the S-R (stimulus-response) model. This model involves the recognition of the stimulus that triggers behavior and leads to a specific response. For example, hunger motivates the acquisition of food, or in a more complex case hunger for something sweet motivates the quest for candy. George Katona, an economist with a psychological flair, has incorporated a substantial amount of psychological content in his research and has concluded, with respect to motivation, that there is a most complex set of events affected by a host of factors. He states: "There cannot be just one economic motive or goal. Motives and goals change with circumstances, with past experiences, and with group belonging."[20] After an examination of the other structural elements which completes this chapter we take a longer look at the essence of this model in the following chapter.

SOCIOLOGICAL ELEMENTS

Concepts of Social Groups

Our approach to the analysis of sociological elements is limited to groups. They are simply one subset of organizations to which an individual belongs.[21] Instead of being concerned with all people belonging to a single income group, for example, which in itself is not always a good predictor of behavior, we use social groups. Social groups are organizations with specific characteristics stemming from social phenomena. For example, a market includes a number of groups with specific attributes which differentiate each from the other. In terms of firms these distinctions can be made on the basis of size or form of legal organization. For social groups the distinctions can be made in terms of a national culture and within such a culture there can be such diverse groups as people living in Oregon or

[18] Stewart H. Rewoldt, James D. Scott, and Martin R. Warshaw, *Introduction to Marketing Management: Text and Cases* (Irwin, 1969), p. 40.

[19] The main criticism of motivational research is that it has a limited population. One method used is the "in-depth" interview. In such cases the individual is put through extensive questioning and asked to describe feelings, fears, needs as they come to mind; the assumption is that several responses will make up for a less detailed but more extensive sampling of a large population. Other methods of gathering information include the projective technique, word association, incomplete sentences, and picture responses.

[20] Katona, *op. cit.*, p. 86.

[21] See, Chapter 4, pp. 108–110.

Vermont or people belonging to one religion or another or voting for one political party or anther.

For purposes of discriminating between groups we can examine the degree to which an individual relates to one in contrast to another. In Chapter 4, we argued that individuals belong involuntarily to some organizations while they voluntarily belong to others. These run the gamut from the family organization to which the individual has at least for some period of time involuntary membership to the consumers' cooperative to which the individual seeks membership on a voluntary basis. Membership in groups or organizations is in the main defined in terms of constraints on action, that is, implicit or explicit rules for entering and maintaining one's membership. The more formal the group, the more definite the rules. They may be as demanding as being born into the group, as the family or the religion, or simply be based on the frequency with which the individual interacts with members of the organization, the extent to which the interacting member defines himself as a member of the group, and the extent to which he is defined by others as belonging to the group.[22] No matter what the conditions of membership, the crucial issue is how much impact the group will have on the actions of the individual member. The degree to which structure of a group affects the individual is the degree to which the individual perceives his security or perceives anxiety with the particular structure. We can best illustrate this point by examination of one such group, namely social class, and relate it to the analysis of buyer structure.

Social Class

Before describing the buyer structure known as social class, it is necessary to make a connection between groups and class; this is completed by understanding reference groups.[23] Reference groups are groups to which the individual compares his actions. They provide structure for buyers in that they offer standards of action to which the individual may aspire. Further, they provide perspectives for the individual which he can execute without having explicit group membership.[24]

Social class as a reference group

Social class in the strictest sense does not conform to the definition of the reference group because of the imprecise definition of the various classes. Social class is a "constructed reference group" because the referent is a social

---

[22] John A. Howard, *Marketing Theory* (Allyn and Bacon, 1965), p. 153.

[23] We have little to say about formal groups in this section, but later sections of the chapter deal with the firm and non-firm establishments.

[24] Tamotsu Shibutani, "Reference Groups as Perspective," *American Journal of Sociology* (May 1955), p. 563, reprinted in Perry Bliss (ed.) *Marketing and the Behavioral Sciences: Selected Readings* (2d ed., Allyn and Bacon, 1967), pp. 255–269.

category lacking a clear framework rather than an actual group or organization such as a family or fraternal association.[25] Further, it is constructed in the sense that it is used by individuals "to structure their social world and to make comparisons and evaluations of their own behavior and that of other people."[26]

Elements of Social Class

Social class is a six part concept according to the investigations of W. Lloyd Warner and Paul Lunt.[27] The six classes are:[28]

1. The upper-upper of "Social Register" Class is composed of locally prominent families, usually with at least second or third generation wealth. Almost inevitably, this is the smallest of the six classes—with probably no more than one-half of one percent of the population able to claim membership. The basic values of these people might be summarized in these phrases: living graciously, upholding the family's reputation, reflecting the excellence of one's breeding, and displaying a sense of community responsibility.

2. The lower-upper or "nouveau riche" class is made up of the more recently arrived and never-quite-accepted wealthy families. Included in this class are members of each city's "executive elite," as well as founders of large businesses and the newly well-to-do doctors and lawyers. At best only one and one-half percent of Americans rank at this level. The goals of people at this particular level are a blend of the upper-upper pursuit of gracious living and the upper-middle class's drive for success.

3. In the upper-middle class are moderately successful professional men and women, owners of medium-sized businesses and "organization men" at the managerial level; also included are those younger people who are expected to arrive at this occupational status level. The motivating concerns of people in this class are success at career (which is the husband's contribution to the family's status) and tastefully reflecting this success in social participation and home decor (which is the wife's primary responsibility).

4. At the top of the "average man world" is the lower-middle class. For the most part they are drawn from the ranks of nonmanagerial office workers, small business owners, and those highly-paid blue collar families who are concerned with being accepted and respected in white-collar dominated clubs, churches, and neighborhoods. The key word in understanding the

[25] Elizabeth Bott, "The Concept of Class as a Reference Group," *Human Relations* VII (1954), p. 226, as reprinted in Bliss, *op. cit.,* pp. 259–285.

[26] *Ibid.*

[27] W. Lloyd Warner and Paul Lunt, *The Social Life of a Modern Community* (Yale, 1941); W. Lloyd Warner and Associates. *Democracy in Jonesville* (Harper & Bros., 1949).

[28] Richard P. Coleman, "The Significance of Social Stratification in Selling," in Bliss, *op. cit.,* pp. 181–183; also in Martin Bell (ed.) *Marketing: A Maturing Discipline* (American Marketing Association, 1961), pp. 171–184.

motivations and goals of this class is respectability, and a second important word is striving. The men of this class are continually striving, within their limitations, to "do a good job" at their work, and both men and women are determined to be judged "respectable" in their personal behavior by their fellow citizens. Being "respectable" means living in well-maintained houses, neatly furnished, in neighborhoods which are more or less on the "right side of town." It also means that members of this class will clothe themselves in coats, suits, and dresses from "nice stores," and save for a college education for their children.

5. At the lower half of the "average man world" is the upper-lower class, sometimes referred to as "the ordinary working class." The prototypical member is a semiskilled worker. He may earn very good money, but does not bother using it to become "respectable" in a middle class way. He is more oriented toward enjoying life and living well from day to day than saving for the future or caring what the middle class thinks of him.

6. The lower-lower class of unskilled workers, unassimilated ethnics, and the sporadically employed is characterized by apathy, fatalism, and a point of view which justifies a "getting your kicks whenever you can" approach toward life, and toward spending money.

Social Class and Income

Social class provides an explanation of buying behavior which income alone does not explain. *"If it were only a matter of income, then individuals with different incomes would merely buy more or less of each item rather than the different items they actually do buy."* [29] For example, if one were to take three families all earning $10,000 a year with other structural elements constant such as age, size of family constant, the buyer behavior of each would differ accordingly to the values of the social class to which each belonged.

An upper-middle class family in this income bracket, a young attorney, is most likely to be found spending a relatively large percent of the family's income on housing, on rather expensive furniture especially in public areas of the house, on clothing from quality stores, and on cultural or social activities. In contrast, the lower-middle class family—headed by a proprietor of a small retail business—probably has a better house but not in a "prestige" neighborhood; it is likely to have as many clothes although not as expensive, and probably as much furniture but not by name designers. Finally, these people almost certainly have a much bigger savings account in a bank.

On the other hand, we must not look to social class as an all-powerful determinant of behavior for there are some purchases which are not related

[29] John A. Howard, *Marketing Management: Analysis and Planning* (Homewood, Illinois: Richard D. Irwin, Inc., 1963), p. 98.

to social class. For example, air conditioners are classless. Thus, in some situations social class is not an element of structure.[30]

Social Class and Structural Change

Class structure is one means of examining the activity of innovation by buyers. However, we must be careful in conceiving of or accepting any simple hypothesis that attempts to relate upper levels to the *status quo,* that is, that tries to show that they are less likely to accept new products than are other classes or if they do it is at a much slower rate. No single class or group of classes will be totally conservative or liberal in reacting to any specific change in an offering. Saxon Graham in a study of class and its relation to product innovation concluded that for some innovations, canasta and television, innovators were along class lines with the former from upper-upper to lower-lower, and the latter from lower to upper.

Further, it was discovered that no single class in the sample displayed conservatism in reacting to all five innovations. The upper classes were conservative in one case, the lower in another, and both in a third instance. And no one of the classes displayed more conservatism than another in reacting to the innovation in health insurance. In light of these findings, it may be concluded that the relation between class and conservatism is much more complex than traditionally supported.[31]

LIFE CYCLE

Definition

Life cycle is the combination of age, marital status, and number of offspring placed in a single structural element. For all practical purposes life cycle is the most dynamic of all the elements so far discussed because it is common to all people. John Lansing and Leslie Kish distinguish seven different stages in life cycle; they are: (1) young single; (2) young married, no children; (3) young married, youngest child under six; (4) young married, youngest child six or older; (5) older married, children; (6) older married, no children; and (7) older single.[32]

Empirical Validation of Life Cycle

In their study, Lansing and Kish correlated family life cycle with six characteristics: home ownership, family debt, working wife, income, purchases of new automobiles and television sets. Family life cycle proved a

[30] Coleman, *op. cit.*, p. 192.

[31] Saxon Graham, "Class and Conservatism in the Adoption of Innovations," *Human Relations* IX (February 1956), p. 100. The five innovations tested were: television, canasta, supermarkets, Blue Cross, and medical service.

[32] John B. Lansing and Leslie Kisch, "Family Life Cycle as an Independent Variable," *American Sociological Review* (October 1957), pp. 512–519.

better predictor of behavior in all cases than age alone. This conclusion is what would be expected from basic social theory because "It is well known that changes occur in people's attitude and behavior as they grow older, but many of these changes may be associated less with the biological process of aging than with the influence of age upon the individual's family member-ships. Thus, the critical dates in the life cycle of an individual may not be his birthday so much as the days when a change occurs in family status, for example, when he marries, or when his first child is born."[33]

We can appreciate the implications of this by looking at the changes which take place as individuals go through such a cycle. A single man typically will spend a greater proportion of income for food eaten out of his home than a married man of the same age; a young couple will spend proportionately less for food away from home than a single person, but proportionately more than a married couple with children, and so on. The same type of relationships are true for other goods and services, for example, furniture, entertainment, and clothing. It is important to note that position in life cycle is also important in pointing to who the decision-maker will be. For example, for the child, up to a certain point, all purchasing decisions will be made by parents; at some point when the child may begin to earn his own spending money, his purchasing discretion will come into force. Much is true at the other end of the spectrum, especially when older people live with their children.

Closely Associated Elements

Closely associated with life cycle as we have seen is the age of the head of the household. Another element which is closely related to the life cycle concept is family size. As would be expected it is not only the change in family size which is important but also the magnitude of the change. The addition of new members without concomitant changes in income places greater pressures on expendable funds. In these types of changes there will be bound to be changes both in the quantity and quality of the goods and services purchased. For example, clothing may be purchased in such a manner that it can serve the needs of several children in a family.

DEMOGRAPHIC ELEMENTS

The demographic elements to be considered are education, national background, religious background, and racial characteristics.

Education

In discussing the concept of education it is important to recognize that it is simply not the measure of the number of years that an individual has

---

[33] *Ibid.*

spent in formal educational institutions though, to be certain, the knowledge acquired in such institutions has a direct effect on the type of occupation one can engage in and hence directly affects the amount of income which may be earned. Education in the broadest context is knowledge and the mechanism by which it is transmitted, namely, language. Language for each culture is different and hence as the individual moves from one culture to another he must learn a new language in order to be able to use his education. We can easily envisage this in terms of removing a college educated American to a primitive tribal setting in Australia. Yet, there are much more subtle aspects, for example, regular coffee in the Far Western part of the United States means black coffee, in Philadelphia, it means two "shots" of cream and in Boston one "shot." What this means is that as the individual is faced with new environments, he must learn ways of handling the situation, and the ability to make this transition is part of education for it is easier to recognize the inherent problems given a level of formal training.

Education affects buying behavior in that it exposes those with more education to a wider variety of ideas and hence a wider group of possible want-satisfying activities. For example, a college educated individual in contrast to a high school educated one may find more pleasure in spending an afternoon in an art gallery. Richard H. Ostheimer discovered that the "some college or beyond" group, with approximately the same number in sample of families as the "did not finish high school group," spent four times as much on photographic equipment.[34]

Nationality Groups

Every individual has a heritage to a specific nationality group although the impact of the group on buying behavior may not be important. The nationality group is usually described in terms of a language or common country or similar cultural systems. Language as we know is the mechanism for transferring knowledge, and language is a function of the culture in which it develops. For example, Benjamin Lee Whorf has shown that some groups of people have languages which reflect the conditions under which they live. Eskimos living in arctic regions have at least a dozen words to describe snow while south sea islanders have none.[35] Linguistic is relativity closely associated with various nationality groups in that we can make distinctions about Germans living in the north of Germany in contrast to those living in Bavaria. In the large cities of the United States such as New York, Boston, and Philadelphia it is quite easy to point to sections such as, respectively, Yorkville, the Northend, and Germantown. As would be expected the offerings in each of the areas reflects the national tastes of the

[34] Richard H. Ostheimer, "Who Buys What? Life's Study of Consumer Expenditures," *Journal of Marketing* XXII (January 1958), pp. 260–272.

[35] Benjamin Lee Whorf, "Science and Linguistics," *Technology Review* XLIV (1940), pp. 229–240.

residents living there. For the individual integrated into the American culture—nationality—stores in such areas are called "old-world."

To the extent that over time individuals loose their national ties, that is, in our case become Americanized, they adopt regional "backgrounds." The example of coffee in the previous section verifies this; also, we can consider dress standards between New York City and Los Angeles and so on.

Religious Elements

Religious characteristics are imprinted on the individual in the same manner as nationality although the rules of behavior which are part of the established religion are much more stringent. Religion transcends boundaries in that behavior of Catholics across national boundaries is more similar than members of different religions within one nation. Religion is perhaps the most formally organized of any institution with specific structures of authority and structures for determining behavior. For example, the Church of the Latter Day Saints prohibits the consumption of stimulants including alcoholic beverages, coffee and tea, and tobacco; Orthodox Jews refrain from eating pork and abide by dietary laws; Christian Scientists regulate their dealings with the medical sciences.[36]

Racial Characteristics

The question of racial difference in buyer analysis has stemmed in part from the revolution aimed at establishing equality among the races that has been in progress in the United States during the past few decades. Part of the interest has been generated from the problems of consumer welfare relating to the issue "Do the Poor Pay More?"[37] The extent to which racial differences directly affect buyer behavior in any given situation are most difficult to determine. To the extent that people of various races use toothpaste, drink scotch, consume rice, or drive automobiles, there is indeed no specific differences directly attributable to race. However, to the extent that racial minorities have been discriminated against and have been deprived of adequate levels of income and acceptable levels of education to survive in the society, and have been forced into certain lines of employment, there is a racial element to be considered. Given this entire set of elements there are grounds for making some statements about the differences in the structure of racial groups.

Marcus Alexis in a study of Negro versus white spending behavior has

[36] Of course religious ethic has had a great impact in the Western World. See R. H. Tawney, *Religion and The Rise of Capitalism* (Peter Smith, 1926), and Max Weber, *the Protestant Ethic and the Spirit of Capitalism* (Scribner, 1930).

[37] Charles S. Goodman, "Do The Poor Pay More?" *Journal of Marketing* 32 (January, 1968), p. 24 and Louise G. Richards, "Consumer Practices of the Poor," *Low-Income Life Styles,* Lola M. Irelan, ed. United States Department of Health Education and Welfare (U.S. Printing Office, 1966), pp. 67–84. *See also* Chapter 16.

suggested, that when income is held constant there are differences. Negroes, as a function of a combination of societal restraints and cultural traditions, tend to underspend, as compared to whites of equal income, in four major categories: housing, automobile transportation, food, and medical care (excluding certain categories of proprietary medicines. See the following table.[38]

TABLE 8.1

NEGRO VERSUS WHITE SPENDING BEHAVIOR CONTROLLED BY INCOME [1]

	Negro spending versus white spending
Food	Less
Housing	Less
Clothing	More
Recreation and leisure	Mixed
Home furnishing	More
Medical	Less
Auto transportation	Less
Non-auto	More
Savings	More
Insurance	Less

[1] Source: Marcus Alexis, "Some Negro-White Differences in Consumption," *American Journal of Economics and Sociology,* 21 (January, 1962), pp. 11–28.

Others have suggested that this is partially explained by the overall desire of the Negro to achieve full membership in the white society. "Because material goods have such an important symbolic role in American society, the acquisition of material goods should be symbolic to the Negro of his achievement of full status. This is not to say that all product categories have such a symbolic function."[39]

BUYER STRUCTURE: THE FIRM AND NON-PROFIT AGENCY

The underlying principles of the previous analysis are relevant when considering the structure of the firm or the nonprofit agency, though there are some specific differences. In part this stems from the fact that the firm and the nonprofit agency are composed of individuals who do not loose their structural characteristics simply because they are placed in another organizational context. However, the firm or nonprofit organization then

[38] Marcus Alexis, "Some Negro-White Differences in Consumption," *American Journal of Economics and Sociology* 21 (January, 1962), pp. 11–28.

[39] Raymond A. Bauer, Scott M. Cunningham, and Lawrence Wortzel, "The Marketing Dilemma of Negroes," *Journal of Marketing* 29 (July, 1965), p. 1.

becomes the focal organization from which the buyer takes his immediate cues. It is the purpose of this section to extend the previous analysis to these types of organizations by focusing on some of the differences which they create in structure.

Internal Structure and Organization Goals [40]

It would be incorrect to assert that there is a one-to-one relationship between the internal structure of the individual and the firm. The major difference between the two is found in the relative clarity with which the observer can discern the goals of the firm or the nonprofit organization in contrast to the motives (goals) of the individual. In the former case the focal organizations is easier to observe while in the latter case, as we have discussed previously, there may be a number of focal organizations from which the individual is taking cues, and depending upon the situation the choice may depend on a number of factors; however, in the case of the firm, it is a simpler relationship, namely, the firm, which is supporting the individual, becomes the primary focal organization. What we see is that the individual in terms of the firm relates much more closely to the structural elements created by that organization than to others in the environment. To be sure, the individual as buyer for the firm may relate to the engineering department or the production scheduling department as different focal points as needs differ.[41] The existence of personal factors notwithstanding, the average individual must relate satisfactorily to the performance criteria established for him by the agency.

A second difference between the individual and the firm or nonprofit agency relates to the degree which specific goals are stated. For the individual these are usually not formally stated. The goals of the business firm are usually stated in terms of producing certain products, realizing certain profits, obtaining certain rates of return on investment, and so on. Those of the Community Chest, as an example of a nonprofit agency, are also stated in raising so much money to help a number of children or provide health services for the elderly. It is not our intention to discuss the origin of goals except to suggest that they are the end result of the interaction of a great number of individuals and groups which make up the firm as well as those who influence it or regulate it from the outside. Among the most important of these are management, workers, stockholders, customers, and governments. Our concern is with four major goals: (1) production, (2) inventory, (3) sales, and (4) profits—defining an internal structure. (A further discussion of firm goals is found in Chapter 10.)

---

[40] This section is based on the following discussion: Kalman J. Cohen and Richard M. Cyert, *Theory of the Firm: Resource Allocation in a Market Economy* (Prentice-Hall, 1965), pp. 331–338. No further notation will be made to this source. For a complete discussion *see* R. M. Cyert and J. G. March, *A Behavioral Theory of the Firm* (Prentice-Hall, 1963).

[41] See Chapter 4, pp. 102–103.

Production

What is to be produced is clearly an internal element of buyer structure in the short run, for it determines what inputs are required. This must be examined in terms of relevant component namely: (1) production at an acceptable level of costs, (2) production which maintains a product of uniform quality, or (3) production which allows a stable employment of resources. For example, a firm which decides to produce typewriter ribbons will necessarily have to purchase the requisite materials at costs which, when combined with those of other inputs at given technologies, will be similar to those of competitors (an external element).

As part of the production goals we must include the concept of maximum use of production facilities. When a firm such as the one in the above example has excess capacity, there might be grounds for changing the nature of the inputs. For example, if excess capacity—the difference between the output that the production facility is capable of producing and the output it is actually producing[42]—arises because current production requires too high a price, the firm might produce a product which costs less to make and hence can be sold at a lower price. Excess capacity, it should be noted, is not unique to production activities. We can use the same concept in retail firms as well. For example, a retail hardware store that has a hundred square feet which is empty would find it in its best interest to add new lines of merchandise.

Inventory Goals

Inventory goals directly affect the quantitative elements of buyer behavior for the firm. Such goals for many firms are a compromise between various functional activities in the firm. For example, marketing may be desirous of avoiding stock-outs at all times, while comptrollers may be interested in minimizing investments in inventory, and production managers might be desirous of maintenance of production schedules. Such requirements have been accounted for in the familiar economic-order-quantity models[43] which proliferate all types of business activity or the "open-to-buy" method which is used by department stores.[44]

---

[42] John M. Cassels, "Excess Capacity and Monopolistic Competition," *Quarterly Journal of Economics* (May 1937), p. 427. K. J. Cohen, "Determining the 'Best Possible' Inventory Levels," *Industrial Quality Control* 15 (October, 1958), pp. 4–10.

[43] Open-to-buy can be stated as follows:

$$B_Y = (I_{Y+1} - I_Y) + S_Y^*$$

where B = open-to-buy for month Y

(I_{Y+1}) = expected inventory (based on seasonal plans) for beginning of month

I_Y = actual inventory at beginning of month

S_Y^* = expected sales

[44] See Chapter 13. Also, see: Robert F. Lanzillotti, "Pricing Objectives in Large Companies," *American Economic Review* (December 1958), pp. 921–940.

Sales and Market Share Goals

Sales and market share goals represent short-run levels of a firm's survival.[45] They are traditionally defined within the context of the firm but their attainment is related to the competitive activities of rivals as well as to the forces in the economy as a whole. Internally, the attainment of goals and hence the purchase of the necessary inputs to reach them are a function of such things as the availability of productive resources, the demands of other parts of the firm for funds, and the ability to assess correctly market potentials.

Gösta Mickwitz, a Finnish economist, has suggested a close relationship between sales goals and the purchase of the various promotional factors which a firm should use in pursuing them. For each of the four periods of a product's life cycle, there is an ordering of the factors which should be utilized. As a product, an electric toothbrush for example, goes through the various stages of its product life cycle, the firm will have to purchase various quantities of the promotional inputs such as service, advertising, changes in product quality, and product differentiation.[46]

Profit

Firms have a profit goal, though it may not be their only goal. This is linked to the accounting control system which necessarily establishes procedures for determining profit and loss. It summarizes (1) demands for accumulating resources in the form of capital investments, dividends to stockholders, and payments to creditors and (2) the demands on the part of top management for favorable performance measures.

The Role of the Purchasing Agent

For purpose of categorization we use the term "purchasing agent" to describe the locus of the purchasing function. As in the family unit, we see specialization of decision-making and purchasing activities in the firm, here however they are more readily identifiable. In the firm we see organizational structures responsible for the procurement of various factors: (1) capital investments, (2) operating supplies, and (3) merchandise for resale, as well as financial and personnel activities.

By capital investments we mean any project which involves an outlay of cash in return for an anticipated flow of future benefits. The future benefits may be monetary as in the case of a new warehouse for a wholesaler or non-monetary in the case of a new tunnel for a state. No matter what the situation, the exchange of present expenditure for future benefits is the dis-

---

[45] Cohen & Cyert, *op. cit.*, pp. 68–69.

[46] Gösta Mickwitz, *Marketing and Competition* (Helsingfors, Finland: Centraltryekeriet, 1959), p. 88. Also, see: Chapter 11.

tinctive feature.[47] Because of the nature of capital investments, they are most often concentrated at the uppermost levels of management of the firm whether it be the operating committee of General Motors or the owner of the corner service station. The characteristics of such acquisitions which place them at this level in the business firm are: (1) the fact that capital expenditures extend into the future for a period longer than items in current operations and (2) the fact that such expenditures are quite often irreversible, because there is little or no secondhand market for many types of capital goods.[48] For the most part such decisions are centralized and are the result of executives representing all of the activities of the firm.

Operating supplies are the factors to the operation of the firm whose time span is comparable to current revenues. They include such items as pencils, lubricants, and hardware, and in general are of low per unit value. Depending on company's organization, these may be purchased by various structures. If the firm is large, a special purchasing department may be responsible for all items. In those situations where firms are composed of several units or where there are special skills required, the function may be decentralized. Such is the case in the acquisitional financial resources or personnel broken away from general purchasing. A similar case exists when transportation is purchased separately from supplies or when production engineers buy raw materials.[49] Merchandise for resale, as we have seen in a previous discussion for many types of retail agencies, is contracted out to specialized independent buyers or is handled through special agencies such as chain store buying offices.[50] For department stores, buying activities are highly specialized by product lines and buyers are also responsible for the promotion and sale of goods in their departments as if they were the owner of one part of the total operation. Here as elsewhere, specific rules are established which provide guidelines as to what products should be purchased, and the means by which products can be deleted from the overall product assortment.[51] Such elements as marketability, durability, productive ability and growth potential form the structure.[52]

The relationship of the individual purchasing agent within the firm is interesting in that it is lateral between divisions performing functions which are given the same level of importance as purchasing. In the main, they establish their own rules in so far as they are not affected by the specific demands of the client departments for whom they work. The degree to

---

[47] G. David Quirin, *The Capital Expenditure Decision* (Irwin, 1967), p. 1. Among the many items which may belong in the capital budget is advertising; *see* Joel Dean, "Does Advertising Belong in the Capital Budget?" *Journal of Marketing* (October 1966), pp. 15–21.

[48] *Ibid.*, pp. 2–3.

[49] George W. Aljian, (ed.), *Purchasing Handbook* (McGraw-Hill, 1958), pp. 1–15.

[50] *See* Chapter 6, pp. 129, 140–142.

[51] Aljian, *op. cit.*

[52] Chapter 11.

which the purchasing department is able to fulfill its twin functions of placement of orders and expediting of orders is directly related to how important its client department view these tasks and how clearly the purchasing agent recognizes what his focal organization should be. Strauss, in a study of purchasing agents, discovered that those who had greatest education tended to view their focal organization as the firm as a whole and hence were more concerned with performing the purchasing functions and even extending them to other activities than did those who did not have the education.[53]

The problem of understanding the role of the purchasing agent becomes most complex when examining the nonprofit organization. Here questions of great magnitude such as national defense reflect the goals of a great number of individuals and groups. In this case, there is first the decision concerning the specific need of any item, an antiballistic missile for example. Then there is the need to determine the contractors, subcontractors and others responsible for its construction. Galbraith in *The New Industrial State* illustrates the complexity involved in this sector:[54]

> This leads the technostructure to identify itself closely with the goals of the armed services and, not infrequently, with the specific goals of the particular service. . . . The technostructure comes to see the same urgency in weapons development, the same requirement for a particular weapons system, the same advantage in an enlarged mission for (say) the Air Force, or Navy, as does the particular service itself.

Obviously, for items of smaller magnitude the elements of structure are less complex although the large organization and especially those related to governmental activities tend to have great influence on the seller in that they require or may require bids, extensive record-keeping activity, and more rigid specifications for merchandise or services purchases.

Budget Constraints

It is necessary to evaluate the financial constraints which are important for the firm and nonprofit organization. Although there are some similarities between these two and the role of income constraints on the individual (or family unit), there are some subtle differences. For the business firm, there is less need to relate current purchasing to current revenue flows. All this suggests that the firm for the most part has greater access to credit, although this depends upon the type of good or service which is being purchased. For example, an automobile parts manufacturer, even with negative income and substantial debt, will more easily be able to purchase sub-units for assembly because of potential demand than an individual in a similar pre-

[53] George Strauss, "Tactics of Lateral Relationships: The Purchasing Agent," *Administrative Science Quarterly* 7 (September 1962), pp. 161–186.

[54] John Kenneth Galbraith, *The New Industrial State* (Houghton Mifflin, 1967), pp. 310–311.

dicament. The potential earning stream for the firm as it converts parts and operating supplies into saleable units creates tangible "goods" against which creditors are willing to take risk.

This is not necessarily true for some nonprofit organizations such as charities which must in the main operate out of current revenue flows much as the individual. It may not be true for the firm or the nonprofit organization in the purchase of assets such as plant and equipment. Both may have internal debt limits imposed either by management or by external elements such as the financial community. For example, debt capacity, the amount of current debt obligations in relation to revenue flows, are established by various financial markets as a means of evaluating various firms in their search for new monies. Similarly, municipalities are rated as to their ability to pay interest on bonds or other financial institutions.

External Elements of Structure

In the same manner in which we recognized the external elements of the individual's structure we can recognize similar elements for the firm; and, the same is true for the external elements. Here we are concerned with how markets affect firms as buyers. In the same way that firms are affected by sellers in the market by their number and size; so are firms affected by the number of buyers in the market. We can classify markets from purely competitive—in the sense that no one buyer can affect price, partially evidenced in capital markets—to the intermediate situation in which there are a number of buyers as for labor in specific geographic areas, to oligopsonistic markets, and finally to the monopsonistic markets, in which there is only one buyer.[55] All of the elements found in the discussion in Chapter 4 come into play.

Let's consider the impact of size on buyer behavior. For example, a small retail druggist may find that trying to purchase from the wholesale druggists at prices competitors, especially large ones, pay is impossible because he simply does not have the volume to generate quantity purchases. Given the fact that a number of such small drugstores exist in any market area, a combination or pooling of purchasing power, some type of voluntary wholesale chain or other type of cooperative activity can provide the means by which the individual buyer can ostensibly purchase his drugs at or near the price being paid by the volume outlet. What is taking place is simply the reflection of the need to create some type of differentiation which will be recognized by suppliers.[56]

[55] William J. Baumol, *Economic Theory and Operations Analysis*, 2d ed. (Prentice-Hall, 1965), pp. 322–323.

[56] Federal Trade Commission, *On the Structure and Competitive Behavior of Food Retailing: Economic Report* (U.S. Government Printing Office, 1966), pp. 41–51. The discussion here is concerned with the same phenomenon in the example except in terms of the food industry.

SUMMARY

Buyer structure is composed of those elements which affect buyer perception and hence behavior. As we will see in the following chapter what needs are recognized and what methods are chosen in the context of a problem solving situation are a function of these elements. Buyer behavior is directly related to structure in that certain elements such as social class have a great influence on the individual buyer. The problem of analysis is that it is most difficult often to divide structure from behavior in that they are almost tautological. To say that some one is unmarried is to say that he is behaving like a bachelor; in the same way to discuss a structural element, educational background, is to expect the individual to act given some empirical beliefs about how someone in that category will act. The problem is more complex in that an individual or marketing agency belongs to a number of groups and has a finite number of structural elements; the only important ones are the ones which are focused on for any specific purchase. Those which are evoked at any time by a participant are known as focal organizations. A positive theory of buyer behavior depends on identifying the relevant structural elements. Of all the structural elements, income defined in the broadest of all perspectives so as to include current as well as expected and the ability to borrow is on average the most important. Income creates an overall limit on behavior. The other elements limit or allow certain types of behavior but in the context of income rather than as first-order factors.

Motives or goals stem from disequilibrium within the structure of the individual or marketing agency. As they recognize these, and we shall have much more to say about this in Chapter 9, specific rules are established for behavior. These rules are thus internalized and hence become part of the internal structure within the individual or organization. They are easier to see within the marketing agency since they tend to be formalized in that the functions such as order placing are delegated; they are nevertheless present for the individual buyer as well.

SUGGESTED READINGS

Books

Harper W. Boyd, Jr. and Sidney J. Levy, *Promotion: A Behavioral View* (Englewood Cliffs, N.J.: Prentice-Hall, Inc., 1967). Chapter 2, "The Audience" provides a brief but complete discussion of the demographic elements of buyer behavior.

Kalman J. Cohen and Richard M. Cyert, *Theory of the Firm: Resource Allocation in a Market Economy* (Englewood Cliffs, N.J.: Prentice-Hall, Inc., 1965), pp. 331–338. The specific section discusses in some detail integral elements of structure.

James F. Engel, David T. Kollatt, and Roger D. Blackwell. *Consumer*

Behavior (New York: Holt, Rinehart and Winston, Inc., 1968). Part 4 of this volume provides one of the most intensive discussions of group influence in marketing. Although the part concentrates on individual and ultimate elements, it does provide the underlying arguments which can be used in other situations.

John A. Howard, *Marketing Management: Analysis and Planning* (rev. ed., Homewood, Illinois: Richard D. Irwin, Inc., 1963). Chapters 2 and 3 present an integrated discussion of structure and behavior within the context of the model developed to a greater extent in the following chapter.

Thomas S. Robertson, *Consumer Behavior* (Glenview, Ill.: Scott, Foresman and Company, 1970).

Articles

Marcus Alexis, "Some Negro-White Differences in Consumption," *American Journal of Economics and Sociology* 21 (January 1962), pp. 11–28. This article provides an interesting example of racial differences and how they are translated into buying behavior.

William B. Bennett, "Cross-Section Studies of Consumption of Automobiles in the United States," *American Economic Review* 57 (September 1967), pp. 841–850.

Robert B. Bretzfelder and Q. Frances Dallavalle, "Personal Income by State and Regions in 1967," *Survey of Current Business* 48 (August 1968), pp. 13–24.

Francis S. Bourne, "The Concept of Reference Group Influence," in Francis S. Bourne (ed.), *Group Influence in Marketing and Public Relations* (Ann Arbor, Michigan: Foundation for Research on Human Behavior, 1956), pp. 1, 2, 7–11. This is a definitive article dealing with the concept of reference groups. Bourne relates specific groups to product purchases and develops a general model. The discussion of the following chapter uses some of this analysis.

Burleigh B. Gardner, "The ABC's of Motivation Research," *Business Topics* (Autumn 1959), pp. 36–37.

Kurt Mayer, "Diminishing Class Differentials in the U.S.," *Kyklos,* (Summer 1959), pp. 605–626.

Richard H. Ostheimer, "Who Buys What? Life's Study of Consumer Expenditures," *Journal of Marketing* XXII (January 1958), pp. 260–272. This article presents a cross-sectional analysis of the consumer date gathered by *Life*. The author relates various purchases to specific groups. Although the data is out-of-date, the method and results are still interesting.

John A. Reinecke, "The 'Older' Market—Fact or Fiction?" *Journal of Marketing* 28 (January 1964), pp. 60–64.

Edward O. Taumann, "Subjective Social Distance and Urban Occupational

Stratification," *American Journal of Sociology* 71 (1965–1966), pp. 26–36.

U.S. Bureau of the Census, *Trends in the Income of Families and Persons in the United States: 1947 to 1960*, Technical Paper No. 8, Washington, D.C.: U.S. Government Printing Office, 1963.

Nathan Wright, Jr., "The Economics of Race," *American Journal of Economics and Sociology* 26 (January 1967), pp. 1–12.

Daniel Yankelovich, "New Criteria for Market Segmentation," *Harvard Business Review* 42 (March–April, 1964), pp. 83–90.

9

Buyer behavior

INTRODUCTION

We have indicated in Chapters 4 and 8 the close relationship between structure and behavior. We now move immediately from buyer structure to buyer behavior, recognizing that it is a somewhat artificial distinction. Of all the topics examined by marketing scholars and practitioners, the subject of buyer (consumer) behavior has received the greatest attention. This attention has been most intense in the post-World War II era as sellers have needed to know more and more about buyers. The need to know more about buyers has not been concentrated only in product markets but has pervaded a wide variety of "markets" including ideas and political beliefs. In general, the study of buyer behavior is a study of *human behavior*. The body of knowledge of buyer behavior hence represents the study by interested persons in a wide range of disciplines from economics, to psychology, to political science, to sociology.[1] The wealth of contributions to buyer behavior means that all of the various concepts cannot be presented within the confines of a single chapter. What we have done, therefore, is to select one aspect of buyer behavior—learning—and examine it within a framework which is sufficiently general to allow some of the other approaches to buyer behavior to be included. Footnotes in the text and the "Suggested Readings" at the end of the discussion provide the reader with a broad assortment of

---

[1] Bernard Berelson and Gary A. Steiner, *Human Behavior: An Inventory of Scientific Findings* (Harcourt, Brace & World, 1964).

additional materials which should be consulted in order to appreciate other approaches to buyer behavior.[2]

PROCESS OF BUYER BEHAVIOR

General Statement

The entire discussion proceeds from "buyer structure"—the elements taken into consideration by buyers. Structure, we recall, affects the choice of goals as well as the process by which one attempts to satisfy his wants.[3] By the process of buyer behavior, we mean the steps, either explicit or implicit, which every buyer goes through in making a decision to accept or reject offerings to fill needs. The process consists of four sequential stages: (1) problem recognition; (2) search; (3) choice; and (4) post-decision evaluation.

PROBLEM RECOGNITION

Perception of Needs

The first step in the buying process is the perception of needs. Like all of the other steps in the process, it is an exercise in problem solving.[4] The problem here is how to recognize needs. It is easy to relate to felt needs arising from physiological imbalance in the individual, such as thirst, or the stock-out of a factor of production by a manufacturing firm. However, there are other needs, such as a vague feeling—a desire—for excitement, which may be perceived but may not be easily translated into action-related activities.[5] By perception of needs we mean the buyer's experience of some type of tension that creates a state of disequilibrium or dissonance in his structure. This state triggers a sequence of events directed toward its source, which the buyer attempts to reduce or eliminate.[6]

Both the kind of need felt and the perception of the need are determined, as we have seen, by the elements of buyer structure. For example, a

[2] For a beginning, see James F. Engel, David T. Kollat, and Roger D. Blackwell, *Consumer Behavior* (Holt, Rinehart and Winston, 1968); and Francesco M. Nicosia, *Consumer Decision Processes: Marketing and Advertising Implications* (Prentice-Hall, 1966); and Ron J. Markin, *The Psychology of Consumer Behavior* (Prentice-Hall, 1969).

[3] The reader may wish on occasion to refer to Chapter 4 for the general argument and to Chapter 8 for buyer structure.

[4] James A. Bayton, "Motivation, Cognition, Learning—Basic Factors in Consumer Behavior," *Journal of Marketing* XXII (January 1958), p. 282.

[5] Philip Kotler, *Marketing Management: Analysis, Planning and Control* (Prentice-Hall, 1967), p. 68.

[6] Bayton, *op. cit.*, p. 283.

desire for excitement felt by an individual in an upper social class, given income levels, education, and the other elements, may be expressed by sailing, while that for someone in the lower-lower social class may be expressed by spending an evening at the local tavern. Here we see that structure has established a learned pattern by which the perceived needs are extinguished. Also, structure affects the perception of the needs; consider the case of an individual of a fundamentalist religion who perceives the need for excitement only to reject it as an unacceptable factor.

Hierarchy of Needs

For the most part needs arise in sets rather than alone. This means the buyer must be able to distinguish among the various needs. A major problem, therefore, is the arrangement of these needs so that they can be solved in order of decreasing magnitude of importance.[7] Given scarce resources, a rational buyer would attend to the most important (greatest tension) needs first. This hierarchy of needs tends to be stable over the long run since they are at the most generic level a function of the basic biological requirements for the individual and a function of the reoccurring operational activities of the agency. Thus, from day to day, the buyer faces many nearly identical needs and hence establishes a pattern for recognizing, ordering, and extinquishing them. "It is this stability that makes possible the prediction of consumer behavior."[8]

Among business firms and nonprofit agencies it is often easier to see the rules and other elements of structure which are established in the organization for the ordering of needs. For example, the business firm has specific organizational units—special planning and control centers—whose function it is to recognize the various needs and provide solutions. A firm that is faced with the need to operate on a day-to-day basis as well as plan for the future will establish mechanisms for both and provide some means by which the priority of the short run and the necessity of the long run are integrated.[9] For example, this can be appreciated by considering the annual production scheduling and introduction of new automobile models. The producer must contend with immediate production needs, labor, parts, and supplies, for a given model but also consider the same needs for future periods. Business firms also have developed more formal means for the ordering of possible solutions for each of the needs in the hierarchy. The purchase of long-use assets, including buildings and operating facilities, as well as the possibly less permanent resources, such as marketing channels,

---

[7] This of course is a major area of analysis in price theory. For a brief review, see William J. Baumol, *Economic Theory and Operations Analysis* (2d ed., Prentice-Hall, 1965), Chapter 9, "Theory of Demand," especially pp. 183–209.

[8] Martin L. Bell, *Marketing: Concepts and Strategy* (Houghton Mifflin, 1966), p. 197.

[9] *See* Herbert Simon, *Administrative Behavior* (Free Press, 1957), a thoughtful discussion of problem solving in organizations.

can be evaluated by rate-of-return on investment[10] or discounted-cash-flow analysis.[11] An analytical tool used as a means of choosing among the several alternative needs in the public area is social-cost/social-benefit analysis.[12] The tools and operating rules of the agencies both help to facilitate the choice of solution, but by their very nature also structure the choice of needs by pointing out which of them can be solved most easily.

For the ultimate buyer, the rules for establishing the order of wants and the methods by which they are to be solved are much more informal, though similar techniques and measurements are used. Obviously, an individual will be much more concerned with ordering the perceived needs in terms of those which lead to biological and psychological well-being at the generic level such as food, clothing, and shelter. How each is solved in a family unit, for example, is a function of that unique structure. For instance, children's ordering of wants are much different from those of their parents (as well as different among families). This is not to suggest that they are necessarily hedonists, but children at most any instant would rather have cookies and toys than clothing and shelter. All one need do to observe this phenomenon is to watch a parent with children shopping in a super-market.[13]

Methods of Recognition

It is important to note other aspects of problem recognition besides the perception of needs. In part the recognition of needs is the result of seller structure insofar as sellers who in any way can differentiate their total product actively campaign on the premise that the present solution to "your problem" is not the optimal one. Continual changes in product attributes (or assertions to that effect)[14] and the communication of such changes, with the implicit argument that the new product is better than the old one, may create the conditions under which buyers recognize problems that they had never thought of before. For example, is it the realization of bad breath on

[10] Kotler, *op. cit.*, p. 405. Other measures are also available. As we discussed earlier, long-run profit maximization may be used as the criterion for selecting profitable products. See John T. O'Meara Jr., "Selecting Profitable Products," *Harvard Business Review* 39 (Jan.-Feb. 1961), pp. 83–89.

[11] Joel Dean, "Does Advertising Belong in the Capital Budget?" *Journal of Marketing* 30 (October 1966), pp. 15–21.

[12] Jerome Rothenberg, *Economic Evaluation of Urban Renewal* (Brookings Institution, 1967).

[13] This is not necessarily "impulse buying" because the children have already made up their minds. However they frequently do not possess the required resources. For a brief study of impulse buying which suggests that for the population examined it is not an important factor, *see* James Duncan Shaffer, "The Influence of 'Impulse Buying' on In-the-store Decisions on Consumers' Food Purchases," *Journal of Farm Economics* XLII (May 1960), pp. 317–324.

[14] See Chapter 3 for a discussion of the uses and misuses of the term "new product."

the part of buyers which activates them to purchase mouth wash, or is it the effect of seller structure which says, "Here is a need you were not capable of recognizing."?

SEARCH

Introduction

Once a problem has been recognized, search comes into play. Buyer search is the activity through which the buyer seeks information about ways of satisfying his need. Essentially, search is the means by which the buyer attempts to reduce risk in the buying process.[15] The amount of effort which is exerted in search activities is in part a function of the level of the satisfaction the buyer has had with his current choice, that is, the degree to which reinforcement and learning have taken place. In those situations in which the buyer has no prior experience, search is a function of the amount of risk inherent in the purchase, that is, the "costs" (including social prestige) should one make a poor choice. Past experience, if it has been favorable, will require one to engage in only a minimal search effort except in those situations in which there are extreme changes in the structure, for example, moving to a new location or a new social context such as "important guests"; or changes in seller structure, such as removal of a product (purchase alternate) from the market. In short, the amount of search will depend on the importance of the purchase to the buyer (as well as his past experiences); clearly, the first time an average buyer purchases an automobile in contrast to, say, a package of breakfast cereal, greater risks are inherent and more energy will be spent in search.

Search effort is reduced by the establishment of rules. Even ultimate consumers have "rules"—although usually in the form simply of habitual attention or response patterns. Although such rules are often more clearly formalized in the context of the marketing agency, as for example specific guidelines for purchasing agents, they are also clearly present for individuals and family units. The purchasing agent may establish a library of catalogs, check with users within his firm, and then call various suppliers or wait for the representatives of suppliers to visit him. The housewife, in setting her own search pattern may, for example, begin with a convenience store, the daily newspaper, women's service magazines, the "yellow pages" or friends. In general, search occurs in response to a problem facing the buyer and is directed by learned rules of associating search activity with particular problems.

Search basically takes four forms; two of which deserve considerable attention: (1) internal search, (2) media search, (3) informal search, and (4) inspection and trial. Internal search is the process by which the buyer

[15] Kalman J. Cohen and Richard M. Cyert, *Theory of the Firm: Resource Allocation in a Market Economy* (Prentice-Hall, 1965), p. 338.

examines the past satisfaction with a given product with the reoccurring need. If past experience has been satisfactory, no further search is necessary so long as the buyer does not perceive any change in the structure. Because this is part of "post-decision evaluation," we postpone the rest of this particular analysis. The last of the forms of search, inspection and trial, is especially important when the buyer has had no previous experience with the good or service under consideration. Inspection provides a low-risk opportunity to observe the product and its qualities. In fact the only buyer risk in inspection is that by inspecting one offering he is losing the opportunity to view others which may be sold to other buyers. One need only consider the case of a person searching for a new house. Trial is also usually a low-risk means of search (ignoring emergency situations) in that the minimum energy and costs are expended in accordance with whether or not the trial is free, as in the case of mass sampling of household detergents, or has minimum cost, as in the case of purchasing a small supply of the product to test.

Media Search

Media search is the activity of buyers seeking information in such media as magazines, newspapers, radio, and television. This search is really double search in that at the same time buyers are searching for information, sellers are searching for buyers needing such information.[16] Although we know a great deal about the search effort of sellers—the frequent result of which is market segmentation—much less is known about buyer search.[17]

Buyer Structure and Search

Media search is a function of structure. Access to and use of various media are related to buyer structure. For example, a housewife in the lower social classes will read the confession (romance) and movie magazines, while women in the middle class read service magazines such as *McCalls* and *Ladies Home Journal*. Women in the upper class read magazines such as *Vogue, Harper's Bazaar,* and *Realities.*[18] Much the same is true for men, whose reading from upper to lower classes, ranges from *Gentlemen's Quarterly* to *Esquire* to *True Adventure*. There are similar structural patterns for business periodicals. Some publications are vertical in that they are aimed at all agencies which buy and sell a particular product while others are horizontal in that they cut across many industries and/or are related to specific functions common to a great number of firms. Examples

---

[16] George R. Fisk, *Marketing Systems: An Introductory Approach* (Harper & Row, 1967), p. 300.

[17] Complete discussion of market segmentation is found in James F. Engel, Hugh G. Wales, and Martin R. Warshaw, *Promotional Strategy* (Irwin, 1967), pp. 77–93; and in Kotler, *op. cit.*, pp. 43–65.

[18] Richard P. Coleman, "The Significance of Social Stratification in Selling," Martin L. Bell (ed.), *Proceedings of the 43rd National Conference of the American Marketing Association* (Chicago: 1960), pp. 171–184.

of horizontal publications are *Business Week, Fortune, Purchasing,* and *Sales Management. American Metals Market* and *Telephony* are examples of vertical publications.

Informal Search

Not to be taken lightly is what is known as informal search. Simply, buyers seek information from others by communicating directly or by observing others—including especially those buyers in the market known to be innovators. The structure-behavior relationship is clearly shown in the following discussion.

"Two-Step Hypothesis"

The "two-step hypothesis" was the result of a voting study in Erie County, Pennsylvania in 1940. The study found that certain members in the voter (buyer) structure were more exposed to the mass media than non-leaders. Tersely stated, "Ideas often flow *from* radio and print *to* the opinion leaders and *from* them to the less active sections of the population."[19] Because of design and execution problems the authors undertook three other studies to test the hypothesis. Of greatest importance for our purposes is the third of these; it examined the ways in which doctors make decisions to adopt new drugs.[20]

The Drug Study

The drug study indicated that the factor most strongly associated with the adoption of the new drug is how frequently a doctor is named by his colleagues as a friend or discussion partner. Secondly, the study showed that the more influential doctors could be characterized in terms of such factors as their more frequent attendance at out-of-town meetings and the diversity of places with which they maintained contact. Finally, influential doctors were more likely to be readers of a large number of professional journals and moreover valued them more highly than did doctors of lesser influence. "But at the same time, they were as likely as other doctors to say that local colleagues were an important source of information and advice in reaching their particular decisions."[21]

---

[19] Paul F. Lazarsfeld, Bernard Berelson, and Helen Gaudet, *The People's Choice* (2d ed., Columbia University Press, 1948), p. 151.

[20] Elihu Katz, "The Two-step Flow of Communication: An Up-to-Date Report on a Hypothesis," in Perry Bliss (ed.), *Marketing and the Behavioral Sciences* (2d ed., Allyn and Bacon, 1967), p. 318. Originally printed in: *The Public Opinion Quarterly* (Spring, 1957), pp. 61–78. The drug study is reported by James Coleman, Herbert Menzel and Elihu Katz, "Social Process in Physicians' Adoption of a New Drug," *Journal of Chronic Diseases* IX (January 1959), pp. 1–19.

[21] Katz, *op. cit.*, p. 331. *See also* James Coleman, Elihu Katz and Herbert Menzel, "The Diffusion of an Innovation among Physicians," *Sociometry* 20 (December 1957), pp. 253–270.

Other Verification

Johan Arndt, in a more recent study, further supported the two-step
hypothesis. In a field experiment involving the diffusion of a new brand of
food product in a university-operated apartment complex, Arndt discovered
that the opinion leaders seemed more influenced by the advertising message
than non-leaders. Further, such leaders were found to be more active com-
municators, both as transmitters and receivers of word-of-mouth communication. More important was the discovery that the content of the word-of-
mouth communication influenced the buying decisions of receivers; "Those
receiving favorable word-of-mouth communications were three times as
likely to buy the new product as were those receiving unfavorable word-
of-mouth."[22]

Innovators

Closely related to opinion leaders and groups as influences on purchasing decisions is the sole of innovators. The concept of innovators is based
on the fact that within groups of buyers we find patterns of behavior by
various members—insofar as some buyers are innovators, pacesetters as it
were, others are early adopters or late adopters, and some are rejecters.[23]
Early analysis established that social classes will accept innovations to the
extent that the innovational features and the cultural characteristics of the
classes are compatible.[24] For example, the acceptance of television was
more readily observable in members of lower classes, apparently due to the
value systems of the upper classes. Rejecters differed greatly from accepters
in that they preferred active, creative recreational activities, such as par-
ticipative sports, serious reading of fiction and non-fiction, while acceptors
confined their efforts to fiction, cursory inspection of the newspaper, or no
reading at all. Further, in the two activities most closely akin to television
—attendance at motion pictures and listening to the radio—accepters were
greater participators than rejectors.[25]

CHOICE

Introduction

The concept of choice recognizes that a buyer has come to a decision
about an offering which he feels specifically will (or will not) satisfy a

[22] Johan Arndt, "Testing the 'Two-Step Flow of Communication' Hypothesis," in Johan
Arndt (ed.), Insights into Consumer Behavior (Allyn and Bacon, 1968), p. 202.

[23] Innovative behavior has been defined in other dimensions, for example, "Innovators,
Early Majority, Late Majority, and Laggards." See Everett M. Rogers, Diffusion of
Innovation (Macmillan, 1962), p. 162.

[24] Saxon Graham, "Class and Conservatism in the Adoption of Innovations," in Bliss,
op. cit., p. 198. Originally printed in: Human Relations IX (1959), pp. 91–100.

[25] Ibid., pp. 200–201. The reader should relate this idea to our discussion of search and
media behavior.

present need. It does not mean that a purchase necessarily will be made. A buyer may not be able to consummate his choice in terms of a transaction for a large number of reasons, all essentially due to some inability of the buyer and seller to "negotiate" a transaction. These reasons may range from the product's being out of stock to the buyer's belief that a given offering costs more than the perceived potential benefits. It should be noted that choice will not always be the end of search. In fact, some buyers make a choice and even a purchase but continue their search in hope of finding a better alternative in future periods.

Conditions for Choice

A buyer is apt to make a choice between several offerings and execute the necessary transaction whenever he is convinced that any one or more of the following is valid.
1. No solutions exist more satisfactory than those already discovered.
2. The effort required to search for additional offerings is not justified in terms of the importance of the need (costs of incremented search exceed incremental gains).
3. The buyer believes that the decision cannot be postponed.
4. The cost of the solution is compatible with income constraints.

Elements of Choice

Choice involves a complex set of elements: offering, brand, and supplier.

Buyer Structure and Product/Brand Choice

The effect of buyer structure and its impact on choice was carefully examined by Bourne. In his analysis of the impact of reference groups he concluded that such groups were exceedingly influential in determining whether a buyer purchases a product, such as a car, and also what particular brand he will purchase. Such an item where both the product and the brand are socially conspicuous he terms a "product plus, brand plus" item.[26] He establishes three other categories: (1) product plus, brand minus; (2) product minus, brand plus, and (3) product minus, brand minus. Various products for each of the categories can be observed in Figure 9.1.

For the product plus, brand minus category, Bourne points to instant coffee, about which he suggests that whether it is served in a household depends in considerable part on whether the housewife, in view of her own reference groups and the image she has of their attitudes toward this product, considers it appropriate to serve it.[27] Type of clothing purchased as an example of product minus, brand plus is heavily influenced by reference

[26] Francis S. Bourne, "Different Kinds of Decisions and Reference Group Influence," in Bliss, op. cit., pp. 271–272. Originally printed in: Revis Lickert and Samuel P. Hayes, Jr., Some Applications of Behavioral Science Research (UNESCO, 1957), pp. 217–224.
[27] Ibid., pp. 272–273.

groups, with each substructure such as teenagers, Ivy League collegians, workers, bankers, and so on setting its own standards and often prescribing within fairly narrow limits, what those who feel related to such groups can wear.[28] For the product minus, brand minus group, product attributes rather than reference-groups dominate. "Reference groups as such . . . exert relatively little influence on buying behavior in this class of items, examples of which are salt, canned peaches, laundry soap and radio."[29]

FIGURE 9.1

PRODUCTS AND BRANDS OF CONSUMER GOODS MAY BE CLASSIFIED BY EXTENT TO WHICH REFERENCE GROUPS INFLUENCE THEIR PURCHASE

Weak –   Reference-group influence relatively   Strong +

	Weak –	Strong +
Strong + (Reference-group influence relatively) +	Clothing Furniture Magazines Refrigerator (type) Toilet soap	Cars* Cigarettes* Beer (prem. v. reg.)* Drugs*
Weak – (Reference-group influence relatively) –	Soap Canned peaches Laundry soap Refrigerator (brand) Radios	Air-conditioners* Instant coffee* TV (black and white)

–   Product   +

Brand or type

1 The classification of all products marked with an asterisk is based on actual experimental evidence. Other products in this table are classified speculatively on the basis of generalizations derived from the sum of research in this area and confirmed by the judgment of seminar participants.

Source: Francis S. Bourne, "Group Influence in Marketing and Public Relations," *Some Applications of Behavioral Science Research*, Revis Likert and Samuel P. Hayes, Jr., ed., (Paris: UNESCO, 1957), p. 218.

Choice is obviously also affected by such factors as income. When funds are not available to the buyer, he must face the problem of obtaining them. The entire problem-solving sequence for funds is similar to that for a commodity. The same principles hold.

Buyer Structure and Supplier Choice

There is little difference between the basic elements in the analysis of the effects of buyer structure on brand and product choice and the choice of supplier. Martineau, who did the basic research on social class, later used

28 *Ibid.*, p. 273.
29 *Ibid.*, p. 274.

the same concepts in evaluating buyer behavior in retail stores. In his analysis he stated that for a woman in a particular social class "some stores intimidate her; others may seem beneath her. A store may be acceptable for one type of good and not for others. A shopper may go to one department store for bargains, children's clothes, or housewares, and to another one for gifts or personal items."[30]

POST-DECISION EVALUATION

Introduction

Post-decision evaluation is the last step in the behavior sequence. It is the process whereby the purchaser compares his purchase to what he had defined in his wants, which, of course, may not have been adequately defined or may have been changed in the search stage. This activity influences choice in subsequent periods, that is, it becomes embodied in the buyer's structure. All things being equal, with a positive post-decision evaluation, the same product will be selected the next time.

Buyer Structure

As one might expect in formal organizations such as business enterprises and government organizations, post-decision evaluation rules are more clearly spelled out than for individuals or informal organizations. For the business firm purchasing raw materials, samples of various parts of the shipments are checked to see if they meet the conditions as to quality, percent of iron content in ore, or other measures. Among marketing agencies whose purchases are for resale, different approaches are taken. For example, actual sales are contrasted with potential or forecasted sales. Many retailers not only make such checks but establish price and promotional adjustments as a means of eliminating merchandise which is not selling to some expected level.[31] Government as a major nonfirm enterprise has established explicit rules for purchase evaluation some of which go so far as to renegotiate contracts, price, and profit levels of firms when evidence indicates *less* value received than was required.

For the ultimate buyer, analysis of post-decision evaluation has been embodied in the concept of cognitive dissonance. Cognitive dissonance arises when expectation is not fulfilled in one of two ways: (1) undesirable

---

[30] Pierre Martineau, "The Personality of the Retail Store," *Harvard Business Review* 36 (Jan.-Feb. 1958), p. 46. *See also* Gregory P. Stone, "City Shoppers and Urban Identification Observations on the Social Psychology of City Life," *American Journal of Sociology* (July 1954), pp. 36–45.

[31] Such price reductions are known as markdowns. A markdown pricing model is described in Richard M. Cyert and James G. March, *A Behavioral Theory of the Firm* (Prentice-Hall, 1963), pp. 140–146.

elements in the product that were known before purchase but were out-weighed by want-satisfying elements when the decision was made; and (2) the introduction of new information after the purchase was made.[32]

LEARNING AND BRAND LOYALTY

Introduction

Definition

Learning is defined as any systematic change in behavior due to the effects of experience. It may not necessarily be adaptive behavior; however, in most buying situations, the dynamic nature of the environment in any period of time means that the buyer will have to adapt to new conditions. Such changes may stem from changes in buyer structure or such phenomena as new products.[33] In the simplest perspective, learning takes place as a buyer experiments with various products to satisfy a want. When the experience has been acceptable, reinforcement takes place. When the same want arises at some later point in time, if all other factors remain constant, the buyer will tend to repeat the same path in the solution of the problem. Hence, the buyer learns (acquires through experience) an acceptable solution.

> "If brand A yields a high degree of gratification, then at some subsequent time, when the same needs arise, the consumer will have an increased tendency to select brand A once again. Each time brand A brings gratification, further reinforcement occurs, thus furthering the likelihood that in the future, with the given needs, brand A will be selected."[34]

The Learning Curve

The learning curve is the representation of the learning process. It is shown graphically in Figure 9.2. The number of experiences (exposures) or, technically trials, are shown on the horizontal axis, and the probability of response shown on the vertical axis.[35] The relationship shown by the

---

[32] Leon Festinger, "Cognitive Dissonance," *Scientific American* 207 (October, 1962), p. 93.

[33] John A. Howard, *Marketing Management: Analysis and Planning* (rev. ed., Irwin, 1963), p. 35.

[34] Bayton, *op. cit.*, p. 282.

[35] Howard, *op. cit.*, p. 36. The equation of the curve is $B = M(1 - e^{-kt})$ where B is behavior, M is maximum brand loyalty, stated probabilistically, t is the number of trials under stable conditions, k is a constant expressing the learning rate, and e is the base of natural logarithms. We are basing the following discussion on Howard's material and will refrain from detailed citation.

curve states that the more experience by the buyer with at least a minimal level of satisfaction, the greater the probability that he will repeat the purchase, assuming, of course, that all other things are constant. Leaving aside the meaning of "all other things" for the time being, we see for example that after three trials the probability of repeating the purchase of the particular item is 0.62. Or in other words, the buyer has a probability of 0.38 of purchasing other brands known to him (including the possibility of not purchasing at all).

FIGURE 9.2

LEARNING CURVE

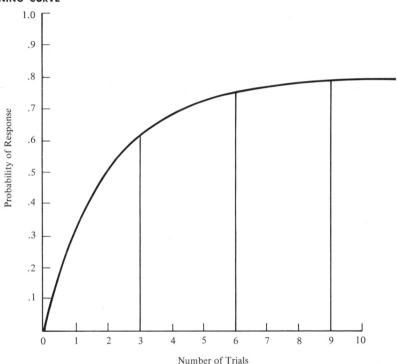

Source: John Howard, *Marketing Management: Analysis and Planning* (Homewood, Ill.: Richard D. Irwin, 1963), p. 36.

Measurement of Learning

Learning is measured by the increase in probability of making a particular response, that is, for example, choosing again a particular product, brand or supplier. As we see, the learning curve is negatively accelerated indicating that as a buyer's experience increases, the amount he learns from each subsequent trial is less than he learned from the previous experiences. That is, the increments to his loyalty are successively smaller. To be certain, this smooth curve is a highly idealized version of reality. Such variation as is found from the smooth curve, however, is explained by changes in buyer structure, environment, and promotional activities of various suppliers.

Reinforcement

When consumption or use of the product leads to gratification of the initial need, we say there is reinforcement. When the same need arises at some future point, the buyer will tend to repeat the process of selecting and obtaining the same item. As defined above, increasing the likelihood that an act will be repeated is *learning*, and for learning to take place, *reinforcement* is necessary.[36]

Reinforcement may originate from pleasant associations with favored brands, enterprises, or products, and unpleasant associations with less favored experiences tend to be forgotten with time.[37] (Frequently there may even be *negative* reinforcement.) Also it may be present as a result of advertising and other promotional efforts.[38] For example, in the post-decision evaluation process for buyers of new automobiles, research indicates that these owners reinforce their decision by reading advertisements of the car they purchased more often than of cars they considered but did not buy and other cars not involved in the choice.[39]

Sellers and Learning

Thus, it becomes the goal of the seller to encourage learning as early as possible—the first try is the ideal, though seldom the fact—so that the buyer does not try other alternatives. Of course, because reinforcement is such an important part of the learning process, the seller attempts to reinforce the experience through advertising. For example, a housewife who purchases coffee only once or twice a month may forget the brand purchased at the last point of need if it were not for continual reminders by the seller, attempting to reinforce his brand of coffee. At the same time, other sellers are attempting to attract new buyers to their brand and establish an experience for the buyer upon which further learning can take place. In extending the prior example, such sellers might attempt a "cents-off deal" as a means of switching buyers, or with a new product, they might heavily

---

[36] Bayton, *op. cit.*, p. 282.

[37] Alfred A. Kuehn and Ralph L. Day, "Probabilistic Models of Consumer Buying Behavior," in Ralph L. Day, *Marketing Models: Quantitative and Behavioral* (International Textbook Co., 1964), p. 53. Originally printed in: *Journal of Marketing* 28 (October 1964), pp. 27–31.

[38] Alfred A. Kuehn, "How Marketing Performance Depends on Other Marketing Variables," *Journal of Advertising Research* 2 (March 1962), p. 3.

[39] Danuta Ehrlich, Isaih Guttman, Peter Schönbach, and Judson Mills, "Post-decision Exposure to Relevant Information," *Journal of Abnormal and Social Psychology* 54 (January 1957), p. 102.

sample a specific geographic area on the premise that a one-time exposure would predispose buyers once the product is used. No matter what the method employed, the end goal of sellers in terms of the buyer learning curve is to increase the slope and the height of the curve and to move the status of the goods from convenience to shopping goods.[40] Obviously ,the ideal situation for a seller, would be learning which, after one purchase, moves immediately to a hundred percent—that is, a *certainty* of a repeat purchase. However, "complete" learning, over *any* length of time, seldom occurs in the real world.

Dynamics of Learning and Problem Solving

Problem solving is a dynamic process because as one problem is solved buyers face new ones. These arise from changes in buyer structure and include such events as the introduction of new offerings or changes in the location of the buyer in time and space. The way in which the multitude of purchasing decisions is handled is by the delegation of responsibilities and the sequential routinization of the buying process. Since we have examined the former, our concern now is with the latter. By "routinization" is meant that as the buyer accumulates favorable experiences, that is, learns about the utility he derives from various specific offerings, he need not explicitly proceed through each of the steps of the buying process. It must be stressed, however, that a single favorable experience or even a number of favorable experiences will not completely routinize the process so that given stimuli will trigger a direct and immediate purchase response. What in fact takes place over time is a reduction of the explicit steps of the process so that as favorable experiences are accumulated by the buyer, fewer and fewer of the steps take place. Because this sequence of the buying process has many possible combinations, it is convenient to state the analysis of the change in steps in more general terms. The three general problem solving conditions in the buyer process are: (1) extensive problem solving; (2) limited problem solving; and (3) automatic response behavior.[41]

Extensive problem solving is characterized by the lack of specificity in the mind of the buyer as to the product or service which will best satisfy his wants. Hence, the buyer will necessarily proceed through each of the several decision steps. This means that there will be a large amount of time and effort expended in considering alternative products, suppliers, and brands. And given the uncertainty it is reasonable to expect a low probability of repurchase. In this situation, the buyer will relate to the most "informative" aspects of his structure. Hence, search of media advertising will be exceedingly important, as will reference or peer groups.

Limited problem solving, as a middle position in the learning spectrum, is characterized by a greater routinization of a given number of steps. For

[40] See Chapter 12.
[41] Howard, *op. cit.*, pp. 45–89.

example, in LPS the buyer knows that a given need can be handled by a particular product class and hence this aspect does not require extensive search. Thus, the probability of purchase within the product class is relatively high though, to be sure, there may be a random probability distribution *among* the various brands until the buyer has had sufficient experience with a number of the alternatives to establish a preference.

Automatic response behavior is the most advanced instance of learning. Here little or no ideation of the purchase process occurs and as stimuli arise they almost automatically trigger class, supplier, and brand choice. At this point in the spectrum, given no chance in buyer or seller structure, the probability of repurchase of brand B for product class C from supplier D approaches 1.00 (certainty). This analysis, it should be pointed out, gives insight into why a given supplier may have specialty, shopping, or convenience characteristics to different buyers. All sellers would of course desire that buyers perceived their offering as a specialty good and thus exhibited automatic response behavior.

BRAND LOYALTY[42]

Definition

Brand loyalty is the preferences held over time by buyers for specific brands. Earlier we exhibited this graphically by the learning curve; however, now we introduce a more complex analysis. To be fully inclusive, any definition of brand loyalty must include the following: (1) brand choice sequence, (2) proportion of purchase accounted for by any brand, (3) repeat purchase probability, and (4) brand preferences over time.[43]

Measurement of Loyalty

Brand loyalty can be measured in several ways. Our discussion will be limited to two specific methods: (1) Markov models, and (2) learning models. In both cases the models are based on the assumption that brand choice in previous periods affects the current purchase.[44]

---

[42] Of course, when we speak of "brand" we are including product and enterprise choice as well. See, for example: R. M. Cunningham, "Brand Loyalty; What, Where, How Much?" *Harvard Business Review* XXXIV (Jan.-Feb., 1956), pp. 116–128; "Customer Loyalty to Store and Brand," *Harvard Business Review* XXXIX (Nov.-Dec. 1961), pp. 127–137.

[43] Engel, Kollat and Blackwell, *op. cit.*, p. 575.

[44] Discussion of brand choice models usually begins with zero-order models. "A zero-order model is one in which the response probabilities (the probability of choosing a particular brand) are not affected or altered by the particular responses that have been made." David B. Montgomery and Glen L. Urban, *Management Science in Marketing* (Prentice-Hall, 1969), p. 56. Also, for an example of its application, *see* R. E. Frank, "Brand Choice as a Probability Process," *Journal of Business* XXXV (January 1962), pp. 43–56.

Markov Models

Markov models presume that the last brand choice affects the current purchase. We can state this in the general form:

State $A =$ brand A was purchased on the last purchase occasion
State $B =$ brand B was purchased on the last purchase occasion
State $C =$ brand C was purchased on the last purchase occasion
State $D =$ brand D was purchased on the last purchase occasion
State $E =$ brand E was purchased on the last purchase occasion

It is postulated that all consumers may be represented by the following first-order transition matrix.

TABLE 9.1

BRAND PURCHASED AT OCCASION t + 1

Brand purchased at occasion t	A	B	C	D	E
A	P_{A_1A}	P_{AB}	P_{AC}	P_{AD}	P_{AE}
B	P_{B_1A}	P_{BB}	P_{BC}	P_{BD}	P_{BE}
C	P_{CA}	P_{CB}	P_{CC}	P_{CD}	P_{CE}
D	P_{DA}	P_{DB}	P_{DC}	P_{DD}	P_{DE}
E	P_{EA}	P_{EB}	P_{EC}	P_{ED}	P_{EE}

where Σ
$j = A_1B_1C_1D_1E$ $P_{ij} = 1$ for $i = A_1B_1C_1D_1E$

The P_{ij}'s are transition probabilities. They represent the probability that a buyer who purchases brand i at purchase occasion t will purchase brand j at purchase occasion $t + 1$.[45] P_{ii} is a measure of a brand's retentive or holding power (loyalty), while P_{ij} is a measure of brand j's ability to attract buyers from brand i. We can see this from the data in Table 9.2.

Brand loyalties are indicated by the underlined data (both absolutes and percents) which are in a diagonal across the matrix. The losses are shown across the rows and gains down the row. For example, Colgate is holding on to 602 of its buyers in period t. Colgate lost 94 buyers to Crest and gained 89 for a net loss of 5. Similar analysis can be made for each of the other brands.

[45] Montgomery and Urban, *op. cit.*, pp. 61–62. For additional discussion *see* F. Haray and B. Lipstein, "The Dynamics of Brand Loyalty: A Markonian Approach," *Operations Research* (Jan.-Feb. 1962), pp, 19–40; Jerome D. Herniter and John F. Magee, "Customer Behavior as a Markov Process," *Operations Research* (Jan.-Feb. 1961), pp. 105–122; J. E. Draper and L. H. Nolin, "A Markov Chain Analysis of Brand Preference," *Journal of Advertising Research* Vol. 4 (Sept. 1964), pp. 33–39; Donald A. Howard, "Stochastic Process Models of Consumer Behavior," *Journal of Advertising Research* Vol. 3 (September 1963), pp. 35–42.

TABLE 9.2

FIRST-ORDER TRANSITION MATRIX [1]

Brand purchased at occasion *t*		Brand purchased at occasion at *t* + 1				
		Colgate	Crest	Ipana	McCleans	Vote
Total	3687(100.0)	872	813	289	715	998
Colgate	947(100.0)	602(63.6)	94 (9.9)	58 (6.1)	102(10.8)	91 (9.6)
Crest	796(100.0)	89(11.2)	562(70.6)	19 (2.4)	77 (9.7)	49 (6.1)
Ipana	267(100.0)	24 (9.0)	25 (9.4)	146(54.6)	47(17.6)	25 (9.4)
McCleans	635(100.0)	75(11.7)	74(11.7)	40 (6.3)	389(61.2)	57 (9.0)
Vote	1042(100.0)	82 (7.9)	58 (5.6)	26 (2.5)	100 (9.6)	776(74.4)

[1] Fictitious data.

The actual prediction by the use of this method is likely to be in error because the impact of structural change in past periods may become operative during the periods being measured. Further, no consideration is made of the impact of changes in the promotional activities in the period. For example, a radical increase in advertising for one product with levels of the competitors held constant may be effective in the shift of a buyer from one brand to another. Likewise, a change in price of one of the products may affect changes. Telser, using consumer panel data, linked prices to transitional probabilities which are functions of the marketing variables prevailing in the market at the time the brand choice is made.[46]

Reasons for Brand Switching

Brand switching can be explained in general by three principles: (1) promotional and price activities by the seller; (2) dissatisfaction with brand in previous periods; and (3) changes in buyer structure. Since we tackle the first two of these principles elsewhere in this chapter, our efforts are concentrated in providing some examples of the last.

One of the more important changes in buyer structure is that of increase in income. One of the effects of changes in levels of income we saw in the last chapter was the change in assortment of goods purchased. Such changes also have impact on the relative quality of items which may be purchased. For example, as income increases for the family, it may switch brands of automobile. Trading-up occurs as a Pontiac is substituted for a Chevrolet, or Mercury for Ford or Dodge for Plymouth.

Brand switching at any one point in time, the first two variables held constant, occurs from changes in the environment experienced by the buyer.

[46] L. G. Telser, "The Demand for Branded Goods as Estimated from Consumer Panel Data," *Review of Economic and Statistics* XXXXIV (August 1962), pp. 300–324.

It may range in simplicity from the family entertaining the boss and being "required" to exhibit products not normally purchased, to the situation where suppliers are out of items and need for the product category prevails over any desire for the usual brand.

Kuehn's Learning Model [47]

Alfred Kuehn used a linear, probabilistic learning model to describe consumer brand shifting.[48] A fundamental aspect of the learning model is the assumption that past purchases affect the probability that the same item will be chosen in the future. An important postulate of this model is the accumulative effect—that is, the probability of purchase depends not only on the last purchase or the last few purchases as in a Markov model, but upon the entire buying history.[49]

Illustration

We can illustrate how this model describes changes in the buyer's probability of purchasing any given brand as a result of his previous purchases of that brand and competing brands. The effect of a four-purchase sequence *XAAX* upon a buyer with the initial probability of $Pa_1{}^1$ is seen by examining Figure 9.3.

The model is defined in terms of four parameters: the intercepts and slopes of the two lines referred to in Figure 9.3 as the purchase operator and the rejection operator. If the brand in question is purchased by the buyer on a given occasion, the buyer's probability of buying the same brand next time the want arises is read from the purchase operator. If the brand is rejected by the buyer on a given occasion, the buyer's probability of buying that brand on the subsequent occasion is read from the rejection operator.[50]

In terms of the model, the buyer begins with purchase 1 with the probability $P_{A,1}$ of buying Brand A. When the consumer chooses another

---

[47] Alfred A. Kuehn, "Consumer Brand Choice—A Learning Process?" in Ronald E. Frank, Alfred A. Kuehn, and William F. Massy, *Quantitative Techniques in Marketing Analysis* (Irwin, 1962), pp. 390–403, originally printed in *Journal of Advertising Research* II (December 1962), pp. 10–17.

[48] This model is a generalized form of stochastic models in William K. Estes, "Individual Behavior in Uncertain Situations: An Interpretation in Terms of Statistical Association Theory," in R. M. Thrall, C. H. Coombs, and R. L. Davis (eds.); *Decision Processes* (Wiley, 1954); and Robert R. Bush and Frederick Mosteller, *Stochastic Models for Learning* (Wiley, 1955).

[49] Montgomery and Urban, *op. cit.*, p. 69.

[50] Kuehn, *op. cit.*, p. 391. Of course, our real interest is understanding why such rejection takes place. As we have stated these are caused in general by changes in structure as well as the effects of post purchase evaluation.

brand (X) on trial 1, however, probability of buying Brand A on purchase 2 $(P_{A,2})$ is obtained from the rejection operator. This results in a reduction in the probability of purchase of Brand A on the next purchase occasion (trial 3). "Continuing in this fashion, the consumer again buys A on trial 3, thereby increasing the probability of purchasing Brand A on trial 4 to $P_{A,4}$. He rejects A on trial 4, however, decreasing his probability of buying A on trial 5 to $P_{A,5}$"[51]

FIGURE 9.3

STOCHASTIC (PROBABILISTIC) BRAND SHIFTING MODEL: LINEAR LEARNING MODEL

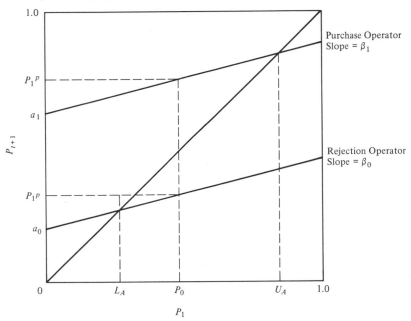

Source: A. A. Kuehn, "Consumer Brand Choice—A Learning Process?", *Journal of Advertising Research,* II December, 1962, © Advertising Research Foundation, 1962.

Empirical Evidence

In his dissertation Kuehn used methodology similar to the linear learning model.[52] He examined more than 15,000 individual purchases of frozen orange juice collected in monthly dairies by the *Chicago Tribune* Consumer Panel in the period 1950 to 1952. Data were analyzed as sequences of five

[51] *Ibid.*, p. 392.

[52] Montgomery and Urban, *op. cit.*, p. 71. Alfred A. Kuehn, "An Analysis of the Dynamics of Consumer Behavior and Its Implications for Marketing Management," unpublished Ph.D. dissertation, Graduate School of Industrial Administration, Carnegie Institute of Technology, 1958.

purchases by means of factorial analysis to ascertain the influence of the buyer's first four brand choices within each sequence upon his choice of a brand on the fifth purchase occasion.[53] The data and analyses are summarized in Table 9.3 where Snow Crop purchases are represented by the letter "S" and purchase of all other brands by the letter "O."

T A B L E 9 . 3

COMPARISON OF OBSERVED AND PREDICTED PROBABILITY OF PURCHASING SNOW CROP GIVEN THE FOUR PREVIOUS BRAND PURCHASES

Previous Purchase Pattern (1)	Sample Size (2)	Observed Probability of Purchase (3)	Predicted Probability of Purchase (4)	Deviation of Predictions (5)
SSSS	1,047	.806	.832	+.026
OSSS	277	.690	.691	+.001
SOSS	206	.665	.705	+.040
SSOS	222	.595	.634	+.039
SSSO	296	.486	.511	+.025
OOSS	248	.552	.564	+.012
SOOS	138	.565	.507	—.058
OSOS	149	.497	.493	—.004
SOSO	163	.405	.384	—.021
OSSO	181	.414	.370	—.044
SSOO	256	.305	.313	+.008
OOOS	500	.330	.366	+.033
OOSO	404	.191	.243	+.052
OSOO	433	.129	.172	+.043
SOOO	557	.154	.186	+.032
OOOO	8,442	.048	.045	—.003

Source: A. A. Kuehn, "Consumer Brand Choice—A Learning Process?", *Journal of Advertising Research*, II, (December, 1962) © Advertising Research Foundation, 1962.

Column 1 represents the purchase sequence; column 2 presents the sample sizes from which the observed and predicted probabilities of purchasing Snow Crop on the fifth occasion were calculated. Column 3 is computed on the basis of the observed frequencies of the five purchase sequence. In pattern SSSO there were 296 responses exhibiting this sequence and

[53] Frank, Kuehn, Massy, *op. cit.*, "Multiple Factor Analysis," pp. 405–460. Especially *see* Roland Harper, "Factor Analysis as a Technique for Examining Complex Data on Foodstuffs," pp. 410–416, originally printed in *Applied Statistics* V (March 1956), pp. 32–48.

Snow Crop was purchased on the 14th occasion in 144 of these. The best estimate of SSSO is 144/296 = 0.486.[54]

Conclusions

Inspection of the data in Table 9.3 suggests that the most recent purchase of the buyer is not the only influence on brand choice. This is in contrast to the analysis of simple Markov models, which assume all purchases are independent events. Other factors which account for the failure of the last purchase to influence greatly the next purchase include (1) the lack of availability of individual brands in stores normally used by the buyer; and (2) infrequency of purchase of the product. For the latter, Kuehn discovered two relations: (1) The probability of a consumer's buying the same brand on two consecutive purchases of frozen orange juice decreases exponentially with an increase in time between those purchases; and (2) Consumers buying frozen orange juice with greatest frequency have the highest probability of continuing to buy the same brand.[55] We would expect that infrequent *consumption* (use) of a durable good would have the same probability-reducing effect as infrequent *purchase* of a nondurable.

Some Differing Results

Frank was first among several to point out the problem of inferring learning effects, that is, changes in brand choices, from previous purchase. He suggested that the learning effects indicated by Kuehn's analysis may be spurious as a result of the aggregation of heterogeneous buyers whose true brand switching processes are zero-order.[56]

McConnell provides another attack on the linear learning model by suggesting that the probability of repurchasing a brand or product may partially depend on time, but more greatly depends on the consumer's perception of the quality of the brand in comparison with other brands.[57] In fact he concludes:

> Models of consumer brand loyalty will have limited predictive power until they incorporate the independent variables such as time and

---

[54] We are not concerned with the origin of column 4 "Predicted Probability of Purchase." Kuehn gives computational form: ". . . the probability of a Snow Crop purchase given the history SOOS is 0.045 (the probability of purchase given OOOO) plus 0.141 or 0.186, the probability given SOOS is 0.045 + 0.141 + 0.321 = 0.507 and the predicted probability given OSSS is 0.045 + 0.126 + 0.198 + 0.321 = 0.691." Kuehn, *op. cit.*, p. 395.

[55] *Ibid.*, p. 397.

[56] R. E. Frank, "Brand Choice as a Probability Process," *Journal of Business* XXXV (January 1962), pp. 43–56.

[57] J. Douglas McConnell, "Report-Purchase Estimation and the Linear Learning Model," *Journal of Marketing Research* V (August 1968), p. 306.

perceived quality on which repeat-purchase behavior is functionally dependent. Perceived quality is an aggregate of many factors; for some product groups it may be represented adequately by price, but more often it includes physical attributes of the brand, the brand image held by the consumer and his peers, advertising packaging, and the type of store selling the brand.[58]

SUMMARY

Buyer behavior consists of four sequential steps: (1) problem recognition; (2) search; (3) choice; and (4) post-decision evaluation. Learning is the key to understanding buyer behavior. The degree to which a buyer explicitly proceeds through each of the steps is a function of how well he has learned about the means for satisfying a particular want. Each time a buyer makes a choice, learning takes place. Learning is the systematic change in behavior due to the effects of experience.

Learning can be influenced. As a buyer makes choices, he is influenced by changes in buyer structure and is bombarded by the various sellers to choose their offerings rather than those of others. The seller chosen attempts to reinforce the attitude of the buyer so that in future periods repeat purchases will take place. At the same time, competitors are attempting to dislodge the buyer from past experiences with new offerings. The degree to which a seller is successful in keeping buyers is known as brand loyalty. It can be measured in a number of ways. Of greatest importance are Markov models and learning models.

The buyer behavior of one period becomes part of the buyer structure for the subsequent period, which in turn, has impact upon choice in the next period as well as other future periods.

SUGGESTED READINGS

Books

James F. Engel, David T. Kollat, and Roger D. Blackwell, *Consumer Behavior* (New York: Holt, Rinehart and Winston, Inc., 1968). A comprehensive integration of consumer behavior concepts and evidence. This volume examines the elements of buyer structure and the decision-making processes; it evaluates much of the relevant material from marketing and the behavioral sciences.

John A. Howard, *Marketing Management: Analysis and Planning* (rev. ed., Homewood, Ill.: Richard D. Irwin, Inc., 1963), Chaps. 3 and 4. These chapters present in great detail the learning theory model proposed in our discussion.

[58] *Ibid. See also* J. Douglas McConnell, "An Experimental Study of the Development of Brand Loyalty," *Journal of Marketing Research* 5 (February, 1968), pp. 13–19. These conclusions relate directly to our definition of price, *see* Chapter 13, pp. 311–316.

George Katona, *Psychological Analysis of Economic Behavior* (New York: McGraw-Hill Book Company, Inc., 1951). This is a classical synthesis of psychology and economics; especially see the discussion of learning.

Ron J. Markin, *The Psychology of Consumer Behavior* (Englewood Cliffs, N.J.: Prentice-Hall, Inc., 1969). The book examines consumer behavior on the premise that it is caused or affected by learning and communication. It intertwines communication theory with consumer behavior.

Francesco Nicosia, *Consumer Decision Processes* (Englewood Cliffs, N.J.: Prentice-Hall, Inc., 1966). This chapter provides and extensive review of the relatively few comprehensive models of behavior and decision-making.

Thomas S. Robertson, *Consumer Behavior* (Glenview, Ill.: Scott, Foresman and Company, 1970).

Articles

Raymond A. Bauer, "Risk Handling in Drug Adoption: The Role of Company Preference," *Public Opinion Quarterly* XXV (Winter 1961), pp. 546–559.

Victor T. Cook, "Group Decision, Social Comparison, and Persuasion in Changing Attitudes," *Journal of Advertising Research* 7 (March 1967), pp. 31–37.

Donald F. Cox and Stewart Rich, "Perceived Risk and Consumer Decision-Making—A Case of Telephone Shopping," *Journal of Marketing Research* 1 (November 1964), pp. 32–39.

Ross M. Cunningham, "Customer Loyalty to Store and Brand," *Harvard Business Review* 39 (Nov.-Dec. 1961), pp. 127–137.

H. Demsetz, "The Effect of Consumer Experience on Brand Loyalty and the Structure of Market Demand," *Econometrica* 30 (January 1962), pp. 22–33.

Gary W. Dickson, "Analysis of Vendor Selection Systems and Decisions," *Journal of Purchasing* 2 (February 1966), pp. 5–17. This article reviews the factors established by firms in selecting alternative suppliers.

A. S. C. Ehrenberg, "An Appraisal of Markov Brand Switching Models," *Journal of Marketing Research* 2 (November 1965), pp. 347–362.

John U. Farley, " 'Brand Loyalty' and The Economics of Information," *Journal of Business* 37 (October 1964), pp. 370–381.

Ronald E. Frank, "Brand Choice as a Probability Process," *Journal of Business* XXXV (January 1962), pp. 43–56.

Herbert E. Krugman and Eugene L. Hartley, "The Learning of Tastes," *Public Opinion Quarterly* 24 (Winter 1960), pp. 621–631.

Bruce Legrand and John Udell, "Consumer Behavior in the Market Place," *Journal of Retailing* (Fall 1964), pp. 32–40.

Vernon G. Lippitt, "Determinants of Consumer Demand for House Furnishings and Equipment," in Irwin Friend and Robert Jones, eds., *A Study of Consumer Expenditures, Income, and Savings: Proceedings of the Conference on Consumption and Savings* (Philadelphia: University of Pennsylvania, 1960), pp. 225–246.

Pierre Martineau, "Social Classes and Spending Behavior," *Journal of Marketing* 23 (October 1958), pp. 121–130.

Frederick E. May, "Buying Behavior: Some Research Findings," *Journal of Business* 38 (October 1965), pp. 379–396. A review article which collates most recent studies of buyer behavior and presents summaries of various empirical contributions. Also has an extensive bibliography.

Omar K. Moore and Donald J. Lewis, "Learning Theory and Culture," *Psychological Review* 59 (1952), pp. 380–388.

Robert W. Pratt, Jr., "Understanding the Decision Process for Consumer Goods: An Example of the Application of Longitudinal Analysis," Peter D. Bennet, ed., *Marketing and Economic Development* (Chicago: American Marketing Association, 1965), pp. 244–260.

James E. Stafford, "Effects of Group Influences on Consumer Brand Preferences," *Journal of Marketing Research* 3 (February 1966), pp. 68–75.

William D. Wells and Leonard A. LoSciuoto, "Direct Observation of Purchasing Behavior," *Journal of Marketing Research* 3 (August 1966), pp. 227–233.

IV   Seller
structure and
behavior

10

Marketing management and information

What is the logic underlying the behavior of sellers? What are the controllable and uncontrollable variables facing a marketing manager? What is "controllability" of variables and what is the role of marketing research in managerial strategy? These and other questions are considered in the present chapter. The following three chapters will analyze the firm's product, marketing channels, promotion, and pricing decisions and some of their implications.

THE NATURE OF THE FIRM

Firms exist because they can provide a demanded good or service at a price acceptable to some or all demanders and equal to or less than the competition. Clearly, if they cannot, they fail. Why do new firms come into being—or what is virtually the same, why do existing firms enter new markets? Firms begin de novo or enter markets because the entrepreneurs believe they can perform the one or more functions more efficiently than the extant firms (if any).

Abstracting from the analysis in Chapter 3, a firm is a collection of productive resources coordinated to satisfy one or more wants. With the exception of financial resources, all productive resources—including managerial knowledge and talent—are flexible but not universal in employment. That is, not all demand is exploitable by a firm. A manager knows more about managing some activities than others; a specific factory is better (or only) suited to produce some types of outputs; a specific machine—for example, a drill press—can produce some types of output and not others; or a specific salesman is better at selling some items than others.

To a firm, creating utility in a product means engaging in certain activities, and incurring the associated costs—hopefully to attain more-than-offsetting revenue. Every activity in a firm incurs a cost. The cost may vary with the output (variable cost) or remain fixed over the output range (fixed cost). But all marketing inputs, just like all accounting, finance, production, or general management resources and activities, have costs associated with them.

The task of the firm is to select those product and geographic markets which will best exploit the range of productive capability the firm possesses *and* afford an opportunity for differential advantage. We will have more to say about firms choosing their target markets. For now, it suffices to say that a firm is a pool of productive resources possessing some degree of output flexibility. The rational manager identifies and selects the product and geographic markets that will permit the firm to use its unique resources most efficiently and thereby more probably attain differential advantage.

Firms' Objectives

What is the objective(s) of the firm? Can we even speak of "objectives" of the firm? In the model of the pure market economy, firms attempt to maximize profits. But, what about in the marketing economy? There is no clear pattern. Some firms give money to the Boy Scouts, some to universities, and some to philanthropic organizations. Some firms court the favor of labor unions and espouse government and business cooperation; some firms are preoccupied in avoiding the clutches of antitrust, whereas other firms take a hard tack with respect to their labor relations and the division between the public and private sectors. Some firms actively engage in public relations, in currying the favor of stockholders, and the general public. Others appear to focus strictly upon the transactions—concerning themselves only with the parties to the market. Implicit in the preceding diversity are a host of objectives. However, there is one which overrides all others—a firm eventually must cover all costs. Whatever activities firms engage in and costs they incur in the short ultimately must be covered by revenues.

It is not inaccurate, therefore, to say that in the marketing economy firms maximize *long-run* profits. An imperfect economic world in which there is imperfect information on all supply and demand conditions, in which there are labor problems, the threat of antitrust action by government plus other government policies, highly concentrated markets (evoking at times a live-and-let-live attitude among sellers), in which there are sharp-tongued critics of capitalism and its various aspects, and customers and suppliers whose loyalty to any brand or buyer respectively is uncertain at best, is a world in which *short-run* profit maximization is perforce the *exception*. The short-run behavior of sellers is better characterized as *highly constrained* profit maximization or simply as "satisficing." But for survival in the long run, profits *are* the central focus, and "long-run profit maximization" is a reasonable characterization of the goal of firms. In our analysis we shall assume a goal of long-run profit maximization.[1] (A more comprehensive expression of the same goal is to say that firms attempt to maximize their present value—a concept that includes both expected future earnings and a risk discount factor.)

PROFIT MAXIMIZATION

Profit maximization may be analyzed in terms of revenues, costs, and differential advantage. Whether a firm sells in but one market or many, it tries in the long run to maximize the difference between total revenue and total cost. Figure 10.1 shows a firm's total revenue and total cost curves. The profit-maximizing output, marginal revenue = marginal cost, is depicted by Q_m, the point at which the TR and TC curves are farthest apart. The equality of MC and MR is indicated by the equal slopes of TC and TR at Q_m.[2]

Profit maximization in terms of average and marginal curves, rather than the total curves is shown in Figure 10.2. P_m is the profit-maximizing price. In the multi-product case if there is complete independence of costs and demands, TR and TC are the sum of the individual product revenues and costs. In most instances, however, multi-market firms experience some common costs as well as demand interrelationships. Thus, the parts of a multi-activity firm typically are not mutually exclusive.

Profit Maximization in Terms of Sales Revenue

What are some implications of revenue for profit? If costs are constant (or decreasing), profits will increase as revenue increases. Increased revenues stem from either an increase in demand or an increase in the inelasticity of demand with an ensuing rise in price.

[1] We gain an understanding of the principles and lose very little realism by assuming a goal of long-run profit maximization. For support of the profit assumption, *see* William L. Baldwin, "The Motive of Managers, Environmental Restraints, and the Theory of Managerial Enterprise," *The Quarterly Journal of Economics*, LXXVIII (May 1964), pp. 253–54; and Philip Kotler, *Marketing Management* (Prentice-Hall, 1967), Chapter 6 and references *passim*.

Two works pointing out the character of firms' short-run objectives and behavior are A. D. H. Kaplan, Joel B. Dirlam, and Robert F. Lanzillotti, *Pricing in Big Business* (The Brookings Institution, 1958), and Richard M. Cyert and James G. March, *A Behavioral Theory of the Firm* (Prentice-Hall, 1963).

[2] The total-revenue curve is convex to the horizontal axis because to sell more requires a lower price, and ultimately, $P \times Q$ yields lower total revenues. The total-cost curve is "S" shaped because of increasing and decreasing returns to variable factors. For a review of these and related concepts *see* for example, Paul A. Samuelson, *Economics: An Introductory Analysis* (McGraw-Hill, 1961), Chapters 24 and 26, or any other basic economics book.

FIGURE 10.1

PROFIT MAXIMIZING OUTPUT: TOTAL COSTS AND REVENUE

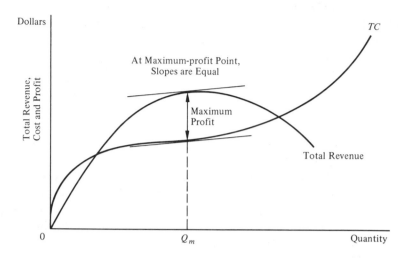

An increase in demand is characterized by an outward shift of the demand curve. With constant or decreasing average costs, an increase in demand produces an increase in profits. All other things being equal, management is always interested in increasing the demand for its products. The manner in which it increases demand (as well as increase in the quantity demanded) is the subject of the subsequent three chapters in this part.

An increase in demand inelasticity implies an increased desire for the product (brand) vis-à-vis competitive offerings. The competitive offerings are perceived by buyers as less substitutable for the subject offering. All other things equal, a firm also desires to increase the demand inelasticity for its products.[3] Over time, the elasticity for any product tends to increase, for the dynamics of seller rivalry typically produce an increase in the number of substitutes within a product or geographic market. Both intra- and inter-industry competition chip away at any firm's current level of market share and differential advantage.

Profit Maximization in Terms of Costs

All other things being equal, a firm maximizes profits by minimizing cost. In general, cost minimization is the least-cost means to attain a given

[3] The reader must remember that elasticity varies along a linear demand curve. The curve is inelastic only where a rise in price results in increased total revenue. Also, as the reader can demonstrate for himself, an increase in demand alters the elasticity of any segment of the linear demand curve. *See* Chapter 13.

For a useful discussion of elasticity *see* D. S. Watson, *Price Theory and Its Uses* (Houghton Mifflin, 1963), Chapter 3. See Chapters 2, 3 and 11–13 of the present book for a discussion of demand, elasticity, and some of their determinants.

goal, or alternatively, attaining the greatest output with a given *budget.*

In Figure 10.3, SS is a simplified example of an equal-output curve showing various combinations of expenditures on advertising and personal selling. For instance, 6 units of personal selling combined with 2 units of advertising yield the same sales as 2 units of personal selling and 5 units of advertising.

FIGURE 10.2

PROFIT MAXIMIZING OUTPUT: MARGINAL AND AVERAGE CURVES

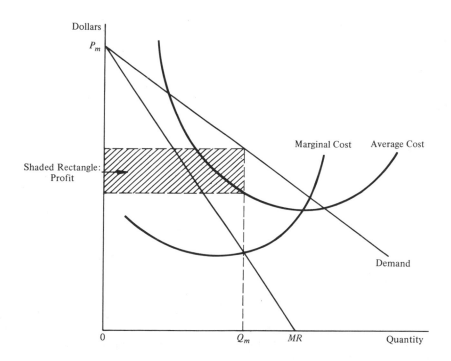

The equal-output curve is convex to the origin for reasons the reader will recall from the theory of production—the decreasing marginal yield of a variable factor. Thus, as one substitutes personal selling for advertising, he must substitute an increasing amount of personal selling for each unit of advertising given up, if he is to attain the desired output level. This declining marginal rate of substitution of one factor for another is typical of trade-offs between many marketing variables. Trade-offs imply that a *combination* of marketing variables is required in most market structures if, all else being equal, revenues are to be maximized, and/or costs minimized.

Figure 10.3, of course, is simply the *physical* relationships between two inputs—advertising and personal selling—and sales. We assume that costs are constant and that a unit of advertising (for example, cost per space or time in a medium) costs $5.00 and a unit of personal selling (for example, total cost per hour of employment) costs $10.00. Figure 10.4 shows the relation between units of advertising and personal selling employed and their respective costs. (The slope of the price lines is 1/2, the ratio of advertising price to personal selling price.)

FIGURE 10.3

AN ILLUSTRATIVE EQUAL-OUTPUT CURVE IN MARKETING. ALL THE POINTS ON THE CURVE REPRESENT THE DIFFERENT COMBINATIONS OF ADVERTISING AND PERSONAL SELLING THAT CAN BE USED TO EFFECT THE SAME TOTAL SALES.

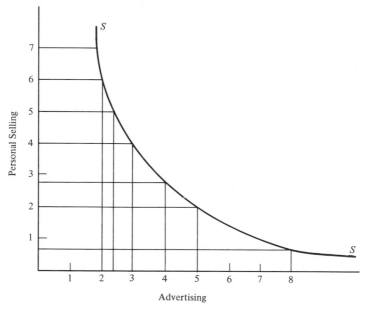

The cost minimization (least-cost) combination of inputs to attain the desired output is shown in Figure 10.5. The single equal-product curve is superimposed on the family of equal-cost lines. Conceptually, the firm will always keep moving along the concave equal-product curve as long as it is able to reach a lower cost line. The firm's equilibrium is where the equal-product curve touches (but does not cross) the lowest equal-cost line.[4] In this analysis we are holding constant all environmental factors such as changes in tastes, the influence of competition, and so on. Formally, the least-cost equilibrium can be defined:

> The marginal physical-product-per-dollar received from the (last) dollar expenditure must be the same for every productive factor.[5]

[4] Samuelson, *op. cit.*, p. 589. This discussion of cost minimization is based on Samuelson, pages 585–91.
[5] *Ibid.*

FIGURE 10.4

EQUAL-COST LINES. EVERY POINT ON A GIVEN LINE REPRESENTS THE SAME TOTAL COST. THE LINES ARE STRAIGHT BECAUSE OF CONSTANT FACTOR PRICES (IN THIS CASE).

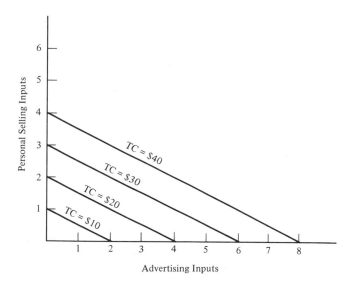

Thus,

$$\frac{\text{Marginal-physical-product of advertising}}{\text{Price of Advertising}} = \frac{\text{Marginal-physical product of P.S.}}{\text{Price of P.S.}}$$

This means simply that a firm in marketing (or any other activity) will redistribute its expenditure among inputs if any one factor offers a greater return for each last dollar spent on it.

A variation of the preceding cost-minimization approach to profit maximization occurs when the budget is *fixed* and the objective becomes one of attaining the greatest sales volume with the given budget. Consider a marketing situation wherein one major problem is deciding between personal selling and advertising inputs. Suppose the fixed weekly budget is $1000. In Figure 10.6 the budget constraint of $1000 is shown by a price line reflecting the ratio of prices of advertising and personal selling.

Figure 10.7 shows a family of equal-product curves using different combinations of the two marketing inputs, that is, the successive sales levels $(S_1, \ldots, S_6)$ attainable by various combinations of personal selling and advertising.

The solution is the tangency between the budget line and the largest attainable equal-sales curve. There are many real-world illustrations of firms approaching their marketing activities with fixed marketing budgets.

The preceding two simplified analyses illustrate the principle of cost minimization in marketing. The reader should conceive of the problem in terms of additional simultaneous inputs such as expenditures on channels of distribution, packaging, product development, trade exhibits and other sales promotion, and so on. He then approaches the real complexity of the revenue-maximization and cost-minimization decisions of marketing management.

FIGURE 10.5

SUBSTITUTING MARKETING INPUTS TO MINIMIZE COST OF ATTAINING A GIVEN SALES TARGET.

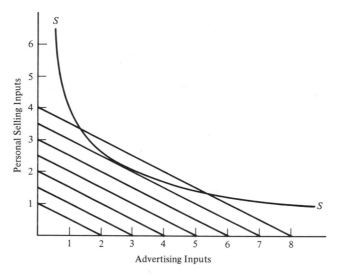

Break-even Analysis

Cost minimization is not necessarily profit maximization, for the lowest point on the average total cost curve may not coincide with the $MC = MR$ output. A downward sloping demand curve typically yields a profit maximization solution at an output *less than* the cost-minimizing output. Also, extra expenditures today may effect lower costs and increased revenues in the future. For example, some types of advertising are expenditures analogous to a capital investment, for these advertising inputs yield a future stream of revenue. Strict cost minimization in this case would *not* be profit maximizing.[6]

In the short run the rational profit-maximizing firm, in deciding on the type and amount of inputs, is interested fundamentally in the increments to total costs and total revenues brought about by each additional unit of output. Thus the rational firm focuses only on incremental or marginal costs and revenues. Fixed costs—those that do not vary with output, such as salaries, rent, and insurance—are irrelevant in determining the type and amount of inputs in the short run. In the long run, of course, all costs must

[6] Advertising as a type of capital expenditure is discussed in Chapter 12.

be covered, but in the short run the issue is the revenue and cost yielded by the last or marginal unit sold. If $MR > MC$, the rational firm will wish to increase output, for an additional unit (or more) sold will realize incremental revenues exceeding the cost incurred.

FIGURE 10.6

THE FIXED MARKETING BUDGET IN THE CASE LIMITED TO ADVERTISING AND PERSONAL SELLING.

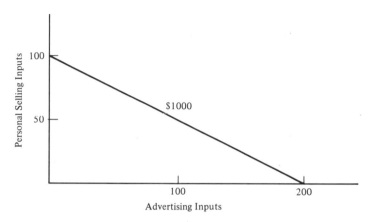

Strictly, the rational firm in the short run must cover only the out-of-pocket or variable costs. Revenues exceeding variable costs apply toward fixed costs and profits. The difference between revenues and variable costs $(R - VC)$ is called the "contribution margin," constituting the contribution to overhead and profits.[7]

Break-even analysis reveals the output point at which total revenues equal total costs. The analysis, by relating the contribution margin to fixed costs, determines the break-even point. Figure 10.8 depicts a simple break-even diagram showing the relationship between total revenue, total cost, total variable cost, and fixed cost. The break-even point occurs at output Q_{BE}. The simplified form shown in Figure 10.8 assumes one given price and

---

[7] Some businessmen erroneously believe that for all products they must set their price to cover total costs rather than pricing in accordance with marginal costs or average variable costs. By contrast, sophisticated price makers relate their prices to both demand and variable costs. Depending on the demand elasticity and the cost structure, the astute pricer may price successfully far above *all* costs on some products and precisely equal to or even less than variable costs on others. These matters are discussed in Chapter 13. Three references to the rationale of blending variable costs and demand in pricing decisions are Donald V. Harper, *Price Policy and Procedure* (Harcourt, Brace and World, 1966), pp. 53–59; Richard Heflebower, "Full Costs, Cost Changes, and Prices," *Business Concentration and Price Policy* (National Bureau of Economic Research, 1955), pp. 361–392; and W. G. Shepherd, "Marginal-Cost Pricing in American Utilities," *Southern Economic Journal*, July 1966.

thus a linear *TR* curve, and also assumes linear cost functions. This form is *not* a profit maximization analysis, but one which shows only the $TR = TC$ point.

FIGURE 10.7

EQUAL-OUTPUT WITH ONLY TWO IMPUTS: PERSONAL SELLING AND ADVERTISING. THE CURVES ARE EQUI-DISTANT (IN THIS ILLUSTRATION), INDICATING CONSTANT RETURNS TO SCALE.

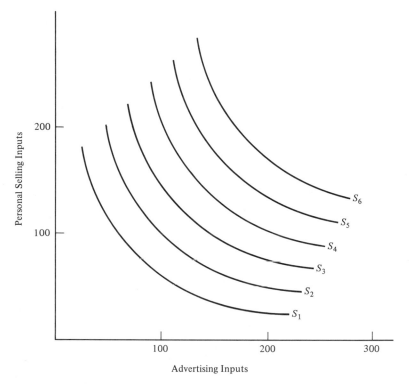

The definition of the break-even point in terms of units and dollars is:[8]

$$\text{BEP (units)} = \frac{\text{Fixed Cost}}{\$ \text{ Contribution-to-fixed-cost-and-profit per unit}}$$

For example, if *FC* are \$50,000 and price is \$1.20 and *VC* \$.80, the \$ contribution/unit is .40. The break-even point in terms of units is $\frac{\$50,000}{.40}$ or 125,000 units. And

$$\text{BEP (dollars)} = \frac{\text{Fixed Cost}}{\dfrac{FC/\text{unit}^{9}}{P/\text{unit}}}$$

[8] \$ Contribution per unit is simply price minus variable cost $(P - VC)$.

[9] $\dfrac{FC/\text{unit}}{P/\text{unit}}$ is $\dfrac{(1 - VC/\text{unit})}{P/\text{unit}}$

FIGURE 10.8

SIMPLE BREAK-EVEN CHART

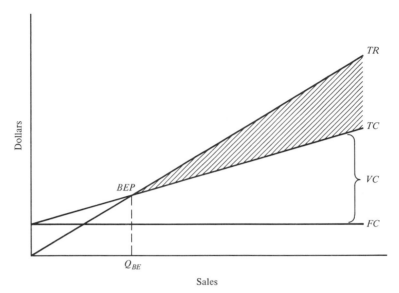

Sales

Using the same data as above, the calculation is $\dfrac{\$50,000}{100\% - 66\%}$ or $\dfrac{\$50,000}{33\%}$

which gives a break-even point in terms of dollar sales of approximately $150,000.

Flexible break-even analysis comes closer to a tool of profit maximization. It incorporates several prices and their corresponding TR curves and relates them to the FC and TC curves.[10] Figure 10.9 shows a flexible break-even analysis. The profit maximizing firm introduces demand considerations in the analysis by estimating the quantity that could be sold at each of the five prices represented by $TR_1, \ldots, TR_5$ in Figure 10.9. The firm selects from the output region beyond BEP the price that maximizes $(TR - TC)$.

Contribution analysis focuses directly on the relevant issue of the difference between TR and variable costs—or some similar concept of costs.[11] Figure 10.10 depicts simple contribution analysis in which the shaded portion is the total contribution to FC and profits. As with break-even analysis, the contribution analysis using a family of prices illustrates the relationships of different combinations of TR, VC, and quantities.

Profit Maximization in Terms of Differential Advantage

Chapter 3 introduced the concept of differential advantage. Only in rivalistic (i.e., other than purely competitive) markets is differential advan-

[10] See E. J. McCarthy, *Basic Marketing: A Managerial Approach* (Irwin, 1968), Chapter 26.
[11] Contribution analysis is discussed in Harper, *op. cit.*, pp. 58–59.

tage a meaningful concept. In Chapter 3, the discussion of matching the want turned largely on presenting an offering designed to match as closely as possible a *given* want. The basic argument advanced was that a condition requiring gratification leads to a demand for a good or service believed by the demander to offer want satisfaction.

FIGURE 10.9

FLEXIBLE BREAK-EVEN ANALYSIS

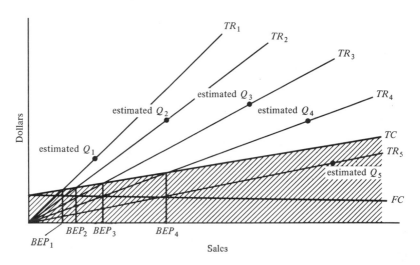

The demander assesses the offerings of sellers vis-à-vis his want. The offering perceived as most fully satisfying the want acquires a differential advantage over the other offerings. The greater the want satisfaction perceived in an offering relative to other offerings, the greater that offering's differential advantage. In the presence of competition, a firm always tries to increase its differential advantage to the extent net profits are thereby increased.

So far then, our argument on differential advantage has been based on maximizing differential advantage with respect to a *given* want. As we shall see, profit-maximizing strategy in the matching of wants is to adjust the offering to the want, *and* insofar as possible adjust the want to the offering.

What are the bases of differential advantage? That is, what does a marketing manager do or try to do to establish a belief in a buyer(s) that the firm's offering possesses more want-satisfying ability than other firms' offerings? As Chamberlin pointed out over thirty years ago, perceived differences—and hence potential differential advantage—may stem from virtually *any* aspect of a firm's structure or operation.

Anything which makes buyers prefer one seller to another, be it personality, reputation, convenient location, or the tone of his shop, differentiates the thing purchased to that degree, for what is bought is really a bundle of utilities, of which these things are a part.[12]

Let us be clear on the important distinctions between physical-product differentiation, total-product differentiation, and differential advantage. As we pointed out in Chapter 3, one can alter his physical product, but this is not necessarily a different *total* product. It is only *total* products which are important, for they are the perceived *total* utility in an offering. Unless and until the total product changes, nothing of marketing significance has occurred. It is the respective total products of all sellers in a market which are assessed by buyers in that market as to which possesses greatest perceived utility, and hence which offering will enjoy greatest differential advantage.

FIGURE 10.10

SIMPLE CONTRIBUTION ANALYSIS

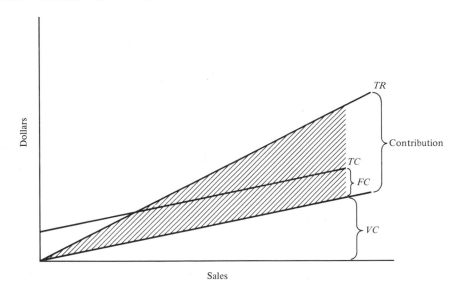

The insightful reader will inquire about the relation between relative efficiency and differential advantage. Remembering that differential advantage inheres in the perception of the buyer, we conclude there is no direct but a very strong *indirect* link between efficiency and differential advantage. By definition, the greater the efficiency with which a firm operates, the greater the resulting savings, that is, discretionary resources. And the greater the discretionary resources a firm possesses, the more it can spend on differentiating its total product to create differential advantage. Therefore,

[12] E. H. Chamberlin, *The Theory of Monopolistic Competition* (8th ed., Harvard, 1962), p. 8 (emphasis added). *See also Ibid.*, pp. 56–57, and Chapter 3 of the present book.

if a firm can perform an activity more efficiently than its rivals, we would expect it over time to exploit opportunities for differential advantage.

As we shall point out in Chapter 13, "price" is closely related to "product." A relatively efficient firm can offer the same physical product at a lower price than less efficient firms. Therefore, in effect, the more efficient firm is offering a larger bundle of utility than the others—creating thereby a differential advantage. Efficiency or comparative economic advantage can manifest itself in many ways in the creation of differential advantage.

Bases for Differential Advantage

From simply casual observation, we concur with Chamberlin that almost anything in a firm is a potential basis for differentiation. We can divide the bases for differentiation into four substantially distinct categories:

1. Technological basis   Technological advantage is evidenced in (1) use requirements, (2) production processes, and (3) marketing methods. As to use requirements, an example of technological advantage is styling a product to meet a particular buyer desire, such as producing golf clubs for left-handed players. Unique assembly-line methods and equipment are examples of a production-process base of differential advantage. With respect to marketing methods, a differential advantage may be obtained by a more efficient distribution, warehousing, or inventory control system.

2. Legal basis   Legal grounds underlie differential advantage due to trademarks, patents, and other absolute or limited legal monopoly elements.

3. Geographic basis   Location leads to differential advantage by way of spatial monopoly or at least high-traffic and/or low-cost location.

4. Enterprise basis   Enterprise differentiation is an extremely important and widespread basis of differential advantage. A firm competing with others in the sale of a necessarily homogeneous physical product such as coal *can* differentiate from the others by adopting distinctive marketing policies as to appeals, product assortment, channels of distribution, timing, and so on. The managerial ingredient is all-importaant in enterprise differentiation, for essentially this type of differentiation depends on creatively combining elements so that although the physical product may be homogeneous, buyers perceive a *distinct*, want-satisfying total product.[13]

[13] The four bases for differential advantage are adapted from Wroe Alderson, *Dynamic Marketing Behavior* (Irwin, 1965), pp. 196–7.

Differentiation and Market Segmentation

There are limits to which a firm can go in differentiating its offering and still remain in the intended product market. Through excessive differentiation, the total product may be perceived as possessing *less* rather than more relevance, for sellers inadvertently may alter their total product to such a degree that they leave the intended product market.

Most frequently, however, the entry into another product market is intentional. As we discussed in Chapter 3, new products and new-product competition are a substantial aspect in seller rivalry. As markets grow in size, demand segments appear. Thus, in the cigarette market, there are relatively distinct market segments—the filter market, the king-size market, the menthol market, plus combinations of these and others. Rather than differentiate further within the initial market, firms may decide to enter a new segment. Thus they enter what is to them a new product or geographic market. The creation and development of a market segment is called "market segmentation," an important managerial strategy and one subtly distinguished from "differentiation." The latter may lead to and develop the former.[14]

Merchandising

A firm attempts to increase its differential advantage over rivals through strategic adaptations, or what we shall call "merchandising." Specifically, merchandising is

> The strategy of innovation in adapting a product or group of products to conform to customers' wants, and adapting demand to conform to effective supply. Frequently it is the *simultaneous* adaptation of supply to demand and demand to supply.[15]

McGarry has stated that there are few concepts in marketing analytically more important than merchandising.[16]

Thus the logic of seller behavior is the creation of differential advantage—effected through merchandising. Merchandising is perceptual adaptation in either or both the offering and the want. Some activities, for example,

---

[14] For a useful discussion of the relationships between differentiation and segmentation, *see* Wendell R. Smith, "Product Differentiation and Market Segmentation as Alternative Marketing Strategies," *Journal of Marketing*, XXI, No. 1 (July 1956).

[15] This discussion of merchandising in part is based on four sources. They are E. A. Duddy and D. A. Revzan, *Marketing: An Institutional Approach* (McGraw-Hill, 2d ed.), Chapter 3; David A. Revzan, *Wholesaling in Marketing Organization* (Wiley), Chapter 11; Edmund D. McGarry, "The Merchandising Function," in Reavis Cox, Wroe Alderson, and Stanley J. Shapiro, *Theory in Marketing* (Irwin, 1964); and Edmund D. McGarry, "Some Functions of Marketing Reconsidered," in Wroe Alderson and Reavis Cox (eds.), *Theory in Marketing* (Irwin, 1950).

[16] McGarry, "The Merchandising Function," *op. cit.*, p. 233.

product development and modification, are designed to adjust one aspect of the total product to match the want more completely. Other activities such as some uses of advertising are intended to orient the demand for the product more completely to the brand of a particular seller. Figure 10.11 illustrates the two-way adjustments in merchandising, showing the increased perceived want satisfaction in period t_2 over that of t_1.

FIGURE 10.11

MERCHANDISING: THE CREATION OF DIFFERENTIAL ADVANTAGE THROUGH ADJUSTMENT OF THE OFFERING TO THE WANT AND THE WANT TO THE OFFERING.

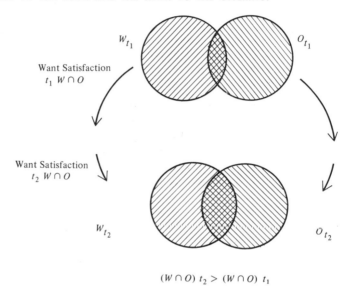

$$(W \cap O) \, t_2 > (W \cap O) \, t_1$$

One can readily agree that some activities in the firm adjust the demand to supply, and other activities adjust supply to demand. But, given all of the elements that comprise a demander's perception of himself and his environment, it is perhaps clear that one cannot neatly label activities in the firm *before the fact* as to the character of their effect.[17] Unexpected results continually occur. Consider a firm that adjusts its physical product, and thereby, it believes, its total product, to match more fully a want for conven-

---

[17] Drawing upon Chamberlin, many analysts in their attempts to assess the social efficiency of marketing, divide all costs incurred in creating utility into a two-fold classification. Marketing efficiency is determined by the ratio of "marketing costs" to market prices. "Production costs" are the complement. Clearly, objective analysis depends on an accurate separation of the two kinds of costs—*if* this is even possible. Chamberlin admits these two costs are "interlaced throughout the price system." Chamberlin, *The Theory of Monopolistic Competition* (Harvard University, 8th ed., 1962), p. 124.

The reader should consider the sources of upward and downward biases in the estimation of marketing efficiency. The matters of productivity and efficiency in marketing will be discussed in Chapter 15.

ience and economy. A case in point is the introduction of low-cost, non-returnable glass as well as aluminum containers for consumer beverages. The unintended effect is to alienate the segment of the beverage market which—although perhaps economy minded—also favors unspoiled nature so strongly that they in protest do not purchase containers which they know will become the non-degradable litter of the masses of thoughtless campers and picnickers.

THE MARKETING MIX AND THE CONTEXT OF MARKETING MANAGEMENT

Independent Variables

Customer perception is the most critical *dependent* variable in seller behavior. A change in a want, a change in a product, a change in the degree of want satisfaction, and a change in the degree of differential advantage all occur *only* from a change in the perception of the buyer.

In Part III, the determinants of buyer behavior were analyzed, and indeed there are a multitude of influences determining the purchasing behavior of buyers. A marketing manager has some degree of control at least in principle over a small number of these independent variables. We briefly discussed in Chapter 3 the controllability of elements of structure. Let us now more extensively consider "controllability."

Controllable and Uncontrollable Variables

A *controllable variable* is an independent variable over which a marketing manager in the relevant decision period has some degree of discretion.

An *uncontrollable variable* is an independent variable over which a marketing manager in the relevant decision period has no degree of discretion.

More specifically, when does a marketing manager have "discretion" or "control" over independent variables? A marketing manager has at least some control over a variable when the market permits him two or more values for the variable.

A rational marketing manager would like everything to be controllable, for then buyers obviously would behave precisely according to his desires: He could precisely predict and anticipate events, and profits would easily be maximized. In most markets, firms continually try to increase their influence over all relevant variables so that demand and inelasticity of demand more easily are increased, and costs of marketing more easily decreased.

Of the total set of influences on buyer behavior, a firm is trying to enlarge the range of discretion it exercises over *any one* variable (for example, the number of different marketing channels and prices from which it may choose) and also the *number* of controllable variables.

There are several determinants of control.

Market Structure.   The market structure may permit no discretion vis-à-vis a variable; hence, there is no control over the variable. In principle, the price one charges for a product is always a controllable variable, for one can arbitrarily assign to his products any particular price he chooses, but is there control *in fact* over this variable? If the price he charges does not correspond to any demand schedule, he sells nothing. There is control over price only to the extent the market permits discretion as to pricing alternatives. In a perfectly competitive market, as we have noted, there is no managerial control over price. In imperfectly competitive markets there is control only if there is a choice of price (which must necessarily correspond to extant demand and reflect competitive forces). If one is to understand controllability of price, for example, the true object of analysis is not the decisions themselves, but rather their reception by the market.[18]

Economic and Calendar Time.   What is uncontrollable in the short run may be controllable in the long run. In the short run, some inputs are fixed in amount: The firm can expand or contract its output only by varying the amounts of other inputs. The output can range from zero if the firm shuts down altogether, to some maximum output permitted by the fixed factors. In the long run all inputs are variable in amount. We live in the short run, and plan in the long run. Examples of the short run in marketing are deciding how to use the present sales force, the present advertising budget, the present channels of distribution, and the price of the present goods and services. The long run is seen in the option of changing the size of the sales force, the size of the advertising budget, the channels of distribution, the product assortment, and so on. There is no specific calendar meaning to short and long run.[19]

There are many "societal" influences on the behavior of buyers over which a firm has no immediate control, let alone in many cases ultimate control. At any instant of time, the world is completely defined: A firm faces given tastes of his customers, competitors, social patterns of society including mores and folkways, government policy in matters such as antitrust, and so on. Time enters into the determination of what is and what is not controllable. In principle, in the long run of society, virtually all human behavior in the economic, political, and social realms is susceptible to influence. Thus, in principle, in the long run virtually everything short of acts of God has a potential element of some controllability. In some market structures "control," if any, is fleeting, for entry of new firms continually

---

[18] For additional aspects of this and related points, *see* M. A. Adelman's trenchant paper, "Pricing by Manufacturers," in *Proceedings of the Conference of Marketing Teachers From Far Western States* (Berkeley: University of California, 1958). *See also* Chapter 13 of the present book.

[19] See for example, Watson, *op. cit.*, p. 164.

injects innovations in the market. On the other hand, a consumer in a monopolized and blockaded-entry market is clearly subject to some control.

Level of Aggregation.   The degree of controllability is a function also of the performing unit. What may be clearly or simply perceived as beyond the influence of a single marketing manager—hence for him, or so he believes, uncontrollable—may be at least partially controllable by a higher-level organization, such as a collection of firms as through trade and industry associations and chambers of commerce. The larger the relative size of the performing unit (including the larger the collection of units), the higher is the possible ratio of controllable to uncontrollable variables. This argument implies some economies of scale. The exact magnitude of economies is an empirical question. Note, however, that a variable may be considered uncontrollable on subjective consideration but in fact controllable when examined objectively. Through imaginative approaches one's scope of activity is frequently seen to be greater than it appears at first.[20]

Summary

A firm is continually trying to maximize its control over the influences impinging on buyers. The greater the control a firm can effect, other things being equal, the greater its differential advantage, and hence profits. The amount of control enjoyed by a firm is evidenced by the number of variables it has discretion over and the range of alternatives open to it within each variable.

The amount of control is determined by:

1. the market structure
2. whether the assessment is made in the economic short run or long run
3. the length of calendar time included in the assessment
4. the performing unit (the level of aggregation).

The Marketing Mix

We turn now to the specific independent variables affecting buyer behavior which are controllable. From discussions in Chapters 2 and 3, we know that form, time, place, and possession utilities must be created for a want to be satisfied. What variables must a marketer utilize if he is both to try to satisfy a want and compete with rival sellers?

The controllable variables can be combined into four variables. First, the variable of good or service we can leave as a separate variable, called "product"; second, price may remain as a variable, "price"; third, physical and ancillary flows may be combined in the comprehensive variable discussed in Part II, "marketing channel"; and fourth, information and persuasion may be combined in "promotion." Thus we come up with what is gen-

[20] See Herbert A. Simon, *Administrative Behavior* (Macmillan, 1958).

erally called the "marketing mix": the strategic controllable variables through which a firm seeks to attain its marketing goals.[21]

Customer Orientation and Controllable and Uncontrollable Variables

The controllable variables must be combined in such a manner that the want is matched, and profits maximized. A useful paradigm showing the centrality of the customer in rational marketing management is presented in Figure 10.12.

FIGURE 10.12

THE MARKETING MIX AND CUSTOMER ORIENTATION*

* The diagram is based on McCarthy, *op. cit.*, p. 38.

The paradigm showing the marketing mix and the customer is a simplification. There are far more uncontrollable than controllable variables influencing the customer, and indirectly, the seller. We have discussed in Part III the environmental psychological, sociological, and economic factors affecting buyers, and have related them to the controllable variables of the marketing manager. A firm gains at best only a small portion of the attention of the customer.[22]

Moreover there are certain influences impinging *directly* upon the seller in addition to the influences that indirectly affect him through the buyer. For example, the antitrust laws are direct constraints upon firms both as sellers and buyers. Governmental fiscal, monetary, and balance of payments policies have elements directly affecting firms. Many elements of a market structure, such as number and relative size of competitors, and conditions of entry are direct influences. There are three sets of structure elements to which the firm in the short run adjusts and in the long run tries to alter: (1) intra-

[21] The four-element marketing mix or close variations thereof are found in virtually all present-day marketing management texts. Three well-known examples are E. J. McCarthy, *Basic Marketing: A Managerial Approach* (Irwin: rev. ed., 1964); John A. Howard, *Marketing Management* (Irwin: rev. ed., 1963); and Philip Kotler, *Marketing Management: Analysis, Planning and Control* (Prentice-Hall, 1967).

[22] See for example, Martin L. Bell, *Marketing: Concepts and Strategy* (Houghton Mifflin, 1966), p. 173.

agency elements of structure such as quality of personnel, budget, and so on; (2) external elements directly affecting the agency such as number and size of competitors, entry conditions, antitrust, and so forth; and (3) external elements indirectly affecting the agency such as influences on the buyer from economic and other conditions. Within the framework of the decision structure (all the elements), the marketing manager tries to select an optimal mix of the four comprehensive "controllables": product, channels, promotion, and price. Figure 10.13 shows the three sets of structure elements and the "controllable" variable,[23] as the firm attempts to match the target want.

FIGURE 10.13

THE ELEMENTS OF STRUCTURE FOR A SUPPLIER AND THE MARKETING MIX. RECALLING THE DISCUSSION IN CHAPTER 4 AS WELL AS THE PRESENT CHAPTER, SOME ELEMENTS OF STRUCTURE ARE "CONTROLLABLE" AND SOME ELEMENTS OF MARKETING MIX ARE "UNCONTROLLABLE," SUCH AS PRICE IN A PURELY COMPETITIVE MARKET.

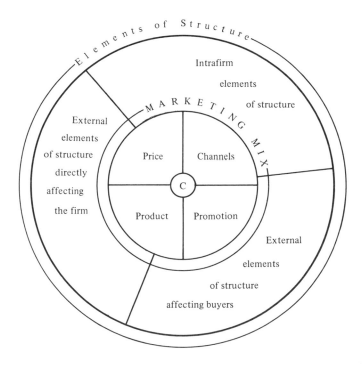

MARKETING RESEARCH AND THE MARKETING MIX

Market conditions are always changing, for the myriad elements in supply and demand are always changing. Whether it be tastes, income,

[23] Figure 10.13 is an adaptation of McCarthy's model. *Op. cit.*, p. 49.

technology, age distribution, competition, or government policy, virtually nothing remains static. It is precisely because of change, and especially complex change, that all participants in the marketing economy—demanders, suppliers, government, and nonprofit agencies—face uncertainty in the marketplace. That is, it is the rare market situation that permits a participant to predict with complete accuracy the outcome of any market decision. More specifically, rare indeed is the customer who knows with certainty the precise satisfaction he will derive from any purchase, and even more rare is the seller who can predict precisely the results of any selling (or buying) decision.

In effect, all participants in marketing, in each and every decision, face a probability distribution of outcomes. For a participant with absolutely no expectation of what the outcome may be (rare), the possible outcomes represent a random distribution. On the other hand, a participant with considerable experience (including knowledge of the characteristics of the elements of his structure) such as a brand-loyal consumer repurchasing the brand, or a seller of a highly differentiated product in a relatively stable market structure, can predict reasonably accurately the approximate outcome of these decisions. To qualify the generalization somewhat, these participants in such situations could predict reasonably well at least the near-term consequences.

If, as we suggest, all participants face probability distributions of outcomes, then we may conclude that a rational participant (whoever he is or whatever he does) in desiring to attain his goals most efficiently, wishes to reduce the *range* of possible outcomes. That is, a rational participant desires either to control the outcome so that it falls at or about some preferred level, or at the minimum, desires to predict more accurately the actual outcome. In either case, the rational participant desires to reduce risk—technically, the variance of outcomes.

It is obvious that a participant fully in control of all elements in his structure could effect outcomes close to his ideal. But aside from a largely fictitious pure (complete) monopolist selling a "required" good and protected by high entry barriers, *complete control* in the real world (other than extremely short lived) is unknown.

The much more interesting and relevant case is the other of the previously mentioned two—namely, *information* about outcomes. The issue is the ability to predict, which as we recall from Chapter 1, implies good theory. As we also know from the discussion in Chapter 4, to predict outcomes one must discover the most important elements of structure and their interaction. Once again, we stress the value of information to demanders, suppliers, and all other participants. Though the procedures differ somewhat in terms of elaborateness and formality, nevertheless in principle, a rational customer has the same basic requirement for, and acquires information just as, a rational seller.

Of course, information in an uncertain world has a cost. It costs one either explicitly or implicitly (for example, forgone opportunities for other uses of one's time) to acquire information. The general principle followed by a rational participant in acquiring information better to forecast or predict events is $MC = MR$. Specifically, an ultimate consumer or a seller or anyone else continues to acquire information until the cost of the last unit of information acquired is equal to the benefit derived from that last unit of information.[24]

A corollary to the $MC = MR$ optimal information rule is that no one can afford to be completely informed. The costs associated with attaining a state of complete information far exceed the benefits to the person acquiring the information. (Recall the U-shaped S-R average cost curve—the result of diminishing marginal returns.) With respect to want satisfaction, a rational, profit-maximizing seller will acquire only enough information on customers' wants to enable him to attain differential advantage. But not one bit more! From this, one sees the many implications for the role of competition. In a market without strong competition, a seller may need to acquire only little information (and in other ways expend little energy) to attain differential advantage. Unfortunately for customers, this may mean relatively little absolute want satisfaction. Accordingly, there is very little consumer sovereignty in such markets.

On the other hand, in markets strongly competitive, a seller is forced to acquire considerable information about what demanders want in order for him to attain differential advantage. In pursuing his own self-interest, a seller in such a market comes much closer to satisfying fully (by knowing more completely) the wants of the demanders. By definition, in such markets consumer sovereignty is considerable.

"Market research" in general relates to the activities of obtaining relevant information in order both to predict outcomes more accurately and, insofar as possible, gain greater control over the elements in one's structure. There is obviously a very close relationship between marketing research and the marketing mix.

We recognize that a decision-maker can be only as rational as the amount and quality of his information. For a seller, information has three major uses. First, information is required for the initial selection of marketing mixes, vis-à-vis the structure. Second, information is required for successful implementation of the decisions. Third, information is required to assess the performance. Immediate revisions in the mix may be necessary, for the market may reject in whole or part the initial set of decisions. Adelman has described the information input and output character of markets:

[24] An excellent technical discussion of information with many implications, though focused in particular on the ascertainment of market price, is George J. Stigler, "The Economics of Information," *The Journal of Political Economy*, Vol. LXIX, June 1961. From a buyer's standpoint, the cost of search is a cost of purchase—with the result that consumption will be smaller the greater the dispersion of prices and the greater the optimum amount of search. *Ibid.*, p. 223.

A market is a system of information on cost and demand, a set of signals which the business firm must learn to read as best he can. . . . The choice in favor of one price or product mix or method rather than another is only the beginning. . . . The next step is to see how far wrong the original decision was. The market is a feedback and corrective information system as well as an original information system.[25]

Figure 10.14 is a simple model portraying the decision-feedback interaction. The decision-maker acquires facts—either employs his own resources to gather them or engages specialists—of all relevant demand and supply elements of structure. On the basis of the information, he next selects the marketing mix which has the highest expected net payout. Upon implementation, he then infers from the market reaction whether the results are sufficiently close to the objectives to warrant the same mix next period, or whether there is such a discrepancy between the objectives and the results obtained that changes are required. If there is a discrepancy between goals and actual performance, the firm determines whether the unexpected result was purely a random happenstance (that is, temporary) or whether a change in the mix of marketing variables is required. This basic cycle of planning, implementation, and feedback continues.

FIGURE 10.14

INFORMATION AND THE DECISION-FEEDBACK CYCLE

We have noted that a market is a feedback and corrective information system as well as an original information system. However, in the real world there is no automatic feedback of market information to provide the basis for decisions.

Market information is extremely imperfect, coming as it does in bits and pieces, full context usually missing, permitting wide latitude in interpretation, and, therefore, offering considerable premiums to those who can read the signals just a little better, or can enforce their reactions

[25] Adelman, *op. cit.*, pp. 147–48.

a little more effectively. The range [of] uncertainty, and the degree of freedom of choice or compulsion to choose, is very wide from market to market, and even within the same firm from product to product.[26]

Because of such imperfections, there is a need for marketing research. It is

> The systematic gathering, recording, and analyzing of data for solutions to problems relating to the marketing of goods and services.[27]

What are some of the techniques of marketing research? Briefly, the techniques used are generally derived from both the physical and social sciences, but chiefly the latter, and are based particularly on the following:

1. *Economics*, for understanding supply and demand, for the concepts of distribution and of utility, and for description of the economy within which the marketing task is performed;
2. *Psychology*, for understanding buyer and seller behavior, and especially for insight into consumer motivation;
3. *Sociology*, for understanding social influences and social groupings, and particularly for the role of class structure as a determinant of consumer behavior;
4. *Statistics*, for the tools and understanding of measurement, and particularly for the mathematical laws governing the conduct and analysis of sample surveys;
5. *Accounting*, for the techniques of cost accounting requisite to measurement of what is profitable, and for evaluation of the costs of distribution;
6. *Industrial Engineering*, to measure the efficiency of the mechanical aspects of marketing (such as transportation and warehousing);
7. *Mathematics*, which provides the basis for representing and analyzing marketing relationships and deriving models of market behavior.[28]

Marketing research, as we have said, is required because of incomplete quality and quantity of information and the dynamic nature of markets. We

---

[26] *Ibid.*, p. 148.

[27] Robert Ferber, Donald F. Blankertz and Sidney Hollander, Jr., *Marketing Research* (Ronald, 1964), p. 4. The interested reader will acquire a good introduction to marketing research from the preceding book plus two other books which Professor Ferber has singly or jointly authored: Robert Ferber, *Market Research* (McGraw-Hill, paperback, 1949); and Robert Ferber and P. J. Verdoorn, *Research Methods in Economics and Business* (Macmillan, 1962). *See also* Philip Kotler, *Marketing Management: Analysis, Planning, and Control* (Prentice-Hall, 1967), Chapter 9.

[28] Ferber, *et al.*, *Marketing Research, op. cit.*, pp. 5–6. *See also ibid.*, Chapter 4, for a discussion of the relevant concepts borrowed from the behavioral sciences.

may think of marketing research as a rational means of coping with risk.[29] For example, the production of many goods and services today requires large capital investments. Within limits there is usually some flexibility in the production and marketing factors as to the precise good or service produced and/or marketed. To protect the investment, marketing research is engaged in to increase the probability that the want will be matched by production and marketing as completely as possible—that is, that the "total product" conforms closely to the want.

One may object that the more marketers know about the wants of demanders, the more they can "manipulate" wants. The issue is real, but an empirical one. Does behavior stem from attitudes? And can attitudes be changed by persuasion? These issues were dealt with briefly in Chapters 3, 8 and 9. We consider them also in Chapter 12, an analysis of promotion. At present, the important point is that wants are either fully articulated by buyers, or they are, in part at least, *deduced* by marketing research. In the latter instance, marketing research *potentially* enhances consumer sovereignty.

SUMMARY

Firms exist because they can provide a demanded good or service at a price acceptable to some or all demanders, and equal to or less than competition. The essential goal of firms is to survive—that is, to cover all costs in the long run. In an uncertain world, this means in essence, a goal of long-run profit maximization.

Profit maximization may be analyzed in terms of revenue maximization holding costs constant; cost minimization holding revenues constant; or differential advantage at the least cost.

Marketing inputs in principle are no different than any other inputs in production, finance, and so on. All types of inputs reveal varying patterns of diminishing returns in the short run, and varying patterns of returns to scale in the long run. The optimal-mix decision with respect to advertising, personal selling, product development, and other marketing inputs is either to maximize their combined output for a given cost, or for a given output, minimize their cost. Conventional production analysis using equal-output curves and budget lines are employed in marketing or any other input-mix optimality analysis.

Merchandising is the effort to increase the offering/want intersection by simultaneously adapting both the offering and want to effect a greater matching.

There are many independent variables affecting buyers. From the standpoint of a seller, some of the variables are "controllable" and some "uncontrollable." A rational firm would desire all structure elements to

[29] See the discussion of risk bearing in the present book, especially Chapter 5.

be controllable—that is, a state in which he can select from two or more values for the variable. Controllability is affected by market structure, economic and calendar time, and level of aggregation of performing units.

The marketing mix is the four comprehensive variables of "product," "channels," "promotion," and "price"—optimally combined in light of all structure elements to maximize profits. As mentioned in Chapter 4, some of the structure elements are within the performing unit, and others are from outside the unit.

Marketing research is the acquisition and use of information to increase predictability of events and decisions. Also insofar as possible, marketing research is used to facilitate gaining greater control over the elements in one's structure.

Specific Consideration of the Marketing Mix

The following three chapters contain specific analyses of the elements of the marketing mix. The reader recalls the discussion of "total product"— that is, *all* of the perceived want satisfying elements in an offering (Chapter 3). It is logical, therefore, to begin the analyses of the marketing-mix variables with "product" in which we discuss the firm's choice of product market and geographic market, and the relation of physical product to total product. Closely related to the choice of physical product (the good or service engaged in), is the set of issues concerning the marketing channel. Drawing upon the previous discussion of functions and flows (Chapter 5) and channels and agencies (Chapter 6), the marketing channel decision is coupled with "product" issues in the first of the three marketing-mix chapters (Chapter 11).

In treating the product-market, geographic-market, and marketing-channel decisions, the basic "total product" context has been set. It is logical then to consider promotion decisions with respect to the product/channel context. This we do in Chapter 12.

Finally, we consider "price" in Chapter 13, an analysis which is the logical capstone to our three-chapter consideration of the marketing mix. As the reader shall see, "price" is as comprehensive as "total product"— and is simply a different perspective of the offering/demander relationship.

SUGGESTED READINGS

Marketing Management

Joel Dean, *Managerial Economics* (Englewood Cliffs, N.J.: Prentice-Hall, Inc., 1951).

Dean is one of the few authors who provides a broad conceptual base for marketing management. From our concept of marketing as essentially all activities both pre- and post-transaction relating to the sale or lease of goods and services, we require an inclusive analytical framework for marketing management. Though now approximately twenty years old, Dean is still one of the best conceptual frameworks for managerial marketing.

John Howard, *Marketing Management* (Homewood, Ill.: Richard D. Irwin, Inc., 1963).

For several years Howard's book stood along with Dean's as the two leading conceptual and analytical marketing-management books. One of the especially useful portions of Howard's book—from which we drew in Chapter 9—is his discussion of the processes of customer learning and brand loyalty. Though several years old now, Howard's book nevertheless remains central in the introductory analytical literature.

Philip Kotler, *Marketing Management* (Englewood Cliffs, N.J.: Prentice-Hall, Inc., 1967).

Kotler's is one of the more analytical of recent texts in marketing management. Kotler, as Dean, usefully employs elementary economic analysis, but in addition, Kotler incorporates considerable behavioral analysis.

Edmund D. McGarry, "The Merchandising Function," in Reavis Cox, Wroe Alderson, and Stanley J. Shapiro, *Theory in Marketing* (Homewood, Ill.: Richard D. Irwin, Inc., 1964).

A useful framework for considering differential advantage.

David B. Urban and Glen L. Montgomery, *Management Science in Marketing* (Englewood Cliffs, N.J.: Prentice-Hall, Inc., 1969).

A relatively sophisticated, analytical book, stressing quantitative models of marketing-management decisions.

Marketing Research

Conceptual Role of Information

Armen A. Alchian, "Information Costs, Pricing, and Resource Unemployment," *Western Economic Journal*, VII, June 1969.

George J. Stigler, "The Economics of Information," *Journal of Political Economy*, LXIX, June 1961.

Two thought-provoking discussions of the role of information in firm behavior. As we have suggested, marketing research in essence is an effort to increase the precision of prediction (reduce unexplained variation). These two articles provide many implications of information for marketing management.

Organization and Techniques of Marketing Research

Seymour Banks, *Experimentation in Marketing* (New York: McGraw-Hill, Inc., 1965).

Robert Ferber, Donald F. Blankertz and Sidney Hollander, Jr., *Marketing Research* (New York: The Ronald Press Co., 1964).

Robert Ferber and P. J. Verdoorn, *Research Methods in Economics and Business* (New York: Macmillan, Inc., 1962).

Paul Green and Donald Tull, *Research for Marketing Decisions* (Englewood Cliffs, N.J.: Prentice-Hall, Inc., 1966).

W. A. Spurr and C. P. Bonini, *Statistical Analysis for Business Decisions* (Homewood, Ill.: Richard D. Irwin, Inc., 1967).

R. E. Frank, Alfred A. Kuehn, and William F. Massy, *Quantitative Techniques in Marketing Analysis* (Homewood, Ill.: Richard D. Irwin, Inc., 1962).

These are a few of the leading books in research design and techniques in marketing research.

11

Product
and channel decisions
and performance

The present chapter analyzes product and channel decisions in the firm. The succeeding two chapters deal with promotion decisions and price decisions respectively. Each of the analyses is concerned with the rationale of the decisions and certain of the effects.

Ideally, one would analyze the marketing-mix decisions *simultaneously*. That is, he would look at the product decision and effects concomitantly with the channel, promotion, and price decisions and effects. Obviously, each of the four "controllable" variables influences as well as in influenced by the other three. However, a simultaneous analysis of the four variables would be extremely complex. The path of least resistance is to analyze each separately, but in so doing to point out the interrelationship of the four controllable variables in the marketing mix.

TOTAL PRODUCT

The logic of marketing management lies in the manipulation of certain variables to effect a total product that so efficiently matches wants that the firm attains its goals. The matching of wants in a manner that provides differential advantage is conceptualized in "merchandising."[1]

[1] Refer to Chapter 10.

254

The most logical beginning in analyzing the marketing mix is the "product." The element most fundamental in a transaction is the offering given up by the seller (lessor) and acquired by the buyer (lessee). It may be a consumer product, or a consumer or intermediate service, or factor of production. In many respects the argument is the same. The owner of a factor of production, good, or service (or combination of them), aware of a current or probable demand for his good or service, determines *if* and *how* he can satisfy the demand and still attain his own goals. Before deciding his asking price, his promotion, and his distribution channels, he must select the basic product markets in which he wishes to participate.[2] For example, one desiring to engage in consumer-appliance manufacturing may choose, in response to perceived demand, to manufacture and market television sets. But, of course, "television sets" embrace a whole spectrum of sizes and attributes. Thus, he would then select the specific product market(s)—that is, further deciding through marketing research as to color and/or black-and-white sets; the quality range; the size range; and so on. Ultimately, in conformance with expressed or inferred demand vis-à-vis supply capabilities, the manufacturer would arrive at precisely what television sets he was going to produce and market. At this point, by carefully analyzing the want, he would shape his total product.[3]

Categories of Products Based on Customer Behavior

All goods and services (including factors of production) in any transaction may be classified by the type of customer into one of two categories: ultimate-consumer, retail transaction; or non-ultimate-consumer, wholesale transaction.[4]

Products in Retail Transactions

The classification of retail offerings is based on the customer perception of and behavior with respect to the offerings. Offerings (including services) sold at retail, classified by buyer behavior, may be separated into three

---

[2] The reader may refer to Chapter 3 to recall the discussion of product and geographic markets and physical product.

[3] The conception of product developed in Chapter 3 is that the total product is determined by buyer perception of a seller's offering, and typically exceeds the "physical product." This important distinction between physical and total product is also made by E. J. McCarthy, *Basic Marketing: A Managerial Approach* (rev. ed., Irwin, 1964), Chapter 11; and by Philip Kotler, *Marketing Management* (Prentice-Hall, 1967), pp. 288 ff.

In the case of completely homogeneous physical units, for example, agricultural commodities within a particular grade, the distinction between physical product and total product is perhaps easier to make. See L. B. Darrah, *Food Marketing* (Ronald, 1967), pp. 5–9.

[4] Refer to Chapter 3 for the definitions.

categories: (1) convenience goods, (2) shopping goods, and (3) specialty goods.[5]

(1) Convenience goods. Goods for which the consumer wishes to minimize effort in acquiring. Included as a convenience good is any good for which the marginal gain in want-satisfaction from searching and comparing alternative offerings is *less* than the marginal cost (in terms of time, effort, and so on) of search. Although the designation of convenience and the other two categories of goods is a matter of personal perception, goods which are considered convenience goods by many consumers are, for example, chewing gum, razor blades, and staple food items.

(2) Shopping goods. Goods for which a consumer believes that to a point there is a net gain in searching and comparing alternatives. Comparison of price and quality are made between two or more offerings. Examples of shopping goods for many consumers are relatively expensive or risky items as stoves, washing machines, houses, automobiles, clothes, especially fashion items, liability and health insurance, and good wines.

(3) Specialty goods. Goods or brands (or sources of supply) for which the consumer will make a specific purchasing effort to acquire (patronize). For many consumers examples of specialty goods are Hickey-Freeman or Brooks Brothers men's suits, Cadillac automobiles, Christian Dior gowns, a specific barber or hairdresser, a particular brand of gasoline, or more particularly, a specific service station. A good (or source of supply) acquires a specialty status whenever a customer manifests an intended *loyalty* toward it.

Every marketer, whether in retail *or* wholesale markets, would like to create a "specialty" status for his total product. With respect to consumer goods, the logic of marketing management is that of a firm attempting to change the customer perception of its offerings from convenience goods (that is, brand indifference) and shopping goods (some relevance of brand) to that of specialty goods (maximum relevance of brand or source).[6]

---

[5] This three-fold classification of consumers' goods is long-standing in the literature of marketing. In 1923, Professor Melvin T. Copeland of the Harvard Business School published an article setting forth the behavioral distinctions of products sold at retail: "Relation of Consumers' Buying Habits to Marketing Methods," *Harvard Business Review*, April 1923, pp. 282–9. Virtually all textbooks in marketing utilize this basic three-way scheme. For two sound elaborations of consumers' goods classifications, *see* Kotler, *op. cit.*, pp. 292–5; and E. W. Cundiff and R. R. Still, *Basic Marketing* (Prentice-Hall, 1964), pp. 39–45.

[6] The latter status is directly related to the concepts of positive customer learning, inelastic demand, and differential advantage.

Products in Wholesale Transactions

Offerings sold in wholesale markets are either purchased by wholesale middlemen or retailers for resale, or they are purchased by industrial or any of several types of institutional customers. Industrial goods are goods used in the production of other goods. Land, labor and capital are the broad categories of "industrial goods." More specifically, other than labor, most industrial goods may be placed into one of four categories: (1) equipment and physical facilities used in producing goods or services; (2) materials entering into the product, (3) manufacturing or service supplies, and (4) management materials.[7]

1. Equipment and physical facilities used in producing goods or services. In this category are included installations, minor equipment, and land and buildings.
2. Material entering into the product. This category of industrial goods includes raw materials, semi-manufactured goods, and fabricating parts.
3. Manufacturing or service supplies. These are goods essential to the business operations of the customers but do not become part of the finished product. Examples are fuel oil, coal, compressed oxygen.
4. Management materials. Included in the category are office equipment and office suppliers.[8]

When one speaks of wholesale transactions, he must remember that the customers range from middlemen, to processors and manufacturers, to institutions, to governments. Also, the offerings range from finished physical industrial goods and services, and range from very costly and durable capital equipment to inexpensive services and supplies. The common characteristic of wholesale transactions is that the customer demand is a demand derived from other markets, or other activities.[9]

Because wholesale-market demand is derived, it is (or becomes more) inelastic. For example, if a retailer faces a substantial consumer demand for a particular good, the retailer in buying will be to some extent less price sensitive than he otherwise might be. Not that he is irrational—recognizing the retail price possibilities, he enters the wholesale market with interest in acquiring the desired good within some price *range*. If a manufacturer perceives a strong demand for a product he will be intensely interested in acquiring all the required inputs for the production of the demanded

---

[7] Cundiff and Still, *op. cit.*, pp. 46–49.

[8] For greater detail of all categories, *see ibid.*, or, for example, McCarthy, *op. cit.*, Chapter 15.

[9] In democracies the government demand for goods may be thought of as a demand derived from constituents' demand. A similar argument may be made for goods demanded by nonprofit philanthropic organizations, and so on.

product. Thus, if he needs grinding wheels to produce the product, his demand for grinding wheels may be relatively inelastic. However, *among the sellers* of grinding wheels, there may be considerable price *elasticity* of demand. Although intent on buying the needed grinding wheels, the manufacturer as a profit maximizer will tend to patronize the lowest-priced supplier, other things being equal.[10]

THE FIRM'S CHOICE OF OFFERINGS AND OFFERING ASSORTMENTS

How does a firm select a good or service to market? Or, with respect to current offerings, how does a firm choose to add or delete from its assortment?

Choice of An Offering

The marketing economy is a large set of specialists, each engaging in a number of productive activities and selling their resulting outputs at prices in the long run exceeding or equal to the costs of production and marketing. A new firm intending to sell a good or service can succeed only if it can produce and market its offering at a price less than or equal to that at which extant firms are selling the *same* product (that is, firms in the same product market).[11] Clearly, it is easiest for a firm if it markets a unique offering for which there is a demand. In such an instance, the firm, for some period at least, will enjoy a monopoly.

A firm, therefore, is a set of productive resources assembled by an entrepreneur in the expectation of performing one or more functions at a net return equal to but preferably greater than the market average. When one can perform an activity at a cost at less than the market, he is especially motivated to engage in the activity. When he cannot be more efficient than the market—unless the activity is a minor subsidiary activity in which production or customer convenience is at stake or unless it serves to lower

[10] The derived-demand and price-inelastic nature of wholesale transactions frequently produces larger price fluctuations in wholesale markets than in retail markets. For an elementary discussion of these phenomena, *see* McCarthy, *loc. cit.*

[11] A classic statement on the economic opportunity for a new firm is that of R. H. Coase, "The Nature of the Firm," *Economica,* New Series, Vol. IV (1937), reprinted in G. J. Stigler and K. E. Boulding (eds.), *Readings in Price Theory* (Irwin, 1952). Another useful basic conceptualization of the firm is in E. A. G. Robinson, *The Structure of Competitive Industry* (University of Chicago Press, 1958, paperback). Robinson's book originally published in 1931, remains relevant today in explaining firms' behavior. *See* George J. Stigler, "The Division of Labor is Limited by the Extent of the Market," *The Journal of Political Economy,* Vol. LIX, June 1951, reprinted in Perry Bliss, *Marketing and the Behavioral Sciences* (Allyn and Bacon, 1963), pp. 262–275. Also refer to the discussion in the present book in Chapters 5, 6, and 10.

average cost or increase demand for other goods—he probably will not engage in it. Firms continually assess each of their various current operations in terms of whether it would be more economical to buy the activity on the market. Purchasing agents in firms evaluate production capabilities within the firm vis-à-vis market conditions to determine whether the firm should make or buy. The comparison of internal and external economies underlies vertical integration—that is, the latter is the perceived greater profitability in performing preceding or succeeding activities within the firm.[12] For example, frequently the decision of a manufacturer of a consumer good to engage in wholesaling and retailing activities is based in large part on the perceived superior long-run efficiency of internal over external performance of the activities.

The one or more pools of productive resources which at any point in time constitute a firm are to an extent flexible as to what those pools of resources can produce (market). Thus, based on its management resource with knowledge of certain production and marketing activities, plant and equipment with particular production capability, and some marketing channel and promotional capability, a firm can vary its output within some finite limits. Hence, some range of demand is exploitable by any given firm. Within the unique capabilities of the set of resources constituting the firm, management attempts to satisfy those wants for goods and services which will utilize the resources most efficiently toward the maximization of profits.[13] As we pointed out in Chapter 10, profit maximization is the maximization of $(TR - TC)$, and hence, management assesses the strength and probable duration of various exploitable demands as well as the relative efficiencies in matching the several wants. The particular product and geographic market(s) selected are those which most probably will provide the maximum long-run difference between total revenues and total costs.

The Offering-assortment Decision

If the world were static rather than dynamic, a firm would select once and for all, one or more offerings to market. The choice of the goods or services which would maximize profits under the given cost and demand conditions would be a one-time decision. From then on, in that neither cost nor demand conditions would change, the optimal marketing mix could be readily determined and maintained.

[12] Vertical integration is a decision typically more complex than merely the existence of *internal economies* exceeding the economies of external specialists. Although not a sufficient condition, internal economies are in the long run certainly a necessary condition. Some evidence that they are not the full explanation of vertical integration is found in Stanley C. Hollander, "Who Does the Work of Retailing?", *Journal of Marketing*, July 1964. *See also* the discussion of external economies in agencies and channels in the present book in Chapter 6.

[13] *See* John C. Narver, "Supply Space and Horizontality in Firms and Mergers," *St. John's Law Reveiw*, Spring, 1970.

The world, of course, is dynamic, not static. Relative profitability of markets changes because cost and demand change. Cost conditions change due to changing technologies, changing supply conditions in factor markets, and emergence of external economies or diseconomies. Similarly, demand conditions change because of elements such as changing customer income and tastes, new government policies, and changes in the intensity and character of the competition.

What is the rationale for adding new offerings to (or deleting some existing offerings from) the assortment? The underlying reason, of course, for adding a new good or service to the line is to increase long-run profits.[14] Virtually all product additions can be conceived of as either (1) utilizing idle capacity within the current production and marketing resources; (2) reducing risk; (3) experiencing a saturation of current markets; (4) exploiting potential economies of scale; and (5) generating demand for current products by adding other products.

1. Idle Capacity.   There are many meanings of "idle capacity." Strictly speaking, idle capacity means the underutilization of a resource, evidenced by an output less than the lowest point on the short-run average cost curve. But focusing on profits rather than solely on costs, a better meaning is underutilization in the sense of total-profit opportunities.

Idle capacity occurs in any production or marketing factor that cannot be exactly and immediately adjusted for short-run output changes. Indivisible inputs make up much of production and to an extent marketing as well; hence, idle capacity is rather pervasive in the firm.

Three substantial sources of idle capacity are (1) secular shifts in demand brought about by competitive firms or changes in requirements of customers; (2) vertical integration in which the firm has at one or more levels an output in excess of its own requirements, or in which the firm must add products if it is fully to respond to customer wants at a given level in the distribution process; and (3) research which creates excess capacity by making current offerings and their production obsolescent, and which also develops new goods and services to absorb excess capacity.[15]

---

[14] Discussions of the conceptual basis of the new-product-addition decision may be found in Joel Dean, *Managerial Economics* (Prentice-Hall, 1951), pp. 115–120; John C. Narver, *Conglomerate Mergers and Market Competition* (Berkeley: University of California, 1967), Chapter 4; and Michael Gort, "Diversification, Mergers, and Profits," in William W. Alberts and Joel E. Segall, *The Corporate Merger* (University of Chicago Press, 1966).

Three other discussions highlighting diversification motives are W. L. Thorp and W. F. Crowder, *The Structure of Industry*, TNEC Monograph 27 (U.S. Government Printing Office, 1941), Part VI; Kenneth R. Andrews, "Product Diversification and the Public Interest," *Harvard Business Review*, XXIX (July 1951); and Thomas A. Staudt, "Program for Product Diversification," *Harvard Business Review*, XXXII (November–December 1954).

See the discussion of the meaning of "new product" in Chapter 3 of the present book.

[15] Dean, *op. cit.*, pp. 116–120.

2. Reduction of Risk.   The reduction of risk is a frequent inducement to add offerings, or to enter new geographic markets. If the demand bases for the firm's offerings is narrow and/or subject to substantial fluctuations, the firm will choose to enter markets in which the demand is either independent of or countercyclical to the demand in extant markets. The spreading of risk by diversifying into a number of markets of *zero* cross elasticity of demand stabilizes the revenue and profit streams in the firm. The assumption is that demand in all markets will not behave identically and simultaneously and in particular, that among the markets, minuses will be offset elsewhere by positive changes.

Stabilized revenues and profit flows can reduce the variance of dividend-payout. More generally, stabilized earnings will tend to increase the discounted present value (market value) of the firm.[16]

Another type of risk, inducing diversification, is the risk of antitrust prosecution for monopolizing a market. Although the issues are complex, one may generalize that firms engaging in interstate commerce and with large market shares recognize the increasing antitrust risk in continuing to further their share of a given product and geographic market. They are induced, therefore, to diversify into other markets. (See the discussion of antitrust in Chapter 14.)

3. Saturation of Current Markets.   Declining marginal profitability in current markets means an increasing opportunity cost in continuing in the present markets. Or, with constant or even increasing marginal profitability in current markets, rapidly growing and accessible new markets may offer profit potential greater than the current markets.

Figure 11.1 depicts a sales curve in which increased marketing inputs yield decreasing sales. For this offering, the market potential has become saturated. The declining marginal productivity of marketing effort means, of course, a rising marginal cost—assuming the firm buys its inputs at a constant unit cost for each unit of advertising, personal selling and other inputs.

Figure 11.2 relates to the sales curve of Figure 11.1 by showing the corresponding decreasing and then increasing marginal costs of marketing— depicted by the decreasing and then increasing slope of the total cost curve. Figure 11.3 shows explicitly the associated average and marginal cost curves, the rising unit costs a direct function of the decreasing marginal productivity of marketing in the given market.

4. Exploiting Economies of Scale.   In some cases a firm may wish to increase its scale of activity to take advantage of lower average costs of production and marketing. Assuming no effects on demand and assuming a situation of substantially increasing returns to scale, a firm as in Figure 11.4 may wish

[16] William W. Alberts, "The Profitability of Growth by Merger," in W. W. Alberts and J. E. Segall, *The Corporate Merger, op. cit.*

to enlarge its scale from that depicted by AC_1 to AC_2. It is rational for a firm to exploit increasing returns to scale (decreasing long-run average cost) only if it will increase its long-run total profit. Figure 11.4 suggests such an increase in total profit, for current profits, *abcd*, are less than profits at the larger scale, *efgh*. The profit-maximizing outputs for the two scales are respectively Q_1 and Q_2. To increase the quantity demanded to correspond to the new production and marketing scale, the firm must reduce its average price from *cj* to *gk*. Figure 11.4 shows only an increase in total profits from a larger scale; however, the figure does not depict a profit-maximizing equilibrium. The latter would be the scale (still larger than AC_2) at which *long-run MC* intersected *MR*. Nevertheless, Figure 11.4 is suggestive.

FIGURE 11.1

A PRODUCT'S SALES CURVE SHOWING INCREASING AND THEN DIMINISHING MARGINAL RETURNS TO MARKETING EFFORT.

An example of adding products to exploit economies of scale is a relatively small grocery store changing its structure to that of a supermarket by enlarging the selling space and adding other food and nonfood related items.[17]

---

[17] Although not dramatic in magnitude, some economies of scale are possible in food retailing. See *Organization and Competition in Food Retailing*, National Commission on Food Marketing, Technical Study No. 7, June 1966, Chapter 7.

The analysis of scale effects in retailing is somewhat complicated, for as firm size increases, the total product (for many consumers) changes. That is, many consumers perceive want-satisfying elements offered by, say, a corner grocery store different from those offered by a large supermarket. Moreover, as we discuss in Chapter 13, it is difficult to compare prices between two different bundles of utility.

FIGURE 11.2

AN OFFERING'S TOTAL COST CURVE SHOWING DECREASING AND THEN INCREASING MARGINAL COST OF MARKETING AS THE MARKET BECOMES SATURATED.

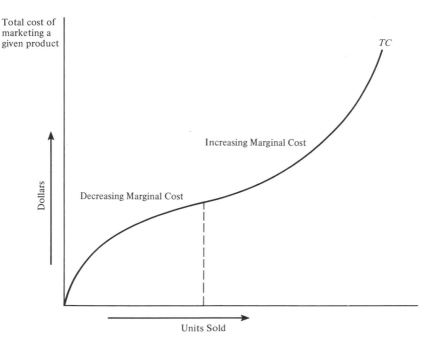

In Figure 11.4, the demand curve, D, represents the total demand for grocery products. The lower price-range segment associated with AC_2 is consistent with empirical data suggesting the lower average prices of supermarkets vis-à-vis smaller independent stores.[18] The profit maximizing outputs for the two scales of activity are respectively Q_1 and Q_2.

5. Generating Demand for Current Products by Adding Other Products. Some products are consumed jointly or at least are closely associated in use. Examples are fishing rods, reels, and lures; beer and pretzels or other snack food; gasoline and motor oil; men's ties and shirts; and pencils and paper. The addition to an assortment of a good or service which typically is used in conjunction with another good or service in the assortment may increase the demand for the original offering. Within a retail agency such as a supermarket, a specialty store, or a department store, a rational manager, insofar as possible, will add jointly demanded goods and services to his assortment. Moreover, he will display the items together to increase the stimulation of wants.

[18] *Ibid.*, Chapters 16 and 17. *See also Special Studies in Food Marketing,* National Commission on Food Marketing, Technical Study No. 10, June 1966, "Retail Food Prices in Low and Higher Income Areas."

FIGURE 11.3

THE AVERAGE AND MARGINAL COST CURVES

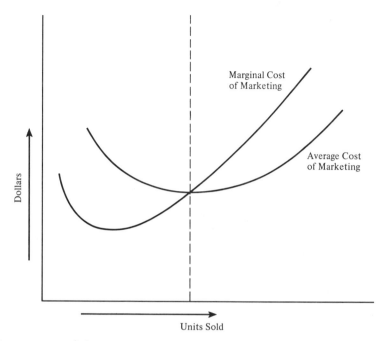

A variation of the preceding is the adding of an offering which because of its strong demand builds traffic for *all other* offerings in the store in the case of a retailer, or in the product line in the case of a wholesaler or manufacturer. In retailing, a "loss leader" (or "profit leader") is a good or service that attracts consumers to the place of business. The increased traffic in the store yields increases in demand for all offerings such as impulse items that are "traffic elastic"—that is, products whose demand rises at least in proportion to the number of consumers. Typically a good or service serving as a traffic builder is a frequently purchased or otherwise well-known shopping good and is offered at a substantially reduced price. In competitive markets a retailer may have several offerings he alternately uses as profit leaders—switching frequently among them to keep the competition off guard.[19]

[19] See Alfred R. Oxenfeldt, "Product Line Pricing," *Harvard Business Review* (July–August 1966); Perry Bliss, "Non-price Competition at the Department Store Level," *Journal of Marketing,* XVII, April 1953. Reprinted in Stanley C. Hollander, *Explorations in Retailing* MSU Business Studies (Michigan State University, 1959); and Richard Holton, "Price Discrimination at Retail: The Supermarket Case," *Journal of Industrial Economics,* VI, October 1957. For a more technical presentation *see* R. H. Coase, "Monopoly Pricing with Interrelated Costs and Demands," *Economica,* N.S. XIII, November 1956.

FIGURE 11.4

PRODUCT ADDITIONS TO EXPLOIT ECONOMIES OF SCALE

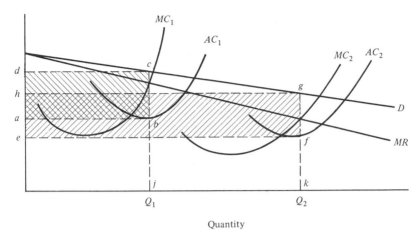

Quantity

Technically, a profit leader is an "externality" to other offerings in the firm's assortment: That is, from this source external to them, one or more other offerings experience either or both a lower average cost or increased demand. Frequently firms in wholesale or retail markets also utilize "attractive" *inputs* in the hope for similar externalities. For example, it is by no means unknown for firms to hire All-American athletes to increase the visibility of the entire product line. The effect, if successful, is to obtain from a given input (whether it be a "sensational" new product or an All-American) a greater than proportionate increase in total sales.

From this example, we see that "product" decisions are at times inseparable from "promotion" decisions. Without much effort the reader can anticipate an equal phenomenon associated with certain "channel" and "price" decisions. Once again we repeat: The total product includes all four "controllable" variables and any one or all may alter customer perception of want-satisfying elements in an offering.

Size of the Offering Assortment

At what point does the firm stop adding offerings and/or cease entering new geographic markets? The profit-maximizing firm will continue to expand operations—whether through horizontal, vertical, or new-market growth—until the marginal cost of the additional sales exceeds the marginal revenue derived from the additional sales. That is, until marginal profits are zero. For example, a retail store will continue to add goods to its line—if it determines that it cannot profitably enlarge its sales of current offerings—until the cost of the marginal unit in the marginal market exceeds the marginal revenue. In the real world, these costs and revenues would be virtually impossible to determine precisely. However, in principle, the firm, upon choosing growth through product and geographic diversification, continues to enter new markets until it encounters approximately the condition of $MC = MR$.[20]

Many firms in diversifying experience a relatively constant MC over a considerable range of output. A flat MC curve implies constant marginal productivity of the production and marketing inputs and non-varying input prices (or equally offsetting changes). The reason for no undue increase in marginal cost is that there is frequently excess capacity in the form of equipment, personnel, and organization through the firm. Moreover, many resources (for example, management, salesmen, and so on) are flexible in what they can produce. Thus, depending on the magnitude of excess capacity and flexibility of resources, the firm may be able to enter a considerable number of product markets without encountering sharply rising marginal cost.[21]

The Magnitude of New Product Additions

It is extremely rare for a firm to sell in only one product market.[22] For the five comprehensive reasons discussed above, firms on the average con-

---

[20] The conceptual argument of a firm entering new geographic or product markets up to the point of $MC = MR$, is presented in Eli W. Clemens, "Price Discrimination and the Multiple-Product Firm," *The Review of Economic Studies*, Vol. XIX (1950–51), reprinted in R. B. Heflebower and G. W. Stocking, *Readings in Industrial Organization and Public Policy* (Irwin, 1958), pp. 262–276.

Clemens believes businessmen have a rather accurate, even though subjective, knowledge of the full marginal costs of increasing their activity. "When [the businessman] says that the profit on a certain additional piece of business is 'not worth his time and trouble,' he is giving expression to a very real concept of marginal cost." *Ibid.*, p. 272.

[21] The technological features described, and which account for the relatively constant MC over a range of output, are common to many manufacturing and merchandising firms: "The primary activities of diversifying firms are technologically related to a vast range of products." Gort, *Diversification and Integration in American Industry, op. cit.*, p. 109. Also, *ibid.*, Chapters 1 and 7 *passim.* Clemens alludes to the same phenomenon; "What a firm has to sell is not a product, but rather its capacity to produce." Clemens, *op. cit.*, p. 276.

Cost structures of high fixed costs and common costs force firms to operate as close to economic capacity as possible. For example, retailers' cost structures are typically those of high fixed costs and common costs. Moreover, retailers and many other diversified firms have interrelated demands (negative cross-elasticities) among products. Thus a multi-product firm which has high fixed and common costs, operates near capacity by entering additional markets and practicing price discrimination. Richard H. Holton, "Price Discriminaton at Retail: The Supermarket Case," *Journal of Industrial Economics*, VI (October 1957); Fritz Machlup, "Characteristics and Types of Price Discrimination," *Business Concentration and Price Policy*, National Bureau of Economic Research (Princeton University Press, 1955), p. 398 and M. A. Adelman, *op. cit.*, "The 'Product' and 'Price' in Distribution," *American Economic Review*, May 1957, especially pp. 268, 269, and 271. See Chapter 13 in the present book for additional comments on price discrimination.

[22] *See* the discussion of diversification in Chapter 3 of the present book.

tinually increase the number of product markets (and geographic markets) in which they sell goods and services. Market diversification, in the sense both of product-market and geographic-market diversification, characterizes modern business.

The data on the extent of diversification are not nearly as complete nor accurate as one would desire. The best source of data on market diversification—although far from perfect—is the U.S. Census which compiles product information at various levels of SIC (Standard Industrial Classification) aggregation. One shortcoming is that Census "products" are not necessarily offerings in the same product market.[23]

Not surprisingly, there are more data on offering assortments of the largest corporations than on smaller firms. To what extent are the large corporations entering new product markets? At the five-digit or "product class" level of detail, data indicate that among the 1000 largest industrial firms there has been considerable product diversification between the years 1950 and 1962. Again, data at the five-digit level tend to understate the true extent of product (and geographic markets) diversification.[24]

As Figure 11.5 indicates, of the 1000 largest industrial firms in 1962, only 49 were selling in but one five-digit category; whereas, in 1950, 78 were selling in only one five-digit category. Similarly, of companies producing two to five offerings, there were 354 in 1950, and 223 in 1962. Thus, in 1962 there were fewer large companies specializing in but one to five offerings. On the other hand, the chart reveals the scope of increased offering assortments, that is, of increased product diversification. Some 477 firms produced six to fifteen products in 1962; whereas, 432 produced this range of products in 1950. An even greater increase was evidenced in numbers of firms which were substantially diversified in terms of the number of product markets. Among the 1000 largest firms, 128 produced sixteen to fifty products in 1950, but this number jumped to 236 in 1962. Finally, between 1950 and 1962, there was almost a one hundred percent increase in the number of firms—eight firms compared to fifteen firms—producing over fifty products.[25]

---

[23] The rationale of the SIC system can be found in U.S. Congress, Senate, Committee on the Judiciary, Subcommittee on Anti-trust and Monopoly, 89th Congress, 2d Session, 1966, *Concentration Ratios in Manufacturing Industry, 1963, Part I*, p. xii.

One who uses Census data should be extremely cautious. Any reader interested in pursuing the matter further, should see *ibid.*, especially the views of Senator E. McK. Dirksen and Senator R. L. Hruska, pp. v-viii. *See also* Joe S. Bain, *Industrial Organization* (Wiley, 1959), pp. 108–118, and Eugene Singer, *Antitrust Economics: Selected Legal Cases and Economic Models* (Prentice-Hall, 1968), Chapter 14.

[24] For example, in the steel industry one five-digit category is "hot-rolled sheets and strip, including tin mill products." Clearly hot-rolled sheets have separate markets from hot-rolled strip, and from tin mill products.

[25] The data in Figure 5 are from the testimony of Harrison F. Houghton, Federal Trade Commission, before the U.S. Senate, Subcommittee on Antitrust and Monopoly, of the Committee on the Judiciary, *Hearings on Economic Concentration, Part I: Overall and Conglomerate Aspects*, 88th Congress, 2d Session, 1964, pp. 156–196.

FIGURE 11.5

DISTRIBUTION OF 1000 LARGEST INDUSTRIAL FIRMS ACCORDING TO NUMBER OF FIVE-DIGIT PRODUCTS, 1950 AND 1962

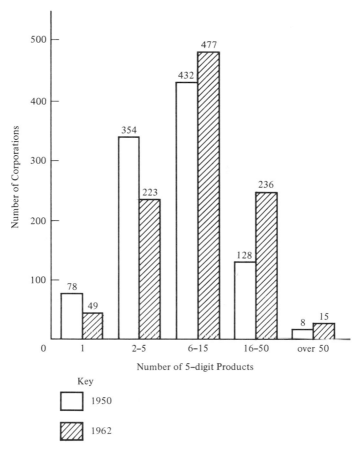

Other studies indicate that increased diversification has characterized *all* of manufacturing and not simply the largest 1000 firms. In the past two decades firms of all sizes have on the average increased the number of product and geographic markets in which they sold goods and services.[26]

Avenues to Adding Offerings

A firm can increase its product assortment—that is, enter a product market new to it—either by internally investing or by acquiring another firm currently producing the product. The latter avenue, merger, is frequently utilized by firms wishing not only to enter a particular product market, but to begin with a share of the market and to begin with an

[26] For an analysis in support of this generalization *see* John C. Narver, *Conglomerate Mergers and Market Competition, op. cit.,* Chapter 2.

on-going production and marketing operations. Mergers taking a firm into product and geographic markets new to it—as we pointed out in Chapter 3— are called "conglomerate mergers."[27] The majority of mergers in recent years have been conglomerate mergers; whereas, in earlier periods, horizontal mergers predominated.[28]

We have indicated five basic reasons for diversification. For what reasons is this accomplished by merger? Empirical studies reveal that firms diversify through merger to (1) take advantage of the fact that it frequently is less expensive to buy a current firm than to build an equivalent operation anew; (2) enjoy greater speed (let alone frequently lower expense) in entering attractive markets such as rapidly growing markets; (3) gain economies of size—that is, attain a more efficient size more rapidly; (4) reduce risks quickly (if an exogeneous change, such as diminution of demand, new competition, and so on, looms ahead in current markets); (5) enter markets with distinctly different technologies (the technical background is, of course, supplied by the acquired firms); (6) acquire key personnel—those of proven ability, therefore adding to the attractiveness of their employing firm as a merger object; (7) achieve the benefits diversification can bring (such as one or more of the reasons for diversification cited earlier) *and* to realize tax benefits such as negative-profit write-offs from acquiring a firm which has experienced net losses; and (8) acquire an under-valued firm—that is, a "bargain." The preceding, although not exhaustive, constitute the major reasons why firms choose to carry out their diversification by means of merger.[29]

Table 11.1 presents the number of mergers and acquisitions recorded by the Federal Trade Commission from a review of selected financial periodicals for the period 1955 to 1966. From Table 11.1, one sees that

[27] To repeat the point in Chapter 3, "conglomerate merger" means simply all market-diversification mergers.

[28] John C. Narver, "Conglomerate Mergers and the Controversy over Conglomerate Mergers," *Journal of Marketing,* July 1967, text at n. 6; and Narver, "Some Observations on the Impact of Antitrust Merger Policy on Marketing," *Journal of Marketing,* XXXIII, January 1969. See Table 11.2 and accompanying text below.

[29] The motives for diversification-by-merger are drawn from Michael Gort, "Diversification, Mergers, and Profits," in W. W. Alberts and J. E. Segall, *The Corporate Merger, op. cit.,* pp. 42–44, W. W. Alberts, *ibid.,* Chapter 11; and John C. Narver, *Conglomerate Mergers and Market Competition, op. cit.,* pp. 69–71. Gort believes that merger is more likely to be attractive for defensive diversification than for the exploitation of opportunities in industries with above-average profits. He defines decisions of a defensive type as those to achieve a more efficient size of firm, to reduce risks, to use spare resources, or to escape from the adverse effects of managerial morale of a decline in firm size, Gort, *loc. cit.*

For a discussion of merger motivations aside from form—that is, not limited to either horizontal, vertical, or conglomerate mergers—*see* references cited in Narver, *ibid.,* p. 71, n. 10; Alberts and Segall, *ibid.,* and Federal Trade Commission, *Economic Report on Corporate Mergers,* 1969.

mergers in total (that is, horizontal, vertical, and diversification) have maintained a level through the 'sixties substantially higher than the average for
the period 1955–1959. But specifically, what about diversification or conglomerate mergers? Table 11.2 shows the relative position of conglomerate
mergers among the total "large" manufacturing and mining mergers (the
acquired firm has assets of ten million dollars or more). We have seen that
firms are continually diversifying into new product and geographic markets,
and in Table 11.1, that mergers in the 'sixties are high both absolutely and
relative to the late fifties. From Table 11.2 we see that conglomerate mergers
of one type or another comprise the vast majority of all large mergers in
manufacturing and mining.

TABLE 11.1

**NUMBER OF MERGERS AND ACQUISITIONS RECORDED, BY MAJOR INDUSTRIAL GROUPING
OF ACQUIRING COMPANY, 1955 TO 1966**

Acquiring company	1955-1959 Total	Annual average	1960	1961	1962	1963	1964	1965	1966
Full acquisitions[1]	4,984	997	1,216	1,592	1,504	1,329	1,519	1,628	1,517
Mining	318	64	48	74	48	79	59	62	55
Manufacturing	3,691	738	918	1,043	985	906	1,006	1,063	1,051
Trade[2]	480	96	127	255	235	186	207	191	188
Services and others[3]	495	99	123	220	236	158	247	312	223

[1] Acquisitions involving more than half of the assets or stock of other independent companies, subsidiaries of other independent companies, and whole divisions of other independent companies.
[2] Wholesale and retail trade combined.
[3] "Others" consists mainly of companies engaged in insurance, warehousing and storage, commercial
farming, contract construction, and extending credit to businesses and individuals (other than banks).
Source: Willard F. Mueller, Director, Bureau of Economics, Federal Trade Commission, Statement
before the Select Committee on Small Business, United States Senate, March 15, 1967, Appendix
Table 1.

In the period 1963–1966, conglomerate mergers comprised 71 percent
of all large mergers in manufacturing and mining. This figure rose to 84
percent in 1967, and to 89 percent in 1968. Product-line extension mergers
accounted for 52 percent of all large mergers in the period 1963–1966 and
61 percent in 1967, but fell to 39 percent in 1968. From the early part of
the 1960s to the present the unrelated or "pure" conglomerate mergers have
increased as a percentage of all large mergers to their peak level of 44 percent of all large mergers in 1968.[30]

[30] Some of the reasons for the rise of these unrelated mergers and certain of their impli-
cations are discussed in Narver, "Some Observations on the Impact of Antitrust Merger
Policy on Marketing," *op. cit.* See also the extensive discussions in FTC, *Economic
Report, op. cit.*

TABLE 11.2

PERCENTAGE DISTRIBUTION OF LARGE ACQUISITIONS (ACQUIRED FIRM ASSETS EXCEED TEN MILLION DOLLARS) MANUFACTURING AND MINING, BY TYPE OF MERGER, 1951-68

Type of Merger	1951-1954	1955-1958	1959-1962	1963-1966	1967	1968
Horizontal	37.0	28.0	17.0	15.0	8.0	4.0
Vertical	12.0	16.0	18.0	15.0	8.0	7.0
Conglomerate	51.0	56.0	65.0	71.0	84.0	89.0
Production extension	37.0	47.0	39.0	52.0	61.0	39.0
Market extension	6.0	4.0	8.0	5.0	1.0	6.0
Pure conglomerate	7.0	5.0	17.0	14.0	22.0	44.0
Total	100.0	100.0	100.0	100.0	100.0	100.0

Source: Narver, "Some Observations on the Impact of Antitrust Merger Policy on Marketing," *op. cit.*, p. 28, and Federal Trade Commission, *Economic Report on Corporate Mergers* (1969), p. 61.

Demand and Input Relationships in Diversification

We will employ the term "commonality" to refer to demand and/or input relationships in diversification.[31] What is the average commonality in character market diversification? Much of contemporary diversification by *internal investment* is into product and geographic markets which are demand-complementary and/or input-related to the firm's current markets and activities.[32]

Table 11.2 shows the high proportion of all large mergers which represent economically related diversification. From the study by Gort as well as from the Alberts and Segall symposium on mergers, the overriding twofold implication is that typically (1) internal investment is a more profitable growth avenue than merger and (2) internal investment on average leads the profit-maximizing firm to diversify into supply or demand related markets. It is not surprising therefore that most diversification mergers and most internal investment diversification are of an economically related type.

There are only two fundamental ways in which a merger can be profitable: (1) pecuniary and real economies—which respectively include lower input prices and/or market power on the one hand, and increased

[31] The definition of "product diversification," given in Chapter 3, is adding a good or service which is perceived by buyers as non-substitutable for the firm's current products. When an added good or service is thus perceived, the addition has no demand positive-cross-elasticity relationship to the firm's other products. It may, however, have negative-cross-elasticity of demand relationships to them, as well as common inputs.

[32] Stigler, among others, believes that in diversification it is unusual not to find some connections in marketing, production, purchasing, research, and other activities. George J. Stigler in "Forward" to Michael Gort, *Diversification and Integration in American Industry*, National Bureau of Economic Research (Princeton University Press, 1962), p. xix. Gort's findings support a conclusion of high-commonality in much of diversification. Gort states that in choosing among diversification alternatives equally attractive, a firm will usually select the one in which there is the greatest relationship to its own primary activity. Gort, *op. cit.*, p. 108, and *passim*.

input productivity on the other; and (2) "bargains" in which the acquiring firm obtains another firm for a price *less* than that firm's fully capitalized future earnings.[33] If the market for firms' assets—the "merger market"— were a market in which all buyers and sellers were fully informed, then bargains would vanish. All firms would sell at their fully capitalized value. However, because the merger market, as most other real-world markets, is not perfect, bargains exist and merger-prone firms scour the horizon for such bargains. As a result, in the late 1960s there was a substantial increase in the number of unrelated conglomerate mergers.[34] In the *absence* of bargains, a merging firm, like an internally investing firm, would be limited to those markets in which it could obtain either or both pecuniary and real economies. If a firm were to realize its maximum profit potential, mergers on average would tend to be in economically related markets.

A careful examination of the five basic motives for adding products listed earlier reveals that at least some minimal commonality would be expected. For example, if in the short run one desires to absorb idle capacity in one or more current activities, or in the long run to exploit a situation of increasing returns to scale, the logical implication is adding one or more offerings which are economically related. Otherwise excess capacity absorption or exploitation of scale economies is impossible.[35] Although merger bargains may take firms all over the economic map, the maximization of profits requires a diversifying firm primarily to exploit input and demand relationships.[36]

Efficiencies in the Diversified Firm

It is clear from the preceding discussion that diversification varies with respect to efficiencies. Market-diversified firms extend along a spectrum with respect to their commonality (economic relationships). The higher the commonality, the greater the opportunities for pecuniary and real economies. At the upper end of the spectrum, market diversification is

---

[33] These points are discussed in Narver, "Some Observations on the Impact of Antitrust Merger Policy on Marketing," *op. cit.*, and references cited therein.

For some empirical data on the relatively low profitability for the acquiring companies in mergers, *see* Michael Gort and Thomas F. Hogarty, "New Evidence on Mergers," *The Journal of Law and Economics* XIII (April 1970) and Thomas F. Hogarty, "The Profitability of Corporate Mergers," *Journal of Business* (July 1970).

[34] FTC *Economic Report, op. cit.*

[35] Logical support for high-commonality diversification in the profit-maximizing firm is found for example in Joel Dean, *op. cit.*, pp. 125–133.

[36] The avoidance of the risk of antitrust may, however, lead some large firms into low-commonality diversification. If it has a large market share in one or more markets it can, of course try to avoid antitrust monopoly complaints by simply ceasing to compete vigorously. However, if it wishes to grow, its safest recourse is to enter other markets. In particular, out of fear of a "conglomerate power" prosecution, it may wish to diversify completely away from any current activity. The sources and implications of conglomerate power are analyzed in Chapter 14 in the present book. *See also* Narver, *Conglomerate Mergers and Market Competition, op. cit.*, Chapter VI.

virtually equivalent to horizontal and vertical growth with respect to both types of efficiency. At the low end of commonality, efficiency is probably very low.[37]

The Offering-deletion Decision

An optimal offering assortment is not always attained *solely* by adding goods and services. Occasionally, the firm will reduce one or more parts of its assortment, shedding those offerings which fail to meet profit expectations.

It is useful to distinguish two contexts of product failures: (1) new products and (2) on-going products. New offerings fail for any of several reasons, ranging from insufficient marketing research on the demand, costs, and competition, to an inability of the firm to provide the desired total product. Whatever the reasons, new-product failures are numerous.

> At least 80 percent of the new products introduced to the market fail to make the grade. Especially high is the failure rate for products which require extreme changes in user [behavior] and user ways of looking at familiar tasks.[38]

Commonality in the Failures of Offerings

Gort's study of large manufacturing firms reveals a general *inverse* relationship between product failures and commonality. The logic of high-commonality diversification is borne out in his findings:

> For a manufacturing enterprise, the likelihood of survival in non-manufacturing operations appears to be distinctly *less* than in manufacturing industries. . . . In manufacturing, the number of abandonments in the 1929–54 period as a whole equaled only 19.0 percent of additions; for non-manufacturing the comparable percentage was 47.0.[39]

---

[37] The relative efficiency of the three major growth patterns is yet to be fully explored empirically. For some additional discussion of efficiencies in diversification *see* John C. Narver, *Conglomerate Mergers and Market Competition, op. cit.,* pp. 71–74; John Kitching, "Why Do Mergers Miscarry?", *Harvard Business Review,* XLV (November–December, 1967), pp. 84 ff; and Narver, "Some Observations on the Impact of Antitrust Merger Policy on Marketing," *op. cit.*

The issues in diversification performance versus diversification-merger performance should be kept separate. Merger, in and of itself, may introduce additional variables such as bargains, the use of convertible securities, and the question of emotional compatibility of the parties to the merger. Thus, one cannot analyze diversification performance per se by looking only at diversification mergers.

[38] C. F. Phillips and D. J. Duncan, *Marketing: Principles and Methods* (5th ed., Irwin, 1964), p. 573 ff. and sources cited.

The criteria of "failure" are in themselves complex. When has a product "failed"? The meaning and considerations associated with failure are well discussed in Joel Dean, *op. cit.,* pp. 133–37; and Philip Kotler, *Marketing Management: Analysis, Planning, and Control* (Prentice-Hall, 1967), pp. 302–312.

[39] Gort, *Diversification and Integration, op. cit.,* pp. 99–100 and pp. 51–57, and n. 16, p. 58; emphasis added. Also see John Kitching, "Why Do Mergers Miscarry?" *op. cit.,* pp. 84 ff; and with respect to real economies in marketing, Narver, "Some Observations on the Impact of Antitrust Merger Policy on Marketing," *passim* and works cited.

AN EXTANT OFFERING ASSORTMENT: SOME ''PRODUCT'' ISSUES

In the preceding sections we elaborated the decision to add product (and geographic) markets to the assortment. The argument given is relevant to both the entirely new firm and the on-going firm. At the present point, the focus shifts to some aspects of a current offering assortment. Thus, the immediate interest in the "product decision" is not in the choice of new products, but in certain implications of the given set of offerings in the firm.

Life Cycle of Products

Most durable goods and many non-durable goods that do not fail initially, go through a growth and decline in sales volume and profits as shown in Figure 11.6. If we assume the curve relates to a single-product firm, it is clear that the firm will need additional new-product profit to sustain growth. The previously mentioned five comprehensive motives for diversification can be inferred from the situation represented by Figure 11.6.

FIGURE 11.6

BASIC LIFE CYCLE OF PRODUCTS

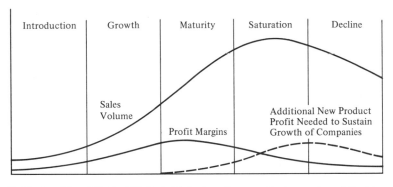

Source: E. W. Cundiff and R. R. Still, *Basic Marketing: Concepts, Environment, and Decisions* (Prentice-Hall, 1964), p. 415, from Booz, Allen & Hamilton, Inc.

The reasons for the respective positions and timing of the sales and profit-margin curves are complex. However, frequently the profit-margin curve peaks earlier than the sales curve because of the entrance of competition resulting in more vigorous rivalry. Clearly, profit margins would tend to fall especially rapidly if, irrationally, price were reduced *in spite of* price-inelastic demand or if promotion were increased *in spite of* promotion-inelastic demand. Moreover an irrational pricing decision by one firm in a concentrated market could well force the others to follow suit.

Another cause of decreasing marginal profitability in a market is saturation of the market. The market may no longer be growing; hence, the additional market share of any one firm is gained at the expense of other competitors—and at increasing marginal costs. Moreover, the learning capacity of the market may be reached. (Recall Chapter 9 and the discussion of learning.) Thus, in such a context the increasing marketing effort of any firm tends at most to fracture somewhat established loyalty patterns without creating new ones. The result is offsetting promotional efforts by all competitors and more or less random pairing of customers and sellers.

Changes in customer tastes in the product market in general contribute to the downturn in total market sales and hence ultimately in any firm's sales. Although the time will vary depending on the product, most goods, as in Figure 11.6, experience a fashion cycle—increasing and then decreasing popularity.[40]

Brands and Branding

In previous sections of the book, we have seen that the logic of marketing management is the attempt to create differential advantage, and thereby maximize profits. Clearly, if customers are completely indifferent to the choice among the offerings of the suppliers in a market, no seller has any advantage over the competition, and buyers and sellers are paired randomly.

Sellers, to the greatest extent possible, identify themselves by attaching distinguishing markings or labels to their products, or, if they are selling homogeneous physical products such as coal, dimension lumber, standard industrial supplies, and so on, they identify and differentiate the enterprise (the source) rather than the offering.[41]

Let us be more specific about the identification of offerings. Generally, identification implies "brand." The definition of brand: "A word, mark, symbol, device, or a combination thereof used to identify some product or service."[42] Examples of familiar brands are "Ford," "Playboy," "Goodyear," and "Sunkist."

There are two broad types of brands: (1) manufacturers' or producers' brands, commonly referred to as "national" brands; and (2) middlemen's brands, usually termed "private" brands. Examples of national brands in canned goods are "S & W" and "Del Monte." Private brands are, for example, the "Town House" brand of Safeway, or the "Eight O'Clock Coffee" of the

---

[40] A *style* is a distinctive mode or method of expression in the field of some art. We have styles of furniture, houses, haircuts, and so on. A *fashion* is a style which is popular at a given time. In short, styles do not change, but fashions do. One of the best introductory discussions of fashion cycles, from which these definitions were taken is C. F. Phillips and D. J. Duncan, *op. cit.*, pp. 91–98.

[41] See the discussion of enterprise differentiation in the present book in Chapters 3 and 10. The logic of sellers reducing random pairing by identifying themselves in the market as relevant sources of supply and by assisting in the specification of customer wants is developed in Wroe Alderson, *Dynamic Marketing Behavior* (Irwin: 1965), pp. 119–137.

[42] C. F. Phillips and D. J. Duncan, *op. cit.*, p. 579. The term "trade mark" is the legal counterpart of "brand" but in ordinary usage the two are considered synonymous. *Ibid.*

Great Atlantic and Pacific Tea Company. Both national brands and private brands may consist of individual brands *or* family (blanket) brands.[43]

Extent of Private Branding

It is extremely rare for a wholesaler or a retailer to sell only his own brand. It is also rare for a consumer-product, integrated manufacturer-distributor to sell only his own brand—although Sears-Roebuck is an example of a retailer whose private label sales account for close to 95 percent of Sears' total sales.[44] On the other hand, there are many small retailers who sell only national brands; however, such agencies do not account for a large percentage of retail sales.

Thus, virtually all retailing and wholesaling firms which own brand names, engage in "dual merchandising." Dual merchandising is the practice by middlemen (wholesale or retail) of simultaneously selling private and national brands. Specifically, dual merchandising relates to buying for resale. The counterpart concept on the selling side is "dual distribution." Dual distribution is the selling of one's brand through his own wholesale or retail outlets as well as selling the same brand to other wholesalers or retailers.[45]

The use of private brands is widespread. For example, private brands account for 30 percent of sales of one automobile appliance chain—and the percentage is increasing all the time. Private label bakery goods, accounting for 11 percent of the market in 1958, increased their share to 20 percent in 1962. For the same period of time, comparable figures for replacement of automobile tires were 15 percent and 39 percent; and for gas ranges, 20 percent to 30 percent.[46]

Dual merchandising is particularly significant in the food industries. The private brand share of total supermarket grocery volume (excluding meats and produce) was estimated in 1960 to be 20 percent—and undoubtedly is higher today. Five-sixths of all grocery chains sell some goods under their own brands.[47]

---

[43] Phillips and Duncan, *op. cit.*, pp. 579–588, discuss several aspects of brand policy, including the intermixing of private and national brands in the offering assortment. Also, they treat the considerations of a manufacturer deciding whether to sell some of his output as private-label items, with the possible result of heightened inter-brand competition between his and the private brands.

[44] Lawrence M. Hughes, "The 'Secret' Hand in Private Brands," *Sales Management*, September 16, 1960, pp. 35 ff.

[45] For a discussion of dual distribution and some of its implications, *see* L. E. Preston and A. E. Schramm, Jr., "Dual Distribution and Its Impact on Marketing Organization," *California Management Review*, VIII (Winter 1965). *See also* Ronald Savitt, "The Dual Distribution Bills: What are they all about?", *California Management Review*, X (Summer 1968).

[46] Phillips and Duncan, *op. cit.*, p. 584. *See also* Louis Stern, "The New World of Private Brands," *California Management Review*, VIII (Spring 1966), pp. 43–50.

[47] Hughes, *op. cit.*,

The National Commission on Food Marketing in its final report stated that private labels were used by every type of food retailer—independents, voluntary chains, cooperative chains, and of course corporation chains. Their most extensive use is by the larger chains. The report concluded:

> In 1964, among all chains of 11 or more stores, retailer brands represented half the sales of frozen fruit juice, frozen vegetables, bakery products, and dairy products. Retailer brands represented one-third of the coffee, bacon, and wieners, and more than one-fourth of canned fruits and vegetables. The use of private labels probably has about stabilized in these areas, and most future growth may come from extension of private labels to new products.[48]

Packaging

The packaging decision involves two fundamental considerations: (1) the need for product protection; and (2) the need for product differentiation and identification. The optimal package is that which provides the least expensive, adequate protection *and* the largest contribution to differential advantage. The package may play a substantial role in merchandising consumer products. For example, if the offering is frequently purchased as an impulse item, or is a shopping good, there are many merchandising implications in the packaging. For most industrial products, however, packaging serves far more in a protection capacity than a merchandising capacity.[49]

CHANNEL DECISIONS

The analysis of channel decision draws substantially upon the preceding offering-decision discussion as well as the analysis of total product, differentiation, flows, channels, and agency and geographic structures.[50] We once

---

[48] *Food from Farmer to Consumer*, Report of the National Commission on Food Marketing, (U.S. Government Printing Office, June 1966), p. 75. The Final Report was a summation and conclusion of a series of technical analyses of various aspects of food marketing. For the detailed special study of private label products in food retailing, see Technical Study No. 10, *Special Studies in Food Marketing*, June 1966, pp. 1–120. See also *Organization and Competition in Food Retailing*, Technical Study No. 7, June 1966, Chapter 6.

[49] For discussions of the complexities in packaging decisions, *see* Cundiff and Still, *op. cit.*, pp. 429–31; Kotler, *op. cit.*, pp. 332–334; and for a more normative treatment, William H. Reynolds, "What Businessmen Need to Know About Industrial Design," *Business Topics*, Summer 1966, pp. 57–66. The requirement to provide information on a package's contents and to avoid misleading shapes and designs are contained in the federal "Truth in Packaging" legislation.

[50] *See* Chapters 3 and 5–7. *See also* Kotler, *op. cit.*, Chapters 16 and 17; Ralph F. Breyer, "Some Observations on 'Structural' Formation and the Growth of Marketing Channels," in Cox, *et al.*, *Theory in Marketing* (Irwin, 1965); and Bruce E. Mallen, *The Marketing Channel: A Conceptual Viewpoint* (Wiley, 1967).

again point out a basic proposition: A rational firm selling any good or service will carefully analyze a want and then draw upon its resources efficiently to create, insofar as possible, a differentiated total product that matches the want.

"Efficiency" we recall means utilizing the marketing-mix inputs to create the total product in a manner that yields a $MC = MR$ condition. Clearly, the latter is the rational solution, but we recognize also that not all firms successfully effect the profit-maximizing condition—either because they have other goals, or they are not rational in their decision-making, or if intendedly rational, they cannot precisely calculate their costs and revenues to accord to the $MC = MR$ solution. The rational profit-maximizing firm will always attempt such a calculation if only a rough approximation. Moreover, difficulty in measuring actual costs and revenues does not in any manner invalidate *seeking* the $MC = MR$ solution.

With respect to channels, the firm selects the channel (the total set of flows and agencies) which contributes most to long-run profits through most efficiently facilitating the effecting of the appropriate total product. We stress the two aspects: *efficiency* and *differentiation* pertaining to the long-run profits of a given good or service, though at times differentiation may be difficult if even possible.

Several implications are immediately apparent. For any good or service, a firm may find on the one hand maximum efficient differentiation through a *vertically integrated* channel in which the firm engages in all the functions and the associated flows. Or on the other hand, the firm may believe maximum efficient differentiation lies in a completely *disintegrated* channel in which the firm, for example marketing a consumer good, employs one or more wholesale middlemen and independent retailers. Of course, the firm may conclude that some combination of partial integration in one or more flows in conjunction with independent agencies in other flows is the channel most probably yielding maximum profits.

An associated implication is that the optimal channel for a good or service at any point in time may not be optimal in a succeeding time period. Changes in buyer and seller market structures—the fact of life in a dynamic world—require continual reconsideration of channel arrangements.

Another implication is that the optimal channel for one good or service may not be optimal for other of the firm's offerings. Typically one finds various channels within the same firm among its various product and geographic markets.

Also one frequently finds that in a given product market, some of the sellers successfully employ a vertically integrated channel, others a combination of integrated and nonintegrated channels, and yet others completely nonintegrated channels.

Among all firms, channels differ because, among other reasons (1), the firms' resources differ; (2) their perceptions of the strengths and weaknesses of those resources differ; (3) their perceptions of the wants differ; (4) their offering assortments differ, requiring special considerations with respect to joint supply and joint demand (discussed in the previous sections of this chapter); and (5) their personal goals and preferences differ. This is simply to say that a rational firm exploits what it believes it can do best vis-à-vis a want. Thus many markets are characterized by small firms and large firms successfully competing, and also by differences in channels and other marketing mix elements among them.

Productivity and Economies in Channels

The essential productivity problem with respect to channels is no different from that of pricing, offering, and promotion. It is to maximize the output of a given set of inputs, or minimize the inputs to attain a given output. Taking into account the costs of various channel alternatives, the marketing manager thus wishes for each offering to select the channel that is most efficient.

We recall the definition of marginal cost, $MC = P_V \left(\dfrac{1}{MP} \right)$ How does a manager decrease the price per unit of channel effort and also how does a manager increase the marginal productivity of channel effort? Consider a manufacturer who decides to use independent wholesalers and retailers in the marketing of consumer goods. If there is considerable consumer loyalty for his brands, the manufacturer may obtain the promotional skills, efforts, and loyalty of the middlemen for lower costs than possible with unknown brands. The middlemen recognize the profit possibilities and accordingly are willing to price their services for less.

The marginal productivity effect on MC is easily seen. First, a manager increases the MP of a channel by training and developing the agencies, so long as developmental effort yields (or promises to) a greater than proportionate increase in output. This may involve instituting new techniques of inventory control and data processing, new methods of inventory handling and physical distribution, new approaches to hiring and motivating the middlemen's salesmen, and so on. However effected, a proportionately greater increase in the MP than in the unit price of channel inputs will necessarily lower MP of channel activity. Also, MP increases, all other things equal, when the same channel inputs handle a greater number of jointly demanded products. Thus, adding complementary products to the same channel without having to expend proportionately more effort obviously increases the MP of the channel. However, one can add products within the same channel and experience an increase in sales only to a point. Total sales ultimately will decline—that is, marginal productivity becomes negative—when one has added so many products within the same channel that the agencies become overwhelmed, causing their effectiveness to decrease. All of this is implicit in the unit sales and marginal productivity curves in

Figure 11.1, typifying the situation of adding units of a variable input in conjunction with some given fixed inputs.

Extensive versus Limited Distribution

The structure of demand in large part determines whether the greatest productivity lies in extensively or limitedly distributing the offering. Among consumer goods, convenience goods are extensively distributed, for consumers desire to minimize their effort to acquire the good. With perhaps the exception of impulse items, one can do relatively little to influence the demand for convenience goods, other than maximize their exposure to consumers. Thus for example, vending machines selling convenience goods are placed in the "path" of consumers.

Shopping goods require selling effort on the part of the brander as well as the retailer (who frequently are identical as we have seen). Consumers desire to compare to some extent in purchasing shopping goods, believing they will obtain a net gain in utility by evaluating alternatives. The implication for channels is that a rational firm selling shopping goods will distribute sufficiently extensively to permit easy comparison shopping but not so extensively that any one retailer is unmotivated to promote the good because too many competitors also carry it. There is thus some selectivity in distributing shopping goods, for the brand owner wants maximum promotional effort at the retail level.

Specialty goods frequently are very limitedly distributed. It is not unusual for exclusive distributorships to be established in which each designated area is served by only one outlet. In exchange for the exclusivity, the retailer who values the franchise, is motivated to devote special effort to maintain the specialty-good image currently held by many consumers. This, of course, benefits both the retailer and the brand owner. In recent years, franchising has grown more rapidly than any other form of distribution.[51] A specific meaning of "franchising" is the relationship in which a firm (the franchisor) with a pattern or formula for the manufacture and/or sale of a good or service, extends to other firms (the franchisees) the right to use the pattern or formula *subject to* a number of restrictions and controls.[52] The popularity of franchising is understandable. A firm short on capital and/or long on risks with a good, service, or trademark for which there is a perceived demand, may by franchising obtain distribution at less than full internal costs by attracting franchisee capital. Franchisees enter willingly believing the costs of the franchisor's imposed restrictions are less than the expected revenue from the franchise arrangement, *and* less than the oppor-

[51] Donald N. Thompson, "Franchise Operations and Antitrust Law," *Journal of Retailing,* XLIV, Winter 1968–69, p. 39.

[52] *Ibid.,* p. 40. The entire issue of *Journal of Retailing,* Winter 1968–69, is devoted to various aspects of franchising. *See also* Ronald Savitt, "Franchising in Trouble," *Diversification and Innovation* (March 1970), pp. 13–22.

tunity costs (that is, engaging completely independently in the given type of good or service).

Industrial goods are distributed in varying degrees of extensiveness depending on the buyer structure and character of demand for the item. Industrial supplies, which typically are frequently-purchased homogeneous items, usually are extensively distributed through wholesale middlemen of one type or another. On the other hand, capital equipment especially when sold as differentiated offerings, is more limitedly distributed—often sold directly by the manufacturer in conjunction with his and the customer's engineers and other technical personnel.[53]

External Economies

With an reference to profit maximization, is a firm better off to integrate vertically and thereby perform some or all of the channel activity itself, or is it more profitable to depend on a channel composed of independent agencies, at the limit a completely nonintegrated channel? (The reader is referred to the discussion of external economies in Chapter 6). The rational firm desiring to maximize long-run profits will in general exploit any economy which permits average costs to decrease proportionately more than average revenues, or revenues to increase proportionately more than costs. The economies may be internal, or as in the case of specialist middlemen, external. Use of middlemen or other outside agencies largely boils down to their relative efficiency in one or more flows.[54] But using lower-cost specialists may confront the firm with a conflict, for uppermost in the firm's mind is the necessity of continually effecting a total product conforming closely to the want. The more dynamic the market, the more true is this generalization. Adjustments in the total product require both control over the marketing inputs, and flexibility as to timing of changes in the mix. Control and flexibility in the marketing mix may be *lessened* by utilizing nonintegrated channels, even though variable costs may be lower.[55] Consequently, the desire for increased control over the total product no doubt accounts for considerable vertical integration *in spite of* lower costs through using independent middlemen. The rationale of ignoring the lower-cost alternative is that the greater control and flexibility over the total product may yield increases in total revenue proportionately greater than increases in total costs *and* that these profits exceed the profits available from the lower-cost alternative.

Interrelationship of Channels and Other Marketing-mix Decisions

The relatively brief analysis of channel decisions in the preceding section in no sense suggests that the channel decision is a simple decision. We

---

[53] See Chapter 6 for a discussion of middleman agencies in retailing and wholesaling.
[54] Kotler, *op. cit.*, p. 389.
[55] *Ibid.*, p. 386.

have pointed out that the channel decision comprehends the issues of choice of product market, functions, flows, channel structures and behavior, and agency and geographic structures. These issues were discussed in Chapters 3 and 5–7 and the current chapter. For the sake of brief exposition, we stress that the reader relate these analyses to the channel-decision framework outlined above, and to the succeeding two chapters as well.

The channels of a firm constitute the marketing context *in which* the product, price and promotion decisions are made. As Kotler has pointed out, "The channels chosen for the company's products intimately affect every other marketing decision."[56] Nowhere is the interrelationship among the marketing-mix variables more pronounced than between channels and the other three variables. Three examples will illustrate the relationship. First the total product of a firm is affected by the type of agencies through which a firm markets its good or service. Is a particular national brand of television set the same total product marketed in a discount house on the one hand and in a high-fashion department store on the other? That is, are the demander perceptions of the total bundle of utility the same?

Second, promotion decisions are affected by the channels chosen by a company. A nonintegrated channel requires promotion effort directed both at the middlemen, to induce their full cooperation, and at the subsequent customers to effect a user demand. Thus nonintegrated channels require both "push" and "pull" promotion of the product through the channel—in contrast to the completely vertically integrated channel, in which the firm directs its promotion effort solely to the user (though at times, the integrated firm may have to do some internal urging).

Third, the "price" of a product is affected by the channel. Price, including the elements of price structure—the terms and conditions of sale for a given good or service—is necessarily different when middlemen are utilized than when the firm is completely vertically integrated. In the former instance, the price chosen must consider the ultimate-user structure as well as middlemen market structures. We recall that the merchant middleman takes title to the offering and thus there are at least three markets (frequently more) in a channel in which a manufacturer of a consumer good markets through a wholesaler as well as a retailer: manufacturer-wholesaler, wholesaler-retailer, retailer-consumer. The manufacturer's price structure must incorporate the retail list price as well as all the functional and other discounts for the middlemen.

The following two chapters discuss the promotion and price decisions. In those chapters additional channel implications will be considered.

SUMMARY

As stated in the previous chapter, the logic of marketing management lies in the manipulation of certain variables to effect a total product that

[56] Kotler, *op. cit.*, p. 386.

efficiently matches wants and, insofar as possible, creates differential advantage. Although customers may perceive utility in any or all elements of an offering—physical product, channels, promotion, and price—the most logical beginning point in analyzing the marketing mix is the *product* variable and the choice of product markets. Until a firm has selected its product markets, it cannot decide anything with respect to channel, promotion or price.

A firm in essence is one or more pools of productive resources assembled in the expectation of providing a desired good(s) or service(s) equally or more efficiently than other firms in the market. Though capable of producing a range of types of offerings, the firm at any time will produce only those goods and services with the highest expected profitability.

Virtually all additions of offerings to a firm's assortment can be conceived of as either or all (1) utilizing idle capacity in production or marketing, (2) reducing risk, (3) responding to a saturation of current markets, (4) exploiting potential economies of scale, and (5) generating demand for current offerings by adding demand-related offerings. The profit-maximizing firm continues to increase activity and/or enter new product and geographic markets to the point of $MC = MR$.

A firm can enlarge its offering assortment either through internal investment or through a merger (acquisition). Mergers taking a firm into product and geographic markets new to it are called "conglomerate mergers"—and in the last few years they have been rapidly increasing as a proportion of all mergers.

Most diversification—either internally or externally—is economically related to the current inputs or demand of the firm. Efficiency in diversification is *directly* related to the amount of economic relationship in diversification, and frequency of failures of new offerings are *inversely* related to the amount of economic relationship in diversification.

Most goods and services that succeed experience a life cycle in which they gain increasing customer acceptance and then ultimately decline. Some of the explanations for such cycles are market saturation, competition, and change in customer tastes.

To attain differential advantage, firms attempt to give a positive distinctiveness to their offerings—which includes use of a label, symbol or other device (all of which are subsumed by the term "brand") to identify the offering. There are two broad types of brands: (1) manufacturers' or producers' brands ("national" brands), and (2) middlemen's brands ("private" brands). Private branding is widespread and increasing. It is common for large retailers to carry both national and their own brands.

The packaging decision involves: (1) adequate protection for the offering, and (2) differentiation and identification. The optimal packaging is that which provides the least expensive sufficient protection *and* largest contribution to differential advantage.

The national firm selects the marketing channel (the total set of flows and agencies with respect to an offering) which contributes most to long-run profits. The optimum channel for some goods may be a completely vertically integrated channel—and for others a completely nonintegrated channel. Frequently, both patterns are found in the same firm, or in the same market among competing firms.

Some offerings are extensively distributed—for example, "convenience" goods and industrial supplies, whereas others are limitedly distributed, such as retail "specialty" goods. Recently, franchising has rapidly increased in the marketing of heterogeneous shopping goods and specialty goods.

The channel decision is extremely interrelated with the other marketing-mix elements. A firm can make virtually no promotion or price decision until the product-market and marketing channel—the basic strategic contexts—are selected.

SUGGESTED READINGS

The Selection of An Offering and Assortment

Kenneth R. Andrews, "Product Diversification and the Public Interest," *Harvard Business Review*, XXIX (July 1951).

Joel Dean, *Managerial Economics* (Englewood Cliffs, N.J.: Prentice-Hall, Inc., 1951), especially, pp. 115–120 and *passim*.

A very useful conceptual discussion of the selection of offerings to produce and market.

Thomas A. Staudt, "Program for Product Diversification," *Harvard Business Review*, XXXII (November-December 1954).

Like Andrews' article, a managerially-oriented article pointing out aspects of the product-diversification decision.

Diversification: Internal and Merger

Stephen H. Archer, "Diversification and the Reduction of Dispersion," *Journal of Finance*, XXIII, December 1968.

A treatment of the basic concept, diversification, and its effects—written with respect to finance but with many implications for product and geographic diversification.

R. D. Buzzell and R. E. M. Nourse, *Product Innovation in Food Processing, 1954–1964* (Boston: Harvard Graduate School of Business Administration, 1967).

A useful empirical examination of many cost and productivity aspects of product development and new products (though defined differently from the present text) in food manufacturing.

Federal Trade Commission, *Economic Report on Corporate Mergers* (1969).

The most extensive examination to date on the structure and

behavior of large-firm diversification both by internal investment and merger.

Henry G. Manne, "Mergers and the Market for Corporate Control," *Journal of Political Economy*, LXXIII, April 1965, pp. 110–120.

A discussion of the many implications of a viable market for firm assets, an important article in that many firms new-product additions have been effected through merging.

D. S. Tull, "The Relationship of Actual and Predicted Sales in New-Product Introductions," *Journal of Business*, XC, No. 3 (July 1967); D. S. Tull and H. C. Rutemiller, "Note on the Relationship of Actual and Predicted Sales in New-Product Introductions," *Journal of Business*, July 1968.

Some empirical evidence of new-product performance.

Brands and Branding

Bjorn Carlson and Bertil Kusoffsky, *Distributor versus Producer Brands* (Stockholm: Economic Research Institute, Stockholm School of Economics, 1966).

National Commission on Food Marketing, *Special Studies in Food Marketing*, Technical Study No. 10, June 1966, pp. 1–120.

A detailed examination of private branding in food retailing.

Louis Stern, "The New World of Private Brands," *California Management Review*, VIII, Spring 1966, pp. 43–50.

A discussion of some aspects of the extensive branding in the economy.

Channel Decisions

Ralph E. Breyer, "Some Observations on 'Structural' Formation and the Growth of Marketing Channels" in Reavis Cox, *et al.*, *Theory in Marketing* (Homewood, Ill.: Richard D. Irwin, Inc., 1964).

A thoughtful article by one of the best-known channel theorists.

R. D. Entenberg, *Effective Retail and Market Distribution: A Managerial Economic Approach* (Cleveland: World Publishing Co., 1966).

A channel book by a long-time student of distribution.

Bruce E. Mallen, *The Marketing Channel: A Conceptual Viewpoint* (New York: John Wiley & Sons, Inc., 1967).

A useful collection of readings pertaining to both positive and normative aspects of channels.

12

Promotion
decisions
and performance

Having considered product and channel decisions in the preceding chapter, we turn now to the activities of participants—sellers and buyers—promoting their interests. One tends to see promotion in terms of suppliers and their goods and services. Sellers by and large are in a position in our economy of trying to gain the attention, interest, and custom of demanders. However, in times of excess demand—scarcity—buyers take the initiative. Much of our discussion of promotion has implications for both supplier and demander promotion, but in the main, we will focus on promotion by *suppliers*.

THE MEANING AND COMPONENTS OF PROMOTION

Definition

"Promotion" is the use of personal and nonpersonal means by demanders and suppliers to inform and persuade in order to effect transactions.

There are three broad types of promotion: (1) advertising, (2) personal selling; and (3) special sales programs. "Advertising" is the use of nonpersonal communication media—television, radio, newspapers, magazines, billboards, telephone, and so on—to inform and/or persuade. "Personal selling" is the use of sales personnel, either one's own employees or agents hired for specific sales periods, for informing and/or persuading current and potential customers. "Special sales programs" are combinations of advertising and personal selling such as trade fairs, retail games, point-of-sale displays, trading stamps, exhibits of new products, and so on. Because of space limitations, personal selling and special sales programs, essentially an amalgam of advertising and personal selling, will not be discussed at any length in this chapter. Our principal focus will be on advertising, but much of what we say about advertising applies to the other two types of promotion.[1] The choice of the *combination* of the three types of promotion to convey the information and persuasion is called the "promotion mix."

Promotion, whether advertising, personal selling or special sales efforts, consists in varying degrees of information persuasion. "Information" means the dissemination of facts with respect to any aspect of form, time, place, and possession utilities. In that the real world consists of imperfectly informed potential buyers and sellers, want satisfaction requires at least minimum levels of information for both the *creation* and *effective performance* of markets. Thus, in the economy for transactions to occur, there must be overt informing of would-be traders. With respect to any profit-maximizing firm or utility-maximizing consumer, the optimal level of information is not, however, complete knowledge; rather, the optimal level of information for firm, nonprofit agency, or individual, is that level for which the cost of securing an additional bit of information equals the value of the additional information.[2]

Sellers and even buyers on occasion persuade as well as inform. "Persuasion" means an attempt to change perceptions, attitudes, and hence behavior to conform to the desires of the persuader. For example, the desire of a seller is to convince, at minimal cost, buyers to buy from him. But, in "sellers' markets,"[3] customers will actively seek out sources of supply, especially if the product sought is a required good. In such circumstances, a buyer would be inclined not only to inform sellers of his interest, but also perhaps to provide reasons why the sellers should sell to the particular

---

[1] For some useful analyses of personal selling and references, the reader is referred to Philip Kotler, *Marketing Management* (Prentice-Hall, 1967), Chapter 19, "Sales-Force Decisions"; and John Howard, *Marketing Management: Analysis and Planning* (rev. ed., Irwin, 1963), Chapter 14, "Promotion Decisions—Personal Selling."

There is a sizeable literature on various aspects of sales promotion, especially some evidence of the economic effects of certain sales promotion devices. Some of the better-known pieces of the literature on sales promotion are Carolyn Shaw Bell, "Liberty and Property, and No Stamps," *Journal of Business*, XL, April 1967; Harold W. Fox, *The Economics of Trading Stamps* (Public Affairs Press, 1968); Federal Trade Commission, *Economic Report on the Use and Economic Significance of Trading Stamps* (1966); "Who Wins Marketing Promotion Games?", *Fortune,* February 1969; and Federal Trade Commission, *Economic Report on the Use of Games of Chance in Food and Gasoline Retailing* (1968).

[2] As Stigler has said, "There is no 'imperfection' in a market possessing incomplete knowledge if it would not be remunerative to acquire (produce) complete knowledge." George J. Stigler, "Imperfections in the Capital Market," *The Journal of Political Economy*, Vol. 75, June 1967, p. 291.

[3] See Chapter 3.

buyer. Many goods and services were in short supply during World War II, and industrial customers and wholesale and retail middlemen used advertising as well as price inducements to acquire the limited goods and services.

Market Structure and Differentiability of the Offering

Market structure and the differentiability of the offering in large part determine the extent to which firms emphasize information or persuasion in their promotion. In general, the greater the interdependence among sellers (that is, the greater the "personalness," of the market), the more firms will tend to persuade. On the other hand, the more a firm is an "independent" decision-maker (that is, enjoys a limited monopoly), the more it will be able merely to employ information in its promotion. (See Chapter 4.) Why, for example, need a monopolist persuade? In principle, it is sufficient for it merely to inform its captive demanders.

Firms selling homogeneous *total* products—for example, a particular grade of wheat or coal—will tend, if anything at all, to emphasize information rather than persuasion in their promotion mix. Recall that a firm selling a homogeneous physical offering, may at times nevertheless effect a differentiated total product and what individual firms cannot do in differentiating products, trade associations sometimes can. If, throughout a market, all firms are perceived as offering identical utility, in effect they sell homogeneous total products. Wheat farmers would be an example. The reason a firm selling homogeneous *total* products does not use persuasion is perhaps obvious: Any one seller of such a product has no control over supply, in that homogeneous total products are perceived by demanders as completely substitutable. Therefore, it is irrational for any one seller of such a product—for example, any one wheat rancher—to promote "his" offering.

However, what is irrational at the firm level, *may not* necessarily be irrational at the industry level.[4] It is in the long-run interest of firms in general and those selling homogeneous physical products in particular to differentiate their offerings, but this is sometimes beyond the province of any firm. Industry trade associations *can* frequently alter the demand for a homogeneous product. Witness the case of oranges, long considered completely substitutable by consumers. High quality oranges bearing the brand "Sunkist" were successfully promoted by the Orange Growers Cooperative Association of California. The demand for this brand of orange became less elastic than the general demand for oranges. Through promotion—information and persuasion—other "commodities" also have become differentiated goods. For example, consider the consumer awareness of "Chiquita" bananas and the now year-round consumption of fresh and frozen turkeys.

---

[4] See the discussion in Chapters 4 and 10 on the meaning and determinants of "control" over elements of structure and marketing variables.

Persuasion will be minimized also if an offering is considered completely a *convenience* good—a good for which a consumer wishes only to minimize effort in acquiring. This, however, may be a relatively unimportant issue, for strictly speaking there probably are only a relatively few goods and services about which a consumer is *completely* brand-indifferent. For example, in a supermarket, a consumer perceives some difference in utility among various types (and brands) of candy and gum, although much less so among shoe laces and buttons. Of course, the more insistent a want, the less a consumer is concerned with brands. Usually, however, brand-indifference stemming from an insistent want are "crisis" circumstances, about which we cannot generalize. Thus at least to a minor degree, most consumer goods probably have a shopping-good character to them, implying thereby that some persuasion to the ultimate consumer is rational. On the other hand many industrial goods are more physically homogeneous— implying in *concentrated* markets the requirement for complex forms of promotion if a seller is to gain differential advantage.

The promotion used in selling to middlemen frequently varies from that employed to appeal to the ultimate consumer, for the manufacturer may *promote* a convenience good *to* middlemen, in terms of the unique profit potential, traffic building or other distinguishing commercial feature, even though the consumer perceives all offerings as the same. Thus, promotion of goods perceived by consumers as convenience or homogeneous shopping-goods may solely emphasize information with respect to promotion content to the ultimate consumer; whereas, promotion of the same goods to various middlemen in the channels will include some persuasion along with information.[5]

Institutional and Product Promotion

"Institutional" promotion is intended to establish goodwill toward a supplier or other agency without necessarily emphasizing any one offering. Examples of institutional advertising are General Electric's "Progress is our most important product"; and Westinghouse's "You can be sure if it's Westinghouse."

"Product" promotion is directed to individual offerings singly or in combination. The sponsor of the promotion may be a trade association promoting the generic product—"seafood," "Douglas Fir Plywood"; "wool"—

[5] It is virtually impossible to determine how much of advertising, let alone promotion, is "informational" and how much is "persuasive." Obviously, facts can be persuasive— hence there is no easy distinction between them. It is roughly estimated the promotional portion is probably less than 50 percent in the U.S. and somewhere around 30 percent in the United Kingdom. Jules Backman, *Advertising and Competition* (NYU, 1967), p. 30. Persuasive advertising in the U.S. is perhaps on the order of 1 percent of national income. See Leonard Weiss, *Case Studies in American Industry* (Wiley, 1967), p. 327 and see also the following section on "Expenditures on Promotion" in the present text.

or a single firm promoting its own brand of seafood, plywood, or wool garment.

Whether the promotion is institutional or product, commercial or non-commercial, the purpose of promotion is the same: to change favorably the recipient's perception and hence behavior to accord more closely to the desires of the sponsor. The intent in promotion is similar in concept whether one is promoting the Peace Corps, Charles Krug Wine, a candidate for public office, Allegheny Airlines, or the preservation of wilderness areas.

EXPENDITURES ON PROMOTION

Advertising is, of course, only one of three types of promotion, but it has the distinction of being the most controversial. In a later section of this chapter we shall consider some of the economic effects of advertising. At present, the discussion will be of trends in advertising expenditures in the economy.

The growth in total advertising expenditures in the economy has paralleled closely the growth of aggregate economic activity as measured by gross national product, personal consumption expenditures, disposable personal income, and total corporate sales. Indeed, nearly 100 percent of the variation in aggregate advertising expenditures may be explained by variations in the four economic aggregates.[6]

TABLE 12.1

THE RELATIVE IMPORTANCE OF ADVERTISING IN THE UNITED STATES ECONOMY INDICATED ON VARIOUS AGGREGATE BASES.[1]

	Advertising as percent of 1965
Personal consumption expenditures	3.54%
Disposable personal income	3.25
Gross national product	2.24
Total corporate sales	1.44

1 Jules Backman, *Advertising and Competition* (New York University Press, 1967), p. 173, p. 182.

Secular-trend comparisons of advertising with total GNP are somewhat misleading, for government is an increasingly important factor in GNP, which means that advertising as a percentage of *total* GNP understates advertising's size in the economy. In general, advertising since the mid-fifties has maintained an approximately constant relative position with respect to the four aggregate measures. In the 1960s total advertising expenditures have been equal to about 3.5 percent of personal consumption

6 Jules Backman, *Advertising and Competition* (New York University Press, 1967), pp. 168–173.

expenditures, compared to 3.0 percent prior to World War II and 2.7 to 3.0 percent in 1929. During the 1950s when the ratio of advertising to personal consumption expenditures was rising from 3.0 percent in 1950 to 3.6 percent in 1960, television advertising increased from .09 percent to .49 percent of personal consumption expenditures. Thus, even if one excludes television advertising, there was still an overall increase from 2.90 percent to 3.18 percent.[7]

Since 1935, *Printers' Ink* has published annual data for total advertising expenditures and for expenditures in eight recognized media—radio, newspapers, magazines, television, farm publications, business papers, outdoor advertising, and direct mail. There is in addition a miscellaneous category, which includes among other items, weekly newspapers. The total amount spent for the eight major types of media advertising in 1965 was $12.3 billion.

Table 12.2 presents a breakdown of advertising expenditures for selected years in the period 1935–1966.

RATIONALE OF PROMOTION

For a seller, we have mentioned that promotion—advertising, personal selling, and special sales programs—is intended to change favorably the demanders' perception of the supplier and his offering, and thereby change the demanders' behavior. Also, recalling the discussion in Chapter 10, promotion may sharpen demanders' perception of their *wants*. Thus, promotion, through information and persuasion (in varying degrees), may alter a demander's perception of both the offering and his want. To the extent promotion facilitates one's specification of his want and facilitates locating relevant offerings, it is socially productive.[8]

In general, a firm through the use of promotion (and the other variables) seeks differential advantage. In terms of demand curves, promotion intends to shift out demand curves and also make them less elastic. For a firm, the increase in inelasticity is obviously sought because every firm rationally desires to obtain at least a limited monopoly. With a limited monopoly, a firm acquires some control over price by means of its partial control over supply. All firms, sellers and buyers, try to escape the rigors of competition to whatever extent possible. Promotion offers one possible means for gaining some insulation from competition.

In terms of the learning curve (brand-loyalty model) discussed in Chapter 9, promotion seeks to increase the slope and the height of the curve (that is, speed and amount of learning). At the limit, promotion in conjunction with one or more other variables would create a *certainty* of brand

---

[7] *Ibid.*, pp. 173–174.
[8] See the discussion of want satisfaction in Chapter 3.

TABLE 12.2

ADVERTISING EXPENDITURES 1935, 1940, 1945, 1950, 1955, 1960-1966 [1]

(Millions of Dollars)

Year	Maga-zines	News-papers	Farm Pub.	Radio Net-work	Radio Spot	Radio Local	TV Net-work	TV Spot	TV Local	Direct Mail	Out-door	Business Papers	Misc.[2]	Total
1935	136	762	4	63	15	35				282	31	51	312	1,690
1940	198	815	7	113	42	60				334	45	76	398	2,088
1945	365	921	12	198	92	134				290	72	204	587	2,875
1950	515	2,076	21	196	136	273	85	31	55	803	143	251	1,125	5,710
1955	729	3,088	34	84	134	326	540	260	225	1,299	192	446	1,836	9,194
1960	941	3,703	35	43	222	428	783	527	281	1,830	203	609	2,328	11,932
1961	924	3,623	33	43	218	423	887	533	270	1,876	180	578	2,321	11,845
1962	973	3,681	34	46	229	461	976	611	311	1,933	171	597	2,359	12,381
1963	1,034	3,804	34	56	238	495	1,025	679	328	2,078	171	615	2,551	13,107
1964	1,108	4,148	33	59	251	537	1,132	780	377	2,184	175	623	2,750	14,155
1965	1,199	4,457	33	60	268	558	1,231	866	412	2,314	180	671	2,959	15,255
1966p	1,295	4,876	34	65	294	642	1,373	931	461	2,454	181	712	3,272	16,545

[1] Jules Backman, op. cit., Appendix Table A-1, pp. 178–179.

[2] Apparently includes cost of corporate advertising departments, signs and advertising novelties, car cards, motion pictures, and artwork, plates, and other mechanical costs. See Neil H. Borden, The Economic Effects of Advertising (Irwin, 1942), p. 54.

repurchase upon an initial purchase. Realistically, however, a certainty of repeat purchase, outside of some few special cases of pure monopolies, is rare. Nevertheless, the firm seeks to acquire maximum customer loyalty at a maximum rate and maintain it at a high level.

Implicit in the learning curve implications, promotion seeks to move goods from the status of convenience goods and shopping goods to that of specialty goods. At the very minimum, the firm desires to alter the conception of convenience goods to that of differentiated shopping goods. However, the preferable state by far is specialty goods—goods which a consumer is willing to make a special effort to acquire. The rationale in industrial goods is identical. In general, promotion seeks to eliminate random pairing of buyers and sellers.[9]

MODEL OF PROMOTION

Promotion, like any other variable input in conjunction with fixed inputs, demonstrates increasing returns and then decreasing returns. This general pattern of increasing and then decreasing returns to a variable input is, of course, representative of all inputs whether they are units of marketing, production, finance or accounting. A typical input-sales curve for promotion is shown in Figure 12.1.

Figure 12.1, shows the pattern of initial increasing sales per unit of promotion followed ultimately by decreasing sales per unit of promotion. The curve, of course, assumes other inputs are constant, thereby revealing only the promotion-sales relationship.

Some obvious reasons for the increasing returns are the cumulative effects of repeat sales, word-of-mouth or "spillover" promotion from satisfied customers, increased efficiency by managers in using media and establishing effective message content, increasing goodwill effected by salesmen, and lastly salesman learning. The marginal productivity of promotion ultimately declines because among other reasons the most likely prospects have been reached and prospects less susceptible for reasons including brand-loyalty to competitive brands are encountered. Also progressive exhaustion of the most accessible geographic areas and/or most efficient media accounts for decreasing and, ultimately, negative returns.[10] Another factor causing a decrease in marginal productivity of promotion inputs is that customers

[9] Advertising's role in facilitating search and minimizing random pairing is discussed in Wroe Alderson, *Dynamic Marketing Behavior* (Irwin, 1965), Chapter 5. Refer to Chapters 9 and 11 in the present book on buyer behavior and product policy.

[10] Joel Dean, "How Much to Spend on Advertising," *Harvard Business Review,* January–February 1951. For a discussion of decreasing *MP* of promotion due to encountering competitors' brand-loyal customers, as well as the associated concepts of "core" and "fringe market," *see* Wroe Alderson, *Dynamic Marketing Behavior, op. cit.*, p. 125 ff.

may have attained the maximum (for them) height on the learning curve—they are "learned up."

It is useful to distinguish between varying marginal productivity of inputs within a given promotion-production function and between two different promotion-production functions. For example, with respect to the same consumers and holding all other inputs constant, X units of television advertising may yield 10,000 units of sales, whereas X units of radio advertising may yield only 4000 units of sales. This comparison is in real terms only—it says nothing about relative efficiency, for nothing has been said of the respective unit costs. It is clear that two different relationships exist between the respective inputs and outputs. Figure 12.2 shows the hypothetical total sales curves, S_t for television and S_r for radio. The X units of radio advertising inputs yield 4000 units of sales, as seen from the S_r curve relating units of radio advertising and units of sales. Similarly, the X units of television advertising inputs yield 10,000 units of sales, as shown by the S_t curve relating units of television advertising and units of sales. It is even conceivable that the two sales curves might cross, due to a higher average productivity of one medium at low levels of intensity of use, and a higher average productivity for the other medium at intensive use levels. The reader should consider for what kinds of products in what kinds of market the average productivity of radio exceeds that of television.

FIGURE 12.1

PROMOTION-SALES CURVE

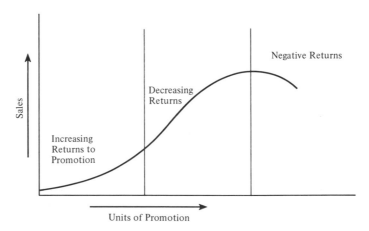

Exogenous factors may increase or decrease the productivity within a given production function. For example, in Figure 12.3, the sales curve S^n relates television inputs and sales for a given product under "normal" economic conditions. Above S^n is curve S^e showing the increase in average productivity of television advertising inputs in a period of economic "expansion." Thus, the demand for the hypothetical product in Figure 12.3 is income elastic—there is a greater tendency to purchase the product in periods of rising incomes. And, of course, an income-elastic good will be purchased much less frequently during periods of falling incomes. The curve S^r shows the low marginal and average productivity of television advertising inputs for the hypothetical product during periods of economic "recession." A given level of inputs, X, is related to the three curves.

FIGURE 12.2

HYPOTHETICAL TELEVISION AND RADIO ADVERTISING-SALES CURVES

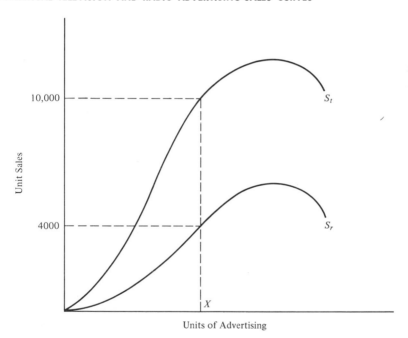

Units of Advertising

Promotion Inputs and Cost Curves

Assuming a constant per-unit price for promotion inputs, the promotion-sales curve translates immediately into the well known curvilinear cost curve, pictured in Figure 12.4. The law of variable proportions, that is, adding a variable factor to a stock of fixed factors, produces first decreasing average cost and then the increasing average cost. Specifically, the curvilinear cost curve in Figure 12.4 indicates that marginal cost and the average cost of promotion decrease and then increase—which is to be expected when variable inputs are increasingly added to some fixed factors. One interesting question is the location of the point at which marginal cost of promotion starts to rise, that is, the point of inflection noted as D in Figure 12.4. The reader will recall that marginal cost depends on the relationship between the marginal product (MP) and the price per unit of variable input (P_v).

Thus, the marginal cost of promotion, other things equal, depends on the MP and P_v of salesmen, sales shows, and advertising.

Clearly, MC of promotion will continue to decrease as long as MP rises proportionately faster than increases in P_v or as long as P_v falls proportionately faster than decreases in MP. If P_v and MP either rise proportionately or fall proportionately, MC of promotion will remain constant. By breaking MC of promotion into its two component parts, the reader recognizes that neither P_v nor MP alone determines MC. A rise in the MP of promotion could be more than offset by a rise in P_v such that MC of promotion *rises*. Similarly, a firm could realize pecuniary economies, that is, a reduction in P_v, but simultaneously experience a reduction in MP such that MC *rises*.

FIGURE 12.3

BUSINESS CONDITIONS AND PROMOTION-SALES CURVES

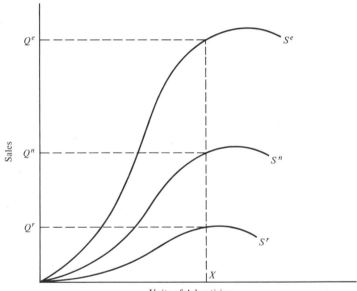

Units of Advertising

The reader should consider hypothetical situations in which P_v and MP increase or decrease at *dis*proportionate rates. It would be rare for simultaneous, equally offsetting and pecuniary real effects.

With respect to P_v, how would economies arise—that is, lower prices for promotion? One obvious situation in which the media suppliers—television, radio, newspapers, magazines, and so on—might reduce their prices for space or time is if one of the media achieves a technological development and offers its services at lower prices. (In this case, a real economy among suppliers produces a pecuniary economy for a firm purchasing advertising time or space.) An external economy such as vocational or educational institutions providing a larger or more qualified pool of sales personnel will lower promotion P_v for firms for fewer costs would be required per salesman. Another reason for a firm gaining a lower P_v of promotion is market power in buying advertising space and time. For example, if a firm is a substantial buyer of network television advertising, the networks may discriminate in price among the buyers, granting the largest buyers a disproportionately lower price.[11] If revenues remain constant, an outward (downward) shift in the total cost curve (Figure 12.4) whether from lower P_v or increased MP, of course, increases total profits.

FIGURE 12.4

TOTAL COST CURVE OF PROMOTION

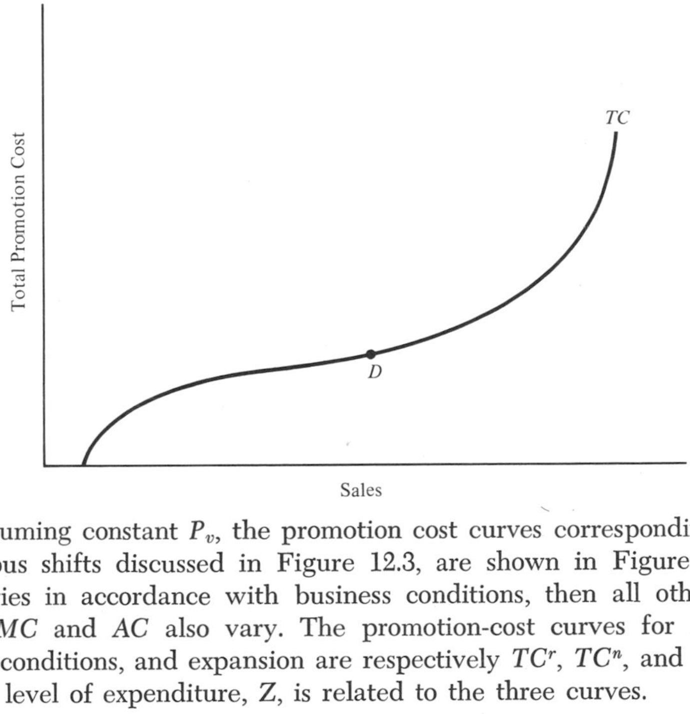

Assuming constant P_v, the promotion cost curves corresponding to the exogenous shifts discussed in Figure 12.3, are shown in Figure 12.5. As MP varies in accordance with business conditions, then all other things equal, MC and AC also vary. The promotion-cost curves for recession, normal conditions, and expansion are respectively TC^r, TC^n, and TC^e, and a given level of expenditure, Z, is related to the three curves.

[11] A reduced advertising P_v, based on purchasing power, was alleged by the Federal Trade Commission in Procter & Gamble's acquisition of Clorox. The contended discriminatory price, the Commission argued, would tend to raise the barriers to entry to anti-competitive levels in the liquid bleach market. For reference to the reduced advertising V_p, see *Trade Regulation Reporter* (Commerce Clearing House), paragraph 16,673, p. 21, 579 ff. For a rebuttal see David M. Blank, "Television Advertising: The Great Discount Illusion, or Tonypandy Revisited," *The Journal of Business*, January 1968, pp. 10–38; and David M. Blank, "Tonypandy Once Again," *Journal of Business*, January 1969. See also John L. Peterman, "The Clorox Case and Television Rate Structure," *Journal of Law and Economics*, XI (October 1968), pp. 321–422.

FIGURE 12.5

BUSINESS CONDITIONS AND PROMOTION-COST CURVES

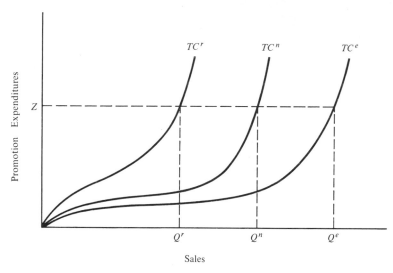

Profit Maximization Level of Promotion

We may now analyze the level of promotion inputs that maximize profits, invoking once again the all-other-things-equal assumption. Using the curvilinear cost curve shown in Figure 12.4 (and Figure 12.5), in conjunction with a revenue curve, it is easy to determine the profit maximizing level of promotion. Figure 12.6 shows a revenue curve, TR, and the promotion cost curve, TPC. We assume a constant price for the offering and thereby show a linear TR curve.

The profit maximizing point, of course, is the output at which $MC = MR$. In Figure 12.6, output Q_m is that point, for at that output, the slopes of TR and TPC are equal. The corresponding promotion level is V_m. Thus, holding all other variables constant, the firm maximizes its profits by utilizing OV_m dollars of promotion. We implicitly combine advertising, personal selling, and special sales efforts; however, the reader may prefer to consider that Figure 12.6 pertains solely to one of the components.[12]

Advertising as An Investment

The preceding analysis of productivity and costs of promotion has implied a relatively near-term relationship between promotion and changes

[12] This productivity, cost, and profit analysis of promotion in many respects is similar to that of Joel Dean, "How Much to Spend on Advertising," *Harvard Business Review*, (January–February 1959). See also John Howard, *Marketing Management* (Irwin, 1963), Chapter 13, and Joel Dean, "Measuring the Productivity of Investment in Persuasion," *Journal of Industrial Economics*, XV, April 1967.

in sales. Some advertising, of course, clearly is of a short input-output character. One example is direct-mail solicitation whereby recipients are urged to respond immediately to some special offer usually within a stated period of time. Quite soon after the mailing, the advertiser is usually aware of the productivity and hence average cost of the effort.[13]

FIGURE 12.6

PROFIT MAXIMIZING LEVEL OF PROMOTION

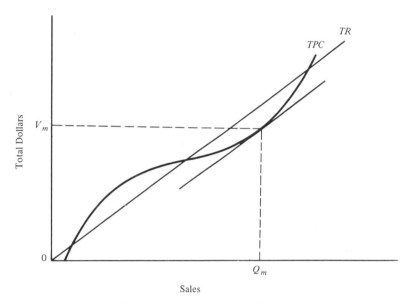

The analysis highlights the principles of short-run promotion productivity and efficiency. An extension of the general argument is to conceive of promotion in terms of an *investment* rather than an accounting "expense." There is straightforward logic in conceiving of expenditures on persuasion as an investment.[14]

An investment is an outlay made at some point in time to achieve benefits in the future. Futurity is the hallmark of an investment, and futurity is precisely of the essence in most promotional outlays. As we have

[13] The short period between inputs and responses in one-shot direct mailings, unlike many advertising efforts, affords relatively easy assessment of the actual effects of the expenditure. This was pointed out from a practitioner's viewpoint, in David Ogilvy, *Confessions of an Advertising Executive* (Dell, 1963).

[14] This section owes much to Joel Dean, "Does Advertising Belong in the Capital Budget?", *Journal of Marketing*, Vol. 30, October 1966. A very clear treatment of capital expenditures from both a positive and normative standpoint is G. David Quirin, *The Capital Expenditure Decision* (Irwin, 1967).

pointed out, promotion expenditures are intended to increase demand for an offering—that is, to increase inelasticity as well as to shift the demand curve upward so that more units will be sold at a given price. To change the demand function means, of course, to alter the perception of the current and potential customers so that they are more favorably disposed toward the offering. As we have pointed out, to change behavior, particularly in the face of entrenched, competitive offerings, may require considerable time and effort by a firm. Thus, the long-range objectives and character of much of promotion frequently render it an *investment*. In principle, advertising, for example, should compete for a place in the firm's capital budget just as any other investment proposals whether for machinery, an expanded lunchroom, or a new research laboratory. Rationally, to select among investment proposals, a firm uses discounted cash flow analysis to determine either the after-tax rate of return or the after-tax present value.[15]

SOME ECONOMIC EFFECTS OF PROMOTION

This section will consider some additional aspects of productivity and costs in promotion. The first portion relates to the productivity of promotion and data on economies in promotion, especially advertising. The second part discusses briefly the principal empirical findings of promotion effects on market structure and performance.

Promotion and Some Economic Effects in the Firm

In analyzing economies of scale in promotion, and in particular advertising, there are two fundamental analytical problems:

(1) To distinguish static and single product economies of scale from dynamic, multi-product, and other spillover effects, and

(2) Even within a static and single product analysis, to distinguish among economies associated with messages, exposures, contacts, and sales.[16]

Simon has argued that increasing returns with respect to messages and exposures are offset by diminishing returns with respect to contacts and sales

---

[15] Most any modern managerial finance text covers the rudiments of present value analysis. Aside from managerial finance texts, the reader may refer to Quirin, *op. cit.* See also the solely literary treatment by Dean, "Does Advertising Belong in the Capital Budget?", *op. cit.*; and Dean's more comprehensive article, "Measuring the Productivity of Investment in Persuasion," *op. cit.*

[16] Lee E. Preston, "Advertising Effects and Public Policy," in the *Proceedings of the 1968 Academic Meetings of the American Marketing Association,* pp. 558–566. *See* Julian L. Simon, "Are there Economies of Scale in Advertising?", *Journal of Advertising Research,* V, June 1965.

so that in the net there are only constant or even decreasing returns to scale. The increasing returns with respect to messages and exposures and the decreasing returns with respect to contacts and sales are depicted in Figure 12.7.

The existence of economies in television advertising—including some derived in part from price discrimination—has been alleged by the anti-trust agencies. The television networks have energetically denied price discrimination, and recently, they have discontinued any quantity discounts in the sale of advertising time.[17]

FIGURE 12.7

ADVERTISING INPUTS AND POTENTIAL RESULTS

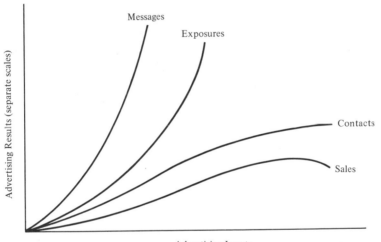

Source: Preston, "Advertising Effects and Public Policy," *Proceedings of the 1968 Academic Meetings of the American Marketing Association,* p. 560.

The issue of television advertising economies is complex when the listed price per minute of time is based on the expected number of viewers. For example, in Winter 1967, NBC's "Tuesday's Movie" cost an advertiser $56,000 per minute; whereas the average nighttime minute was $40,000. The more popular the program, the higher the *total* cost per minute. However, the *average* cost (cost per thousand viewers) may stay approximately the same. In 1967, the cost of reaching each thousand nighttime TV viewers remained at $1.90.[18] Predicted audiences are only estimates. If a program is watched by more viewers than the network expected when it set its adver-

---

[17] *See* the references cited in note 11 above.

[18] *Business Week,* June 29, 1968, pp. 118 ff.

tising rates, the advertiser enjoys a large coverage yielding a lower price-per-thousand cost. The networks ultimately bring the price back in line to accord to the revised program ratings.

A general conclusion with respect to economies in advertising in *all* media is that any tendency for advertising/sales ratios to fall with magnitude of advertising may be either (1) offset by a tendency of firms to grow by product multiplication, or (2) over-exploited by many large firms which continue to expand into regions of diminishing returns. Therefore, there is no general and pervasive tendency for large scale advertising activity to be accompanied by the achievement of sizeable economies of scale, either in terms simply of unit cost or more complexly as measured by advertising/sales ratios.[19]

Promotion and Some Market Effects

Promotion, like price, product and channels of distribution—the other three primary controllable managerial variables—may affect market structure and thereby market performance. Promotion may alter market structure in two ways: (1) by creating differential advantage for the firm or for groups of firms and products vis-à-vis other extant competitors, and/or (2) by creating barriers to entry. These two effects, though closely related, are not the same.[20]

They are separable as follows: Large-scale advertising could create entry barriers and simultaneously *increase* the demand elasticity facing individual firms or brands in a market. An example may be retail gasoline marketing. On the other hand, advertising might substantially *decrease* the elasticity of demand, yet not create entry barriers, so that the increased inelasticity would not necessarily yield higher price-cost margins for individual firms. Advertising in the liquor industry suggests a possible example.[21]

The relationships between advertising, demand elasticities and barriers to entry are not easily analyzed. As a result, there has been an understandable tendency to resort to analysis of rather gross effects, specifically, the relationships among advertising activity, market structure (especially firm size and concentration), and market performance (especially profitability and market share stability).

There is a decided mixture of results in the analysis of the relationship between advertising, market concentration, and market share stability. Some studies show no statistically significant correlation between advertising

[19] Preston, *op. cit.*

[20] This section draws from Preston, *op. cit.* Recall also the discussion of market structure in Chapter 4 of the present text.

[21] James H. Ferguson, "Advertising and Liquor," *The Journal of Business,* XL, October 1967, pp. 414–434.

intensity and market concentration; whereas others find a significant association between level of advertising and concentration.[22]

A comprehensive analysis of the market effects of advertising investigated interindustry differences in profit rates (rate of return on equity after taxes) for 41 consumer goods industries, 1954–1957. The study concluded:

> Industries with high advertising outlays earn, on average, at a profit rate which exceeds that of other industries by nearly four percentage points. This differential represents a 50 percent increase in profit rates. It is likely, moreover, that much of this profit rate differential is accounted for by the entry barriers created by advertising expenditures and by the resulting achievement of market power.[23]

Although the Comanor-Wilson study is persuasive, some caution is advised in interpreting the results. The findings indicate a statistical relationship between advertising intensity and profit rates. However, these associations are not observed in all cases nor always in significant magnitude, and moreover, a statistical association does not prove causation. Nevertheless, from these and similar findings, it is highly probable that intensive advertising contributes to concentration and profitability. Quite possibly, high concentration tends to *increase* advertising intensity, either because a firm with large market share tends to gain more from generic demand expansion, or because oligopolists tend to shift competitive effort to more complex forms and/or jointly to use advertising as a barrier to entry of new competitors.

Conclusions of the Market Effects of Promotion

To conclude this brief discussion of market effects of promotion, the evidence is that there tends to be some association between high levels of advertising activity and certain elements of market structure and perform-

[22] The leading studies are cited in Preston. The best known investigation finding little or no association between advertising and concentration is Lester G. Telser, "Advertising and Competition," *The Journal of Political Economy*, LXX (October 1962), pp. 471–499.

Two studies of the Telser model producing results diametrically *opposed* to his findings are H. M. Mann, J. A. Henning, and J. W. Meehan, Jr., "Advertising and Concentration: An Empirical Investigation," *The Journal of Industrial Economics*, XVI (November 1967), pp. 34–45; and C. Y. Yang, "Industrial Concentration and Advertising," Hearings of the Subcommittee on Antitrust and Monopoly, Committee on the Judiciary, in *Concentration and Divisional Reporting*, Part 5, U.S. Senate, 89th Congress, 2d Session, U.S. Government Printing Office, 1966, Appendix 8.

An important major study finding a strong association between advertising and performance is "The Degree of Product Differentiation and the Condition of Entry in Food Manufacturing Industries," *The Structure of Food Manufacturing*, Chapter 3, Technical Study No. 8, Natural Commission on Food Marketing (June 1966).

[23] W. S. Comanor, and T. A. Wilson, "Advertising, Market Structure, and Performance," *The Review of Economics and Statistics*, LXIX, November 1967, pp. 423–440.

ance. In some markets, advertising appears to lead to more concentrated markets and hence frequently to higher profit levels. For large and continuous advertisers, advertising is not specifically less expensive, but it is probably more profitable over the long term for them than for smaller and less consistent users.

One reason for the somewhat inconclusive relationship between advertising, concentration, and profit rates, is that advertising is only one of three promotion variables by which a firm may effect differential advantage. There might be stronger associations if all three promotion elements were included. Moreover, a firm can differentiate itself not only by means of promotion but also through adroit use of its product, channel and price variables as well. We recall that the "total product" of a firm is a demander's total set of percepts of an offering, and these percepts are affected by more than advertising alone. It may well be that beyond some point advertising becomes anti-competitive, that is, it leads to high level of concentration, barriers to entry, and excessive profits. However, this relationship if true, has yet to show up clearly in statistical analyses. We have not as yet any conclusive demonstration, given all that comprises total product and the bases for differential advantage. We may conclude that the associations found in the studies to date *are* suggestive, but they do not answer all the questions.

On the Social Welfare Implications of Promotion

We shall comment briefly on some social implications of promotion; the reader should also see Chapter 16, "Consumer Welfare." Persuasion is part of man's apparatus to adapt his way of life to change. Without some stimulus to action, man tends to be indifferent and apathetic to change, frequently unwilling to exert spontaneously the effort which change requires. For most people, preconditioned routines are preferred and habitual responses retained. Thus, change, whether it be to support the UN, the local symphony, or a new brand of soap, comes only by some stimulus to induce change. In civilized society, this stimulus is persuasion in the form of the written, spoken, or "viewed" word.[24]

Some critics raise important criticisms of advertising, claiming that it corrupts tastes, creates wants, and is wasteful of economic resources. Often it *is* tasteless and banal, but there are perhaps even more important issues. The alleged power of advertising to convert nonbelievers into captive customers has become an article of faith among some observers and commentators, among them, Professor John Kenneth Galbraith.[25] According to Galbraith in *The New Industrial State*, promotion's control over demand and certain technological imperatives, produce bigness and planning in our

[24] Some of these points are taken from Edmund D. McGarry, "The Propaganda Function in Marketing," *Journal of Marketing*, October 1958.

[25] See *American Capitalism: The Concept of Countervailing Power* (Houghton Mifflin, 1952); and *The New Industrial State* (Houghton Mifflin, 1967).

society in the form of large industrial firms, which he claims have largely supplanted the market mechanism. But opposition—both theoretical and empirical—to Galbraith is abundant.[26]

We have argued that advertising and other similar promotional variables do stimulate behavior, but one may distinguish between "stimulation" and "creation." Denying none of the stimulative power of advertising, there is considerable question whether, in the absence of an underlying psychological or physiological need, advertising can truly *create* much of anything.[27]

We should recall Stigler's observation that it is not necessarily logical to blame the menu or the restaurant waiter for one's own obesity. Or is it?

There is some evidence suggesting that advertising's (or any other outside "persuader's") power to affect behavior is *inversely* proportional to the importance of the purchase. Thus, in purchases such as many low-cost shopping goods there is only a relatively small economic risk, for only a small proportion of one's resources is committed in such a purchase. With financial commitment or social risks relatively low, one resists less (or thinks less about) the entreaties of an advertiser. The purchase of a house or an automobile *is* a risky decision and one typically draws upon his own attitudes and cognitive powers in such decisions. In general, the influence of advertising decreases in proportion to the importance the customer attaches to the matter.[28]

In unimportant purchases, one's beliefs and attitudes are not substantially involved; whereas they are involved in important purchases. Advertising can influence behavior in important decisions only by first changing underlying beliefs and attitudes—which requires advertising messages that *coincide* with one's perception of himself and his environment. That is, advertising that proceeds through one's perception of himself, by moving with the current, has some chance of modifying behavior.[29] But that is far different from an "outside" persuader simply creating de novo whatever behavior he desires.

Another theme with respect to advertising allegedly creating wants is that advertising turns one's aspirations to objects that he would not naturally think of. Thus, because of advertising we desire certain goods and services which in the normal course of events are not intrinsic wants. We are led to aspire to such things as clean teeth, higher education, a minimum of offensive odors, the symphony, and the Peace Corps. Are wants necessarily without merit simply because they have been acquired under the pressures of advertising? Each of us resents anyone else passing judgment on the

[26] See the discussion in Chapter 14, "Marketing and Public Policy."

[27] The reader is encouraged to review the discussion in Chapter 3 on the distinction between needs and wants.

[28] George Katona, *The Mass Consumption Society* (McGraw-Hill, 1964), p. 58 ff.

[29] Irving S. White, "The Functions of Advertising in Our Culture," *Journal of Marketing*, XXIV, July 1959.

quality of our own tastes and wants. Thus, to question the validity of others' wants (whether or not evoked by advertising), borders on impudence— a point emphatically made by Professor Harry Johnson:

> All economically relevant wants are learned. Moreover, all standards of taste are *learned*. It is, therefore, both arrogant and inconsistent to assume that those who have acquired their standards from general culture and advanced education can choose and pass judgments according to standards possessing independent validity, while those who have acquired their standards from social pressures and advertising can neither understand nor learn to understand the difference between good and bad taste.[30]

Let there be no mistake. To point out the illogic of some who attack the influencing of other's tastes as well as to point out the potential social usefulness of some advertising, is *not* to condone the obvious excesses and tastelessness so frequently a part of advertising. Persuasive advertising to young children is especially indefensible from an ethical standpoint.

However, in a free society, the right to persuade and be persuaded is also one of the essential freedoms. In our opinion, we must ensure that each of us has the facts and at least some minimum level of education in order to choose rationally—to accept or reject what he hears or reads. With sufficient facts and rational ability, society will be amply protected, as it must be, from any excesses by persuaders.

As with all other aspects of a free society, there are risks. The free exchange of ideas with persuasive intent is one necessary risk of a free society. Also, we have seen that advertising may lead to higher market concentration, barriers to entry, and excess profits. All the while preserving, insofar as possible, the right to persuade, one may find cause for some public policies against advertising if advertising preys on the defenseless— the uneducated and the young—or induces monopoly (especially if monopoly losses are as large as estimated, 2 to 6 percent of national income).[31]

SUMMARY

Promotion is the use of personal and nonpersonal means by demanders and suppliers to inform and persuade in order to effect transactions. There are three broad types of promotion: (1) advertising, (2) personal selling,

---

[30] Harry G. Johnson, "The Consumer and Madison Avenue," reprinted in Perry Bliss, *Marketing and the Behavioral Sciences* (Allyn and Bacon, 1963), p. 122 (emphasis added).

[31] Weiss estimates monopoly profits at about 2 to 4 percent of national income. Leonard Weiss, *Case Studies in American Industry* (Wiley, 1967), p. 318. David R. Kamerschen estimates them to be on the order of 6 percent of national income. "An Estimation of the 'Welfare Losses' from Monopoly in the American Economy," *The Western Economic Journal*, IV, Summer 1966.

and (3) special sales program. Advertising is the use of nonpersonal communication media—television, radio, newspapers, magazines, billboards, telephone, and so on—to inform and/or persuade. Personal selling is the use of sales personnel, either one's own employees or agents hired for specific sales periods, for informing and/or persuading current and potential customers. Special sales programs are combinations of advertising and personal selling, such as trade fairs, retail games, trading stamps, exhibits of new products, point-of-sale displays, large-scale sales demonstrations, and so on.

Promotion, whether it be advertising, personal selling, or special sales programs, consists in varying degrees of information and persuasion.

Institutional promotion is intended to establish goodwill toward a supplier or other agency without necessarily emphasizing any one offering. *Product* promotion is directed to individual offerings singly or in combination. The intent in promotion is similar in concept whether one is promoting a public service organization, a wine, a candidate for public office, an airline, or low-sudsing detergent.

The market structure and the differentiability of the offering determine in large part the extent to which firms emphasize information or persuasion in their promotion. In general, the greater the interdependence among sellers the more firms will tend to persuade. On the other hand, the more a firm is an "independent" decision-maker the more it will be able merely to employ information in its promotion. Persuasion will be minimized also if an offering is considered completely a convenience good. Similarly a seller of homogeneous supplies enjoying relative independence from his competitors, will use relatively little persuasion. But this same firm selling its homogeneous supplies in *concentrated* markets, in order to gain independence, will be forced to seek any and all possible avenues of differentiation—which means necessarily a greater proportion of persuasion in its promotion.

The promotion used in selling to middlemen frequently varies from that employed to appeal to the ultimate consumer. A manufacturer, for example, may *promote* a convenience good to middlemen in terms of the unique profit potential or other distinguishing commercial features, even though the consumer perceives all offerings as the same.

In 1969 advertising was approximately 3.5 percent of national personal consumption expenditures, 3.25 percent of disposable personal income, and 2.24 percent of gross national product. The growth in total advertising expenditures in the U.S. economy has paralleled closely the growth of aggregate economic activity as measured by these macro-indicators.

Promotion as any other variable input used in conjunction with fixed inputs demonstrates increasing returns and then decreasing returns. Increasing returns are due in part to the cumulative effects of repeat sales, word of mouth or other spill-over promotion from satisfied customers, increased efficiency by managers in using media and establishing effective message content, increasing goodwill effected by salesmen, and salesman learning. The marginal productivity of promotion declines because, among other reasons, the most likely prospects have been reached and prospects less susceptible, for reasons including brand loyalty to competitive brands, are encountered.

Promotion will vary in its effect on sales according to business conditions in general. In times of economic recession, promotion has much less effect (elasticity of response) than in times of economic expansion.

Advertising can be seen very realistically as an investment rather than a short-run expenditure. Frequently, it takes a considerable period of time for the results of a promotional expenditure to occur.

There is little evidence of persistent or substantial economies of scale in advertising. Increasing returns with respect to messages and exposures are probably completely offset by diminishing returns with respect to contacts and sales, so that in net there are only constant or even decreasing returns to scale for advertising. Such economies of scale as have been alleged by some are probably due in largest part to price discrimination in the purchase of advertising time.

There is some evidence that promotion tends to increase barriers to entry and consequently reinforce high concentration in some markets. As a result of intensive promotional effort in some markets with high concentration, there is a tendency for higher than normal profits.

Persuasion is part of man's apparatus to adapt his way of life to change. Without some stimulus to action man tends to be indifferent and apathetic to change, frequently unwilling to exert spontaneously the effort which change requires. There is some evidence suggesting that the ability of advertising (or any other outside persuaders) to affect behavior is *inversely* proportional to the importance of the purchase.

In a free society the right to persuade and be persuaded is also one of the essential freedoms. To protect society from any possible excesses from advertising or other promotion, each of us must have the facts and at least some minimal level of education in order to choose rationally, that is, to be able to accept or reject what one hears or reads.

SUGGESTED READINGS

Advertising

Wroe Alderson, *Dynamic Marketing Behavior* (Homewood, Ill.: Richard D. Irwin, Inc., 1967), Chapter 5.

> A conceptual treatment of advertising's role in facilitating search and minimizing the random pairing of buyers and sellers.

Jules Backman, *Advertising and Competition* (New York: New York University Press, 1967).

A sizeable study of advertising's implications for competition, financed by the Association of National Advertisers.

The book is useful for certain data combined in one place, though the study curiously doesn't touch upon some issues, such as economies of scale in advertising.

Raymond A. Bauer and Stephen A. Greyser, *Advertising in America: The Consumer View* (Harvard Business School, 1968).

The most comprehensive measurement and evaluation of public attitudes toward advertising to date.

Neil H. Borden, *The Economic Effects of Advertising* (Irwin, 1944).

A well-known study of the economic implications of advertising.

W. S. Comanor and T. A. Wilson, "Advertising, Market Structure, and Performance," *The Review of Economics and Statistics*, LXIX, November 1967, pp. 423–440.

Comanor and Wilson investigated interindustry differences in profit rates for 41 consumer goods industries, and found that high advertising outlays earned significantly higher profit rates than other industries.

Joel Dean, "How Much to Spend on Advertising," *Harvard Business Review*, January-February 1951.

A discussion of the marginal productivity of advertising and the reasons for increasing and decreasing returns to advertising effort.

———, "Measuring the Productivity of Investment in Persuasion," *Journal of Industrial Economics*, XV, April 1967.

Dean argues that much of promotion is on investment, and he points out several implications of such a perception of promotion.

John C. Peterman, "The Clorox Case and Television Rate Structures," *Journal of Law and Economics*, XI (October 1968), pp. 321–422.

A detailed examination of the issue of discrimination in the sale of TV advertising time with respect to the Federal Trade Commission complaint against Procter & Gamble's acquisition of Clorox.

Lee E. Preston, "Advertising Effects and Public Policy," *Proceedings of the 1968 Academic Meetings of the American Marketing Association,* pp. 558–566.

A useful summary and implications of data on economies of scale and market-structure effects of advertising.

Lester G. Telser, "Advertising and Competition," *The Journal of Political Economy*, LXX (October 1962), pp. 471–499.

A well-known study finding little or no association between advertising and reductions in competition.

John J. Wheatley, *Measuring Advertising Effectiveness* (Homewood, Ill.: Richard D. Irwin, Inc. 1969).

Possible Anticompetitive Effects of Sale of Network TV Advertising,

Hearings before the Subcommittee on Antitrust and Monopoly of the
Committee on the Judiciary, U.S. Senate, 89th Congress, 1966.
Parts 1 and 2.

Sales Promotion

Federal Trade Commission, *Economic Report on the Use of Games of
Chance in Food and Gasoline Retailing* (1968).

Federal Trade Commission, *Economic Report on the Use and Economic
Significance of Trading Stamps* (1966).

Harold W. Fox, *The Economics of Trading Stamps* (Public Affairs Press,
Washington, D.C., 1968).

Two substantial efforts to appraise the real cost and benefits of
trading stamps.

Personal Selling

Edward L. Brink and Wm. T. Kelley, *The Management of Promotion:
Consumer Behavior and Demand Stimulation* (Prentice-Hall, Inc.,
1963).

John Howard, *Marketing Management Analysis and Planning* (Irwin, Rev.
Ed., 1963), Chapter 14, "Promotion Decisions—Personal Selling."

Philip Kotler, *Marketing Management* (Prentice-Hall, 1967), Chapter 19,
"Sales-Force Decisions."

13

Price decisions
and
performance

"Price" and "product" are closely interrelated, and "price," as we shall see, cannot be discussed separately from "product." In this chapter we consider carefully several aspects of price—including its meaning, the meaning of "price competition," pricing in response to changes in costs and demand, and pricing to effect changes in demand as well as to increase quantity demanded.

As with other analyses, the present chapter is limited by space. Accordingly, we shall present only the major aspects of pricing analysis, suggesting additional sources which the interested reader should consult for further details.

THE MEANING OF PRICE

We define "price" as the total resources expended by a buyer or lessee in acquiring a given good or service.

For a transaction to occur a rational demander obviously must perceive utility in the good or service *greater than* the utility of the scarce resources he must give up to acquire the offering, and the seller (on the average) must anticipate net revenue exceeding the net value of retaining the offering.

But what specifically are these "total (scarce) resources" expended by a buyer or lessee? "Price" in a transaction consists both of what the buyer explicitly pays the seller in exchange for a specified good or service *and*, in that for many people time and effort have a cost equivalent, *also* the resources expended by the buyer in terms of purchase time, travel effort and other associated tasks and inconveniences. Thus the "total resources expended by a buyer or lessee in acquiring a given good or service" include *all* types of the demander's scarce resources expended in the transaction. Obviously the meaning of "scarce" depends on the individual. A busy college student will impute a considerable cost to his time involved in a transaction, and hence for him the price of a given good or service will be higher than the price of the same good or service at the same store for, say, a retired individual who has few or no alternative demands on his time. Indeed, the latter person may *derive* utility from the act of shopping, as a pleasant way to use time.

Aside from price consisting of both explicit and implicit expenditures of scarce resources, we see from the definition that price in terms of utility consists of two parts: (1) a demander's total scarce resources expended in acquiring a specified good or service, and (2) the specified good or service— that is, a specific bundle of utility.[1] Hence, price is the relationship between what is given up and what is obtained. Price, therefore, can be expressed elementally:

$$\text{Customer's scarce resources} \gtrless \text{bundle of utility.}$$

A simple example will help clarify the twofold nature of price. What is the actual price in a sale in which a customer must acquire the good at the seller's warehouse? First of all, a customer is aware of the sale because he recognizes that the listed dollar cost is less than the level at which this seller and other sellers normally sell the good. This dollar cost, however, to this customer is *not* necessarily a lower price. The relevant question to the customer is precisely how many scarce resources he must consume in acquiring the desired good. Moreover, is the good at the warehouse sale substantially the same *total product* as that which he would obtain in purchasing at the regular terms in the regular retail store? With respect to the expenditure of scarce resources, there should be included the imputed cost of one's time, automobile gasoline and parking, or bus fare, and so on. Moreover, there are other costs to be borne before the customer derives *use* utility—that is, transportation, assembly, learning to use the product, and so on. As to the product itself—bundle of utility—in a warehouse sale it may be smaller in that there is usually no privilege to return unsatisfactory goods, the goods sometimes are partially unassembled, and so on.

---

[1] The reader may wish to refer to Chapters 3 and 11 for a review of offerings as bundles of utility. The present discussion in part is adapted from that of E. J. McCarthy, *Marketing: A Managerial Approach* (3d ed., Irwin, 1968), Chapter 24. There is ample theoretical and empirical support for this inclusive concept of "price." *See* for example, George J. Stigler, "The Economics of Information," *The Journal of Political Economy*, LXIX, June, 1961, p. 223 and *passim*.

Thus, a rational customer will purchase at the "sale" only if the *net* increase in utility from the warehouse sale exceeds the *net* increase in utility from purchasing at the regular terms and from the regular outlet. This says merely that in the perception of a customer the warehouse sale is desirable if his total expenditure of scarce resources *declines* relative to the utility he wishes to acquire.

The meaning of price increases and decreases is complex. We turn now specifically to these issues.

Price Increases and Decreases: The Meaning

We urge the reader always to consider price in terms of the "total scarce resources/bundle of utility." Only then can one determine actual price increases and decreases.

A "price increase" occurs when the amount of the resources expended rises relative to the utility received. The increase of scarce resources relative to the bundle of utility occurs in two ways. First, even with an increase in the bundle of utility—such as extra product features—if a customer must expend proportionately more resources than the product enlargement, then the price has risen. Second, even with a decrease in the amount of expended scarce resources, if the bundle of utility decreases proportionately more, then the price has risen.

A "price decrease" occurs when the necessary scarce resources fall relative to the bundle of utility. Even if the bundle of utility decreases, there is nevertheless a price decrease if the scarce-resource expenditure declines proportionately more. A price decrease occurs also if an increase in the amount of scarce resources a customer must expend is offset by a proportionately greater increase in the bundle of utility. An obvious example of a price decrease in which a customer's scarce resources remain unchanged is a "two-for-one" sale. Or another example: A manufacturer of candy bars desires to keep the stated retail price of his product at five cents. He could nevertheless effectively price-compete by offering larger or higher quality bars for the five cent price. (Candy lovers lament that recent years have seen largely the reverse: The five cent price was maintained but smaller and smaller bars were offered.) An example of a price decrease in which a customer expends more resources for even greater satisfaction is a lover of chamber music who purchases a front-row seat at twice the price of a back-row seat—and triples his enjoyment.

In passing, we note that a "bargain" is simply a price decrease larger than some "normal" level. Clearly, for a transaction to be worthwhile to a customer, there must be a "sufficient" positive utility differential. Precisely what constitutes a sufficient utility gain is a personal matter, a function of subjective evaluation. People with many constraints on their time may have a larger "normal differential" if they are to transact than, say, someone with more time at his disposal and more inclined to enjoy shopping as an end in itself. (For this second person there are obviously two sources of utility.)

It is against a "normal differential" that some price decreases are perceived as bargains—that is, something beyond one's personal standard, utility inducement. This conceptualization of bargains as values greater than normal levels is applicable to demanders in all markets. For firms, the standard in investments may be their cost of capital.[2]

The concepts of price increase or decrease are meaningful only in a given *product market*. That is, disproportionate changes in required scarce resources and bundles of utility constitute "price changes" as long as the offering remains in the same product market. But if a seller alters his offering or changes the scarce resources required of the demander so much that the demander no longer perceives a relationship between the offering and his want, there is not a price change but a different product.[3]

"Price," "Product" and "Price Competition"

The preceding discussion of price as including both the customer's total scarce resources expended *and* a given good or service, points up the close relationship between the concepts "price" and "product." Also, based on customers' perceptions of *net* utility, it suggests there is no useful distinction between "price competition" and "nonprice competition." An inclusive definition of price, as is ours, is simply the obverse of total product.

It is merely a matter of choice whether one expresses a price reduction as a decrease in expended scarce resources relative to utility received, or as an increase in utility received relative to expanded scarce resources. For example, consider the simple two-for-one sale. One can see this in terms of a 50 percent reducation per unit in (at least part of) the scarce resources expended by the customer. Or, one can see it in terms of a substantial (at the limit, 100 percent) increase in utility relative to one's expenditure of resources. A second simple example is a retail store instituting free delivery service (usually on purchases exceeding some dollar level). A customer whose normal purchases of the same goods and services now qualify for free delivery may see this either as fewer scarce resources required (he can now avoid the costs of travel to the store), or as enhanced utility (the convenience of not having to go to the store).

We cannot stress too much the grave error in any price analysis that ignores the product and looks only at the expenditure of scarce resources, or, worse yet, looks only at the price-tag portion of a customer's resource expenditure.

In addition, to focus solely on the listed price is simplistic for a second

---

[2] For a useful discussion of bargains for firms with respect to acquiring on-going assets —mergers—*see* W. W. Alberts and Joel E. Segall, *The Corporate Merger* (Chicago University Press, 1966), Chapter 11.

[3] The reader may wish to review Chapter 3 on the relationship among wants, offerings, and product markets. We discuss pricing that radically changes perception of offerings (hence, effects new products), later in this chapter.

reason: In industrial markets, especially, there is frequently a difference between the list price and the transaction price. This difference may be sizeable, for in some markets there is considerable price shading, that is, special concessions to favorite and valued buyers. For many homogeneous industrial products, the difference between the list price—which is published or otherwise generally available—and the actual transaction price points up the fiction of list price. Concentrated oligopolies selling homogeneous total products in industrial markets are the most frequent setting for off-list pricing.[4]

For us, any meaningful distinction between "price" and "(total) product" or similarly "price competition" and "nonprice competition" is virtually impossible. Strictly speaking, competition among sellers is all about increasing the satisfaction of demanders who, of course, have only finite resources. Hence, competition among sellers obviously comes down to increasing perceived utility relative to the required outlay of resources. *Perceived utility relative to perceived resource expenditure*—that is the whole of competition. If utility rises relative to resources expended, there is a price decrease—call it price or nonprice competition. We hasten to add two clarifications.

First and foremost, for real competition—strenuous rivalry—to exist, there must be a sufficient number of firms to ensure essentially independent decision-making and hence real alternatives for customers. Only in this context will firms most probably seek to increase the differential between utility and customers' total outlay of resources.

Second, to say as we do that all competitive effort that is meaningful—that is, increases perceived utility relative to expenditures—is "price competition," is also implicitly to acknowledge that much that firms do is *meaningless*, that is, much advertising, personal selling, and other forms of sales promotion as well as many product and channel activities have *no* effect on the perceived utility of a good or service. They are wasted resources.[5] Moreover, continued zero (or very low) marginal productivity of any activity may (through cost pressure) ultimately lead to a price increase. Hence, meaningless competitive effort in two ways is an unproductive use of society's resources.

To summarize, we recall that "total product" includes all utility elements. "Price" is a utility relationship. Thus, price and total product are the same concept with different emphases. All of competition relates to utility-scarce resources differentials; hence all competition, necessarily, may be conceived as "price competition" or equally, "total product competition."[6]

---

[4] *See* George J. Stigler, "Administered Prices and Oligopolistic Inflation," *Administered Prices: A Compendium on Public Policy,* Subcommittee on Antitrust and Monopoly, Committee on the Judiciary, U.S. Senate, 88th Congress, 1st Session, 1963.

[5] Recall the discussion in Chapter 3 of the meaning of "new product."

[6] Some readers with a strong economics background may find "real price" a useful synonym for our two-fold concept of price.

Prices and Discounts

Vertical price structures show the terms and conditions of sale, including the discounts granted to the members of the channel. A functional discount is a total-resource reduction granted in exchange for performing one or more functions that the seller would have to perform himself.[7]

Functional Discount Illustrated

A typical functional discount is illustrated in the following table. The table is interesting for it shows the price structure for more than one marketing channel. For example there is a direct channel between the seller and a retailer pharmacy. This channel exists for the retail drugstore that purchases 1000 or more tablets. It shows that when the retailer buys in sufficient volume, he is entitled to the functional discount accorded to the wholesaler. The second channel and its concomitant price structure is the one of manufacturer-wholesaler-retailer.

TABLE 13.1

UPJOHN PRICE SCHEDULE FOR ORINASE IN 0.5 GRAM TABLETS, BOTTLES OF 50 TABLETS

Item	Price
Production costs per 1000	$ 13.11
To Wholesaler per 1000	83.40
To Retailer per 1000 [1]	100.00
To Consumer per 1000	140.00

1 Retailers can purchase at the wholesaler price-level if they purchase $100.00 worth of merchandise per year. Source: U.S. Congress, Senate Committee on the Judiciary, *Report Administered Prices: Drugs*, 86th Congress, 1st session, 1961, p. 20.

Thus, we see that functional discounts are "reductions" in price granted in exchange for specified services performed by the customer, such as a retailer promoting the seller's product, or an industrial customer performing the transportation function in place of the seller. Seasonal and quantity discounts have analogous bases.

How do these functional discounts relate to the price equation? Obviously a discount means that fewer resources must be given up—but, we should ask, fewer resources in exchange for what? In the presence of competitive forces, the price equation maintains an approximate equality—which necessarily means a seller reduces the total product in proportion to the "resource" reduction granted the buyer.

Consider the case of a buyer performing the transportation function: When the buyer picks up the product from the seller's plant, the transportation costs are shifted to the buyer, and the total product is reduced. The

[7] See E. T. Grether, *Marketing and Public Policy* (Prentice-Hall, 1966), p. 63.

explicit amount paid the seller is of course lower, but there is a net saving to the buyer *only if* the buyer's cost of self-delivery is less than the discount granted by the seller.

THE BASIC RATIONALE OF PRICING

Most products with the possible exception of "prestige" goods in other than purely competitive markets, face downward sloping demand curves. A lower price increases the quantity demanded. The rational firm, in order to maximize profits, sets price to yield an equality of marginal revenue and marginal cost. Figure 13.1 shows the profit-maximizing price, P_m, and the corresponding profit-maximizing sales, Q_m, for a hypothetical single-product firm. The rectangle $ABEF$ is the total revenue, and the rectangle $DCEF$ is the total cost associated with selling output Q. The total profit is the rectangle $ABCD$.

FIGURE 13.1

PROFIT-MAXIMIZING PRICE FOR A FIRM SELLING A DIFFERENTIATED SINGLE PRODUCT

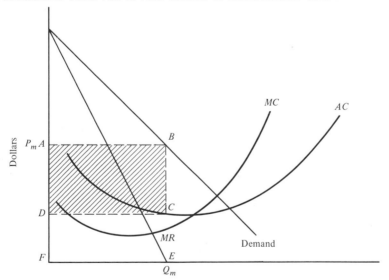

In Figure 13.1 MC changes dramatically with changes in output. MC is of course simply the change in total variable cost, for in the short run, some costs are fixed. Thus, the greater the proportion of fixed costs to total costs, the relatively smaller will be MC with increased output. For example, the MC to a supermarket in adding another product to its shelves is virtually zero. What increase in variable costs arises from a supermarket selling an additional consumer product? It will typically not require additional stock personnel, markers or checkers. Hence there is virtually no increase in variable costs and thus MC for all practical purposes is zero. The condition of zero MC implies that a firm is still at a level of output corresponding to the downward or horizontal portion of its AC curve.[8]

If average costs in the short run do not change appreciably with moderate changes in output, the firm may focus primarily on the demand curve in determining price. (Throughout the immediate discussion we omit explicit analysis of competition, simply assuming that competition is fully reflected in the shape of the demand curve.)

Pricing and Elasticity

With respect to a given product demand curve, and all other things being equal, a rational manager lowers price if demand is elastic and raises it if demand is inelastic. In both cases total revenue will increase. Obviously a firm that is a profit maximizer rather than a revenue maximizer will increase revenue only to the output at which the increment in total revenue is equal to the increment in total cost, that is, $MR = MC$.

Profit-maximizing pricing does not necessarily lead to high prices. Rather, profit-maximizing pricing leads to high prices only *if* demand is highly inelastic. The extreme case is a firm with a completely inelastic product demand curve—absolutely vertical. A completely inelastic demand indicates that the firm could continue to raise price over some range and it would experience no decrease in units sold. This situation, however, is neither a frequent nor interesting case, for any such monopolist selling a product that is in any sense a "necessity" would soon come under public regulation. A hypothetical example is a private monopolist of ferry service between a well-populated but small offshore island and the mainland. On the other hand, a product that was not a necessity, above some price would obviously lose sales to substitute products.

A normative addage in the retail trade is "Charge what the traffic will bear." This retail rule of thumb is the commonplace expression of our preceding more formal rule: Rational firms raise price until they encounter the elastic portion of the demand curve. Retailers who know their clientele are amazingly accurate in estimating the price that constitutes, in effect, the upper end of the inelastic portion.

---

[8] *See* Richard Holton, "Price Discrimination at Retail: The Supermarket Case," *Journal of Industrial Economics,* VI, October 1957; and also Holton, "Scale Specialization and Costs in Retailing," *American Economic Review,* LI, May 1961. Marginal cost depends on two elements: (1) the price of variable inputs and (2) the marginal product of the variable inputs. For a clear discussion of production and cost theory *see* C. E. Ferguson, *Microeconomic Theory,* (Irwin, 1966), Chapters 6–8.

For an interesting analysis of idle capacity leading to market diversification, *see* Eli Clemens, "Price Discrimination and Multi-Market Firm," *Review of Economic Studies,* XIX, (1950–51), pp. 1–11. *See also* the discussion of diversification in Chapter 11 of the present book.

If a retailer sells a completely homogeneous good about which consumers are well informed, and if there are many competitors, he faces a
completely elastic demand curve. His only substantive decision is whether
and how much of the item he wishes to stock, for in this situation he has
no discretion over price. As the model of pure competition indicates, he
simply must sell at (or if foolish, below) the market price.

Let us consider some complexities in demand-oriented pricing in firms
selling differentiated products (that is, firms with sloping demand curves).
Assuming constant or falling costs, an increase in demand would provide
the firm selling with two options. With the outward-shift of the demand
curve, it could increase price to the point of selling the same amount at the
higher price, or by maintaining the same price, it could increase output.
The firm would raise price only if it could thereby increase profits more
than from merely increasing output at the old price.

Assuming MC is constant, it is a *fiction* that a demand increase will
necessarily lead a firm to increase its price. When demand increases, if the
new demand is more elastic than the old, a rational profit-maximizing firm
will *lower* price. Figure 13.2 illustrates a demand increase with D_1 and MR_1
the old demand and marginal revenue curves respectively, and D_2 and MR_2
the new curves. D_2 is more elastic than D_1; accordingly, P_2 is lower than P_1.[9]
A possible example of increased demand with increased elasticity is the
demand for generic drugs sold in retail drug stores. The *physical* product
is homogeneous, but the *total product* is somewhat differentiated owing
to differences in marketing mixes, location, and so on among stores. With
increased awareness by consumers of the equal merits of generic and
branded drugs, but higher prices of branded drugs, the increased demand
D_2, could be more elastic. Another example of an increase in elasticity
concomitant with a demand increase is a retail gasoline market which is
growing rapidly, hence the shift in demand; but also in which there is sharp
competition between private branders and the major brands, thus the
increase in demand elasticity.[10]

"Cost-oriented" Pricing

In some market structures sellers arrive at a price by first calculating
all costs and the target profit they wish to realize, from which they then
determine the price. Of course, unless price falls somewhere on the product
demand curve, a firm will sell nothing. For this reason, it is unrealistic to
make any hard and fast distinction between total reliance on demand and
total reliance on costs in pricing. In many instances, close inspection of
so-called "cost-oriented" pricing reveals it to be pricing which *is* fully

[9] *See* Watson (2d ed.), *op. cit.*, p. 315 ff. and p. 42 for a discussion of point elasticity.
[10] *See* Ralph Cassady, Jr., "The Price Skirmish—A Distinctive Pattern of Competitive
Behavior," *California Management Review*, Winter 1964, pp. 11–16.

responsive to demand. The price generally is sufficient to cover variable costs (especially direct costs), but the additional margin is sensitive to demand.[11]

FIGURE 13.2

LOWER PRICE FROM AN INCREASED, MORE ELASTIC, DEMAND

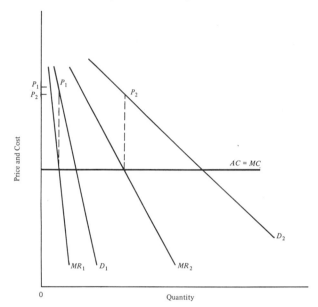

What is the principle of full-cost pricing? The concept is that of pricing to cover total unit costs (including a target profit) at some assumed volume rate. In full-cost pricing, the firm's average total cost curve (*ATC*) constitutes its various offering prices. To establish a price, a firm estimates the quantity it will sell this period, and *then* relates costs to this quantity, and arrives at a price. Note that in this procedure the price maker essentially "ignores" demand. Realistically, this would imply a market in which demand is extremely inelastic. Figure 13.3 shows a hypothetical *ATC* curve which includes target profit as well. The height *gh* indicates the average unit cost associated with the estimated total sales for the next period, 50,000 units. P_1 is the corresponding asking price. Total costs are the rectangle *adgh* and total revenue is the same rectangle, *adgh*. But suppose demand is less than estimated? That is, the demand curve shifts in, resulting in sales of 40,000 at price P_1. The firm obviously does not cover all costs, for the average cost at 40,000 units is *bf*, but the price is, of course, P_1. Thus the firm experiences total costs indicated by rectangle *abef*, total revenue of *abcd*, and, therefore, realizes a net loss of *cdef*.

[11] Richard Heflebower, "Full Costs, Cost Changes, and Prices," *Business Concentration and Price Policy* (NBER, 1955).

FIGURE 13.3

HYPOTHETICAL FULL-COST PRICING

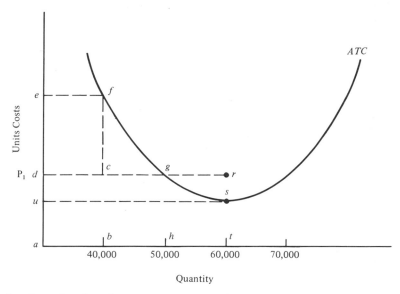

Quantity

On the other hand, suppose actual sales at price P_1 were 60,000 rather than the estimated 50,000. Because the firm is still on the downward sloping portion of *ATC* it derives a windfall profit from an outward shift of demand. At price P_1 the sales of 60,000 leads to total costs indicated by the rectangle, *aust*, and to total revenue, *adrt*. The firm realizes windfall profits (for target profits were already included in the *ATC*) of *drsu*.

Why might a seller use something akin to full-cost pricing? Two suggested answers are (1) simplicity, in that, costs are more in nature of facts than is demand, and thus, a seller can simply add a profit margin to the costs to arrive at price; and (2) a seller knows that in the long run he must cover all costs if he is to remain a viable firm. His anxiety about this may induce him to try to cover all unit costs and unit profit on each item sold.

In what markets might a seller successfully use full-cost pricing? Successful use would be in those markets in which there is relatively inelastic demand—some type of a limited monopoly—whereby customers have no alternative sources of supply to compare, or whereby for whatever reason, customers do not consider it worth their while to shop elsewhere. In the latter instance, the seller enjoys a spatial monopoly. For example, a consumer attracted to a particular department store because of a substantial sale on appliances might purchase other items not on sale, willingly paying a much higher ticket-price for them over that of competitor stores.[12]

---

[12] The successful retail merchant is frequently one who knows and exploits demand elasticities and interrelationships. *See* for example, Richard Holton, "Price Discrimination at Retail: The Supermarket Case," *op. cit.*

A conventional hardware store presents an example of full-cost pricing, for many conventional retailers such as hardware stores and corner grocers historically have been prone to employ a fixed percentage markup to each item. As a result, the total product of such stores has emphasized personal service elements rather than a reduction in the scarce resources required of a customer. Remember: In the view of *some* consumers, this may not be a higher price, but for many other customers it is. Discount hardware stores and supermarkets have cut deep inroads into the market shares of stores employing full-cost pricing, for many customers were immediately attracted to the price-cutting outlets.[13] To these customers, the new outlets' price was a price decrease. That is, the reduction somewhat in total product at the discount house (less personal service, and so on) was *more than offset* by the reduction in the scarce resources expended.

Full-cost pricing is quite clearly the procedure used in cost-plus contracts with the federal government. On the other hand, contractors competitively bidding for a particular government job are aware of the cost structures of their competitors and frequently will keep their bid below some maximal full-cost level. However, if there is but one bidder or if there is collusive bidding in which identical bids are submitted by "competitors," it is more likely that price will tend to maximal levels.[14]

We need not elaborate the irrationality of ignoring demand in pricing. If demand is elastic and a firm prices only in accordance with costs and target profit, the firm may either miss the demand curve completely or relate only to the upper end of the demand curve. Secondly, aside from the issue of elasticity of demand, cost-oriented pricing is backward looking, using as guides historical average costs and sales. The new price, P_2, is based on last period's costs which in turn were determined by the level of output attained. But in that output is a function of last period's price, P_2 is determined by P_1, which does not necessarily relate to current supply and demand. Thirdly, if demand is less than last period, actual costs rise, and the procedure leads the firm unwisely to raise prices as a result of decreasing demand! And just as irrationally, in the face of increasing demand, the procedure suggests lowering price (assuming the firm is on the downward portion of this short-run ATC curve). Both of these are opposite in direction to what common sense would suggest.

[13] *See* Stanley C. Hollander, "The Wheel of Retailing," in Perry Bliss (ed.), *Marketing and the Behavioral Sciences* (1st ed., Allyn and Bacon, 1963).

[14] Lack of competition in government contracts or in other markets has a considerable social cost. For example, some $22.7 billion in new contracts, amounting to 52.7 percent of all Defense Department contract awards in fiscal year 1967, were negotiated by the Department *without* any form of competition. "The Antitrust Laws and Government Contractors," *Antitrust and Trade Regulation Report* (Bureau of National Affairs), May 21, 1968, B-1 ff. *See also* Chapter 15 "Marketing and Public Policy" in the present book.

A sizeable price conspiracy among electrical contractors led to high prices to the government, and hence the public. See John Fuller, *The Gentlemen Conspirators: The Story of the Price Fixers in the Electrical Industry* (Grove Press, 1962).

As we shall discuss later, firms in the real world react more to changes in costs than demand. Many are the businessmen who are inclined to try to raise prices when costs have risen. It is a brave but also wise man who, confronted by rising costs, excess capacity, and *elastic* demand, *lowers* price to increase quantity demanded and thereby lower his unit costs.[15] Let us remember also that much that is called full-cost pricing has only in part a standard markup—the remainder being a demand-sensitive margin.

PRICING AND COMPETITION

Strong competitive forces will maintain approximate balance in the price equation. There are two fundamental conditions required for competitive forces to be present: (1) Potential suppliers and potential customers must be well informed as to supply and demand opportunities, and (2) Barriers to entry must be low so that new suppliers and demanders can enter and exit in response to supply and demand changes.

For example, under pure competition if demand exceeds supply, price would be bid up to an equilibrium, or supply would increase to establish a lower equilibrium, in either case eliminating excess demand. It is the same for markets characterized by downward-sloping product demand curves. An increase in demand, all else being equal, provides any firm a potential to increase price, or maintain price—but in either case to realize an increase in profits.

A firm will raise or maintain price depending on the elasticity of demand, the interrelationships the product may have with other of the firm's products, and its relative short-run and long-run preferences. The profits, in general, and an imbalance in the price equation in particular, is an open invitation to potential competitors to enter the market. The new competition seeks some of the excess profits being earned by present suppliers. The new entrants attempt to win customers by offering greater value, and thereby they begin the process of reestablishing equality in the price equation at a normal profit level.

On the other hand, if entry is not possible for new competitors, firms currently enjoying excess profits are protected from new resources entering to compete away their profits. For this reason, the monopolist with high

---

[15] Another form of cost-oriented pricing is marginal-cost pricing in which price is equated to marginal cost. This pricing basis is frequently argued as legitimate for public utilities and other government regulated enterprises, for it allocates resources efficiently: The price paid is equal to the added cost of the output. The issues are complex and will not be discussed here. *See* Watson, *op. cit.*, pp. 320–322; and W. G. Shepherd, "Marginal Cost Pricing in American Utilities," *Southern Economic Journal,* July 1966, pp. 58–70; and J. R. Nelson, "Practical Problems of Marginal-Cost Pricing in Public Enterprises: The United States," in A. Phillips and O. Williamson (ed.) *Prices: Issues in Theory, Practice, and Public Policy* (Pennsylvania University Press, 1967).

barriers to entry leads that quiet life we all would enjoy (but which we nonmonopolists never attain short of judicious marriage or some such event).

Similarly, competitive forces can correct excess profits on the buying side of the market. For example, when there is strong market power on the buying side, there can be coercive pressure for discounts with no accompanying reduction in the total product. The result is that a customer with monopsony power may obtain a price reduction strictly from his economic strength.

How long can the buyer continue to exact monopoly returns from the seller or sellers? He can continue to receive this favored treatment until either new resources enter as competitors on the buying side and thereby compete away some of his market power, or until he runs afoul of the antitrust laws—which happens if it can be demonstrated his discriminatory treatment either *has* or *may* lessen competition. Under current law, discriminatory pricing is illegal only if it may tend to lessen competition among the buyer's customers, suppliers, or his own competitors. Prolonged price discrimination generally is anticompetitive, but nonsystematic, sporadic price discrimination can be strongly procompetitive.[16] We turn now more specifically to these and related issues.

Price Discrimination

"Price discrimination" is selling the same product at different percentage markups over cost. Let us be clear: Price discrimination is *not* necessarily simply a difference in price for the same product. For example, there is price discrimination if a seller of a certain product to customers A and B experiences no differences in costs in selling but nevertheless sells at different prices to the two customers. In such a case there is clearly a different percentage markup over cost. Obviously, the same price but different costs is also price discrimination. On the other hand, if the seller incurs different costs in selling to customers D and E, the same percentage applied to each cost base will, of course, result in different prices. But because the same *percentage markup* has been applied, there is no price discrimination—each buyer is paying the same price in proportion to the seller's costs realized in selling to him.[17]

In passing, we shall point out a couple of the *procompetitive* aspects of nonsystematic, sporadic price discrimination. First, a seller of a new product will begin to make profits on the product only when he has enlisted the interest and achieved the loyalty of numerous customers. And, of course, all of this takes time and expenditures. To elicit interest in the product

---

[16] Price discrimination and the antitrust laws are treated in Chapter 14 "Marketing and Public Policy."

[17] The technical aspects of price discrimination are briefly and clearly treated in Watson, *op. cit.*, Chapter 17; and a more detailed discussion is found in Fritz Machlup, "Characteristics and Types of Price Discrimination," *Business Concentration and Price Policy* (National Bureau of Economic Research, 1955), pp. 397–440.

among customers whose attention currently is upon other goods and services requires a seller to present his new product at a price which encourages trial use. It is clear that for a while costs will exceed price—the product in its early period, in trying to gain a foothold in a new market, necessarily will incur losses or at least, varying markups. Thus, there may be different percentage markups for a while. The flow of new offerings into new geographic markets would be rudely damped if price discrimination of this procompetitive type were not permitted. Firms with excess capacity— operating on the downward-sloping portion of their average total cost curves—seek additional markets in which to sell as long as price exceeds or equals marginal cost. Thus, they will sell in increasingly distant markets as long as $P \geqq MC$.[18] Firms' invasions of geographic markets will reduce pockets of monopoly. However, as we have seen, successful interpenetration of markets necessarily requires price discrimination.

In passing, we note that the prime public policy issue with respect to price discrimination is twofold: (1) to determine the most meaningful and measurable concept of price discrimination; and (2) to determine the conditions in which price discrimination is decidedly undesirable from a total social standpoint. The latter may best be considered the criteria of *unreasonable* price discrimination.

General Issues in Pricing When Firms Are Interdependent

Firms in concentrated markets are interdependent in that a gain in market share by one firm is felt immediately by one or more competitors. If shares are approximately evenly distributed among the competitors—a symmetrical oligopoly—retaliation upon loss of market share is frequently swift.[19]

Figure 13.4 shows firm interdependence in terms of a kinked demand curve, *abc*. Any demand curve is simply a summary schedule of responses to changes in price. Whether oligopoly demand curves are actually "kinked" is irrelevant—the important point is that a firm raising its price above the equilibrium price, P_e, will experience the response denoted by segment *ab* if all other firms do not similarly raise their prices. If all firms raise their prices to the same level as the initiator, then all firms will move up along the straight line *a'bc*. The nature of the want as well as the condition of entry in the market will determine the amount of inelasticity in curve *a'bc*.

---

[18] *See* Eli W. Clemens, "Price Discrimination and the Multiple-Product Firm," *Review of Economic Studies*, XIX (1950–51), pp. 1–11; R. H. Holton, "Price Discrimination at Retail: The Supermarket Case," *op. cit.*; and Lee E. Preston, "Markups, Leaders and Discrimination in Retail Pricing," *Journal of Farm Economics* (May 1962), pp. 291–306; *see also* Joel Dean, *Managerial Economics* (Prentice-Hall, 1951), Chapter 9, "Price Differentials."

[19] We are not suggesting that firms try to maximize sales revenue or market share. The point at present is that in terms of market share or any similar criterion, tight oligopolies demonstrate interdependence.

On the downward side, if a firm cuts its price and if all other firms match the price cut, all firms will move down the segment *bc*. As drawn in Figure 13.4, the price reduction is not expanding the total market—the demand is inelastic. This means, of course, that among firms selling homogeneous total products, as in our example, if customers are generally informed of the prices asked by the several sellers, no seller can fail to match a lower price. When the demand is inelastic, each firm upon reducing its price to match a lower price experiences a smaller total revenue.

A secret price concession, to the extent it can be effected in highly concentrated markets, is depicted by segment *bc'*. A "secret concession" is a reduction in tag price the existence of which is unknown to competitors (which is almost impossible in a concentrated market). To the extent a firm can reduce its price, either by requiring fewer scarce resources of customers or by increasing the bundle of utility, and *escape* matching by competitors, that firm happily will move along segment *bc'*.

And this observation forces us to consider the manner in which much of real world competition takes place. Most firms selling at wholesale and many at retail have some *close* competitors. Thus, oligopoly (interdependence) of one degree or another is the prevailing structure in manufacturing and distribution in our economy.[20]

For the reasoning brought out above and implicit in Figure 13.4, firms wishing to enlarge their volume in many markets of our economy cannot simply lower their price—*unless* they are certain that a lower market price will expand the total market—that is, that total market demand is elastic. If firms in concentrated markets (or firms which, across several markets, are interdependent with other firms) generally cannot reduce price without inviting self-defeating retaliation, one deduces that the major portion of price competition is of a complex rather than simple form.[21] For example, a diversified firm wishing to improve its position in market M_1 might exploit demand complementarity by cutting the price of other of its products in other markets, but which are also used by customers in M_1, all the while maintaining the price in M_1. In the short run, competitors in M_1 who were

[20] How much of our economy is oligopolistic is beyond precise ascertaining, for we have yet to devise means of precisely measuring real world markets. Careful estimations of the amount of oligopoly in the real world are available. For some estimates *see* Willard F. Mueller, *Status and Future of Small Business,* Hearings before the Select Committee on Small Business, U.S. Senate, 90th Congress, 1st session, March 15, 1967; and W. G. Shepherd, "Trends of Concentration in American Manufacturing Industries, 1947–58," *The Review of Economics and Statistics,* May 1964. See also "White House Task Force Report on Antitrust Policy," *Antitrust and Trade Regulation Report,* No. 411, Special Supplement, No. 411, May 27, 1969.

[21] *See* Perry Bliss, "Non-Price Competition at the Department Store Level," in S. Hollander, *Exploration in Retailing* (East Lansing, Michigan, MSU, 1959), pp. 182–193. Also refer to our discussion of merchandising in Chapter 10 an *see* Alfred R. Oxenfeldt, "Product Line Pricing," *Harvard Business Review* (July–August 1966).

not similarly diversified could not respond in kind. Although, one would suppose that if the joint-pricing plan yielded economies, other firms would begin engaging in the particular combination. Until such time, however, the one firm would have achieved a differential advantage.

FIGURE 13.4

INTERDEPENDENCE IN OLIGOPOLY PRICING

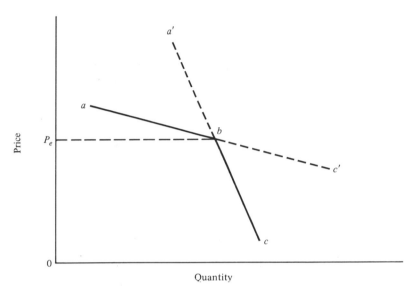

Aside from the risk of competitive matching of a "naked" price cut, there are other reasons why firms typically do not cut price without also changing one or more nonprice aspects, and also, why they do not cut it often. A firm may inadvertently induce customers not to purchase immediately, if the customers have reason to expect further price cuts; moreover, a customer of a firm known for frequent price cuts may be uncertain whether there is another location at which the seller is asking less for the same product.

SOME ADDITIONAL COMMENTS AND COMPLEXITIES OF PRICES AND PRICING

On Understanding Price Levels and Changes

Though the marketing economy differs from the pure market economy, are supply and demand as price setting forces somehow absent in the real world? No. Supply and demand exist in both the pure market economy and the real world. But in the real world, the patterns of demand and supply include and reflect the degree of competition and monopoly in any market.

Thus the idea of a price other than that set by supply and demand is simply a misunderstanding. "Price is always set by supply and demand, but either or both may be under monopoly control."[22]

There is such frequent comment on the subject that we pointedly emphasize supply and demand's role in real-world pricing:

> [A] price is determined in a market, and a market is a system of information on cost and demand, a set of signals which the business firm must learn to read as best he can. . . . [T]he choice in favor of one price or product mix or method rather than another is only the beginning of the pricing process. The next step is to see how far wrong the original decision was. The market is a feedback and corrective information system as well as an original information system.
>
> It is not, therefore, the price *decision* which is our true object, but rather its reception by the market. There is a considerable vogue today of asking business men how they set prices, and their answers, when they are not mere public relations—as is usually, I fear, the case— are heavily oriented to cost.[23]

Adelman points out two differing examples. The petroleum and steel industries contrast radically in the ability to pass along costs in higher prices. With respect to petroleum, at the start of 1957 the prices of crude oil rose an average of 30 cents per barrel. The price composite of refined products immediately was also raised 30 cents per barrel. However, by July of 1957, the increase in the prices of refined products had crumbled away, and by April 1958, the composite had deteriorated another 30 cents. It then regained some 20 cents. As a result the refiners' margin was squeezed by 30 cents, then 60, and finally 40, despite complete market information and rational advice that if everybody together would only cut back refinery runs and hold the line, all refiners would gain. This quite sensible monopoly advice was not followed: There was too much individual self-interest at work. Because of excessive inventories on first one product and then another,

---

[22] M. A. Adelman, "Pricing by Manufacturers," D. J. Duncan (ed.), *Conference of Marketing Teachers from Far Western States* (Berkeley: University of California, 1958), p. 147.

The term "administered prices" simply refers to prices set in markets where supply and/or demand is under some control. Adelman, *op. cit.*, p. 153. *See also* George J. Stigler, "Administered Prices and Oligopolistic Inflation," *Journal of Business*, January 1962; printed also in *Administered Prices: A Compendium on Public Policy*, Subcommittee on A. T. & Monopoly, Committee on Judiciary, U.S. Senate, 88th Congress, 1st session, 1963. In addition, *see* M. A. Adleman, "A Commentary on 'Administered Prices,'" *Administered Prices, ibid.*, but on the other hand, consider Walter Adams and Robert F. Lanzillotti, "The Reality of Administered Prices," *ibid.*

[23] Adelman, *op. cit.*, pp. 147–148 (emphasis in original). An example of the interview approach is A. D. H. Kaplan, Joel B. Dirlam, and Robert F. Lanzillotti, *Pricing in Big Business* (Brookings, 1958). Refer to Chapter 2 of the present book.

prices grew soft, and regular price concessions became routine, finally to be published. (Recall the discussion in Chapter 4 on interfirm organization.)

Raw material costs of course *do* effect prices—but the relationship between raw materials costs and prices is loose, or at least so general that it usually tells us nothing about a specific problem. Contrast the example of steel to that of oil. The last whisper of winter ushers in the annual justifications about the need for price rises in steel—justifications quite in advance of any wage increases. However, for that matter, the expected higher wages doubly "justify" price increases. All of this starts in about March, and by July, every company is on record either in favor or at least not opposing. In recent years there have been some deviations among the leading steel companies, but how much of this is due to admonitions from the White House, how much to "industrial statesmanship," and how much to market structure is debatable.[24] At any rate, by the end of July, prices are up. Adelman puts it well:

> Those who think that the higher wages "explain" the higher prices, as well as their opponents, chiefly in the labor unions, who try to demonstrate that the price increase is greater than is "justified" by the wage boost, avoid the more basic question as to whether the wage boosts would ever be granted in the first place if it were not known that prices would be boosted to cover the cost.[25]

To what may we attribute the difference between price behavior in steel and petroleum products? The difference is found not in the particular method of price decision or any such matter—it is found in the *market structures* of the two industries, that is, the control over supply. In 1956 when the price increases in steel became effective, steel production was at about 55 percent of capacity. Clearly, even before the price boost, any steel company could have produced considerable output at incremental cost less than incremental revenue at the then prevailing price. And even more so at the higher price. Interestingly this seemingly irresistible temptation was not yielded to by any firm. The reason is that each firm had complete assurance that everybody else would refrain from independent action. Such mutual self-restraint, obviously the best course for the industry as a whole, is simply a case of joint monopoly—the example of steel clearly evidencing a closely organized group of suppliers.

Neither the steel industry nor any other industry can continue indefinitely to increase price. There is, of course, the possibility of raising prices over some range—but only until other industries develop adequate *substi-*

---

[24] Consider the breakaway by Inland Steel in the President Kennedy-steel confrontation in 1961, and the roll-back (partial) by Bethlehem Steel in the President Johnson-steel face off in 1968.

[25] Adelman, *op. cit.*, p. 149.

tutes for steel, thereby inducing steel customers to switch to them; or until steel *imports* constrain domestic price rises in steel. One example of substitute products is aluminum cans which have tended to set a lower ceiling over tin plate prices.

The link between raw materials costs and product prices is sometimes virtually untraceable because the supply-demand conditions in a firm's market may be quite different from what they are for his suppliers and his customers. It is clear why prices of raw materials and finished goods can move in opposite directions. Also, the wider a firm's gross margin, the greater the room for divergent trends between its prices and those of a supplier or commercial customer.

Competitive Pricing Responses to Changes in Costs and Demand

In formal analysis of economic theory, equal importance is ascribed to the roles of cost and demand curves in determining price. However, taking real world markets as systems of imperfect signals, there perhaps is a considerable difference in the reliability of data as between demand and cost.[26] Data on cost, particularly on changes in cost are in the nature of facts, being largely based on quantified experience. But changes in demand depend on too many variables and too many types of market and product structures to be predictable with the same approximate accuracy of costs.

How does a firm know that "demand has shifted to the right," which would mean that the market would accept a higher price? A judgment that demand has increased is based on the evidence that inventories are below "normal" and unfilled orders are above normal; on inquiries or orders from other than one's usual customers; on salesmen's reports and trade reports, and so on.

When a decision is made to raise price, the moment of truth has arrived. The market reception is, as we have said, the all important aspect of pricing. Will the price rise stick? Businessmen face a dilemma: Out of rational self-interest, they correctly do not wish to price below the profit-maximizing price, but when they increase the price they want to be sure it sticks. There can be substantial economic loss connected with a price rise that has to be rescinded. For example, unsuccessful price increases may lessen customer goodwill, and involve considerable communication expenses. Also in a concentrated market, customers of items frequently purchased will be aware of price differences and switch to the lowest-priced offering. Thus, an unsuccessful price rise loses some customers and those that remain loyal become restless at the minimum.

Because of the difficulties of guessing at demand and because of the associated risk in raising prices, there frequently is a considerable lag

---

[26] Much of this section is from Adelman, *op. cit.*

between the first evidence that demand has increased and a firm actually raising the price.

On the other hand, price increases in a perfectly adjusting market, one in which demand increases are immediately reflected in a new price, describes a smooth line rising to the right.

As we have suggested, in actual markets prices frequently *hang* from the theoretical line of price increase such that there is a constant lag in arriving at the new profit-maximizing price. Figure 13.5 shows the real world lag of price increase to increases in demand. The subject hypothetical firm is not a pure monopolist; rather, it has achieved some differentiation in a market with many strong competitors. Three demand curves are shown. D_1 is the current demand; D_2 is the first demand increase, and D_3, the second increase. MC is the marginal cost curve for the firm, and MR_1, MR_2, and MR_3 are the three marginal revenue curves associated with the three demand curves.

The current price is P_1 which with D_1 yields sales of A. If demand shifts to D_2, P_1 now yields sales of B. The firm, sometime later convinced that demand has in fact increased, increases price, thereby moving back along D_2 to arrive at P_2—the price yielding C sales equating MR_2 and MC. Similarly, when demand increases to D_3, P_2 yield sales of E; and when the firm is certain of the permanency of the demand increase, it then raises price to P_3, the profit-maximizing price determined by the equality of MR_3 and MC. The lagged pricing describes a price increase path of a stair-step appearance, namely, $ABCDE$. The "perfect" adjustment path is described by connecting points A, C, and E.

One may also find price rises in *anticipation* of demand, increases. Compare this to the preceding discussion of pricing in the steel industry. Not surprisingly, there are unique risks in anticipatory price rises. If demand did not quickly increase to the expected level, there would be a "kink" in the product demand curve of the price raiser, for unless all other firms followed the leader, his higher price would stand alone, inducing his customers to switch to the competition. Even in non-oligopolistic markets, a price rise considerably ahead of a demand increase is irrational unless product demand is price inelastic. But if in fact it is inelastic and if average costs are constant or decreasing, the firm should have raised price *regardless* of any anticipated increase in demand.

Anticipatory price rises take the graphic form of a stair step above the "true" price increase expansion line. The actual price increase path $GHIJK$ is a stair-step extending above the perfect expansion path GIK, shown in Figure 13. 6. P_1 yields output G. The firm, anticipating the demand increase to D_2, raises price to P_2. Prior to the demand increase the price rise merely moves the firm back along D_1 to yield sales of H. However, the firm with astute foresight has set P_2 at the profit maximizing level with respect to the increased demand, D_2. Similarly, the firm anticipates the demand shift to D_3, by raising price to P_3 immediately prior to the increase in demand.

Figure 13.5 showed price rises lagging behind increases in demand. The intermediate pattern is that of the actual price and the ideal price continually crossing: A firm hangs back in raising price until it is virtually certain of the demand increase. It then not only meets the level supportable by the new level of demand, but goes above it, anticipating an immediate further rise in demand.

FIGURE   13.5

PRICE INCREASES LAGGING IN RESPONSE TO DEMAND INCREASES

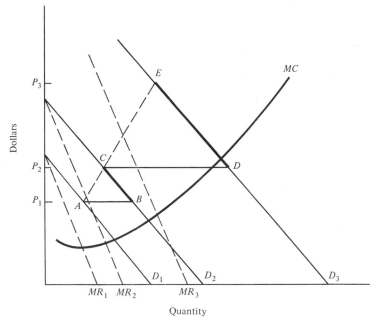

The analytical implications of price lags and leads with respect to changes in demand or cost are several. Most important is that evidence on prices can be ambiguous. An industry which has, by purely chance reasons, lagged in pricing so that its belated increase meets with no resistance obviously has lost profits which it might otherwise have earned. However, the uncautious observer, who notices only the final instant when the price rises, might conclude there exists some "power" to raise prices freely. That is, by looking only at the moment and disregarding all else, one can develop false theories of price making—the unfortunate result whenever analysis ignores the total marketing structure.

On the other hand, rigid prices are equally complex. The absence over some period of time of price rises does not necessarily imply no difference between the actual price and the true price line; nor does it necessarily indicate an absence of "pricing power." Why would a firm *not* raise price upon recognizing a "gap" between the actual price and the true price or upon recognizing inelastic demand? In relatively concentrated markets current sellers may wish not to attract new competitors. Thus, regardless of a price gap or demand inelasticity, they may engage in *keep-out* pricing whereby they deliberately maintain prices lower than the short-run profit maximizing level. If entry is neither free nor completely blockaded—that is, there are some costs associated with successful entry—the extant sellers with their unit-cost advantage will price sufficiently low to deter the most efficient potential entrant.[27] In short, in keep-out pricing, the firms substitute in keep-out pricing, the firms substitute long-run profits for short-run gain, long-run profits for short-run gain, by declining to exploit opportunities for short-run profit increases.

FIGURE 13.6

PRICE INCREASES IN ANTICIPATION OF DEMAND INCREASES

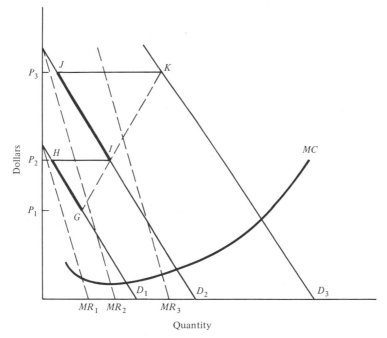

[27] The concept of keep-out pricing has been insightfully discussed in Joe S. Bain, *Barriers to New Competition* (Harvard, 1956), and in Bain, "A Note on Pricing in Monopoly and Oligopoly," reprinted in A. E. A. *Readings in Industrial Organization* (Irwin, 1958). *See also* Paolo Sylos Labini, *Oligopoly and Technical Progress* (Harvard, 1962); Franco Modigliani, "New Developments on the Oligopoly Front," *Journal of Political Economy*, LXVI, June 1958, pp. 215–232; and the theory advanced by Robert Smith, "A Barrier Theory of Markets: A Long Run View," paper presented at Western Economic Association Meetings, 1968.

Prices and Effecting Demand Shifts

Pricing can shift demand curves. (The typical conception is merely that price moves along a given demand curve.) Price shifts demand curves by two processes: First, in a multiple-product firm, there frequently are demand complementarities such that a price reduction in A increases the quantity of A demand *and* increases the demand for B. An example of demand complementary products is beer and pretzels (or other snack food). A reduction in the price of beer increases the demand for pretzels.[28]

Demand interrelationships are developed and exploited in all rational firms, but *par excellence* in supermarkets. The concept of profit-leader is that of building consumer traffic in the store. If the leader is sufficiently attractive not only will there be a considerable increase in consumers but the savings on the leader item may be such that the consumers feel it worth their while to do additional shopping while in the store. Thus, the supermarket enjoys a limited spatial monopoly. Items that are traffic elastic—sales more than proportionate to traffic—enjoy an increase in demand from the traffic generated by the profit-leaders.[29] Specifically all impulse items benefit, as well as many staples.

The second means by which price can increase demand is if a price change alters a customer's perception of an offering. Retailers are well aware of certain price lines to which consumers have grown accustomed. Within these price lines such as men's ties at $1.50, $2.50, $3.50, and $4.50 and up, and within price points such as nickel (and now dime) candy bars, consumers hold certain perceptions. Thus, products priced within a perceptual range are imbued—at the outset at least—with characteristics and expectations associated with that price level category.[30] Price changes that purposively (or involuntarily) change the product can and do occur in all types of markets—not merely retail.

Aside from habitual perceptions of price lines, many customers quite explicitly rely on price as an indicator of quality. Products today frequently are complex and technical, and thus many consumers are hopelessly at sea with respect to understanding the intrinsic quality of a vast number of contemporary products. The day has long passed in which a consumer knew personally the majority of suppliers of goods and services. As a result, in large part born of desperation and lack of detailed information, consumers rely on price to indicate relative quality. This is much less true for indus-

---

[28] The application of demand interrelationships in pricing are well treated in Alfred R. Oxenfeldt, "Product Line Pricing," *Harvard Business Review* (July–August 1966). A useful analysis is found in R. H. Coase, "Monopoly Pricing with Interrelated Costs and Demands," *Economica*, N.S. XIII, Nov. 1956.

[29] *See* Holton, "Price Discrimination at Retail: The Supermarket Case," *op. cit.*

[30] *See* Stanley C. Hollander, "Customary Prices," *Business Topics*, Summer 1966. *See also* Harold J. Leavitt, "A Note on Some Experimental Findings about the Meaning of Price," *Journal of Business*, July 1954, pp. 205–10; and Benson P. Shapiro, "The Psychology of Pricing," *Harvard Business Review*, July–August 1968. *See also* Donald Harper, *Price Policy and Procedure* (Harcourt, Brace, and World, 1966), pp. 280–3.

trial customers whose job is to know actual quality differences. Of course, after initial use, a consumer gains some first hand knowledge of the merits of any product. The first hand knowledge reinforced by comments from positive reference groups and opinion leaders affect the speed of one's learning vis-à-vis a brand, as discussed in Chapter 9.

The paradoxical aspect of judging quality by price is what it may portend for price competition.[31] It may turn price competition around such that sellers are inclined not to push for the lowest price for fear of the customer perception of low quality associated with low prices. However, so far at least, it appears unlikely that low prices acquire any blanket negative meaning—especially because the consumer movement, including federal legislation, has increased the amount of objective information a seller must supply about his product. Agencies such as Consumers Union which test various brands of products and report their findings facilitate more rational purchasing by consumers. Nevertheless, the fear of price-quality association prompts some firms to support resale price maintenance. (See the discussion below.)

Conspicuous-consumption items such as high-quality automobiles as well as furs and diamonds appear for some consumers to have a positive relationship between price and quantity. In the vernacular, these items have a certain "snob appeal" inducing certain consumers to purchase them simply because the items are high priced.[32] Some goods and services, especially if their high price and hence "exclusivity" is widely communicated, may experience from a price rise both increased quantity demanded and increased demand.

Resale Price Maintenance

Resale price maintenance, frequently known as "fair trade," is the widely discussed and disputed practice by which the brander of products requires resellers to offer them at minimum or stipulated prices.[33] The issues

[31] See Tibor Scitovsky, "Some Consequences of the Habit of Judging Quality by Price," *Review of Economic Studies* XII (2) (1944–45), reprinted in Perry Bliss (ed.), *Marketing and the Behavioral Sciences, op. cit.*; and Andre Gabor and C. W. J. Granger, "Price as an Indicator of Quality," *Economica*, New Series, February 1966.

[32] See McCarthy, *op. cit.*, pp. 549–551.

[33] J. R. Gould and L. E. Preston, "Resale Price Maintenance and Retail Outlets," *Economica* XXXII (August 1965), p. 302. Some discussion and analyses of resale price maintenance are B. S. Yamey, *The Economics of Resale Price Maintenance* (London: Pitman, 1954); L. G. Telser, "Why Should Manufacturers Want Fair Trade," *Journal of Law and Economics* (October 1960); P. W. S. Andrews and F. A. Friday, *Fair Trade* (Macmillan, 1960); B. S. Yamey (ed.), Resale Price Maintenance (Aldine Publishing Co., 1966); "Fair Trade: The Problem and Issues," U.S. Congress Hearings reprinted in S. Hollander, *Explorations in Retailing* (Michigan State University: 1959), also in U.S. House of Representatives Report 1292, 82nd Congress, 2d session, 1952, pp. 7–15; J. R. Gould and B. S. Yamey, "Professor Bork on Vertical Price Fixing," *The Yale Law Journal* LXXVI, March 1967, pp. 722–730; Robert H. Bork, "A Reply to Professors Gould and Yamey"; *ibid.*, pp. 731–745; and E. T. Grether, *Price Control Under Fair Trade Legislation* (Oxford University Press, 1939).

are complex and will not be developed here; however, analyses suggest that the use of resale price maintenance by a manufacturer or other brander tends to increase the number of retail outlets, to increase the service content in the total product of such outlets, and to increase price over what it would be in the absence of resale price maintenance.

A firm wishes insofar as possible to control supply and demand and thereby to increase profits. Thus, the desire to engage in price maintenance is understandable from the manufacturers' or other branders' standpoint *if* such practice does not reduce profits from what they would be without fair trade. Convenience goods—in particular, impulse and emergency items—as well as specialty goods may yield the manufacturers more profits under price maintenance, for they are items for which price is not typically a factor. Of course, the structure of the market would be a constraining factor. The higher the maintained price relative to costs, the more are sellers induced to carry the item, thereby increasing the revenues of the manufacturer at a less than a proportionate increase in cost. However, from the standpoint of competitive retailers selling a price-maintained good, the guaranteed retail price may attract so many additional retailers that each retailer's market area and demand is reduced until each realizes only a normal profit in spite of higher retail price. That is, each retailer is forced to operate at a less efficient (higher average cost) level of output.

It is sometimes argued that with the possibly higher margins under resale price maintenance, retailers will offer more services to the consumer, thereby increasing utility. However, this is rational behavior and socially desirable only if one assumes all consumers prefer more service to lower prices. If price maintenance is uniformly practiced in a market by all retailers, a consumer is denied a choice between more service and lower price. All in all, the evidence suggests that under fair trade the total price is higher.[34]

Social Aspects of Prices and Pricing

In the contemporary economy, two overriding social issues of pricing are (1) price levels and practices in low-income areas such as urban ghettos, and (2) downward pressure on prices across all markets as induced by competition. The issue of price levels in low-income areas, including credit practices of ghetto merchants, are discussed in Chapter 16; competition—its maintenance and implications for price levels—is treated in Chapter 14.

SUMMARY

For a transaction to occur, there must be a perception of gain by both the demander and supplier. The customers must perceive a net

[34] A related set of issues is the responsiveness of prices in nonintegrated channels of distribution as opposed to vertically integrated changes. A useful general analysis is Hawkins, "Vertical Price Relationships" in R. Cox and Wroe Alderson, *Theory in Marketing* (Irwin, 1950).

increase in utility, and the seller (on the average) must anticipate net revenue exceeding the net value of retaining the offering.

"Price" is the total resources expended by a buyer or lessee in acquiring a given good or service. Thus, price is a two-part concept, consisting of both the resource expenditure of the customer and a good or service acquired. The resources expended include both what the buyer explicitly pays the supplier and all indirect acquisition costs such as the time and effort involved in acquiring the offering.

A "price increase" occurs when the amount of the customer resources expended rises relative to the bundle of utility. A "price decrease" occurs when the resources expended fall relative to the bundle of utility. Price increases or decreases may be conceived of either in terms of disproportionate changes in required resources relative to utility received, or vice versa. Thus "price" and "(total) product" are essentially identical concepts—with merely different emphases. Accordingly, based on customers' perceptions of *net* utility among various offerings, there is no useful distinction between "price competition" and "non price competition." Open, vigorous competition is the effort by sellers to increase utility relative to resource expenditures. And, competition among buyers has a parallel intent. Thus, by whatever aspect of "price" or "(total) product," successful competition is that which demonstrates to demanders a greater utility-resource margin from one firm than another.

Profit-maximizing pricing in the short-run is pricing to effect an equality between marginal revenue and marginal cost. Profit-maximizing pricing leads to higher prices only insofar as demand is inelastic. On the other hand and assuming constant costs, if an increase in demand also increases the elasticity, the new price will be lower than the previous price. Undue emphasis on cost in pricing is irrational and may lead to prices having little bearing to demand and thus to profits.

Price discrimination is selling the same product at different percentage markups over cost. It is *not* necessarily a difference in price for the same product. Nonsystematic price discrimination tends to be procompetitive.

Many real markets are characterized by interdependency among the firms. Hence, pricing is frequently of a complex nature (complex adjustment of the utility-resource differential) to preclude easy emulation by competitors.

Prices are always set by supply and demand—but either or both may be under monopoly control. Firms adjust prices in response to major changes in both demand and costs. However, costs are more in the nature of facts to firms. Thus firms may tend to respond more quickly to cost changes than to demand changes. There may even be a considerable lag before a firm is convinced that demand has changed sufficiently to warrant a price change.

Some price changes shift demand curves both for the reason of demand interrelationships among products in a product line, and because a customer's perception of a product's utility may be a function of the price. So-called "snob appeal" is a well-known example of a positive association for some customers between the price and desirability of a product. Short of any snob appeal, some customers may rely on price as an indicator of quality, especially when the product is technically complex.

"Resale price maintenance" is the practice by which a brander of products requires resellers to offer them at no less than stipulated prices. Some implications of resale price maintenance are that it tends to increase the number of retail outlets, to increase the service content in the total product, and also to increase price over what it would be in the absence of resale price maintenance.

Two contemporary social issues in pricing are (1) price levels for goods sold to low-income consumers, and (2) competition as a force compelling lower prices and more efficiency. Price levels in low-income areas are considered in Chapter 16, and the maintenance of competition, in Chapter 14.

SUGGESTED READINGS

The Meaning of Price and the Context of Pricing

M. A. Adelman, "Pricing by Manufacturers," in D. J. Duncan (ed.), *Conference of Marketing Teachers from Far Western States* (Berkeley: University of California Press, 1958).

An extremely thoughtful paper discussing the essential meaning of price, the role of market structure in pricing, and the aspects of cost and demand to be considered in price analysis. A point of view stressing the impossibility of distinguishing between production and selling costs.

———, "The Product and Price in Distribution," *American Economic Review*, May 1957.

An analysis of the close relationships between product and price with implications for pricing analysis in all markets. The serious reader should carefully consider both of the Adelman articles.

Perry Bliss, "Non-Price Competition at the Department Store Level," *Journal of Marketing* XVII (April 1953), pp. 357–365.

Through illustrations of department store practices, Bliss demonstrates the difficulty of separating price competition from non-price competition, in that what any firm sells is a bundle of utility. He points out the various situations when, either from demand interrelationships or changes in customer perception, price changes shift demand curves, rather than merely move along demand curves.

Conceptual and Empirical Analyses of Pricing and Performance

Joe Bain, "Note on Pricing in Monopoly and Oligopoly," *American Economic Review* (March 1949), pp. 448–464.

A well-known discussion of limit pricing to avoid attracting new firms into the market.

R. Cassady, Jr., "The Price Skirmish—A Distinctive Pattern of Competitive Behavior," *California Management Review*, Winter 1964, pp. 11–16.

A discussion of some market-structure situations in which there were outbreaks of explicit price changes. The article considers the determinants of such behavior and the manner in which the markets regained an equilibrium.

Norman Collins and Lee Preston, *Concentration and Price-Cost Margins in Manufacturing Industries* (Berkeley: University of California Press, 1968).

A comprehensive survey and analysis of certain market-level elements of structure and their relationship to market performance.

R. Cyert and J. March, "Organizational Structure and Pricing Behavior in an Oligopolistic Market," *American Economic Review*, March 1955, pp. 129–139.

A useful analysis of unit-level elements in the total marketing structure—elements frequently overlooked in efforts to explain the total determinants of pricing behavior.

Costs, Prices, and Pricing

Richard Heflebower, "Full Costs, Cost Changes, and Prices," in *Business Concentration and Price Policy*, (National Bureau of Economic Research, 1955), pp. 361–92.

A consideration of the meaning and role costs in pricing. Heflebower, among other points, suggests that "cost-oriented" pricing may be more demand sensitive than is sometimes assumed. See the discussants comments, pp. 392–96.

Fritz Machlup, "Characteristics and Types of Price Discrimination," in *Business Concentration and Price Policy*, National Bureau of Economic Research (Princeton: Princeton University Press, 1955), pp. 397–434.

Machlup discusses the meaning and types of price discrimination, offering an extensive classification system. The reader will find value in considering Machlup's paper in the light of the comments of two discussants, Ronald Coase and Andreas Papandreou, pp. 435–440.

W. G. Shepherd, "Marginal-Cost Pricing in American Utilities," *Southern Economic Journal*, July 1966, pp. 58–70.

The question considered by Shepherd is the extent to which firms in regulated industries employ marginal-cost pricing.

Inter-product Cost and Demand Relationships

Ronald H. Coase, "Monopoly Pricing with Interrelated Costs and
    Demands," *Economica*, New Series, XIII, November 1946.
Joel Dean, *Managerial Economics* (Englewood Cliffs, N.J.: Prentice-Hall,
    Inc., 1951), Chapter 8, "Product Line Pricing."
R. H. Holton, "Price Discrimination at Retail: The Supermarket Case,"
    Journal of Industrial Economics, (October 1957), pp. 13–32.
A. R. Oxenfeldt, "Product Line Pricing," *Harvard Business Review*
    (July–August, 1966), pp. 137–44.
Lee E. Preston, "Markups, Leaders and Discrimination in Retail Pricing,"
    Journal of Farm Economics, (May 1962), pp. 291–306.

    A sample of articles conceptually and empirically pointing up
many aspects of pricing of cost and/or demand-related products.

Vertical Pricing Including Vertical Price Fixing

J. C. Darnell, "The Impact of Quality Stabilization," *Journal of Marketing
    Research* (August 1965), pp. 274–82.
J. R. Gould and L. E. Preston, "Resale Price Maintenance and Retail
    Outlets," *Economica* (August 1965), pp. 302–12.
E. R. Hawkins, "Vertical Price Relationship," in R. Cox and W. Alderson,
    (eds.), *Theory in Marketing* (Homewood, Ill.: Richard D. Irwin,
    Inc., 1950).

    A careful and very useful conceptual examination of several
aspects of vertical price relationships. Notable for its uniqueness
in the literature.
Stanley C. Hollander, *Explorations in Retailing* (East Lansing: Michigan
    State University, 1959), pp. 230–41.

    Summarizes the points pro and con resale price maintenance.
This paper and those by Gould and Preston and Yamey present
conceptual and empirical analysis of some of the implications of
resale price maintenance.
B. S. Yamey, *Economics of Resale Price Maintenance* (London, 1954).

Pricing and Customer Perception

Andre Gabor and C. W. J. Granger, "Price as an Indicator of Quality,"
    Economica, New Series, February 1966.
Stanley Hollander, "Customary Prices," *Business Topics*, Summer 1966,
    pp. 45–56.
Harold J. Leavitt, "A Note on Some Experimental Findings about the
    Meaning of Price," *Journal of Business*, July 1954, pp. 205–210.
J. Douglas McConnell, "The Price-Quality Relationship in an Experimental
    Setting," *Journal of Marketing Research*, V, August, 1968.
Tibor Scitovsky, "Some Consequences of the Habit of Judging Quality
    of Price," *Review of Economic Studies* XII (2) (1944–45).

This sample of five articles includes analysis of customer expectations of "appropriate" price levels, experimental analysis of perceptions of quality conditioned by price levels, and discussions from both a private and social standpoint of the implications of demanders judging quality by price. The reader considering these materials will want to remember the basic connection between "price" and "product (total)," and note the role for market information as a partial solution to the tendency for customers otherwise uninformed to rely on price as a proxy for quality.

V Social perspectives of the marketing economy

14

Marketing
and public policy

We have defined marketing as "All activities in any way related to transactions of ownership or use rights to any factor, good, or service."[1] The reader recognizes that so defined, marketing is pervasive in the economy, for wherever there is a market, there is marketing.[2] We recall the structure of the market or the fungibility of the good or service in no way changes the *fact* of marketing—although the particular patterns of buyer and seller behavior vary depending on the structural characteristics of the market.[3] Thus among markets, differing characteristics of structure change only the form not the substance of marketing.

PUBLIC POLICY IN MARKETING

What is the meaning of "public policy in marketing?" Remembering the supply-and-demand-inclusive meaning of marketing, we define public policy in marketing as: Any governmental policy at the federal, state, or local level which in any way affects the supply of or demand for goods and services. The definition in essence says that any governmental policy that

[1] See Chapter 1.

[2] As discussed in Chapter 3, a market is "the contact between suppliers and demanders for transferring title or use rights."

[3] Refer to Chapter 4 and Parts III and IV of this book.

affects supply or demand—that is, markets—necessarily affects marketing; hence, it is public policy in marketing. Clearly, this definition covers most government economic policies. Virtually every government economic policy affects the supply of or demand for some factor of production, product, or service. We list below some of the principal types of policies subsumed by public policy in marketing.

Some Illustrations of Public Policy in Marketing

From the definitions of marketing and public policy, the following types of policies fall within the ambit of public policy in marketing:

1. Antitrust. "Antitrust" is a set of policies at the federal level, and in many states as well, designed to maintain competition. The maintenance of competition means, in general, the maintenance of rivalry among sellers and among buyers in a market. In particular, maintaining competition means diffusing economic power, thereby to increase rivalry and value to consumers. (Competition was discussed in Chapter 3.) Understandably, among industrial organization and antitrust scholars, measurement techniques and policy emphases vary. However, competition as the diffusion of economic power is a generally accepted meaning.[4]

2. Regulation. Economic regulation, unlike antitrust, is the explicit *controlling* of specific activities of firms. Examples of regulated industries are the utilities such as electricity and appliance gas; ground, sea, and air transportation; radio and television broadcasting; and commercial banking and insurance. In general, regulated industries are exempt from the antitrust laws. The pressures for efficiency come not from other firms, but come *in principle* from a regulatory agency or commission.

    There is considerable pressure to return some of the regulated industries, or aspects of them, to the competitive sector and the purview of antitrust.[5]

---

[4] See George Stigler, "Imperfections in the Capital Market," *The Journal of Political Economy*, Vol. 75, June 1967, p. 289. A more explicit emphasis on the size structure of firms is in the meaning of competition illustrated by Abe Fortas (later, Associate Justice of the U.S. Supreme Court.) A still different emphasis is the focus on consumer welfare and its putative relationship to the quantity of output in a market. The latter viewpoint, vigorously argued by Professor Robert Bork, appears with Fortas' comments in a "Symposium on the Impacts of Present-Day Antitrust Policy on the Economy," 23 *American Bar Association, Antitrust Section* (1963).

    Antitrust is discussed in some detail in subsequent portions of this chapter.

[5] For an extensive introduction to regulation, *see* Clair Wilcox, *Public Policies Toward Business* (Irwin, 1960), pp. 539–778. *See also* Charles F. Phillips, Jr., *The Economics of Regulation—Theory and Practice in the Transportation and Public Utility Industries*

3. Consumer protection. Consumer protection is the set of policies by which the federal, state, or local governments—alone or in conjunction with nongovernment organizations—assist the consumer in buying and using products. Some components of consumer protection are:

a. Consumer education
b. "Truth in lending"
c. "Truth in packaging"
d. Food and drug inspection and labeling
e. Control of deception practices

Consumer protection and guidance in markets have recently been elevated to a subcabinet level in the federal government. President Johnson established the President's Committee on Consumer Interests in 1964.[6]

4. Government procurement policies. The policies followed by federal state, and local government in purchasing goods and services as well as in letting contracts for research and development are clearly a part of public policy in marketing. The purchasing practices of government have many economic and social implications. For example, a re-structuring of an industry on grounds other than efficiency may result from a persistent policy of government contract-letting on bases other than competitive bidding and lowest *total* cost. For example, some $22.7 billion in new contracts amounting to 52.7 percent of all Defense Department contract awards in fiscal year 1967, were negotiated by the Department without any form of competition.[7] Obviously, noncompetitive bidding may not reward the most efficient firms.

(Irwin, 1965); and Carl Kaysen and Donald F. Turner, *Antitrust Policy* (Harvard, 1959), Chapter VI.

Comments on the efficacy and desirability of regulation are found in "A Critical Evaluation of Public Regulation by Independent Commissions: A Symposium," *American Economic Review,* Vol. 48, May 1958, pp. 527–567; "Re-evaluation of the impact of present-day antitrust policy on the economy," 23 American Bar Association, Antitrust Section (1963) *passim*; and "Senate Antitrust Unit to Check Whether Regulated Industries are over-protected from Competition," *Antitrust and Trade Regulation Report* (Bureau of National Affairs), May 9, 1967, pp. A-1, A-2, and A-11–A-13.

[6] Consumer protection and services programs in the federal government are summarized in the *Guide to Federal Consumer Services,* (Executive Office Building, Washington, D.C.: President's Committee on Consumer Interests, 1967). Over 50 federal agencies and departments are listed. Consumer protection as an aspect of consumer welfare is further discussed in Chapter 16 of the present book.

[7] "The Antitrust Laws and Government Contractors," *Antitrust and Trade Regulation Report* (Bureau of National Affairs), May 21, 1968, B-1 ff. *See also* Carl Kaysen and Donald F. Turner, *Antitrust Policy* (Harvard, 1959), pp. 221–229.

5. Direct and indirect subsidization. Government at federal, state, and local levels has subsidized private enterprise in one form or another throughout the nation's history. In some cases it has made outright gifts of public land or payments from the Treasury. More frequently in trying to attract industry, federal and state governments by rendering services for which they make no charge, sell goods and services for less than they are worth, and exempt some industries and firms from taxes that others must pay. Subsidized enterprises, in effect, are removed from the full force of competition and are granted some of the privileges of uncontrolled monopoly. From a total social view not all subsidizations are necessarily undesirable, for some types, such as facilitating investments in urban ghettos, can be socially justified.

An especially controversial tax favor was the 27.5 percent depletion allowance for many years granted the oil and gas industry. Percentage depletion reduced an oil company's liability under the corporate income tax from the 52 percent paid by concerns in other industries to only 26 percent. The deduction, moreover, could be made each year, even though every dollar invested in the property was written off many times. This program deprived the Treasury of hundreds of millions of dollars of revenue and in addition stimulated the development of mineral properties and speeded their eventual exhaustion.[8]

6. International and interregional trade policies. Trade policies, both international and intranational, affect both the supply of and demand for goods and services. Since 1932 there has been a gradual declining trend in the ratio of tariffs to dutiable imports, declining from 32 percent in 1941–1945, to 16 percent in 1946–1950, to 12 percent in 1960, to 6 percent in 1966. Multilateral talks under the auspices of GATT (General Agreement on Tariffs and Trade) and the Kennedy Trade Act of 1962, which led to the "Kennedy Round" of tariff negotiations in 1966–1967, were primarily responsible for effecting the reduction.[9]

With respect to intra-U.S. trade barriers, a national market is

---

[8] A useful introductory discussion of government promotion and subsidization of private enterprise is found in Wilcox, op. cit., pp. 429–452. In 1965, oil companies were able to deduct $3 billion from their income before paying federal income taxes; however, pressure is building for reforms. The Washington Post, September 28, 1968, p. C7.

Additional comments on subsidizations are found in the section "The Scope of Antitrust in The Economy," pp. 353–355.

[9] Heinz Kohler, Scarcity Challenged: An Introduction to Economics (Holt, Rinehart and Winston, 1968), p. 466. See also Wilcox, op. cit., Chapter 12; and Carl Kaysen and Donald F. Turner, op. cit., pp. 231–33.

a reality for most goods of a relatively high specific value in that transportation is a small percentage of revenue and intranational trade barriers are few. Nevertheless, a number of states retain tax programs and other means of preferential treatment discriminatory to outside firms by which they attract industry to their state and enhance the competitive position of firms domiciled in their state. See the preceding comments and references on subsidization by government.

7. Fiscal and monetary policy. Fiscal and monetary policies are logically a part of public policy in marketing, for fiscal policies, such as a change in income taxes or government spending, and monetary policies, such as a change in the interest rate, obviously affect among other things, disposable income and its use.

The list of public policies in marketing could easily be continued, for example, to include policies such as those of the Post Office Department which by affecting the ability to sell and buy through the mails affect geographic markets; the Agriculture Department which inspects and grades various commodities; and the local building code and zoning authorities whose policies obviously affect the sale of construction materials, the geographical distribution of businesses and houses, and the sale of real property. All of these and more are included in public policy in marketing.[10] The reader is encouraged to conceive of additional public policies in marketing and to think of major government economic policies that do *not* somehow affect marketing. The latter are relatively few.

In a political democracy, policies are continually undergoing scrutiny both by those who administer them and those to whom the policies are directed. Some current public policies in marketing are old: The Sherman Antitrust Act was passed in 1890. And some are relatively young, such as the Fair Packaging and Labeling Act (1966) and the Truth in Lending Act (1968).

We turn now to a detailed consideration of one set of public policy in marketing—antitrust, the policies relating to maintaining competition. Let us not forget: Antitrust is only one of several important areas of public policy in marketing. It is singled out at present because it is one of the most significant and complex public policies relating to marketing.

ANTITRUST: MAINTAINING COMPETITION

Antitrust is the attempt to maintain rivalry among both buyers and sellers in markets by diffusing economic power so that the impersonal mar-

[10] For a discussion of additional public policies, see Kaysen, *op. cit.*, Chapter VII.

ket forces will be maximized. The rationale is that firms *independently* pursuing their self-interest most probably will generate real economies and increases in consumer welfare. Specifically, independent behavior is most likely to lead to goods and services in which the "price" and "nonprice" elements are so combined that wants are substantially satisfied. We see then that antitrust—the maintenance of rivalry—is all about the maintaining of independent behavior among firms.[11]

Antitrust as the Antithesis of Public Control

Antitrust is but one of three fundamental public policy alternatives with respect to markets and market behavior. The three alternatives are (1) antitrust; (2) public regulation and ownership; and (3) complete "noninterference." [12] The empirical support for and justification of noninterference, an alternative which necessarily condones concentrated oligopoly and private monopoly, are by far the weakest of the three. In a hypothetical world, such as the pure market economy for example, complete governmental noninterference is not only desirable but a logical requisite. But in the satisfaction of wants in the real world, in particular the real world of the United States and other marketing economies, democratic processes over many decades have developed institutions *dependent* on government intercession through either antitrust or regulation. There is therefore an immense burden of proof upon anyone asserting that noninterference in our complex world will guarantee consumer satisfaction. For example, in the absence of some type of government action what would prevent (or punish) firms from agreeing on prices and sharing markets? Witness the electrical conspiracy in 1961 in which leading electrical equipment manufacturers conspired to fix prices in the sale of certain products.[13]

The relevant debate today, therefore is not the question of noninterference, but the character of "interference." For many social goals aside from competition, such as pollution control for example, government activity will increase. Moreover, even in markets, government *participation* is a foregone conclusion in industries in which there is a "natural monopoly" (for

[11] The conclusion that independent action by firms is directly related to consumer satisfaction is derived from the analysis in Chapter 3 of competition and differential advantage, and the evidence in Chapter 4 of the general tendency for markets to become less competitive as seller concentration and barriers to entry reach high levels. See the references cited therein, and consider the behavior aspects of marketing structure in Chapters 13 and 15.

[12] For an introductory discussion of the three positions and bibliographical references, *see* David R. Kamerschen, "A Critique of the Status Quo Approach to Public Policy," *The Antitrust Bulletin*, Vol. 9, 1965, pp. 747–760.

[13] *City of Philadelphia* v. *Westinghouse Electric Corp.*, 210 F. Supp. 483 (E. D. Penn., 1962). *See* John G. Fuller, *Gentlemen Conspirators: The Story of the Price Fixers in the Electrical Industry* (Grove Press, 1962); and R. A. Smith, "The Incredible Electrical Conspiracy," *Fortune*, April 1961 and May 1961.

example, postal service), or in which there are issues of public health and safety. In general, to those who desire a maximum of *private* decision making in the economy, antitrust is the answer. Other people, in general, on economic and/or political grounds prefer *public control* of the nation's scarce resources. Let us look further into the philosophy of antitrust versus public control or regulation. ("Public control" and "regulation" will be used as synonyms for the *totality* of regulation and public ownership.)

The Philosophy of Antitrust

Advocates of antitrust reject both private monopoly and public control. Although their preferences as to approach may differ, all supporters of antitrust are united in preferring the impersonal market forces generated and reinforced by strongly competing private firms, to monopoly of either the private or public variety.

Professor Walter Adams, a vociferous proponent of free markets, represents the general consensus of antitrust on the desirability of diffusing economic power:

> [P]ublic regulation and public ownership suffer from the same basic drawback as private monopoly, viz., the concentration of power in the hands of a few. Such power may be used benignly or dangerously, depending on the men who possess and control it. They may be good men, benevolent men, and socially minded men; but society still confronts the danger of which Lord Acton so eloquently warned: Power corrupts, and absolute power corrupts absolutely.[14]

There is, of course, government "interference" even in antitrust, but it exists *in principle* only as a *temporary* intercession required to alter market structure or anticompetitive conduct. It should be made clear that in antitrust, as distinct from government regulation or ownership, government enters through a due-process procedure, and then only temporarily, to effect a change in market structure or conduct.

The antitrust philosophy—free, impersonal markets—was clearly uppermost in the most recent major antitrust legislation. The arguments in favor of a 1950 amendment to strengthen the merger law illustrate the desire to maintain impersonal markets through antitrust, rather than permit economic concentration as enhanced by mergers to increase to the point of either a private oligarchy or public control. The original legislation, the 1914 Clayton Act, omitted mergers in which the acquiring company purchased only the assets rather than the equity stock of another company. Subsequently, in arguments favoring plugging the "assets loophole," the proponents pointed out that the quantity of unreachable mergers was such

---

[14] Walter Adams in Walter Adams (ed.), *The Structure of American Industry* (3rd ed., Macmillan, 1961), p. 554. *See also* Lee Loevinger, "Regulation and Competition as Alternatives," *Antitrust Bulletin,* January–April 1966, pp. 101–40.

that in the absence of corrective legislation, fewer and fewer companies would own more and more of the productive assets of the economy—until there was simply either private socialism or, equally undesirable some type of government control.[15]

Antitrust in the Hierarchy of Public Policies

Both the Congress and the Supreme Court during the 1960s strongly reaffirmed that antitrust is one of our most important public policies. Vigorous antitrust enforcement can play a substantial role in maintaining a vital, responsive economy. In the second merger case brought before it under the amended Section 7 of the Clayton Act, the Supreme Court stated:

> Subject to narrow qualifications, it is surely the case that competition is our fundamental national economic policy, offering as it does the only alternative to the cartelization or governmental regimentation of large portions of the economy.[16]

The Joint Economic Committee, composed of members of both the House of Representatives and the Senate, consistently emphasizes the vital role to be played by antitrust. For example, in its 1967 Report, the Committee said: "Antitrust must be assigned a central role in national economic policy of no less significance than monetary and fiscal policy."[17]

Not only is antitrust a major public policy in our marketing economy, but clearly, it is closely related to the objectives and roles of other major policies such as fiscal and monetary policy. For example, the continuing battle against inflation can be assisted by strong antitrust policies along with fiscal and monetary policy. The reader will recall the discussion in Chapter 4 of the association between marketing structure (especially cer-

[15] The Congressional arguments, some admittedly rather emotional, pointed up the classical liberalism in the economics and politics of antitrust. The distaste for both private and public agglomerations of power and the preference for a decentralized economy and society are found throughout the history of the 1950 Celler-Kefauver Amendment to Section 7 of the Clayton Act. The legislative history and intent of Congress in the 1950 Section 7 Amendment may be found in *Brown Shoe* v. *U.S.*, 370 U.S. 294 (1960) (the first merger decision by the U.S. Supreme Court under the amended Section 7); David D. Martin, *Mergers and the Clayton Act* (University of California Press, 1959); Willard F. Mueller, "The Celler-Kefauver Act: Sixteen Years of Enforcement," a staff report to the Antitrust Subcommittee, Committee on the Judiciary, House of Representatives, October 16, 1967.

[16] *U.S.* v. *Philadelphia National Bank*, 374 U.S. 321, 372 (1963). The first case reviewed by the Court under the revised Section 7 was no less emphatic on the need for maintaining competition: *See Brown Shoe* v. *U.S.*, 370 U.S. 294 (1960).

[17] *Joint Economic Report* on the 1967 Economic Report of the President, 90th Congress, 1st Session, Report No. 73, March 17, 1967, p. 25. See the parallel emphasis in the section on "Competition and the Growing Concentration of Economic Power," in the 1968 *Joint Economic Report* of the Committee, 90th Congress, 2d session, Report 1016, March 19, 1968, pp. 37–38, and also the supplementary views of Representative Wright Patman, pp. 39–41.

tain elements of market structure) and price-cost margins, profit levels, and so on.[18] It follows then that antitrust policy that curtails excessive market power and monopolizing conduct will assist in damping some aspects of inflation.[19]

The Scope of Antitrust in the Economy

What percentage of the economy is neither directly regulated nor specifically exempted from antitrust such as agriculture and foreign trade? The question is *not* the percentage of markets in which there is strong competition, for that important issue relates to the economy's workability, enhanced, we trust, by our economic policies.[20] The question for now simply is the percentage of the economy nominally within the scope of antitrust.

Accurate estimates of the proportion of the economy outside of antitrust are difficult to obtain, for the exempted and regulated portions are continually changing. For example, commercial banking is a regulated industry under partly separate and partly concurrent control of the Comptroller of the Currency, the Federal Deposit Insurance Corporation, the Federal Reserve Board, and state regulatory agencies. The Department of Justice's Antitrust Division nevertheless has successfully brought suit against several bank mergers, even subsequent to passage of the Bank Merger Act of 1966 which provided a community "convenience and needs" defense.[21]

The "exempt sector" means that part of the economy to which antitrust policy does not apply because of legislative exemptions, expressed or implicit.[22] Exemptions are not always complete, and in some cases the legislation exempting an industry contains anti-monopoly provisions. Nevertheless, the competitive standard typically applied by regulators is substantially

[18] Consider again the relationship between marketing structure and performance summarized in Norman Collins and Lee Preston, *Concentration and Price-Cost Margins* (University of California Press, 1968).

[19] *See* "Antitrust and Anti-inflationary Policies," Study Paper No. 2, *Report of the President's Cabinet Committee on Price Stability* (January 1969).

[20] For some discussion of the extensiveness and social cost of monopoly, see the section on Mergers and Oligopoly, later in this chapter.

[21] The Bank Merger Act is Public Law 89-356, 80 Stat. 7. A list of the F.T.C. and Department of Justice complaints including Justice complaints against bank mergers during the period 1950–1967 is found in Willard F. Mueller, "The Celler-Kefauver Act: Sixteen Years of Enforcement," *op. cit.* Other exemptions in addition to regulated industries from the antitrust laws are receiving increasing scrutiny. See the text and references on Economic Regulation earlier in this chapter.

[22] This discussion is based in large part on Carl Kaysen and Donald F. Turner, *Antitrust Policy: An Economic and Legal Analysis* (Harvard, 1959), pp. 41–43. *See also* the discussion on exceptions to antitrust in Clair Wilcox, *Public Policies Toward Business* (Irwin, 1960), pp. 361–369; and the rationale of the exemptions in Kaysen, *op. cit.*, Chapter VII.

Exemptions from the antitrust laws are, in effect, no less than subsidizations to the exempted industries. The exemptions, shielding the firms from the rigors of competition, permit cooperation and in varying degrees other types of monopoly benefits. (*See* the discussion above of "Direct and indirect subsidization.") This does not imply all exempted

lower than that contained in the antitrust laws, so that exemptions in combination with the approach of the regulatory agencies give in varying degrees a monopoly character to these markets.

Table 14.1 lists the major industries which we may classify as exempt, as well as their shares of national income for 1954. The total of *measured* exemptions in 1954 was 18.4 percent of national income. Let us note: Table 14.1 is *not* exhaustive, for it omits minor local public utilities such as rubbish disposal which are regulated in some states and cities. It also excludes the smaller natural resource industries, such as Colorado molybdenum, which are subject to state conservation laws. Also omitted are patents, Webb Pomerene associations (foreign trade exemptions), and retail price maintenance—exemptions so dispersed over the economy that one cannot treat them in the context of a separate exempt sector. For similar reason, the labor market, which is also exempt from antitrust, is excluded.

Moreover, Table 14.1 underestimates because industry size, as a single datum, *understates* the economic importance of many exempt industries. For example, transportation, an exempted industry, is a cost incurred by almost all industries, and the price structure of transportation helps determine location of industries, firms, and size of geographic market structures. Also, electric power, the economy's principal energy input for firms and households is more important than its small share of national income would indicate. The same may be said for both commercial banking, the major source of short-term credit and a major source of the nation's money supply, and insurance companies, which originate only one percent of national income but are a major source of investment funds.[23]

The total exempt sector, based on both what is listed *and* what is omitted from the Table 14.1, is clearly *large* relative to the total economy.[24]

---

industries (or regulated industries for that matter) are thereby necessarily more profitable. But it *is* to imply there could possibly be more total (private *and* social) benefits if some industries were to be removed from their exempted or regulated status.

For other discussions of antitrust exemptions see Phillip Areeda, *Antitrust Analysis: Problems, Text Cases* (Little, Brown, 1967), pp. 49–59; "Antitrust Exemptions," XXXIII *Antitrust Law Journal* (1967), pp. 1–110; Richard Caves, *American Industry: Structure, Conduct, Performance* (Prentice-Hall, 1967), Chapter 5; and with respect to export-association exemptions from antitrust, Willard F. Mueller, "The Nature and Scope of Webb-Pomerene Associations," Statement before the Subcommittee on Antitrust and Monopoly, Committee on the Judiciary, U.S. Senate, June 26, 1967.

[23] Four kinds of summary information about each of the regulated industries listed in Table 14.1: primary regulatory agency, extent and nature of regulation, present market structure, and probable market structure in the absence of regulation, are found in Kaysen and Turner, *op. cit.*, pp. 289–91.

[24] A discussion of recent trends in the scope of antitrust in the economy is E. T. Grether, *Marketing and Public Policy* (Prentice-Hall, 1966). *See also* the papers by Professors Grether and Ben Lewis and the discussions, all with respect to consistencies, inconsistencies, and trends in regulated and unregulated sectors of the economy in *American Economic Review*, LIII, May 1963, pp. 26–64.

TABLE 14.1

MEASURABLE PERCENTAGE OF NATIONAL INCOME ORIGINATING IN SECTORS EXEMPT FROM THE ANTITRUST LAWS, 1954.

Exempt sector		Percentage of national income, 1954
Agriculture		5.5
Transportation		4.6
Railroads	2.2	
Highway freight carriers	1.3	
Local and highway transportation	0.5	
Water transportation	0.3	
Air transportation (common carrier)	0.2	
Pipeline transportation	0.1	
Local and communication utilities		3.7
Electricity and gas	1.9	
Telephone and telegraph	1.5	
Radio broadcasting and television	0.2	
Local utilities (n.e.c.)	0.1	
Commercial banking and insurance		2.5
Commercial banking	1.5	
Insurance	1.0	
Natural resource industries		0.9
Crude oil and natural gas	0.8	
Anthracite coal	0.1	
Total, exempt private industries		17.2
Government enterprise		1.2
Federal	0.8	
State and local	0.4	
Total, exemptions that can be measured		18.4

Source: Carl Kaysen and Donald F. Turner, *Antitrust Policy: An Economic and Legal Analysis* (Harvard, 1959), p. 42.

An estimate of exemptions in 1966—though not completely comparable to Table 14.1—is found in Willard F. Mueller, *A Primer on Monopoly and Competition* (Random House, 1970), p. 130.

Approaches in Antitrust

In antitrust, there is some disagreement not surprisingly on the approach and extent of action required to effect and increase competition— markets which yield continual increases in real economies and consumer welfare.[25] One school of thought we may call the "structure-performance" school.[26] The primary focus is on market *structure* as both the basic cause of behavior *and* the appropriate focus for remedial action under the antitrust laws. The structure-performance school considers seller and buyer concentration and entry conditions (including numbers and strength of potential competitors) as the most important determinants of competition.

Antitrust enforcement over the past decade may be characterized in the main as being oriented toward structure-performance. This is especially true with respect to mergers in which a showing of an incipient tendency for an anticompetitive market structure was sufficient to strike down the merger.[27]

There is a second school of antitrust thought, which we may call the "output" school. It is distinguished from the structure-performance school in believing that actual market structures cannot be measured, and, more importantly, that aside from occasional collusion and deception, the real world *does* yield approximately the same results as the pure competition model.[28] A corollary argument of the output school is that for the most part,

[25] We maintain the important distinction between real economies, the situation in which fewer inputs are required per unit of output, and *pecuniary* economies, a lower price per unit of input or, as with market power, revenue exceeding payment to all inputs including a normal profit. Real economies are of the most value to society, for having to do with the physical productivity of society's scarce resources, they free resources for employment elsewhere in the economy; whereas pecuniary economies frequently reflect only relative bargaining strengths in buying and selling markets. Real economies are at once social economies; pecuniary economies are at once private economies, but may *possibly* induce real economies.

[26] *See* Chapter 4 in the present text with respect to market structure elements. A cross-section of views within the structure-performance school are Collins and Preston, *op. cit.*; Caves, *op. cit.*; Carl Kaysen and Donald F. Turner, *op. cit.*, Chapter 3; Willard F. Mueller, "Status and Future of Small Business," *Hearings before the Select Committee on Small Business*, U.S. Senate, 90th Congress, 1st session, April 6, 1967; George J. Stigler, "The Case Against Big Business," *Fortune*, May 1952; Corwin Edwards, *Maintaining Competition* (McGraw-Hill, 1949); Walter Adams, "Public Policy in a Free Enterprise Economy," in Walter Adams (ed.), *The Structure of American Industry* (3rd ed., Macmillan, 1961); and Joe Bain, *Industrial Organization* (Wiley, 1959).

President Johnson's special ad hoc Commission on antitrust policy was strongly "structural" in its recommendations. *See* the July 5, 1968, *Report of the White House Task Force on Antitrust Policy*, reprinted in *Antitrust and Trade Regulation Report*, No. 411, May 27, 1969.

[27] For example, *U.S.* v. *Brown Shoe*, 370 U.S. 294. *See* the discussion of antitrust merger policy below.

[28] The measurability issue and the problems of market-structure analysis are squarely raised by Yale Brozen, "Significance of Profit Data for Antitrust Policy," in J. Fred Weston and Sam Peltzman, *Public Policy Toward Mergers* (Goodyear Publishing Co., 1969). Strong opposition to the structure-performance school is also found in "Task Force on Productivity and Efficiency," *Antitrust and Trade Regulation Report* No. 413, June 10, 1969.

agency and market structures are simply manifestations of economies. In short, the output school holds that "the market" works; and in the main resources *are* allocated efficiently. Believing much of market behavior simply is a reflection of economies, this school holds that there is a direct relationship between consumer welfare and the quantity of output in a market.

The output school should not be confused with the strict noninterference point of view. The output school has no emotional attachment to *either* private bigness or public ownership and regulation. Both the structure-performance and output schools place little faith in the prospects for benign use of *power* whether it be private or public.

The output school claims that its approach, focused on market performance, is more singularly *economic* than that of the structure-performance school. The latter, they argue, seeks both the economic and social ends associated with diffusion of power which are not always consistent goals and may lead to contradictory policies.[29] There is, of course, the *possibility* the structural emphasis will inadvertently sacrifice economies. Has the frequently employed structure-performance approach interfered with real economies? This question in turn raises the question of the frequency of large-firm economies, an empirical question to which we now turn.

Antitrust and Economies

Antitrust enforcement with a structure emphasis involves occasional breaking up of mergers and firms intendedly to change market structure to yield more effective competition. Some opponents of this approach rail against virtually any structural change for fear of upsetting economies of scale. Of course, it would frustrate our general economic goal of resource efficiency if restructuring markets sacrificed economies. However, the evidence appears to go the other way. As we indicate in Chapters 4 and 15, there is *no evidence* of any "technological imperative" requiring ever-larger firms in order to capture all possible economies. As one student of the sub-

---

[29] The broader goals of the structure-performance school were evident in the 1950 Amendment to Section 7 of the Clayton Act. *See* Narver, *Conglomerate Mergers and Market Competition, op. cit.,* Chapter 3, and John Blair, "Conglomerate Mergers—Theory and Congressional Intent," in Weston and Peltzman, *op. cit.* Strong opposition to the broader goals of the structure-performance school are found in Robert H. Bork and Ward Bowman, "The Crisis in Antitrust," *Columbia Law Review,* Volume 363 (1965); Robert H. Bork, "The Goals of Antitrust Policy," *American Economic Review,* May 1967; and Kenneth S. Carlston and James M. Treece, "Antitrust and the Consumer Interest," *Michigan Law Review,* Vol. 64, March 1966.

The output school is not beyond criticism, for at times it appears to reason largely from abstract economic models—at the limit, reasoning entirely within pure theory, an approach described by Professor Fritz Machlup as "extreme apriorism," in C. E. Ferguson, *Microeconomic Theory* (Irwin, 1966), p. 4 ff.

ject says: "In fact, we do not know of a single instance of *empirical support* of the scale argument." [30]

Leaving aside monopoly issues, large firms with no cost advantage may *nevertheless* remain in certain industries and sectors of the economy. The reader need only consider the distorting influences which we have mentioned, for example, government procurement policy, exemptions from the antitrust laws such as regulated industries, so-called military-industrial complexes, tax loopholes, and other preferential treatment.[31] The evidence suggests that a vigorous antitrust *structural* focus to diffuse economic power *will not* sacrifice economies; rather, it will serve the interests of consumers by providing more alternatives *and* promote efficiency through the rivalry of the more numerous viable firms.

Professor George Stigler, a well-known advocate of private enterprise and competition, provides a concluding passage to the subject of a structural focus in maintaining competition and economic freedom:

> The dissolution of big business is only part of the program necessary to increase the support for a private, competitive enterprise economy, and reverse the drift toward Government control. But it is an essential part of this program, and the place for courage and imagination. Those conservatives who cling to the status quo do not realize that the status quo is a state of change, and the changes are coming fast. If these changes were to include the dissolution of a few score of our giant companies, however, we shall have done much to preserve private enterprise and the liberal-individualistic society of which it is an integral part.[32]

---

[30] Kamerschen, *op. cit.*, p. 754 (emphasis in original), and see *ibid.* plus Chapters 4 and 15 in the present book for references to empirical studies. The absence of evidence of scale economies beyond some penultimate size of firm runs counter to one of the major themes of John K. Galbraith in *The New Industrial State* (Houghton Mifflin, 1967). Professor Galbraith was opposed by three well-known economists of the "structure-performance" school, all three of whom challenged Galbraith with substantial evidence refuting his premise of general increasing returns to scale. For the debate *see Planning, Regulation, and Competition,* Hearing before Subcommittees of the Select Committee on Small Business, U.S. Senate, 90th Congress, 1st session, June 29, 1967. *See also* Bain, *Industrial Organization, op. cit.*

[31] President Eisenhower's warning against the military-industrial complex taking on a disproportionate role in our society will long be remembered. However, the only aspect of the President's warning of relevance to the current discussion is the implication it holds for increases in firm size and lessening of competition for reasons unrelated to *real* economies.

[32] George J. Stigler, "The Case Against Big Business," *Fortune*, Vol. 45, May 1952, p. 123 ff. Another fundamental criticism by Stigler is that big business encourages and justifies bigness in labor and government. *Ibid.*

The Machinery and Statutes of Antitrust

There are federal and state antitrust laws, enforced by government agencies at the respective levels. In addition to government suits, there is also provision under the antitrust laws for private-party, treble-damage suits.[33]

Three statutes and their amendments comprise the backbone of antitrust at the federal level: (1) The Sherman Act, dealing with collusion, monopoly, and intent to monopolize; (2) The Clayton Act, covering price discrimination, exclusive and tying contracts, interlocking directorates, and anticompetitive mergers; and (3) The Federal Trade Commission Act, which pertains to unfair methods of competition and deceptive practices.

The federal antitrust laws are enforced by two agencies: the Antitrust Division of the Department of Justice and the Federal Trade Commission. The Antitrust Division has sole jurisdiction over the Sherman Act and joint jurisdiction with the FTC over the Clayton Act. The FTC has the sole responsibility for enforcing the FTC Act.

To be more specific, we shall briefly summarize the prohibitions contained in the federal antitrust laws.[34] It is illegal:

1. To enter into a contract, combination, or conspiracy in restraint of trade (Sherman Act, Section 1);
2. To monopolize, attempt to monopolize, or combine or conspire to monopolize trade (Sherman Act, Section 2).

In situations in which the effect *may be substantially* to lessen competition or tend to create a monopoly in any product and geographic market, it is illegal:

3. To acquire the stock or the assets of corporations, regardless whether the acquiring and acquired firms are competitors, vertically related or conglomerate (Clayton Act, Section 7, as amended in 1950);
4. To enter into exclusive and tying contracts (Clayton Act, Section 3):
5. To discriminate among purchasers to an extent that cannot be

---

[33] There were approximately 2000 treble-damage suits initiated immediately after the defendants pleaded guilty in the 1961 electrical price-fixing conspiracy.

[34] The present section is from Wilcox, *op. cit.*, pp. 59–60. The reader interested in details of illegality and records of complaints and cases may acquire a general background in Wilcox, *op. cit.*, pp. 49–337. For current reports on antitrust actions and the most recent interpretations of the laws, refer to Commerce Clearing House, *Trade Regulation Reporter; Antitrust and Trade Regulation Report* (Bureau of National Affairs); and the annual reports of the Federal Trade Commission and Department of Justice, Antitrust Division; a brief, thoughtful treatment of some major legal issues is Sumner Marcus, *Competition and the Law* (Wadsworth, 1967).

justified by a difference in cost or as an attempt made, in good faith, to meet the price of a competitor (Clayton Act, Section 2 as amended by Robinson-Patman Act, Section 2-a).

In general it is also illegal:

6. To pay a broker's commission if an independent broker is not in fact used (Robinson-Patman Act, Section 2-c);
7. To provide supplementary services to a buyer or to make allowance for services rendered by a buyer unless such concessions are equally available to all buyers (Robinson-Patman Act, Sections 2-d and 2-e);
8. To give larger discounts than those given others buying the same goods in the same quantity, or to charge lower prices in one locality than in another (Robinson-Patman Act, Section 3);
9. Knowingly to induce or receive an illegal discrimination in price (Robinson-Patman Act, Section 2-a);
10. To serve as a director of competing corporations (Clayton Act, Section 8);
11. To use unfair methods of competition (Federal Trade Commission Act, Section 5);
12. To employ unfair or deceptive acts or practices (Federal Trade Commission Act, Section 5 as amended by Wheeler-Lea Act, Section 3).

In largest part these provisions are designed to maintain competition and prevent monopoly. However, some of them have other purposes. For instance, one purpose of the Robinson-Patman Act is to preserve the small firm. It is the purpose of Section 5 of the Federal Trade Commission Act not only to prevent unfair practices that may lead to monopoly, but to preclude the employment of such methods where no danger of monopoly exists. The purpose of the Wheeler-Lea amendment is not to maintain competition, but to protect the consumer against deceptive practices.[35]

MERGERS AND OLIGOPOLY: THE MOST CRITICAL CONTEMPORARY ISSUES

Market power and oligopoly have constituted the most critical issues in the performance of markets for the past couple of decades. Other issues such as collusion, price discrimination, reciprocity, and tying arrangements are merely manifestations of either or both oligopoly and market power. For example, collusion can succeed only in concentrated markets

[35] Wilcox, *op. cit.*, p. 60.

and reciprocity and tie-ins require market power in buying and selling markets respectively. Thus, market concentration and barriers to entry are *the* most critical issues and focuses for antitrust. The bulk of the present discussion will be on mergers, but first, some brief attention will be given directly to the general issues of oligopoly and market power.

Market Power and Oligopoly

Not all industries and markets are highly concentrated, but some of our economically most important industries are extremely concentrated. Automobiles and steel are two industries whose pricing and other decisions affect millions of consumers and whose annual revenues amount to hundreds of millions of dollars. In 1963 the largest four U.S. automobile manufacturers accounted for 99 percent of the sales of passenger cars (SIC 37171) by U.S. automobile manufacturers. The four-firm sales totaled $16.7 billion. (Obviously, however, one must include imported cars to determine net competition.) Steel, in general, is also a concentrated industry, although among product classes the concentration varies. One of the more concentrated product classes in 1963 was steel ingot and semifinished shapes (SIC 33122) in which the leading four firms shipped 70 percent of the total domestic sales.[36] The marketing structures in these two industries permit and perhaps encourage coordination among the domestic suppliers.

In the U.S. we have grown to expect an annual hassle between the White House and Congress on the one hand and automobile and steel producers on the other, with respect to price increases. The jawbone economics by means of pleadings and pressure from Washington, possibly yield a "socially responsible" increase in prices. In the process, however, charges and counter-charges fly. Consider the Kennedy-steel confrontation in 1961, and also the crunch in 1968 between President Johnson and the steel and automobile industries. Does all this represent the impersonal play of market forces? Not at all; but under the particular market structures *we could not expect otherwise.* The marketing structure in these two markets leads to an "organization" of the firms, and thus outside pressure is deemed one means of getting satisfactory performance. As a result, there is very little difference between these nominally *nonregulated* industries and *regulated* industries. The essentially public-utility character that these concentrated and critical industries have increasingly taken on was pointed out by Professor Stigler in 1952. It is even more true today.

More and more, big businesses are being asked to act in "the social interest," and more and more, government is interfering in their

---

[36] *Concentration Ratios in Manufacturing Industry 1963*, Part I, Table 4, Subcommittee on Antitrust and Monopoly of the Committee of the Judiciary, U.S. Senate, 89th Congress, 2d session, 1966.

routine operation. The steel industry . . . what with Congressional review of prices and presidential coercion of wages, is drifting rapidly into a public-utility status.[37]

The optimal marketing structures for the economy are those which encourage impersonal forces—independent action by competitors. Market power or control over supply, whether held by one firm or several, increases personalness in the market. Where a few firms in a market have considerable market power, personalness *and* interdependence are increased. How extensive is market power in the economy? Low-level oligopoly is widespread in the economy, in addition to which, as we have noted, there are pockets of high concentration such as steel and automobiles. There is substantial concentration especially in such sectors as manufacturing, transportation, public utilities and some areas of finance. One study of the SIC two-digit manufacturing groups revealed that in fifteen of these twenty broad groups the eight largest firms accounted for roughly one-third or better of the total value added of the industry. And there were similar results at the SIC four-digit or "industry" level.[38]

Welfare Loss from Monopoly

One may ask whether the fact of extensive market power is an important social problem, for perhaps after all, the welfare loss produced by monopolistic misallocation of resources is minimal. Apparently, however, the welfare loss due to monopoly is *not* small. In contrast to previous studies showing welfare losses of two to four hundred million dollars per year, or

---

[37] Stigler, "The Case Against Big Business," *op. cit.,* p. 164. M. A. Adelman contrasts the market power of steel to the less oligopolistic and more independent character of the petroleum industry. See "Pricing by Manufacturers," in *Conference of Marketing Teachers from Far Western States* (University of California, 1958). Other aspects of oligopoly and market power in steel are discussed in Walter Adams and Joel B. Dirlam; "Big Steel, Invention, and Innovation," *Quarterly Journal of Economics,* LXXX, May 1966.

[38] David R. Kamerschen, "A Critique of the Status Quo Approach to Public Policy," *The Antitrust Bulletin,* Vol. 9, 1965, p. 753, and *see also* other works cited in Kamerschen's article. The critical role of market structure in the contemporary economy is the primary emphasis, as we have mentioned, in recent antitrust decisions in merger cases. The significance of structure—especially with respect to concentration and market power— has been extensively analyzed and documented. In addition to references cited in Chapter 4 and elsewhere in this chapter, *see* in particular, the discussions of the magnitude, persistence, and implications of concentration in *White House Task Force on Antitrust Policy, op. cit.;* FTC, *Economic Report on Corporate Mergers* (1969); W. G. Shepherd, "Conglomerate Mergers in Perspective," *Antitrust Law and Economics Review,* II, Fall 1968; and the rich source of data and opinions on trends and implications of marketing structure in *Hearings on Economic Concentration,* U.S. Senate, Subcommittee on Antitrust and Monopoly, Part 1–6 (1964–67).

less than 1 percent of national income—a recent study estimated the annual loss at more than $25 billion or about 6 percent of national income.[39]

Most firms face downward sloping product demand curves, due to differences in customer perceptions of offerings in a market, and thus most firms have some degree of market power. The basic social concern is not market power as such, but excessive and persistent or "unreasonable" market power.

The general policy implications of unreasonable market power are dissolution. Anything less than a structural solution yields only the frustrations we well know such as the annual "coping" with steel and automobile pricing. We have already indicated the *low* social cost of breaking up large firms. Moreover, the resulting increased competition would yield considerable *social benefits*. The solution, therefore, with respect to monopoly power is not for public agencies to coerce good social behavior from firms. Rather the solution is to "promote market *structures* which will *compel* the conduct and performance which is in the public interest." [40]

Some observers hold that rather than having to break up existing market power, it is better to prevent it from developing in the first place. Thus, given the virtual absence of evidence of any scale economies for the largest firms, there is logic in pursuing a vigorous antitrust program against any merger that may substantially (or, in concentrated markets, even slightly) increase concentration or entry barriers.[41] Let us stress that the rationale of a stringent *large* merger policy is that (1) unreasonable market power is already extensive, (2) it is from an equity standpoint more difficult to break up existing concentrated power, and (3) there is very little evidence of any increasing returns to scale for large firms.

[39] Kamerschen, *op. cit.*, p. 756. Also, David R. Kamerschen, "An Estimation of the 'Welfare Losses' from Monopoly in the American Economy," *Western Economic Journal* (Summer 1966). Another author estimates monopoly profits at about 2 to 4 percent of national income. Leonard Weiss, *Case Studies in American Industry* (Wiley, 1967), p. 318. *See also* Collins and Preston, *op. cit.*, p. 109.

[40] Walter Adams, *Planning, Regulation, and Competition, op. cit.*, p. 16, (emphasis in original). For some additional comments in favor of dissolution of leading firms with monopoly power, see Walter Adams in W. Adams (ed.), *The Structure of American Industry, op. cit.*, pp. 554–561; Joe S. Bain, *Industrial Organization* (Wiley, 1959), pp. 609–610; Carl Kaysen and Donald F. Turner, *Antitrust Policy* (Harvard, 1959), pp. 44–99; Joseph F. Brodley, "Oligopoly Power under the Sherman and Clayton Acts: From Economic Theory to Legal Policy," *Standard Law Review*, Vol. 19, January 1967; W. G. Shepherd, "Conglomerate Mergers in Perspective," *op. cit.*; and White House Task Force, *op. cit.*

[41] James M. Buchanan and Gordon Tullock point out the importance of concentrating upon the prevention of monopoly rather than its elimination after it has been created. "The 'Dead Hand' of Monopoly," *Antitrust Law and Economics Review*, Summer 1968. *See also* John C. Narver, "The Impact of Antitrust Merger Policy on Marketing," *Journal of Marketing*, January 1969.

Mergers

An important distinction between internal growth and merger growth is that internal growth is always procompetitive because it always adds capacity. Mergers *may* be procompetitive; however, any competition-increasing effect of *merger* is problematic rather than automatic for it is not certain if and when capacity will be added.

A merger alters competition, if at all, by altering marketing structure. All three types of mergers—horizontal, vertical, and conglomerate—can lessen competition, and all three can increase competition.[42] The merger law, unlike the law on monopoly, is probabilistic. That is, the Sherman Act in dealing with monopoly requires evidence of a certainty of effects; whereas the merger law, Section 7 of the Clayton Act, does not require demonstration of the certainty of anticompetitive results in a merger. Rather, it only requires evidence that the merger "may tend substantially to lessen competition." Thus, the merger law is based on the "reasonable probability" of anticompetitive effect.[43]

If the antitrust agencies were required to show *actual* substantial lessening of competition in order to challenge a merger, the court cases would be even longer than at present and there would unavoidably be considerable inequity to private parties.[44] Most vexing of all would be the unscrambling of mergers whose anticompetitive effects came into view only a considerable time after the merger. Reestablishing separate firms on an equitable basis to the owners is considerably difficult under the present probabilistic law, not to mention what it would be under any "certainty-of-effect" law.

Public Policy with Respect to Mergers

Horizontal Mergers

When concentration and/or barriers to entry are already moderate to high, a horizontal merger involving a market leader very well may tend substantially to lessen competition in that market. In recent years, horizontal-merger policy has developed to the point where no two competitors, other than relatively very small firms, can merge if the market is concentrated or is becoming more concentrated. Horizontal-merger policy is thus ex-

---

[42] Definitions of the three types of merger are found in Chapter 11 of the present text.

[43] *Brown Shoe* v. *U.S.*, 370 U.S. 294, 356–7 (Justice Clark, concurring). A complete citation of all merger complaints under revised Section 7, 1950–67, is in Willard F. Mueller, "The Celler-Kefauver Act: 16 Years of Enforcement," *op. cit. See also* Betty Bock, *Mergers and Markets* (National Industrial Conference Board, 1964), and Bock, *Mergers and Markets: 7* (NICB, 1969).

[44] For example, the Federal Trade Commission issued a complaint against Procter & Gamble's acquisition of Clorox (liquid bleach) at the time of the merger in 1957. The final decision was rendered in 1967 in a Supreme Court decision ordering divestiture. *FTC* v. *Procter & Gamble*, 386 U.S. 568.

tremely stringent—yet, as we have pointed out, the social benefits in such a policy appear to exceed the social cost.[45]

Vertical Mergers

Vertical mergers may lessen competition either by competitors at the supplier's level being foreclosed from access to a substantial share of the buyers; or by competitors of the buyer being foreclosed from a substantial share of supply. The competitive implications of a vertical merger depend in large part on the height of entry barriers and the level of concentration in the markets of either or both the supplier and customer. Foreclosure in vertical mergers, as with share of market in horizontal mergers, may be judged in violation of Section 7 even when the percentages are small. The Supreme Court declared that the merger of Brown Shoe Co. and Kinney Shoe Co. in which Brown had 4 percent of U.S. production and Kinney 1.6 percent of all retail shoe store sales was illegal on both vertical and horizontal grounds.[46]

Conglomerate Mergers

Conglomerate mergers may create less competitive market structures in three principal ways: (1) by eliminating potential competition with respect to concentrated markets; (2) enhancing opportunities for coercive reciprocity (that is, reciprocity enforced by market power); and (3) raising barriers and/or concentration by implementing conglomerate power. "Conglomerate power" is the number of competitive options possessed by large, diversified, profitable firms—which means simply more resources (on hand or available) than the competition and more markets from which to derive as well as in which to allocate the resources.

Taking a long-run view of firms, relatively few "intermarket" mergers are in fact purely conglomerate. The competitive implications of a firm, or a merger, cannot fully be determined by analyzing only the particular manner in which the resources of a firm(s) are used at any specific time. Most inputs in a firm are flexible—their particular short-run utilization is a managerial choice. The critical aspect of a firm or a merger, for purposes of competitive implications, is what that pool of resources *could* easily engage in, not merely in what it currently is engaged. Seen in this light,

---

[45] The leading horizontal-merger precedents under the amended Clayton Act Section 7 are *Brown Shoe* v. *U.S.*, 370 U.S. 294; *U.S.* v. *Philadelphia National Bank*, 374 U.S. 321; *U.S.* v. *Von's Grocery Co.*, 384 U.S. 270; and *U.S.* v. *Pabst Brewing Co.*, 384 U.S. 546. For an example of enforcement policy within a particular industry, see Federal Trade Commission, *Enforcement Policy with Respect to Mergers in the Food Distribution Industries*, January 3, 1967.

[46] Leading vertical merger precedents are *Brown Shoe, supra*; and with respect to policy within an industry, FTC, *Enforcement Policy with Respect to Vertical Mergers in the Cement Industry*, January 3, 1967.

many "conglomerate" mergers combine similar productive resources—and are thus actually horizontal mergers.[47]

SUMMARY AND CONCLUSIONS WITH RESPECT TO PUBLIC POLICY IN MARKETING

Public policy in marketing is *any* governmental policy at the federal, state, or local level which in any way affects the supply of or demand for goods and services. Accordingly, public policies in marketing include antitrust, economic regulation, consumer protection, government procurement, government subsidization of business, international and interregional trade policies, fiscal and monetary policy, zoning laws, postal regulations, and so on. Virtually all major governmental economic policies are a public policy in marketing for virtually all affect markets and transactions.

Competition, the independent rivalry of business firms, yields increases in efficiencies and value to consumers. The maintenance of competition is the concern of public policies known as antitrust. To maintain competition, the antitrust agencies continually must diffuse economic power, for economic theory suggests and empirical studies confirm that highly concentrated markets in conjunction with other structural variables lead to excess profits. The annual welfare loss of monopoly may have run as high as $25 billion in the mid-sixties or approximately 6 percent of national income. The diffusion of power is effected by antitrust policy in two ways: (1) changes in market structures to yield more rivalry; and (2) preclusion of conduct which may create monopolistic market structures.

Antitrust is "pro-business," for it is the private-enterprise alternative to either private monopoly or government control. Market *structure* to the largest extent must be the primary focus of antitrust policy, for merely to prohibit specific types of conduct—such as collusion

---

[47] This point is central to the discussion of definitions of markets in Chapter 3 of the present text. For detailed analysis and policy considerations, *see* John C. Narver, "Supply Space and Horizontality in Firms and Mergers," *St. John's Law Review*, XLIV Spring 1970. A discussion of the competitive implications and legal actions pertaining to conglomerate mergers are found in Narver, *Conglomerate Mergers and Market Competition op. cit.*; and Donald F. Turner, "Conglomerate Mergers and Section 7 of the Clayton Act," *Harvard Law Review*, LXXVIII (May 1965). An aggressive policy against leading-firm conglomerate mergers is argued in J. S. Campbell and W. G. Shepherd, "Leading Firm Conglomerate Mergers," *Antitrust Bulletin*, Winter 1968.

The leading precedent for "product-extension" mergers is *FTC* v. *Procter & Gamble*, 386 U.S. 568. (At issue was Procter's acquisition of Clorox Inc., a manufacturer of liquid bleach, a product Procter did not make or sell at the time of acquisition.) For enforcement policy with respect to "conglomerate" mergers within one specific industry, see FTC, *Enforcement Policy with Respect to Product Extension Mergers in Grocery Product Manufacturing*, May 15, 1968.

and coercive reciprocity—is to contend with only a *symptom*, not
a cause. Monopoly power (market power) is the fundamental problem.

Market structures must be assessed in conjunction with performance;
neither is sufficient alone. Although there is mounting evidence linking
market structure and performance—that is, the theory is getting more
accurate—a strict structural criterion might condemn out of hand some
markets in which there was vigorous competition. On the other hand, to
concentrate soley on market performance as the indicia for antitrust action,
is an invitation for nonenforcement. A judicious blend of structure-
performance analysis is required, with the primary emphasis on
structure.[48]

Antitrust, particularly in merger policy, has probably not precluded
many *real* economies. Large firms, the most frequent object of antitrust
merger attack, can attain virtually all real economies through internal
investment. No doubt there is some inconvenience and private cost when
a merger is precluded, but as Adelman has said, with respect to the
social and private costs of a strong merger policy, "[T]he worst [even]
a wrong merger decision can do is to force a company to build rather
than buy." [49]

There is no precise measurement of the "effectiveness" of antitrust
policy and enforcement. It is, however, safe to say the American economy
is more competitive today than it would be in the absence of antitrust.
With no antitrust, agreements in restraint of trade and restrictive
arrangements no doubt would proliferate, as they have in other industrial
countries having no antitrust programs. There have been some dramatic
court cases in which defendants were broken up, or as the case may be,
forced to divest themselves of an acquired firm. However, most of the
real effects of antitrust occur not at any visible level, but rather
in the offices of corporate counsel and in the deliberations of management.
For example, the merger movement discussed in Chapter 11, almost
certainly has changed direction as a result of strict enforcement of
horizontal mergers. Market concentration in many markets is not as high
as it would be in the absence of antitrust or under other antitrust

[48] These points are well discussed, if only briefly, in Edward S. Mason, "Preface" to
Carl Kaysen and Donald F. Turner, *Antitrust Policy, op. cit.* Another student of industrial organization and antitrust similarly argues the need for breaking up some of the
most concentrated oligopolies, a task he considers as important as conglomerate merger
enforcement, with social benefits far exceeding social costs. William G. Shepherd, "Conglomerate Mergers in Perspective," *op. cit. See also* references to market structure and
real economies in the present chapter and Chapters 4 and 15.
[49] *The Celler-Kefauver Act, op. cit.,* p. 26; *see also* R. B. Heflebower, "Corporate
Mergers: Policy and Economic Analysis," *Quarterly Journal of Economics,* November
1963, p. 558; and John C. Narver, "Some Observations on the Impact of Antitrust
Merger Policy on Marketing," *Op. cit.*

policies. As a result, consumers are better off due to the greater range of alternatives demands.[50]

Some summary conclusions, in abbreviated form, are (1) We as consumers desire continual increases in efficiency and real value in goods and services; (2) To ensure continual increases in efficiency and real value, our society relies on vigorous competition; (3) Competition will be most vigorous when resources can move easily into and out of markets, especially by internal investment—which automatically increases capacity and hence, competition—and therefore there must *not* be resource barriers other than *real* economies; (4) We as producers desire the freest possible hand to respond to demand and supply conditions, and to offer whatever price *and* nonprice combinations are required to effect differential advantage; (5) The freest possible hand means *impersonal* markets, which means in turn, vigorous antitrust—and especially, an antitrust approach emphasizing market structures; and (6) Only be effecting market structures that *compel* desirable performance will consumers be continually well served.[51]

SUGGESTED READINGS

Antitrust, Economic Regulation, and Public Enterprise: Books

Phillip Areeda, *Antitrust Analysis: Problems, Text, Cases* (Boston: Little, Brown & Company, 1967).

A leading casebook in the law of antitrust, containing as well, some introductory economic analysis.

Joe S. Bain, *Industrial Organization* (New York: John Wiley & Sons, Inc., 1959).

A well-known treatment of the analytics of market structure, conduct, and performance, and antitrust policy. Bain focuses in large part on market structure as both the basic determinant of market behavior and the appropriate object for antitrust policy.

E. T. Grether, *Marketing and Public Policy* (Englewood Cliffs, N.J.: Prentice-Hall, Inc., 1966).

Grether has limited his analysis of public policy in marketing to the issues pertaining to maintaining competition and maintaining a

---

[50] *See* Mason, *op. cit.*, Abe Fortas in "Symposium on Reevaluation of the Impact of Present Day Antitrust Policy on the Economy," 23 American Bar Association Antitrust Section (1963), p. 325 ff; John C. Narver, "Some Observations on the Impact of Antitrust Merger Policy on Marketing," *op. cit.*; George J. Stigler, "The Economic Effects of the Antitrust Laws," *Journal of Law and Economics*, Vol. 9, October 1966; and "The Effectiveness of the Federal Antitrust Laws: A Symposium," *American Economic Review*, Vol. 39 (1949), p. 689 ff.

[51] The interested reader may wish at this point to preview the discussion of consumer welfare in Chapter 16.

viable, responsive marketing system. The author, a long-time student of marketing and antitrust, provides in this short book many thoughtful considerations.

Carl Kaysen and Donald F. Turner, *Antitrust Policy: An Economic and Legal Analysis* (Cambridge, Mass.: Harvard University Press, 1959).

The authors combine economics and legal training in this assessment of existing antitrust policy, and recommend new directions for coping with excess market power.

Sumner Marcus, *Competition and the Law* (Belmont, Cal.: Wadsworth Publishing Company, 1967).

A compact, useful discussion of contemporary issues in antitrust, intended to stimulate critical analysis of emerging issues.

Willard F. Mueller, *A Primer on Monopoly and Competition* (New York: Random House, 1970)

An analysis of contemporary market structure and behavior and recommendations for antitrust policy, by the former Chief Economist of the Federal Trade Commission.

Lee E. Preston, *Social Issues in Marketing* (Glenview, Ill.: Scott, Foresman and Company, 1968).

A book of readings on productivity, efficiency, antitrust policy, and consumer welfare.

William G. Shepherd, *Market Power and Economic Welfare* (New York: Random House, 1970).

A relatively detailed review of market structure studies.

Werner Sichel, *Industrial Organization and Public Policy: Selected Readings* (Boston: Houghton Mifflin Company, 1967).

A readings book that combines analytical industrial organization readings on various aspects of market structure and behavior, and policy points of view.

Eugene M. Singer, *Antitrust Economics: Selected Legal Cases and Economic Models* (Englewood Cliffs, N.J.: Prentice-Hall, Inc., 1968).

A concise treatment of the foundations of antitrust and antitrust in both single-product and multiple-product contexts. The book juxtaposes legal and economic analyses of antitrust issues, and considers some complexities in defining and measuring market concentration.

J. Fred Weston and Sam Peltzman, *Public Policy Toward Mergers* (Goodyear, 1969).

A collection of papers analyzing a structural approach to antitrust, and also analyzing other aspects of contemporary antitrust policy.

Studies by the Staff of the Cabinet Committee on Price Stability (Washington, D.C.: U.S. Government Printing Office, 1969).

This book is the Staff Study Papers of President Johnson's

Cabinet Committee on Price Stability. The papers examine the long-term problems of inflation in the economy and examine the inflation implications of the job market and manpower policy; industrial structure and competition policy; construction; and the unemployment-inflation problem.

Social Welfare: Books

Warren G. Magnuson and Jean Carper, *The Dark Side of the Marketplace: The Plight of the American Consumer* (Englewood Cliffs, N.J.: Prentice-Hall, Inc., 1968).

Senator Magnuson, Chairman of the Senate Commerce Committee and long-time advocate of consumer interests, discusses the issues of deception, fraud, and product testing and safety in the contemporary marketing economy.

Clair Wilcox, *Toward Social Welfare* (Homewood, Ill.: Richard D. Irwin, Inc., 1969).

An economist's analysis of the problems of and appropriate policy for dealing with poverty, insecurity through old age or loss of job, and inequality of opportunity stemming from racial discrimination and other bases.

15

Marketing performance: productivity and efficiency

INTRODUCTION

Our purpose in this chapter is not to justify or condemn the marketing system by attempting to answer the age old question: "Does distribution cost too much?" [1] Rather, it is to evaluate two aspects of unit and market performance, namely, efficiency and the related concept of productivity.[2] We are not attempting to avoid these issues but rather provide some insights into the relevant techniques and measures.

Further, our analysis is limited to the unit level and market level, and does not include systems of markets or the entire economy. To extend this analysis to the entire economy would require the examination of the complex relationships in and between the political and economic aspects of the society and the comparisons between various solutions to the same problem.[3] These are obviously beyond the scope of the present volume.

[1] Several authors have attempted to analyze marketing in terms of costs, *see* Paul W. Stewart and J. Frederic Dewhurst, *Does Distribution Cost Too Much?* (Twentieth Century Fund, 1938); Harold Barger, *Distribution's Place in the American Economy since 1869* (Princeton, 1955), and Reavis Cox in association with Charles S. Goodman and Thomas C. Fichandler, *Distribution in a High-Level Economy* (Prentice-Hall, 1965).

[2] See Chapter 5, pp. 112–113. Another aspect of the result of market conduct is in Chapter 16.

[3] *See* Heinz Kohler, *Scarcity Challenged: An Introduction to Economics* (Holt, Rinehart, and Winston, 1968); and Joseph A. Schumpeter, *Capitalism, Socialism, and Democracy* (Harper & Row, 1942).

RELATIONSHIP OF PRODUCTIVITY TO EFFICIENCY

In our discussion, the term "productivity" is defined as the ratio of output to the energy used in producing it or simply as output divided by input. Engineers typically define efficiency as output/input. We will use "productivity" as synonymous with engineer's efficiency. Economists speak of "efficiency" as including *both* productivity *and* the price of inputs.

Productivity can be illustrated by the valuation you make after the completion of this chapter. What you must do is to relate the benefits (the output) received from reading the chapter to the work (the input) which it took to perform the task. If the benefits were high in relation to the energy expended, then we can say that there was great productivity. If, on the other hand, the ratio is low, then, the activity is not very productive.[4] Thus,

$$\text{Productivity} = \frac{\text{Output}}{\text{Input}}$$

It is obvious that if input prices remain constant or decline, an increase in productivity *is* an increase in economic efficiency.

Productivity Measures

Productivity can be measured in terms of (1) value of shipments per employee; (2) value-added per employee; (3) value of shipments per production worker man-hour; and (4) value-added per production worker man-hour.[5] "Value-added" is simply the payment to an agency for furnishing the product or service or both.[6] It is calculated by subtracting the cost of materials from the value of shipments.[7]

Measurement Problems

Although at the outset there seems to be a common base in these measures, we need to recognize certain limitations. For example, in the

[4] Stanley C. Hollander, "Measuring the Cost and Value of Marketing," in Perry Bliss (ed.), *Marketing and the Behavioral Sciences* (2d ed., Allyn and Bacon, 1967), p. 499. Originally printed in: *Business Topics* (Summer 1961), pp. 17–27. See the discussions of unit-level productivity and efficiency in Part IV of the present book.

[5] Betty Bock and Jack Farkas, *Concentration and Productivity: Some Preliminary Problems and Findings, Studies in Business Economics No. 103* (National Industrial Conference Board, 1969), p. 14.

[6] M. A. Adelman, "The 'Product' and 'Price' in Distribution," *American Economic Review: Supplement* (May 1957), p. 269.

[7] Bock and Farkas, *op. cit.*, p. 9. Cost is defined as the direct charges paid for items put into production during the year, excluding discounts, but including freight charges. Also excluded are the cost of such services as advertising, insurance, developmental research, and consulting as well as overhead, depreciation, rent, interest, royalties, materials, machinery and equipment used in plant expansion, and capitalized repairs which are chargeable to fixed assets accounts.

use of labor there is need to recognize that not all labor hours are homogeneous. Some firms employ skilled workers to perform the same tasks that unskilled workers do for other firms. The same is true when we convert labor hours to money costs because various firms combine labor and capital in different proportions and not all firms have the same cost of capital.[8] The problem becomes even more complex when we include the consumer into the productivity measure as should be the case. This is perhaps the most difficult task because we possess little information as to (1) what the consumer wants from the marketing system and (2) how much he participates in it. Alderson for one has suggested a measure for including the consumer; his logic is:[9]

(1) Unit sales per shopping hour
$$= \frac{\text{Number of marketing unit sales}}{\text{Number of shopping hours}}$$

(2) Man-hour equivalents
$$= \frac{\text{Total expenses of marketing}}{\text{Average hour wage rate}}$$

(3) Productivity
$$= \frac{\text{Index of unit sales per shopping hour}}{\text{Index of manhour equivalents}}$$

If there were no marketing system at all, essentially each consumer would have to perform all of the functions of marketing. In principle, actual productivity may be compared against this standard of very low productivity and the difference represents the productivity of marketing. However intriguing this appears as a method of evaluation, it is complicated by the problems of aggregation and definition. Thus, the one useful measure of marketing productivity is value-added, for it offers the advantages of simplicity and accuracy; it mirrors all the forces of demand and cost which impinge upon a firm's operation; and it permits us to measure costs, prices, and output over time. Even with all its benefits, value-added has certain problems.[10]

1. It is an aggregate measure for the unit and disregards specific differences between product and service assortments.
2. On a time basis, it does not fully recognize changing patterns of functions in the marketing channel.
3. It does not clearly allow comparison between changes in "production" activity and those in "marketing" activity. For example, with considerable increase in general productivity over time, the value of a unit of any factor in marketing would increase because its value in other uses had increased. The gross margin and apparent output

[8] Hollander, op. cit., pp. 503–504.

[9] Wroe Alderson, "A Formula for Measuring Productivity in Distribution," Journal of Marketing XII (April 1948), pp. 442–444.

[10] Adelman, op. cit., p. 269.

would also increase although there was in fact no real increase in the quantum of services rendered.

4. The abandonment of direct price comparisons makes it more difficut to reach a judgment about the nature of competition in a market.
5. An adjunct to the previous point is the need to realize that value-added data may be distorted by the inclusion of monopoly gains.[11]

In economic literature, efficiency has been equated with market outcomes generated by perfect competition. Under these conditions the interaction of sellers and buyers leads to the establishment of a unique market price in which the marginal cost equals the marginal satisfaction obtained by buyers; costs are everywhere minimized, and no market participation can gain without loss to another. "This Pareto-optimal outcome has come to be regarded as *the* efficient one from the resource allocation viewpoint, and the failure of social markets to meet the requirements of perfect competition has been said to bring about inefficiency." [12]

Efficiency as an absolute concept is the optimum use of resources. As a relative concept, we talk about efficiency or inefficiency insofar as marketing structures approximate or fail to approximate this optimum level. "The underlying principle is that no resource or other commodity should be used in any way if there is another use for it of greater social value."[13]

Efficiency can be measured in other terms. Dean has suggested four indicators:[14]

Additional Views of Productivity and Efficiency

1. Increasingly rapid changes in marketing techniques indicate gains in efficiency. Implicit is a wider range of consumer choice among services and end products.
2. Increased intensity in competition is indirect evidence of efficiency since competition prods managers into better use of resources, eliminates the unfit, and thereby improves the average level of efficiency.
3. The increasing relative importance of an activity in generating national income is another indication of efficiency. A higher share of resources devoted to marketing activities, for example, "a rising cost of distribution" does not imply lower efficiency. In fact, it indicates just the opposite since resources allocated to marketing

---

[11] *Ibid.*, pp. 269–270.

[12] Lee E. Preston and Norman R. Collins, "The Analysis of Market Efficiency," *Journal of Marketing Research* III (May 1966), p. 155.

[13] Robert Dorfman, *Prices and Markets* (Prentice-Hall, 1967), p. 114.

[14] Joel Dean, "Marketing Productivity and Profitability," in Bliss, *op. cit.*, p. 521. Originally printed in *Productivity Measurement Review* (1960), pp. 47–55.

could increase only if the marginal utility of a unit of input is increasing relative to the marginal utility of a unit of resources devoted to production.

4. Growth in relative patronage for a particular firm is usually a good indication of efficiency. Thus, the growth of the retail grocery chains' share of food retailing may be an indicator of their efficiency. (Recall, however, market structure implications in Chapter 4—a reminder that market share increases could reflect either relative efficiency or market power.)

Efficiency Measure

Our basic performance measure of efficiency is related to the basic theory of production and cost.[15] It is worthwhile to review this. The center of analysis is breaking marginal cost into its component parts:

$$MC = Pv \left(\frac{1}{MP} \right)$$

where Pv is the price paid per unit of a variable input and MP is the marginal product of the variable input, that is, the increment in total output produced by an additional unit of input.

Some Relationships

MC is affected by changes in either Pv or MP. A change in MP is a "real" economy because it is based on a physical relationship between inputs and outputs (whether they be units of labor, advertising, channel expenditures, marketing research, and so on). Real economies are social economies because they directly release scarce resources for employment elsewhere. A reduction in Pv (or an increase in the difference between output price and marginal cost) is a "pecuniary" economy because it is based on input and output prices. It is a private phenomenon and only possibly a social economy, for only possibly will it engender somewhere an increase in productivity. A pecuniary diseconomy occurs when one firm causes a rise in the price of certain inputs, making it more expensive in money terms for other firms who use the inputs. However, it does not increase the social cost of their production because this production requires no larger input quantities or expenditures of time and effort than before. For example, "increased use of leather by a shoe manufacturer may raise leather prices and

---

[15] One of the authors in a recent article observed that production and cost theory are noticeable by their absence in most marketing books. John C. Narver, "Some Observations on the Impact of Antitrust Merger Policy on Marketing." *Journal of Marketing* XXXIII (January 1969), p. 25, footnote 2. We have not followed tradition. A treatment of production and cost theory exceptional for its detail and clarity is C. E. Ferguson, *Microeconomic Theory* (Irwin, 1966), Chapters 6–8.

hence the money costs of other shoe firms, but it need not make it any harder for them to make shoes." [16]

Efficiency and Profitability

If one makes certain assumptions, profits are one of the best indexes for measuring efficiency among individual firms or types of firms. This is so because profits reflect the management's ability to supply desired marketing activities relative to the costs of the combinations of inputs.[17] The use of profits to measure "real" efficiency, however, is beset with difficulties: (1) profit data is usually published only for a company as a whole and not for specific operating divisions which possess greater homogeneity; (2) in tabulations ranging from the smallest to the largest size of corporation, profits for the former tend to be understated, as many entrepreneurs of small corporations frequently remove a substantial part of "real" profits as salary; (3) profit figures published in annual reports may be mistated; and, (4) high profit rates themselves may be the result not of greater economic efficiency but of substantial monopoly or monopsony power.[18]

Although the impact of the fourth can not be minimized, the effects of the first three can be. Analyses of firms can be confined so as to exclude those Standard Industrial Classification (SIC) three-digit industries in which the leading producers are most extensively and conspicuously engaged in other industries. Also it can exclude the small corporation and use an average of several years to minimize pecularities or misstatements arising from unusual factors in any given year.[19]

MARKET-LEVEL PERFORMANCE

In our analysis of market level performance we examine real and pecuniary efficiency. The overriding framework for this is market structure and especially the impact of concentration on various aspects of performance.

Market-level Real Performance

Real performance needs to be examined in two dimensions. The first is the increase in marginal productivity given no qualitative changes in

[16] William J. Baumol, *Economic Theory and Operations Analysis* (2d ed., Prentice-Hall, 1965), p. 369.

[17] Hollander, *op. cit.*, p. 520.

[18] *Hearings on Economic Concentration*, Subcommittee on Antitrust and Monopoly, Committee on the Judiciary, U.S. Senate, 89th Congress, 1st Session, Part 4, *Concentration and Efficiency*, testimony of John M. Blair, Chief Economist, Subcommittee on Antitrust, p. 1551, referred to hereafter as *Hearings on Concentration*. For a useful discussion of the limitations of profit data as indicators of efficiency and competition, *see* Yale Brozen, "Significance of Profit Data for Antitrust Policy" in J. Fred Weston and Sam Peltzman, *Public Policy Toward Mergers* (Goodyear, 1969).

[19] *Hearings on Concentration, op. cit.*

the good or service. The second is the change in marginal productivity associated with qualitative changes in output whether they are larger product assortments offered by sellers, better quality of goods, more efficient ways of performing functions, or a host of other ways.

The first of these we measure in changes of output per unit of input as enumerated earlier, while the latter is measured in terms of the rate of invention, innovation, and technological change as evidenced by patents, for example.

Changes in Productivity

The results of a recent study by the National Industrial Conference Board suggest that there are relationships between firm size, concentration and productivity, namely, that:

> On the average, the top companies in an industry had higher rates of productivity than the remaining companies in the same industry— regardless of the number of companies or the measure of productivity used. It also shows that the industries with the highest productivity tended, on the average, to have high concentration ratios and those with the lowest productivity tended to have low concentration ratios— regardless of how productivity and concentration were measured.[20]

and,

> If we examine the industries in the top and bottom productivity quartiles, the relation between concentration is even more marked, because the industries with the highest productivity are, in general, those with highest concentration ratios and those with the lowest productivity are those with low concentration ratios—whatever the measure of productivity and concentration used.[21]

If indeed these conclusions are valid they hold major public policy implications. If correct, they suggest that the existing pattern of market concentration is the product of large scale production and that the very large companies in an industry are generally considerably the more efficient. This latter inference thus suggests that

> (a) economies of large scale are likely to promote further increases in concentration among the top companies, and hence, merger and

---

[20] Bock and Farkas, *op. cit.,* p. 4. For a brief discussion, *see* "Bigness Means Efficiency," *Business Week* (February 22, 1969), p. 162, ff.

[21] *Ibid.,* p. 21. "Top-companies refer to concentration ratio derived as follows: the denominator is derived by assigning to the industry the total value of shipments of each plant classified in the industry on the basis of products accounting for the largest proportion of the plant's value of shipments. The numerator of the ratio is derived by first combining all the plants reported under common ownership or control and classified in the industry and aggregating the total shipments of these plants to company-level totals."

other antitrust policies interfering with this trend must necessarily be at the expense of economic efficiency and progress; and (b) efforts to increase competition through deconcentration are likely to result in serious economic costs to society.[22]

Willard F. Mueller in his analysis of the NICB study suggests that although there may be some statistical association between concentration and productivity there is no reason to accept the conclusion of causation. He argues that many industries are exceedingly unconcentrated simply because they have low entry barriers which means that frequently they are labor intensive and hence by definition would tend to have low levels of productivity. Further, he argues that the measures of productivity used in the NICB study includes noncompetitive profits and greater advertising outlays which permeate the more concentrated industries.[23] What we have then is the hypothesis that productivity is related to levels of market concentration, and that high productivity stems from high concentration, but the available data does not fully support the assertion. Obviously, this is an area which deserves attention to discover indeed what measures of productivity and efficiency might be used in evaluating concentrated industries.[24] Until these are more fully developed other hypotheses will have to be made on an industry by industry basis with a clear recognition of the factors which *cause* large operations, economies of scale, and levels of concentration.

Changes in Technological Aspects

In general, we do not find the same clear-cut pattern when we turn our attention to technological aspects. Part of this is due to the fact that the type of data necessary to make similar comparisons are not available. Beyond that we do find that industry concentration is not linked clearly to technology. As we will see in a subsequent section on the unit level, technology and change are a function of some factors in addition to market concentration.

Concentration and Technology

In 1958 the most concentrated industries included aircraft propellers, primary aluminum, locomotives and parts, flat glass, electric lamps, tele-

---

[22] Willard F. Mueller, "Competition, Efficiency, and Antitrust: A Policy Maker's View," in National Industrial Conference Board, *Competition, Efficiency, and Antitrust: Compatibilities and Inconsistencies* (NICB: March 6, 1969), p. 19. This is the viewpoint of John Kenneth Galbraith in *The New Industrial State* (Houghton Mifflin, 1967), but this thesis of Galbraith was seriously challenged by three leading economists in a vigorous debate.

[23] Mueller, *op. cit.,* p. 20.

[24] For the extent to which price-cost margins have a close association with market structure, *see* Norman R. Collins and Lee E. Preston, "Price-Cost Margins and Industry Structure," *The Review of Economics and Statistics* LI (August 1969), pp. 271–286.

phone service and equipment, safes and vaults, to name a few. To be certain, not all of these industries are regarded commonly as leaders in technology; some spend little on research while others spend a great amount. When industry groups are ranked from highest to lowest in terms of concentration, it is difficult to argue that they retain the same ranking in terms of their interest and accomplishments in research. "Clearly, particular industries of low concentration such as apparel and furniture are not research conscious, but neither are such concentrated industries as tobacco and dairy products. Some industries of relatively low concentration, notably scientific instruments, insecticides and fungicides, and plastic materials are technically active.[25] We can see this evidence in Table 15.1.

When we add concentration of patents to the discussion, once again we find that sales are much more concentrated among the largest firms than either research and development or patents. For example, the largest 30 firms by sales volume, corresponding roughly to those with one billion dollars or more sales in 1955, accounted for 49 percent of the sales of all 352 corporations on which comparable data were available, but only 45 percent of the research and development employment and 43 percent of the patents. "The implication is that among firms, big enough to appear on *Fortune*'s 1955 list, the largest firms supported inventive and innovative activity less intensely relative to their size than did the smaller firms." [26]

Market-level Profit Performance

Profit performance is measured in two ways. The first of these is the profit rate, after taxes, as a percentage of net worth. The second measure is that of price-cost margins which are the difference between average price and average costs, expressed as a percentage of average price.

Concentration and Profitability

In analysis of 290 manufacturing companies as a group in the period 1959–63 there was no discernible relationship between profitability and company rank (assets). However, when the group of 290 firms were analyzed in an industry-by-industry basis, for each of the 30 industries, there were three groups with respect to a relationship between profitability and concentration. In group I there were seven industries in which there is a positive (direct) relationship between size and profitability. In Group II there was an inverse realtionship. In the third group containing 16 industries there was no significant relationship. between size and profitability.[27]

---

[25] *Hearings on Concentration,* Part 3, *op. cit.,* p. 1083, Statement of Richard Stillerman, Chicago, Illinois.

[26] *Ibid.,* p. 1194. Statement of Dr. F. M. Scherer, Department of Economics, Princeton University.

[27] *Hearings on Concentration,* Part 4, *op. cit.,* p. 1553. Testimony of John M. Blair.

TABLE 15.1

PERCENTAGES OF TOTAL RESEARCH AND DEVELOPMENT PERFORMANCE FUNDS AND TOTAL FEDERALLY FINANCED RESEARCH AND DEVELOPMENT ACCOUNTED FOR BY THE 4, 8, AND 20 COMPANIES WITH THE LARGEST DOLLAR VOLUME OF RESEARCH AND DEVELOPMENT PERFORM- ANCE, BY INDUSTRY, 1959

Industry	Percent of R & D performance			Percent of federally financed R & D		
	1st 4 com- panies	1st 8 com- panies	1st 20 com- panies	1st 4 com- panies	1st 8 com- panies	1st 20 com- panies
Food and kindred products	37	55	78	(1)	(1)	(1)
Textiles and apparel	58	70	82	(1)	100	100
Lumber, wood products, and furniture	42	55	71	(1)	(1)	(1)
Paper and allied products	44	58	77	(1)	(1)	(1)
Chemicals and allied products	45	56	73	86	91	97
Industrial chemicals	63	79	92	87	92	97
Drugs and medicines	45	67	93	79	94	100
Other chemicals	28	45	70	(1)	57	96
Petroleum refining and extraction	50	73	95	62	66	100
Rubber products	85	91	96	90	99	100
Stone, clay, and glass products	51	70	83	45	71	100
Primary metals	44	58	81	47	73	85
Primary ferous products	59	76	96	(1)	(1)	91
Nonferrous and other metal products	56	72	92	(1)	88	97
Fabricated metal products	48	65	78	62	89	98
Machinery	48	58	69	64	79	86
Electrical equipment and communication	63	77	87	64	81	94
Communication equipment and electronic components	60	77	88	63	80	93
Other electrical equipment	89	91	93	97	98	98
Motor vehicles and other transportation equipment	90	94	98	93	98	99
Aircraft and parts	50	71	95	51	71	96
Professional and scientific instruments	62	70	85	71	81	94
Scientific and mechanical measuring instruments	75	83	92	92	95	100
Optical, surgical, photographic, and other instruments	64	79	94	63	81	97
Other manufacturing industries	60	66	78	57	66	73
Nonmanufacturing industries	33	40	51	69	73	84

1 Not available.

Source: *Hearings on Economic Concentration* Subcommittee on Antitrust and Monopoly, Committee on the Judiciary, U.S. Senate 89th Congress 1st session, p. 1355, from the National Science Foundation: "Funds for Research and Development in Industry," 1959, '62–3, app. A, table A-11, p. 62.

Among the seven industries in Group I the most conspicuous example of tendency for profit rates to rise with increasing concentration and increasing size is business machines. IBM, largest manufacturer, with more than five times the assets of the industry's second largest company, has the industry's highest average rate of return, which exceeds that of the most profitable by six percentage points. On the other hand, it is interesting to note that the computer industry with the top four firms controlling 67 percent of the total output, were nearly 60 percent lower on the basis of shipments per employee than the next four, which shared only 13 percent of the output.[28] The increasing returns characterizing Group I do not necessarily imply economies of scale—rather, they may just as logically imply increasing market power.

In the seven industries included in Group II, the general tendency is for rates of return to decline as company size increases. We can observe this in the data in four of the seven industries in Table 15.2. This tendency is most clearly observable in the distilled liquors group. The five smallest— each less than one-tenth the size of National Distillers & Chemicals—had substantially higher profit rates than either the leader or the next two ranking firms, Seagram and Schenley.

In order to unravel concentration, firm size and efficiency, analysis must be carried one step further. If we assume there are asymmetric oligopolistic industries, the leader is likely to possess substantially greater monopoly power than other firms. Where the leader is much larger than its rivals, the chances are that it will possess greater monopoly power than if all firms were of relatively similar size. If this assumption is true—and in over half of the 30 industries studied the total assets of the leader exceeded the assets of the second by more than 40 percentage points—the expectation would be that, all else being equal, they would tend to show a higher profit rate than their lesser rivals. "Since a higher rate could be the result of either superior efficiency or greater monopoly power, the failure of the companies with presumably the greatest monopoly power to earn the highest rates suggests the possibility that they may be even less efficient than their smaller rivals." [29]

---

[28] Bock and Farkas, op. cit., p. 83. Appendix A: Basic Value of Shipments Data. This is most puzzling as Business Week points out. "International Business Machines—which is the subject of a recent monopoly case that charges it has unfair advantages over competitors—says that it's completely mystified by the figures." p. 166.

[29] Hearings on Concentration, Part 4, op. cit., p. 1555. Other studies also provide similar conclusions. J. S. Bain, "Relation of Profit Rate to Industry Concentration: American Manufacturing, 1936–49," Quarterly Journal of Economics LXV (August, 1951), pp. 293–324; C. R. Fuchs, "Integration, Concentration, and Profits in Manufacturing Industries," Quarterly Journal of Economics LXXV (May 1961), pp. 278–291; D. Schwartzman, "The Effect of Monopoly on Price," Journal of Political Economy LXVII (August, 1959), pp. 352–362; L. W. Weiss, "Average Concentration Ratios and Industrial Performance," Journal of Industrial Economics XI (July, 1963), pp. 237–254.

TABLE 15.2

AVERAGE ANNUAL RATES OF RETURN FOR 290 CORPORATIONS IN 30 MANUFACTURING INDUSTRIES, 1959-1963

GROUP II: INDUSTRIES SHOWING DECREASING RATE OF RETURN WITH INCREASING ASSET SIZE

Meat Products				
1. Swift & Co.	$609,559	100	4.4	H
2. Armour & Co.	454,917	75	7.3	E
3. Wilson & Co.	149,093	24	7.1	F
4. John Morrell & Co.	86,933	14	7.5	D
5. Oscar Mayer & Co.	79,983	13	10.3	B
6. Geo. A. Hormel & Co.	70,848	12	9.1	C
7. Cudahy Packing Co.	59,074	10	2.3	I
8. Hygrade Food Products Corp.	56,042	9	5.0	G
9. Rath Packing Co.	46,657	8	.8	J
10. Tobin Packing Co.	23,156	4	12.6	A
Sugar				
1. American Sugar Co.	256,800	100	7.0	G
2. Great Western Sugar Co.	111,609	43	10.6	C
3. S. Puerto Rico Sugar Co.	76,329	30	6.5	H
4. American Crystal Sugar Co.	74,007	29	3.9	I
5. National Sugar Refining Co.	68,097	26	2.9	J
6. Utah-Idaho Sugar Co.	67,265	26	8.0	E
7. Holly Sugar Corp.	61,811	24	8.5	D
8. Amalgamated Sugar Co.	54,305	21	12.1	B
9. U.S. Sugar Corp.	44,642	17	18.7	A
10. Sucrest Corp.	35,247	14	7.4	F
Malt Liquors				
1. Anheuser Busch, Inc.	215,871	100	10.2	E
2. Jos. Schlitz Brewing Co.	181,545	84	7.0	H
3. Pabst Brewing Co.	123,573	57	6.0	I
4. Falstaff Brewing Co.	76,578	35	14.0	D
5. General Brewing Corp.	40,027	18	8.3	G
6. Drewry's, Ltd U.S.A. Inc.	30,334	14	8.8	F
7. Olympia Brewing Co.	28,162	13	18.3	B
8. Pearl Brewing Co.	23,374	11	21.9	A
9. Duquesne Brewing Co.	16,617	7	3.1	J
10. Lone Star Brewing Co.	13,910	6	16.8	C
Distilled Liquors				
1. National Distillers & Chemical Co.	632,921	100	7.0	G
2. Jos. E. Seagram & Sons, Inc.	509,071	81	4.9	H
3. Schenley Industries, Inc.	452,436	71	3.6	J
4. Brown Forman Distillers Corp.	93,734	15	12.5	D
5. Glenmore Distilleries Co.	38,531	9	4.5	I
6. James B. Beam Distilling Co.	48,239	8	21.0	A
7. Heublein Inc.	45,561	7	16.5	C
8. American Distilling Co.	44,688	7	10.8	E
9. Barton Distilling Co.	43,417	7	18.0	B
10. "21" Brands, Inc.	13,220	2	9.5	F

Source: *Hearings on Concentration*, Part 4, p. 1756.

Relation of Profits and Real Performance

According to one point of view, profits and real performance in terms of research and development are linked in that only very large firms in concentrated industries are able to finance the research and development needed to invent new products and processes and to coordinate the complex activities required by the invention and innovation process. According to this view large size carries with it both the added incentives and resources to be innovative and to introduce such innovations into markets. "It is further argued that market concentration provides a stimulus to inventive activity because (1) the higher profits derived from concentration enable firms to finance more research and (2) the avoidance of price competition in highly concentrated markets creates a drive to seek new and improved products as a method of competition." [30]

Price-cost Margins

The hypothesis that certain key features of industry structure are closely associated with variations in the price-cost dimensions of market performance is strongly supported by recent evidence.[31] Specifically, in an analysis of data for a cross-section of 32 food manufacturing industries, Collins and Preston examined and accepted the hypothesis that average price-cost margins are positively related to the degree of concentration. We see this in Figure 15.1. The relationship between price-cost on the vertical axis and concentration ratios on the horizontal takes a form which means that price-cost margins increase at a faster rate with higher levels of concentration.[32]

> Reading from the figure, we note that no systematic increase in margins accompany [sic] increases in concentration in the lower ranges; in those industries for which four-firm concentration is under, say 30 percent, price-cost margins average about 12 percent with no apparent pattern. However, above the 30 to 40 percent concentration level, increases in concentration are systematically associated with increases in price-cost margins, and equal increases in concentration with ever

[30] Cabinet Committee on Price Stability, *Studies by the Staff of the Cabinet Committee on Price Stability*, 1969 Study Paper Number 2, "Industrial Structure and Competition Policy," p. 64.

[31] *Hearings on Concentration*, Part 2, *op. cit.*, p. 719. Testimony of Dr. Norman Collins, Department of Agricultural Economics and School of Business Administration, University of California, Berkeley. *See also* Norman R. Collins and Lee E. Preston, *Concentration and Price-Cost Margins in Manufacturing Industries* (University of California Press, Berkeley and Los Angeles, 1968). Recall the discussions of this and similar aspects of market structure-performance in Chapter 4, Part IV, and Chapter 14 of the present book.

[32] *Ibid.* The relationships between these two variables were found to be continuous and curvilinear.

larger increases in margins. As concentrations reach, say, 60 percent, the price-cost margin has risen to about 25 percent, and—continuing to increase at an increasing rate—when the concentration level reaches 85 percent, the price-cost margin has an expected value of about 45 percent.[33]

FIGURE 15.1

NET REGRESSION RELATIONSHIP BETWEEN PRICE-COST MARGINS AND FOUR-FIRM CONCENTRATION LEVELS

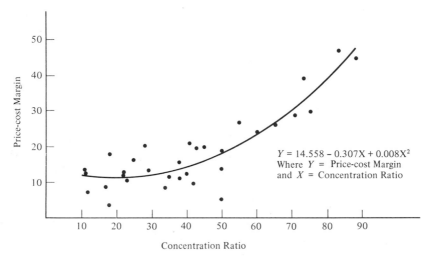

$$Y = 14.558 - 0.307X + 0.008X^2$$

Where Y = Price-cost Margin and X = Concentration Ratio

Source: *Hearings on Concentration,* Part 2, p. 718.

All other things equal, competition tends to force profit levels to equality among all markets (risk included). Of course, in purely competition markets in long-run equilibrium, firms gain only normal profits (the opportunity cost of owner's capital). As we have suggested, market structure-performance analyses help point out differences in competition, all the while recognizing the complexities of profit data.

Earlier in this chapter we suggested that intensive competition was an important stimulus for increases in efficiency. Innovations in business methods are one temporal measure of the efficiency a firm or group of firms in the same industry—assuming all are under similar competitive structures. Examples are numerous. Among leading illustrations are what "department stores did unto specialty shops as discount houses were to do to them; the old-fashioned grocery store was largely displaced by the economy store and it by the supermarket; while the impact of the mail-order house has been recorded for all time in the invective of its rivals." [34]

[33] *Ibid.*, p. 718. See also Federal Trade Commission, *Economic Report on the Influence of Market Structure on the Profit Performance of Food Manufacturing Companies* (1969).

[34] Adelman, *op. cit.*, p. 272.

UNIT LEVEL PERFORMANCE

"Scale" can be measured as the rate of output per unit of time which a firm or plant is designed best to produce, that is, the rate of output which it can produce more economically than any other size of plant or firm. Technically, the long-run average cost curve is the scale curve. A firm operating at a given scale will have a cost per unit which is similar· to those of other firms in the *same* industry. The important consideration is whether larger or smaller plants will have lower or higher costs and if so in what pattern will they be found?

The traditional explanations of economies of large-scale plant emphasize the real savings of the use of specialized machinery, and of further specialization of labor and management. Strictly pecuniary economies (in input *or* output) usually are not included, perhaps because of the assumption that a single plant will not ordinarily be large enough to take advantage of these economies.[35]

Size and Costs

The question which must be asked is how does size affect *costs*? (Note that this is not the question of how size affects *profits*, for profits may include both real and pecuniary economies.) Implicit in the analysis of economies of scale is the assumption that there is an optimum size unit and that units below that size can improve performance by increasing their size. Such pressure upon firms in an industry to increase the size of operating units may be an important cause of structural change within the industry.

Costs may be significantly affected also by the extent to which facilities are utilized. If costs go up steeply as the degree of utilization declines, large incentives may exist to emphasize merchandising and selling efforts. Individual competitors strive for higher volume in order to get better utilization of their facilities. In these ways, the behavior of costs represents an important determinant of structural change and competitive behavior within the industry.[36]

Economies of Scale in Food Retailing

In recent studies on efficiency in food retailing the National Commission on Food Marketing concluded that while store size had little effect on store costs, store utilization, that is the sales per square foot, had a very significant effect on store costs. In terms of the economies of size of store, the total range of variation is somewhat less than 2¢ from stores of 4000 square feet of selling area to stores of 16,000 square feet of selling area.

[35] Joe S. Bain, *Barriers to New Competition* (Harvard, 1956), pp. 56–57.
[36] National Commission on Food Marketing, *Organization and Competition in Food Retailing, Technical Study No. 7* (June 1966), p. 139.

However, for low rates of utilization increases, cost levels decline first and then begin to flatten out.[37] This relationship is presented in Figure 15.2.

FIGURE 15.2

SCATTER DIAGRAM OF STORE EXPENSE AND SALES PER SQUARE FOOT, FOR STORES OF 7000 TO 8000 SQUARE FEET CORRECTED FOR VARIATION IN WAGE RATES

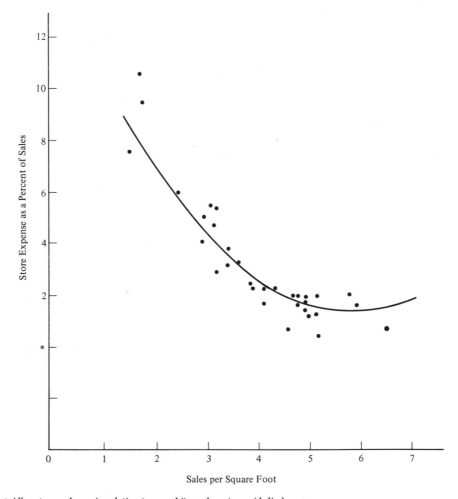

Sales per Square Foot

1 All costs are shown in relation to an arbitrary base to avoid disclosure.

Source: *See* National Commission on Food Marketing, *Organization and Competition in Food Retailing, Technical Study Number 7* (June 1966), Table 5, p. 141.

The Commission conducted nine tests to evaluate space utilization and economies of scale for thousands of retail food stores. The typical relation between utilization and economies of scale is shown in Figure 15.3. There "reverse J" shaped lines show how costs varied with sales per square feet

[37] *Ibid.*, p. 141.

for four different sizes of store. In these cases, the relationship was downward sloping and curvilinear, and the straight line connecting the minimum points of the four curves shows how costs declined when the size of the store increased. Note that sales per square foot of selling space were kept constant. Even though the expense ratios declined with increases in store size, the difference in costs between the largest and the smallest stores rarely amounted to more than 2 percent of sales. This is substantially less than the average 10 percent reduction in costs which was associated with increased sales per square foot of selling space. It was discovered, in general, that a 20 percent increase in sales concomitant with a greater utilization of space would reduce store costs by 1 percent of sales.

FIGURE 15.3

A COMPARISON OF UTILIZATION AND SCALE ECONOMIES FOR FOOD STORES, TEST NO. 4

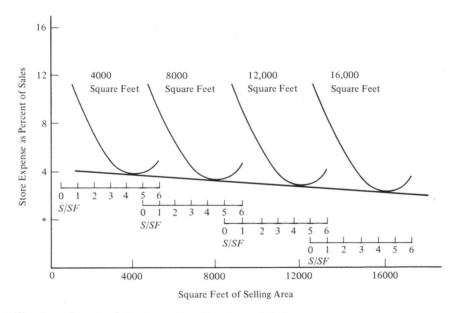

1 All costs are shown in relation to an arbitrary base to avoid disclosure.

Source: *See* National Commission on Food Marketing, *Organization and Competition in Food Retailing, Technical Study Number 7* (June 1966), Figure 2, p. 141.

Economies in Retailing

It should be clearly noted, however, that no one optimal size exists across all retailing agencies. For example, if we use profitability in terms of size, we discover that the most profitable firms vary in size from one line of trade to another. The most profitable general merchandise firms were over $1.5 billion sales (1956–57) while the most profitable food corporations had less than a half billion dollars in sales. Following were the medium-sized corporations—apparel and accessories and drug—with "best sizes of about

$50–100 million annually. Finally, the other types—furniture and house furnishings, building materials and hardware, automobiles and gasoline stations, eating and drinking, and others—tended to be small with maximum profits and sales volumes of $10–25 million." [38]

Size and the Possibility of Other Aspects of Scale Economies

Scale economies in several forms, aside from those mentioned, may arise from size. One of the most important of these relates to the ability of large-scale retail units, single or multiple operations, to operate warehouses. The Food Commission from somewhat scattered data concludes that warehouses for retail food chains have increased in size over the past several years. "While there are economies of operating a large warehouse unit, a major reason for increasing warehouse size has been the increasing number of items handled.[39]

Other economies which accrue from size are such things as manufacturing grocery items, private label programs, and buying of perishables. However, exceedingly large size of the units is required to realize the benefits. For example, "There may be some economies beyond a half billiion in some very minor items manufactured by food retailers, [but] the magnitude of such savings would be small." [40]

Single versus Multiple Activities

The actual economies arising in the firm depend upon its structure, size, management, and access to factor and product markets, and the nature of its offerings. The large firm whose operations are carried out at one centralized location can expect different economies from those of the firm whose activities are in widely dispersed establishments.[41]

There is no shortage of reasons which can be assembled to support the proposition that common ownership and control results in greater efficiency.

Thus, it may be claimed that if the plants are of varying degrees of efficiency, the poorer ones will be brought up to the level of the best. This could be done, for example, by shutting down the more efficient plants and concentrating production in the most productive plants. Or it may be contended that selling and distribution costs can

[38] Edna Douglas, "Size of Firm and the Structure of Costs in Retailing," in Lee E. Preston (ed.), Social Issues in Marketing (Scott, Foresman, 1968), p. 88. Originally printed in Journal of Business XXXV (April 1962), pp. 158–190. We clearly recognize that the measures are not fully compatible, however, the relatively scattered data require this.

[39] National Commission on Food Marketing, op. cit., 140–149.

[40] Ibid., p. 152.

[41] H. G. Hunt, Industrial Economics (Pergamon, 1965), p. 91.

be spread over a greater number of units and are thus lower when a variety of different products are sold by the same organization.[42]

On the other hand, there is no shortage of reasons to suggest that multi-unit operations may be expected to result in diseconomies or be no more efficient than single units at one location. It can be argued that supervision problems, lack of response to changes in supply and demand or the fact that the multi-unit company is susceptible to a variant of Parkinson's Law all support this proposition.[43]

On the question of whether the possible economies outweigh the possible diseconomies, available evidence appears to be negative. Bain found in six industry groups out of 20 that multi-plant economies were nonexistent and for four others for which he could obtain data, multi-plant economies as a percent of total costs were small, or ranging up to only three percent.[44]

Higher profit rate of the multi-unit firms may not be the result of greater efficiency but of monopoly power. For example, in retailing the inherent differentiation because of location of units, the inelasticity of demand with respect to the price of retail service which is only a fraction of total price, and the inertia and ignorance of the individual buyer are the elements of monopoly power which is subtantial in the short run.[45] The ability to exercise such monopoly power leads to larger size firms. "Large firms may develop, however, in those merchandise lines where multistore ownership and/or vertical integration offer sufficient economies or other marketing advantages." [46]

Adoption of New Business Methods

At the unit level one can observe firms and enterprises adopting new business methods not only in forms of operation but in terms of new products offered by sellers (see Chapter 3). Within a short space it is, of course, impossible to review all the various changes which have taken place as possible evidence of greater efficiency: Hence of necessity we have been selective.

Food Distribution.   One of the areas where numerous new business methods have been introduced and have shown increases in firm productivity is food distribution. Most important of these is the change brought about by inte-

---

[42] *Hearings on Concentration,* Part 6, *op. cit.,* p. 2968. Statement John M. Blair.

[43] *Ibid.,* p. 2969. Blair's variation: "The tendency of costs of an organizational unit to rise so as to consume the funds allocated to it."

[44] *Ibid. See* J. S. Bain, "Economies of Scale, Concentration, and Conditions of Entry in Twenty Manufacturing Industries," *American Economic Review* XLIV (March 1954), pp. 15–39; and J. S. Bain, *Barriers to New Competition* (Harvard, 1956), pp. 110–113.

[45] Adelman, *op. cit.,* p. 271.

[46] Douglas, *op. cit.,* p. 88.

gration of the food chain into the wholesale activities. As the large retail food chains adopted the new technologies in physical handling of products including palletized loading, conveyor systems, motorized carts and fork lifts, and even unit trains (complete trains consigned to a single shipper), efficiency and productivity have increased.[47]

One measure of increasing efficiency is the rate of inventory turnover which for the members of the Supermarket Institute was a median increase of nearly 28 percent.[48] Another index in retail chain warehouses is tons handled per man-hour. In the period 1954 to 1965 in Table 15.3, we see that the amount has risen from 1.85 average tons in 1954 to 2.26 in 1965.[49]

T A B L E   1 5 . 3

TONS HANDLED PER MAN-HOUR IN RETAIL CHAIN WAREHOUSES, 1954-1965

Year	Annual average tons handled per man-hour [1]
1954	1.85
1955	1.90
1956	1.87
1957	1.95
1958	2.02
1959	2.08
1960	2.11
1961	2.08
1962	2.12
1963	2.11
1964	2.26
1965	2.26 [2]

[1] Average of 33 reporting companies.

[2] Preliminary.

Source: National Commission on Food Marketing, *Organization and Competition in Food Retailing, Technical Study No. 7,* June 1966, p. 229.

Drug Distribution.   While wholesale druggists have also adopted similar warehouse operating methods, they have also attempted to reverse the buying patterns of retail pharmacists as a means of improving performance. Small retail druggists for many years made their purchases on a hand-to-mouth basis. This practice forced wholesalers supplying them to stock items in large quantities, which slowed down warehouse operations. Druggists who were buying in 1/12 or 1/6 dozen lots forced the wholesaler to absorb

[47] National Commission on Food Marketing, *op. cit.,* p. 227.

[48] *Ibid.*

[49] *Ibid.,* p. 229.

larger costs of order preparation as well as inventory because odd lot items required specailized handling.[50] With this problem in mind some drug wholesalers have offered retail druggists corresponding discounts if they concentrate their purchases in uniform lot sizes.[51]

Firm Size and Technology

Is there any positive relationship between firm size and real productivity in the form of technology? The answer is not clear-cut since there are at the same time large firms and nonfirm enterprises contributing to new technology as well as small firms. At the one extreme are the major systems developments including ballistic missiles, communication satellites, and electronic telephone systems; at the other end are the thousands of components, instruments, chemical compounds and simple mechanical devices produced by individuals working alone or by small firms.[52]

The Steel Industry

The American steel industry has been the center of attention with respect to the introduction of new processes. Adams and Dirlam attempted to test the hypothesis that large firms with substantial market shares have both greater incentives and more ample resources for research and development. They selected the oxygen steelmaking process as a means of testing the hypothesis.[53] Evidence showed that the basic oxygen process was introduced not by the major producers but the smaller ones, namely, Kaiser Steel and McLouth.[54] However, the reasons for the introduction of the new process was not totally attributable to the size of the firms involved as evidence suggested that the production costs for oxygen method and the traditional open-hearth method were similar. Rather, the cost-of-capital was a factor which made the adoption of the new process more advantageous.[55]

[50] E. L. Newcomb, *Fair, Equitable, and Low Distribution* (National Wholesale Druggists' Association, 1940), p. 26.

[51] Ronald Savitt, *Market Competition and Dual Distribution: The Ethical Drug Industry* (Unpublished Ph.D. dissertation, University of Pennsylvania, May 1967), p. 230.

[52] *Hearings on Concentration*, Part 3, *op. cit.*, p. 1189. Statement of Dr. F. M. Scherer.

[53] Walter Adams and Joel B. Dirlam, "Big Steel, Invention, and Innovation," *Quarterly Journal of Economics* LXXX (May 1966), pp. 167–168. *See also* Alan K. McAdams, "Big Steel, Invention and Innovation, Reconsidered," *Quarterly Journal of Economics* (August 1967). Walter Adams and Joel B. Dirlam, "Big Steel, Invention and Innovation: A Reply," *Quarterly Journal of Economics* (August 1967).

[54] I. E. Madsen, "Developments in the Iron and Steel Industry during 1954," *Iron and Steel Engineer* (January 1955), p. 124.

[55] Hearings of the Subcommittee on Antitrust and Monopoly, *Administered Prices: Steel*, Part 3, 85th Congress, 1st Session, 1958, p. 783, 787. Testimony of Mr. John Vaughan Grover, on behalf of McLouth Steel Corporation.

It is necessary to point out some of the factors which influence the rate at which any new process takes place and hence why there are variations in patterns in the introduction of technology by firms of varying size. Specifically for the oxygen process these were:

1. Economic conditions in this country were not conducive to adoption of BOP steelmaking.
2. Substantial improvements were made to existing open hearths at relatively low cost.
3. Rapid improvements in BOP technology favored those companies which could wait.
4. Ingot cost savings were frequently too little to warrant replacing existing open hearths with BOPs.
5. Capital cost savings involve numerous complex factors which vary widely from case to case.

FIGURE 15.4

AVERAGE 1959 PATENTS PER BILLION DOLLARS OF SALES BY SIZE AND TECHNOLOGY GROUPS

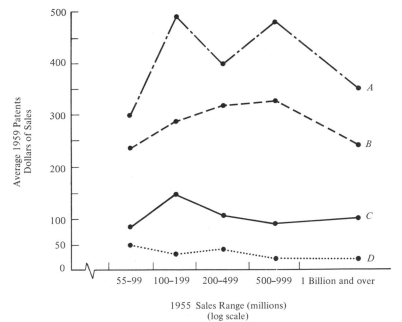

Group A: Electrical Equipment and Communications
Group B: Basic Chemicals and Drugs
Group C: Petroleum, Rubber, Stone-Clay-Glass, Fabricated Metal Products, Machinery, and Transportation Equipment (including Aircraft)
Group D: Food, Tobacco, Textiles, Apparel, Paper, and Primary Metals
Source: *Hearings on Concentration*, p. 1197.

6. Alternative uses of funds were frequently evaluated to be more attractive than BOP projects.
7. Replacement of existing technology takes many years.[56]

Size and Research and Development

In a recent study Scherer examined the average patenting and average research and development per billion dollars of sales for 352 corporations placed in the following categories: (1) electrical equipment and communications, (2) basic chemicals and drugs, (3) petroleum, stone-clay-glass, fabricated metal products, machinery, and transporting equipment, and (4) food, tobacco, textile, apparel, paper, and primary metals. The four technology groups were then subdivided into five size classes. Results for the most active group, electrical industry, are more irregular, although the highest patents-to-sales and R & D-to-sales ratios occur for firms in the $100 to $199 million range. The basic chemicals and drugs group is an exception showing a slight but also irregular tendency for inventive activity to rise with firm size. "Altogether, in six cases out of eight, the highest average rates of patenting and R & D development per billion dollars of sales are found for firms with 1955 sales of less than $200 million." [57] Figure 15.4 provides such evidence.

SUMMARY

It is most difficult to make any conclusive statements about the efficiency of marketing in the United States. It is possible to argue that indeed the system could be more efficient than it is, given that we have some notion of an ideal. Hence we must say the present system has room for improvements. It is of little value to compare our level of efficiency with that found in other economies for no other is on the same scale. Productivity and prices differ, and no other country has precisely the same goals. Distinctions can be made between various industries saying that one uses less input for its output, but this too is very misleading unless we specify exactly the technological relationships between industries. It is of little value to say that the data processing industry is more efficient than the food services industry because both have different combinations of labor and capital and have different marketing structures. And it is of little value to say that a large integrated food food service firm is more efficient than the family running a cafe somewhere on the side street in a large city. There are certain non-quantifiable values such as the ability to enter, operate, and even leave an industry which must be weighted with efficiency.

---

[56] David R. Dilley, "Oxygen Steelmaking: Fact vs. Folklore," in *Hearings on Concentration,* Part 6, *op. cit.,* p. 3145. Introduced by Senator Dirksen.
[57] *Hearings on Concentration,* Part 3, *op. cit.,* pp. 1195–1197.

In general, it can be said that there appear to be some economies to some types of large enterprises, though exact specifications cannot be set for all firms or industries; there are always the exceptions. In those instances, for example, where there are high profits and high concentration, it is most difficult to determine whether high profits result from efficiency from size or simply from monopoly power. In some areas it is easier to perceive changes in productivity and efficiency. There are numerous examples in the distributive trades, wholesaling and retailing, for a wide variety of product groups. To conclude, however, that these changes reflect productivity—either a function of it or a cause of increases in it—would be misleading. We simply have no standard against which to compare. Indeed, the issues are quite complex. A supermarket might show great strides in increasing the number of items handled in a warehouse with given resources, but at the same time customers might spend more time in check-out lines. Has there been an increase in productivity? To whom is it granted? It is these types of problems which must be considered in order to understand this topic.

Comparisons of efficiency then become meaningful at the level of the individual firm when one can compare and contrast similar sized firms in the same industry to see if one is able to combine its inputs in a more efficient manner than the others given that difference in conditions are taken into consideration. Even if extreme differences in the two firms are found, there is no requirement that one firm, the inefficient one, be purged from the market. Consumers may be willing to pay for inefficiency as part of the convenience of having the firm there willing to serve them—which simply reminds us that input efficiency may be far different from perceived value or consumer satisfaction. One need only consider the pleasure of being able to walk to a corner drugstore in the midst of winter to purchase aspirin or other medicines rather than have to exert additional energy to travel some distance for the same item. The latter may be inefficient by the standards of the large-integrated chain drugstore, but in serving a need it, in other senses, is also efficient.

SELECTED READINGS

Books

Harold Barger, *Distribution's Place in the American Economy Since 1869* (Princeton, N.J.: Princeton University Press, 1955).

This is the classic study on the costs and production of the marketing sector. Although Barger's analysis is quite simple, in that he accounts only for a limited number of marketing channels, it does represent the first systematic attempt to measure efficiency in marketing.

Reavis Cox in association with Charles S. Goodman and Thomas G. Finchandler, *Distribution in a High-Level Economy* (Englewood Cliffs, N.J.: Prentice-Hall, Inc., 1965).

This book attempts to examine how large a role distribution plays in the American economy and how well does it perform the functions. It raises some interesting issues though it too is hampered by some problems in definition and measurement.

Margaret Hall, John Knapp, and Christopher Winsten, *Distribution in Great Britain and North America: A Study in Structure and Productivity* (London: Oxford University Press, 1961).

This volume attempts to identify various structures for marketing firms for several countries and then measure their productivity. It examines the results across three economic systems: Canada, Great Britain, and the United States.

Paul W. Stewart and J. Frederic Dewhurst. *Does Distribution Cost Too Much?* (New York: The Twentieth Century Fund, 1939).

Roland S. Vaile, E. T. Grether, and Reavis Cox. *Marketing in the American Economy* (New York: The Ronald Press Co., 1952), Chapter 31 and 32.

Articles

James V. Cook, "1970—Can Marketing Measure up?" in George L. Baker, Jr., Ed., *Effective Marketing Coordination* (Chicago: American Marketing Association, 1962), pp. 21–27.

Reavis Cox, "Broad Social Forces and the 'Cost Squeeze' in Retailing," in Lynn H. Stockman, ed., *Advancing Marketing Efficiency* (Chicago: American Marketing Association, 1959), pp. 215–21.

———, and Charles S. Goodman, "Marketing of Housebuilding Materials," *Journal of Marketing* XXI (July 1965), pp. 36–61.

This is a classic article in the measurement of efficiency in marketing channels.

Edna Douglas, "Size of Firm and the Structure of Costs in Retailing," *Journal of Business* 25 (April 1962), pp. 158–90.

Richard D. Lundy, "How Many Gasoline Service Stations are 'Too Many'?" in Reavis Cox and Wroe Alderson, eds., *Theory in Marketing* (Chicago: Richard D. Irwin, 1950), pp. 323–336.

This article raises some interesting issues about the age old accusation that there are too many middlemen in markets. Lundy examines some alternatives in relation to consumer effort and welfare.

David A. Revzan, "Evaluation of Channel Effectiveness," *Wholesaling in Marketing Organization* (New York: John Wiley and Sons, Inc., 1961), pp. 151–155.

Horace M. Gray, "Small Business: The Institutional Environment," *A-T Law and Economic Review*, Vol. 1, No. 1 (July-August 1967). (Paper presented to Senate Selection Committee on Small Business, March 8, 1967.)

> The author suggests it is folklore that big business is necessarily more efficient and superior to small business in many industries.

Willard F. Mueller, "Competition, Efficiency, and Antitrust: A Policy Maker's View," in National Industrial Conference Board, *Competition, Efficiency, and Antitrust: Compatibilities and Inconsistencies* (New York: NICB: March 6, 1969).

Joe S. Bain, "Survival-ability as a Test of Efficiency," *American Economic Review*, May 1969, pp. 99 ff.

> Also see discussion by Lester Telser, pp. 119 ff.

Additional Books

Wroe Alderson, Vern Terpstra, and Stanley J. Shapiro, *Patents and Progress: The Sources and Impact of Advancing Technology* (Homewood, Ill.: Richard D. Irwin, Inc., 1965).

> A useful collection of papers dealing with the sources and competitive and other implications of technological change and patents.

Betty Bock and Jack Farkas, *Concentration and Productivity: Some Preliminary Problems and Findings*, Studies in Business Economics No. 103 (New York: National Industrial Conference Board, Inc., 1969).

Richard F. Gift. *Estimating Economic Capacity* (Lexington: University of Kentucky Press, 1968).

> Mr. Gift provides a conceptual framework within which a meaningful interpretation of the diverse definitions and measures of productive capacity can be made.

Hearings on Economic Concentration, Subcommittee on Antitrust and Monopoly, Committee on the Judiciary, U.S. Senate, Parts 1–6 (1964–1967).

> An extremely rich source of data on the relationships among firm growth, mergers, concentration, productivity and efficiency.

Edwin Mansfield. *Industrial Research and Technological Innovation: An Econometric Analysis* (New York: W. W. Norton, for the Cowles Foundation for Research in Economics at Yale University, 1968).

> A macroeconomic study using some U.S. data. Presents brief conclusions on such topics as the determination of the rate of technological change, the amount of research and development in the U.S., the determinants of industrial research and development expenditures, and the relationship between such expenditures and invention output.

Thomas Marchak, Thomas Glennan, and Robert Summers. *Strategy for R & D: Studies in the Micro-economics of Development* (New York: Springler-Verlag, 1967).

The authors are interested in the nature of the development process and the alternative strategies that are available to a developer. The book summarizes and brings together a good deal of the work on military development carried out at the Rand Corporation under the general guidance of Burton Klein, whose ideas concerning development strategy had an important influence on this work. Like the book by Nelson, Peck, and Kalachek, this book is devoted largely to the analysis of policy problems; but the problems dealt with here are at the level of the individual project, and the analysis is much more formal and mathematical.

Richard Nelson, Merton Peck, and Edward Kalacheck. *Technology, Economic Growth, and Public Policy* (Washington, D.C.: Brookings Institution, 1967).

Their book is primarily a synthesis and interpretation rather than a statement of new results, and brings together the many diverse trends of fact and argument pertaining to this subject that are scattered among various journals and books, and relates the results to problems of public policy. In contrast to Schmookler, much of their attention is devoted to policy questions.

Jacob Schmookler, *Invention and Economic Growth* (Cambridge, Mass.: Harvard University Press, 1966).

The book is concerned with the causes of variations in invention over time in a given industry and at a moment of time between industries.

W. J. J. Smith and Daniel Creamer. *R & D and Small-Company Growth: A Statistical Review and Company Case Studies.* The Conference Board Studies in Business Economics No. 102 (New York: National Industrial Conference Board, 1968).

Undertaken at the suggestion of, and funded by, the National Science Foundation, this volume deals with case studies of 27 companies in the machinery, chemical, and electronics industries, employing between 100 and 999 people. It is based primarily on interviews with management personnel, in the period 1963–1964, and special tabulations of census data. Analyzes the extent of small company participatin in R & D, the effect on growth, and conditions necessary for permanent R & D programs, as well as the constraints on small company programs.

16

Marketing performance: consumer welfare

Woe unto them that join house to house, that lay field to field, till there be no place

Isaiah 5:8

These issues [preventing the dehumanization of mankind] are the control of population and encouragement of a less consumptive economy . . . divesting ourselves of the fallacy that bigger means better

Paul Sears, *Science Digest*, August 1960.

Long before the stomach dies, the man will die
Rienow and Rienow, *Moment in the Sun* (Dial Press, 1967), p. 25.

THE ANALYSIS OF CONSUMER WELFARE

We come now to the final and in many senses, the most important analysis of the entire book. In this chapter we shall consider the welfare of the consumer in the marketing economy. We are fundamentally interested in the ways in which and the extent to which the marketing economy provides satisfaction for the consumer. This analysis in part will be normative.

Our conclusions with respect to consumer satisfaction are dependent on two underlying questions: (1) *Which aspects* of a consumer's life are we to include with respect to the satisfaction the marketing economy provides; and (2) What is the meaning of *satisfaction* in regard to those aspects?

In order to answer the first question, let us review briefly some characteristics of a market-based economy such as ours. In the pure market economy and, in principle, in the marketing economy, consumers' wants are detected by potential suppliers who then offer a good or service that completely matches the want. We thus describe a first-order effect, namely, a demander who is supplied a product which fulfills his want. Virtually all of our analysis in this book, and as well, the vast majority of received economic theory, deals with first-order effects—a firm selling in one or more intermediate or ultimate markets, and a demander buying in one or more intermediate or ultimate markets.

Thus, if in our analysis of consumer welfare we include only first-order effects, then the analysis and conclusions relate only to the well-being of consumers as they seek products to satisfy their *immediate* wants. Such analysis deals with "first-order" welfare, and the analysis perforce would ignore externalities or higher-order effects in the process by which these wants are satisfied. Thus, the only social costs that the "first-order" analysis includes are society's scarce resources utilized in the first-order activity.

The social benefits, of course, are the utility yielded to the customers and the income yielded to the factors of production.

The magnitude and growth of gross national product—the *quantity* of society's output—has been the logical macro complement to first-order-effect analysis.[1]

Ignored in first-order analysis are such external effects as air, water, or noise pollution emanating from the industrial process through which the immediate consumer want was satisfied; or anti-competitive conduct by a firm. These are higher-order effects than the satisfaction of the immediate want, and they are certainly social costs, for they subtract from the original quantity and/or quality of society's scarce resources. Historically, external effects—external diseconomies in the present context—for reasons of legal loopholes, measurement problems, as well as lack of public concern, typically have been borne predominantly by society rather than by the firm who is polluting, and so forth.[2]

Thus consumer welfare in terms of first-order effects is the prime focus of much of economic and marketing analysis—for by-and-large it is the historic focus in our society. Such analysis, based essentially on the quantity and variety of goods and services in markets, is clearly evident in contemporary antitrust policy and implicit in the analysis of marketing productivity

[1] *See* Robert Bork's focus on output *quantity* as the criterion of consumer welfare, in which he singularly ignores higher-order effects. Robert H. Bork, "The Goals of Antitrust Policy," *American Economic Review*, May 1967.

[2] Only recently, with the advent of broad-scale concern over the crises of our environment has there been a wholehearted effort to begin to shift the costs of pollution from society back to the polluter—thereby to *equalize* private costs and social costs. For example, consider Maine's stringent 1970 law requiring compensation for accidental oil spillages.

and efficiency.[3] And in terms of first-order effects—the direct satisfaction of wants for specific goods and services—the marketing economy probably scores rather well. These passing marks relate only to *effective demand*, and ignore income distribution and the millions of hungry and ill-housed Americans.[4] First-order achievement is apparent from the discussion of the effects of antitrust in Chapter 14 and the appraisal of productivity and efficiency in Chapter 15.

By now it is abundantly clear to the reader that the alternative answer to the question of "which aspects" of a consumer's life to include in appraising the market economy and consumer welfare, is to include *all* aspects— that is, first-order *and* higher-order effects. Essentially this inclusive view of consumer welfare boils down to the total *quality of life* of consumers within the marketing economy.

Obviously "quality of life" is in part *subjective*, for as we discussed in Chapter 3, wants, products and want satisfaction are personal-perceptual concepts. But the "quality of life" of consumers is also in part *objective*. Such things as frustration and poor health, for example, congestion, and air, water, or noise pollution *can* be measured. Thereby one can *directly indicate* with respect to *these* aspects, the welfare of the consumer.[5] At least

---

[3] We have stressed in Chapter 14 that public policy in marketing includes a range of policies from antitrust to consumer protection. It is obvious that all public policies *ought* to complement each other toward the overall goal of maximizing the total well-being of consumers, that is, the citizens of the country. Accordingly, all public policies should be shaped by a concern not only for first-order but higher-order effects as well. Clearly, this may not always be the case. Antitrust, for example, tries to keep competitors apart, that is, keep markets impersonal. In principle, keeping competitors apart on all matters could deter development of safer products. However, the social costs of antitrust's singular focus may be slight. Thus, it is not clear that with more inter-firm cooperation the automobile manufacturers would have introduced antipollutant devices on automobiles or the cigarette manufacturers, low-tar cigarettes any sooner. We offer the antitrust-consumer protection illustration only to suggest that a strict adherence to maximizing first-order effects could frustrate some other aspects of consumer well-being. We insist that the *total* impact on the welfare of the consumer must be the *overall guide* in the totality of public policies in marketing. Certain issues in competitor cooperation are well discussed by Donald F. Turner in a speech, "Cooperation among Competitors," at the Northwestern University School of Law, October 13, 1966.

[4] For some estimations of the poverty problem in America, *see Report of the National Advisory Commission on Civil Disorders* (U.S. Government Printing Office, 1968), and Michael Harrington, *The Other America* (Crowell-Collier and Macmillan, 1963).

[5] Among many others one could cite, one well-researched and useful discussion of the deteriorating quality of the American environment is Robert Rienow and Leona Train Rienow, *Moment in the Sun* (Dial, 1967). For other important discussions pertaining to many citizens' total economic and social environment in our marketing economy, see *Report of the National Advisory Commission on Civil Disorders, op. cit. See also* Federal Trade Commission, *Economic Report on Installment Credit and Retail Sales Practices of District of Columbia Retailers* (1968); and David Caplovitz, *The Poor Pay More* (Free Press of Glencoe, 1963).

from scientific studies one can objectively state the probable health hazards —to both one's physical and psychological state—from unsafe products, meaningless product warranties, crowding and congestion, racial and other forms of discrimination in obtaining employment, housing, or other goods and services and so on.[6]

Considering consumer satisfaction in terms of the total quality of life, means of course, that "consumer sovereignty" is a very complex issue. Consumer sovereignty, as we recall from Chapter 2, means simply that consumer demand determines what a society produces. The extent to which consumers today are sovereign—that is, actually determine what goods and services are produced—is of course an empirical question. If we remember that consumers as citizens have "votes" both in the marketplace and in the political voting booth, then *if* markets and politicians are responsive to actual desires, consumer sovereignty with respect to the "quality of life" could be considerable. We, however, reserve judgment on the responsiveness of markets and politicians—uring that the reader *continuously* judge for himself. In our brief discussion, we can offer only bits of evidence.

The second question underlying the analysis of consumer satisfaction posed at the outset of this discussion relates to the meaning of "satisfaction." As in the discussion in Chapter 3, "complete" customer satisfaction in the first-order sense means that every element in one's want is fully matched by a corresponding element in an offering. However, if all aspects of a consumer's life are to be included in analyzing consumer welfare, then of course "satisfaction" is a comprehensive concept. In principle, the meaning is clear: "Complete" consumer satisfaction with respect to the total quality of life means a fulfillment of all elements in a want *as well as* an absence of harmful (physically or psychologically) second- or higher-order effects.

It is perhaps clear that in an uncertain and in other ways incomplete world (Chapter 2), *complete* satisfaction in the "first-order" sense, let alone the "quality-of-life sense" is the exception rather than the rule. Hence, we understand "satisfaction" to be a relative rather than an all-or-nothing concept.

In summary, we urge that the correct framework for assessing consumer welfare in the marketing economy is the consumers' total quality of life. Accordingly, one should be more concerned with the total *quality* than the quantity of the gross national product. Though this inclusive con-

---

[6] We suggest that a *substantive* meaning of the "social responsibility of business" is an awareness of and facing up to the second-, third-, and fourth-order effects of one's own activity. Daniel Moynihan, White House Counselor on Urban Affairs, has stated that one basis of business-government friction is that typically business' concern was with first-order effects of technology—whereas, government's outlook was primarily oriented to second- and higher-order effects. Business-government rapport could increase if business paid more attention to higher-order effects, and government, both for understanding and use in its own operations, paid more attention to first-order effects of technology.

cept is the relevant criterion for judging the total performance of the marketing economy, first-order effects are nevertheless more readily observable and measurable. Thus, for reasons of simplicity, we shall discuss some first-order welfare issues in the marketing economy, with implications for the more fundamental question—consumers' *total quality of life* in the marketing economy.

We turn now to several aspects of consumer welfare in the marketing economy. We shall consider first the "consumer movement"; secondly, prices in different income areas; thirdly, price differences among some physically identical goods; and finally some additional comments on consumer sovereignty. In conjunction with the present discussion, the reader may wish to review the portions of Chapter 15, dealing with consumer protection and a "consumer perspective" in antitrust.

THE CONSUMER MOVEMENT

The consumer movement is a diverse group of activities intended to make the consumer a wiser buyer and user of goods and services.[7] The movement, a loose collection of interested parties and activities rather than a tightly coordinated whole, turns on increased information and legislation curbing deception and fraud, for the protection and benefit of consumers. By restricting misleading practices as well as educating consumers, it may be looked upon as a set of efforts to make market information more complete and thereby to make markets more responsive.

Some components of the consumer movement at the federal government level are (1) the Special Assistant to the President for Consumer Affairs, a position held by Mrs. Esther Peterson and Miss Betty Furness in the Administration of President Johnson and Mrs. Virginia Knauer, in the Administration of President Nixon; (2) the President's Committee on Consumer Interests,[8] composed of 50 government agencies whose operations have implications for the consumer; (3) the Consumer Advisory Council, under the Council of Economic Advisors, established by President Kennedy;[9] and (4) the Federal Trade Commission, a regulatory agency established in 1914 whose duties, in addition to antitrust, include discovering

---

[7] E. A. Duddy and D. A. Revzan, *Marketing: An Institutional Approach* (2d ed., McGraw-Hill, 1953), Chapter 8.

[8] Executive Order 11349, May 1, 1967 (32 Fed. Register 6759), and Trade Regulation Reporter (No. 306, May 9, 1967, p. 5). *See also Consumer Protection Activities of Federal Departments and Agencies*, U.S. Congress, House of Representatives, 8th Report by the Committee on Government Operations.

[9] *See Consumer Advisory Council: First Report, October 1963* (Executive Office of the President). The Council, existing only by Executive Order, consists of appointed private citizens and special assistants for consumer affairs from government agencies.

and enjoining deceptive practices of firms in interstate commerce and the District of Columbia, as well as administering the Truth in Lending and Truth in Packaging Acts.[10]

At the state level, consumer movement activities are seen for example in departments of consumer affairs or consumer protection frequently located in the office of the state attorney general. California, New York, and Washington are three of many states with established programs and procedures for state assistance in consumer protection.

Increasingly, large cities in the U.S. have established offices or departments of consumer affairs. One of the most active of these is New York City's Department of Consumer Affairs in the office of the Mayor. This department deals with various matters of interest to consumers including a clearing house and coordination of all municipal agencies such as electric utilities, water, garbage, food and health inspection, transportation, and so on. Consumer complaints and grievances are solicited and then followed up for appropriate action, including the possibility for law suits in the victim's behalf.[11]

Much of the thrust of the consumer movement comes from private individuals and organizations. One well-known example is the Consumers' Union which, among other activities, tests products and publishes in their publication *Consumer Reports* the performance of various brands of goods and services ranging from moving and storage companies to electric toasters. Credit unions provide employees information on budgeting and financial planning in addition to loans.[12] Consumer cooperatives are another nongovernment component of the consumer movement. They are agencies in

[10] The Truth in Lending Act is Consumer Credit Protection Act, Public Law 90-321, May 29, 1968 and the Fair Packaging and Labeling Act is Public Law 89-755, November 3, 1966. Specifically with respect to consumer protection, the Commission investigates and curbs deceptive trade practices including false and misleading advertisements and promotional activities of a deceptive nature. It also enforces the wool, fur, and textile labeling laws, and analyzes and measures the tar and nicotine content of cigarettes and publishes its findings.

The Commission conducts extensive economic investigations of industries and marketing activities, for example, *Economic Report on Installment Credit and Retail Sales Practices of District of Columbia Retailers* (March 1968) and *Staff Report on Automobile Warranties* (November 1968), both of which pertain directly to consumer interests.

Also, in 1968 the FTC held several hearings on consumer protection. See *National Consumer Protection Hearings, Federal Trade Commission* (U.S. Government Printing Office, 1967). Mary Gardiner Jones has been one of the most active consumer-oriented Commissioners at the FTC in recent years. See for example, her speech "The Consumer's Interest in Urban Society," May 23, 1969, available upon request at the FTC.

[11] See "Curbing Fraud: New York City Fights Shady Merchandisers With New Legal Curbs," *Wall Street Journal*, January 9, 1970, p. 1.

[12] One textbook dealing extensively with various aspects of personal finance is Arch W. Troelstrup, *Consumer Problems and Personal Finance* (McGraw-Hill, 1965).

various areas of retailing which are owned and directed by consumers. Members receive patronage dividends based on their personal volume of purchases.[13] Consumer cooperatives engage in many types of consumer education programs, including shopping tips, guides to borrowing money, personal safety in the use of various goods, and consumer oriented social action such as political lobbying.

Better Business Bureaus, which are local-level private organizations devoted to encouraging ethical practices among local businesses, are another component of non-government assistance in behalf of consumers. Also, to an extent, trade and industry associations play a similar role; however, self-regulation leaves much to be desired, for it is understandable that businessmen hesitate to police each other when their own gains would be larger if all firms cooperated rather than were in conflict. Yet, it is precisely this type of cooperative tendency among "competitors" that leads to price fixing and other collusive arrangements. Thus, self-regulation, enlarging inter-firm contact as it does, is hardly a guarantee of protection for consumers.

PRICING AND MARKUPS IN DIFFERENT INCOME AREAS

The issue of whether the poor pay more is one that has been investigated in several areas including food. The prices and margins found in low-income areas versus higher-income areas were investigated by the National Commission on Food Marketing in six large cities: Atlanta, Chicago, Washington, D.C., Houston, Los Angeles and New York. The comparisons involved chain stories, large independents ($300,000 annual sales or greater) and small independents (less than $300,000 annual sales). The question was whether similar type stores charged more in areas of low income than higher income, and the conclusions were that on balance there were no indications that any one type of firm exhibited significantly higher prices for similar food items in low-income areas than in higher-income areas.[14]

To find that stores of the same type on the average do not charge higher prices in low-income areas does *not* demonstrate that the poor pay no more than the more affluent. The important added questions are whether there is any difference in price level of different *types* of stories, and whether higher-price types are more prevalent in the ghettos and other low-income

---

[13] *See* Ellis Cowlins, *A Short Introduction to Consumers Cooperation* (Washington, D.C.: The Cooperative League of the U.S.A., 1948); and Jerry Voorhis, *American Cooperatives* (Harper & Bros., 1961).

[14] Organization and Competition in Food Retailing, Technical Study No. 7, National Commission on Food Marketing, *op. cit.*, p. 337, and passim Chapter 17 "Prices and Margins in Different Income Areas." The entire study of prices and income areas is part of *Special Studies in Food Marketing* Technical Study No. 10, National Commission on Food Marketing, 1966.

areas. In the same study cited above, price levels of chains, large independents, and small independents were compared. The comparisons indicated that chain prices are generally lower than independents. Specifically, large independents' prices are about 1 percent higher than chains' and small independents' are more than 3 percent higher.[15] Moreover, chain stores—the lowest-price type of outlet—were least frequently found in the low-income area. The study found that in general the chain stores avoided the lower-income areas, and offered their greater consumer advantages to communities of higher income, higher education, and lower unemployment.[16]

The study indicated that stores serving the low-income area were typically small, dirty, and poorly maintained. The quality of perishables such as ground beef, beef steak, pork chops, chickens, lettuce, and potatoes, was lower in the low-income areas. The quality variation was greatest in independent stores.[17]

Our definition of price (Chapter 13) is customers' total scarce resources expended for a bundle of utility. The National Commission on Food Marketing study reveals that price to low-income consumers was higher on two counts: (1) Because of the prevalence of independents, customers expended more money per unit than if more chains were present; and (2) The average quality level was lower, and hence, for these customers their price was higher also because the poorer quality meant a smaller bundle of utility per scarce-resource expenditure, (including direct money and time and effort).

Costs of operation are higher in the lower-income areas. With respect to leading food chains with stores in low-income and higher-income areas, the gross margins were slightly higher for the low-income stores, but the net margin, in terms of percent of sales, was substantially different—2.73 for the low-income area stores and 3.99 for stores in the higher-income areas.[18]

The National Commission on Food Marketing's findings on prices and profit levels in low-income and higher-income areas are supported in part and refuted in part by other studies and investigations. A Special Study Subcommittee of the Committee on Government Operations, House of Representatives, raised a series of additional questions pertaining to prices and price behavior of firms selling to the poor. The Subcommittee attempted

---

[15] Technical Study No. 7, *loc. cit.*

[16] *Ibid. See* the similar conclusions in more recent studies: FTC, *Economic Report on Food Chain Selling Practices in the District of Columbia and San Francisco* (1969), and U.S. Department of Labor, *Retail Food Prices in Low and Higher Income Areas* (1969).

[17] Technical Study No. 7, *op. cit., passim.* Some of the lower-quality produce in the stores may have been distress-sale items the stores purchased from wholesalers at low prices. *See also* Charles S. Goodman, "Do the Poor Pay More?" *Journal of Marketing* 32 (January 1968), pp. 18–24.

[18] Net margin includes contribution to warehouse expense and overhead. *Ibid.,* Table 17-4, p. 340.

to shed light on possible price discrimination by chains in which they allegedly raised prices in low-income areas coincidental to the issuance of welfare checks. As we have pointed out in Chapter 13, price discrimination is a difference in *percentage* markup over cost. If costs are higher in the low-income area, a constant percentage markup would yield higher prices in the low-income area. Thus, there could be different prices between the two areas, but no price discrimination. As to the alleged first-of-the-month increases in prices, the evidence is mixed as to whether one or more chains systematically engaged in such behavior.[19]

The Federal Trade Commission conducted a study of installment credit and sales practices involving household furnishings and appliances in the District of Columbia. Retailers who primarily used installment contracts rather than selling on a cash basis were the major focus of the report. Such retailers were divided into two groups: Those appealing primarily to low-income customers and those appealing to a more general market.[20]

The findings as to prices on installment credit versus cash transactions, as well as prices in low-income and higher-income areas were rather clear-cut. First, low-income market retailers used installment credit in 93 percent of their sales; whereas general-market retailers used installment credit in 27 percent of their sales.[21]

Without exception, low-income retailers had higher average markups and prices. On the average, goods purchased for $100 at wholesale sold for $255 in low-income market stores, in contrast to $159 in general market stores. When viewed in terms of specific products, contrasts between markups of low-income and general-market retailers are most apparent. One striking example the study found was as follows: The wholesale cost of a portable TV set was about $109 to both a low-income market and a general-market retailer. The general-market retailer sold the set for $129.95, whereas the low-income market retailer charged $219.95 for the same item. A clothes dryer was another dramatic example. It wholesaled at about $115, and was sold by a general-market retailer for $150 but for $300 by a low-income market retailer.[22]

The net profit picture was similar to that of the Food Marketing study: Net profit rate was about the same for retailers in and out of the low-income area. In particular, despite their substantially higher prices, net profit on sales for low-income market retailers was only slightly higher and net profit

---

[19] For testimony and discussion of these and other points, see *Consumer Problems of the Poor: Supermarket Operations in Low-Income Areas and the Federal Response,* Committee on Government Operations, U.S. House of Representatives, 90th Congress, 2d Session, Report No. 38, 1968.

[20] FTC, *Economic Report on Installment Credit and Retail Sales Practices of District of Columbia Retailers,* March 1968.

[21] *Ibid.,* p. ix.

[22] *Ibid.,* pp. x–xi.

return on net worth was considerably lower compared to general market retailers. Other interesting findings are (1) that low-income market retailers unlike their general market counterparts, typically do not sell their installment contracts to banks and finance companies; (2) there were relatively low credit costs among low-income retailers, for many of the finance charges were in effect *included* in the purchase price; and (3) there was extensive use of the courts by low-income retailers to enforce their claims against consumers. Eleven of the 18 low-income market retailers received 2690 court settlements in 1966—ending in 1568 garnishments and 306 repossessions. For this particular group of low-income merchants, one court judgment was obtained for every $2200 of sales. Unlike general-market retailers who may take legal action as a last resort with respect to delinquent customers, some low-income retailers utilize legal action as a normal practice of business.[23] The added burden and cost to all citizens when the court system is used in this manner is obvious.

These two studies provide some facts and insight, but more hard facts clearly are needed. From these and other completed studies, there is evidence that in some instances at least, the poor do pay more.[24] What can be done so that the poor do not pay more? In principle, if the higher prices meant higher profits as well, the higher prices would be eroded over time as a result of competitive incursions and innovation. Outside firms would move in to reap some of the profits. However, frequently in spite of the higher prices, there is insufficient profit to attract outsider firms. Costs of many types are higher in the ghettos and low-income areas, and in a time of civil unrest, there may be some unique risks associated with building new stores in the heart of the low-income areas. Private enterprise has not necessarily failed—rather it simply has not been fully and imaginatively employed in bringing in more efficient operations and lower prices to low-income areas. Some combination of community cooperatives, black capitalism, imaginative and sensitive big business as well as imaginative and sensitive government programs at the federal, state, and local level should be able to find solutions.[25]

[23] *Ibid.*, pp. xi–xiii.

[24] *See* the discussion in *Report of the National Advisory Commission on Civil Disorders, op. cit.*

[25] For a variety of ideas on improving the plight of the low-income consumer see the *National Consumer Protection Hearings, Federal Trade Commission, op. cit. See also* a detailed article by Eric Schnapper, "Consumer Legislation and the Poor," *The Yale Law Journal,* Vol. 76, March 1967. For additional discussions see "Dealing the Negro In," *Business Week* (Special Report) May 4, 1968; the several thoughtful discussions in Kermit Gordon (ed.), *Agenda For the Nation* (Brookings Institution, 1968), and Burton A. Weisbrod, *The Economics of Poverty* (Prentice-Hall, 1965); and for appropriate initiatives by business, *see* Alfonso J. Cervantes, "To Prevent A Chain of Super-Watts," *Harvard Business Review,* September–October 1967.

Pricing and Markups between Branded and Non-branded Physically Identical Goods

In discussions of products, brands, and want satisfaction, we have continually stressed that "reality" to a consumer is what he *perceives* as the utility of the offering and the character of his want. And he willingly expends scarce resources if the perceived utility of the good or service sufficiently exceeds the utility of what he gives up. Accordingly, if a consumer perceives a greater net increase in utility from offering A than from B (even between two brands of a *physically homogeneous* good), then the rational consumer will be willing to pay some amount more for offering A. Preferring one brand of "identical" good over another is rational and consistent with aggregate consumer welfare if, but only if, the consumer is completely (in the economic sense) informed and markets are vigorously competitive.[26]

Aspirin is a well-known illustration of a physically homogeneous product differentiated through promotion such that, for example, the retail price for a given quantity of Bayer's Aspirin is considerably higher than for other brands. There is nothing unethical about any of this—*as long as* consumers are not misinformed of the composition of the offerings. If with full information they still perceive higher utility from one brand than another then clearly some consumers are expressing a preference which a rational manager may manifest in a higher price. We repeat that the cornerstone of our argument is that consumers be "fully" informed of the products' substantive components. If in the presence of complete information, a persistent preference ensues, then we readily concede that to some consumers one brand provides more satisfaction than another.

Considerable controversy has erupted in the drug industry with respect to prescription drugs and the prices of the identical drug when sold by brand name rather than by generic name. In hearings on the drug industry, the Senate Small Business Committee's Monopoly Subcommittee uncovered some extreme differences in prices for the same physical offering. One example is Meticorten, the Schering Corporation's brand of prednisone— an anti-inflammatory hormone much used by, among others, rheumatoid arthritics. Meticorten sold to druggists in the United States for $17.90 per hundred tablets, but was sold by the same firm to druggists in Bern, Switzerland for $4.34 and in Rio de Janeiro for $5.30.[27] In contrast, when sold under its *generic* name, prednisone sells in the United States for $2.20 per hundred and as inexpensively as $.59 per hundred. The hearings on drug

---

[26] Complete information, recalling our discussion in Chapter 10, is information up to the point that the gain from the last bit of information equals the cost of the last bit ($MR = MC$). No one can afford to be absolutely completely informed. "Vigorous competition" (Chapter 14) means especially that suppliers and demanders are informed and there are no artificial or high barriers to entry in the market.

[27] Statement by Senator Lee Metcalf printed in *Congressional Record*, September 6, 1968, p. E7723, and in part from Morton Mintz, "The Great Drug Robbery," reprinted in *ibid.*, E7724-E7725.

pricing may have had an effect. Parke, Davis & Co., selling its brand of prednisone under the name Paracort at $17.88 per hundred, on January 3, 1968, after the revelations of the hearings cut the price of Paracort by 80 percent to $3.45 on a hundred. The Schering Corporation followed by cutting the price of Meticorten, its brand of prednisone, by 40 percent to $10.80 per hundred.[28]

In his March 4, 1968, health message to Congress, President Johnson cited prices ranging from $1.25 to $11.00 for the same quantity of twelve offerings of drugs of the same formulation and dosage. The President pointedly stated,

> The taxpayer should not be forced to pay $11.00 if the $1.25 drug is equally effective. To do this would permit robbery of private citizens with public approval.[29]

Further implications of control over branded drugs were brought to light in a price-conspiracy case decided in December 1967.[30] The firms were convicted of conspiring to fix the prices of three "wonder" antibiotics (tetracycline; Pfizer's Terramycin, or oxtetracycline; and Cynamid's Aureomycin, or chlotetracycline); of conspiring with each other and with the Upjohn Company and the Olin Mathieson Chemical Corporation (Squibb) to monopolize a $100 million a year market for the products which are effective against a broad range of infections. The case disclosed that the cost of producing 100 tablets of tetracycline in the 250 milligram dosage is as low as $1.52. But from 1953 to 1961, the period covered by the indictment, the price to druggists was $30.60, and to consumers $51.00.[31]

Pricing and profits of the prescription drug industry in large part reflect a lack of competitive forces. The basic problem is one of market structure, in particular, product-differentiation barriers to entry. Investigations conclude there is simply too much control over supply in the ethical drug market to produce more competitive pricing in the U.S.[32]

[28] Statement of Senator Stephen Young in *Congressional Record*, September 20, 1968, pp. S11174-S11176. Other examples are cited by Senator Young. See also Mintz, *op. cit.*, and statement by Senator Thomas McIntyre, "The High Cost of Prescription Drugs," in *Congressional Record*, October 12, 1968, pp. S12704-S12717.

[29] Reprinted in Mintz, *ibid.*, p. E7724, and Statement by Senator Stephen Young, *Congressional Record*, September 20, 1968, p. S11174.

[30] Pfizer, American Cyanamid Company, and Bristol Myers.

[31] In the 6 years ending in 1955, Cyanamid's sales of antibiotics totaled $407 million, with gross profits totaling $342 million or only $65 million less. Profits, at an annual rate, were between 82.6 and 85.7 percent. From Morton Mintz, "The Great Drug Robbery," reprinted in *Congressional Record*, September 6, 1968, p. E7724.

[32] These conclusions are those of the Task Force on Prescription Drugs, a Department of Health, Education, and Welfare unit. The Task Force's findings as reported in the *Washington Post* by Morton Mintz, appear along with comments by Senator Joseph Montoya in the *Congressional Record*, September 16, 1968, pp. S10800-10801.

Similar conclusions were reached by Dr. Willard F. Mueller, Director of the Bureau

The pricing possibilities with respect to *branded* versions of generic drugs permit large profits which necessarily come in part from those who can least afford high prices—the elderly. Although the elderly comprise less than 10 percent of the population, they account each year for 23 percent— about $1 billion—of spending at retail for prescription drugs. The HEW Task Force on Prescription Drugs revealed that more than 90 percent of the elderlies' prescriptions were written for brand name drugs.[33] To the extent that prescriptions are filled on a brand name rather than generic basis, there clearly may be a substantial cost to society, borne in particular by the elderly.

CONSUMER SOVEREIGNTY IN THE MARKETING ECONOMY

How sovereign is the consumer in the U.S. marketing economy? That is, is he the ultimate formulator of which goods and services are produced? And in this assessment, are we speaking of first-order sovereignty or sovereignty with respect to total quality of life? By this point, the reader will concede that the important question of consumer sovereignty at either of the two levels cannot be answered in terms of a simple yes or no.

of Economics, Federal Trade Commission, in testimony before Senator Gaylord Nelson's Hearings on the Drug Industry, Senate Small Business Committee, Subcommittee on Monopoly, Part V, 1968.

For a counter-view to which Dr. Mueller was responding, see G. R. Conrad and I. H. Plotkin, *Risk and Return in American Industry—An Econometric Analysis* (Arthur D. Little, 1967), and their testimony in *Hearings, loc. cit.*

[33] Mintz, in *Congressional Record*, September 16, 1968, p. S10801. The Task Force indicated some of the reasons why many doctors prescribe by brand rather than generic name. First, the drug industry spends an estimated $3000 per year *per doctor*—on 20,000 salesmen who promote the firms' products, about 1100 mailings a year of free samples of drugs, and on advertising in medical journals, many of which are in large part dependent on the advertising revenues from the drug industry. Second, many doctors cannot keep up with the volume of new drugs, and must rely on claims made by the drug companies and their representatives. Third, many doctors are not fully aware, of the price differences at retail between certain prescriptions filled by brand name rather than generic name. *Ibid.*

The drug industry did not relish all the prominence the hearings and controversy created. The industry's public image is poor, a conclusion readily drawn from a Roper Research Associates, Inc., poll showing that of the persons sampled, 97 percent were critical of the profits and pricing practices of the drug industry. Fully 100 percent of the male respondents in the poll cited the drug industry negatively on one or more of six questions. Mintz, in *Congressional Record*, September 6, 1968, p. E7724.

Two Milwaukee, Wisconsin, newspapers reported that the doctors and representatives of the drug industry contributed heavily to the unsuccessful campaign of the opponent of Senator Gaylord Nelson in the latter's 1968 Senatorial race. See "Drug Industry Seeks to Defeat Senator Nelson," comments by Senator Wayne Morse in *Congressional Record*, September 24, 1968, p. S11318.

First-order Wants and Consumer Sovereignty

Taking only the first-order want satisfaction, in the model of the *pure* market economy, the consumer is sovereign, but in the actual marketing economy there are some markets in which he would also appear to be sovereign, whereas in others he appears to have little sovereignty.[34]

A consumer in a low-income area, at least with respect to some goods and services, does not have the opportunity to choose from a large number of substantive alternatives. His immobility, lack of information, and scarcity of supply alternatives render him to a position of taking or leaving what his immediate retail agencies offer him. On the other hand in markets in which competition is strong, with new entry possible for viable firms, and in which both demanders and suppliers are well informed, consumers may well be sovereign in the sense that any profitable demand will be responded to by appropriate total products. There may be considerable want satisfaction in these markets.

To be more specific, we can cite some pressures which would tend to increase consumer sovereignty with respect to first-order wants.

Some Pressures for Increases in Consumer Sovereignty

1. New Product Development. New product development may represent improvements such that prices decrease (that is, a decrease in the ratio of customers' scarce resources expended to utility received). New products alone are *not* necessarily evidence of proportionate increases in consumer sovereignty, for many "improvements" may not in fact alter consumers' perception of utility.[35] Two aspects of product development may provide implications for consumer sovereignty: (1) the volume of new products introduced into any given market;[36] and (2) the rate of failure of new products—an admittedly ambiguous variable.[37]

   We suggest that a *medium* failure rate of new products would be consistent with, although certainly no proof of, consumer sovereignty. A high persistent failure rate could imply (1) that current offerings were completely satisfying consumers; thus they had no desire for new products; (2) or the opposite—that markets were

---

[34] The issues to which we address ourselves go far beyond the issue of whether wants can or are "created." Refer especially to Chapters 3 and 12 for discussions of the ability of outside persuaders to "create" wants. It would appear that "want creation" may not be the most important question in appraising consumer sovereignty.

[35] Refer to Chapter 3 and the discussion of the meaning of "new products."

[36] In a 5-year period in the 1960s drug stores and other members of the Toiletry Merchandisers' Association were offered 10,000 new products.

[37] At least 80 percent of new products introduced fail economically. Of course, a product that never gets off the ground is a failure different from one that loses out after a couple of years. See the discussion of failures of offerings in Chapter 11.

completely monopolized so that new, even better offerings simply could not get opportunity in such markets; (3) or that whether the new products were better or worse, marketing management poorly handled the introduction of the new offerings so that current products held their position irrespective of their relative merits.

By contrast, a medium failure rate would imply that consumers perceived some new products as improvements, that markets were not completely monopolized and blockaded, and that management was reasonably efficient in designing and introducing new total products.

2. Mixture of Price and Nonprice Competition. We have discussed the complexities of price and how any aspect of competitive effort—including advertising—can in principle impart value to an offering. Whenever a customer perceives an increase in *value*, for whatever reason, any arbitrary distinction between "price" and "nonprice" competition ceases.[38] Moreover, the price of which we speak is, of course, the transaction price rather than the list price, for changes in the latter may be illusory with respect to actual price changes.

3. The Consumer Movement In Its Various Aspects and Forms. Increasingly, the consumer in low- as well as higher-income areas will benefit from the concerted actions of government and private organizations which we combine under the consumer movement. Whether it is hearings and public concern over automobile safety, wholesome meat and fish, drug prices and practices, consumer credit and protection, truth in packaging, promotional games, or new antitrust legislation, the increased information will tend to make markets more complete, responsive, and more able to yield benefits to consumers. The force of the consumer movement varies among industries, and thus the consumer is not equally benefited from the movement in all industries. To the extent the consumer movement yields better and/or safer products for the consumer and also makes him a wiser buyer and user of products, his sovereignty will have increased.

4. Antitrust and the Market Concept. The marketing concept, which we discussed in Chapter 10, is the approach to designing total products in which the firm carefully assesses the want and only then chooses the combination of price, product, channels, and promotion with which to respond to the want. To the extent that the marketing

[38] Refer to Chapter 13.

concept is implemented and is not simply an alluring after-dinner topic, the consumer will be benefited. Clearly, *if* a firm through careful research is discovering and responding precisely to the elements of a want, then the consumer enjoys considerable sovereignty. But a firm will, of course, minimize expenditures to attain its desired ends. If it can effect the transaction without really knowing what is wanted, it will do so. But this is simply a recognition that competition is very weak in that market. Thus, if competitive pressures are weak or nil, then the firm will not be under pressure to provide the consumer with any more than a minimal amount of utility. We see, therefore, that the so-called marketing concept provides implications for consumer sovereignty *only insofar* as competitive pressures are present. No one should expect profit maximizers to be irrational. Impersonal market forces must provide the insistent pressure—without which the "marketing concept" is merely talk. We come once again to the vital role of complete market information and nonblockaded markets so that competition continually will push for increased value and thereby yield more sovereignty to consumers in the marketing economy.

Quality of Life and Consumer Sovereignty

Unlike consumer sovereignty with respect to first-order want satisfaction in which one can cite certain pressures which may tend to enhance consumer sovereignty, the issues are more complex when one speaks of consumers' total quality of life. The points discussed in the preceding section apply, but there is obviously much more.

The marketing economy, as the pure market economy par excellence, is able *in principle* to provide consumer sovereignty vis-à-vis first-order wants. However, the marketing economy at present probably *cannot* provide consumer sovereignty with respect to the total aspects of consumers' lives. Burgeoning population and vast, frequently complex technological and industrial processes simply result in many externalities—such as air, water, noise pollution, congestion, and other side-effects of one type or another.

Once all these dangers to body and mind are recognized, there may be a sufficient demand for their elimination. If we perceive this demand as simply many respective markets, we can envisage suppliers ultimately providing appropriate goods and services to satisfy the wants. By this reasoning, the marketing economy *could* yield consumer sovereignty with respect to the total quality of life. However, it is *unlikely* to do so for the simple reason that effective demand is not present in these markets and time is running out. We have so contaminated our environment (consider the long duration of DDT concentrations and that of other chlorinated hydrocarbons)[39] and we have so polluted our waters (consider Lake Erie, believed beyond recovery by many, as well as Lake Michigan, the Hudson River and many others in virtually every section of our country)[40] that action is required now to save for posterity what remains relatively unspoiled. If left solely to "the market" for correction, the response time could be too long. Moreover, the marketing economy—assuming no additional controls—could well continue creating ever more pollution of one form or another, just as it attempted to solve to extant problems.[41]

For consumer sovereignty in regard to the total quality of life, the consumer must be both a demanding consumer and a demanding citizen. The marketing economy alone can only partly provide the solution. The aroused citizens, must as *consumers* make their voices heard in "the market" and as *citizens*, their voices heard in the political arenas. Firms must be made aware of and held responsible for their second- and higher-order

---

[39] Then Secretary of the Interior Stewart Udall said in 1963, "the unnerving fact is that pesticide residues have been found in virtually every type of warm-blooded animal across the land. . . . Man himself is slowly building up in his body small, but relentlessly cumulative traces of chemicals." Rienow & Rienow, *op. cit.*, p. 157.

To date, we know the most about the dangerous effects of DDT—only one of many types of chlorinated hydrocarbons which have the distinction of being extremely long-lived and mobile. Carried by winds, birds, animals, and water, chlorinated hydrocarbons such as DDT are now found not only in the flesh of isolated tribes but even in arctic penguins, seals, and in the flesh of fish that live 100 miles out in the sea. *Ibid.*

The cumulative effect is pronounced as higher-order animals in the food chain feed on lower-order animals whose fatty tissues contain concentration of chlorinated hydrocarbons. Many of DDT's effects are well documented. For example, the Interior Department reveals that one part of DDT in one billion parts of water kills blue crabs in eight days. In more understandable terms, one part per billion is the same as, for example, one ounce of chocolate syrup in 10 million gallons of milk. But DDT is far from the most toxic. Endrin, another chlorinated hydrocarbon used as a pesticide, and so on, is listed by the Department of Interior as "about 50 times more toxic than DDT. The other pesticides—dieldrin, aldrin, chlordane, and toxophene—fell in between." *Op. cit.*, pp. 156–157.

[40] If Lake Erie is already "a dying lake," Lake Michigan is close on its heels. For fifty years fifteen major and thirty-five minor industries plus many cities and towns bordering Michigan have relentlessly poured their wastes into the large, very deep lake, until now according to a federal study, the pollution is "practically irreversible." Rienow, *op. cit.*, p. 106.

One survey revealed that 2000 principal sources of pollution pour contaminants into New York State's waterways. Included were 1167 communities and 760 large industrial sources dumping raw or half-treated sewage and industrial wastes into its streams. Added to these are many institutions, homes, farms, and boats, not to mention all the herbicides and pesticides that wend their way into the waterways. *Ibid.*, p. 107 and *passim.*

[41] As Peter Blake stated so strongly in the "Preface" to his book, *God's Own Junkyard* (Holt, Rinehart & Winston, 1964), p. 7:

> [This book] is a deliberate attack on all those who have already befouled a large portion of this country for private gain, and are engaged in befouling the rest.

effects, and our elected representatives, similarly, must be made sensitive to and concerned about all effects of economic activity.

In this way the marketing economy and our total social system can jointly yield a sovereignty to consumers. With respect to the total quality of life, it has never been more true that the economic and social orders are very much intertwined.

SUMMARY

Consumer welfare means the extent to which the marketing economy provides satisfaction for consumers. One can take a limited focus and consider only the satisfaction of immediate wants, that is, first-order effects. Or one can include *all* aspects of a consumer's life, that is, the total quality of his life in the marketing economy.

Considering consumer satisfaction in terms of the total quality of life is a very complex issue. In principle, "complete" consumer satisfaction—complete consumer sovereignty—with respect to total quality of life means a fulfillment of all elements in a want *as well as* an absence of harmful (physically or psychologically) second- or higher-order effects.

The consumer movement is a diverse group of activities intended to make the consumer a wiser buyer and user of goods and services. The movement, a loose collection of government and private agencies, is engaged in both information and legislation to curb deception and fraud, and thereby enhance want satisfaction.

Studies of food prices and margins in low-income areas versus higher-income areas reveal that in many product and geographic markets, the poor do pay more. The reason the lower-income consumers pay more is *not* that super-market chains and other branch-store operations generally price discriminate; rather, it is because there are more relatively inefficient stories in the ghettos and other low-income areas than in the more affluent areas. Also, the quality of produce and meat is frequently lower in the low-income stories. Other studies show that ghetto retailers of durables, especially with the use of "easy" credit, have much higher prices than downtown retailers of the identical items.

A fully informed consumer perceiving a greater net increase in utility from one brand of physically homogeneous offerings than another is not necessarily irrational. Nor is there anything unethical about this, *as long as* consumers are *informed* about the composition of the offerings. In the prescription drug markets, however, some price differences between branded and unbranded offerings of the *same* drug have not been due to preferences of fully informed consumers. Rather, some very substantial price differences between branded and generic forms of identical drugs have been due to incomplete consumer information, high barriers to entry, and strong control over supply.

With respect to first-order want satisfaction in the marketing economy, the consumer would appear to be well served in many but not all (for example, low-income) markets. Yet, in many markets his "sovereignty" is considerable because competition is keen.

The marketing economy is able in principle and largely in fact to provide consumer sovereignty with respect to many first-order wants. However, the marketing economy at present probably *cannot* provide consumer soverignty with respect to the total quality of consumers' lives. Burgeoning population and vast, frequently complex industrial processes result in many externalities—such as air, water, noise pollution, congestion, and so on. The pollution and contamination continue apace, much of which is considered irreversible. The "market solution" alone would probably be too slow. Thus the economic, social, and political orders are closely interrelated in effecting not greater quantity but a truly high quality of life for consumers in the marketing economy.

SUGGESTED READINGS

A Cross-Section of Readings on the Quality of Life of Consumers

Carolyn Shaw Bell, *Consumer Choice in the American Economy* (New York: Random House, Inc., 1967).

John Kenneth Galbraith, *The New Industrial State* (Boston: Houghton Mifflin Company, 1967).

Kermit Gordon, ed., *Agenda for the Nation* (Washington, D.C.: The Brookings Institution, 1968).

Michael Harrington, *The Other America* (New York: Crowell-Collier and Macmillan, Inc., 1963).

George Katona, *The Mass Consumption Society* (New York: McGraw-Hill, Inc., 1964).

Robert J. Lavidge and Robert J. Holloway, ed., *Marketing and Society: The Challenge* (Homewood, Ill.: Richard D. Irwin, Inc., 1969).

Senator Warren G. Magnuson and Jean Carper, *The Dark Side of the Marketplace: The Plight of the American Consumer* (Englewood Cliffs, N.J.: Prentice-Hall, Inc., 1968).

National Consumer Protection Hearings, Federal Trade Commission (Washington, D.C.: U.S. Government Printing Office, 1969).

1967 New York State Bar Assoication Antitrust Law Symposium (Special symposium on consumer protection; reprinted in Commerce Clearing House Trade Regulation Reports).

Lee E. Preston, ed., *Social Issues in Marketing* (Glenview, Ill.: Scott, Foresman and Company).

Report of the National Advisory Commission on Civil Disorders (New York: Bantam Books, Inc., 1968).

Robert Rienow and Leona Train Rienow, *Moment in the Sun* (New York: The Dial Press, 1967).

E. B. Weiss, "Marketers Fiddle While Consumers Burn," *Harvard Business Review*, July–August, 1968.

Clair Wilcox, *Toward Social Welfare* (Homewood, Ill.: Richard D. Irwin, Inc., 1968).

James Harvey Young, *The Medical Messiahs: A Social History of Health Quackery in Twentieth-Century America* (Princeton, N.J.: Princeton University Press, 1967).

Some Readings on Income Differences and Pricing

David Caplovitz, *The Poor Pay More* (Glencoe, Ill.: Free Press of Glencoe, 1963).

Federal Trade Commission, *Economic Report on Installment Credit and Retail Sales Practices of District of Columbia Retailers* (1968).

FTC, *Economic Report on Food Chain Selling Practices* (1969).

Charles S. Goodman, *Do the Poor Pay More?* (Philadelphia: Wharton School of Finance and Commerce, University of Pennsylvania, 1967.

National Commission on Food Marketing, *Organization and Competition in Food Retailing*, Technical Study No. 7 (June 1966), especially Chapters 16 and 17.

Retail Food Prices in Low and Higher Income Areas, Bureau of Labor Statistics, U.S. Department of Labor, February 1969.

Subject Index

Accumulation, 45, 47, 50
Advertising,
  defined, 120
  effects in markets, 302–304, 307
  effects in the firm, 300–302, 307
  expenditures, 290–291
  as an investment, 298–300, 307
  as part of selling, 120
  and promotion, 287
Agency,
  See Firm
Agents and brokers, 141
Allocation, 45, 47, 50
Aluminum Corporation of America, 138
American Express, 126
Antitrust,
  defined, 346
  and economics, 357–358
  effectiveness, 367–368
  machinery and statutes, 359–360
  and market structure, 367
  philosophy, 351–352
  pro-business, 366–367
  and public policy, 352–353
  scope of, 353–357
Assemblers, 142

Associated Press International, 126
Assorting, 45, 47, 50
Assortment,
  defined, 43
  discrepancy of, 47, 48
  size of, 265–266

Bank AmeriCard, 126
Basing point pricing, 154
Boise Cascade Corp., 71
Brand,
  defined, 275
  and pricing, 408–410
  private branding, 276
  as product, 61
  types of, 275–276
Brand loyalty,
  defined, 213
  measurement, 213–220
Brand switching,
  and buyer structure, 215
  reasons for, 215–216
Break-even analysis,
  defined, 234
  flexible, 235

Buyer behavior,
  approach to, 16
  choice, 205–208
  general statement, 199
  post-decision evaluation, 208–209
  problem recognition, 199–205
  process, 199
  and structure, 220
"Buyer learning," 93
Buyer structure,
  and brand switching, 215
  and buyer behavior, 220
  and choice, 207–208
  defined, 109
  and media search, 203–204
  and post-decision evaluation, 208–209
Buying,
  defined, 119
  as a marketing function, 119–120
  related to selling, 119

Champion Paper Corporation, 72
Chevrolet Division of General Motors, 93
Chicago Board of Trade, 78
Choice,
  and buyer structure, 207–208
  conditions for, 206
  defined, 205
  elements of, 206
Clayton Act,
  Section 3, 359
  Section 7, 359, 364, 365
  Section 8, 360
Cognitive dissonance, 178, 208
Colgate-Palmolive, 75
Command solution, 32–33, 49
Communication,
  as a function, 126–128
  an integrating force, 126
  as an instrument of control, 126
  related to advertising, 126
Competition,
  and antitrust, 349–360
  defined, 75, 80
  direct and potential, 75–76
  imperfect, 38–39
  inter-industry, 69
  monopolistic, 38–39
  nonprice, 75
  price, 75

Conduct,
  defined, 104
  group, 112
  marketing, 111
  unit level, 111
Consumer movement, 17, 402–404
  components, 402–403
  defined, 402
Consumers' Union, 107
Consumer welfare,
  defined, 398
  and efficiency, 400
  first order analysis of, 399, 411–413
  and pricing, 404–407
  and productivity, 399
Contact,
  meaning of, 57–58
Contribution analysis,
  defined, 235
  example, 237
Convenience,
  goods, 164, 212, 256, 280, 289
  stores, 144
Crown Zellerbach Corp., 71

Decision-making,
  defined, 86
  human, 113
  nature of, 94
  role of research in, 247–250
  and time, 94
Defense Department, 107
Demand,
  cross-elasticity of, 68, 68n, 73
  problem, 29–31
Demanders,
  defined, 57
  same product market, 69
Demographic elements, 185–188
Department of Agriculture, 126
Differential advantage,
  bases of 236–237, 238, 283
  defined, 76, 80
  and merchandising, 239
  and profit maximazation, 227
Diners' Club, 126
Diversification,
  data on, 267
  defined, 73
  market, 80, 267
  reasons for, 269, 269n

Division of labor, 23, 24, 41
Double-funnel, 46

Economies of scale,
    in channels, 279–280
    exploiting, 261–263
    external, defined, 135–137, 137n, 148–
        149, 281
    in food retailing, 385–388
Economy, 22–23, 49
    impure, 39–40
    mixed, 39–40
    pure, 38–39
Efficiency,
    and consumer welfare, 399
    defined, 278, 374
    measure, 375
    and profitability, 376
    relationship to productivity, 374
Engel's Law, 175–176
Enterprise differentiation,
    defined, 77
    as part of differential advantage, 238
    principle of, 137
European Economic Community, 135
Exclusive dealing contracts,
    channel control, 147
    related to vertical integration, 138
External economies, 135
    example, 135
    and marketing channels, 148–149

Facts, defined, 7
Federal Housing Authority, 125
Federal Reserve Board, 130
Federal Trade Commission Act, 359–360
Financing,
    example, 136
    as a marketing function, 124–125
Firestone Rubber and Tire Company, 138
Firm,
    defined, 134, 250, 283
    functions to perform, 135–138
    internal structure and organizational
        goals, 189–190
    nature of, 225–226
    objectives, 226
    and profit maximization, 227, 240
Flows,
    defined, 118, 128, 132
        measurement, 130–132
        relation to functions, 129–130
Ford Motor Company, 41
Franchising agreements,
    related to vertical integration, 138
Functionalism, 12, 105
Functions,
    defined, 118, 132
    of exchange, 119–121
    facilitating, 124–128
    of physical supply, 121–124
    relation to flows, 129–130
    relation to marketing channel, 147–148
    See also. Buying, Selling, Transporta-
        tion, Standardization and grading,
        Financing, Communication, and Risk-
        bearing

Garrard of Great Britain, 119
Georgia-Pacific Corp., 71
Gravity Models, 164–166
    Reilly's "Law of Retail Gravitation,"
        165–166
Groups,
    market and intermarket conduct, 112
    market and intermarket performance,
        112
    nationality, 186–187
    reference, 181–182
    of sellers and buyers, 114
    social, 180–181

Heterogeneity,
    defined, 43
    meaningful, 44
    meaningless, 44
Homeostasis, 178
Home Owners Loan Corporation, 125
Horizontal integration,
    defined, 138
    and vertical integration, 139
Howard Johnson, 139

Idle capacity,
    defined, 260
    sources of, 260
Impurities, 40, 41, 42, 43
Income,
    and consumption, 175
    changes in, 175–176
    permanent, 176

and social class, 183–184
transitory, 176
Information,
cost of, 247n
and decision-making, 247
and marketing research, 247–248
optimal, 247
and promotion, 287
Innovators, 205
Institution,
component, 42
defined, 41
InterBank, 126
Interdependency, 24, 25
International Paper Co., 71
In transit privileges, 159
Investment,
advertising as, 298–300
defined, 299

Jones and Laughlin Steel Company, 100

Kiefer-Stewart, Inc., 141
KLH Research and Development Corporation, 119

Learning,
defined, 209
curve, 209–210
measurement, 210
models, 213, 216–218
and problem solving, 212
and promotion, 291–293
and sellers, 211–212
Lever Brothers, 75
Life cycle,
definition, 184
other elements, 185
product, *see* Product
Ling-Temco-Vought, 100
Lorenz curve, 29, 30n

"Make or buy" decisions, 107, 139, 149
McDonald's Hamburgers, 139
Manufacturers sales branches and offices, 141
Market,
and buyer structure, 109
defined, 57, 67, 79
diversification, 72–73, 80
economy, 33

geographic, 79–80
and information, 248
price, 49
purely competitive, 99
segmentation, 239
and seller structure, 109–110
solution, 33–34, 39
See also Market areas, Markets
Market areas,
boundaries for, 156–158
defined, 151
extension of, 160
and transportation, 122
Marketing,
approaches to study of, 12–20
analytical, 18–20
functional, 15
industrial organization, 13–14
institutional, 14–15
managerial, 12–13
other, 16–17
behavior, 111–112
channel, 145–149
defined, 4, 113, 345
channel, 145–149
conduct, 111–112
forces, 34–35
institution, 41
performance, 112
and public policy, 345–349
sources of structure
structure-behavior, 85–86
See also Marketing channel, Marketing mix, Marketing research, Marketing variables
Marketing channel,
decisions, 277–282
defined, 145
discussed, 145–149
and marketing mix, 281–282
and productivity, 279–280
vertically integrated, 278
Marketing mix,
and controllable variables and products, 254–255
defined, 251
and marketing channels, 281–282
and marketing research, 247
Marketing research,
defined, 249, 251
Marketing variables,
controllable, 241, 243–244

and marketing mix, 254–255
and marketing structure, 242
uncontrollable, 241
Markets,
buying and selling, 78
factor, 5
geographic, 72, 73, 79
as organizations, 98
product, 72, 79
retail, 77
time aspects of, 77–78
wholesale, 77
See also Market
Markov models,
and brand loyalty, 213, 214
Matching, 56–57, 254
Merchandising,
defined, 239, 250
and differential advantage, 239
dual, 276
and total product, 254
Merchant wholesalers, 140–141
Mergers,
and antitrust, 364–366
conglomerates, 100, 270, 365–366
horizontal, 270, 364–365
motives, 269n
numbers of, 269
profitability, 271–272
vertical, 270, 365
Middlemen agencies,
reasons for, 139–140
Monopoly,
price, 91
welfare loss from, 362–363
Motivation,
defined, 179
research, 179–180

National Wholesale Druggists Association, 126
Needs,
affectional, 177
biogenic, 54
defined, 54, 79
ego bolstering, 177
ego defensive, 177
hierarchy of, 200–201
perception of, 199–200
psychogenic, 54
recognition of, 201–202

New York Stock Exchange, 78
New York Times, 121
Normative science, 9n

Offering,
altering, 70
defined, 61
deletion decision, 273
firm's choice, 258–274
and market structure, 288–289
new, 260–265
separate geographic markets, 152
size of assortment, 265–266
Oligopoly, 95
bilateral, 147
tight, 99
Open-to-buy, 190n
Organization,
focal, 102–103, 195
formal, 100–102
industrial, 13–14
informal, 97
markets as, 98
structure and, 114
theory of, 19, 96n

Packaging,
nature of decision, 277
Perception,
defined, 199
Performance, 104
unit level, 112
Persuasion,
defined, 287
and differentiability of the offering, 288–289
Positive science, 9n
Petroleum Bulkplants, Terminals, and LP Gas Facilities, 141
Post-decision evaluations,
and buyer structure, 208–209
defined, 208
Price,
changes, 327–334
cost margins, 383–384
decrease, 313
defined, 311, 337
and demand changes, 334–335
discrimination, 324–325, 337
equilibrium, 35

and markets, 152–154
and nonprice competition, 75
and products, 314–315
rationale of, 317–323
social aspects, 336, 404–410
Pricing,
  basic rationale of, 317–323
  "cost oriented," 319–320
  and competition, 323–327
  and consumer welfare, 404–407
  and elasticity, 318
  full-cost, 320–322
  social aspects of, 336, 404–410
Principle of massed reserves, 139–140
Principle of minimum transactions, 140
"Principles" of marketing, 17
Problem solving,
  automatic response behavior, 212, 213
  conditions of, 212
  extensive, 212
  and learning, 212
  limited, 212–213
Procter & Gamble, 71, 75, 107
Product,
  defined, 60–61, 79
  and demanders, 69
  different, 62–63
  life cycle, 191, 274–275
  market, 67, 67n, 68–69
  and marketing mix, 254–255
  new, 74–75
  and suppliers, 69–70
  total, 61–62, 77n, 315
  want satisfaction, 64
Production problem, 26–29
Productivity,
  changes in, 377–378
  and channels, 279–280
  and consumer welfare, 399
  defined, 112, 372, 373
  measurement of, 372–374
  relationship to efficiency, 374
Profit maximization,
  and differential advantage, 227
  and pricing, 318–319
  and promotion, 298, 299
  in terms of costs, 228–230
  in terms of revenues, 227–228
Profitability,
  and concentration, 379–382
  and efficiency, 376

Promotion,
  defined, 286, 306–307
  expenditures, 290
  institutional, 289
  as an investment, 299–300
  model of, 293–300
  product, 289–290
  rationale, 291–293
  social implications, 304–306
Public policy,
  defined, 345–346
  in marketing, 345–349
Purchasing agent, 191–193
Psychological elements, 176–180

"Rationality,"
  limits of, 87n
  and marketing management, 76
  and structure, 101
Reilly's "Law of Retail Gravitation," 165–
  166
Reinforcement,
  defined, 211
Resale price maintenance, 147, 335–336,
  338
Retail,
  classifications of establishments, 142–145
  sales defined, 6
  transactions and products, 255–256
Rights,
  transfer of, 57
Risk,
  defined, 128, 128n
  of interdependency, 24–25
  reduction of, 261
  research as risk reduction, 250
Risk-bearing,
  as a function, 128
Rivalry, 75, 80
Robinson-Patman Act, 360

St. Regis Corporation, 71
Search,
  buyer, defined, 202
  and buyer structure, 203–204
  cost of, 247n
  forms of, 202
  informal, 204–205
  media, 203
Sears & Roebuck, 107

"Seller learning," 93
Selling,
    defined, 120
    as related to buying, 119
Set, defined, 56
Search, 120
Sherman Act,
    Section 1, 359
    Section 2, 359
Shopping goods, 164, 212, 256, 280
Shopping stores, 145
Simplification,
    defined, 124
Small Business Administration, 3, 155
Snap-on-tools, 139
Social class, 181–184
Sorting out, 44–45, 46–47, 50
Sorting process, 43, 44
    by performance, 47
Specialty goods, 164, 256, 280
Specialty stores, 145
Standardization,
    defined, 123–124
    example of, 147
    as a function, 123–125
    reduction of risk, 124
    related to simplification, 124
Stimuli,
    defined, 178–179
    S–R model, 180
Storage,
    defined, 122
    example, 136
    as a function, 122–123
Structure,
    buyer, 109, 174
    complexity of, 93–95
    controllable aspects of, 90–93
    defined, 88, 88n, 113
    elements of, 90–93, 199
    external aspects of, 194
    implications of, 88n
    and individuals, 106–110
    markets, 242, 288–289
    and media search, 203–204
    and organization, 114
    uncontrollable aspects of, 90–93
    unit buyers and, 106–107
    unit sellers and, 107–108
Structure/Behavior,
    dynamics of, 115

examples of, 104–105
    influences, 113
    relation between, 103–106
Suppliers, defined, 57
    same product market, 69–72
Supply and demand, 35, 50
    laws of, 36

Theory,
    defined, 7, 8
    in marketing, 10
    normative, 9
    state of in marketing, 10–11
    relationships between positive and normative, 9–10
Tradition solution, 31–32, 49
Transactions, 4
    bases for, 58–59
    by description, 58–59
    and functions, 119
    by inspection, 58
    retail, 255–256
    by sample, 58
    and transportation, 121
    wholesale, 257–258
Transportation,
    defined, 121
    example of, 136
    and market areas, 122
    as a marketing function, 121–122
Truth in Lending Bill, 17
Truth in Packaging Bill, 17
"Two-Step Hypothesis,"
    defined, 204
    examples, 204, 205

Unit,
    buyer structure at, 106
    seller structure at, 107
U.S. Antitrust Division, 100
U.S. Plywood Corporation, 72

Venn diagram, 57, 64
Vertical integration,
    defined, 138–139
    and functions, 138–139
    and marketing channels, 278
    by merger, 270, 365
    and profit maximization, 281
    related to firms, 138, 259n

related to flows, 128
and sorting process, 46
Veterans' Administration, 125
Wants,
  defined, 54, 61
Want satisfaction, 22, 40, 41, 50, 56–57,
  64
  perceived, 65–66, 79
Warehouses,
  chain store, 129
  circumstances favoring, 161

private, 160
public, 160
Weyerhauser Corp., 71
Wheeler-Lea Act, 360
Wholesale,
  buying cooperatives, 141
  definition of sales, 6
  kinds of establishments, 140–142
  transactions and products, 257–258
Wholesome Meat Act, The, 17

Name Index

Abraham, W. I., 131n
Adams, K. A., 150
Adams, W., 39n, 351, 351n, 356n, 362n, 363n, 391, 391n
Adelman, M. A., 35n, 82, 138n, 242n, 248n, 266n, 328, 328n, 329n, 330n, 336n, 362n, 372n, 373n, 384n, 389n
Alberts, W. W., 260n, 261n, 269n, 271, 314n
Alchian, A., 82, 252
Alderson, W., 11n, 12, 12n, 15, 16n, 43, 43n, 48n, 51, 52, 54n, 55, 55n, 76n, 90, 90n, 91n, 105, 105n, 116, 117, 122n, 145n, 238n, 239n, 275n, 277n, 293n, 309, 336n, 373, 373n, 395, 396
Alexis, M., 187, 188, 189n, 196
Aljian, G. W., 192n
American Marketing Association, 6
Andrews, K. R., 284
Andrews, P. W. S., 335n
Archer, S. H., 284
Areeda, P., 354n, 368n
Arndt, J., 205, 205n

Backman, J., 289n, 290n, 309
Bain, J., 14n, 76n, 88n, 106n, 110n, 112n,
115, 267n, 333n, 339, 356n, 363n, 368, 381n, 385n, 389n, 396
Baldwin, W. L., 227n
Baligh, H. H., 149
Baker, G. L., 395
Banks, S., 252
Barger, H., 371n, 394
Bartels, R., 52
Bauer, R., 188n, 221, 309
Baumol, W. J., 166, 166n, 169, 194n, 200n, 376n
Bayton, J. F., 54n, 80, 179n, 199n, 209n
Beckman, T. N., 18n
Bell, C. S., 287n, 416
Bell, M. L., 13n, 54n, 182n, 200n, 203n, 244n
Bennett, P., 222
Berelson, B., 198n, 204n
Berry, J. L., 161n, 162, 162n, 163, 163n, 166n, 169
Blackwell, R. D., 17n, 195, 199n, 213n, 220
Blair, J. M., 376n, 379n
Blake, P., 414n
Blank, D. M., 297n
Blankertz, D. F., 249n, 252

427

Bliss, P., 24n, 54n, 115, 182n, 204n, 205n, 258n, 265n, 306n, 322n, 326n, 338, 372n
Bock, B., 364n, 372n, 377n 381n, 396
Bogue, D. J., 157n
Bonini, C. P., 253
Borden, N. H., 309
Bork, R. H., 335n, 346n, 357n, 399n
Bott, E., 182n
Boulding, K. E., 20, 21, 258n
Bourne, F. S., 206, 206n
Bowman, W., 357n
Boyd, H. W., 195
Breyer, R. F., 145, 277n, 285
Brink, E. L., 310
Brodley, J. F., 363n
Brozen, Y., 356n, 376n
Buchanan, J. M., 363n
Bucklin, L. P., 150
Bush, R. R., 216n
Buskirk, R. H., 13n
Buzzell, R. D., 284

Cannon, W. B., 178n
Caplovitz, D., 400n, 417
Carlson, B., 285
Carlston, K. S., 357n
Carper, J., 17n, 370, 416
Cassady, R., Jr., 141n, 319n, 339
Cassels, J. M., 190n
Caves, R., 14n, 88n, 106n, 110n, 112n, 115, 354n
Cervantes, A. J., 407n
Chamberlin, E. H., 51, 62n, 77n, 80, 81, 237n, 240n
Cherington, P. T., 15n
Clark, C. P., 52
Clark, F. E., 52
Clark, J. M., 70n
Clemens, E. W., 266n, 319n, 325n
Clewett, R. M., 150
Coase, R. H., 92n, 135n, 264n, 340
Cohen, A. R., 178n
Cohen, K. J., 18n, 21, 81, 189n, 190n, 191n, 195, 202n
Coleman, J., 109n, 182n, 184n, 203n, 204n
Collins, N., 14n, 101n, 102n, 110n, 115, 339, 353n, 363n, 374n, 378n, 383, 383n
Comanor, W., 14n, 110n, 303, 303n, 309

Conrad, G. R., 128n
Converse, P., 165n
Cook, J. V., 395
Cook, V. T., 221
Coombs, C. H., 216n
Copeland, M. A., 82
Copeland, M. T., 256n
Cowlins, E., 404n
Cox, D., 221
Cox, R., 11, 11n, 12, 12n, 15n, 52, 58n, 108n, 129n, 130n, 131n, 132, 137n, 145n, 152n, 157n, 169, 239n, 277n, 285, 336n, 371n, 395
Craig, R., 133
Creamer, D., 397
Crowder, W. F., 260n
Cundiff, E. W., 256n, 257n
Cunningham, R. M., 213n, 221
Cunningham, S. M., 188n
Cyert, R. M., 18n, 21, 81, 92n, 96n, 98n, 102, 102n, 106n, 115, 116, 189n, 191n, 195, 202n, 208n, 227n

Darnell, J. C., 340
Darrah, L. B., 255n
Davidson, P., 176n
Davidson, W. R., 18n
Davis, R. L., 216n
Day, R. L., 211n
Dean, J., 70n, 201n, 251, 260n, 284, 293n, 298n, 299n, 300n, 309, 325n, 340, 374, 374n
Decker, W. S., 166n
Demsetz, H., 221
Dennis, C. C., 153n, 156n
Dewhurst, J. F., 371n, 395
Dickson, G. W., 221
Dilley, D. R., 393n
Dirksen, E. McK., 267n, 393n
Dirlam, J. B., 227n, 328n, 362n, 391, 391n
Dooley, P. C., 100n
Dorfman, R., 9n, 23n, 33n, 39n, 51, 374n
Douglas, E., 165n, 388n, 389n, 395
Draper, J. E., 214n
Duddy, E. A., 14n, 15n, 33n, 58n, 77n, 96n, 105n, 108n, 117, 119n, 124n, 125n, 128n, 132, 160, 160n, 169, 239n, 402n
Duncan, D. J., 18n, 43n, 52, 273n, 275n, 276n, 328n, 388n

Ehrenberg, A. S. C., 221
Ehrlich, D., 211n
Emmer, R. E., 21
Engel, J. F., 17n, 195, 199n, 203n, 213n, 220
Entenberg, R. D., 285
Estes, W. K., 216n

Farkas, J., 372n, 377n, 381n, 396
Farley, J. U., 221
Farris, J. E., 150
Farris, P. L., 132
Federal Trade Commission, 116, 194n, 269n, 270n, 284, 310, 405n, 417
Ferber, R., 249n, 252, 253
Ferguson, C. E., 135n, 318n, 357n, 375n
Ferguson, J. H., 302n
Festinger, L., 178n, 209n
Fetter, F. A., 156n
Finchandler, T. C., 131n, 371n, 395
Fisk, G., 15n, 128n, 176n, 203n
Fortas, A., 368n
Fox, H. W., 287n, 310
Frank, R. E., 109n, 116, 213n, 216n, 218n, 219, 219n, 253
Friedman, M., 9n, 51, 176, 176n
Friend, I., 222
Freud, S., 177
Fuchs, C. R., 381n
Fuller, J. G., 101n, 322n, 350n
Furness, B., 402

Gabler, W. K., 52
Gabor, A. 335n, 340
Galbraith, J. K., 26n, 39n, 90, 193, 193n, 304, 305, 358n, 378n, 416
Garoin, L., 138n
Gaudet, H., 204n
Gibbs, J. P., 157n
Gift, R. F., 396
Glennan, T., 397
Goldstucker, J., 166n
Goode, W. J., 7n, 8n
Goodman, C. S., 130n, 131n, 132, 186n, 371n, 395, 417
Gordon, K., 407n, 416
Gort, M., 70n, 137n, 260n, 269n, 271n, 272n, 273n
Gould, J. R., 335n, 340
Gouldner, A. W., 23n, 31n, 51
Gouldner, H. P., 23n, 31n, 51

Graham, S., 184, 184n, 205n
Graig, D. R., 52
Granger, C. W. J., 335n, 340
Gray, H. M., 396
Green, H. L., 157, 157n
Green, P., 253
Greene, M. R., 132
Grether, E. T., 11, 11n, 12n, 15n, 21, 39n, 52, 58n, 77n, 108n, 129n, 132, 137n, 152n, 169, 316n, 335n, 354n, 368, 395
Greyser, S. A., 309
Guttman, I., 211n

Haire, M., 96n
Hale, R. D., 138n
Hall, M., 139n, 140n, 163, 163n, 395
Hancock, R., 139n
Haray, F., 214n
Harper, D. V., 233n, 334n
Harrington, M., 55n, 400n, 416
Hartley, E. L., 221
Hartman, L. M., 170
Hatt, P. K., 7n
Hawkins, E. R., 82, 336n, 340
Haveman, R. H., 23n, 25n, 29n, 30n, 38n, 51, 75n
Hayes, S. P., Jr., 206n
Heflebower, R. C., 147n, 233n, 266n, 320n, 339, 367n
Heilbroner, R. L., 23n, 24n, 25, 25n, 26n, 27n, 29n, 34n, 38n, 51
Henry, J., 178n
Herniter, J. D., 214n
Hirchleifer, J., 82
Hobbes, T., 177
Hogarty, T. F., 272n
Hollander, S. C., 137n, 145n, 258n, 264n, 322n, 334, 335n, 340, 372n, 373n, 376n
Hollander, S., Jr., 249n, 252
Holloway, R. J., 416
Holton, R., 70n, 264n, 266n, 318n, 321n, 32, 334n, 340
Hotchkiss, G., 51
Houghton, H. F., 267n
Houthakker, H. S., 176n
Howard, D. A., 214n
Howard, J. A., 13n, 181n, 183n, 196, 209n, 212n, 220, 244n, 252, 298n, 310
Hruska, R. L., 267n

Huff, D., 166, 166n, 167n, 169
Hughes, L. M., 276n
Hunt, H. G., 388n

Ide, E. A., 166, 166n
Irelan, L. M., 187n
Isard, W., 169

Johnson, H. G., 306, 306n
Johnson, L. B., 17n
Johnson, O., 77n
Jones, M. G., 403n
Jones, R., 222
Jones, W. L., 141n
Jung, A. F., 165n

Kalacheck, E., 397
Kamerschen, D. R., 306n, 350n, 358n,
    362n, 363n
Kaplan, A. D. H., 227n, 328n
Katona, G., 55n, 175n, 180, 180n, 221,
    305n, 416
Katz, E., 109n, 204n
Kaysen, C., 154n, 347n, 348n, 349n, 353n,
    356n, 363n, 367n, 369
Kelley, W. J., 310
Kemeny, J. G., 56n, 65n
Kendall, M. G., 174n
Kennedy, J. N., 174n
Keynes, J. M., 9n, 175, 175n
Kish, L., 184, 184n
Kitching, J., 273n
Knauer, V., 402
Knapp, J., 163, 163n, 395
Knight, F., 96n, 128n
Knopf, K. A., 23n, 25n, 51, 75n
Kohler, H., 348n
Kollat, D. T., 17n, 195, 199n, 213n, 220
Kotler, K., 13n, 21, 177n, 199n, 201n,
    227n, 244n, 249n, 252, 255n, 277n,
    281n, 282n, 287n, 310
Kriebel, C. H., 132
Krugman, H. E., 221
Kuehn, A. A., 109n, 116, 211n, 216, 216n,
    217, 217n, 218n, 219, 219n, 253
Kusoffsky, B., 285
Kuznets, S., 52

Labini, P. S., 333n
Lansing, J. B., 184, 184n
Lanzillotti, R. F., 190n, 227n, 328n

Lave, L., 101n
Lavidge, R. J., 416
Lazarsfeld, P. F., 109n, 204n
Leavitt, H. J., 334n
Legrand, B., 222
Leven, C. L., 132
Levy, S. J., 195
Lewis, B., 354n
Lewis, D. J., 222
Lewis, E. H., 139n
Lickert, R., 206n
Lippitt, V. G., 222
Lipstein, B., 214n
Loeb, B. S., 176n
Loevinger, L., 351n
LoSciuoto, L. A., 222
Lundy, R. D., 395
Lunt, P., 182, 182n

Machlup, F., 266n, 324n, 339, 357n
Madsen, I. E., 391n
Magee, J. F., 160n, 170, 214n
Magnuson, W. G., 17n, 370, 416
Malinowski, B., 31n
Mallen, B. E., 43n, 146n, 150, 277n, 285
Mann, H. M., 110n, 303n
Manne, A. S., 170
Manne, H. G., 285
Mansfield, E., 396
Manzel, H., 109n
March, J. G., 18n, 86n, 87n, 88n, 90n,
    92n, 93n, 94n, 96n, 98n, 106n, 115,
    116, 189n, 208n, 227n, 339
Marchak, T., 397
Marcus, S., 359n, 369
Markin, R. J., 199n, 221
Marks, N. E., 122n
Marshall, A., 177
Martin, D. D., 352n
Martineau, P., 207, 208n, 222
Mason, E. S., 368n
Maslow, A. H., 179, 179n
Massy, W. F., 109n, 216n, 217n, 253
May, F. E., 222
McCarthy, E. J., 13n, 235n, 244n, 245n,
    255n, 257n, 312, 335n
McConnell, J. D., 219, 219n, 220n, 340
McGarry, E. D., 132, 239, 239n, 252, 304n
McIntyre, T., 409n
McKie, J., 14n
McNulty, P. J., 82

Meehan, J. W., Jr., 303n
Menzel, H., 204n
Metcalf, L., 408n, 409n
Mickwitz, G., 191, 191n
Miller, R. A., 150
Mills, J., 211n
Mintz, M., 408n, 409n, 410n
Modigliani, F., 333n
Montgomery, D. B., 213n, 214n, 216n, 217n, 252
Montoya, J., 409n
Moore, H. L., 150
Moore, J. R., 116
Moore, O. K., 222
Morse, W., 410n
Morton, N., 122n, 123n
Mossman, F. H., 122n, 123n
Mosteller, F., 216n
Moynihan, D., 401n
Mueller, E., 175n
Mueller, W. F., 39n, 68n, 128n, 138n, 326n, 352n, 356n, 364n, 369, 378, 378n, 396, 409n, 410n

Narver, J. C., 70n, 81, 100n, 259n, 260n, 268n, 269n, 270n, 272n, 273n, 358n, 363n, 366n, 367n, 368n, 375n
National Commission on Food Marketing, 130n, 131, 148n, 262n, 263n, 277, 277n, 285, 303n, 385n, 390n, 404n, 417
National Industrial Conference Board, 372, 377, 378, 378n
Nelson, G., 410n
Nelson, J. R., 323n
Newcomb, E. L., 391n
Nicosia, F. M., 16n, 17n, 43n, 221
Nolin, L. H., 214n
Nourse, R. E. M., 284
Nutter, G. W., 52

Olgilvy, D., 299n
O'Meara, J. T., Jr., 201n
Ostheimer, R. H., 186, 186n, 196
Oxenfeldt, A. R., 13n, 264n, 326n, 334n, 340

Parsons, T., 23n, 51
Pashigian, B. P., 14n
Patman, W., 352n
Pavlov, I. P., 177

Peck, M. J., 138n
Peltzman, S., 356n, 357n, 369, 376n
Penrose, E. T., 134n, 178n
Peterman, J. L., 297n, 309
Peterson, E., 402
Phillips, A., 92n, 96n, 101n, 102n, 116, 276n, 323n
Phillips, C. F., 18n, 273n, 275n
Phillips, C. F., Jr., 346n
Pirenne, H., 51
Plotkin, I. H., 128n
Pratt, R. W., Jr., 222
Polanyi, Karl, 33n, 34n, 51
Pred, A. R., 132
Preston, L. E., 9n, 10n, 14n, 101n, 110n, 161n, 276n, 300n, 309, 325n, 335n, 339, 340, 353n, 363n, 369, 374n, 378, 383, 383n, 388n, 416

Quirin, G. D., 192n, 299n, 300n

Reilly, W. J., 165, 165n
Rewoldt, S. H., 180n
Revzan, D. R., 8n, 9n, 11n, 14n, 33n, 43n, 52, 58n, 77n, 78n, 96n, 105n, 108n, 117, 119n, 124n, 125n, 128n, 132, 145n, 147n, 155n, 160, 160n, 163, 164n, 239n, 395, 402n
Reynolds, R. B., 165n
Reynolds, W. H., 277n
Rich, S., 221
Richards, L. G., 187n
Richartz, L. E., 149
Rienow, L. T., 400n, 414n, 417
Rienow, R., 400n, 414n, 417
Robertson, T. S., 174n, 196, 221
Robinson, E. A. G., 140n, 258n
Rogers, E. M., 205n
Rothenberg, J., 201n

Sammett, L. L., 153n, 156n
Samuelson, P. A., 8n, 9n, 27n, 29n, 30n, 35n, 51, 64n, 68n, 227n, 230n
Savitt, R., 276n, 280n, 391n
Scherer, F. M., 379n, 393
Schmookler, J., 397
Schnapper, E., 407n
Schönbach, P., 211n
Schramm, A. E., 276n
Schumpeter, J. A., 371n
Schwartz, G., 165n
Schwartzman, D., 381n

Scitovsky, T., 335n, 340
Scott, J. D., 180n
Scott, W., 88n, 90
Sears, P., 398
Segall, J. E., 260n, 261n, 269n, 271, 314n
Shaffer, J. D., 201n
Shapiro, B. P., 334n
Shapiro, S. J., 11n, 145n, 239n
Shepherd, W. G., 233n, 323n, 339, 363n, 367n, 369
Sherwood, C., 150
Shaw, C. B., 17n
Shibutani, T., 97n, 109n, 181n
Sichel, W., 369
Simon, H. A., 18n, 40n, 86n, 87n, 88n, 90n, 93n, 94n, 96n, 97n, 115, 126n, 200n, 243n
Simon, J., 300, 300n
Singer, E. M., 138n, 267n, 369
Smelser, N., 23n, 51
Smith, A., 43n, 49n
Smith, P., 132n
Smith, R., 333n, 350n
Smith, W. J. J., 397
Smolensky, E., 175n
Spurr, W. A., 253
Stafford, J. E., 222
Stanton, W. J., 13n
Staudt, T. A., 260n, 284
Steiner, G. A., 198n
Stern, L. W., 150, 285
Stewart, P. W., 371n, 395
Stigler, G., 24n, 43n, 102n, 135n, 245n, 252, 258n, 271n, 287n, 312, 315n, 346n, 356n, 358, 358n, 362n, 368n
Still, R. R., 256n, 257n
Stillerman, R., 379n
Stinchcombe, A. L., 96n
Stocking, G. W., 21, 68n, 266n
Stone, G. P., 208n
Strauss, G., 107n, 193n
Summer, R., 397

Tawney, R. H., 187n
Taylor, R. M., 122n
Telser, L. G., 215, 215n, 303n, 309, 335n, 396
Terpstra, V., 396
Thompson, D. N., 280n
Thorp, W. L., 260n
Thrall, R. M., 216n

Tolley, G. S., 170
Treece, J. M., 357n
Troelstrup, A. W., 403n
Tucker, W. T., 177n, 179n
Tull, D. S., 253, 285
Tullock, G., 363n
Turner, D., 39n, 347n, 348n, 353n, 356n, 363n, 366n, 367n, 369, 400

Udall, S., 414n
Udell, J., 222
Urban, G. L., 213n, 214n, 216n, 217n, 252

Vaile, R. S., 15n, 58n, 60n, 108n, 129n, 132, 137, 152n, 169, 395
Vaughan, J., 391n
Verdoorn, P. J., 249n, 252
Vining, R., 170
Viner, J., 52
Voorhis, J., 404n

Wales, H. G., 203n
Wales, T. J., 156n
Wallace, D., 138n
Walsh, R. G., 116
Warner, W. L., 182, 182n
Warshaw, M. R., 180n, 203n
Watson, D. S., 37n, 68n, 228n, 319n, 323n, 324n
Weiss, E. B., 417
Weiss, L., 289n, 306n, 363n, 381n
Weisbrod, B. A., 407n
Wells, W. J., 222
Weston, J. F., 133, 356n, 357n, 369, 376n
Wheatley, J. J., 309
White, I. S., 305n
Whorf, B. L., 186, 186n
Wilcox, C., 346n, 348n, 359n, 360n, 370, 417
Williamson, O., 92n, 96n, 102n, 323n
Wilson, T. A., 14n, 110n, 303, 303n
Winsten, C., 163, 163n, 395
Wolf, A. J., 165n
Wolfe, P., 169
Wortzel, L., 188n

Yamey, B. S., 335n, 340
Yang, C. Y., 303n
Young, J. H., 417
Young, S., 409n

Zusman, P. A., 133